Microsoft Azure

Planning, Deploying, and Managing Your Data Center in the Cloud

Marshall Copeland

Julian Soh

Anthony Puca

Mike Manning

David Gollob

Apress®

Microsoft Azure: Planning, Deploying, and Managing Your Data Center in the Cloud

ISBN-13 (pbk): 978-1-4842-1044-4

ISBN-13 (electronic): 978-1-4842-1043-7

Managing Director: Welmoed Spahr
Lead Editor: Gwenan Spearing
Development Editor: Gary Schwartz
Technical Reviewer: Thomas LaRock
Editorial Board: Steve Anglin, Mark Beckner, Gary Cornell, Louise Corrigan, Jim DeWolf, Jonathan Gennick, Jonathan Hassell, Robert Hutchinson, Michelle Lowman, James Markham, Susan McDermott, Matthew Moodie, Jeffrey Pepper, Douglas Pundick, Ben Renow-Clarke, Gwenan Spearing, Matt Wade, Steve Weiss
Coordinating Editor: Melissa Maldonado
Copy Editor: Tiffany Taylor
Compositor: SPi Global
Indexer: SPi Global
Artist: SPi Global

Distributed to the book trade worldwide by Springer Science+Business Media New York, 233 Spring Street, 6th Floor, New York, NY 10013. Phone 1-800-SPRINGER, fax (201) 348-4505, e-mail orders-ny@springer-sbm.com, or visit www.springeronline.com. Apress Media, LLC is a California LLC and the sole member (owner) is Springer Science + Business Media Finance Inc (SSBM Finance Inc). SSBM Finance Inc is a Delaware corporation.

For information on translations, please e-mail rights@apress.com, or visit www.apress.com.

Apress and friends of ED books may be purchased in bulk for academic, corporate, or promotional use. eBook versions and licenses are also available for most titles. For more information, reference our Special Bulk Sales–eBook Licensing web page at www.apress.com/bulk-sales.

Any source code or other supplementary material referenced by the author in this text is available to readers at www.apress.com. For detailed information about how to locate your book's source code, go to www.apress.com/source-code/.

Contents at a Glance

Contents

About the Authors

Marshall Copeland is a cloud solution architect at Microsoft with expertise in cyber security. His work is customer-facing, and in 2008 he began directly supporting US state and local government accounts architecting Microsoft's private cloud. He now focuses on Microsoft Azure Public Cloud, Government Cloud, and Hybrid Cloud for both Windows Server and Linux system workloads. Marshall's career also includes architecture consulting for many Fortune 500 companies supporting technologies such as Active Directory enterprise architecture, systems management, and Cisco network engineering. Marshall is completing his Masters of Science in Information Assurance (MSIA) degree in cyber security from Dakota State University. He has presented at Microsoft TechReady, Microsoft TechEd, and Microsoft Management Summit. Marshall co-wrote *Microsoft Azure: Planning, Deploying, and Managing Your Data Center in the Cloud* and *Microsoft Office 365 Administration Inside Out* first and second editions. When not working, Marshall and his wife enjoy spending time with family and friends in Colorado.

Julian Soh, a principal architect at Microsoft, works with customers to evaluate, understand, plan, and adopt cloud-based technologies, such as Microsoft Azure and Office 365. Prior to joining Microsoft, Julian spent many years in the IT industry, spanning the private, public, education, and defense sectors in both leadership and technical roles. At Microsoft, Julian previously covered productivity technologies, such as SharePoint, Lync (now Skype for Business), Office, and Windows. Julian is also an author for the *Microsoft Office 365 Administration Inside Out* series.

Anthony Puca is a Microsoft datacenter solution specialist. Anthony has been consulting with US state and local government accounts on Microsoft Windows Server, System Center, Private, Public, and Hybrid Cloud Technologies for the last five years. His IT career started 24 years ago as a mainframe librarian for American Express. Anthony has been a consultant for Perot Systems, Avanade, and EMC Corporation with responsibilities for enterprise architecture, system engineering, network engineering, and database administration. In the last eight years, he has presented at Microsoft TechReady, Microsoft TechEd, Microsoft Management Summit, Microsoft Security Summit, VMworld, and various CIO summits across the United States. Anthony co-wrote three MOF whitepapers on change, configuration, and release management. He also authored the SAMS/ Pearson book *Microsoft System Center Configuration Manager 2007 R2 Unleashed*, focusing on inventory management, software distribution, and operating system deployments; the O'Reilly book *Microsoft Office 365 Administration Inside Out*, and the Apress book *Microsoft Azure: Planning, Deploying, and Managing Your Data Center in the Cloud*. Anthony received Microsoft's Most Valuable Professional (MVP) seven times, from 2004–2010. These MVP awards were for datacenter monitoring with Microsoft's System Center Operations Manager and Windows Management Instrumentation. Anthony's customer demographics over the last decade include vehicle rental, retail, financial services, food processing, manufacturing, mining, healthcare, government, and energy.

Mike Manning in a Microsoft Certified Master in Exchange 2007 and Exchange 2010 with over four years of Office 365 deployment experience and two years of Microsoft Azure experience. Mike has been working in information technology for over 20 years, and he is very passionate about technology and the Microsoft cloud focus and direction. Mike's other interests outside of information technology include his family, hockey, and baseball.

David Gollob has over 30 years of experience working in database and analytics systems. After receiving his degree in math and computer science at the University of Denver, Dave worked as a principal consultant for numerous Fortune 100 companies, helping them to develop enterprise business solutions, highly scalable OLTP systems, and data warehouse and analytics systems. Dave's vendor tour started with Sybase, where he participated in two patents for his work at TCI Corporation focused on billing and distributed systems design. At Sybase, Dave also spent one-and-a-half years in Switzerland as the principal architect. In 1996, Dave joined Microsoft, where he remains today. Dave's work at Microsoft includes his delivery as both a principal consultant as well as a managing consultant, where he founded the Microsoft Telecom Practice. Dave has presented and participated in numerous industry events, panel discussions, Microsoft technical events, and product review and feedback cycles. Today, Dave travels the western states visiting state and local government customers, evangelizing and assisting with data (big and small) architecture planning, advanced analytics, and solutions design. Dave enjoys his time with his family as well as mountain biking, skiing, hiking, and fishing in Colorado.

About the Technical Reviewer

Thomas LaRock is a head geek at SolarWinds and a Microsoft Certified Master, SQL Server MVP, VMware vExpert, and Microsoft Certified Trainer. He has over 15 years' experience in the IT industry in roles including programmer, developer, analyst, and database administrator.

LaRock has worked in numerous IT roles over the past 15 years with much of his career focused on database administration, leading to his role as technical evangelist for Confio. While at Confio, his research and experience helped to create the initial versions of the software now known as SolarWinds Database Performance Analyzer.

LaRock joined the SolarWinds family through the acquisition of Confio in 2013. His many Microsoft accreditations include SQL Server MVP, MCSM, MCM, MCT, MCITP, MCTS, MCDBA, and MCP—whew!

LaRock is also president of the Professional Association for SQL Server (PASS) and is an avid blogger, author, and technical reviewer for numerous books about SQL Server management. He now focuses his time working with customers to help resolve problems and answer questions regarding database performance tuning and virtualization for SQL Server, Oracle, Sybase, and DB2, making it his mission to give IT and data professionals longer weekends.

Foreword

This team of authors do an excellent job of explaining Microsoft Azure and its many components and features. IT managers, IT architects, project managers, business analysts, and systems administrators can all benefit from the content included in this book. You will enjoy the book's logical flow and layout: it starts at a high level, helping you to understand the landscape, concepts, nomenclature, and moving parts of Azure, and then drills down into the ever-changing core services and features.

This book is like your own personal tour guide to Azure. Build and experiment with your own free Azure subscription as you follow along step by step, experimenting with the services as they are described to you in detail. This book consolidates information that would take you months to pull together and digest from disparate blogs and web sites and will accelerate your learning and help you to avoid pitfalls and blockers that might otherwise slow you down.

As a 10-year Microsoft Valued Professional (MVP) and CEO of a highly decorated Microsoft partner specializing in Azure, I can tell you that this book is a must-read for people involved in the transformation of their IT infrastructures. Knowledge is critical to making educated decisions, and the content in this book will provide you with an Ivy League education in Azure.

One of the other key differentiators in this book is its inclusion of government challenges, compliance requirements, and Azure-specific solutions. Those involved in governmental decision making or influence positions will find the information in this book particularly beneficial.

Open your mind as you pick up this book: it will help you understand multiple Azure features, scenarios, and services. It covers everything from Azure web applications to networking, VMs running in IaaS, Azure identity management, high availability, disaster recovery, migration options, and monitoring and reporting. This book is jam-packed with everything you need to know about Azure. Have fun on your journey!

—Rory McCaw, CEO, Infront Consulting Group, September 2015

Acknowledgments

I want to thank my wife, Angela Copeland, for putting up with all the late nights I spent working on this project in my "spare time." Thank you to my family—Bonnie, Anita, Andy, and Joe—and to Mark and Carla Hilley and Matthew and Elizabeth Jacobs for your support. A big thank you to the Apress team for all of their hard work and long hours. A special thank you to Gwenan Spearing for guiding us from idea to publication. Thank you Melissa Maldonado for keeping us on track and to Gay Schwartz and Thomas LaRock for excellent feedback and great insight to help make this a much better book.

I could not have completed a single page of this book without the support of Keith Olinger, my manager and a great person who supported me with many insightful conversations. Thank you to my fellow authors, Julian Soh, Anthony Puca, Mike Manning, and David Gollob. I am lucky to call you friends, and I could not have completed this book without your skill and dedication.

To Mark Russinovich, thank you for being a friend and for suggesting Microsoft Azure as a topic. I have great appreciation and respect for the amazing work completed by the Microsoft Azure Engineering team.

Thank you to an amazing and supportive account team: Tori Locke, Dean Iacovelli, Steve Finney, Able Cruz, Mark Wernet, Chris Wilch, Steve Kirchoff, Ben Callahan, David Stewart, Brent McCarthy, Tara Larson, and Steven Fiore.

—Marshall Copeland

Undertaking the writing of a book is a demanding but rewarding experience that extends far beyond an author's personal time. It requires the understanding and support of the important people in the author's life. As such, I would like to extend my heartfelt gratitude for the support of my wife Priscilla and daughters Jasmine and Makayla. The times they put up with my absence from family activities in order to complete this book represent a big sacrifice on their part. I would like to thank my dad, Soh Kim Wat, and my mom, Betty, for providing me the opportunity through education to be successful in my chosen career. I am also very grateful to have had the opportunity to continue to work with my co-authors Marshall Copeland, Anthony Puca, Michael Manning, and David Gollob. I am humbled by your professionalism and very thankful for your friendship and partnership. You are truly the best in the industry.

Last but not least, I want to extend my appreciation to the great folks at Microsoft for supporting and helping us with this project, especially Michael Donlan, Tori Locke, John Bunn, Javier Vasquez, Keith Olinger, Dean Iacovelli, Kelly Cooper, Peter Zalkind, Darren Carlsen, Steve Read, Jeff Langford, Scott Wold, Mark Ghazai, David Zarling, Tom Moen, and the extended Microsoft Azure team, Office 365 team, and Account Teams. Without your support and input, this project would not have been successful.

—Julian Soh

Writing a book requires a lot more time and effort than you might imagine. Although it's fairly easy to write about what you know, it's quite difficult to cover a topic like Azure that is so large and so broad. We frequently found ourselves thinking that we could write an entire book on what we cover in any single chapter. That level of effort to stay in lockstep with the Microsoft Azure Engineering Team and share what is available today and right around the corner was a large task. I would like to thank my beautiful wife Laura for her patience and for starting many dinners alone throughout my third book project. The compounding of life, work, and loved ones made the little free time I had that much more valuable.

Special thanks to the other authors: Marshall Copeland, Mike Manning, Julian Soh, and David Gollob. Without them, this book would not have been completed. Each one of them stepped up at various times to make sure we stayed on track and kept moving forward. Their unique insights into the various aspects of Microsoft Azure solutions provides an eloquent summary of some very complex technologies. I don't think anyone has ever said it, so thank you to Marshall for all the "Chapter Status?" e-mails to the team.

Working at Microsoft has exposed me to a large array of clients, the huge pool of challenges they face in their day-to-day business, and some of the brightest and most passionate IT professionals I have ever met. Thank you to Keith Olinger and his Datacenter Specialist team, a talented pool of individuals who continuously keep me and each other on our toes. Thank you to my Account Teams: Mark Starr, Nathan Beckham, Jed Zercher, Will Fahim, Elisa Yaros, Adam Loughran, Todd Strong, Bobby Bliven, and Nicole Deprey, and their manager, Kelly Cooper. This group keeps the customers' business needs and challenges in the foreground and reminds me of the value these things provide to the customers and public. Finally, a big thank you to Scott Wold for always being a resource I can count on to help me or our customers. Your assistance with many Azure-related items was very appreciated.

—Anthony Puca

When I first started working on this book, I didn't realize the time commitment I was taking on. A book project is equally challenging and rewarding. Anyone who has worked with the Microsoft Cloud technologies has seen the pace of change that is happening. The time and effort required to keep up with these rapid changes while continuing to meet regular work and family commitments can sometimes be overwhelming.

With that in mind, I would like to thank my wife, Arlene, and my children, Kevin and Nicole, for their understanding and support while I took time away from them to work on this book. Without their patience and support, I would not have been able to complete this project.

I would also like to thank my manager, Stanley Lum, for supporting me as I continued to meet my work commitments while working on this book. Finally, I would like to thank Anthony Puca, David Gollob, Julian Soh, and Marshall Copeland, my co-authors, for their efforts in writing, proofreading, fact-checking, and keeping us on track to complete this project.

—Mike Manning

I want to acknowledge and thank my authoring peers and friends Marshal Copeland, Anthony Puca, Julian Soh, and Mike Manning for inviting me to participate in writing this book. This is my first book, and I could not have asked for a better team to indoctrinate me and show me the ropes. Thanks to my good friend Mike Wilmot for his inspiration and critical thinking around machine-learning topics and business model strategies. I am humbled by the brilliant team of data scientists and engineers who design, develop, and continuously advance Azure machine learning. These people are tireless and incredibly passionate, truly representing the new Microsoft. If it wasn't for this team, led by Vice President Joseph Sirosh, we wouldn't have this game-changing platform. I want to thank my manager, Keith Bauer, for his unwavering support and for being an amazing sounding board. I want to thank and express deep gratitude to my brothers Steve and Ken, who always push the limits and challenge me to do the same. And, of course, thanks to my wife and kids for putting up with my late nights while I worked on this book.

—David Gollob

Introduction

Think about the first time you heard the term *cloud computing* a few years ago (or longer). There are accounts and reports as far back as 2006 of the term being used to describe some of the larger virtualization initiatives for companies like Google, Amazon, and Microsoft. If you search for more tangible evidence, you can find a report dated 1996 from the offices of Compaq Computer, where a group of technology executives who were intrigued by the future of Internet business published a report titled "Cloud Computing." Fast-forward 20 years into the future to learn about cloud computing services.

The discussions in this book should help you understand the need to improve your organization's maturity to support a formal cloud strategy that includes broad deployment options to support applications, infrastructure, and networking extensions. In addition to using cloud computing as another business-support initiative, corporations need to create new policies in support of cloud computing's greater security compliance to more easily enable line-of-business applications.

Thought leaders in many companies read the industry researcher reports from Gartner, Forrester, IDC, and others that show the growth from traditional datacenters to include cloud computing. They present different statistics and timelines, but they all agree that the IT industry and businesses are migrating to the cloud. Workloads drive business; and enterprise customers that review IT spending are realizing the technology efficiencies and automation of cloud-enablement.

Decision makers including CIOs, CTOs, and IT managers are using cloud-based IT to become agile and efficient in responding to business requests made by the CEOs and CFOs. Azure is a global cloud service; it is engineered to build on current IT skill sets using ITIL best practices in support of SMBs and enterprises with traditional constraints that prevent IT from achieving better alignment to the business. Cloud computing enables any size IT department to quickly respond with solutions for business to reach consumers with products and services in a global market.

What This Book Covers

This book provides deep insight into cloud services offered today by Microsoft Azure. It should help IT administrators, IT architects, business decision makers (BDMs), and small and large business leadership teams to quickly evaluate the cloud services available in Azure to improve their IT agility. In these chapters, you discover how this public cloud provider uses *commodity computing* to allow your business to extend into these readily available services.

This book is different than many books on cloud computing in that it follows two main themes: typical business problems that many companies face and that have cloud solutions, and step-by-step examples that help IT and technical team members to evaluate Azure services quickly. A few other publications provide insight into specific Azure topics, but this book provides a well-rounded understanding of a broad array of Azure cloud services to support you as you connect the dots to achieve IT agility.

Each section presents several key topics. These topics help you fully understand the Microsoft Azure services discussed and how to implement the features. This book is designed to assist you by using the following methods:

- Using a conversational style that helps to raise questions about features and answer those questions, including focused, step-by-step exercises to help you achieve deeper understanding

- Providing information with detailed explanations to help fill knowledge gaps as you continue to expand your learning about cloud computing

- Creating a foundation around cloud services that helps you move traditional IT to a cloud computing approach that provide solutions to "what if" scenarios

How to Use This Book

Although the book and the exercises in each chapter can be used independently, you are not required to read from beginning to end. The four parts group topics in a way that can make learning easier, but the exercises in the individual chapters stand as independent guides for you to follow.

The chapters of the book are organized into four sections. Part 1 is useful for anyone new to the Azure Cloud Services platform and is necessary reading if you want an overview of Azure's capabilities. The chapters are as follows:

1. "Microsoft Azure and Cloud Computing": Business discussions specific to growth today and tomorrow

2. "Overview of Microsoft Azure Services": A high-level look at Azure services and their value to both businesses and IT

3. "Azure Real-World Scenarios": How large and small businesses use Azure to solve problems for their companies and IT

4. "Planning Your Azure Deployment": Considerations for extending the traditional datacenter model to a cloud platform

Part 2 is a fast-moving section that provides a fast ramp-up for IT pros:

5. "Getting Started with Azure Web Apps": Easily building web sites while using features like auto-scaling (up and down)

6. "Getting Started with Azure Virtual Machines": Templates to use, including Linux, Windows, Oracle, SQL, MySQL, and your own customized versions

7. "Understanding Azure Storage and Databases": BLOB storage, how to create storage services, and how to secure access to these services

Part 3 bridges the gap between traditional datacenters and cloud services. You learn about the networking extensions needed to securely communicate with cloud properties:

8. "Extending Your Network with Azure": Virtual private networks that extend networks securely into Azure

9. "Identity Management with Azure Active Directory": How Azure Active Directory creates accounts, providing access for cloud services

10. "Extending Azure Active Directory": Controlling authentication from on-premises while allowing single sign-on for more than 2,500 cloud apps such as Salesforce, Google Apps, WebEx, and Twitter, and customizing your own applications

11. "Clusters, Regional VNets, High Availability, and Disaster Recovery": Features you can use to create solutions that are highly available while using Azure Site Recovery to back up VMware

12. "Migrating Your Virtual Machines to Azure": Using PowerShell to copy your VMs to Azure, convert VMDK to VHD, and create templates from your customized images

13. "Monitoring and Reporting": Azure services that provide real-time monitors for applications, services, and VMs with enterprise reporting features

Part 4 covers Azure services that may seem futuristic but give today's businesses analytic insight via the first cloud-based machine learning service. You develop the agility to use cloud-enabled Hadoop, to securely manage mobile devices while supporting partner collaboration through documents without the loss of intellectual property, and more:

14. "Microsoft Azure Machine Learning": Predictive cloud-based analytics using the R development language, Python, and drag-and-drop capabilities

15. "Data Management and BI with HDInsight": Hadoop services in Azure to scale in the support of volume, velocity, and verity of data

16. "Working with Intune and RMS": Azure services that support managing Apple, Android, and Microsoft mobile devices and tablets and use digital certificates to protect documents

Hardware and Software Requirements

The requirements to connect and use all Microsoft Azure cloud services from the Azure Portal are very broad, to better support the diversity of companies, IT administrators, network administrators, and developers. The Azure Portal can be accessed and managed through many supported browsers, including these:

- Safari (version 7 or the latest for best security)
- Chrome (latest version for best security)
- Firefox (latest version for best security)
- Edge (Windows 10 with the latest security updates)
- Internet Explorer (Version 11 or higher with the latest security updates)

The Azure Portal runs well on modern hardware for most PCs, Macs, and tablet devices. Although mobile phones and their browsers may connect, they currently are not supported by Microsoft Premier Services. The minimum PC hardware recommendations are as follows:

- Processor, 1GHz or faster
- 2GB RAM (4GB or more recommended for PC)
- 64GB hard disk (or higher for PC)
- Network connection (wired or wireless)

To complete some of the more advanced exercises, you are required to use a Microsoft Windows operating system (OS) that supports PowerShell 5.0 (or higher). PowerShell 5.0 is included in Windows 10 and can be installed as a free upgrade from Windows 8.1. An additional free Azure PowerShell module is required to complete all the advanced exercises.

▒ **Note** You can download and install Azure PowerShell using the Microsoft Web Platform Installer at `http://go.microsoft.com/fwlink/p/?linkid=320376&clcid=0x409`.

This book does not provide in-depth exercises that require Visual Studio Online, Visual Studio 2013, or Visual Studio 2015 for development. We encourage you to sign up for a free trial subscription or use your MSDN subscription for development and search Apress.com for Microsoft Azure development titles. The Azure APIs support a large number of development languages, including Java, Ruby, .NET, PHP, Node.js, and Python, just to name a few.

Who This Book Is For

The book's intended audience includes IT professionals such as IT administrators, IT architects, IT support staff, and business systems integration team members as well as TCP/IP networking professionals. The chapters are written to help novice IT admins ramp up, with feature discussions and expert guidance using specific exercises. The content supports an audience that includes business administrators or developers interested in enabling IT agility by extending your on-premises datacenter into cloud services. Our intended readers are interested in gaining deeper insight to add greater levels of service availability and investigate disaster recovery (DR) solutions for VMware and Hyper-V virtual environments, including enterprise DR for physical servers that need to support business continuity.

This book is also intended for business personnel responsible for IT budget planning and IT executives investigating ways to lower operating costs such as life-cycle hardware replacement, increasing datacenter power and cooling costs, and recurring costs for datacenter security audits. In addition, it's for anyone interested in Azure cloud computing—it is a great reference if you require more detail before you invest and begin integrating your business using Azure cloud services.

## PART I

Introducing Microsoft Azure

■ ■ ■

## CHAPTER 1

Microsoft Azure and Cloud Computing

What Is Microsoft Azure?

Microsoft Azure is an overarching brand name for Microsoft's cloud-computing services. It covers a broad, and still growing, range of services that often form the foundational elements of cloud computing.

If you are reading this book, chances are that you are an information technology (IT) professional and have some basic knowledge of Azure. This book was written for the IT professional interested in using cloud-computing services. Some of the topics that may interest you include lowering operating costs, increasing agility, developing better disaster recovery (DR) strategies, accessing unlimited storage, and foregoing responsibility for future hardware refreshes.

Although Azure is considered a fairly new cloud service, it has grown by leaps and bounds in terms of capabilities and offerings during its brief history. Azure is also so diverse that it is not uncommon for IT professionals to be familiar with only a specific subset of Azure services.

■ **Note**   Azure may seem to have a short history, but it should not be mistaken for a new or immature technology. Azure is based on mature Microsoft technologies such as Windows Server Hyper-V, Active Directory services, SQL Server, System Center, and so on.

The Azure/Office 365 Connection

Azure was introduced as Windows Azure in 2008. Prior to 2008, Microsoft primarily focused on another cloud service that was well known as Business Productivity Online Standard Suite (BPOS). BPOS consisted of Exchange 2007, Microsoft Office SharePoint Server 2007, Office Communications Online, and Microsoft Office Live Meeting. In 2011, Microsoft rebranded BPOS to Office 365. Office 365 is a software as a service (SaaS) offering that provides customers with access to Microsoft's top productivity tools without having to implement and maintain significant on-premises infrastructure. Office 365 delivers Exchange Online to provide turnkey e-mail services, SharePoint Online to provide collaboration capabilities, Lync Online for instant messaging (IM) and virtual meeting spaces, and Office Pro Plus for productivity tools for desktop and mobile users.

3

In order to provide SaaS capabilities for customers, Microsoft had to build datacenters to host the BPOS and then Office 365 productivity suite offerings. The datacenter infrastructure is provided and managed by a special team within Microsoft known as *Global Foundation Services (GFS)*. As a result, customers now have the option to use Microsoft's productivity and collaboration tools without the added complexity of managing them.

Other core benefits of Office 365 are its scalability, high availability, and associated service-level agreement (SLA). Providing these requires more datacenters, geo-redundancy (redundant services in different geographic regions), and a highly trained operational workforce. The investment made by Microsoft in GFS is beyond the means of many organizations. As a result, even small businesses can now enjoy enterprise-level SLAs and performance.

Anyone who has installed and configured Exchange, SharePoint, or Lync on-premises knows there are myriad required dependent technologies. Active Directory services for identity management is one such technology. To ensure that the services are performing well, monitoring tools such as System Center Operations Manager are required. To provide Office 365 subscribers with unlimited OneDrive for business storage space, a vast and comprehensive storage solution had to be adopted by GFS. Remember too that these services and benefits need to be cost competitive, so economies of scale and efficiency of operations are important topics that Microsoft and GFS continuously need to manage.

It is well known that the birth of cloud computing resulted from the realization that it is possible to monetize excess computing capabilities. What differentiates Azure is that it was built specifically to provide cloud services. It is not the result of excess computing capabilities that were designed for other purposes. It was designed from the ground up to support Office 365. Because other non-Office 365 services can take advantage of foundational services, such as Active Directory, Azure makes acquiring these services possible.

▓ **Note**   The scalability, elasticity, and reliability of Office 365 SaaS is highly dependent on the Azure infrastructure.

IaaS, PaaS, and SaaS

We have identified Microsoft Office 365 as a SaaS. Other types of cloud services are classified as *infrastructure as a service (IaaS)* or *platform as a service (PaaS)*.

Because Azure provides computing power for Office 365 foundational services, such as Active Directory, it is easy to identify the IaaS nature of Azure. In fact, Azure is most recognized for its IaaS offering. Examples of Azure IaaS offerings include Azure virtual machines and virtual networks, Azure storage solutions, and Azure recovery services. However, Azure is most often mistaken to be only an IaaS, when in fact it has a large portfolio of PaaS offerings. Examples of its PaaS offerings include Azure SQL Database, Azure websites, Azure Content Delivery Network (CDN), Azure BizTalk Services, and Azure Mobile Services.

As you can see, the Azure portfolio of services is much more significant than better-known Office 365 SaaS offering. Subsequent chapters cover key Azure services. For now, the important takeaway is that, as far as cloud computing goes, Microsoft has demonstrated that it is betting its future as a cloud-computing services provider. No other technology company has the *combination* of mature technologies, infrastructure, and financial commitment to package a complete SaaS, IaaS, and PaaS offering. In fact, with the changing of the guard in Microsoft's corner office, CEO Satya Nadella has made cloud computing part of the company's mission—mobile first, cloud first. It also helps that Mr. Nadella was the executive responsible for inventing and developing the Azure business.

When Microsoft reported its earnings for the quarter ending September 2014, cloud-computing services grew by 128% over the previous year, and they contributed to the bulk of the company's $14.93 billion in revenue.

These developments are important if you are shopping for an IT partner to provide cloud-computing services, because you are handing off a very important piece of your IT operations. Knowing that a company has built its comprehensive cloud-computing services from the ground up and that it has a strong financial portfolio, has leadership committed to the service, and is an industry leader should buoy the confidence of any CIO making this decision.

Security, Compliance, and Privacy

As a service offering, Azure is a follow-up act to Microsoft Office 365. This is important because Microsoft implemented many industry-required security standards and regulatory compliance requirements when building the Office 365 business. Furthermore, through Office 365 operations, Microsoft has built a cloud-specific, service-oriented organization to address operational requirements including sales and licensing, incident management, and customer support.

For Office 365, Microsoft introduced the concept of a *Trust Center*. A Trust Center is Microsoft's one-stop shop on the Web for all things related to security, compliance, certifications, SLA metrics, and privacy. It is basically everything a customer needs in order to trust a service. Therefore, like Office 365, there is a Trust Center for the Azure cloud service, known simply as the *Microsoft Azure Trust Center* (http://azure.microsoft.com/en-us/support/trust-center). Figure 1-1 shows the Microsoft Azure Trust Center.

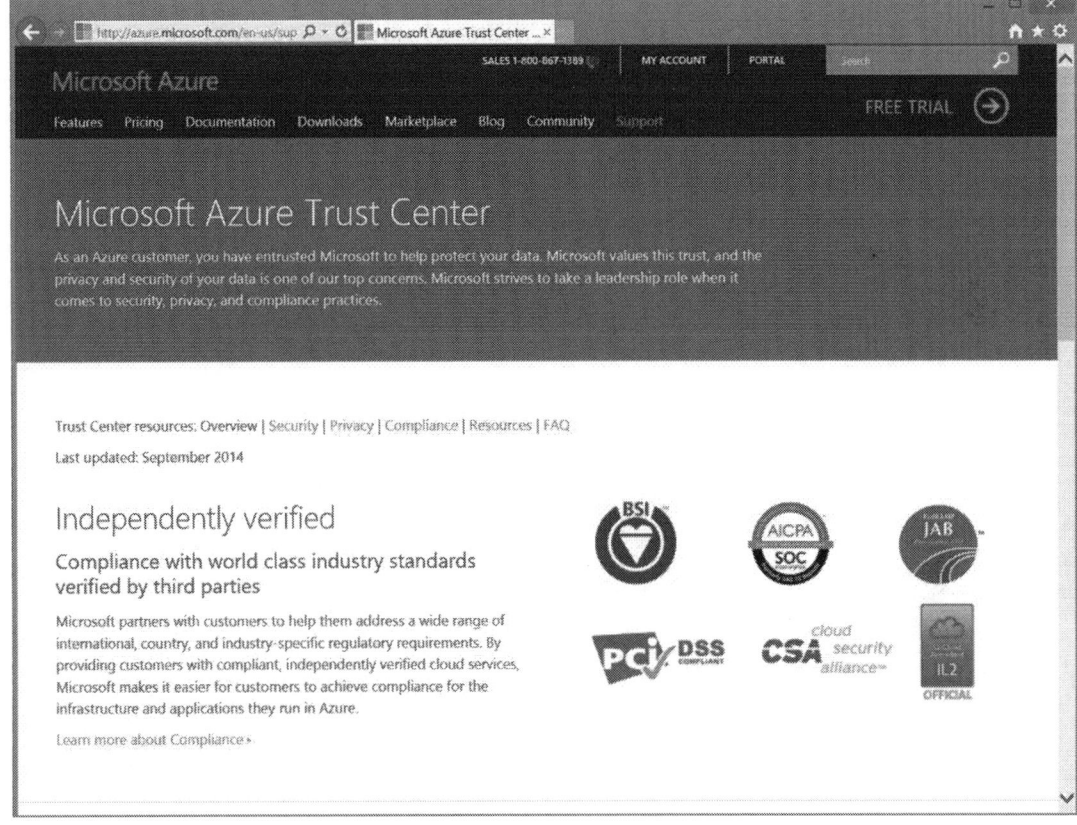

Figure 1-1. *Microsoft Azure Trust Center*

> ■ **Note**   The Microsoft Azure Trust Center is a one-stop shop for everything related to security, compliance, trust, and privacy. It is located at http://azure.microsoft.com/en-us/support/trust-center.

Addressing Security

Microsoft adopted a multipronged approach when it comes to addressing security in the Azure platform. In addition to standard 24×7 monitoring of the service, other core elements of the approach are discussed in the following subsections.

Using Existing Resources across the Organization

Instead of reinventing the wheel, Microsoft used and enhanced existing resources to secure Azure. By relying on the combined experiences of the **Digital Crimes Unit** , the Malware Protection Center, and Microsoft Research, and with visibility to security threats on a global scale through services such as Windows Update, Xbox Live, and Office 365, Microsoft is in a great position to have early knowledge to address threats. Microsoft has also proven to be relentless in prosecuting hackers and shutting down rogue hosting providers.

Adhering to an Evolving Security Development Life Cycle

Microsoft aggressively patches its cloud-computing platform and has been following a disciplined Security Development Life Cycle (SDL) that was introduced in 2004 to develop more secure code. Because Microsoft is the developer of nearly the entire technology stack, from the Hypervisor on up, the company is in the best position to be agile in making code changes. Microsoft engineers have been trained to adopt an "assume a breach" mindset and to address potential issues aggressively.

Machine Learning

One of the most interesting approaches to security is Microsoft's use of machine learning (ML). Machine learning is based on complex algorithms developed by Microsoft Research, and it serves three purposes:

- It is used as the technology that drives consumer services like Xbox, Bing, and Cortana.

- As an Azure service, it allows customers to use it to mine data.

- It is used as the technology that mines data and logs to identify threats.

Microsoft also uses rules to trigger suspicious activities. For example, if a user logs in successfully from Singapore and then attempts to log in from Seattle a few minutes later, this triggers a security event. Even though this could technically be accomplished via remote access, the security event is still triggered because of the "assume a breach" mentality.

Previewing New Security Features

Another practice adopted by Microsoft is involvement of the user community. This began with the early preview program for the Windows desktop OS, much like the Windows 10 preview program in place at the time of this writing. This practice has been extended to the introduction of new features in the Azure platform, including those related to security. Figure 1-2 shows new security features being previewed in Azure Active Directory at the time of this writing.

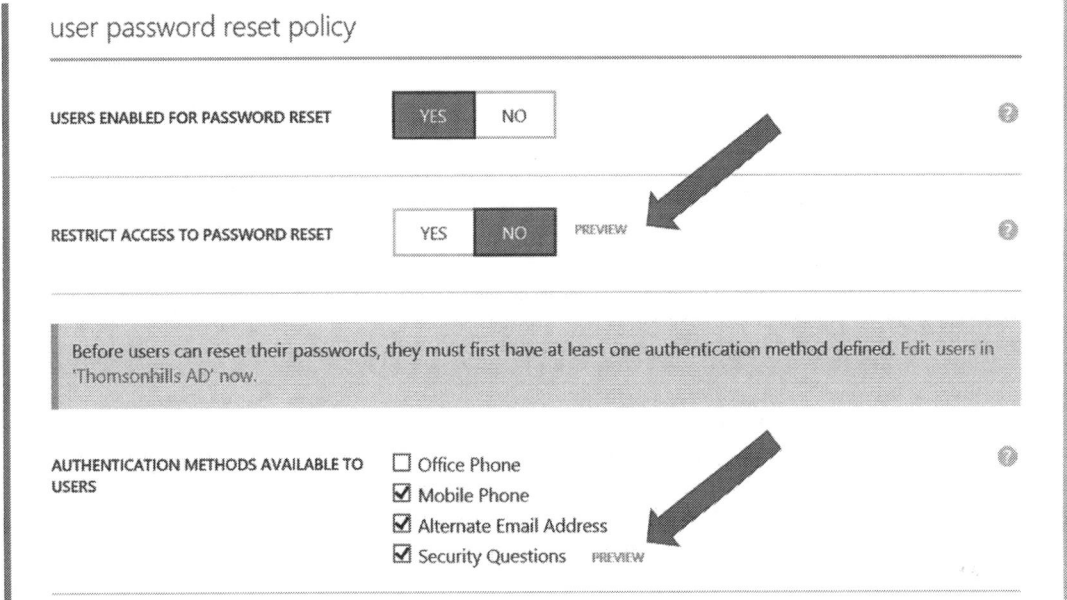

Figure 1-2. *Preview of new user password security features in Azure Active Directory Premium*

Penetration Testing

Penetration testing is a standard part of any robust security program. As part of standard operations, Microsoft conducts regular penetration tests against the Azure platform. Moreover, the program goes a step further by incorporating a *white hat* feature that allows customers to conduct their own penetration testing. Customers are required to agree to the terms of penetration testing, submit a request form, and receive approval before conducting such tests. The terms and the request form can be found on the Microsoft Azure Trust Center or at `https://security-forms.azure.com/penetration-testing/terms`.

Certifications and Industry Standards

Azure is also built to meet industry standards for IT and specifically for cloud-computing services. Industry-recognized certifications have been obtained for Azure, including the following:

- ISO 27001/27002

- SOC 1/SSAE 16/ISAE 3402 and SOC 2

- Cloud Security Alliance CCM

- PCI DSS Level 1

Azure is also certified by international standards because it is a global service. Examples of international certifications for Azure include the following:

- United Kingdom G-Cloud

- Australian IRAP

- Singapore MTCS

- EU Model Clauses

Prominent industry-specific certifications are also applicable to Azure, such as these:

- HIPAA

- Food and Drug Administration 21 CFR Part 11

- FERPA

The full list of certifications for the Azure platform is located at the Microsoft Azure Trust Center: http://azure.microsoft.com/en-us/support/trust-center/compliance.

Certifications govern the suitability of Azure for specific industry use, and they form the basis of customer trust. Third-party auditors, who are recognized by the certification bodies, independently verify each certification. There is also a requirement for recertification and periodic audits to ensure compliance with all certifications.

Microsoft is a member of the advisory committees of many of the certification bodies, and it provides feedback and recommendations on proposed changes. This allows Microsoft to have visibility into many upcoming changes in order to incorporate them into the Azure platform in a timely manner.

Microsoft Azure Government

Shortly after Office 365 debuted, Microsoft realized that there are specific requirements unique to government entities. This was initially most applicable to the United States federal government and extends to US state and local governments that interact and share data with the federal government. As such, the concept of a US government-only cloud was conceived, which led to the release of the Office 365 Government Community Cloud (GCC). Customers under the Office 365 GCC model must be US federal, state, or local government entities. Today, there are separate GCCs for non-US governments.

Like Office 365, Azure was initially released as a public cloud platform; but in October 2014, Microsoft Azure Government, which is the government edition equivalent to the GCC, was soft-launched for a select number of early government customers. On December 9, 2014, Microsoft publicly announced the general availability of Azure Government. It is considered a rolling deployment, and although not all capabilities and services in Azure are available in Azure Government, there is a roadmap to identify when a capability becomes available.

For more information about Azure Government, check out http://azure.microsoft.com/en-us/features/gov/.

Azure Government is significantly different from other cloud services providers because it specifically addresses technical and mandatory regulatory requirements, such as

- FedRAMP

- FISMA

- FBI Criminal Justice Information Systems (CJIS)

Often, these government-specific requirements make it difficult for cloud services providers to scale up. They may also make it riskier for cloud services providers because of special SLAs and compliance requirements that can cause providers to be penalized for noncompliance. For example, the FBI CJIS standard requires that the cloud service provider's personnel be background-checked and fingerprinted. At the time of this writing, Azure Government is the only major service that can meet all the requirements in FBI CJIS.

▓ **Note**   Standards such as CJIS apply to all customers using Azure Government. Therefore, even if a government entity using Azure Government does not require Microsoft personnel to be background-checked and fingerprinted, the same personnel would be responsible for the service, and therefore the government customer would default to this higher standard requirement.

Privacy

Microsoft strongly believes in customer privacy and that content in Azure belongs to the customer. Microsoft draws a clear line separating consumer services from enterprise services, with Azure falling in the latter category where no customer data is mined, sold, or shared with marketers or third-party partners.

Microsoft also promotes privacy by making sure it is transparent about how information is managed. For example, Microsoft published a white paper entitled "Protecting Data and Privacy in the Cloud" to explain how it handles privacy as it relates to cloud-computing services. Microsoft also publishes its datacenter regions, and it goes into detail regarding if, when, and how data is transferred between regions.

When it comes to privacy, the European Union (EU) has the most stringent requirements to govern the handling of personal data, as extensively covered under the EU Data Protection Directive (95/46/EC). Microsoft adheres to the US-EU Safe Harbor certification, which allows data to be transferred outside of the EU to Microsoft for processing purposes.

The Microsoft Azure Trust Center has a section on privacy at
http://azure.microsoft.com/en-us/support/trust-center/privacy.

▓ **Note**   You can download t he "Privacy in the Cloud" whitepaper from
http://go.microsoft.com/?linkid=9694913&clcid=0x409.

It is a good practice to search the Microsoft Azure Trust Center and set a favorite for the important information you find. This simple approach has been one of the best practices adopted by Microsoft, and it helps to provide answers quickly to many of the questions that contribute to the uncertainty of adopting a cloud-computing service.

Why Microsoft Azure?

Now that you have a basic understanding of Azure and a sense of how it meets security, regulatory compliance, and privacy requirements, the next question is, "Why Microsoft Azure?"

The bigger question, though, is "Why cloud computing?" The promise of cloud computing, regardless of whether it is of the SaaS, IaaS, or PaaS variety, is the ability to use economies of scale to drive down the costs associated with IT operations. It also allows any organization to achieve a high degree of availability and resiliency at a truly geo-redundant level.

Furthermore, the highly elastic nature of cloud computing provides customers with the ability not only to scale up in real time, but also to scale down when services are not needed, ultimately paying only for utilization. Acquiring hardware and software in the traditional way meant being able to meet peak utilization, if scoped correctly, but it also led to idle usage most of the time.

Cloud computing provides all the attributes to maximize the efficiency of IT operations from a financial standpoint as well as from a service-delivery standpoint. Azure possesses all of these attributes, with the added benefit of being fully integrated into the Office 365 SaaS offering, thereby making Microsoft one of the most comprehensive providers of cloud-computing services.

The Azure Portal

The Azure Portal, or simply the Portal, is the web management interface for all Azure resources. At the time` of this writing, the web address of the Portal is `https://manage.windowsazure.com`. You see the Portal referenced extensively in this book, because this is how you manage Azure.

■ **Note** At the time of this writing, the Portal is also undergoing an update and a new Portal is being previewed. You can access the new Portal at `http://portal.azure.com`. Where possible, this book references the new Portal.

How Azure Is Licensed

Before embarking on a discussion of licensing, you need to become familiar with two Azure terms: *Azure account* and *Azure subscription*. These are the logical containers that differentiate one customer from another.

Azure Accounts

As the name implies, an Azure account is the first step to acquiring Azure services. The Azure account requires a unique identity known as the *Microsoft Azure account name*. This name uniquely identifies a particular customer, and there is usually a one-to-one relationship between the customer entity and the account name.

There are three ways to set up an Azure account:

- By creating a new Microsoft account or use an existing Microsoft account

- Via an Enterprise Agreement (EA)

- Via an existing Office 365 tenant

Creating an Azure Account

You can use a Microsoft account, formerly known as a Microsoft Live ID, to create a new Azure account. Follow these steps to sign up for an Azure account with a Microsoft account. We assume that you already have a Microsoft account or know how to sign up for one, so we do not go through those steps here.

■ **Note** You can sign up for a Microsoft account by visiting `https://signup.live.com/signup.aspx`.

SIGNING UP FOR AZURE WITH A MICROSOFT ACCOUNT

This exercise walks you through the process of setting up a new Azure account:

1. Go to `https://account.windowsazure.com/signup`.

2. Sign in with a Microsoft account.

3. Sign up for the free 30-day trial. Figure 1-3 shows the Sign Up form, which requires a credit card for verification purposes only. You use the same credit card to pay for Azure after the trial.

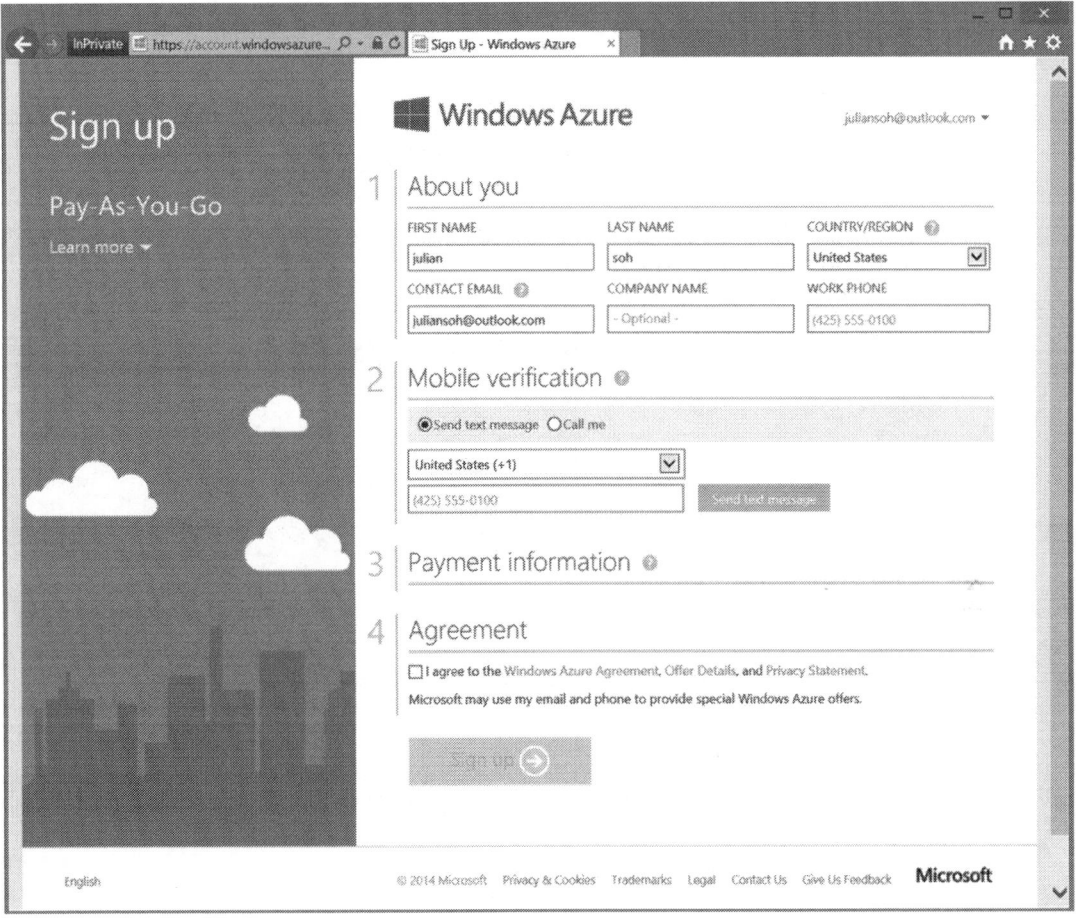

Figure 1-3. Windows Azure pay-as-you-go 30-day free trial signup

4. After you enter a phone number for mobile verification, click Send Text Message.

5. Enter the verification code, and click Verify Code.

6. Once the code is verified, you are prompted for a credit card number for verification purposes.

7. After the credit card number has been verified, click the check-mark button to create the Azure account.

Once you have an Azure account, you can add a subscription. You go through the process of adding a subscription later in this chapter.

Going through the previous steps creates a unique Azure account name. You can determine the Azure account name by following the steps in the next exercise.

DETERMINING YOUR AZURE ACCOUNT NAME

This exercise walks you through the process of determining your Azure account name:

1. Log in to the Azure Portal at `http://manage.windowsazure.com` if you are not already logged in.

2. In the menu on the left, scroll down and select Active Director, as shown in Figure 1-4.

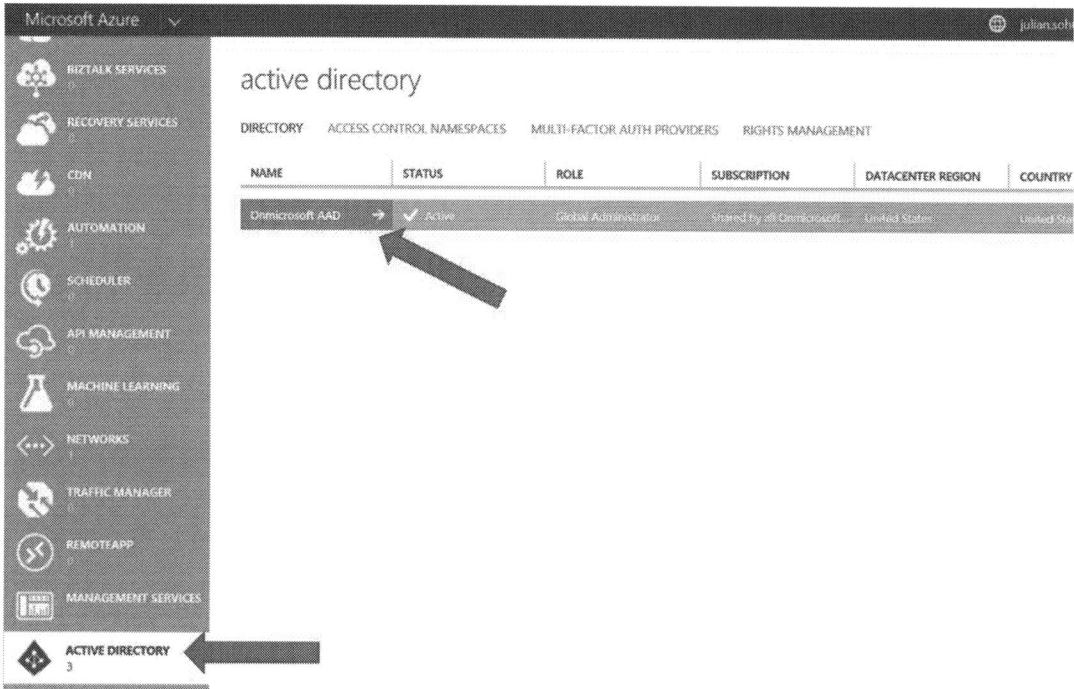

Figure 1-4. *The Active Directory menu option in the Azure Portal*

3. A single default directory should be listed, as shown in Figure 1-4. Click the arrow next to the directory's name.

4. Click Domains on the top menu, as shown in Figure 1-5.

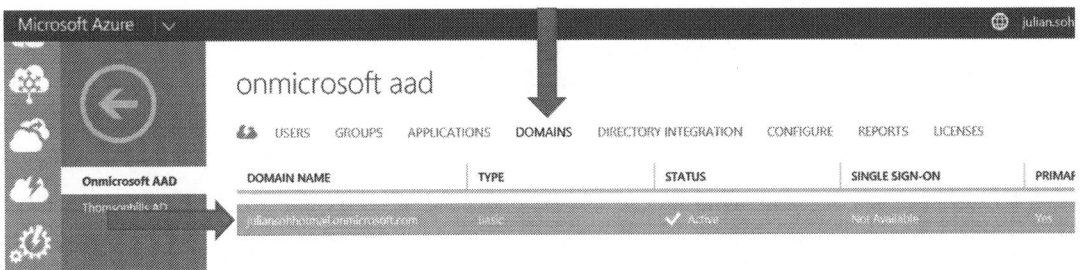

Figure 1-5. *Finding your Azure account name in the Portal*

5. As you can see in Figure 1-5, the Domain Name column shows your Azure account name, which has a `.onmicrosoft.com` extension: for example, `myazureaccount.onmicrosoft.com`.

Take note of your Azure account name, because you need to reference it whenever you interact with Microsoft or a Microsoft Certified Cloud Partner.

If instead of using a Microsoft account your organization purchases Azure through an Enterprise Agreement, your Microsoft account team will help you sign up for an Azure account.

If your organization already has an Office 365 subscription, you can create an Azure account based on the same tenant name as your Office 365 subscription. Follow the steps in the next exercise to create an Azure account based on an existing Office 365 tenant.

CREATING AN AZURE ACCOUNT FROM AN EXISTING OFFICE 365 TENANT

This exercise walks you through the process of activating an Azure account from an existing Office 365 tenant:

1. Go to `https://account.windowsazure.com/signup`.

2. Click Sign In With Your Organizational Account, as shown in Figure 1-6.

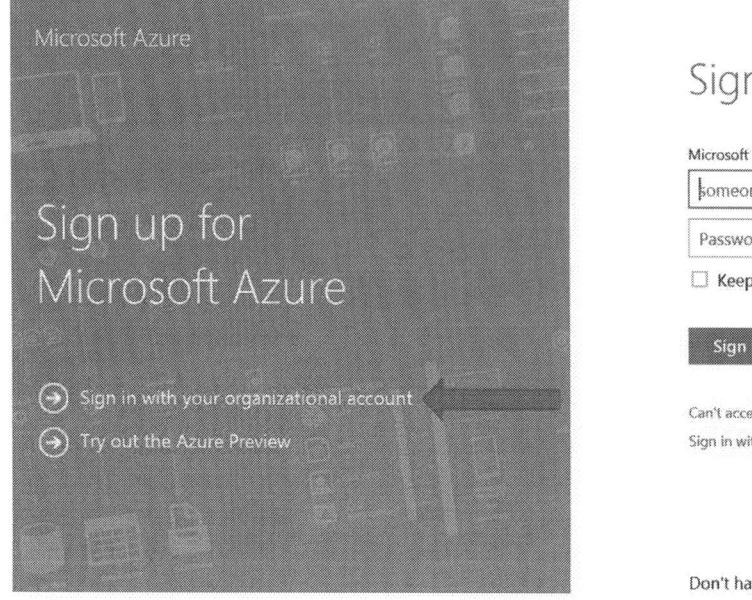

Figure 1-6. *Signing up for Azure with an organizational account*

3. Log in with your Office 365 tenant administrator account.

4. An Azure account is associated with your Office 365 tenant; the Azure account name is the same as your Office 365 tenant name. You are then prompted to add a subscription, as shown in Figure 1-7. Click Sign Up for Windows Azure.

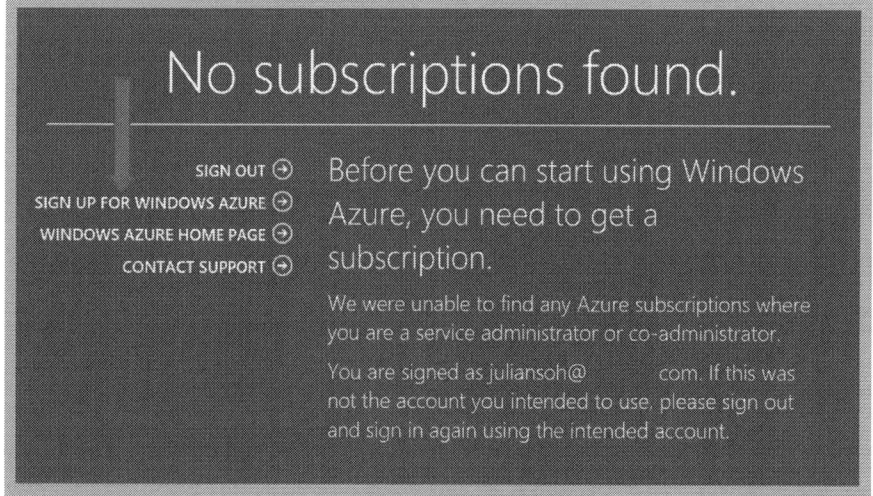

Figure 1-7. *Adding a subscription to a new Azure account*

5. You are prompted to select a subscription, as shown in Figure 1-8. Select a subscription type, and follow the instructions to purchase the subscription. Upon completion, the subscription is added to your Azure account. Take note of the different types of subscriptions.

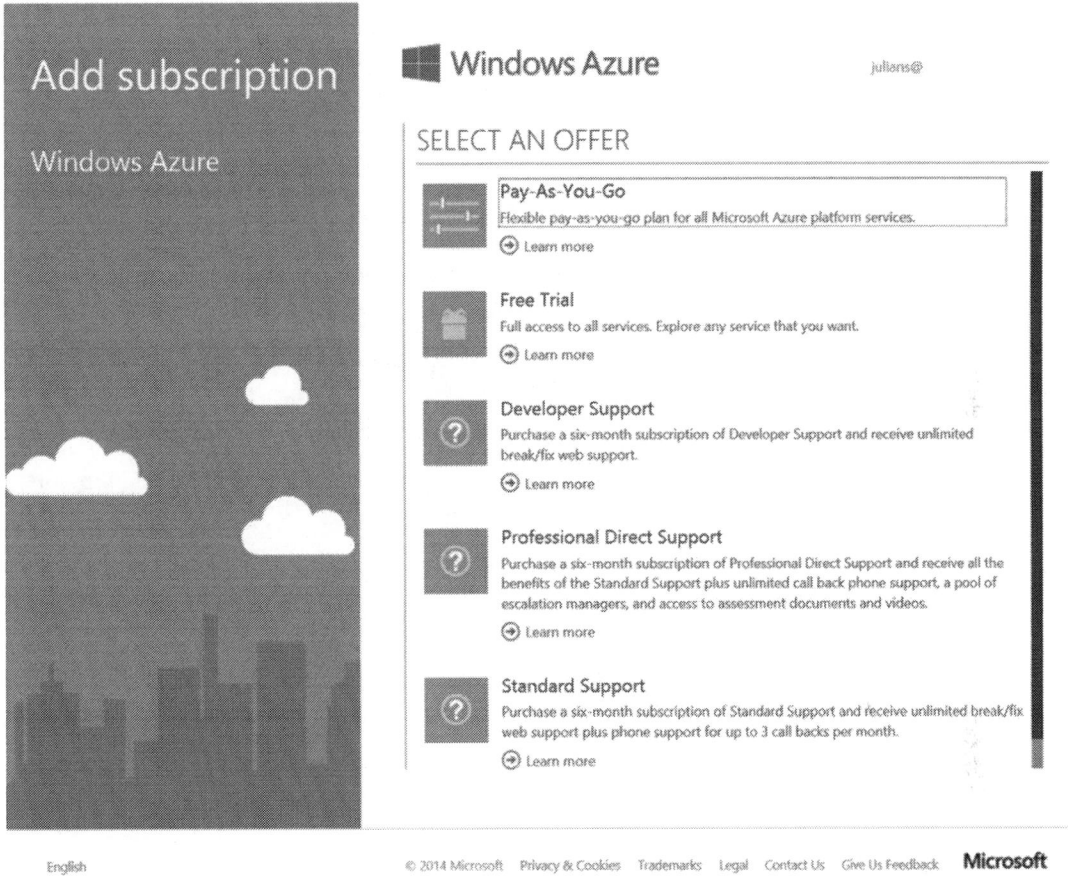

Figure 1-8. *List of available types of Azure subscriptions*

Azure Subscriptions

We just walked you through the process of adding a subscription in the previous section. Once you have an Azure account, you need to add one or more Azure subscriptions to the account.

■ **Note**   One Azure account can have multiple Azure subscriptions associated with it.

As mentioned earlier, Azure is a collection of many cloud-computing services. As such, each service may have its own licensing and utilization model. For the services covered in the following chapters, a section addresses licensing issues and costs specific to that Azure service. However, as an introduction, it is sufficient to know that there are primarily three types of utilization models in Azure:

- Azure pay-as-you-go via credit card

- Azure monetary commitment

- Azure Client Access Licenses (CALs)

Depending on the type of Azure service, one or more of these models will be applicable.

An *Azure subscription* is the primary consumption vehicle for Azure services, which are charged based on utilization. An example of Azure utilization is Azure virtual machines (VMs). Azure VMs are charged based on uptime. Another example of an Azure service that is billed based on use is storage.

The pay-as-you-go option via credit card, as the name implies, allows services such as Azure VMs to be charged to a credit card on a monthly basis. When you create Azure VMs, you can pick the specific Azure subscription against which such use is billed. You see this throughout the book as you create different Azure services.

Azure monetary commitment is designed for large enterprises to pay for Azure services on an annual basis. This is usually tied to an EA, which is also renewable on an annual basis. Such an organization estimates its use for the year and pays that amount as part of the EA renewal. Once a monetary commitment subscription has been created, Azure services can start drawing down from that subscription amount. Azure monitors daily consumption trends to determine whether there are enough funds in a monetary commitment subscription to last until the annual renewal date. If not, the global and billing administrators are notified, and the organization can add funds to the Microsoft subscription. This simplifies billing and facilitates budget planning and allocation for enterprises.

However, not all Azure services are based on consumption. Some Azure services are based on traditional server licensing or CALs. Examples of Azure services that rely on the CAL model are Azure Active Directory (AAD) Premium and the Enterprise Mobility Suite (EMS). To use such services, a customer pays only for the required licenses. All Azure license-based services are subscriptions, and they are usually priced per user or instance per month. Later chapters cover services such as AAD Premium and EMS.

Multiple Azure Subscriptions

Azure's ability to support multiple subscriptions per Azure account makes it easier to do separate billing. This is especially useful in bill-back scenarios.

SETTING UP MULTIPLE AZURE SUBSCRIPTIONS

This exercise is based on a scenario in which an organization wants to create multiple Azure subscriptions. You are the IT Director for ThomsonHills Inc., and your staff has just created an Azure account. The company is interested in adopting Azure for cloud-computing services rather than refreshing the on-premises datacenter. You are responsible for providing IT services in the form of application servers that support line-of-business (LOB) applications to different departments. Each department has its own operating budget and needs to pay for the IT services rendered to it. You need to manage each department's IT expenditure separately. For starters, you need to on-board the Human Resources department and the Marketing department to Azure:

1. Log in to your Azure Portal at `https://manage.windowsazure.com`.

2. Click your login name in the top-right corner, and select View My Bill from the drop-down menu, as shown in Figure 1-9.

Figure 1-9. *Viewing your bill from the Azure Portal*

3. On the Account page, on the Subscriptions tab, you see all the Azure subscriptions associated with the Azure account. Click the Add Subscription option, as shown in Figure 1-10.

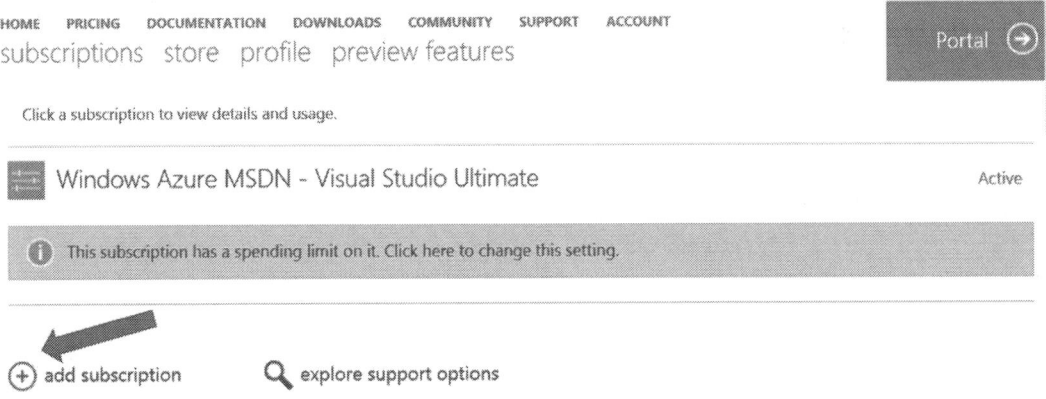

Figure 1-10. *Adding an Azure subscription*

4. On the next screen, select a pay-as-you-go subscription, and follow the instructions to add it to the Azure account.

5. Repeat steps 3 and 4 to add another pay-as-you-go subscription. After you are done, you should see two pay-as-you-go subscriptions on the Account page, similar to what is shown in Figure 1-11.

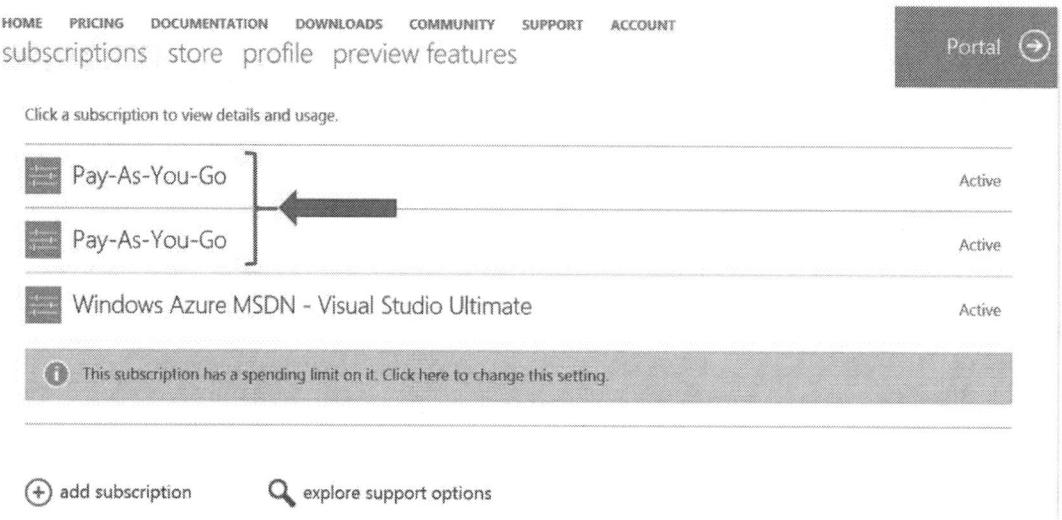

Figure 1-11. Multiple Azure subscriptions in one Azure account

6. Select the first pay-as-you-go subscription.

7. On the details page for the Azure subscription, take note of the available information and options, and then click Edit Subscription Details, as shown in Figure 1-12.

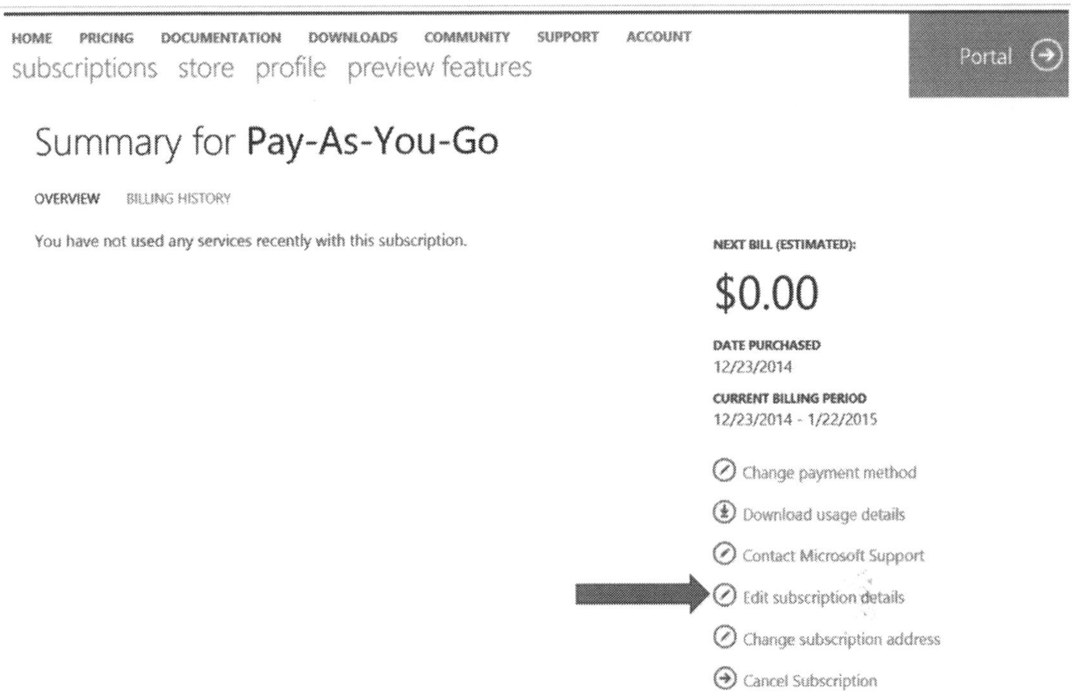

HOME   PRICING   DOCUMENTATION   DOWNLOADS   COMMUNITY   SUPPORT   ACCOUNT

subscriptions store profile preview features

Portal →

Summary for **Pay-As-You-Go**

OVERVIEW   BILLING HISTORY

You have not used any services recently with this subscription.

NEXT BILL (ESTIMATED):

$0.00

DATE PURCHASED
12/23/2014

CURRENT BILLING PERIOD
12/23/2014 - 1/22/2015

⊘ Change payment method

⊕ Download usage details

⊘ Contact Microsoft Support

⊘ Edit subscription details

⊘ Change subscription address

→ Cancel Subscription

Figure 1-12. *Editing Azure subscription details*

8. Type **Human Resources Consumption (Pay-As-You-Go method)** in the
   Subscription Name box, as shown in Figure 1-13, and then click the check-mark
   button.

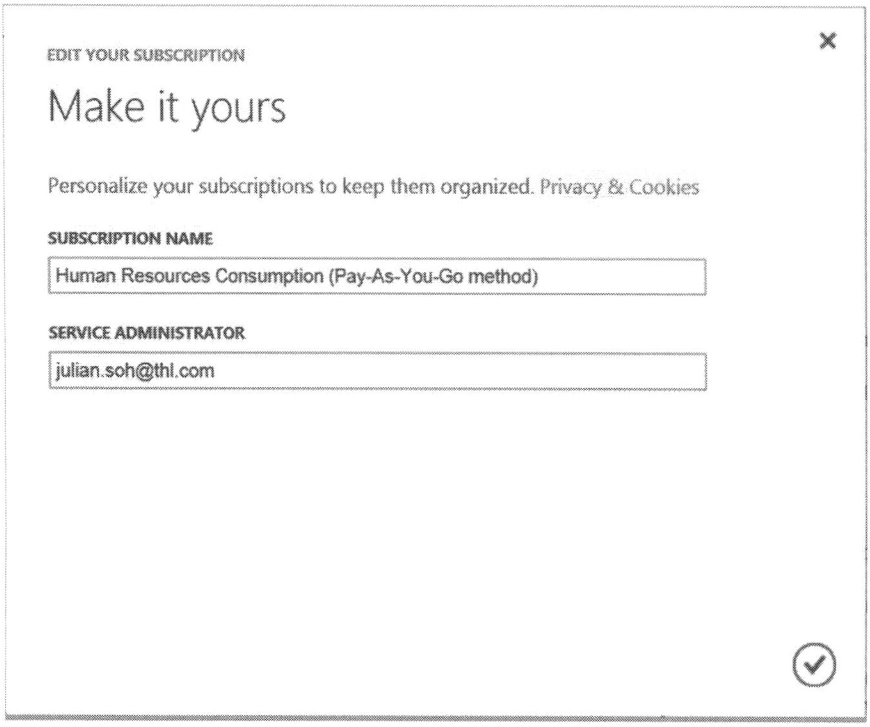

EDIT YOUR SUBSCRIPTION

Make it yours

Personalize your subscriptions to keep them organized. Privacy & Cookies

SUBSCRIPTION NAME

Human Resources Consumption (Pay-As-You-Go method)

SERVICE ADMINISTRATOR

julian.soh@thl.com

Figure 1-13. *Changing the subscription name*

9. Repeat steps 6–8 for the second pay-as-you-go subscription, and name it **Marketing Department (Pay-As-You-Go method)**.

10. When you are done, you should see two different subscriptions against which Azure services can consume. Thanks to the subscription name changes, you can easily identify which subscription to use when creating Azure resources. Your screen should look similar to Figure 1-14.

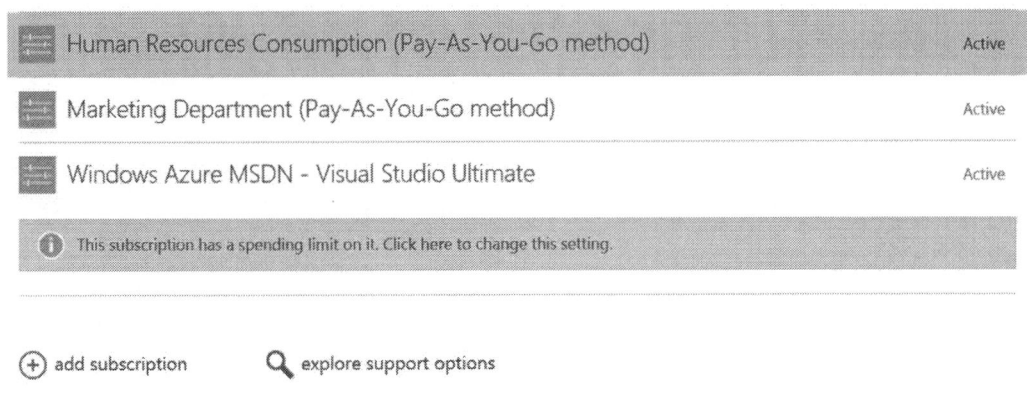

Figure 1-14. Renamed Azure subscription descriptions

This exercise demonstrated a scenario that warrants multiple Azure subscriptions. It also showed you how to add such subscriptions and rename them for easy identification.

■ **Note**   Consider putting the billing method as part of the Azure subscription's description, as shown in the exercise. This enables you not only to identify the subscription, but also to know how the subscription is being funded.

When you have multiple Azure subscriptions in your Azure account and have created different Azure resources that consume against their respective subscriptions, you can use the subscription filter to display only the resources associated with any of the subscriptions. The subscription filter is located in your Azure Portal, as shown in Figure 1-15.

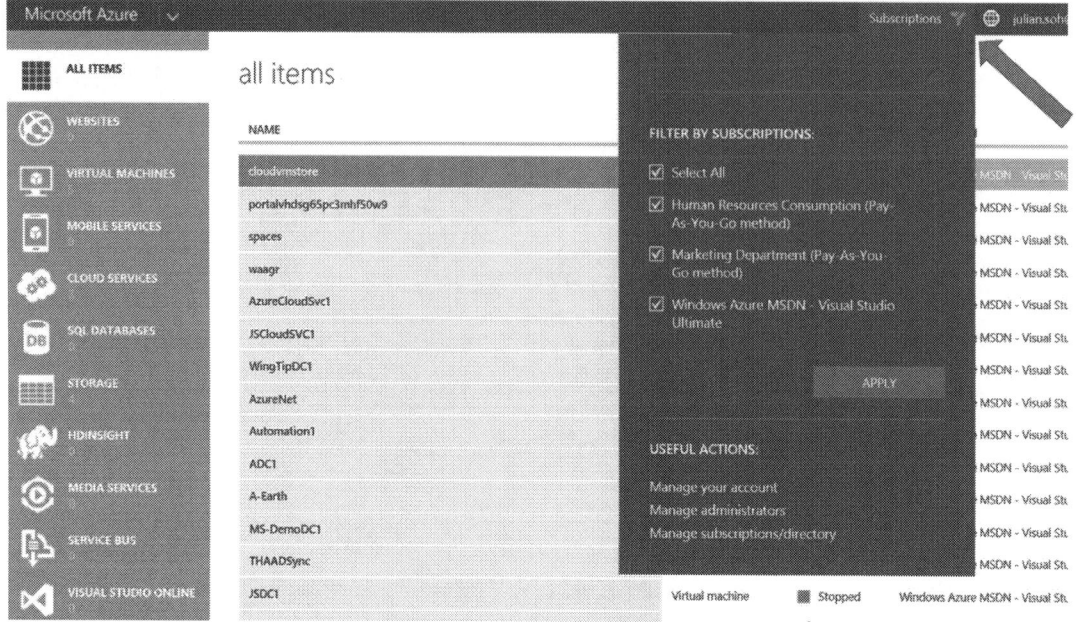

Figure 1-15. *The subscription filter in the Portal*

Scoping Azure

Now that you understand the concept of Azure accounts and subscriptions and have worked through the exercises to create them, it is time to determine how many Azure resources you consume. Under the pay-as-you-go model, you want to forecast your charges. Under the monetary commitment model, you need to know how much to commit for the upcoming year. Therefore, you need a way to come up with an estimate.

If you are an Enterprise customer and have a Microsoft account team, you can work with the account team to come up with that estimate. If you do not have an account team assigned to your organization, you can work with a Microsoft Certified Cloud Services partner or use the Azure Pricing Calculator.

Accessing the Azure Pricing Calculator

The Azure Pricing Calculator is located at: `http://azure.microsoft.com/en-us/pricing/calculator`. You can also access it from the Portal by following these steps:

1. Log in to the Portal at `https://manage.windowsazure.com`.

2. Expand the Microsoft Azure menu by clicking the chevron next to the Microsoft Azure logo at top left, as shown in Figure 1-16.

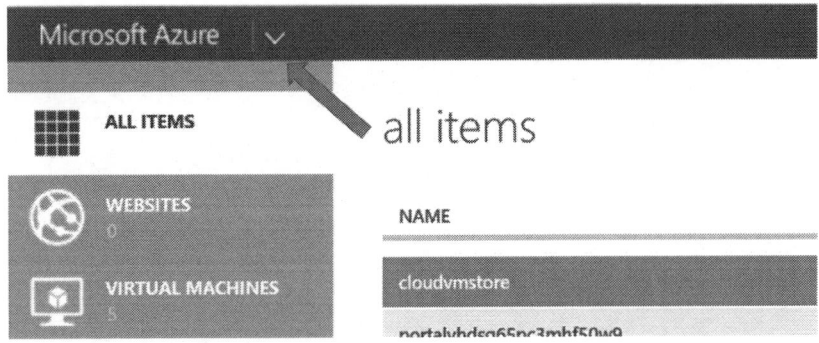

Figure 1-16. *Expanding the Microsoft Azure menu*

3. Select Pricing from the expanded menu, as shown in Figure 1-17.

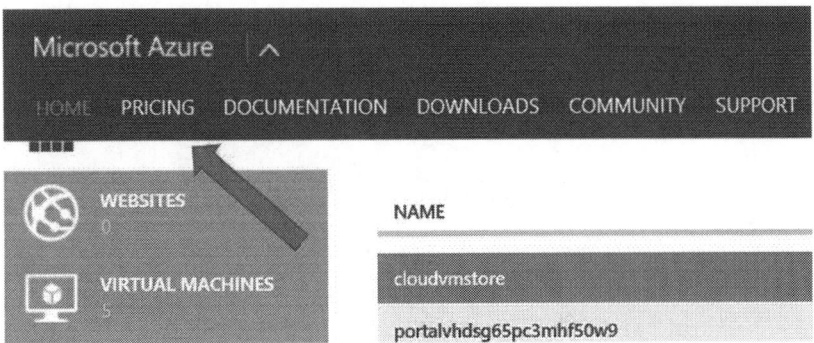

Figure 1-17. *Select Pricing from the expanded menu*

Using the Azure Pricing Calculator

The Azure Pricing Calculator is intuitive and easy to use. You can select from the different Azure service categories, such as web sites, VMs, storage, and so on, along the top. Figure 1-18 shows the Azure Pricing Calculator.

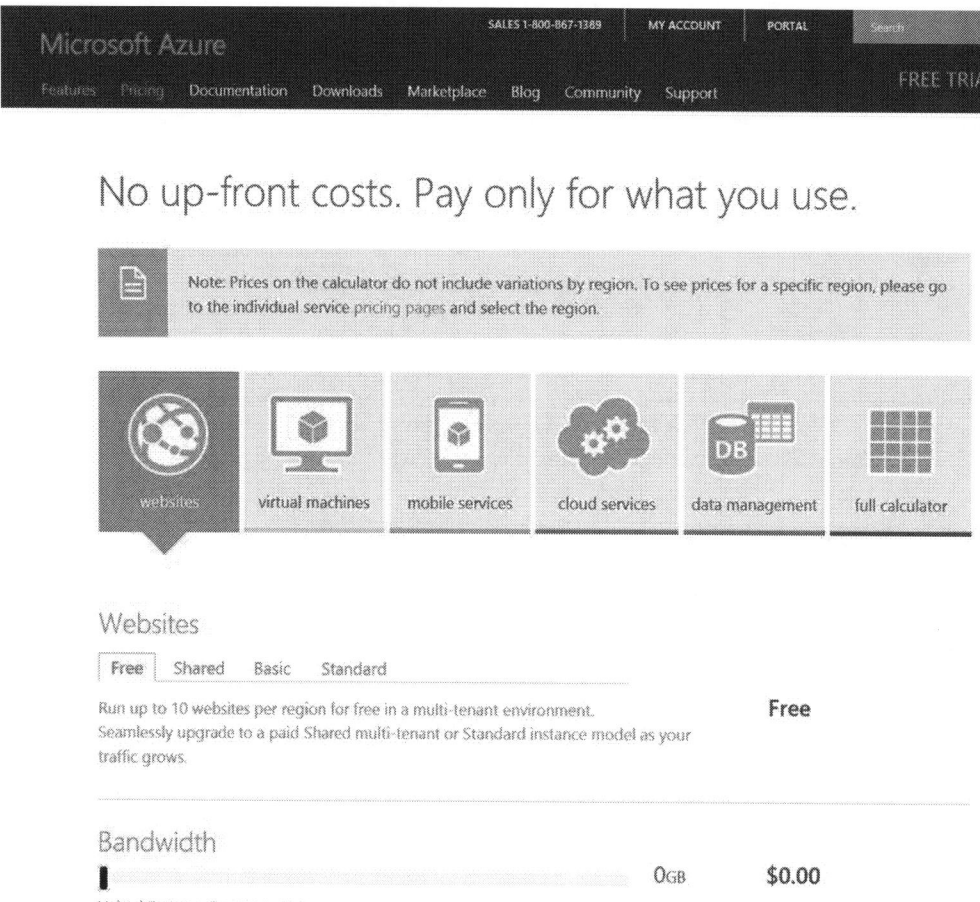

Figure 1-18. *The Azure Pricing Calculator*

Once you have selected a category, the options for that category are displayed. Use the sliders next to an Azure resource to determine the number of units that you require.

USING THE AZURE PRICING CALCULATOR

This exercise will help you quickly learn how to use the Azure Pricing Calculator:

1. Access the Azure Pricing Calculator at: `http://azure.microsoft.com/en-us/pricing/calculator` or via the Portal.

2. Click the Virtual Machines box.

3. Hover over the question mark to get help on the resource type, as shown in Figure 1-19.

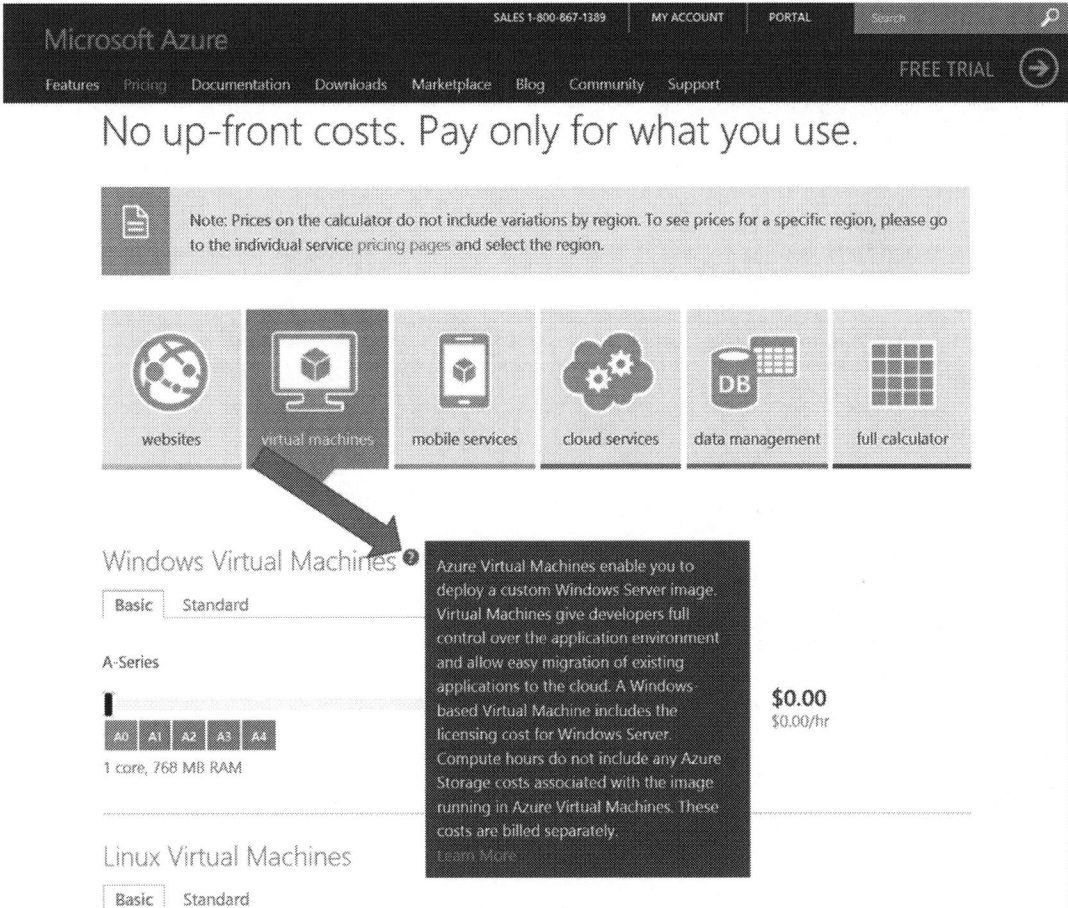

Figure 1-19. Getting help and information on an Azure resource

4. Select A0, A1, A2, and A3 VMs, and note the number of cores and RAM for each VM.

5. Click the Standard tab to get more VM options, and read the description of the difference between a standard VM and a basic one.

6. Use the slider to select the number of instances of the VM that you require, and note the hourly rate for that VM, as shown in Figure 1-20.

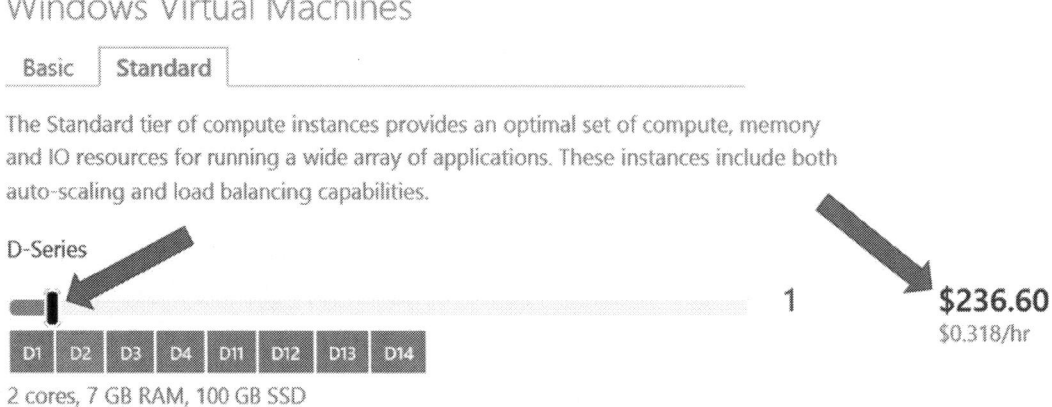

Figure 1-20. Selecting the number of units of D2 VMs

In addition to the individual categories of Azure resources, note the option to display the full calculator. This option combines all Azure resources on a single page. When you are done selecting all the different Azure resources you need and their quantities, the calculator provides you with a total cost. This is the value you can use as an estimate.

▦ **Note**   It is sometimes difficult to get the right value by using the slider, because some mice and trackpads are very sensitive. We have found it easier to use the left and right arrow keys on the keyboard to increase or decrease the number of instances.

Summary

This chapter was designed to get you started with Microsoft Azure. It introduced you to the various Azure services and how this cloud-computing platform addresses security, regulatory compliance, and privacy concerns.

You were also introduced to key Azure technologies, such as the Azure Portal, Azure accounts and subscriptions, and the different ways that Azure services can be billed. Finally, we introduced the Azure Pricing Calculator as a tool to assist you in estimating how much Azure services will cost you.

Chapter 2 introduces the different Azure Services. Later chapters explore some of these services in greater detail, including use-case and deployment scenarios.

■ ■ ■

Overview of Microsoft Azure Services

Microsoft Azure Services

As you saw in Chapter 1, Microsoft Azure represents computing capabilities. What does that mean? That Azure strives to be the foundation of modern computing and continues to evolve. The services presented are a snapshot in time, and you should expect new services to be introduced at an accelerated pace.

This evolution is currently manifested by monthly releases of new capabilities. As of this writing, Azure addresses 25 categories of services.

This chapter goes through all these services at an introductory level. Furthermore, by working your way through this chapter, you will become more familiar with the Azure Portal. The chapter should be used as a quick reference guide to the different Azure services, their intended audience, and the benefits of each.

The Azure Portal

Azure services are managed and accessed primarily via PowerShell or the Azure Portal. This chapter focuses on using the Azure Portal to introduce the different Azure services.

At the time of this writing, the Azure Portal is in transition. Figure 2-1 shows the current Azure Portal interface, and Figure 2-2 shows the new interface that was introduced in the spring of 2015. The current portal is accessible via `https://manage.windowsazure.com`, the new Preview Portal is accessible at `https://portal.azure.com`. In both cases, an existing Azure subscription is required to log into the Portal.

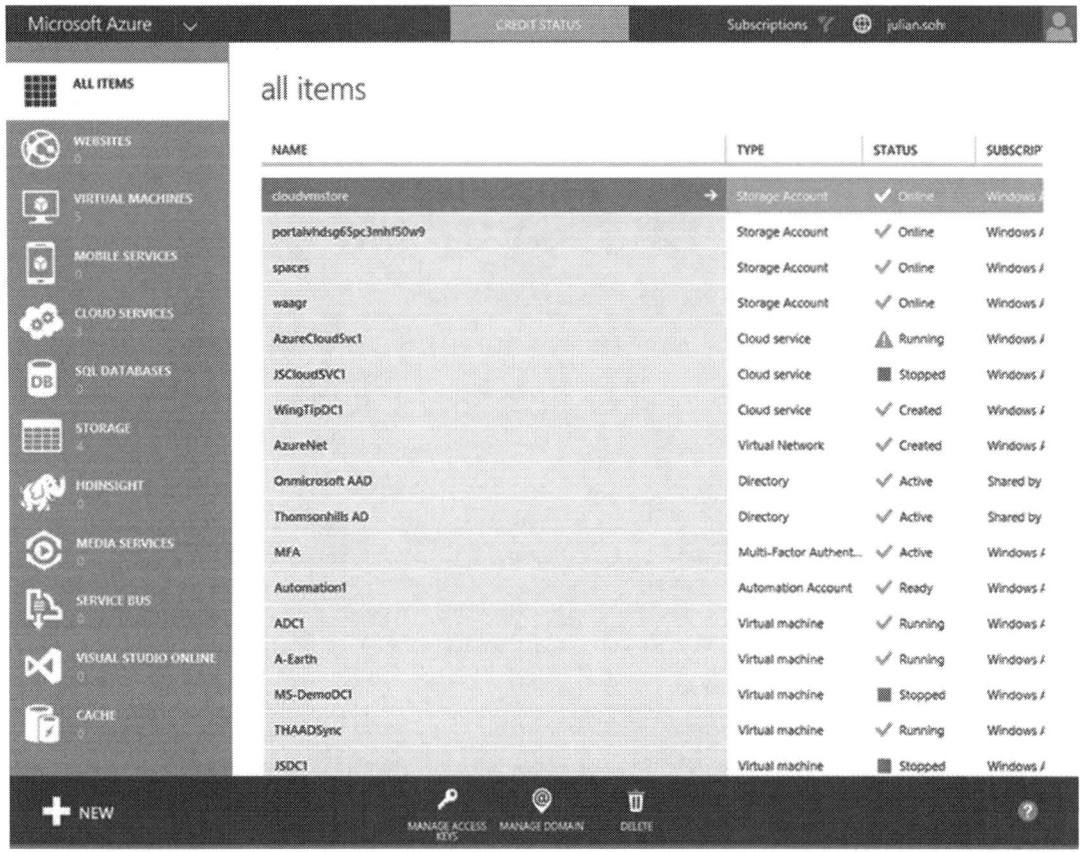

Figure 2-1. *The current Azure Portal interface*

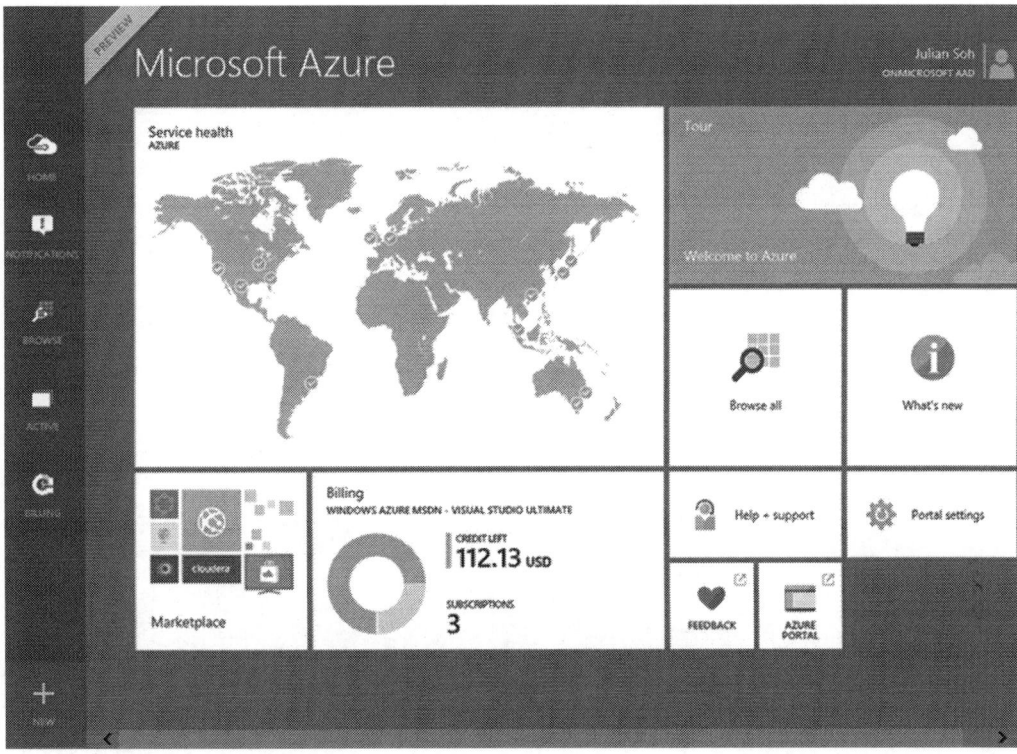

Figure 2-2. *The new Azure Portal interface*

The original Azure Portal interface is sometimes known as the Full Azure Portal. If you are at the Full Azure Portal and would like to switch to the new Portal, simply click the user icon at upper left and select Switch to New Portal from the drop-down menu, as shown in Figure 2-3. You can switch back to the Full Azure Portal from the new Portal interface in the same way.

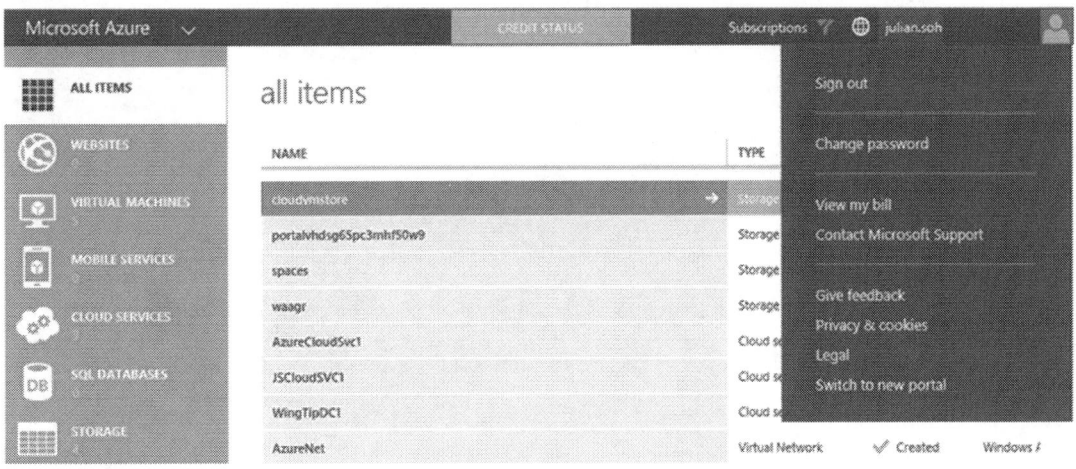

Figure 2-3. *Switching to the new Portal from the original Portal*

Because the new Portal is imminent, the remainder of this chapter and the book, where applicable, focus on the new Portal interface.

■ **Note**　At the time of this writing, the new Azure Portal interface is in preview. The final release of the new Portal may be slightly different from the preview version. Furthermore, not all Azure services are shown in the preview version of the new Portal—for example, Visual Studio Online, HD Insight, and so forth. If you do not see a service in the new Portal, you may have to switch to the Full Azure Portal. There may also be new Azure services that appear in the new Portal but not in the existing Full Azure Portal. Because of this transition period, which may stretch through calendar year 2015 and part of 2016, you need to be familiar with both Portals.

In order to view the different Azure services from the new Portal, click Browse in the left margin and select Everything, as shown in Figure 2-4.

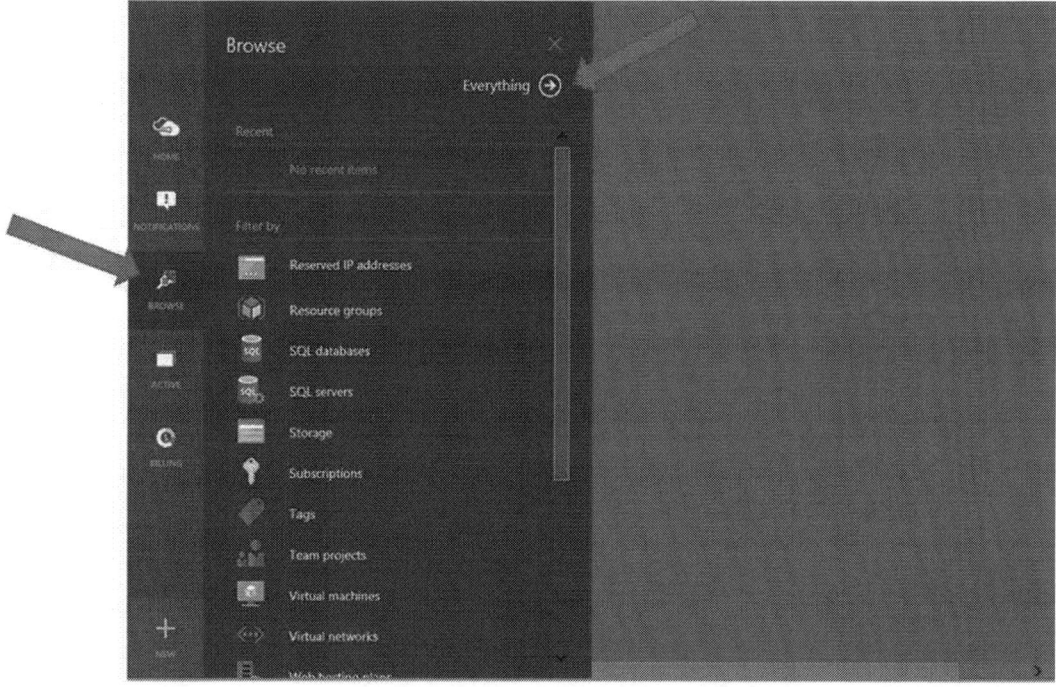

Figure 2-4.　*Browsing Azure services from the new Portal*

Because most Azure services are currently accessible via the Full Azure Portal, this chapter uses it to describe these services (refer again to Figure 2-3). The first service on that list is Websites, followed by Virtual Machines, Mobile Services, and so on. Let's go down the list and explore each of these services; each description defines the service, indicates the most relevant audience to whom the service is applicable, and highlights the service's benefits and capabilities.

Websites

Azure Websites is an Azure service that provides the platform for building and hosting your website.

What Is It?

Azure Websites is classified under the provider as a service (PaaS) category. It is essentially a fully managed platform that enables you to build and deploy websites and web-based applications in seconds.

Audience

The target audience for Azure Websites is application developers and hosting providers.

Benefits and Capabilities

From an operational point of view, there are no web servers to maintain or patch. Websites and apps deployed on Azure Websites also benefit from the scalability of the service, including the ability to auto-scale. This lets organizations focus solely on the site's look and feel and the application code. Azure is fully responsible for the infrastructure, the operating system (OS), and the web server publishing platform.

■ **Note**   Relying on Azure Websites to manage the infrastructure does not mean giving up total control. Azure Websites provide real-time monitoring, alerts, and analytics so that you and your team are informed of any issues.

Azure websites and data can be automatically backed up so that your sites' code and data have disaster recovery built in as part of the deployment. Rapid deployment of websites and web-based applications is achieved by providing fully managed Microsoft and non-Microsoft platforms. For example, popular publishing platforms such as WordPress, Joomla, and Drupal are available for content management.

In the likely event that you need to access data sources, Azure Websites can access Azure-based databases as well as databases running in your on-premises datacenters. Developers can use Visual Studio, which has built-in integration with Azure services and allows for a full application development lifecycle that includes the continuous publishing of web applications as well as multiple testing and staging environments that can be isolated from each other.

The anticipated end result is a quicker and more efficient way to publish and update websites. Because IT no longer needs to provision hardware or patch software because the infrastructure is handled by Azure, published websites and applications have improved uptime and better security.

References

Azure Websites is explored in detail in Chapter 5. You can also find more information at
http://azure.microsoft.com/en-us/services/websites/.

Virtual Machines

Azure Virtual Machines is probably the most recognized Azure service. It falls under the infrastructure as a service (IaaS) category.

What Is It?

As an IaaS, Azure Virtual Machines provides customers with a quick and easy way to deploy and manage virtual machines (VMs).

With Azure VMs, customers are responsible for managing the guest OS and the software installed on the VMs, including patching and securing the VMs. Azure is responsible for the underlying hardware, the hypervisor, and the datacenter environment, such as power, cooling, physical access security, redundancy, and disaster recovery.

Audience

The target audience for Azure Virtual Machines includes datacenter operations and infrastructure providers, such as central IT for organizations, as well as customers looking to get out of the datacenter operations business but who still require enterprise class servers and databases to host their applications and other software assets.

Benefits and Capabilities

Managing datacenters is essentially a high-cost and complex facilities-management project. Datacenters house the IT backbone of many organizations, and the disruption of such services usually means significant loss of revenue. In some cases, it is a matter of life and death. Thus it is not an overstatement to say that the datacenter is a mission-critical component of any industry.

Local and Geo-Redundancy with Service Level Agreements (SLAs)

There are essentially three types of datacenter infrastructure:

- Legacy and/or out-of-capacity, single-location datacenter
- Modern single-location datacenter with spare capacity
- Modern geo-redundant datacenter

Azure datacenters fall into the third category, with each location having excess capacity and the ability to scale up and out quickly. In terms of *geo-redundancy*, Azure datacenters can be hundreds of miles apart. By default, in a datacenter, VMs are provisioned on three physically separate infrastructures that are located in different parts of the facility. This is known as *local redundancy*. As an Azure customer, you have control over whether the VMs are replicated to geographically separate datacenter facilities located a distance apart from one another. Geo-redundancy occurs in addition to local redundancy—it is not a substitute. Therefore, for many organizations, the greatest benefit of hosting VMs in Azure is its built-in local and geo-redundancy capabilities. This is even more important if an organization's datacenter infrastructure falls into the first legacy category: an out-of-capacity type of facility. Local and geo-redundancy help organizations meet their disaster recovery (DR) and high availability (HA) requirements.

Azure VMs that have two or more instances deployed in the same availability set come with a financially backed 99.95% service-level agreement (SLA). Availability sets are covered in more detail in Chapter 11.

Open Architecture

Azure VM infrastructure is built to support Microsoft and non-Microsoft technologies. An organization can choose to use certified images from the Azure VM gallery or upload its own images. Figure 2-5 and Figure 2-6 show the VM image gallery in the Full Azure Portal and the new Azure Portal, respectively. Note that the VM image gallery contains Microsoft and non-Microsoft technologies that are certified on Azure.

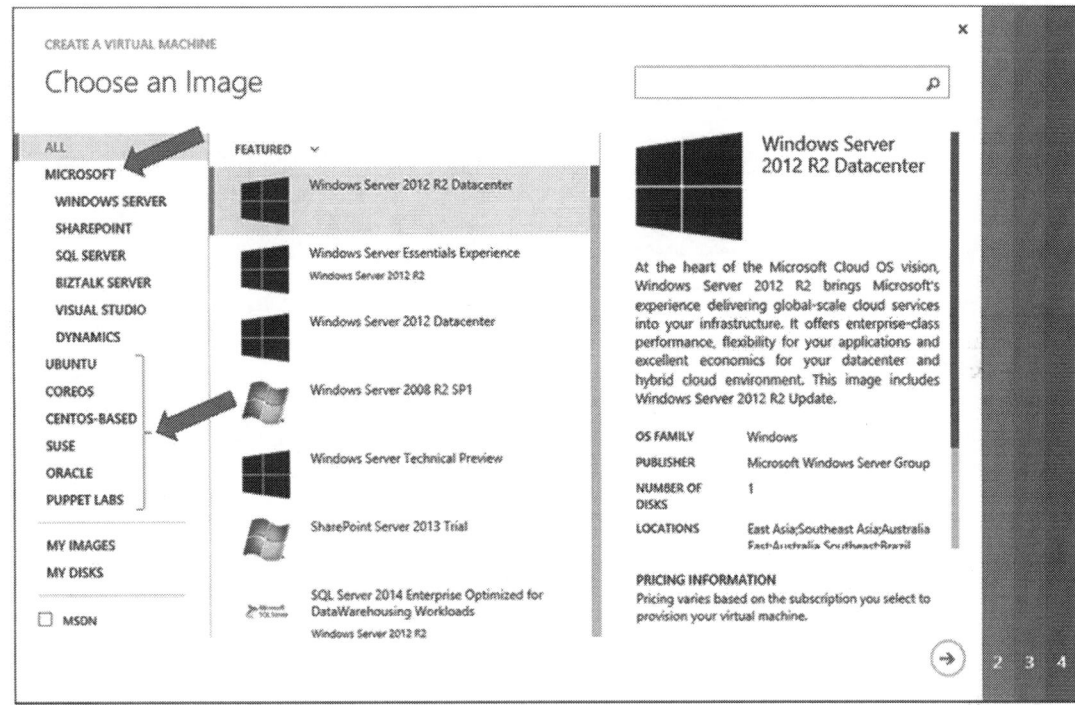

Figure 2-5. *Azure VM image gallery in the Full Azure Portal*

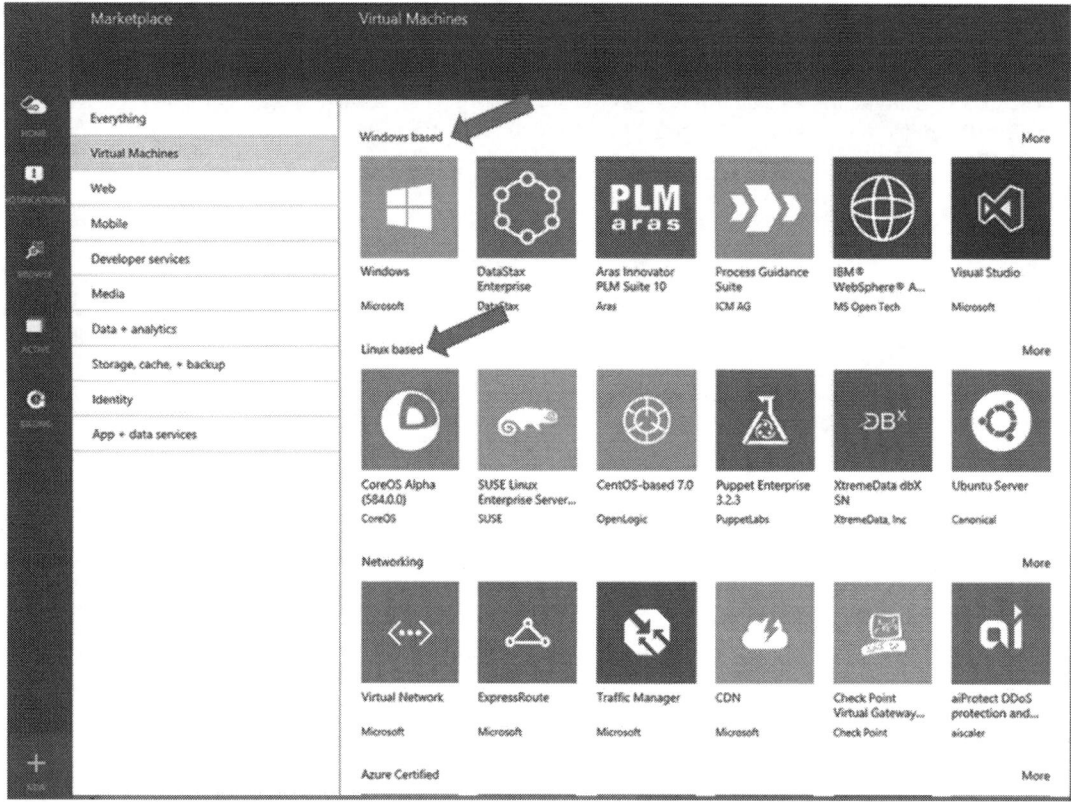

Figure 2-6. *Azure VM image gallery as seen in the new Azure Portal*

Modern and Always Up-to-Date Hardware

Azure VM customers no longer need to replace and update hardware. They no longer experience racking of servers and waiting for hardware orders to be processed. Azure VM customers have access to the latest hardware, and they only need to know the number of processor cores, the amount of memory, and the type of storage.

There are many options for VMs, A-series with high performance, enterprise drives, and D-series with solid state drives (SSDs). In January 2015, Microsoft announced a new class of VMs touted as the "largest VM in the cloud," known as the G-series. The G-series VMs provide the most memory, the highest processing power, and the largest local SSD storage of any VM currently available. The G-series VMs are based on the latest Intel Xeon processor E5 v3 family.

■ **Note** For information about the different VM sizes, see the Virtual Machine and Cloud Service Sizes for Azure at https://msdn.microsoft.com/en-us/library/azure/dn197896.aspx If you are interested in comparing the different VMs, visit this blog: http://blogs.msdn.com/b/igorpag/archive/2014/11/11/ azure-a_2d00_series-and-d_2d00_series-consistent-performances-and-size-change-considerations.aspx.

Flexibility

Requirements change, and, as such, the infrastructure on which an application depends tends to grow or shrink. With earlier virtualization technology, applications were based on physical infrastructure and remained locked in. Therefore, it was difficult to scale up or down in response to a business's needs. The ability to change the VM type for applications provides the flexibility to supply the best architecture at the time and to maximize IT operational budgets. The ability to schedule shutdowns for VMs manually or automatically further maximizes operations budgets, because it allows IT departments to pay only for what they use and when they need the VMs.

You have seen that VMs are charged based on utilization. As long as the VM is running, it is incurring charges. This model can also extend to licensing. The guest OS in a VM is included as part of the VM runtime charges. In some cases, certain software in the VM is covered under the same licensing model. For example, the SQL and Oracle VMs provide licenses that are part of their respective VM runtime charges. Alternatively, customers that own licenses can still use their own licenses and install them on the VM. Bringing an existing license reduces the VM runtime charges accordingly. Therefore, the flexibility extends from the hardware to the licensing of software.

References

Azure VMs are explored in greater detail in Chapter 6. For more information about Azure VMs, visit http://azure.microsoft.com/en-us/services/virtual-machines/.

Mobile Services

Azure Mobile Services falls under the PaaS category. It is a platform designed to build and publish mobile apps.

What Is It?

Azure Mobile Services provides a platform to rapidly build and deploy apps for iOS, Android, Windows, and Macs. Specifically, it provides the following key capabilities that are associated with mobile apps:

- Authentication

- Push notifications

- App data stored in the cloud or on premises

Audience

The target audience for Azure Mobile Services includes application developers and organizations that need to provide native mobile apps that are responsive and scalable.

Scalability and Performance

Just as with Azure Websites, customers can focus solely on designing and developing mobile apps and let Azure manage the delivery mechanism. Like all the other Azure services, mobile apps deployed on Azure enjoy good performance, high availability, scalability, and the ability to support natively all the popular mobile platforms, not just Microsoft's. The ability to store data on premises or in the cloud, and to be able to cache data, lets developers balance security and performance requirements.

Real-Time Analytics

Azure Mobile Services provides app owners with real-time analytics to help determine customer behavior through app interaction. This gives organizations the ability to fine-tune or even segment user experiences. In-app push-notification capabilities further provide a rich experience that allows organizations to interact with users.

Social

Mobile apps deployed on Azure can be connected to social websites such as Facebook, Google+, Microsoft, and Twitter. Identity information can be connected to these social platforms to provide a single sign-on solution for more seamless integration between the app and the social websites preferred by the user.

References

For more information on Mobile Services, visit `http://azure.microsoft.com/en-us/services/mobile-services/`.

SQL Databases

As the name implies, Azure SQL Databases handles the provisioning of databases in the cloud. However, SQL databases are available as PaaS and IaaS offerings.

What Is It?

Azure SQL Databases provides Microsoft SQL Server technologies in the cloud. SQL databases fall into the PaaS and IaaS categories because they can be provisioned either way.

As an IaaS, Microsoft SQL Server is installed on a VM. In this model, organizations are responsible for maintaining and patching the guest OS and the SQL database engine and other roles.

As a PaaS, Azure SQL Databases allows you just to provision a fully managed relational database service that includes built-in high availability. With this model, organizations are not responsible for any hardware or software infrastructure—just the contents and the size of the databases.

Figure 2-7 shows the difference between provisioning Azure SQL Server (IaaS) versus a SQL database (PaaS).

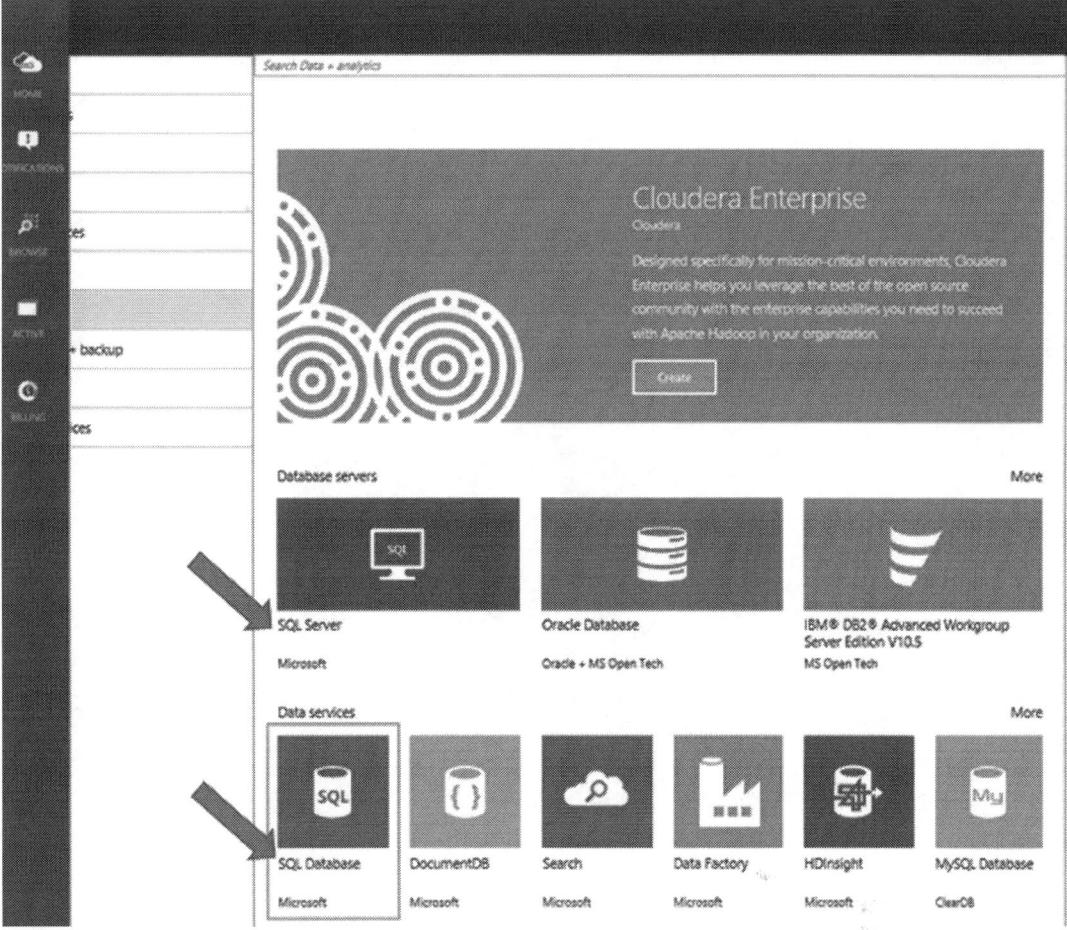

Figure 2-7. *SQL Server (IaaS) vs. SQL database (PaaS), as shown in the new Azure Portal*

Audience

The target audience for Azure SQL Databases includes application developers who need to use databases as a storage medium and non-developers who want to consume database services.

Benefits and Capabilities

Databases are mission-critical components on which applications rely. Over the years, Microsoft SQL Server technology has made big strides in terms of performance, scalability, and high availability (HA). SQL Server Availability Groups is a recent technology that has taken HA to a new level. Still, many of these technologies are most effective when they are built on a geo-redundant infrastructure. Azure SQL Databases is designed to allow for technologies such as AlwaysOn to provide databases with HA capabilities.

References

For more information on Azure SQL Databases, visit http://azure.microsoft.com/en-us/services/sql-database/.

Azure Storage and StorSimple

There are several types of storage options in Azure. Azure SQL Databases is one of four major types, as shown in Figure 2-8.

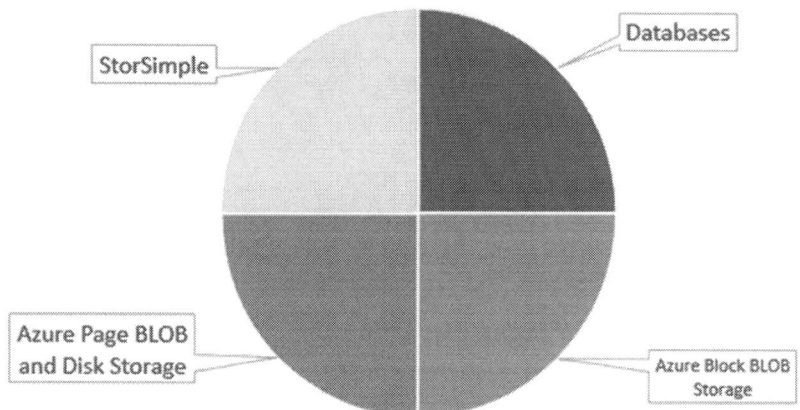

Figure 2-8. *The four major storage options in Azure*

What Is It?

Azure Storage is essentially hosted hard drive space in the cloud. You may be familiar with consumer versions of these storage options such as OneDrive, DropBox, ShareFile, Google Drive, and iCloud. Azure Storage is the commercial and enterprise equivalent of such storage solutions, and it includes capabilities that are not available in consumer cloud storage, such as DR, HA, and audit capabilities. Azure Storage solutions are also designed to work seamlessly with enterprise workloads, including servers and applications. This section introduces the three additional storage options shown in Figure 2-8: Azure Block BLOB Storage, Azure Page BLOB and Disk Storage, and StorSimple managed storage.

Audience

The target audience for Azure Storage and StorSimple is IT operations personnel who manage storage options and organizations that are looking at replacing or expanding storage capacity. Recent events have also resulted in new business initiatives that may lead to a significant spike in storage needs. For example, law enforcement videos from body cameras (bodycams) and the expanded use of rich media for training and communications may accelerate the need for additional storage availability.

Benefits and Capabilities

Azure Storage provides many options for storing and managing your data in Azure. StorSimple provides an integrated solution for managing storage tasks between your on-premises devices and Azure cloud storage.

Agility and Price

The biggest benefit of Azure Storage is the ability to scale up or down in seconds and only pay for what is being used. Because Azure has the benefit of economies of scale when purchasing hard drives, the savings are passed along to customers.

■ **Note** You may hear the terms *thin provisioning* and *thick provisioning* when configuring Azure Storage. *Thin provisioning* refers to the allocation of space dynamically as needed; whereas thick provisioning means allocating a certain amount of predefined space, like a fixed volume, regardless of current demand. Thick provisioning immediately allocates space, and it is thus considered consumed and incurs storage charges immediately on provisioning.

High Availability and Redundancy

Like all Azure services, storage in Azure has built-in HA and DR. At a minimum, storage is allocated as locally redundant storage (LRS), where it is replicated across three different infrastructures in the same datacenter. Customers have the option to provision geographically redundant storage (GRS), which expands an LRS instance to a second geographically separated Azure datacenter, hundreds of miles away. Figure 2-9 illustrates selecting the storage redundancy level as seen in the new Azure Portal when provisioning storage.

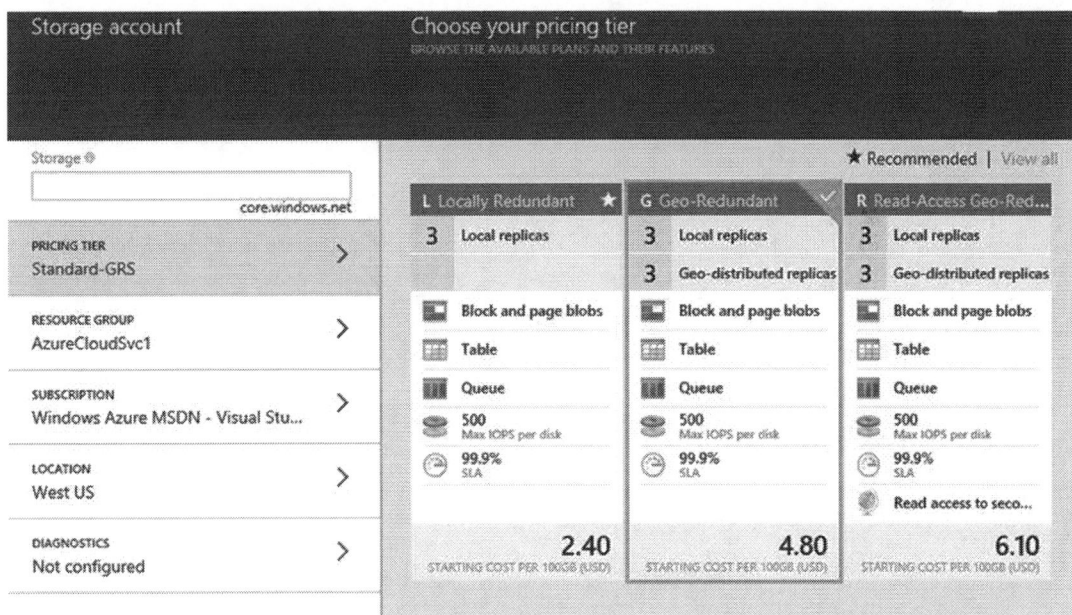

Figure 2-9. *The various redundancy levels as seen in the new Azure Portal when provisioning storage*

There are also options to take snapshots of Azure storage so that customers have timely copies of files in case there is a need to revert to a previous state. Traditional strategies that reduce storage downtime, such as striping, RAID, mirroring, and replication can be designed based on Azure Storage.

Innovative Approach to Storage

Azure introduced new and innovative ways to provision and manage storage. Solution providers, such as SoftNAS, can provide software-based NAS that uses Azure Storage.

Azure StorSimple is based on a 2U physical rack-mountable device that is installed on premises. A StorSimple device provides the ability to overflow into the cloud through content aging, compression, and deduplication. Instead of a disk-to-disk-to-tape concept, a StorSimple device provides a disk-to-disk-to-cloud approach. Each StorSimple device has SSDs for low-latency tier one data, traditional spinning drives for tier two data, and connectivity to Azure for tier three data. StorSimple is a good example of a hybrid cloud model as it pertains to storage. Chapter 7 covers it in detail.

References

Azure Storage and StorSimple are discussed in detail in Chapter 7. For more information about Azure Storage, visit http://azure.microsoft.com/en-us/services/storage/. For more information about StorSimple, visit http://azure.microsoft.com/en-us/services/storsimple/.

HDInsight

HDInsight is a Hadoop distribution powered by Azure.

What Is It?

Hadoop is a Java-based programming framework designed to process large data sets by using a distributed computing infrastructure (nodes). Azure meets the classic distributed cloud computing model, and, as such, it is a great candidate to be a Hadoop platform. HDInsight is a version of Hadoop provided in Azure. It can process large amounts of data, scaling from terabytes to petabytes, and it has the ability to spin up as many nodes as necessary to process the data.

Audience

The target audience for HDInsight includes data warehouse developers, data scientists, and analysts who need to process large amounts of data. HDInsight is also applicable to organizations that have business intelligence or advanced analytics initiatives.

Benefits and Capabilities

The flexibility and scalability of Azure make it easy to spin up as many nodes as necessary to process data efficiently. When processing data, exponentially more space is normally necessary than would be required by the raw data itself, because of the need to replicate data and store information that will be required for analysis. Therefore, Azure's access to petabytes of storage is an important requirement in order for Hadoop in HDInsight to work. HDInsight also allows developers to use their preferred language, including C#, Java, .NET, and more. In addition, HDInsight supports hybrid configurations, so it can be connected to other Hadoop clusters that may be located on premises or in other clouds.

References

HDInsight is covered in detail in Chapter 15. For more information, visit `http://azure.microsoft.com/en-us/services/hdinsight/`.

Azure Media Services and Content Delivery Network (CDN)

Azure Media Services is a set of capabilities designed to handle rich content, specifically audio and video. The *Content Delivery Network (CDN)* is a distributed computing model designed to stream content efficiently worldwide, thus offloading organizations' network and bandwidth load.

What Is It?

Audio and video files have special handling requirements, such as storage, encoding and decoding (CODEC), conversion, editing, meta-tagging, and playback. Azure Media Services is designed to provide all of these capabilities so that audio and video content can easily be consumed in different form factors and on different devices. In certain scenarios, there may be the need to create metatags for rich content automatically in order to facilitate indexing and searching.

Azure Media Services works closely with Azure CDN in that the latter is the delivery mechanism for vast numbers of viewers located across the globe. Streaming bandwidth-intensive videos from a single source is less efficient than a global delivery network, which provides a better experience for end users and relieves the need for organizations to install expensive high-bandwidth, low-latency networks specifically designed for streaming.

Benefits and Capabilities

Audio and video content can take up a lot of storage space. Therefore, all the benefits of Azure Storage are applicable when dealing with rich media content. Azure Media Services can process rich content and make it easy to consume. Furthermore, Azure Media Services and Azure Storage provide the ability to integrate with third-party video management system (VMS) providers as well as third-party video capture device manufacturers. Figure 2-10 shows the Azure Media Services technology stack.

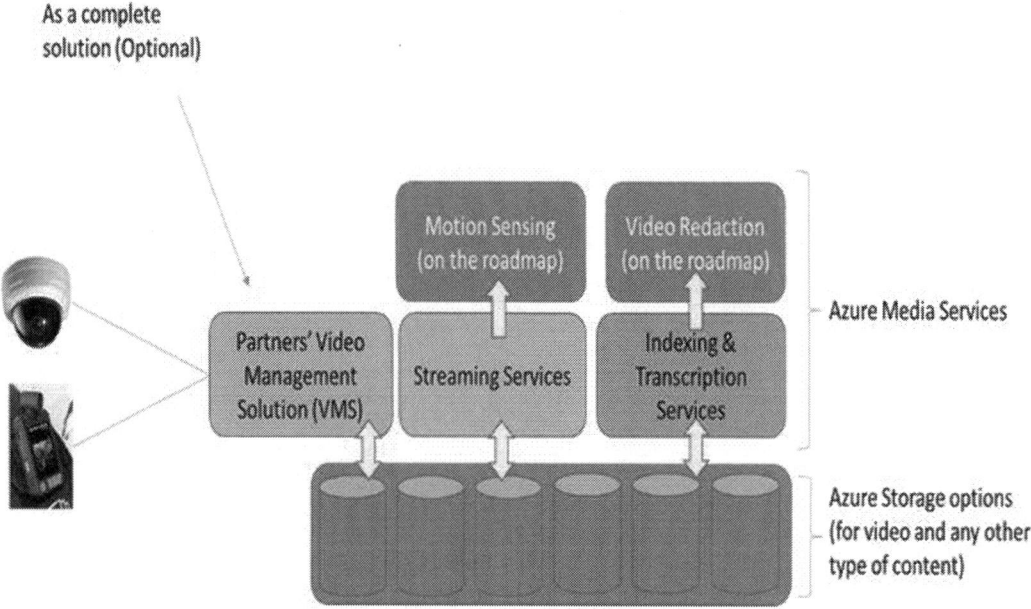

Figure 2-10. *Azure Media Services technology stack and integration with partner solutions*

■ **Note**   At the time of this writing, the ability to detect motion in a video and the ability to auto-detect content patterns are still in development. However, they are part of the roadmap of capabilities that Microsoft is seeking to deploy. Justice, law enforcement, surveillance, and public safety customers are most interested in this set of capabilities.

The ability to transcribe audio and video content in order to create a transcript enhances the ability to index and search content. It also provides the ability to meet Americans with Disability Act (ADA) requirements. Azure Media Services Transcription Service processes videos by playing them in their entirety in order to create the transcript. This is done in the background and does not require anyone to sit through the entire playback. Furthermore, organizations can choose to process only those videos that require transcription, so this saves time and cost.

Another goal of Azure Media Services is to accept and recognize a wide array of video types, such as MP2, MP3, MOV, AVI, and many more. It will then be able to repackage them into the common H.264 format for easier consumption across the broadest array of devices. Azure Media Services also boasts *adaptive streaming*, which means in the event that an end user's network degrades, the quality of the video resolution may change in order to preserve smooth streaming.

■ **Note**   Recently Microsoft Office 365 introduced Office 365 Videos, which is based on SharePoint Online. The architecture behind Office 365 Videos is Azure Media Services. SharePoint Online is configured to use a specially built connector to access Azure Media Services. This is all preconfigured and done transparently, and it is an example of how other solutions can be built to use Azure Media Services.

References

For more information on Azure Media Services, visit http://azure.microsoft.com/en-us/services/media-services/. For more information on Azure CDN, visit http://azure.microsoft.com/en-us/services/cdn/.

Service Bus

Azure Service Bus is a queue-based messaging system for connecting applications and services.

What Is It?

One of the key requirements for applications is the ability to interact with other applications or services. The most common way for applications to communicate with other applications is via a message queue. Fundamentally, Azure Service Bus is that message queue.

Audience

The target audience for Azure Service Bus includes application developers who need to incorporate a robust and highly available inter-application messaging system, regardless of whether the application resides on premises or in the cloud.

Benefits and Capabilities

Azure Service Bus provides one-directional or bidirectional communications channels between applications. It can also act as a relay for messages or as a message broker with subscription and filtering capabilities. Often, when an application queue is not available, there are delays in data processing or notifications. Azure Service Bus provides a highly available system. Furthermore, Azure Service Bus enables on-premises applications to communicate with services and other applications in Azure and vice versa. This allows organizations to adopt a modern hybrid datacenter approach.

References

For more information on Azure Service Bus, visit http://azure.microsoft.com/en-us/services/service-bus/.

Visual Studio Online

Visual Studio Online provides developers with tools to manage development projects and to store code in Azure.

What Is It?

Visual Studio Online combines capabilities from Visual Studio, Team Foundation Server (TFS), and cloud services to make it easier for developers to manage development projects. With Visual Studio Online, development teams should no longer need to deploy servers dedicated to software project management, testing, or storing code.

Audience

The target audience for Visual Studio Online includes application developers and development teams.

Benefits and Capabilities

Instead of deploying and maintaining servers dedicated to source control, organizations can use Visual Studio Online as a code repository. The redundancy provided by Azure significantly reduces the risk of losing valuable code-based intellectual property (IP). Furthermore, Azure's HA capabilities ensure that there is minimal impact to development timelines as a result of the downtime associated with outages or the unavailability of traditional code repositories.

Visual Studio Online also supplies robust control that securely supports the development efforts of a range of developers—from just a few to thousands—through capabilities such as advanced branching, merging, and visualization. To promote communication, Visual Studio Online provides the ability to comment and reply to code edits and changes between team members.

References

Developer tools such as Visual Studio Online are beyond the scope of this book and are better served by reference material dedicated to this topic. For more information about Visual Studio Online, visit http://azure.microsoft.com/en-us/services/visual-studio-online/.

BizTalk Services

BizTalk is Microsoft's business-to-business (B2B) tool for enterprise application integration.

What Is It?

BizTalk Server has been around as a standalone technology for quite some time, with the primary role of providing enterprise application integration. Azure BizTalk Services is the hosted version of BizTalk.

Audience

The target audience for Azure BizTalk Services includes developers and system integrators (SIs) who need to integrate enterprise applications and line-of-business (LOB) applications that are based on disparate technologies.

Benefits and Capabilities

Azure BizTalk Services provide all the benefits of BizTalk Server without the need to deploy and maintain any infrastructure. Key capabilities of Azure BizTalk Services include out-of-the-box connectors to integrate SAP, Oracle EBS, SQL Server, and PeopleSoft. Azure BizTalk Services also provides the ability to integrate applications founded on standards-based communication such as HTTP, FTP, and SFTP. In addition, Azure BizTalk Services supports B2B integration between applications that are housed on premises and those hosted in the cloud, thus supporting the modern hybrid datacenter initiative.

References

For more information about Azure BizTalk Services, visit http://azure.microsoft.com/en-us/services/biztalk-services/.

Recovery Services

Disaster recovery in Azure is provided through Azure Recovery Services for protection of corporate data and to provide availability for application workloads.

What Is It?

Azure Recovery Services consists of two distinct services:

- Azure Backup
- Azure Site Recovery Services

A key component of the service is its *vaults*, which are used to store and protect data based on the services that are most needed by a particular business. Vaults store backups of applications and configuration settings for VMs. They provide the options to fail over, from site to site or site to Azure, and replication from on premises to other locations.

Audience

The target audience for Azure Recovery Services includes IT administrators and server-management personnel. It also includes Chief Information Security Officers (CISOs) who are responsible for DR and business continuity.

Benefits and Capabilities

The term *natural disaster* is often used to prepare for personal and business disaster-recovery efforts. Disasters may include hurricanes, tornadoes, earthquakes, and so forth. They can cause billions of dollars in damage and untold hardship for individuals and families. On the financial side, a business that took a lifetime to build or generations to grow can be destroyed in hours or even minutes.

AZURE BACKUP

Azure Backup lets you back up Windows servers easily. The simplicity of this service gives small and large businesses peace of mind. Only a few steps are required, to start and complete a backup plan:

1. Create a backup vault from the Full Azure Portal. In the Azure Recovery Services view, select the Create a New Vault option, and click the arrow to start the wizard. For this example, choose Backup Vault, provide a unique business name and the Azure region in which to create the storage vault, and click the checkmark at bottom right in the window, as shown in Figure 2-11.

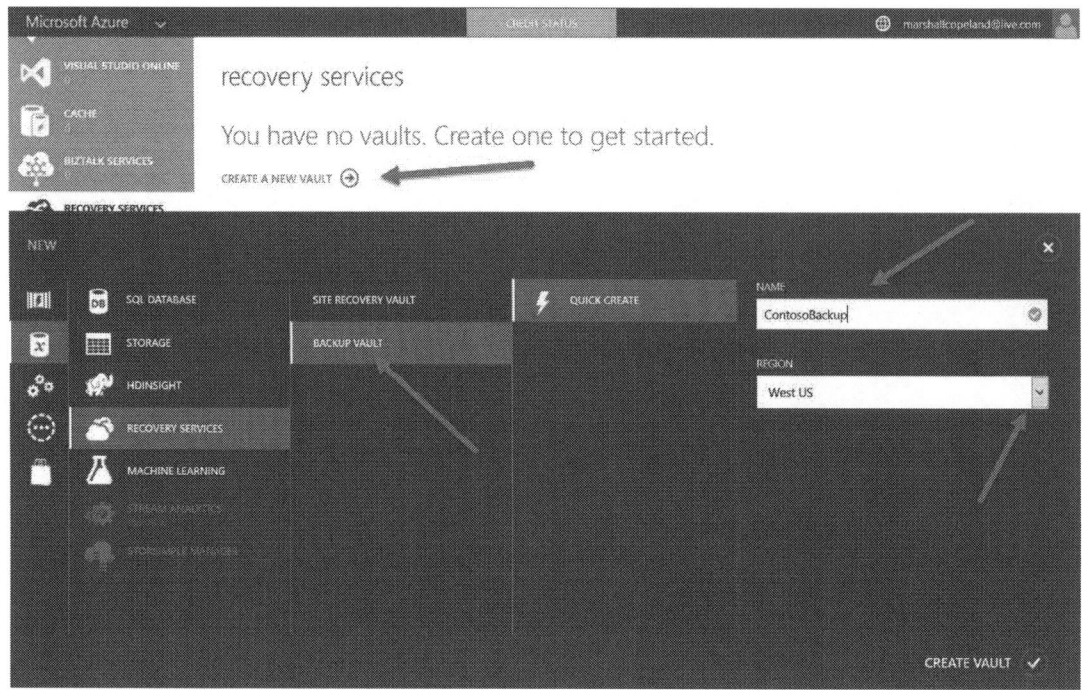

Figure 2-11. *Use the Full Azure Portal to create a backup vault or site recovery vault, and locate the storage vault in an Azure region*

2. Once the vault is created in your Azure subscription, the simplicity of this backup process is evident. Select the name of the backup (in this case, ContosoBackup), and download the vault credentials (at right) needed to register your server with your Azure backup vault (just created).

3. Download and install the backup agent. Once the agent is installed, use the management interface to create a backup policy. (*Ingress* data, or data moving into the vault, incurs a cost.)

■ **Note**   Azure supports Windows Server 2012 and System Center 2012 SP1 Data Protection Manager, or Windows Server 2012 Essentials. The management interface to enable backup from that server is different: Server 2012 Management Console, Data Protection Manger Console, or Windows Server Essentials Dashboard.

The vault credentials created includes the vault name and current date, which you can download using the Save As option in the Portal. These vault credentials cannot be edited. This example uses the vault credentials, which can be downloaded from the right side of the console (see Figure 2-12). An alternate server-authentication method is to manage certificates, as shown in the center at the bottom of the Portal. Once the backups are started, you can return to this screen and select Protected Items to view the recovery points and backup details.

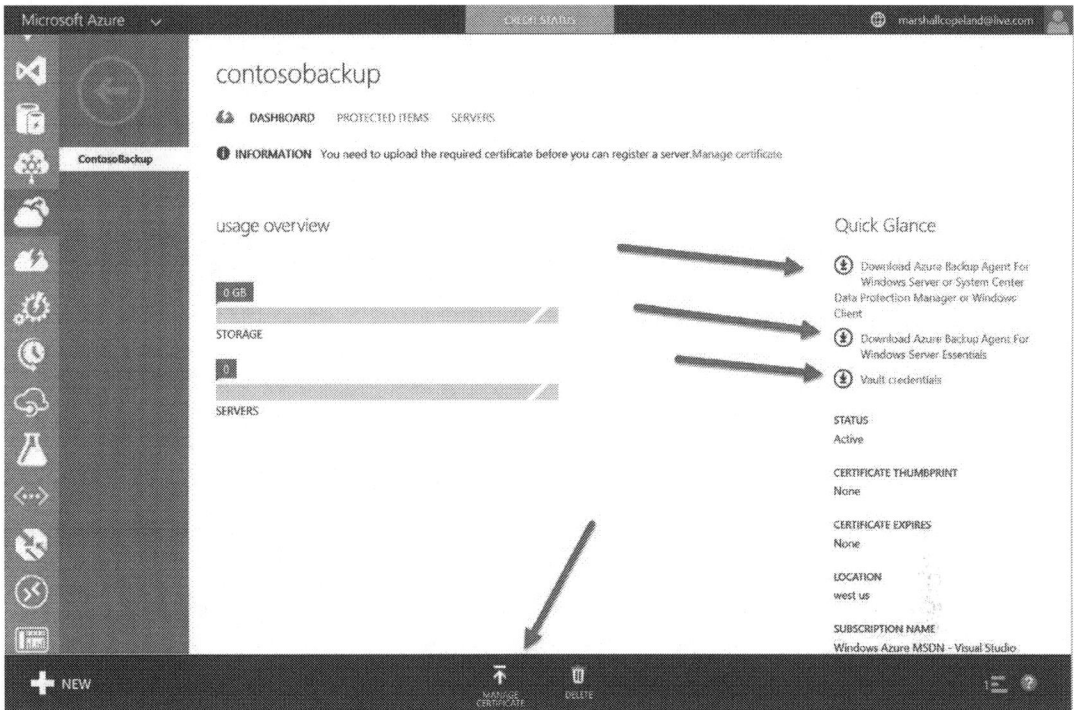

Figure 2-12. *Azure Backup details designed to support disaster recovery by backing up servers from on premises to Azure*

Azure Site Recovery

This is the recovery model built by Azure customers who requested specific recovery scenarios. This support model is the broadest set of features to support most medium and large business needs. The specific scenarios include the following:

- On-premises to Azure (Virtual Machine Manager (VMM) + Hyper-V)

- On-premises to on-premises (VMM + Hyper-V to VMM + Hyper-V)

- On-premises to on-premises (SAN replication + VMM)

- On-premises VMware to on-premises VMWare using InMage

■ **Note**   InMage is a Microsoft acquisition that enables real-time replication between VMware sites. The requirements have changed based on customer feedback, but currently InMage is available as a separate product via a subscription to Azure Site Recovery services.

The first Azure Site Recovery scenario is to back up on-premises servers into your Azure subscription using System Center VMM and Microsoft Hyper-V (virtualization hypervisor). The steps to complete this start when you create an Azure vault (as in the previous exercise), install the provider on the VMM server, add the Azure storage account, and install agents that allow applications to use System Center VMM to store in your Azure vault. Additional steps include using the VMM console to enable protection in the Azure cloud, mapping networks from VMs to Azure networks, and testing the deployment.

References

For more information about Site Recovery Services, visit `http://azure.microsoft.com/en-us/services/site-recovery/`. For more information about Azure Backup, visit `http://azure.microsoft.com/en-us/services/backup/` and `http://azure.microsoft.com/en-us/documentation/services/site-recovery/`.

Automation

This Azure service for automation provides reputable and reliable processes to do work automatically for almost any Azure or third-party cloud service.

What Is It?

Automation in Azure uses Microsoft's PowerShell workflows, called *runbooks*, to communicate through an exposed API for cloud management to create, deploy, monitor, and maintain your Azure properties.

Audience

The target audience for Automation includes Azure administrators, IT administrators, developers, and SIs who need to automate repetitive processes for VMs, web services, Azure Storage, SQL Server, enterprise applications, and LOB applications.

Benefits and Capabilities

Over the years, Microsoft PowerShell interactive scripting language has continued to add new commands to support administration and management. However, the strength of using PowerShell is not in the individual cmdlets but in when they are enabled through a business process flow in the runbook workflows.

AZURE AUTOMATION

Azure Automation runbooks can be created and customized based on the system tasks needed to provide useful work. Automation runbooks take input parameters, provide output, and can even call child runbooks. Azure work, in the form of runbooks, can be created or chosen from the preconfigured runbooks in the gallery. Follow these steps:

1. In the Full Azure Portal, select the Automation view, and click Create an Automation Account. Provide a unique name, and select the Azure region with which the account should be associated. Click the checkmark in the lower-right corner to finish this step (see Figure 2-13).

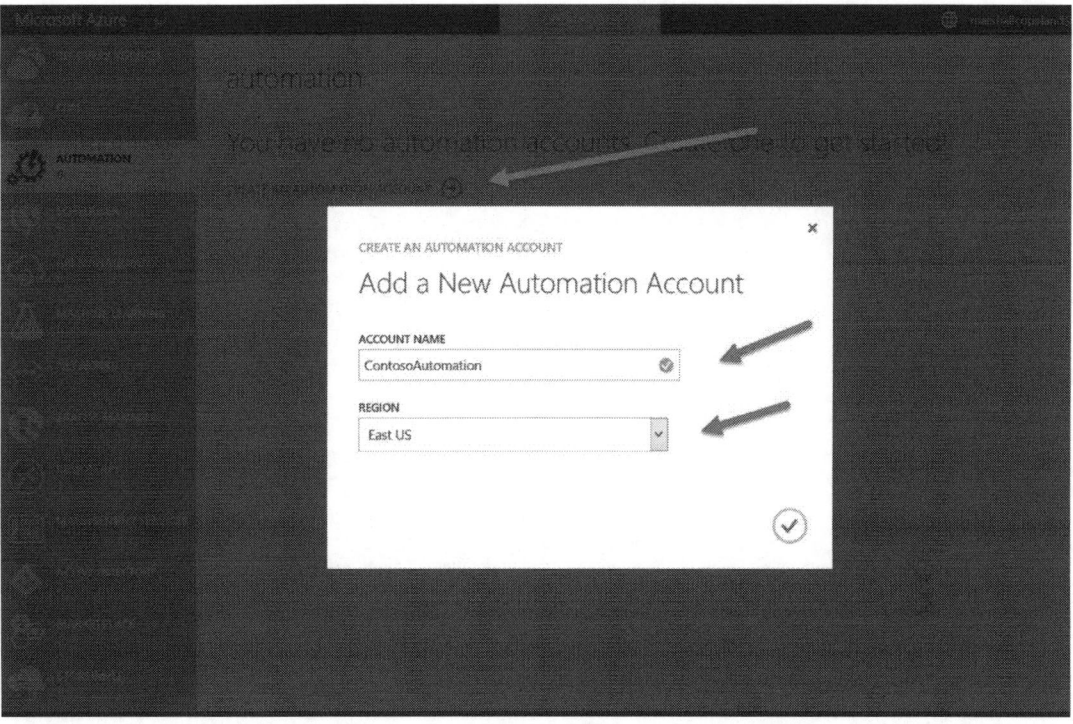

Figure 2-13. *The Full Azure Portal requires an automation account before any runbooks can be imported and modified*

■ **Note** There are two subscription-pricing models for automation accounts. The Free model supports a total job run time of up to 500 minutes, and the Basic model supports job run times at $0.002 cents per minute.

2. Once the account is created, you need to create a runbook or select a preconfigured runbook to use for automation requirements. For this example, select a runbook from the Runbook Gallery by going back to the Automation view, selecting the account created (ContosoAutomation), and clicking runbooks.

    The runbooks are created by the community, by individual contributors (like Charles Joy MSFT) or, in this example, the System Center Automation Product Team. Each runbook from the gallery provides a description so you can better understand the automation task.

3. The gallery enables different views based on the runbook. Once you have selected a runbook, click the arrow at bottom right to move through the wizard (see Figure 2-14).

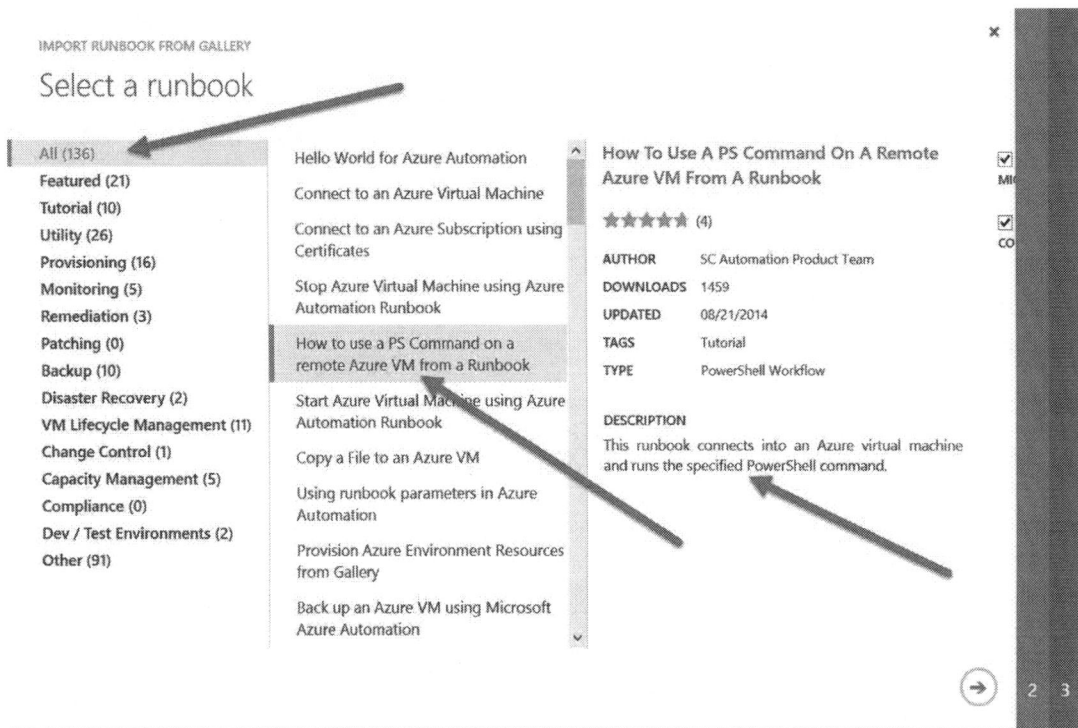

Figure 2-14. *Preconfigured runbooks from the current gallery. Views help separate automation features based on work topics*

4.   When the wizard screens' options are completed, go back to the Automation account that you created and edit the runbook to provide the automation task specific to your business needs. In this example, `invoke-pscommandsample`, select the option to enable editing in this runbook, as shown in Figure 2-15. Notice the options to test this runbook after automation and then to publish it into production.

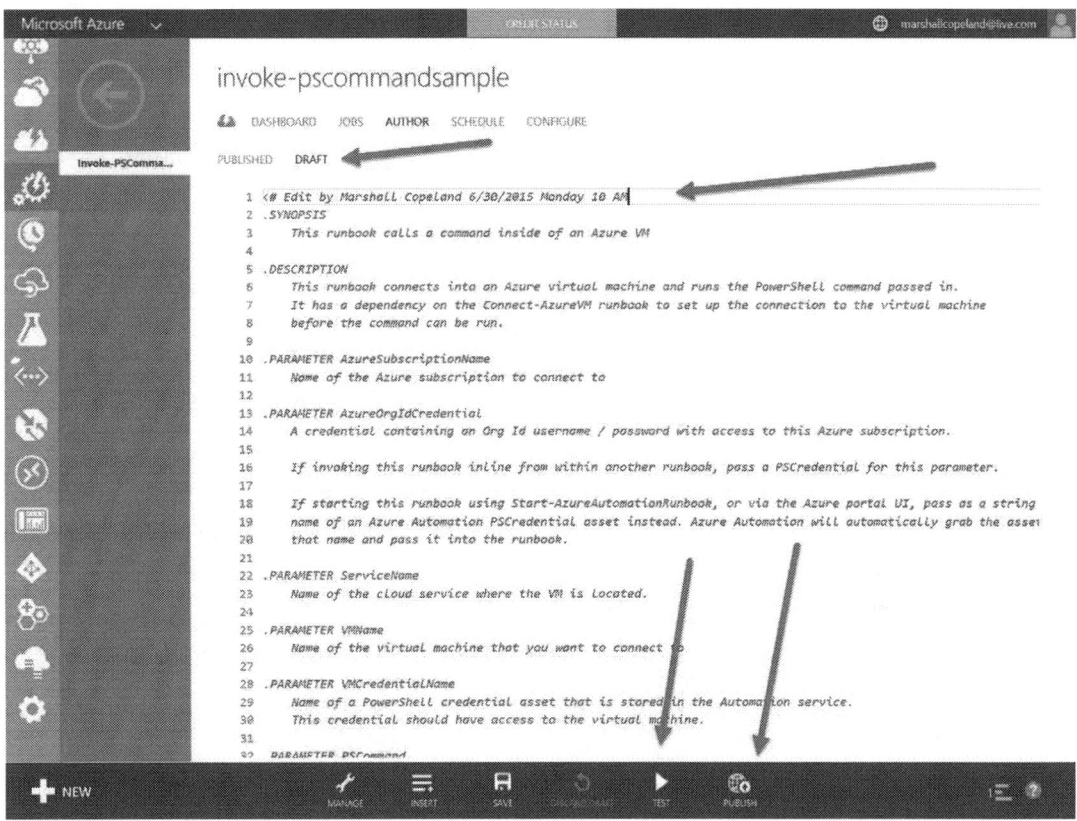

Figure 2-15. *Editing the runbook PowerShell script after the runbook has been imported into the Automation services*

References

For more information on Azure Automation, visit http://azure.microsoft.com/en-us/services/automation/ and http://azure.microsoft.com/blog/2014/08/12/azure-automation-runbook-input-output-and-nested-runbooks/.

Scheduler

Azure Scheduler is designed to run jobs in the cloud once or on a recurring basis to take action using HTTP or HTTPS endpoints. For example, a recurring action to gather website data and put in in a spreadsheet can be scheduled to run daily.

What Is It?

Azure Scheduler is a process or framework that uses the Scheduler API to schedule jobs programmatically. This feature is used to invoke work on a recurrent or calendar basis using the REST API to manage communication to HTTP, HTTPS, or a storage queue.

Audience

The target audience for Scheduler includes developers of Azure Mobile Services, to enable them to create scheduling scripts, Azure websites, and WebJobs for production; test/dev; and many others that need scheduling services.

Benefits and Capabilities

Developers of company resources use this feature with HTTP commands such as GET, PUT, POST, DELETE, and others. Creating jobs both inside and outside of Azure properties is a key benefit. One example would be to pull down a Twitter feed and gather data that could be used in a company's social marketing efforts.

AZURE SCHEDULER

1. From the Full Azure Portal, select the Scheduler view, and click Create a New Job (in this example, ContosoJob). Name the job, select the action type and method from the drop-down lists, input a URI (contoso.com), and click the arrow to move to the next page. Choose to configure the job as a one-time job or a recurring job. If the job is a recurring job, set the schedule for how often the job should run, including a start and end date/time. Click the checkmark in the lower-right corner to complete the wizard.

2. Once the job is completed, select it to review the details and examine statistics, such as the number of jobs enabled, errors, and other details, as shown in Figure 2-16.

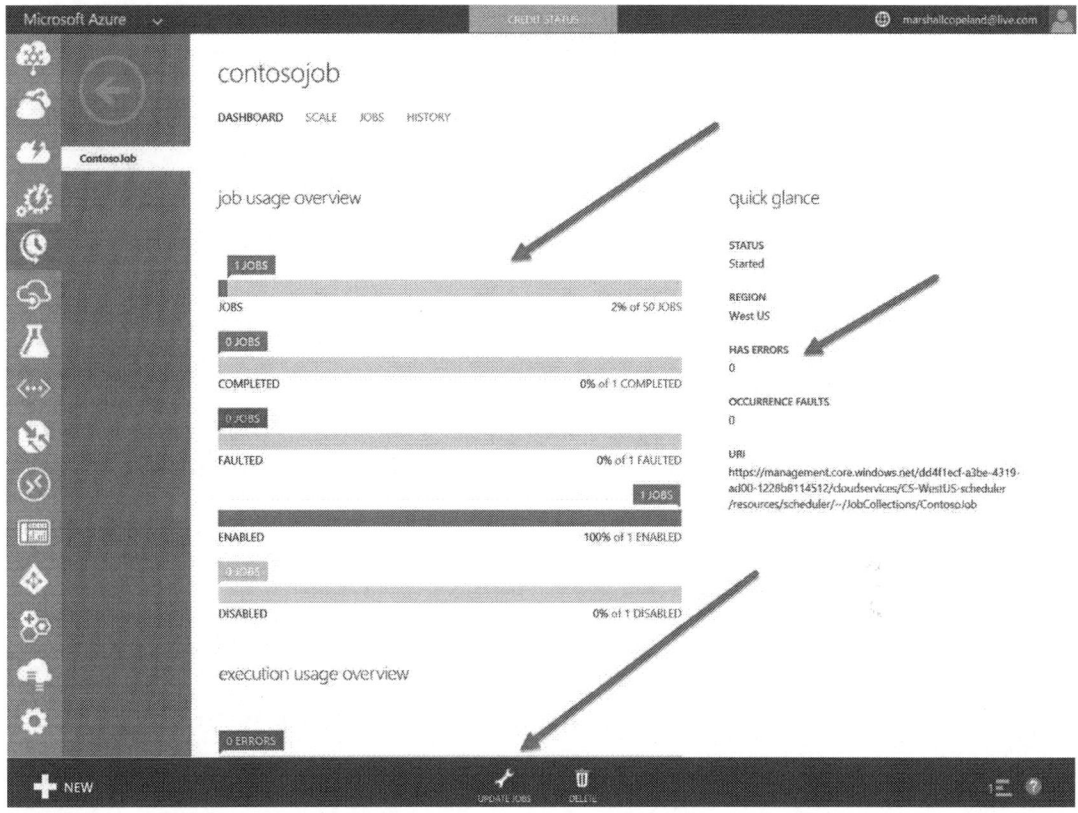

Figure 2-16. *Azure Scheduler job dashboard, which you can use to review the details of jobs, including job errors*

References

For more information on Scheduler, visit http://azure.microsoft.com/en-us/services/scheduler/.

API Management

This Azure feature provides a framework to manage custom, public, or proprietary application program interfaces (APIs) for development. It provides a secure service so that other companies or communities can build applications using APIs that you make available.

What Is It?

One way to accelerate the adoption of a developer platform is by enabling an API management process, which is integrated into Azure. This service more easily streamlines the process for developers to share, manage, and secure their API intellectual property.

Audience

The target audience for API Management includes developers who are building applications that can use this Azure cloud service to better their customers support or to attract new customers and other developers to their platform.

Benefits and Capabilities

Azure API Management allows businesses to grow by enabling other businesses, customers, partners, and private developers to use your APIs. Selling digital assets enables businesses to become more agile by securely publishing an API set to the developer community. This service helps to streamline production platforms and create new content channels for products and services.

From the Azure Portal, you can configure any of your current APIs on the Portal back end. These may be public, private, or partner APIs. You enable features in your *public* Azure Portal, such as caching, security, and others needed to enable consumption of the API set. Developers then subscribe and register at your Portal, which is automatically created by Azure API Management, and then start using your exposed API to build tools and services.

API Management provides the framework for development of your APIs by supplying configurable proxy features, forms, and protocols to expose only the property that you select by enabling quotas, rate limits, and valuation.

References

For more information on API Management, visit `http://azure.microsoft.com/en-us/services/api-management/`.

Machine Learning

Azure Machine Learning (ML) cloud services allow companies to create advanced analytic solutions using the nearly unlimited Azure resources. ML is a powerful cloud-based predictive analytics service that can use any data including unstructured HDInsight data.

What Is It?

Azure Machine Learning allows a user with a web browser to drag and drop gestures and data-flow graphs to build and connect any data, anywhere, in order to share complex analytics in minutes. No coding is required, but it is optional to use current resources.

Audience

The target audience for Azure Machine Learning includes businesses who want to know more about their customer's habits, requirements, and purchasing preferences with the goal of operationalizing this data. Analytics are used to target e-mail and/or direct mail campaigns more precisely based on large amounts of data. Your company may also choose to sell the analytic insight created with Azure Machine Learning by publishing its analytic web services through the Azure Marketplace.

Benefits and Capabilities

Companies and businesses can make better decisions and function more efficiently based on the diagnosis and understanding of the analytics provided by Azure Machine Learning. You need two parts to take full advantage of it:

- Azure Machine Learning (introduced earlier)

- Azure Machine Learning Studio

AZURE MACHINE LEARNING STUDIO

The Azure Machine Learning Studio provides an interactive workspace in which you can develop and drag and drop data from sources and enable statistical functions, as shown in Figure 2-17. This studio provides a sandbox for testing your predictive analysis model. No programing is required. Follow these steps:

1. Create a Machine Learning workspace in your Azure subscription, and select the option at far right to sign in to Azure Machine Learning Studio, which is automatically associated with your Azure subscription.

2. The first time you are in the studio, select the Experiment Tutorial to become more familiar with the drag-and-drop features.

3. Rename and save your work so you can come back later to improve or create new analytic models.

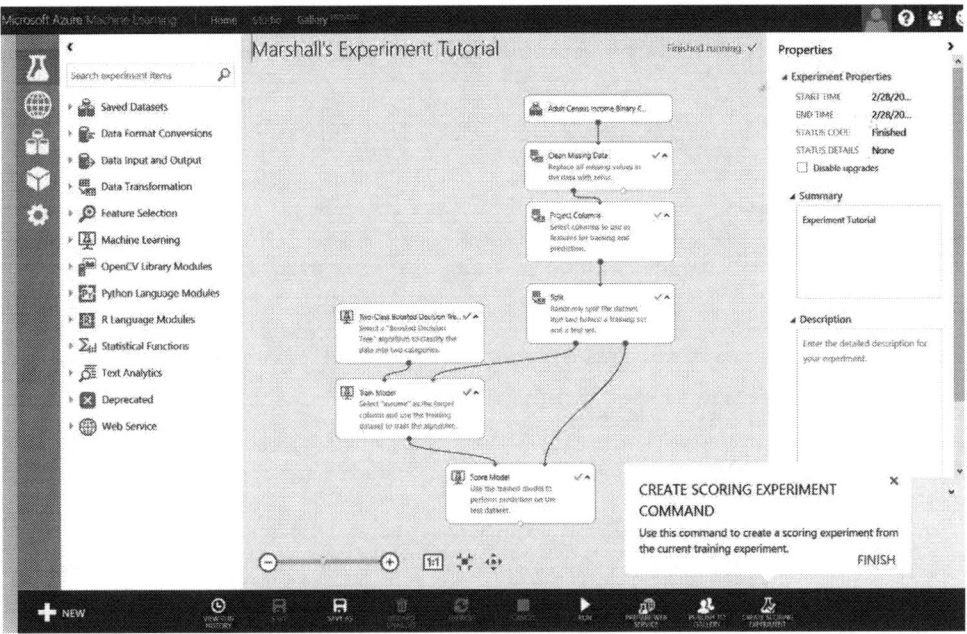

Figure 2-17. The Machine Learning Studio view of the default tutorial, which is designed to teach drag-and-drop features for analytics

■ **Note** When you are ready to publish models that you create, they become visible to the public and are not limited to the view from within your Azure subscription.

References

Azure Machine Learning Studio is further explored in Chapter 14. To see more information, visit http://azure.microsoft.com/en-us/services/machine-learning/.

Networks

As the name implies, Networks handles the provisioning and management of virtual networks in Azure.

What Is It?

Like all things that connect to the Internet, Azure VM cloud services need IP addresses. These IP addresses and IP classes are based on virtual network segments in Azure. Virtual networks allow IT administrators to group VMs in order to control accessibility and security, just like on-premises networks and VLANs.

Azure Networks also lets organizations define networks that are on premises in order to establish connectivity between virtual networks in Azure and these on-premises networks via a secure gateway.

Audience

The target audience for Azure Networks includes IT administrators who want to enable IaaS and business owners who want to enable disaster recovery in Azure or for a datacenter managed through Azure. In addition, the audience includes network team members who need to extend their TCP/IP network into Azure virtual networks for production application and on-premises DNS look up.

Benefits and Capabilities

Azure Networks provide the ability to connect on-premises infrastructure to Azure datacenters in order to extend and create true hybrid datacenter architectures. This allows administrators to manage Azure-based VMs as they would on-premises VMs. The three network-connection methods—point-to-site virtual private network (VPN), site-to-site VPN, and ExpressRoute—are explained next. These connections are then made to Azure gateways that are created, managed, and monitored by the customer organization's IT or network staff, the same way they would any network device.

The networking options to connect Azure are scalable, persistent, and secure so that the Azure network is seamlessly integrated with your on-premises datacenter. Azure Networks forms the foundation on which many Azure services can easily be made available. Figure 2-18 illustrates a site-to-site VPN tunnel connecting an on-premises datacenter network to an Azure virtual network via an Azure gateway. The on-premises networking equipment is configured to communicate and establish a secure VPN with the Azure gateway's IP address, which is provided when the gateway is created.

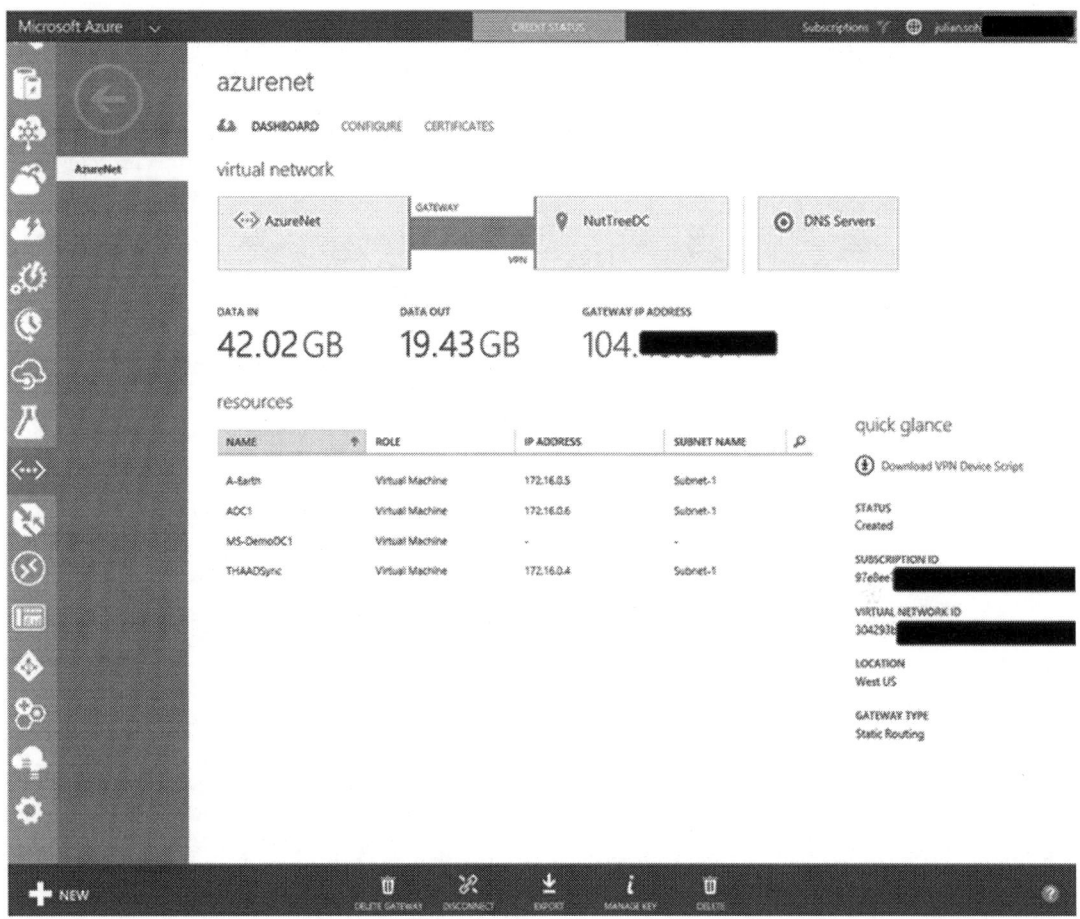

Figure 2-18. *Connection of an on-premises datacenter to an Azure network via the gateway and VPN tunnel*

Point-to-Site VPN

A point-to-site VPN lets you set up a VPN from an individual machine to Azure virtual networks. Point-to-site VPNs are generally used in a development environment where individual machines need to connect to VMs that are hosted on an Azure network. The more common scenario is a site-to-site VPN.

Site-to-Site VPN

A site-to-site VPN provides the connection between on-premises network segments and Azure virtual network segments. This allows traffic to be fully routable between both network segments via the Border Gateway Protocol (BGP). This is the typical architecture for extending an organization's network into Azure. On-premises VMs can then communicate with VMs in the Azure virtual network segment. This communication uses the Internet to connect to the Azure gateway, and it is secured via a persistent VPN tunnel.

ExpressRoute

A more traditional, albeit more expensive, method of connecting two remote datacenters is via a dedicated network circuit. *ExpressRoute* enables the provisioning of a multiprotocol labeling system (MPLS) circuit to connect an on-premises network with Azure's network. An ExpressRoute circuit is provisioned via worldwide partner ISPs and telecom providers that support Azure, such as AT&T, Level-3, BT, Tata, SingTel, Equinix, and many more.

References

Azure Networks is discussed in detail in Chapter 8. For more information about Azure Networks, visit `http://azure.microsoft.com/en-us/services/virtual-network/`. For more information about ExpressRoute, visit `http://azure.microsoft.com/en-us/services/expressroute/`.

Traffic Manager

This service is used to distribute user traffic to Azure services in one or more datacenters.

What Is It?

Traffic Manager controls IP and web traffic by load-balancing with DNS name resolution across different methods to different endpoints (for example, cloud services and websites) in Azure datacenters.

Audience

The target audience for Traffic Manager often includes the typical team that uses load balancing in a collaboration between the website team and the network team. With the help of Traffic Manager, when creating profiles in the Azure Portal, the website team and business owners can easily distribute the load from inside Azure.

Benefits and Capabilities

Traffic Manager is currently available only in the Full Azure Portal for configuration. It does appear as an option in the Preview Portal, but profiles cannot yet be created. Traffic Manager supports load balancing without the added cost of expensive routers or the expense of employing networking engineers.

With traditional hardware load balancing, there are rules that need to be configured using network commands. Azure Traffic Manager handles the configuration rules by using an *intelligent policy engine* and applying to Domain Name System (DNS).

A key component to understand about Traffic Manager, and what sets it apart from traditional load-balancing hardware, is that no end-point traffic is moved or routed through it. The (software) profile that is created uses a DNS query to route traffic to the appropriate end point.

After you create and deploy the Azure services (that is, Azure Cloud Services and Azure Websites), those are the end points. Then you can create a profile by selecting Create a Traffic Manager Profile in the Traffic Manager view, as shown in Figure 2-19. This enables the New Network Services option, with Traffic Manager and Quick Create preselected. Be sure to enter a unique name for the DNS prefix.

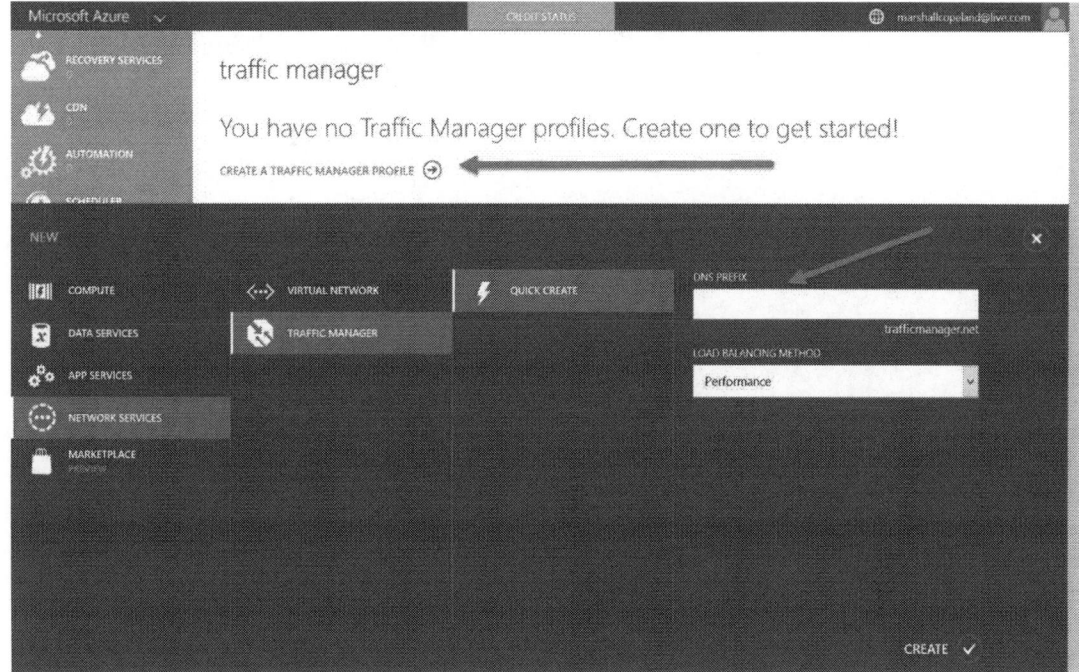

Figure 2-19. *Create a new Traffic Manager profile by selecting Create a Traffic Manager Profile in the Traffic Manager view*

The DNS name in this example could be ContosoMainWebsite.trafficmanger.net. Notice that only the first part of the DNS name can be edited. Technically, this process creates a lookup for the resource record (CNAME) in the DNS services. The next option is to select the end points for this profile at the top of the Traffic Manager Profile view, as shown in Figure 2-20.

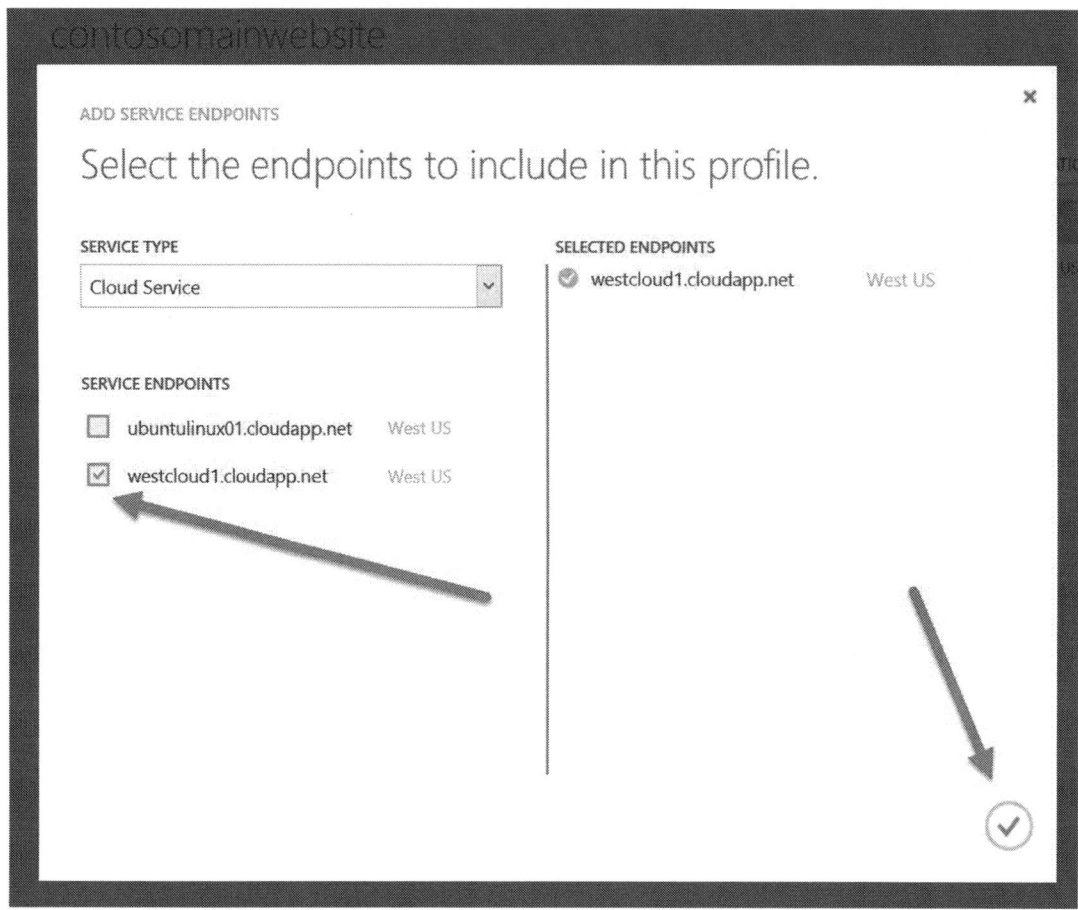

Figure 2-20. *Select the specific end points to add to this profile for querying DNS. Click the check mark at lower right to configure the profile*

You can configure additional options for each profile to support the end points, such as DNS time to live (how long does the query remain valid?) for each query. Additional settings include the type of load balancing, performance (default), round robin, and failover. These are all major load-balancing features in high-end and high-cost hardware.

References

For additional information about Traffic Manager, visit http://aka.ms/matm.

RemoteApp

The RemoteApp service provides your company's core applications hosted on Windows servers in Azure, and it allows access by users with tablets like Microsoft Surface, iPad, and various Android devices.

What Is It?

Using the RemoteApp service, IT can enable a massively scalable Remote Desktop Service for Windows with applications running on Azure cloud services in about an hour. This service scales dynamically, enables global access from almost any device, and is configured from the Full Azure Portal.

Audience

If your CEO has visions of a successful deployment of virtual desktop infrastructure (VDI), Azure RemoteApp enables global deployment of servers hosting Windows applications. The target audience for the RemoteApp service also includes IT organizations that struggle with agility, resources, or the ability to scale up and down based on user demand. IaaS teams can take advantage of the pre-built application collections in Azure, or they can integrate existing on-premises services using the Microsoft Remote Desktop Session Host.

Benefits and Capabilities

Microsoft Windows has provided Remote Desktop Services (RDS) as part of the OS for many years. Customers are challenged by the cost and location of IT server hardware that allows scaling to support virtual hosted applications. Azure RemoteApp is ready to use instantly with tens of thousands of preconfigured servers, which removes the complexity of on-premises configuration.

Use of Azure RemoteApp is provided in two, easily consumable models: cloud collection and hybrid collection. A *cloud collection* is ready to go with minimal configuration from the Azure Portal. This includes all the applications and data stored in Azure cloud services. Companies that have enabled synchronization between on-premises Active Directory and Azure Active Directory can sign in using their corporate credentials.

Azure RemoteApp *hybrid collectio*n includes all the applications running in the Azure cloud; it also stores data in Azure. However, this model further allows users to access information and resources on the company's local network. Corporate accounts are used to log in to access these Azure applications if federated services between on-premises and Azure are enabled.

Azure administrators and business owners with privileges in Azure subscriptions can start a RemoteApp trial by selecting one of the Microsoft Office applications that are preinstalled and ready to share with all end users in your organization.

AZURE REMOTEAPP SERVICE

To use the Azure RemoteApp service, follow these steps:

1. From the Full Azure Portal, select the RemoteApp property, and click the Create a RemoteApp Collection arrow in the center of the screen to start the wizard. Some of the required decisions include the unique name of the collection, what Azure region to use, Basic or Standard plan, and what preconfigured Office application to use during the trial.

2. Click the Create RemoteApp Collection check mark in the lower-right corner, as shown in Figure 2-21.

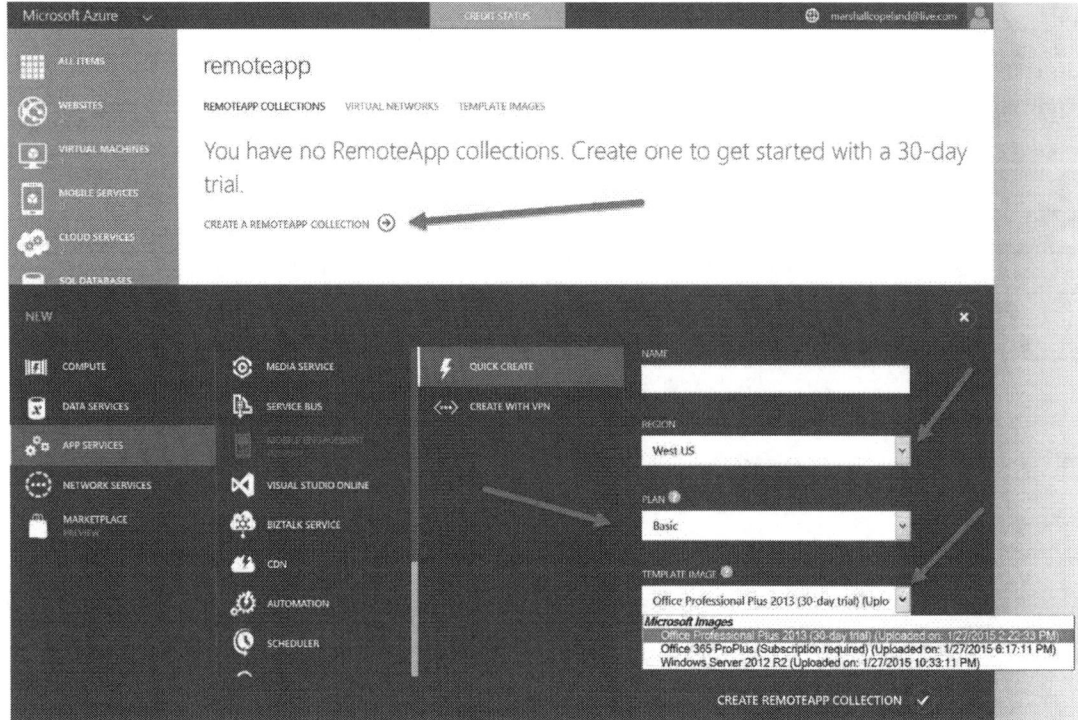

Figure 2-21. *RemoteApp trial enabled using the Full Azure Portal. This allows the quick-create wizard to use preconfigured Microsoft Office applications*

There are two plan choices, and the cost of each plan is about the same for traditional types of users, task workers, and information workers. The Basic plan includes using lightweight remote applications for 0.18 cents per hour, and the Standard plan includes using productivity applications for 0.20 cents per hour.

■ **Note**   Pricing is not the only reason to choose a cloud solution. It is important, however, because we've seen over time that changes in Azure actually help control, if not reduce, customer costs.

The hybrid collection for Azure RemoteApp requires the on-premises IT team to complete connections supporting IaaS network connections, so a few more technical steps are required to enable other applications. The major steps include creating a custom template image for the RemoteApp service, creating the RemoteApp collection (described earlier), enabling the on-premises network with Azure virtual networks, and publishing your company's RemoteApp applications to Azure.

References

For more information and step-by-step details required to create either of the two Azure RemoteApp services, visit http://azure.microsoft.com/en-us/documentation/articles/remoteapp-whatis/.

Management Services

Azure Management Services supports alerts and notification components for any of the services used in the Full Azure Portal.

What Is It?

In the simplest form, Azure Management Services issues alerts based on overages or an anomaly in components configured in your subscription. This feature specifically supports the creation of active rules based on Azure metrics to send out notifications about any threshold violations.

Audience

The target audience for Azure Management Services includes Azure administrators, technical team members, application owners, and business solution owners. Preemptive alerts are sent by e-mail and report any degradation in performance that may impact availability. Alerts are created using a two-step wizard to support these types of notifications.

Benefits and Capabilities

Azure Management Services provides e-mail notifications in real time when issues are uncovered and performance breaches thresholds established using the built-in Azure metrics. Specific metrics vary based on the Azure workloads and are exposed through the Full Azure Portal.

AZURE MANAGEMENT SERVICES

One example of such a notification uses the wizard to configure an alert for an Ubuntu server:

1. Click the Management Services property, and click Add Rule at bottom center in the Portal to start the wizard, as shown in Figure 2-22.

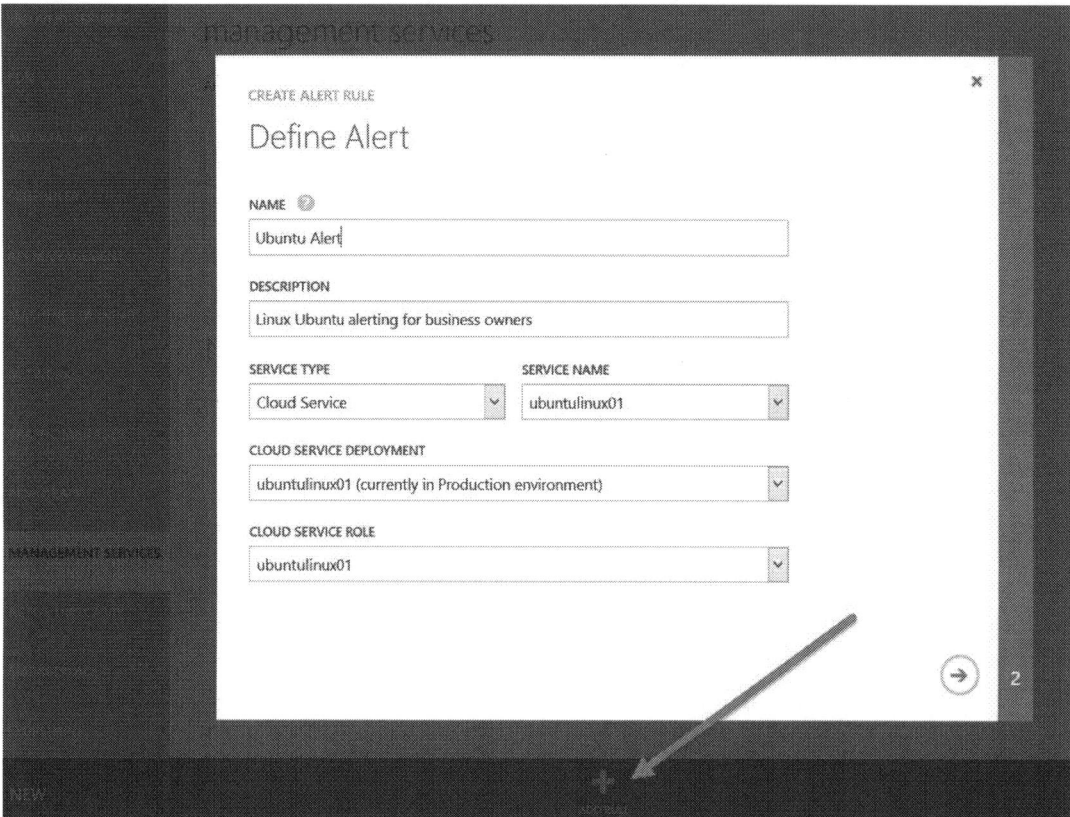

Figure 2-22. *Create a new alert by clicking Add Rule at bottom center in the Management Services view*

2. Add a name and description, and use the drop-down arrow to select the service type. In this example, Cloud Service is selected for the Ubuntu Linux server. Other service types include Mobile Services, SQL Databases, Storage, Virtual Machines, and Websites. The service type selected may prepopulate data in the wizard, as is the case in this example. The Cloud Service Deployment data and Cloud Service Role are created automatically.

3. Click the arrow at bottom-right to move to the second page of the wizard, shown in Figure 2-23. The default Metric is CPU Percentage, so you need to add a Threshold Value and check two options: "Send an e-mail to the service administrator and co-administrators" (default Azure admins) and "Specify the email address for another administrator." Enable Rule is checked by default. If you click the down arrow to the right of the CPU Percentage metric, you can select other metrics. These include Disk Ready Bytes / Second, Disk Write Bytes / Second, and Network In and Network Out.

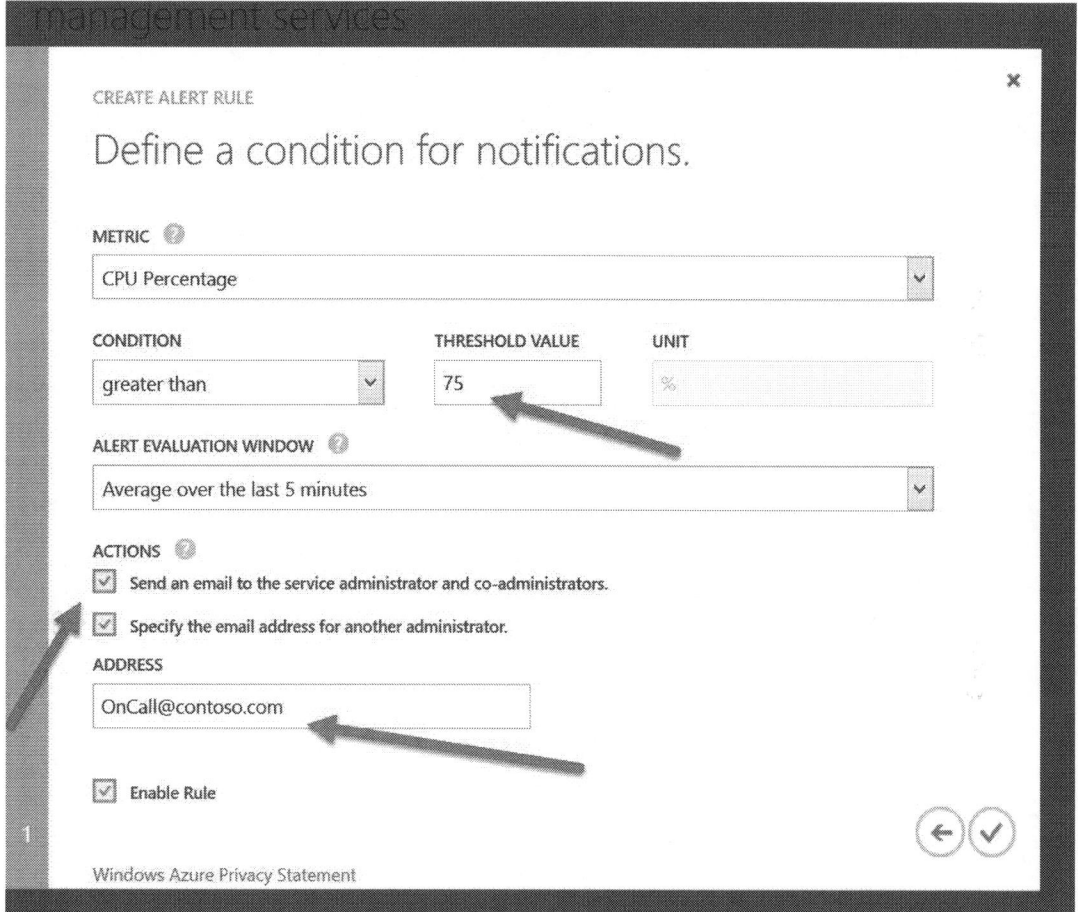

Figure 2-23. *Complete the creation of a new alert by adding a threshold values, enabling e-mail actions, and validating Enable Rule, which is checked*

The second Action, "Specify the email address for another administrator", enables the Address text box; enter OnCall@Contoso.com. This address can be a distribution list so that more than one e-mail recipient can be alerted at the same time. You can easily enable automation by using System Center Orchestrator to monitor the e-mail account OnCall@contoso.com, pull the exact user e-mail that is on call from a SQL database or Excel worksheet (for example, Anthony.Puca@Microsoft.com), and automatically e-mail that individual and not the entire team.

4. Click the check mark at bottom right to complete this alert. It appears on the main screen in the Management Services view in the Portal.

Let's look at one more example to help you understand the power of these services and how better to take advantage of the alerting feature. In this case, you want to set an alert for one of your websites:

5. Click Add Rule at the bottom of the Management Services view. Just as before, provide a Name and Description, but this time select one of your websites as the Service Type.

6. Click the arrow at the bottom of the page to move t the second page, shown in Figure 2-24.

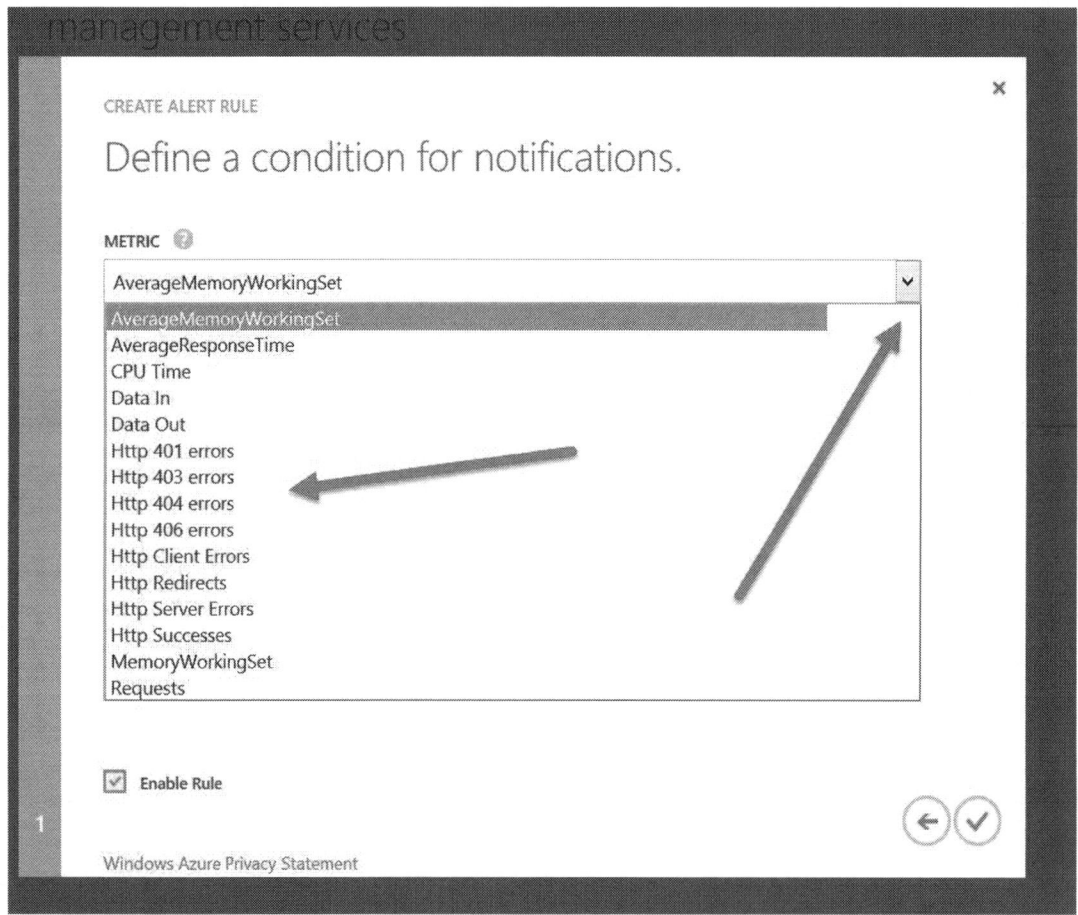

Figure 2-24. Second page of the wizard after selecting Website. The default Metric is AverageMemoryWorkingSet. Click the drop-down arrow to explore additional metrics

In this example, Service Type (from the first page of the wizard, as you saw in Figure 2-22) was changed to Website and the Contoso Company Website was selected. Now you can customize alerts based on HTTP error codes. When web administrators make changes to the website, links to pages may be missed or misconfigured; by enabling multiple alert notifications, you can more easily identify corrections.

One final thought regarding the types of alerts possible with this example: you could create an alert based AverageResponseTime in the Metric drop-down list. If you select this metric, the response time threshold is measured in milliseconds. This alert could be set for 3,000 milliseconds or 3 seconds, (1 second = 1,000 milliseconds), which is an eternity for some websites to render the main page of your company portal.

References

Alerting in Management Services is easy, and it can be customized based on resources including all the different services. For more information about alerting and monitoring using Azure Management Services, visit https://msdn.microsoft.com/en-us/library/azure/dn306639.aspx.

Azure Active Directory (AAD)

Azure Active Directory (AAD) is identity management (IDM) in the cloud.

What Is It?

AAD is Active Directory in the cloud. It is intended to extend on-premises Active Directory (AD) and provide modern IDM capabilities, such as claims-based authentication and out-of-the-box federation with popular third-party software-as-a-service (SaaS) apps like Salesforce, Dropbox, and ServiceNow. AAD strives to be a feature-rich advanced directory-as-a-service (DaaS) offering in Azure, and it is currently one of the most rapidly adopted Azure services.

Audience

The target audience for AAD includes application developers who need authentication services for apps, IT administrators managing AD or other IDM solutions, SIs who need to provide single sign-on (SSO) capabilities to disparate third-party SaaS, and CISOs who are interested in providing advanced IDM features such as multifactor authentication (MFA) and Rights Management Services (RMS).

Benefits and Capabilities

AAD is already the IDM for Office 365 customers. Through AAD, Office 365 services can provision mailboxes and grant access to SharePoint Online sites because user accounts that are locked in AD are not synchronized to AAD. A good resource on Microsoft Office 365 administration is *Microsoft Office 365 Administration Inside Out* by Anthony Puca, Julian Soh, and Marshall Copeland (Microsoft Press, 2013). This book addresses how and why AD is synchronized to AAD.

AAD is now unlocked for non-Office 365 uses as well. Azure sells the expanded capability of AAD via a SKU known as *Azure Active Directory Premium*, which is also part of a suite known as the *Enterprise Mobility Suite (EMS)*.

For Office 365 customers, the benefit of expanding the use of AAD includes the ability to take advantage of all the integration work that has been done for Office 365, such as Directory Synchronization (DirSync) and Active Directory Federation Services (AD FS) for SSO.

For non–Office 365 customers who use on-premises AD, extending into Azure with AAD delivers the capability to use all the security profiles that have been implemented in AD for claims-based applications, provide SSO, and implement advanced authentication services such as MFA and RMS.

Figure 2-25 shows the application gallery in AAD. At the time of this writing, AAD provides SSO for more than 2,400 out-of-the-box pre-federated apps.

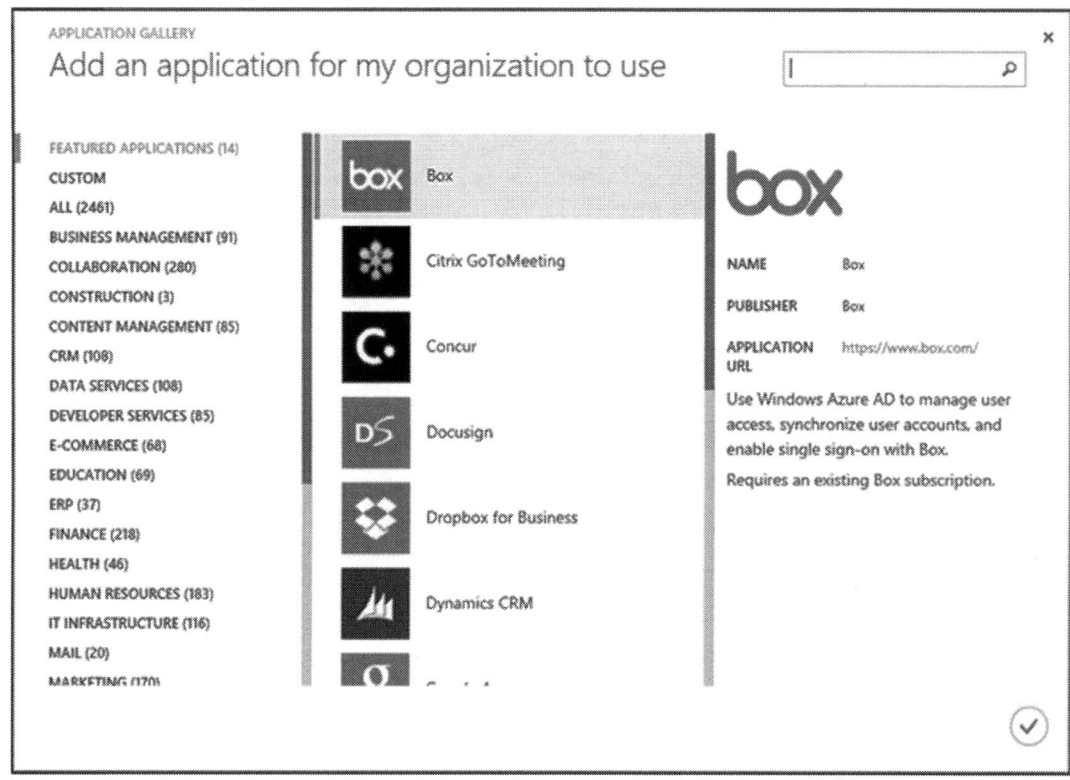

Figure 2-25. *Adding a pre-federated third-party SaaS from the application gallery in AAD to provide SSO*

References

AAD is covered in detail in Chapter 9. For more information, visit `http://azure.microsoft.com/en-us/services/active-directory/`.

Summary

This chapter was designed to increase your familiarity with all the different Azure Services available today. You should expect the number of services to increase over time. As you can see, Azure is a collection of many services for different business requirements, and it covers all aspects of IT operations—from networks to IDM and access control to application development. From here, you can choose to go directly to the chapter that dives deeper into the configuration and use of each specific Azure service.

In the next chapter, you gain the deep insight necessary for planning Azure services. Planning provides guidance to ensure that services are created effectively based on business requirements. Read the planning section to understand how specific configurations may be used and how potentially unwanted configurations may be avoided.

CHAPTER 3

■ ■ ■

Azure Real-World Scenarios

Real-World Scenarios

Previous chapters provided a detailed introduction to the more than 1,500 Microsoft Azure services, in order to give you a good foundation in Azure's capabilities. To complete this first part of the book, this chapter examines some real-world scenarios in which Azure is being used, although the customers and organizations remain anonymous.

The goal of this chapter is to tie Azure's capabilities together in order to solve business problems. This sets the stage for the next part of the book, which dives into these selected Azure services in detail. The scenarios discussed here are designed to help you visualize how Azure can help you to meet similar business needs in your organization.

At the time of writing, these are some of the common workloads being deployed in Azure:

- Identity management and authentication

- Rich content storage and processing, specifically audio and video files

- Testing and development environment

Identity Management and Authentication

Microsoft Active Directory (AD) is the long-standing identity management (IDM) platform for Microsoft Windows servers and networks. It is a mature technology that has been in use for nearly two decades. There are many AD roles, such as Active Directory Domain Services (AD DS), Active Directory Federation Services (AD FS), Active Directory Lightweight Domain Services (AD LDS), and Active Directory Certificate Services (AD CS). There are also AD tools and dependencies, such as Microsoft Identity Manager (MIM), AD Domain Name Services (AD DNS), and so on. Collectively, these technologies provide for management of identities, networked resources, locations, and access to applications and services.

In the scenario addressed here, the specific AD capability you examine is authentication. This is important because without the ability to authenticate, users can't access resources on the corporate network. Without the proper trusts in place, users may be overwhelmed by the incessant need for redundant authentication as they traverse from one service to another.

Business Drivers: Building a Claims-Based Authentication Infrastructure

Because software as a service (SaaS) is provisioned from external networks and datacenters that are not part of the corporate IT environment, they need to be integrated with AD in order for the customer not to have to re-authenticate to the SaaS if they have already been authenticated by AD. You can do this by using claims-based authentication capabilities such as AD FS, which provides a single sign-on (SSO) experience for users. Furthermore, organizations do not want to trade the benefits of SaaS for the burden of managing multiple IDM systems, which increases cost and risks.

Challenges

Building an AD FS infrastructure, or adopting a third-party solution to provide claims-based authentication and using traditional AD, is already a mature approach. However, one of the benefits of SaaS solutions like Office 365 is the service-level agreement (SLA) that provides guaranteed availability and uptime beyond the reach of most organizations. Relying on on-premises authentication availability means the SLA for the SaaS can be only as good as the availability of the claims-based authentication infrastructure.

Organizations that have deployed Office 365 with SSO have occasionally discovered that an outage with AD FS hosted on-premises resulted in users being unable to log in to Office 365. And in setting up AD FS for the first time, some organizations realize that they lack the necessary claims-based authentication infrastructure and must acquire additional hardware.

Solution Description

Building or moving a claims-based authentication infrastructure such as AD FS from on-premises datacenters to Azure improves the SLA for SaaS solutions. This assumes that Azure's SLA provides higher availability than the on-premises SLA, which is often the case. In addition to higher availability, the claims-based authentication infrastructure benefits from better georedundancy, and therefore it meets or exceeds many disaster-recovery (DR) requirements.

For organizations that are considering acquiring new hardware in order to implement AD FS or a third-party claims-based authentication infrastructure, alternatively building the environment up in Azure enables these organizations to avoid hardware acquisition and future hardware-refresh cycles. Building a georedundant and highly available claims-based architecture using this approach uses the Azure infrastructure as a service (IaaS) offering.

In addition to IaaS, Azure offers identity as a service (IDaaS) in the form of Azure Active Directory (AAD), which provides claims-based authentication to Office 365 and other SaaS solutions. AAD allows organizations to manage users in AD, and it creates such users in SaaS if needed. Therefore, you no longer need to manage users manually in a fragmented SaaS environment where each SaaS may require its own IDM.

Solution Reference

Chapter 11, "Clusters, Regional VNets, High Availability, and Disaster Recovery," provides detailed information about Azure IaaS to assist you in building a high-availability, georedundant AD FS infrastructure. Detailed information about AAD as an IDaaS extension for AD is covered in Chapter 10, "Extending Azure Active Directory."

Rich Content Storage and Processing

Rich content refers to video, audio, and high-quality graphic files. Generally, these types of files differ from documents because they can consume large amounts of network bandwidth, storage space, or both.

Business Drivers: Body-Worn Video Cameras

At the time of this writing, one rich content real-world scenario is the trend to require police officers to wear body-worn video cameras in order to make law-enforcement activities more transparent. Body-worn video cameras create a new source for content that needs to be stored, processed, and viewed on different types of devices.

Challenges

Organizations that have to store audio and video files may find it difficult to estimate the amount of content that will be generated and thus the amount of storage space required. In this scenario, the audio and video content generated may vary based on the volume and frequency of incidents, and thus the storage needs are difficult to predict. Furthermore, once content is created, there is a potential need to convert it into other compatible formats for playback purposes, and the level of effort required to convert content may be significant.

Solution Description

Azure provides two types of services with respect to audio and video files:

- A scalable, elastic, and redundant storage medium

- Processing and streaming of audio and video content

At the minimum and most simplistic level, Azure as a scalable and elastic storage medium is very well suited for unpredictable workloads. Azure's default *locally redundant storage (LRS)* provides a level of redundancy that meets or exceeds many organizations' requirements. Alternatively, if more redundancy is required, organizations can elect to use *geographically redundant storage (GRS)*.

Once the audio and video content is stored in Azure, you can use additional value-added capabilities. This takes the form of Azure Media Services. Azure Media Services is a set of video-processing and analyzing capabilities that includes

- Conversion of videos into streaming formats for ease of consumption

- Speech-to-text transcription, known as the *Indexing Service*

Figure 3-1 shows all the supported streaming formats into which Azure Media Services can convert an audio/video file.

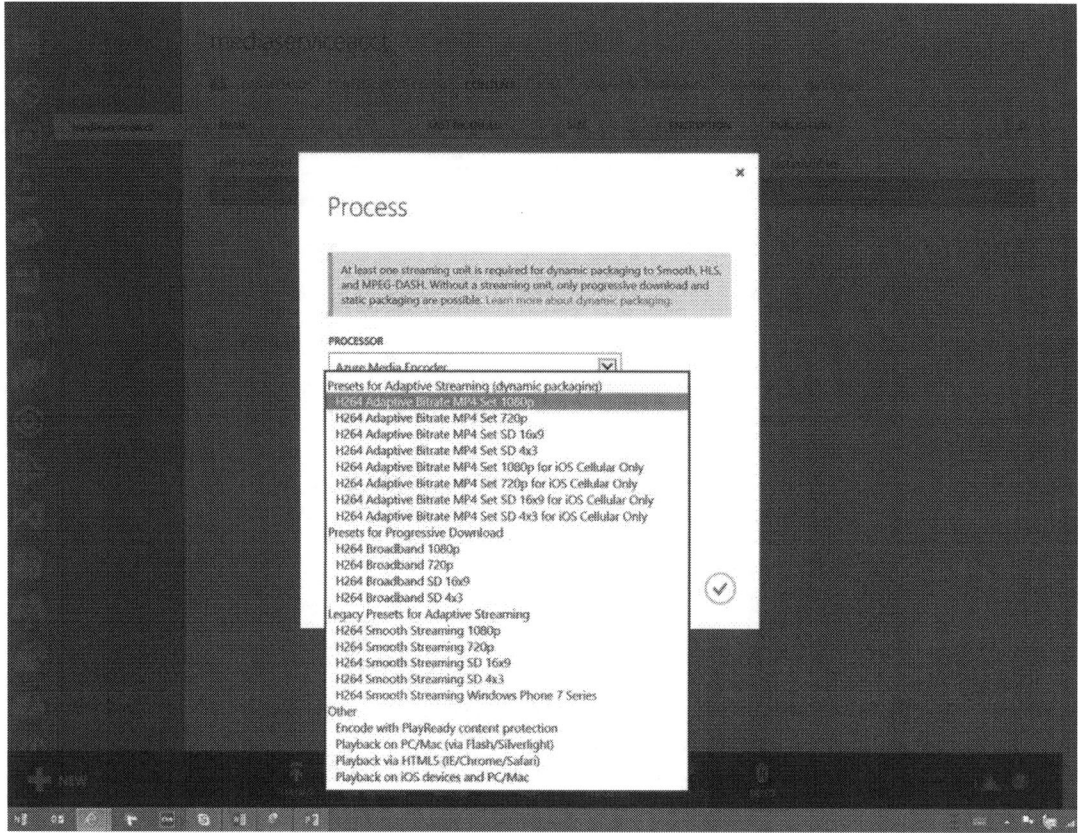

Figure 3-1. *Streamable formats to which Azure Media Services can convert a media file*

When the Indexing Service processes a video, an XML-based file, also known as a *text transcription markup language (TTML)* file, is created. Figure 3-2 shows a TTML file created by the Indexing Service. Notice that the first and second columns are the start and stop times of the transcribed speech.

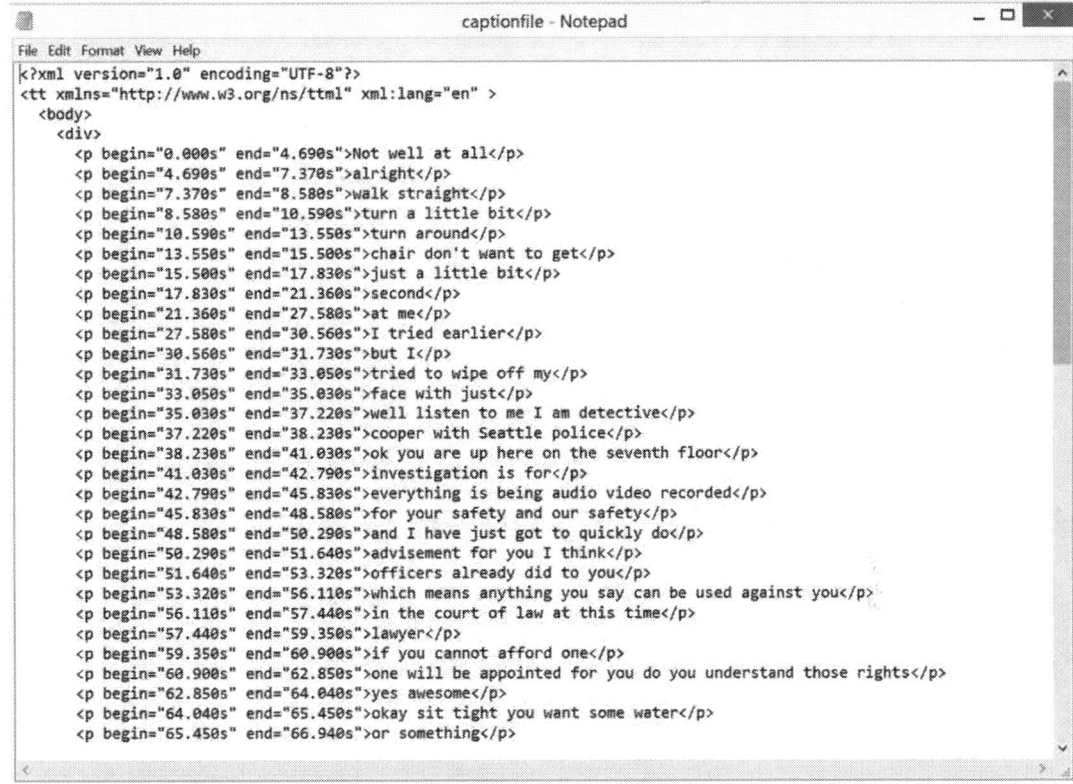

```
                          captionfile - Notepad                          _ □ ✕
File  Edit  Format  View  Help
<?xml version="1.0" encoding="UTF-8"?>
<tt xmlns="http://www.w3.org/ns/ttml" xml:lang="en" >
  <body>
    <div>
      <p begin="0.000s" end="4.690s">Not well at all</p>
      <p begin="4.690s" end="7.370s">alright</p>
      <p begin="7.370s" end="8.580s">walk straight</p>
      <p begin="8.580s" end="10.590s">turn a little bit</p>
      <p begin="10.590s" end="13.550s">turn around</p>
      <p begin="13.550s" end="15.500s">chair don't want to get</p>
      <p begin="15.500s" end="17.830s">just a little bit</p>
      <p begin="17.830s" end="21.360s">second</p>
      <p begin="21.360s" end="27.580s">at me</p>
      <p begin="27.580s" end="30.560s">I tried earlier</p>
      <p begin="30.560s" end="31.730s">but I</p>
      <p begin="31.730s" end="33.050s">tried to wipe off my</p>
      <p begin="33.050s" end="35.030s">face with just</p>
      <p begin="35.030s" end="37.220s">well listen to me I am detective</p>
      <p begin="37.220s" end="38.230s">cooper with Seattle police</p>
      <p begin="38.230s" end="41.030s">ok you are up here on the seventh floor</p>
      <p begin="41.030s" end="42.790s">investigation is for</p>
      <p begin="42.790s" end="45.830s">everything is being audio video recorded</p>
      <p begin="45.830s" end="48.580s">for your safety and our safety</p>
      <p begin="48.580s" end="50.290s">and I have just got to quickly do</p>
      <p begin="50.290s" end="51.640s">advisement for you I think</p>
      <p begin="51.640s" end="53.320s">officers already did to you</p>
      <p begin="53.320s" end="56.110s">which means anything you say can be used against you</p>
      <p begin="56.110s" end="57.440s">in the court of law at this time</p>
      <p begin="57.440s" end="59.350s">lawyer</p>
      <p begin="59.350s" end="60.900s">if you cannot afford one</p>
      <p begin="60.900s" end="62.850s">one will be appointed for you do you understand those rights</p>
      <p begin="62.850s" end="64.040s">yes awesome</p>
      <p begin="64.040s" end="65.450s">okay sit tight you want some water</p>
      <p begin="65.450s" end="66.940s">or something</p>
```

Figure 3-2. TTML file created by the Indexing Service

In this case, the TTML file can be used for captioning in order to meet American Disabilities Act (ADA) requirements for the hearing impaired or to search in the audio or video file, because the start and end times of the transcribed text are also produced in the TTML. Figure 3-3 shows a simple HTML 5 player that uses the TTML file along with the associated video file.

HTML5 Video Caption Maker

This demo allows you to create simple video caption files. Start by loading a video in a format your browser can play. Then alternately play and pause the video, entering a caption for each segment.

If you have a saved WebVTT or TTML caption file for your video, you may load it, edit the text of existing segments, or append new segments.

Figure 3-3. *HTML 5 video player with caption file*

■ **Note** You can see the HTML 5 player used in the example in Figure 3-3 and other standards at http://dev.modern.ie/testdrive.

Microsoft Azure datacenters in Canada are now available to support the greater security requirements for video and other workloads for the Canadian Government and Canadian citizens. You can read more about Azure in Canada at the Microsoft Blog: http://blogs.msdn.com/b/make_it_better/archive/2015/06/02/microsoft-azure-canada-datacenters-yay.aspx.

Solution Reference

Azure Storage is covered in detail in Chapter 7, "Understanding Azure Storage and Databases." You can find more information about Azure Media Services at http://azure.microsoft.com/en-us/services/media-services.

Creating a Preproduction Sandbox

Any organization that undertakes custom in-house software development provisions its architecture for development and testing purposes. Even if no custom in-house software development activities are involved, it is not uncommon for organizations to have a testing environment to check configuration changes to commercial off-the-shelf software (COTS) prior to implementing the changes in the production environment.

Business Drivers: Creating a Testing and Development Architecture

Building a testing and development architecture requires the acquisition and maintenance of hardware. Sometimes the testing and development environments are separate. When added to the production environment, this translates to three separate environments that an organization must manage and maintain. Whenever there is a hardware upgrade in the production environment, the old production environment may trickle down into the testing and development environments.

Nonetheless, there may be instances when the hardware in the testing and/or development environments needs to be kept up-to-date along with the production environment. If such a need exists, then the testing and development environments must go through an upgrade whenever the production environment is upgraded. Most organizations try to keep the testing environment identical to the production environment; the only difference between the two is that the production environment may have greater redundancy and be larger in scale.

The primary business driver when there is a need to maintain testing and development environments is the cost of acquiring and maintaining hardware in the two or three separate environments.

Challenges

In addition to the cost of maintaining hardware in two or three separate environments, there is also the challenge of agility and scalability. *Agility* describes the ability to provision hardware quickly for the testing and development environments. *Scalability* describes the ability to add more hardware in order to expand the testing and development environments.

The traditional approach to acquiring hardware usually takes a lot of time, and thus it is not an agile or cost-effective method. Furthermore, if hardware is acquired in order to scale out a testing or development environment, it is a permanent action. Unless an organization is leasing or can return the hardware, it is usually not easy to scale back down if the need for the larger environment is temporary and no longer required.

Solution Description

Using Azure Virtual Machines and Virtual Networks for testing and development purposes is one of the most popular reasons for adopting IaaS:

- Organizations new to IaaS feel more comfortable experimenting with the cloud in their testing and development environments because these are usually less mission-critical.

- The flexibility to scale up and down quickly in Azure, which is based on consumption, provides a compelling cost model.

- Each Microsoft Developer Network (MSDN) subscription comes with a monthly Azure allowance. This is ideal for developers who need to have an environment with servers for development projects.

Solution Reference

Using and migrating to Azure Virtual Machines is covered in detail in Chapter 6, "Getting Started with Azure Virtual Machines," Chapter 11, "Clusters, Regional VNets, High Availability, and Disaster Recovery," and Chapter 12, "Migrating Your Virtual Machines to Azure." For more information about using MSDN with Azure, visit `http://msdn.microsoft.com`.

Small and Mid-Sized Businesses

According to the US government, businesses with fewer than 250 employees fall into the small business category; medium-sized businesses have fewer than 500 total employees. Small and mid-sized businesses (SMB) focus on providing goods and services for their "niche markets," which many big corporations are not willing to supply. These businesses may struggle to ensure that they achieve sufficient sales, more than break-even, and possibly have a greater profit. Even if the yearly sales and number of employees are less than those of a "big box" store, many SMB owners are faced with IT challenges similar to those of the larger corporations.

The almost-daily IT challenges faced by SMB organizations are just as critical to the longevity of the business as those of larger organizations, even though the business owners may not have a budget to support one or more IT staff employees.

Business Driver: We're Not in the Datacenter Business

One example is a local real estate services team that has very little invested in datacenter infrastructure. Employees are mobile with phones and laptops, and the few servers the company uses an email from their local service provider (`business@someCableCompany.com`) needs are located in an office closet and under the desks of office workers. With more than one office, there are servers in each office storing all the customer data, property listings, contracts, and payroll information. Microsoft Azure provides the necessary infrastructure for businesses including:

- High Speed TCP/IP Networking

- Virtual Machines on demand

- Email as a service (Office 365)

- Cross Collaboration as a service (SharePoint)

For email communication, the company previously used an email service provided by a local Internet service provider (ISP), but it recently moved to Microsoft Office 365 to share documents with OneDrive. The company can now view sales employee calendars to confirm appointment times.

Another example is a small printing company that produces customized notecard stock used by amateur photographers. The company has grown over the years to include products like display stands, plastic sleeves, and personalized stamps for customers. This company has two major storefront locations in the United States: one in Denver, Colorado and one in Portland, Oregon. Each location has servers tucked away in corners of the rented storefronts, and the company use leased network lines from the phone company to link the two locations together to share business data. In the Portland location, a web server provides Internet sales and marketing services for the store. It is consistently unresponsive due to either network traffic or power issues in the building. Data on the servers includes sales transactions, employee information, product inventory, and raw materials used to build the notecard stock.

Both of these companies focus on sales, products, and employees, but not on IT infrastructure. They may never have prepared for the effects of a natural disaster or a catastrophe created by a disgruntled employee. They don't have the funding to invest in building out the necessary data networks, purchasing servers for redundancy, and implementing a disaster recovery (DR) plan—they simply back up servers to tape. They both use Microsoft Hyper-V server for virtualization because it is included as a server role in the Windows Server operating system. The business owners may have contacted a local ISP to rent space in their colocation facility, but the long-term contract and high up-front cost were not in their budgets.

Challenges

Many SMB owners know they should invest in core business IT infrastructure, but they lack the in-house expertise and up-front funding needed to purchase redundant servers for their business. Small Businesses need to improve disaster preparedness, server redundancy, and application-recovery systems.

Businesses need to perform datacenter-level recovery for critical business workloads in the event of a server failure. Backups need to be automated and easily managed so that they remain in order without manual intervention.

DR plans need to be created in case a natural disaster or manmade disaster destroys critical server operations at any location. The need to perform multi-tier application and individual server-level recovery of critical workloads should be part of the DR plan.

Both of the example businesses need to minimize capital and operational expenses. They should consider reducing the number of aging existing on-premises servers by using Azure Virtual Machine services and move other applications, such as web servers, into a robust environment that expands automatically based on customer traffic.

The nature of sensitive data, including customer data, partner data, and payroll information, and the security and privacy of their infrastructure is critical. Data is highly sensitive and competitive in nature for each business.

Both business examples are cost conservative in terms of the overall solution, but they want to create a process that is automated and provides redundant services, quick testing, and validation for recovery plans.

Solution Description

The Azure pay-as-you-go model can help these two example businesses invest in IT by taking advantage of services as commodities. Azure provides two key areas for companies to use for business strategies when it comes to daily backups and DR preparedness—Azure Site Recovery and Azure Backup:

- Azure Site Recovery with Azure as a DR site

- Planned, unplanned, test failover, and failback on the servers, application, and data with Microsoft System Center VMM

- Azure Backup agent installed for all on-premises Windows servers

- Restore of both physical servers and virtual servers without relying on offline tape storage

- Site-to-site VPN between the servers in the offices or datacenter to the Azure virtual network

Azure Site Recovery with a recovery site in Azure offers the ability to perform planned and unplanned recovery and testing with minimal disruption to production. It provides orchestration and failover and failback processes to support the applications starting in the correct order.

Security is a priority for Azure, and many processes have been put in place in support of the many security-compliance requirements, such as PCI, HIPAA, FedRAMP, and ISO 27001 to name just a few:

- Data replicated to Azure as part of Azure Site Recovery is encrypted during transit, and businesses have the option to enable encryption at rest.

- VPN hardware is not an expense, because an SMB may look at enabling Microsoft Server RRAS, which is included in the server OS.

- Azure supports SMB virtual servers to be copied up to Azure, providing connectivity so that local aging server hardware is never an issue.

Applications running in Azure provide additional benefits that address redundancy, auto-scaling, and cost factors:

- Web sites running in Azure provide auto-scale-out based on performance metrics, and they auto-scale-down when no longer needed.

- Applications, VMs, and other servers are locally redundant in Azure, and businesses with critical applications have options to enable georedundancy to another Azure datacenter.

Figure 3-4 shows the network connectivity required to support Azure Site Recovery for mid-sized companies and Azure Backup for small or medium-sized businesses that require DR options.

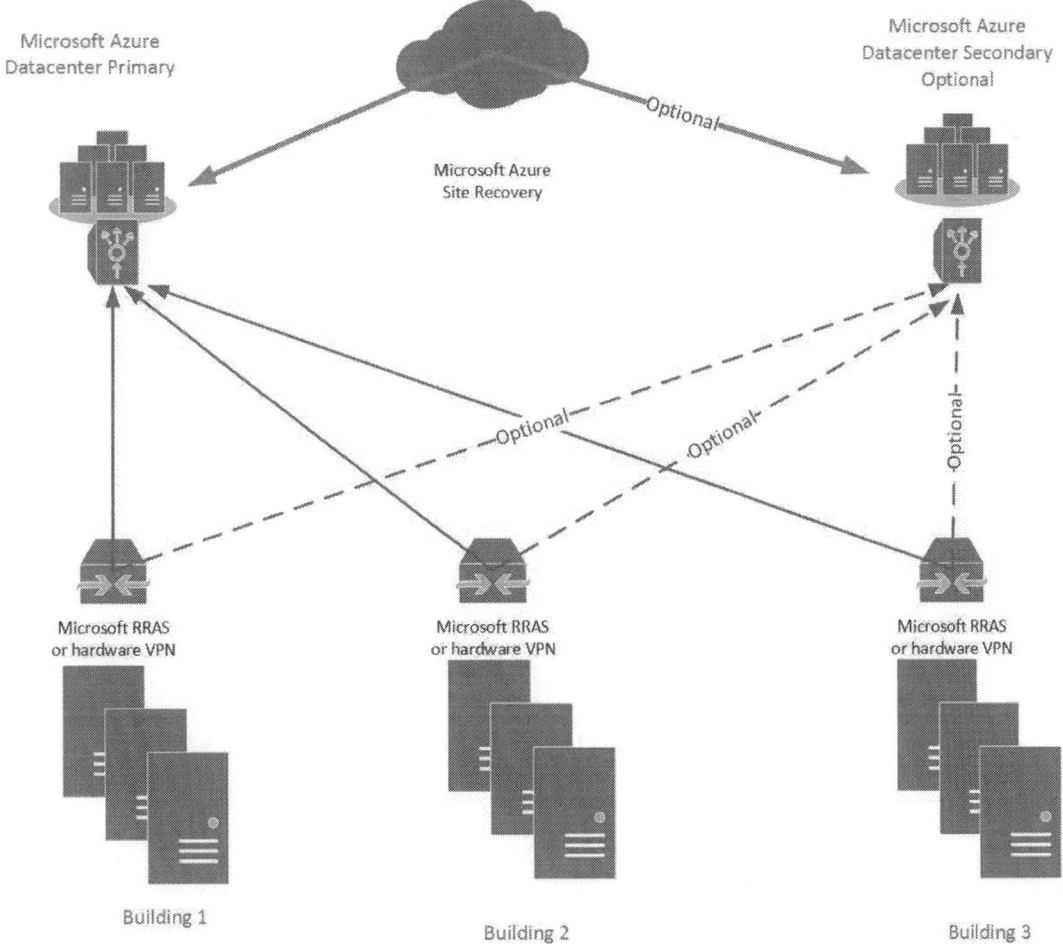

Figure 3-4. *Azure Site Recovery and Azure Backup diagram*

Solution Reference

Exercises covering the Azure services described in these real-world examples are provided in Chapter 5, "Getting Started with Azure Web Apps," Chapter 6, "Getting Stared with Azure Virtual Machines," Chapter 8, "Extending Your Network with Azure," and Chapter 11, "Clusters, Regional VNets, High Availability, and Disaster Recovery." Additionally, you can find the step-by-step deployment processes for VPN devices and Windows Server 2012R2 RRAS on the MSDN network, with detailed guidance at http://msdn.microsoft.com/en-us/library/azure/jj156075.aspx.

Large Business, Corporations, and Government Agencies

Multinational corporations and government agencies with locations both in the United States and across Europe have a global reach and are supported by large IT departments. Often, very large organizations have teams of IT personal who specialize either in given functions or in separate areas, such as networking, operating systems, applications, monitoring, and security.

One of the major IT challenges for large corporations is a global mobile workforce. A robust communications infrastructure and secure network connectivity into the corporate network are always at the forefront of any change in architecture. Mobile users who are based all over the world also have home offices. They take their work home with them and on the road. These users often have more than one mobile device, and most have residents across the country, not in the region in which they work, live, and support local businesses.

Corporations often host systems at colocation facilities in different world geographies, and the business model often requires all IT operations to have specific security compliance. In the United Sates, companies are continuously providing resources to achieve SOC1, SOC2, PCI, and other compliance to protect both intellectual property (PI) and personally identifiable information (PII) data.

As government agencies and large corporations grow both in the United States and Europe, there is a need to scale, automate, and simplify IT management. As these large organizations move to Azure, they focus on associated IT spending, minimizing cost, greater utilization of flexible resources, and reducing up-front capital expenditures. Moreover, every corporation is singularly focused on IT and network security.

Business Driver: Grow the Business, Scale Out Infrastructure, Reduce IT Budgets, and Maintain Security

Large corporations may have 15,000 to 50,000 or more employees on multiple continents. The products and services they sell vary based on their business and customer base. As the companies continue to grow, both the business divisions themselves and IT require the ability to scale up quickly as different system loads increase and to reduce spending based on customer activity.

Division and department managers are challenged to deliver contained hosting and operational costs for both IT and business facilities. With so many employee devices, there is a need to isolate corporate systems from Internet-facing systems. As the demand for laptops, tablets, and mobile phones increases, corporate access requires continued support for virtual private network (VPN) access.

As IT networks expand into different states, regions, and countries, best practices are used to simplify the duplication of successful processes and to maintain current security compliances. However, in countries across Europe and Asia, different security compliance requirements need to be put in place and processes designed to address the security statutes of the particular country. New datacenter locations require different security configurations and more IT auditing to provide services for customers and employees in those locations.

The EU's Article 29 Working Party for contractual commitments is part of the EU's Standard Contractual Clauses to protect all data for EU countries. Japan requires IT datacenters to maintain standards for financial industry information systems (FISC) for banking, computer systems, information system audits, contingency planning, and security policy development.

Businesses expanding into Australia require digital data storage to be certified by the Australian Signals Directorate (ASD) for the processing of "unclassified" data. The Ministry of Public Security in China requires auditing compliance with a multi-level protection scheme (MPLS) for data pertaining to Chinese businesses or citizens. In addition, businesses in China are required to maintain the Trusted Cloud Service certification developed by the China Cloud Computing Promotion and Policy Forum (CCCPPF).

Corporations expanding datacenters into the United Kingdom are required to achieve and maintain the UK Government G-Cloud certification. Meanwhile, back in the United States, any company that provides products or services to federal or local law enforcement agencies accessing the FBI's Criminal Justice Information Services (CJIS) database must adhere to the Criminal Justice Information Services (CJIS) Security Policy.

Azure maintains rigorous third-party audits to enable Azure services to meet a very broad set of international and industry-specific compliance standards, so corporations may quickly and globally extend IT services globally using an Azure tenant, all with a simple mouse click.

Challenges

Large corporations expanding into new markets and foreign countries have evaluated the business drivers for their corporate growth. Extending the business IT network and datacenter presence requires extensive planning and focused attention on the compliance and privacy requirements of each nation.

Datacenter colocations and expanding into existing buildings for new IT network connectivity may not be ideal because of specific datacenter needs, such as structural integrity to maintain the weight of racks of servers; uninterruptible power distribution units (PDU), which channel electricity to power the servers; and the need for physical security. In the event of a power outage at large organizations, the datacenter requires additional facilities storage for fixed-position backup batteries in order to maintain power to the servers while the diesel backup generators start up, reach capacity, and then enable electricity network failover.

Other global businesses may decide to build a new datacenter, which could involve a very lengthy time period for construction that impedes the business from growing quickly. New building construction requires the purchase of land for the datacenter, with a variable cost per square foot for the new building based on the country's available land. Other considerations include local construction company experts for datacenters—not just any residential builder or commercial builder is qualified to build a datacenter. Some countries require a percentage of the workers to be local citizens, so bringing in a complete seasoned construction crew on visas may not be permitted.

As the construction of the datacenter approaches a finished and usable facility, additional key support structures are needed, such as large humidifiers and separate air-conditioning units for maintaining constant cooling required for the server hardware to run optimally. Businesses are required to limit physical access to these facilities based on full-time employees and contractors who have validated security background checks, in order to adhere to the specific country's security compliance requirements. Only after the miles of copper or fiber network are in place, servers are racked and stacked, and the operating systems and applications are installed can the IT auditing process begin.

Solution Description

Large global corporations are moving their workloads to Azure in order to expand into new business markets quickly, because all compliance with privacy laws in the US, UK, EU, and Asia are satisfied by Azure. US corporations migrate their business services to Azure Virtual Machines (VMs) using a topology that secures data at rest and in transit. In addition, note the following:

- The corporate IT deployment experience is unchanged by implementing independent Azure VMs, enabling migration directly in a process called *lift and shift*.

- VMs in Azure have firewall rules allowing specific TCP connections and TLS needs to be configured using the appropriate security certificates installed for web sites.

- Azure web sites can be enabled to host external data collection, whereas internal web sites are enabled with the most recent release of the corporate web application. The internal web sites are configured with a network security group to prevent external traffic.

- Company web applications used to access data should use Active Directory domain credentials so that passwords are not stored in web configuration files on the application servers.

- Corporate web sites are restricted to traffic in the virtual network, and no public endpoint is exposed to the Internet.

- Access to public websites listening for Transport Layer Security (TLS) connections on port 443 can be directly supported by Azure load balancers.

Communications are secured from the corporation's current on-premises datacenter by enabling a VPN that is configured for site-to-site connections. As with local datacenter networks, similar configurations are used:

- Azure virtual networks (VNets) use industry standard Internet Protocol Security (IPsec) to secure all communication traffic between a corporate VPN gateway and Azure.

- Application tiers of service can be separated by networking subnets.

- Web front-end VMs can be placed in one subnetwork and the database back-end VMs can be placed in a different subnetwork.

- Multiple networks enable security boundaries that can be further enhanced with firewalls and intrusion-detection systems used to spot suspicious traffic.

Customers new to Azure are often surprised at the number of infrastructure-automation conveniences built into the Azure services:

- VMs created using the Azure portal wizard provide a step to enable anti-malware extensions for Microsoft, Symantec, and Trend Micro.

- Anti-malware extensions include antivirus, anti-malware, firewalls, and intrusion detection.

- Additional security features may be enabled by third-party services, such as data encrypting using SecureVM by CloudLink.

Additional benefits for customers using Azure are included with all the Azure subscriptions and tenant access. Customers that need to scale up or scale out IT network services can take advantage of the following:

- The Azure VM auto-scale feature is based on a number of different metrics such as CPU utilization, network connectivity, and so on.

- PowerShell automation is supported through the Azure Portal.

- End-to-end compliance is achieved by using Azure in addition to the current corporate IT compliance processes and procedures.

- Azure regional datacenters support data sovereignty by maintaining sensitive data in the network boundaries of the corporation. They only exchange data with third-party counters that meet the data-protection requirements of the country of origin.

- Microsoft does not transfer customer data outside of the geography of the customer's network enablement, with the exception of providing customer support, troubleshooting issues, and complying with legal requirements.

- Corporations have complete control over their data and their customer's data in specific geographic areas and regions supported by the Microsoft datacenters.

- The Azure platform undergoes rigorous regular auditing to maintain and support new compliance requirements for different industries.

- Validations for US businesses include government (FISMA and FedRAMP), financial services (SCO1, SCO2, PCI, and DSS), healthcare (HIPAA), and many more.

The reference example, shown in in Figure 3-5, provides high-level considerations for security that separates public properties from back-end corporate VMs and services. Figure 3-5 shows the network overview and one of the possible ways to increase security with parameter fencing using more than one network security group (NSG).

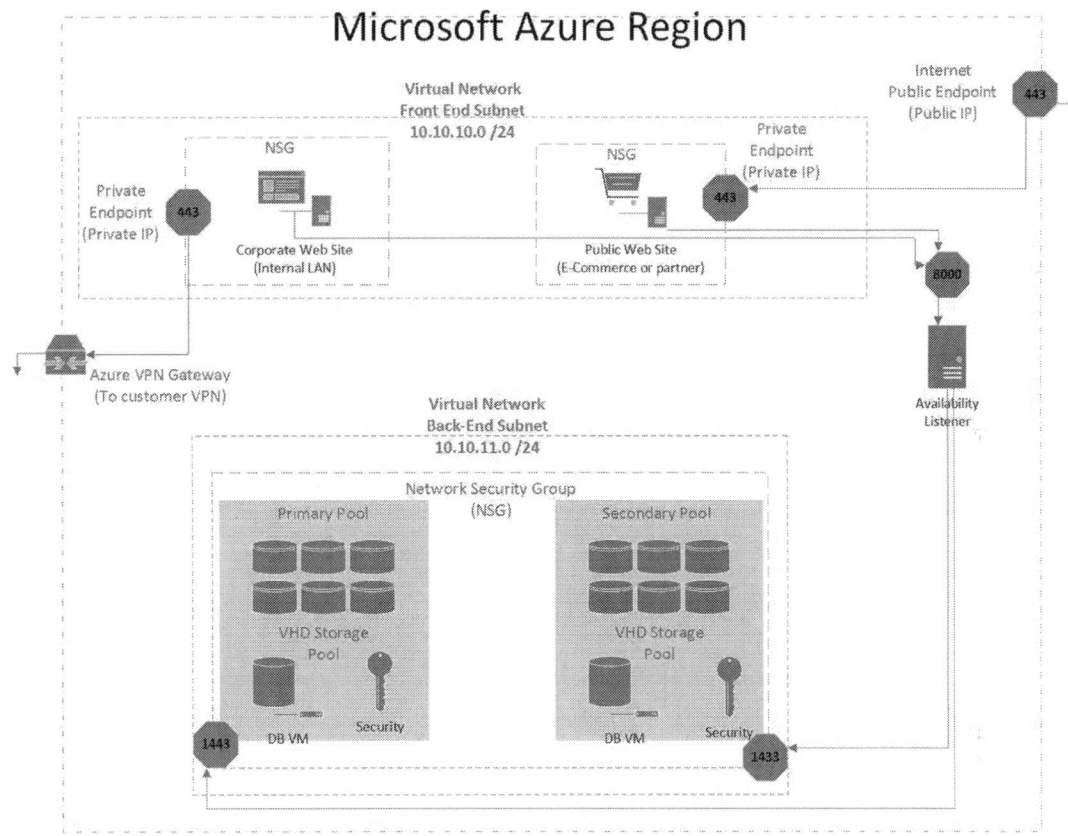

Figure 3-5. *Azure security separates front-end and back-end IP subnets*

Solution Reference

This book provides many examples that are directly applicable to creating network boundaries in large corporations in the step-by-step exercises covering Azure services. Detailed information and guidance can be found in Chapter 5, "Getting Started with Azure Web Apps," Chapter 6, "Getting Started with Azure Virtual Machines," Chapter 7, "Understanding Azure Storage and Databases," and Chapter 8, "Extending Your Network with Azure." If you have additional questions regarding current Azure compliance standards, visit the Azure Trust Center at http://azure.microsoft.com/en-us/support/trust-center/compliance.

Summary

This chapter described several real-world scenarios of how Azure is used. It also provides a foundation through several examples of customer scenarios for your consideration. Guidance to the relevant chapter exercises is provided at the end of each example.

The next chapter builds on the information you've learned in the previous chapters. Chapter 4 ends Part 1, "Introducing Azure." Part 2, "Microsoft Azure Quick Start," provides you with hands-on exercises that let you start using some of the major Azure workloads, including web sites, VMs, and storage.

CHAPTER 4

■ ■ ■

Planning Your Azure Deployment

Planning Concepts

Chapters 1 and 2 introduced the different Azure services as well as the business drivers for considering Azure as part of an organization's IT portfolio. As with most IT initiatives, the main business driver is cost, which includes tangible and intangible costs.

Previous chapters focused primarily on intangible costs, such as service-level agreements (SLAs), agility and scalability, disaster recovery (DR), high availability (HA), and security. These are important concepts, and, in some cases, an organization may have a real number associated with such costs. For example, some organizations develop business continuity plans that include the costs associated with per-hour outages in terms of revenue and opportunity losses.

This chapter focuses on the tangible operational costs associated with Azure services and also introduces tools and approaches you can use to evaluate such costs.

The Online Azure Pricing Calculator

In Chapter 1, you worked through an exercise that showed you how to use the online Azure Pricing Calculator. This section provides a brief refresher, because the Pricing Calculator is an integral part of Azure planning. You can choose to skip this section if you are already comfortable with the online Azure Pricing Calculator.

Figure 4-1 shows how to use the slider to determine bandwidth consumption for a web site. The first screen in the figure defines bandwidth utilization, followed by two screens that use the slider to determine the cost associated with various amounts of bandwidth the web site might use.

Figure 4-1. *Definition of bandwidth, and using the slider to determine the cost associated with the amount of bandwidth used by a web site*

■ **Note** As a reminder from Chapter 1, it may be easier to click the slider and then use the keyboard's left and right arrow keys to move it. A mouse may be too sensitive to drag the slider, thus making it more difficult to determine a precise value.

There are several ways to use the Azure Pricing Calculator. You can obtain pricing for each service or, alternatively, click the full calculator, as shown in Figure 4-2, so that all Azure services are listed and are not broken down by categories. After doing so, you can select all the required Azure services for a project and the quantities you need, and get the total cost by scrolling down to the bottom of the page.

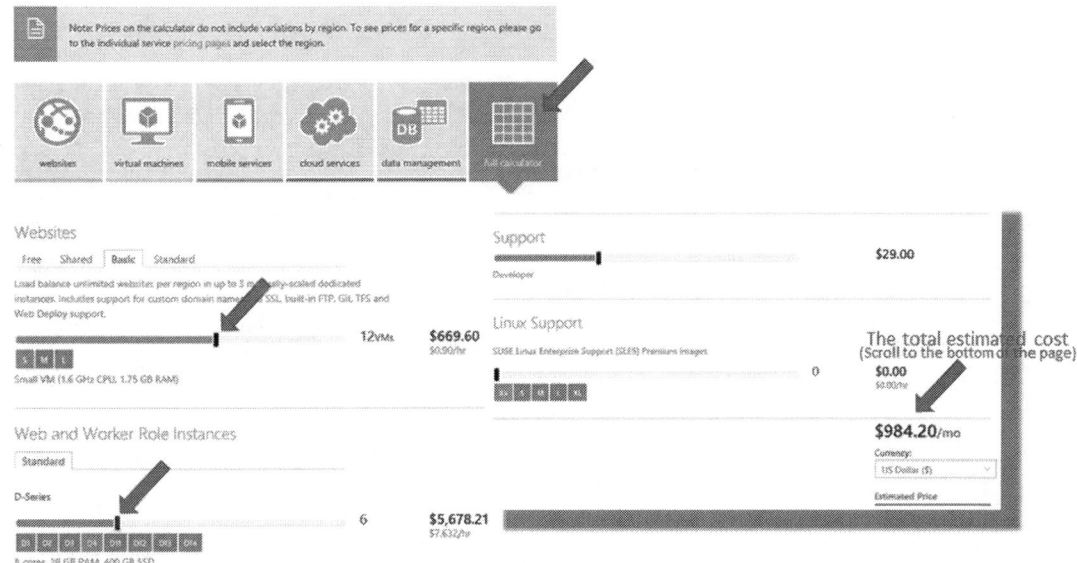

Figure 4-2. *The full calculator, and the total shown at the bottom of the page*

■ **Note**   Organizations that have access to a Microsoft Account Team should contact the account executive to assist in cost modeling for Azure. The Microsoft Account Team has other tools available and can develop a more accurate model based on geographical factors and special pricing considerations. The Azure Pricing Calculator is a good starting point for preliminary budget-planning purposes.

Azure Cost Estimator Tool

The Azure Cost Estimator Tool is an alternative to the online Azure Pricing Calculator; you can download it from `www.microsoft.com/en-us/download/details.aspx?id=43376`. The primary difference between the online Azure Pricing Calculator and the Azure Cost Estimator Tool is that the latter is a full desktop client and has scenario-based capabilities. Figure 4-3 shows the two options provided by the Azure Cost Estimator Tool.

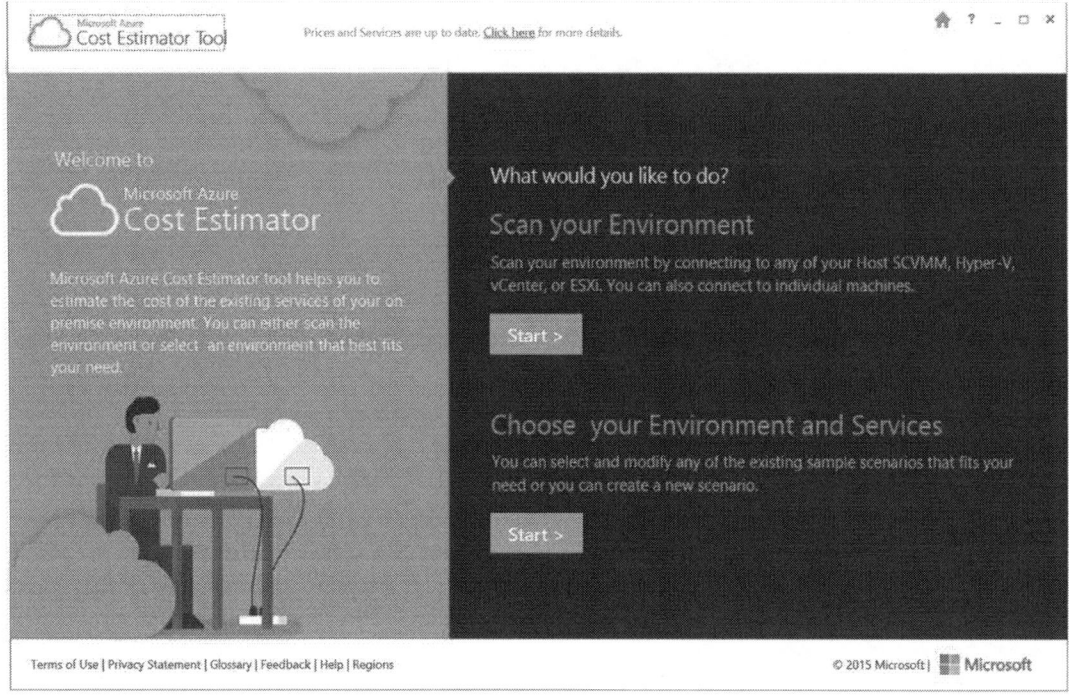

Figure 4-3. Microsoft Azure Cost Estimator Tool's welcome screen

Scan Your Environment

Clicking the Start button under the Scan Your Environment option launches a wizard that guides you through scanning a physical machine, virtual machine (VM), Hyper-V host server, or vCenter. A report of the scanned machines is then produced.

■ **Note** There is no menu or back button in the Azure Cost Estimator Tool. To go back to the previous screen, click the Microsoft Azure Cost Estimator Tool logo in the top-left corner.

Choose Your Environment and Services

Scenario-based options are an alternative method for using the Azure Cost Estimator Tool. Click the Start button under the Choose Your Environment And Services option to build scenarios. You can create multiple scenarios and add services from the Services tab to a scenario in order to estimate the cost of running that setup in Azure. There are also sample scenarios under the Sample Scenarios tab, as shown in Figure 4-4.

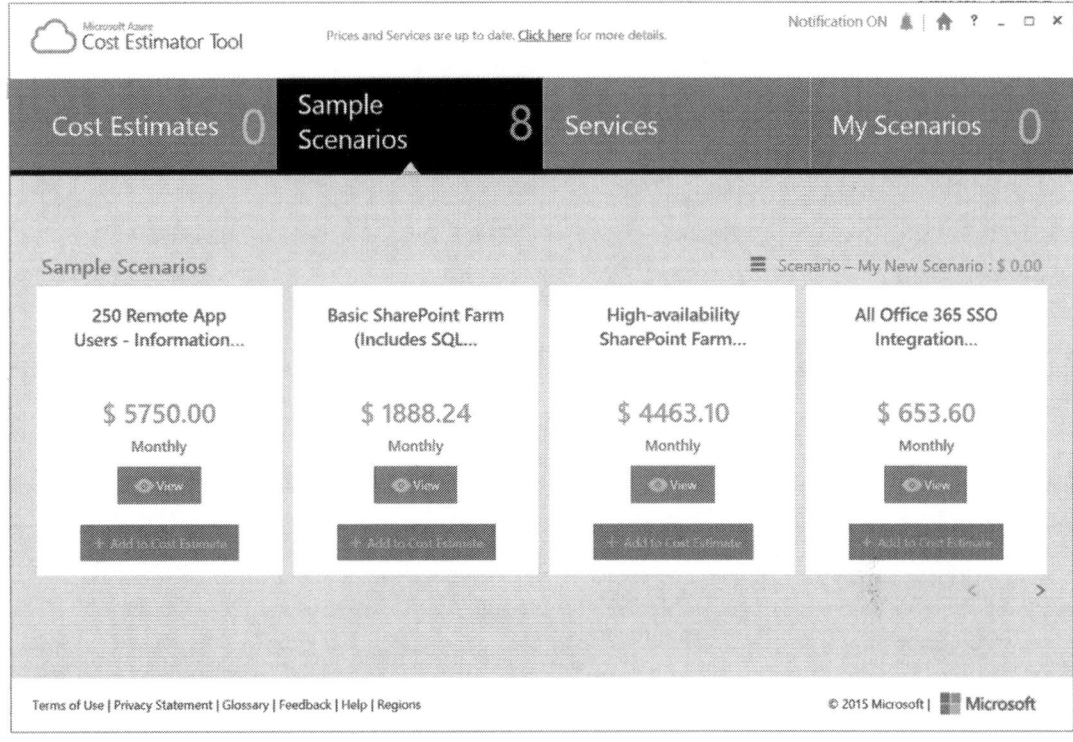

Figure 4-4. *Sample scenarios in the Azure Cost Estimator Tool*

■ **Note** You can find features and release information for the Azure Cost Estimator Tool by clicking the link in the center top of each page within the tool. The tool can and should be updated with the latest Azure pricing information. To do this, go into Choose Your Environment And Services under the My Scenarios tab, create a new scenario, and click the Get Latest Price button.

Geographical Factors Affecting the Cost Model

Microsoft Azure provides services from datacenters located around the world. As such, one of the most important factors to note is that the location from which services are provisioned may affect the cost.

At the time of writing, there are 17 Azure datacenter regions. Each region is served by datacenters within that region. Table 4-1 lists the current regions and their locations. As Azure continues to expand, you can visit http://azure.microsoft.com/en-us/regions/ for updated information.

Table 4-1. *Azure Regions and Datacenter Locations as of January 2015*

Azure Region	Location
Canada	Toronto, Quebec City
Central US	Iowa
East US	Virginia
East US 2	Virginia
US Gov Iowa	Iowa
US Gov Virginia	Virginia
North Central US	Illinois
South Central US	Texas
West US	California
North Europe	Ireland
West Europe	Netherlands
East Asia	Hong Kong
Southeast Asia	Singapore
Japan East	Saitama Prefecture
Japan West	Osaka Prefecture
Brazil South	Sao Paulo State
Australia East	New South Wales
Australia Southeast	Victoria

It is also important to note that not all Azure services are available in all regions. Furthermore, certain regions are reserved: for example, services in the US Gov regions are reserved for US government entities only; the regions were created in order to address special regulatory compliance issues specific to US government organizations. Additional verification is required for organizations that sign up to use the US Gov regions where Microsoft Azure Government services are being provisioned.

Aside from such restrictions, nothing prevents an organization from provisioning Azure out of any region. Because pricing may be affected based on regions, an organization may not automatically want to choose the closest region and datacenter location. For example, if the majority of an organization's customers are located in a different region, it may make sense to provision Azure services out of the region that is closest to the customers instead of out of one that is closest to the organization's corporate headquarters. This should be taken into consideration when planning for DR and HA, or if your organization has a worldwide business model that "follows the sun."

Microsoft Assessment and Planning (MAP) Toolkit

Microsoft introduced the Microsoft Assessment and Planning (MAP) Toolkit to help customers plan, deploy, and adopt Microsoft technologies. It is designed to be a multi-product toolkit, and Azure was recently added as a MAP Toolkit capability.

The MAP Toolkit for Azure is designed to help organizations plan and migrate to Azure. The latest version of the MAP Toolkit for Azure can be downloaded from `https://technet.microsoft.com/en-us/solutionaccelerators/gg581074.aspx`.

Installing and Starting MAP

One of the most important capabilities of the MAP Toolkit for Azure is the ability to conduct an in-depth inventory of an organization's environment. This is carried out through an agentless discovery service that discovers Windows OS platform versions, SQL databases, VMs, and even applications. Data collection and inventory is an important step in any planning process. The MAP Toolkit creates and maintains an inventory database, which is the step of the wizard when the tool is launched, as shown in Figure 4-5.

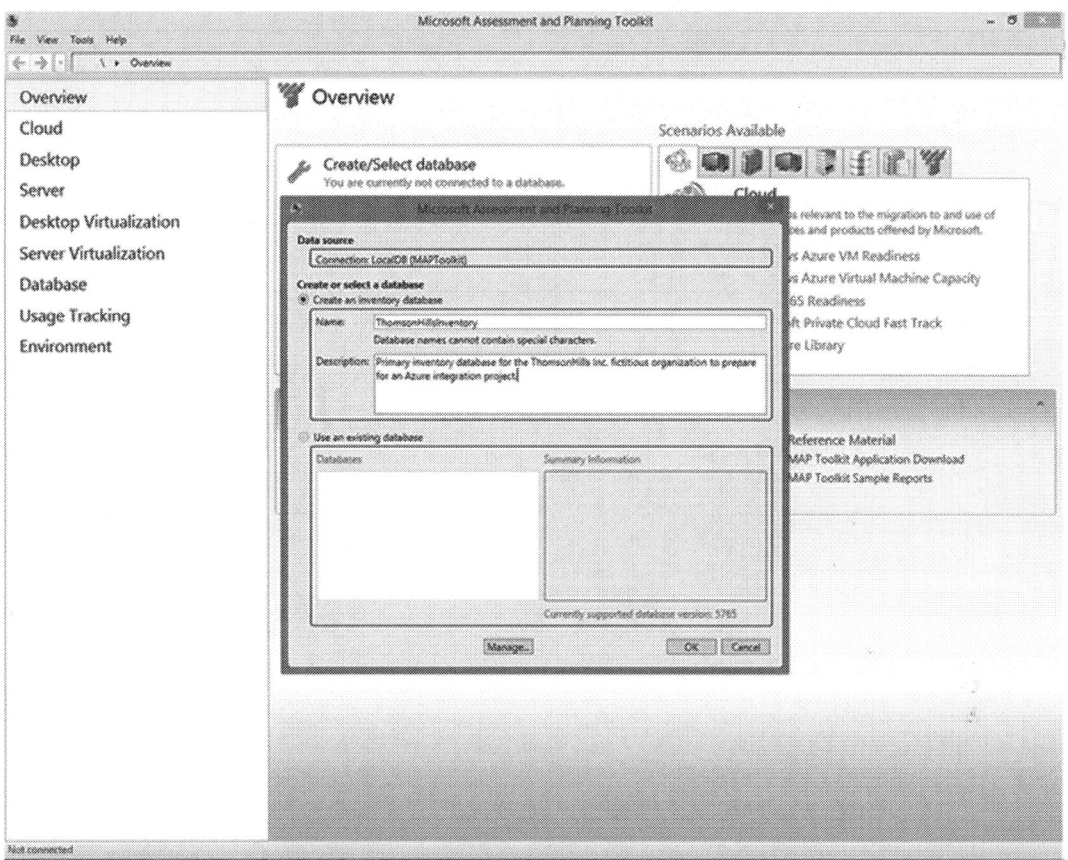

Figure 4-5. *MAP Toolkit prompting the user to create a new inventory database or to connect to an existing one*

Once the inventory database has been created, the Azure assessment capabilities are located on the Cloud screen, as shown in Figure 4-6. The MAP Toolkit also provides a guided step-by-step process to conduct the assessment.

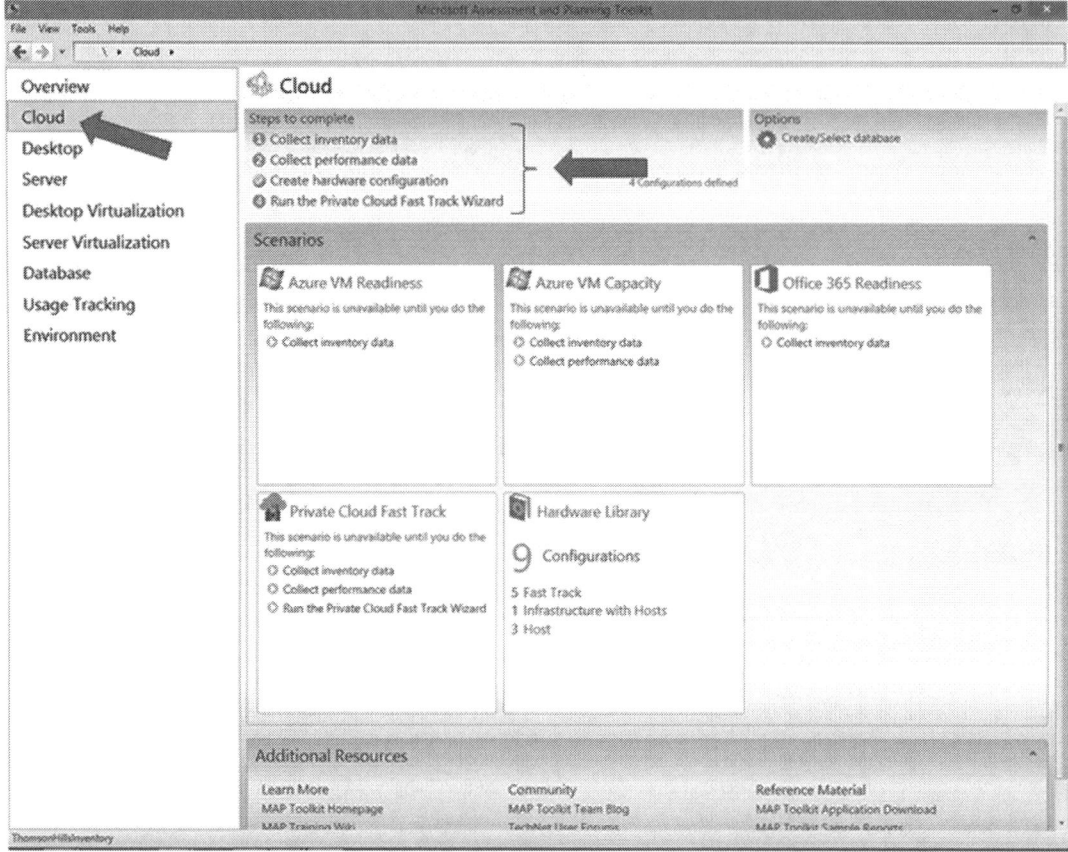

Figure 4-6. *MAP Toolkit for Azure and the step-by-step guide*

Inventory

With your database set up, follow these steps to inventory your environment.

INVENTORY AND ASSESSMENT WIZARD

Inventorying Your Environment

Start the inventory by launching the Inventory and Assessment Wizard:

1. Select Cloud from the MAP Toolkit's left navigation pane, and click Collect Inventory Data, as shown in Figure 4-6. Doing so launches the Inventory And Assessment Wizard, shown in Figure 4-7.

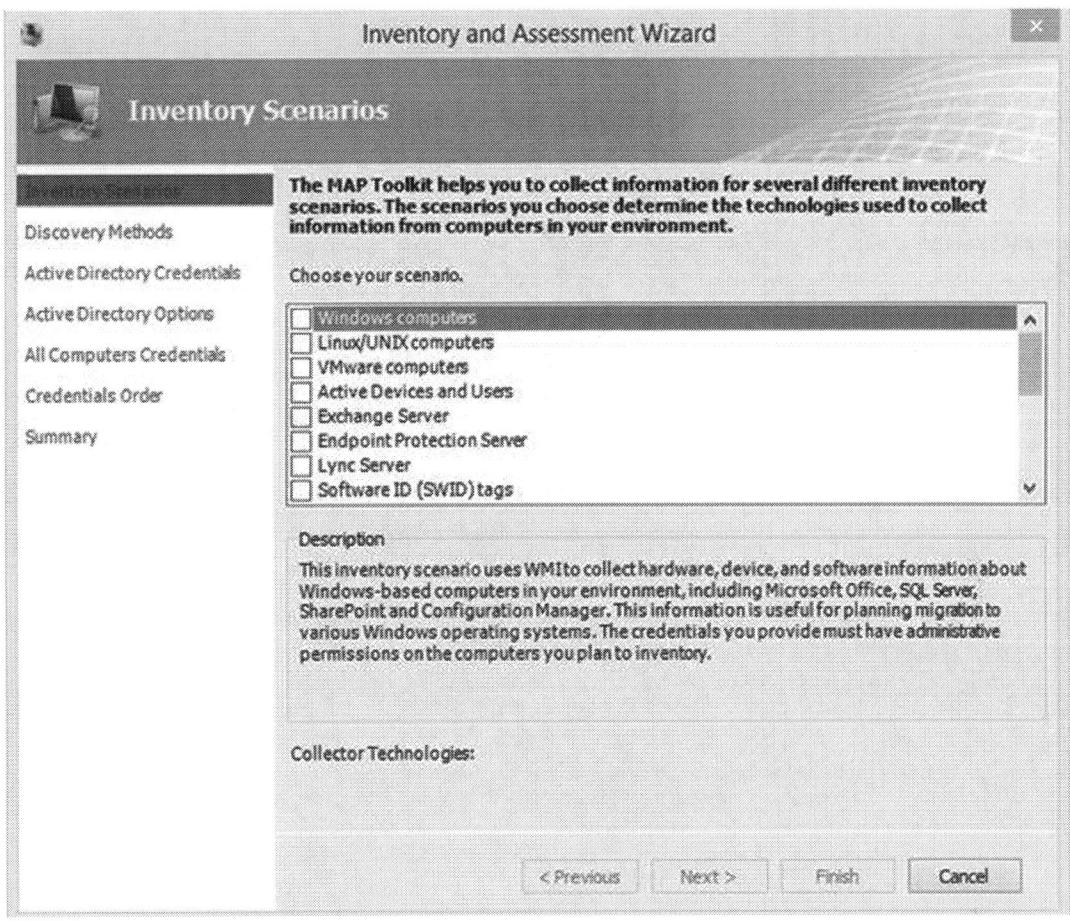

Figure 4-7. Inventory And Assessment Wizard

2. Select Inventory Scenarios, and note the description of each scenario. Be sure to select and read the description for the Windows Azure Platform Migration scenario.

3. Click Next when all the applicable scenarios have been selected.

4. Specify the discovery methods, and click Next.

5. Specify your Active Directory credentials, and click Next.

6. Specify whether you want to inventory the entire AD or just certain organizational units (OUs), and click Next.

7. Click Create, and enter the AD administrator credentials to be used when logging in to computers in the domain, as shown in Figure 4-8. Repeat this step to add other admin credentials if required. Click Next when you're finished.

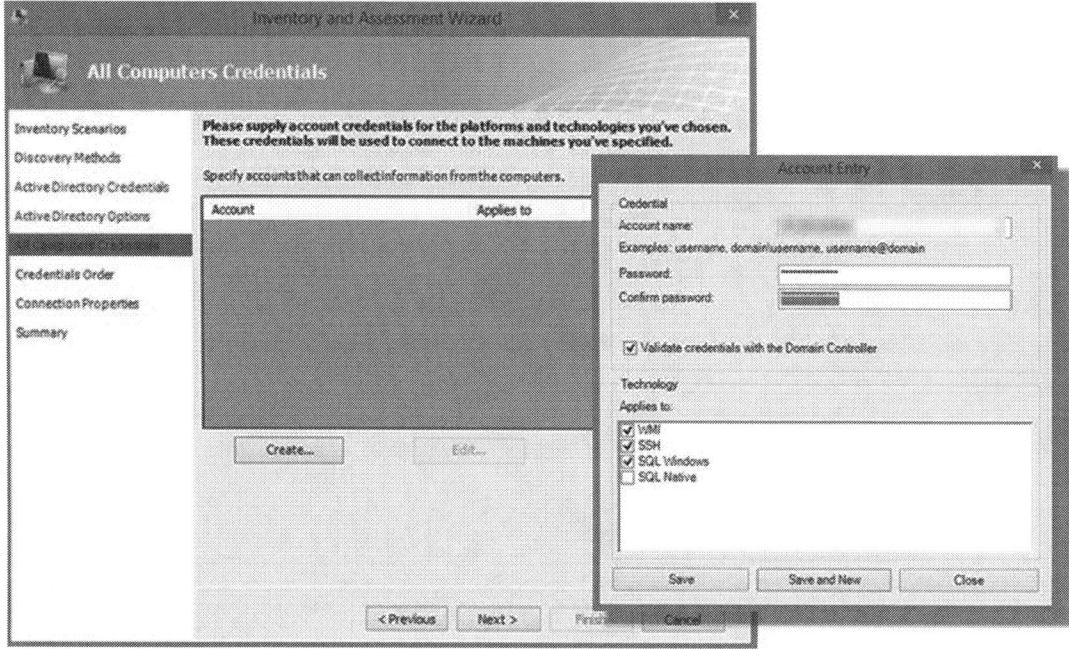

Figure 4-8. Enter the administrator credentials to use when logging in to machines

8. If you created more than one administrator credential in step 7, you can prioritize the order of credentials that MAP will use to try to log in to machines. Click Next when you're finished.

9. Some methods, like SSH, use ports to connect to a machine. Modify the port if necessary. Click Next.

10. On the Summary screen, review the configuration information that the Inventory And Assessment Wizard has collected based on your answers from the previous steps. Click Finish to begin the inventory process.

11. As the Inventory And Assessment process is running, click Details to get more information. The inventory process is finished when the status switches from Running to Completed, as shown in Figure 4-9.

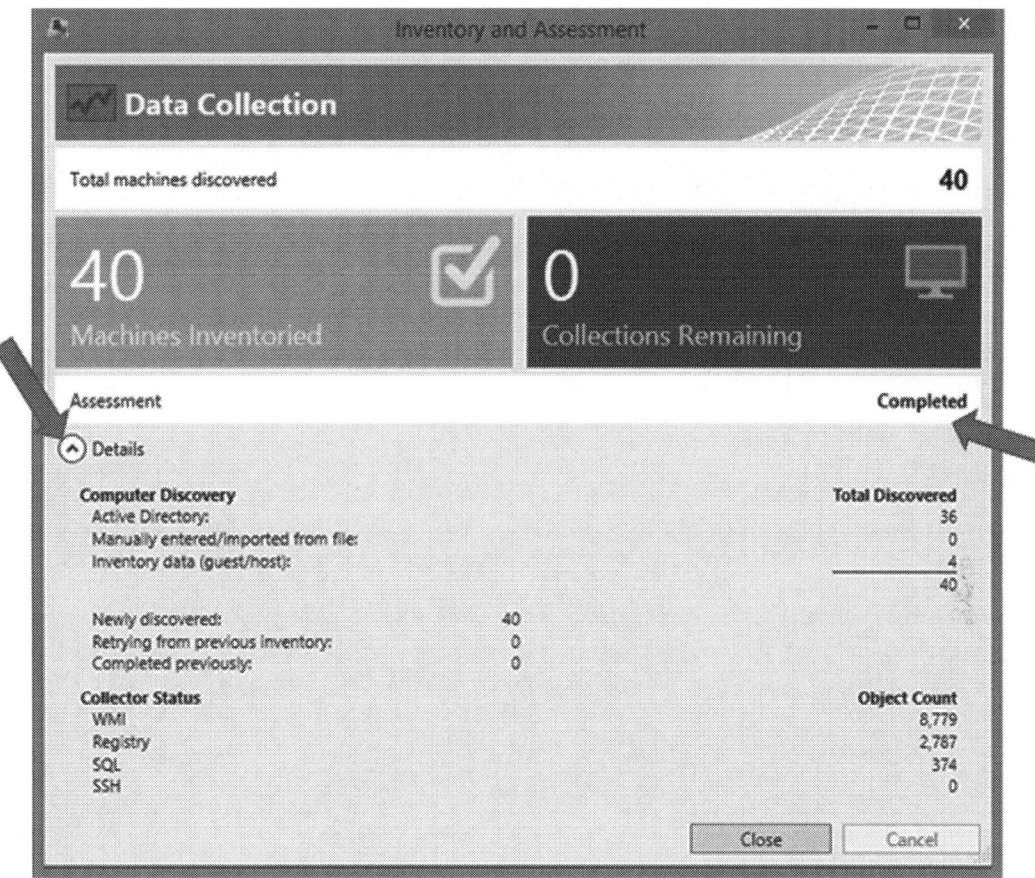

Figure 4-9. *The inventory progress report*

12. Review the information that has been collected, and then click Close.

13. On the main page of the MAP Toolkit, note that a scenario that estimates VM capacity is not available until performance data is collected, as shown in Figure 4-10.

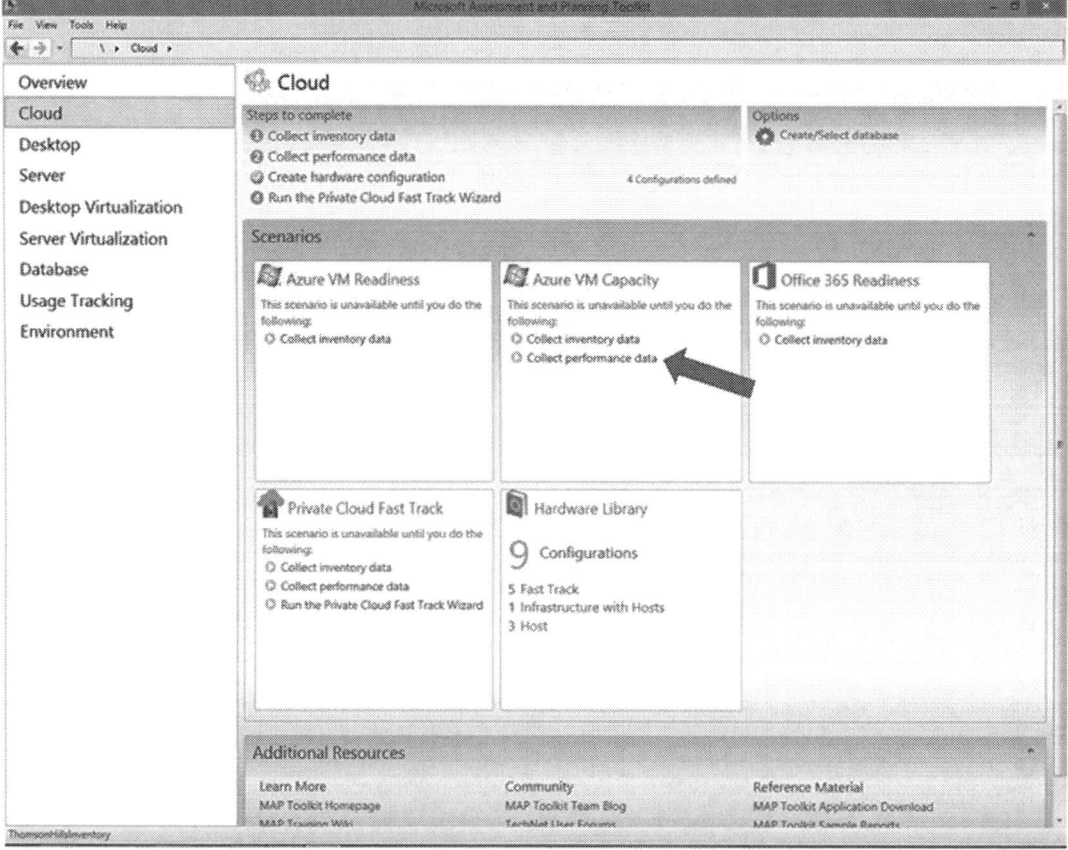

Figure 4-10. *Collect performance data to explore VM capacity scenarios*

14. Under Steps To Complete at the top of the screen, click step 2, Collect Performance Data.

15. Follow the prompts in the wizard, select the VMs for which you want to collect performance data, and then start the process. Note that it may take some time for performance data to be collected, especially if you selected a larger timeframe from which to collect that data.

16. When MAP is done collecting performance data, as shown in Figure 4-11, click Close.

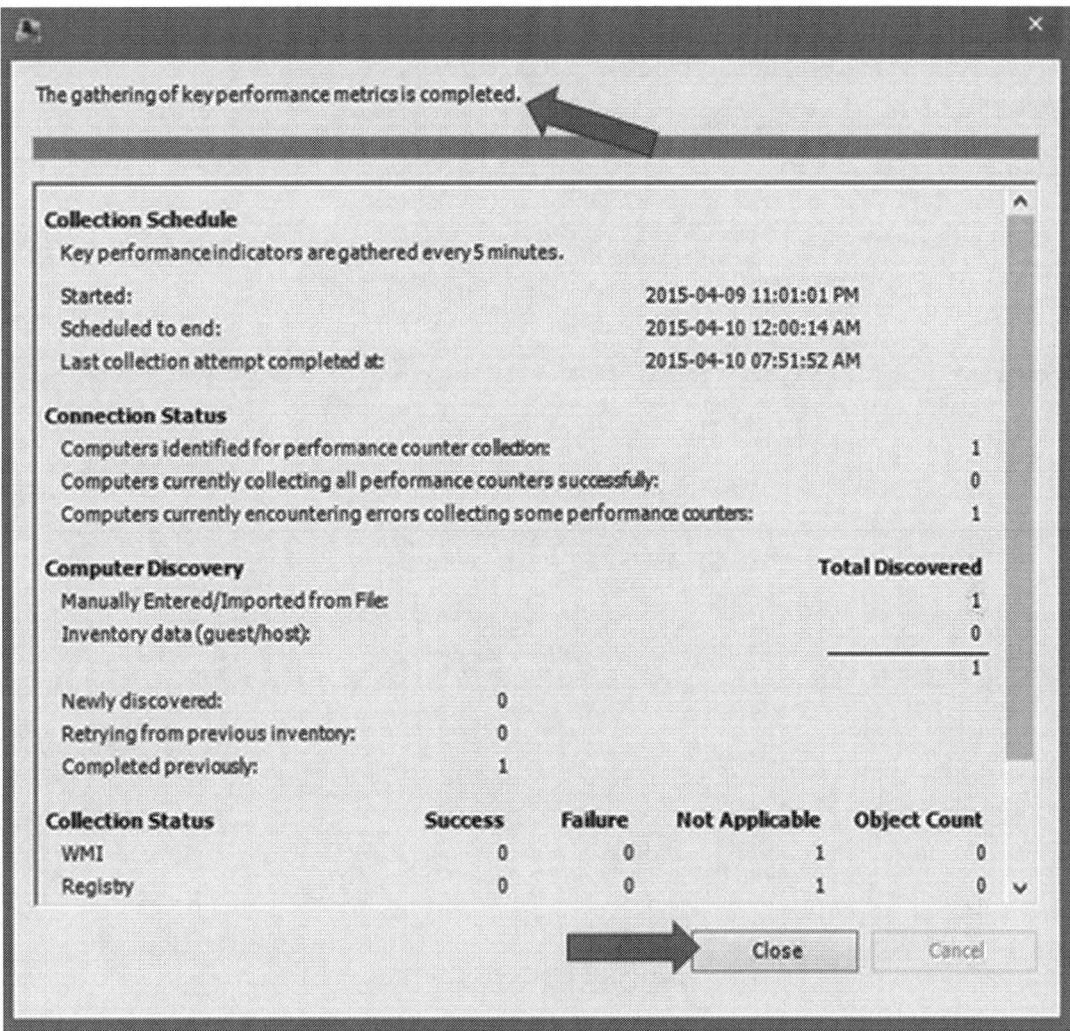

Figure 4-11. *MAP has finished gathering performance data*

17. On the main page of the MAP Toolkit, Azure VM Capacity should now display the number of VMs that have been properly sized, as shown in Figure 4-12.

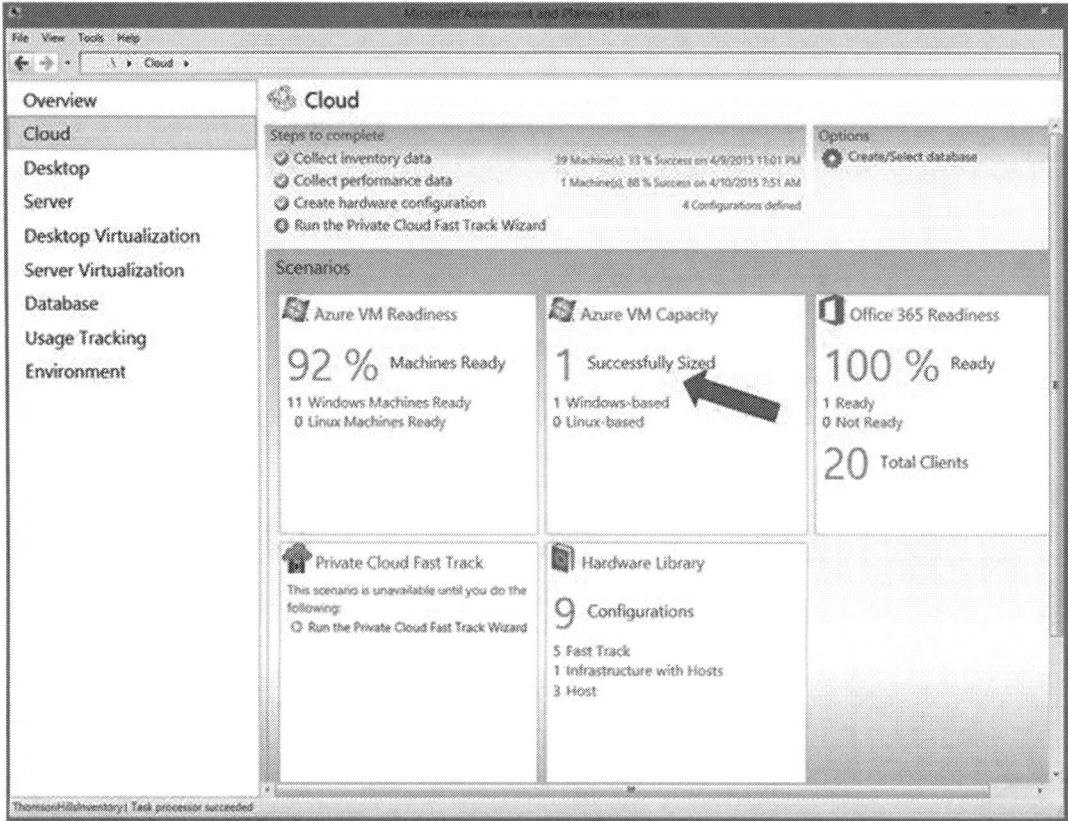

Figure 4-12. *Azure VM Capacity tile showing the number of successfully sized VMs*

18. Click the Azure VM Capacity tile to open the full VM sizing report, as shown in Figure 4-13. The information can also be exported to an Excel workbook.

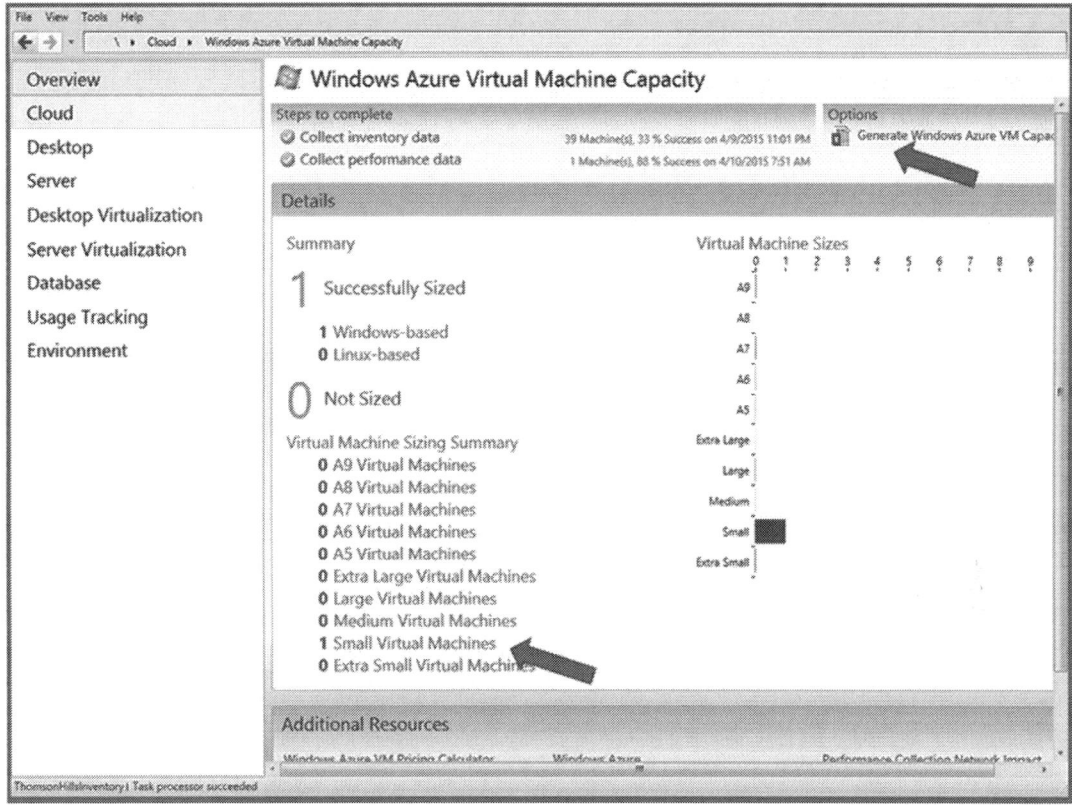

Figure 4-13. *Azure VM Capacity report*

The MAP Toolkit also provides other types of analysis. You can use the information gathered and interpreted by the MAP Toolkit to estimate the consumption level in Azure and what it will cost.

■ **Note** Both the MAP Toolkit and the Azure Online Calculator are provided for analysis and preliminary budgeting purposes. The MAP Toolkit provides information on what types of VMs you will need in Azure. That information should then be fed into the Azure Online Calculator to determine the cost. For the final cost, you should work with a Microsoft Account Representative or a reseller.

Microsoft Azure Trial

One good approach for a deployment or evaluation plan is to take advantage of a Microsoft Azure trial. A trial provides important insights into the viability of using Azure for specific scenarios.

IMPLEMENTING A MICROSOFT AZURE TRIAL

Recently, a software development company was hired to rewrite a legacy pension-management system. The system required new hardware and software for development, testing, and an eventual move to production. New capabilities would be introduced—for example, the ability for subscribers to access the system and manage their retirement funds through the Internet—but there was no historical data regarding how much traffic the system would generate as a result. In this scenario, the Microsoft Account Team recommended an Azure Trial account to help ensure that the new system could run in Azure and had the capability to scale accordingly.

There are several types of Azure trials, but generally they are free and provide fully functional Azure accounts that are limited only by duration and consumption level. The Azure Enterprise Trial is a one-month trial account with a $200 limit. Any workloads built in this trial account are billed against the $200 credit limit. After the one-month trial, the Microsoft Azure Enterprise Trial account can be converted to a paid production account without having to rebuild the Azure workloads.

Microsoft Azure Enterprise Trial

The easiest way to take Azure on a test drive is to sign up for the Enterprise Trial account at www.microsoft.com/Azure. Click the Try For Free link, as shown in Figure 4-14.

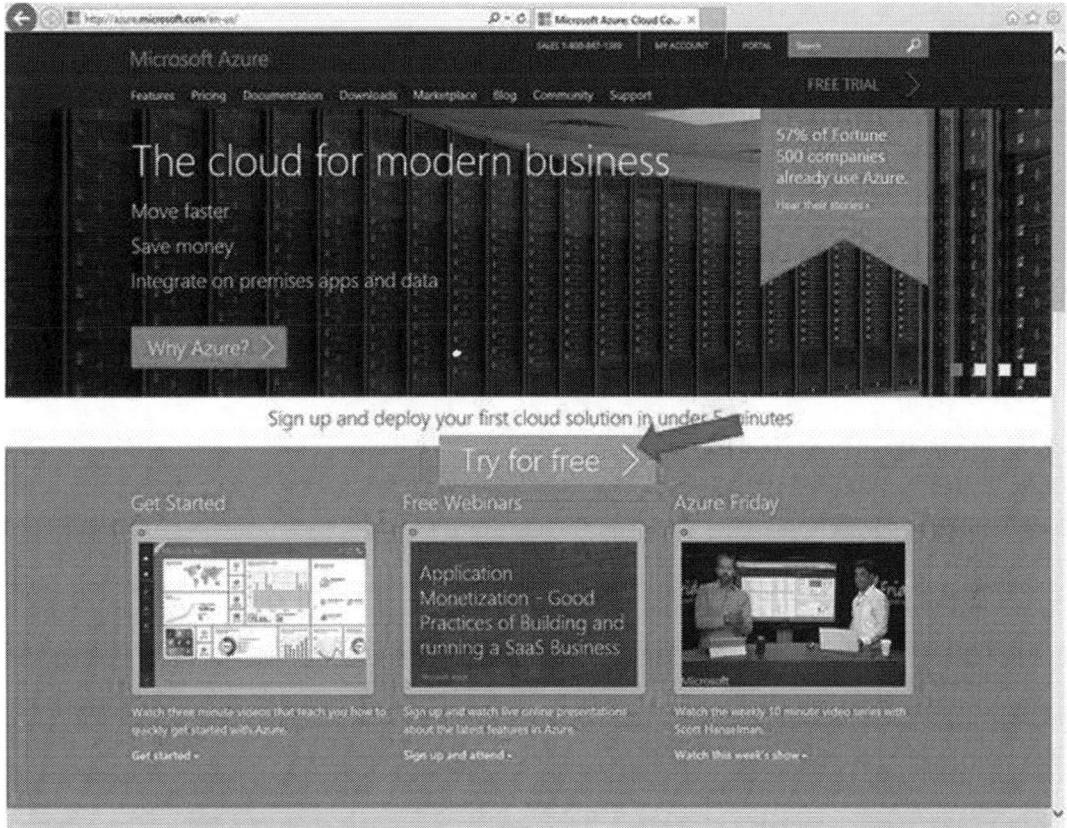

Figure 4-14. *Trying Azure for free at www.microsoft.com/azure*

■ **Note** You can find frequently asked questions (FAQs) regarding the Microsoft Azure Enterprise Trial at
http://azure.microsoft.com/en-us/pricing/free-trial-faq/.

Microsoft Azure Government Trial

As mentioned in Chapter 1, several flavors of Azure accounts have unique requirements to meet regulatory and compliance needs. One example is the Microsoft Azure Government account, which is available only to public sector entities in the United States. As such, in order to sign up for a Microsoft Azure Government Trial account, the Microsoft Account Team for the public sector customer must nominate and submit the request. The Microsoft Account Team has the necessary paperwork for the US public sector entity to complete, and the Microsoft representative also submits the paperwork to authorize and provision the Microsoft Azure Government Trial account.

Like the Microsoft Azure Enterprise Trial account, a Microsoft Azure Government Trial account can be migrated to a paid production account without having to rebuild the Azure workloads that were deployed during the trial period. At the time of this writing, a Microsoft Azure Government Trial program provides a 90-day trial account with a $200 credit limit per month.

Azure Service-Specific Trials

The credit limit for most trials applies to Azure workloads that are based on consumption, such as VMs and storage. However, some Azure services are not based on consumption, such as Azure Active Directory Premium (AADP). These services are based on Client Access Licenses (CALs) and, as such, cannot use the monetary amount (credit or paid) available in an Azure account. Trials for services such as AADP can be activated in the Azure Portal, as shown in Figure 4-15.

Figure 4-15. *Activating the Azure Active Directory Premium and EMS trial*

▪ **Note** AADP can provide single sign-on (SSO) for third-party SaaS apps. Chapter 10 explores this in detail. As part of the planning process, if you need to discover what types of SaaS apps your organization uses, you can use a free Cloud App Discovery tool provided by Microsoft. Visit `https://appdiscovery.azure.com` to download and learn more about this tool.

Microsoft Developer Network (MSDN)

As mentioned in Chapter 1, MSDN subscribers get a $150 per month credit subscription in a Microsoft Azure account. Unlike the other Azure trial accounts, MSDN Azure accounts do not have an expiration date. The $150 credit renews every month for as long as the MSDN subscription is valid. However, the $150 does not roll over from month to month; if any part of the $150 is not used, it is lost, and a new $150 is allotted at the start of the next month.

If the $150 limit is exceeded, workloads in the MSDN Azure account are suspended. MSDN subscribers can choose to remove this restriction and keep a credit card on file to support workloads so they continue to work after the $150 credit is used up.

Planning for Network Performance

Microsoft Azure is the datacenter in the cloud, and the idea is that computing and storage resources will eventually migrate there, so the importance of network reliability, bandwidth, and latency cannot be overstated. As such, planning for Azure—or any cloud provider, for that matter—should include an analysis of the current location's network performance as compared to Azure datacenters.

Azure Throughput Analyzer

Microsoft Research provides a desktop utility that measures the upload and download throughput achievable from an on-premises client machine to Azure storage.

USING THE AZURE THROUGHPUT ANALYZER

Analyzing Upload and Download Throughput to Azure Storage

Follow these steps to run a test to determine the network throughput level from an on-premises client machine to Azure storage:

1. Download the Azure Throughput Analyzer tool at `http://research.microsoft.com/en-us/downloads/5c8189b9-53aa-4d6a-a086-013d927e15a7/default.aspx`.

2. Install the Azure Throughput Analyzer tool, and then launch it.

3. Go to the Azure Management Portal at `https://manage.windowsazure.com`, create a new storage account or access an existing storage account, and then select keys, as shown in Figure 4-16.

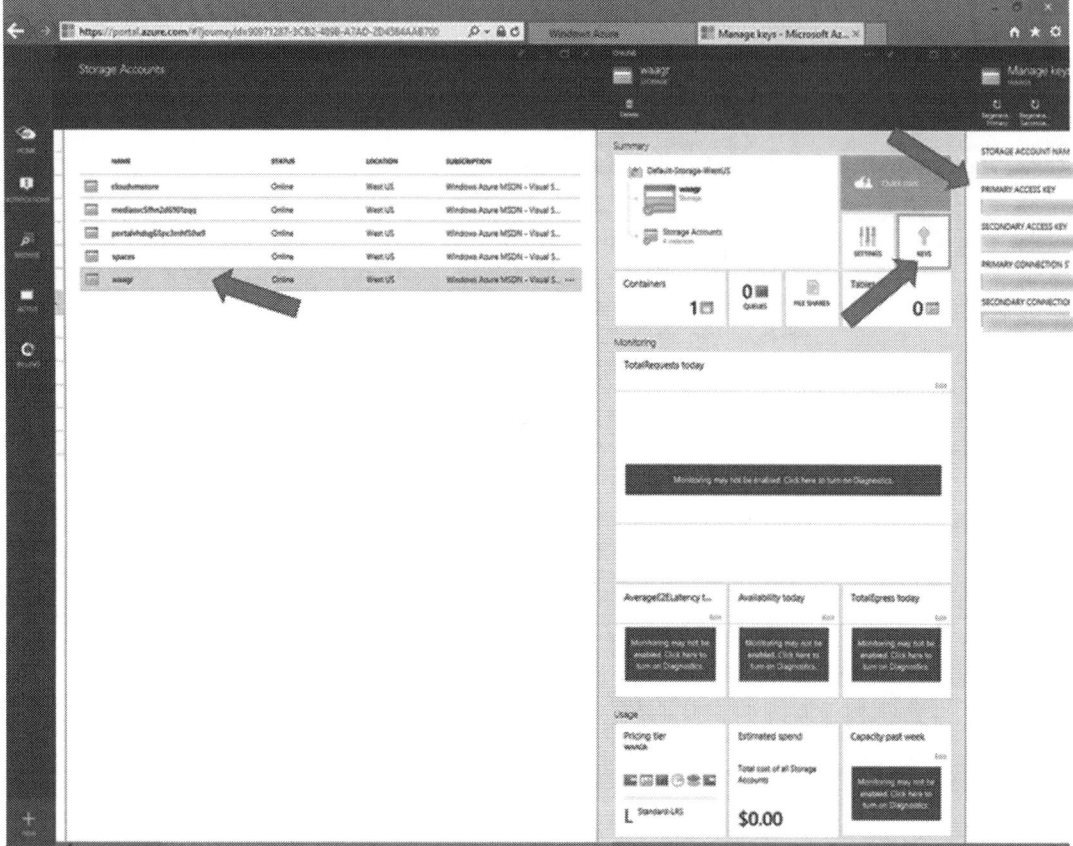

Figure 4-16. *Getting the keys for an Azure storage account*

4. Copy the Primary Access Key to the clipboard.

5. Go to the Azure Throughput Analyzer tool, and select Tools ➤ Storage Settings, as shown in Figure 4-17.

6. Provide a Name to describe the storage settings (we used "Test" in this exercise), and paste the Account Key information and the Account Name from the Azure Portal, also shown in Figure 4-17.

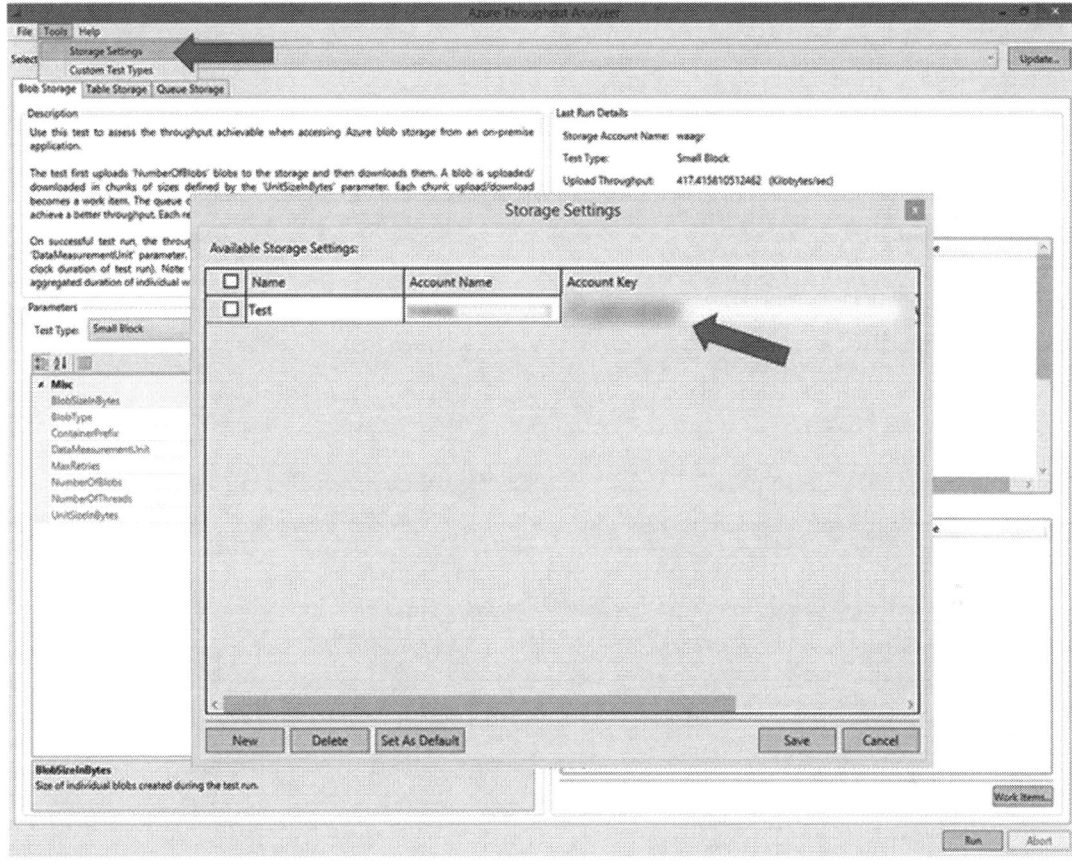

Figure 4-17. Setting the storage settings in the Azure Throughput Analyzer tool

7. Click Save.

8. Select the storage account setting you just created, and click Run, as shown in Figure 4-18.

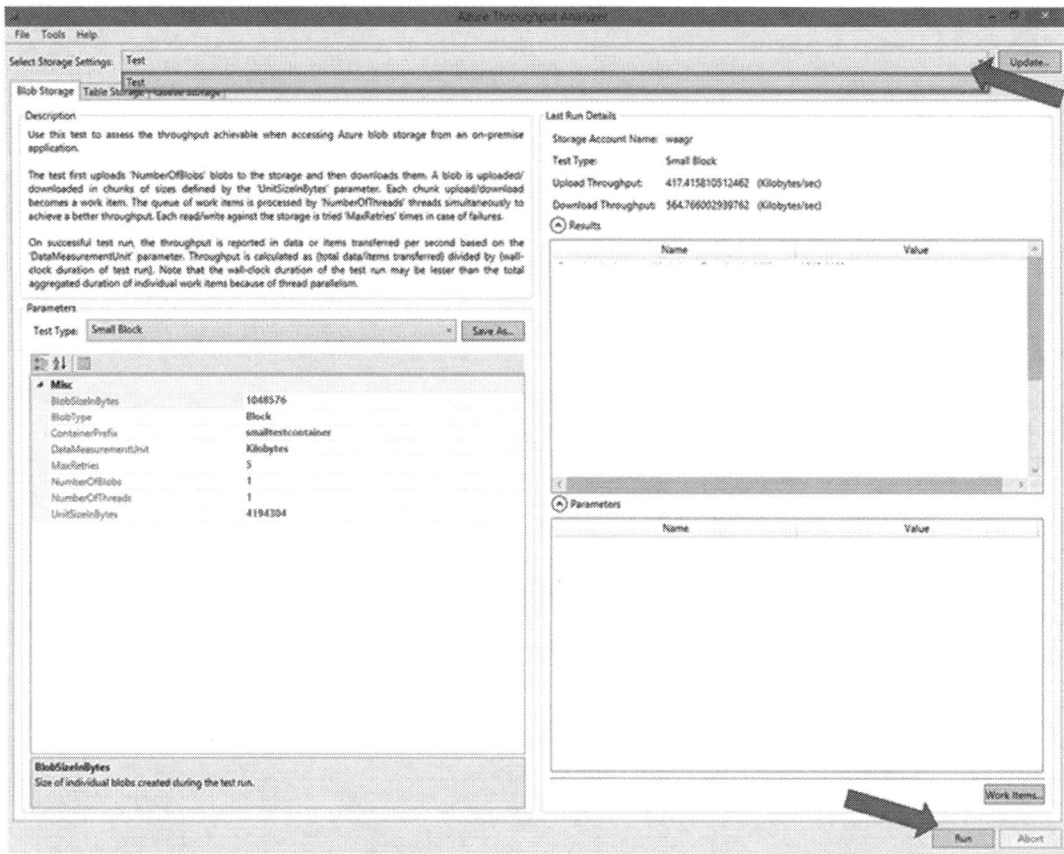

Figure 4-18. *Selecting a storage account setting, and running the analysis*

9. After the analysis is complete, information about data-transfer performance is displayed in the Results pane. The parameters used for the test are displayed in the Parameters pane, as shown in Figure 4-19.

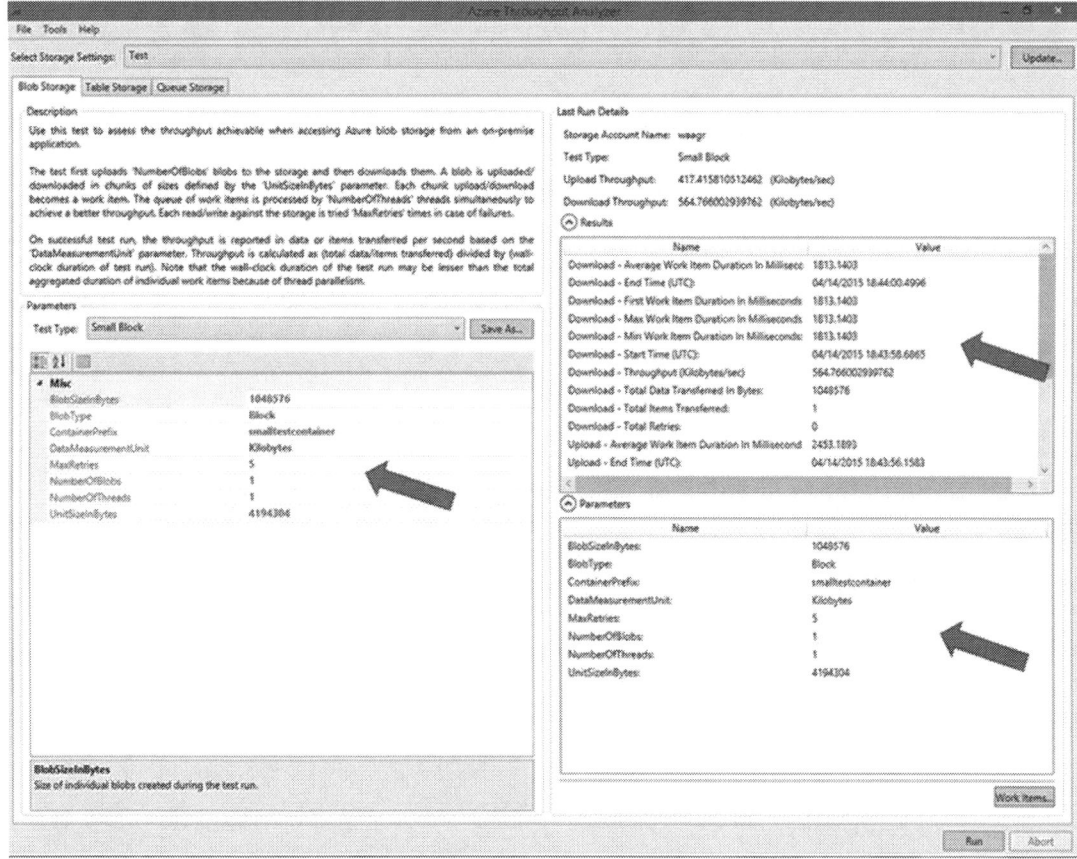

Figure 4-19. *Results from the throughput test*

The Azure Throughput Analyzer can test additional parameters and different storage types (Blob, tables, and queue storage) and different sizes (small blocks, large blocks, and so on). This free tool should provide you with some insight on the performance of your network with respect to data transfers.

Third-Party, Web-Based Network Latency Test

As an alternative to installing a client-based application like the Azure Throughput Analyzer, you can use an online-hosted network test tool located at www.azurespeed.com. This third-party tool provides similar network-performance information that you can use during the planning process. Figure 4-20 shows the Azure Storage Latency Test screen displaying the network performance of different Azure datacenters from the on-premises client's browser.

Figure 4-20. *Azure Storage Latency Test results from* `www.azurespeed.com`

Like the Azure Throughput Analyzer tool, the Azure Storage Latency Test should be run from different on-premises locations in order to determine each location's network performance.

Summary

This chapter provided you with some tools to help plan your Azure deployment. With these tools, you can better evaluate Microsoft Azure by discovering the types of SaaS apps your organization is using, determining network performance and VM sizing, and translating that information into Azure workloads. You can use the Online Calculator to determine the cost to run the workloads in Microsoft Azure.

Chapter 4 looks at a few real-world scenarios in which Azure is being used and the business drivers behind each scenario. After that, the next section of this book discusses some key Azure services in detail.

## PART II

Microsoft Azure Quick Start

CHAPTER 5

■ ■ ■

Getting Started with Azure Web Apps

The Azure Web Apps service provides the lowest bar of entry into the Azure cloud-computing world. It's the easiest way to get started with Azure. It's a platform as a service (PaaS) solution that helps you quickly deploy web-based apps that easily scale to meet the demands of your customers. Azure Web Apps supports most of the current popular development platforms and APIs in use today.

The Azure operations team takes care of managing the infrastructure, availability, maintenance, security, and patching of Azure to ensure reliable and secure performance, freeing you to focus on delivering your web app. Azure Web Apps also lets you scale up or out quickly, so that your apps can handle the load your customers put on the system. The Azure Portal allows you to configure the number and size of your VMs manually or to configure autoscaling so your VMs scale automatically to meet load demands on schedule.

The Azure Web Apps service gives you all you need to establish a global web presence for your web site. Regardless of the size of your organization, you need a robust, secure, and scalable platform to drive your business, brand awareness, and customer communications. Azure Web Apps can help maintain your corporate brand and identity with Microsoft's financially backed business continuity service-level agreements (SLAs).

Use the Tools You Know

Azure Web Apps embraces the entire array of cross-platform tools and services that you already know and need to create a great web app experience. It lets you collaborate, deliver, and scale quickly across the entire development and operations lifecycle for continuous deployments.

With Azure Web Apps, you can quickly create new sites from the Azure gallery, which provides templates from popular web site content-management systems (CMSs) such as Orchard, WordPress, Drupal, Umbraco, DNN, and many other third-party web applications in the Azure marketplace. You can bring your existing web assets to Azure Web Apps from a variety of languages and frameworks. Azure Web Apps supports open source framework like .NET, Java, PHP, Node.js, and Python.

Azure Web Apps makes it easy to choose from various database backends to meet your needs for use with your apps. It includes support for many backend databases, including Microsoft SQL, MySQL, DocumentDB, Search, MongoDB, Redis, and Azure Table Storage. You can also use a SQL or MySQL database to test your apps at no cost.

Moving your apps to Azure Web Apps is pretty easy. You can use the familiar FTP tools or your source control management system. Azure Web Apps supports direct publishing from popular source control options, such as Visual Studio, Visual Studio Online, and GitYou, to help you move existing sites to Azure Web Apps easily with an online migration tool.

Quick Start: Creating a New Web App from the Portal

Azure Web Apps allows you to create a powerful new web site in seconds. It starts with simplicity at the core. It's very simple to deploy a web site in Azure because you don't need any tools to get started. Everything you need is available through the Portal.

Once you've created your Azure account, you can sign in to the Azure Portal to begin creating your new web app. In the Portal, select New ➤ Web + Mobile ➤ Web App, as shown in Figure 5-1.

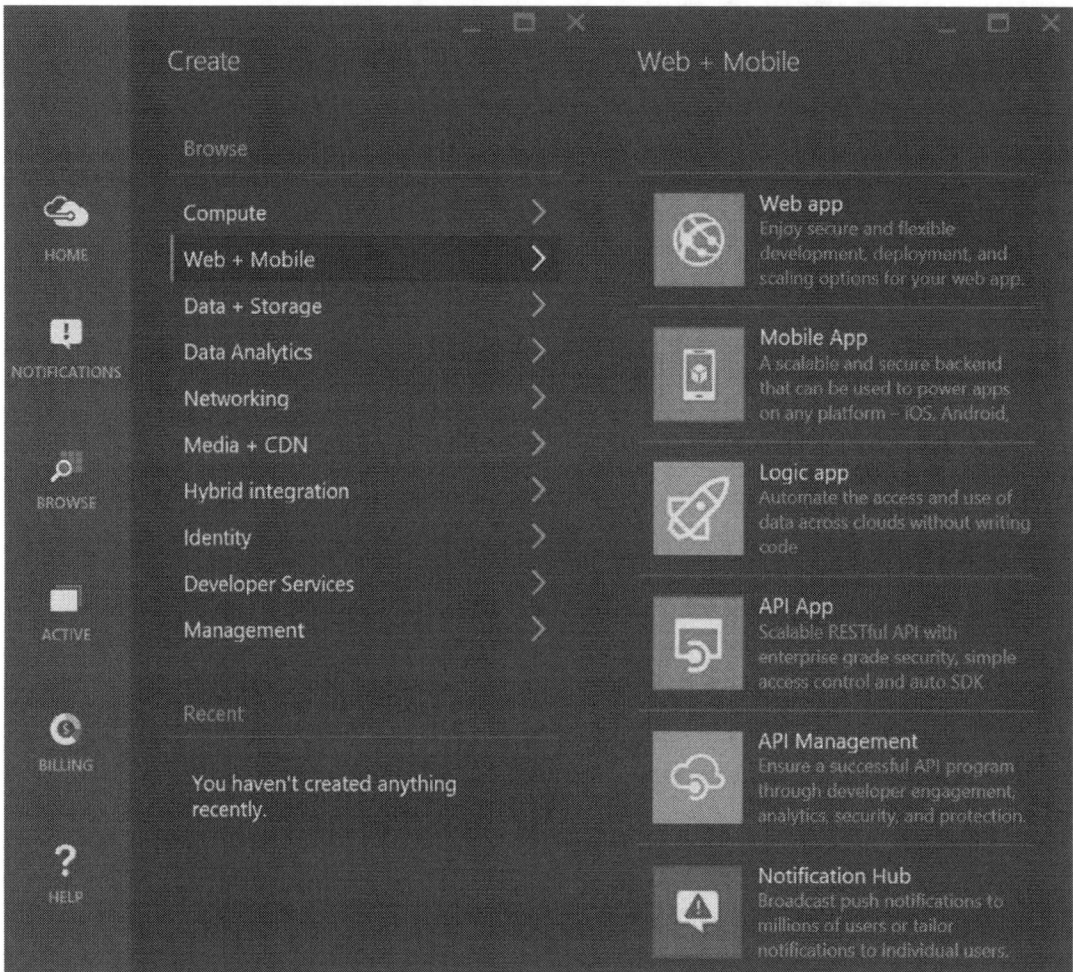

Figure 5-1. *Creating a new web app*

As shown in Figure 5-2, when the Web App pop out appears, enter the URL for your web site. The URL must be unique; `azurewebsites.net` is appended to it.

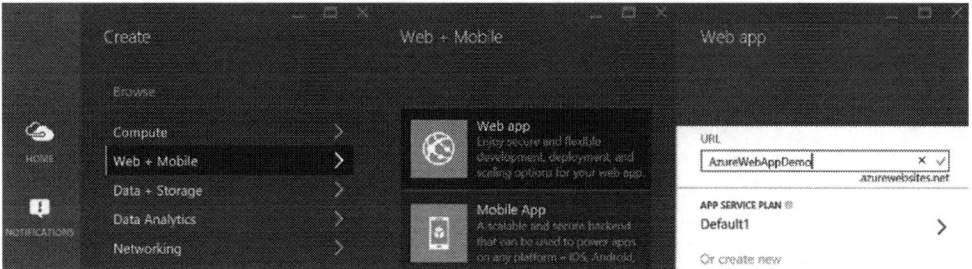

Figure 5-2. *URL and other settings to get started*

When creating your web site, you can choose from many pricing options. In this example, create your web site using the Free tier. If you want to change the web-hosting plan to a higher-priced tier, you can select from a list of available pricing options that include additional processor cores, more memory, and location, as shown in Figure 5-3.

Figure 5-3. *Different pricing tiers add functionality and scale to your web app*

After entering the URL for your web site and choosing the tier you want to use, select an existing resource group or create a new one. As shown in Figure 5-4, for this example, create a new resource group, giving it the same name as your URL so that you know its purpose.

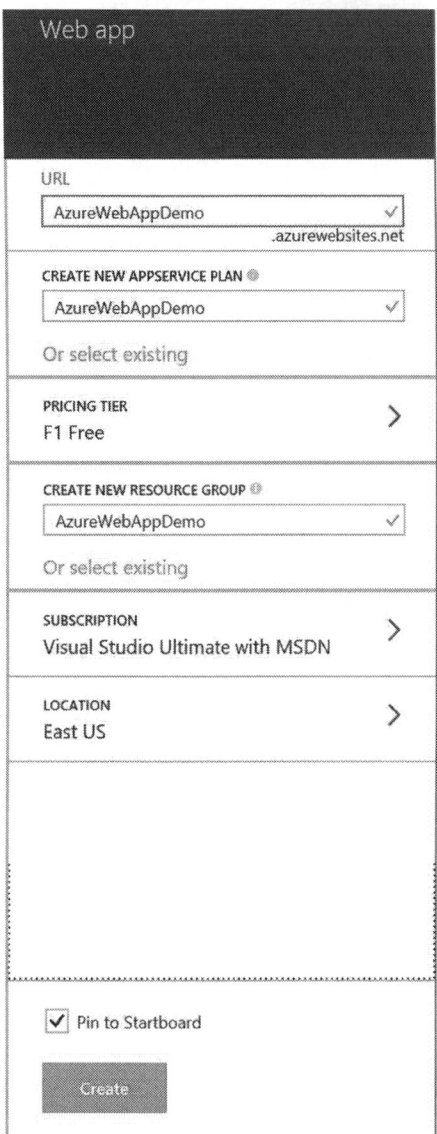

Figure 5-4. *Azure web app pricing tier and resource groups*

The final steps in creating your web app are to choose a subscription, if you have more than one, and setting the location of your app. It's recommended that you set the location close to the part of the world from which you expect most of your web traffic to emanate. Doing this will improve the app's performance, because traffic will have to travel a shorter distance when users are browsing your site.

When you have completed the settings, click Create (as shown at the bottom of Figure 5-4). If you wish to pin the app to your Startboard, select the check box before clicking the Create button. When the new app is created, you will see it on your Startboard on the main page of the Azure Portal, as shown in Figure 5-5.

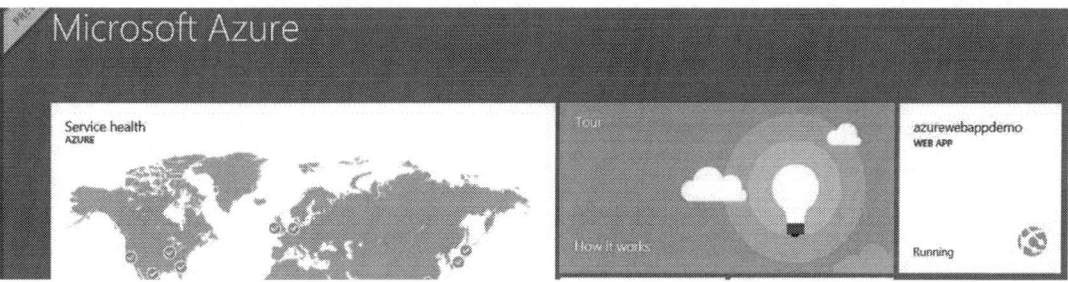

Figure 5-5. *Azure Portal*

Clicking the app opens the app window. As shown in Figure 5-6, you can see the app's settings and perform traffic monitoring.

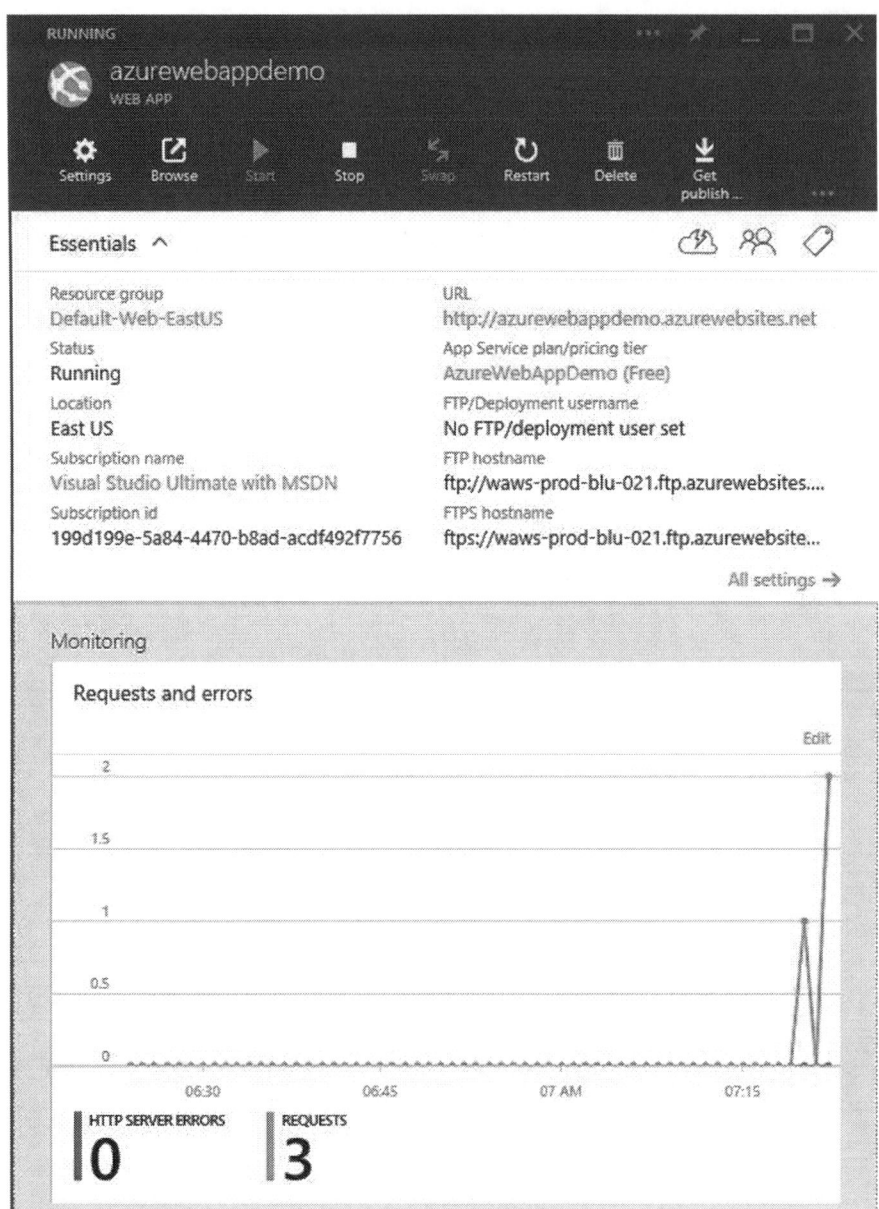

Figure 5-6. Azure web app settings and performance

You can view a lot of useful information about the app's availability and performance by scrolling through the rest of the web app page and clicking sections. Some of the additional items shown are as follows:

- Storage usage

- Performance

- Scale (turn autoscale on or off, and set the scaling parameters)

- Monthly spend (the monthly cost of the site for which you will be billed when not using the Free tier)

- Events

- Alerts

- Deployment slots (used to test new app code in a staging environment)

Creating a Web App from the Marketplace

Alternately, you can create your web app from the Azure Marketplace. The Marketplace offers prebuilt, open source, and community-contributed projects that are made available in the gallery.

To get to the Marketplace, click the Home icon on the left side of the Portal to return to the Startboard. From there, click the Marketplace icon, as shown in Figure 5-7.

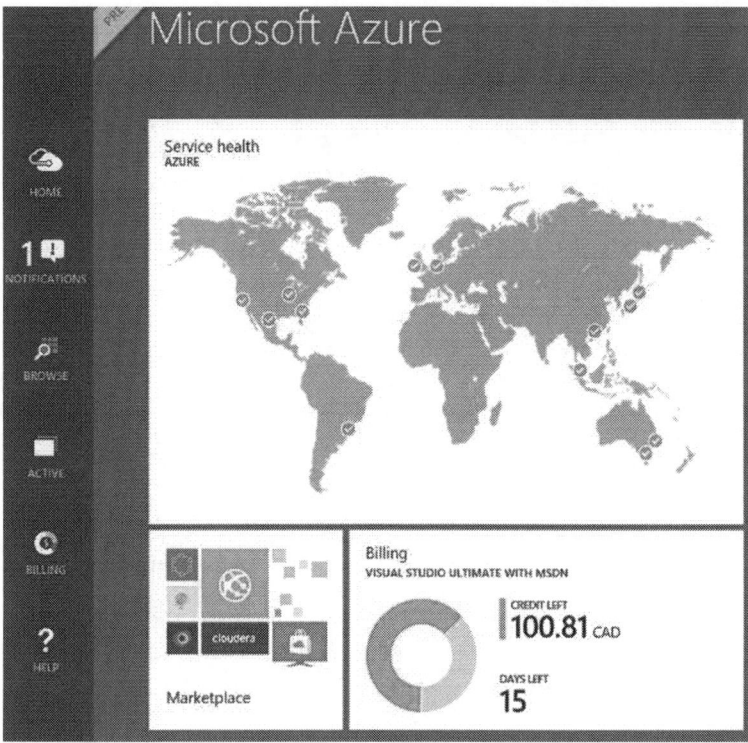

Figure 5-7. *Azure Startboard in the Portal. You can pin frequently used objects here*

After selecting the marketplace, you can select a project from the various categories, as shown in Figure 5-8. In this example, click Web + Mobile and then select an ASP.NET empty site to get started quickly.

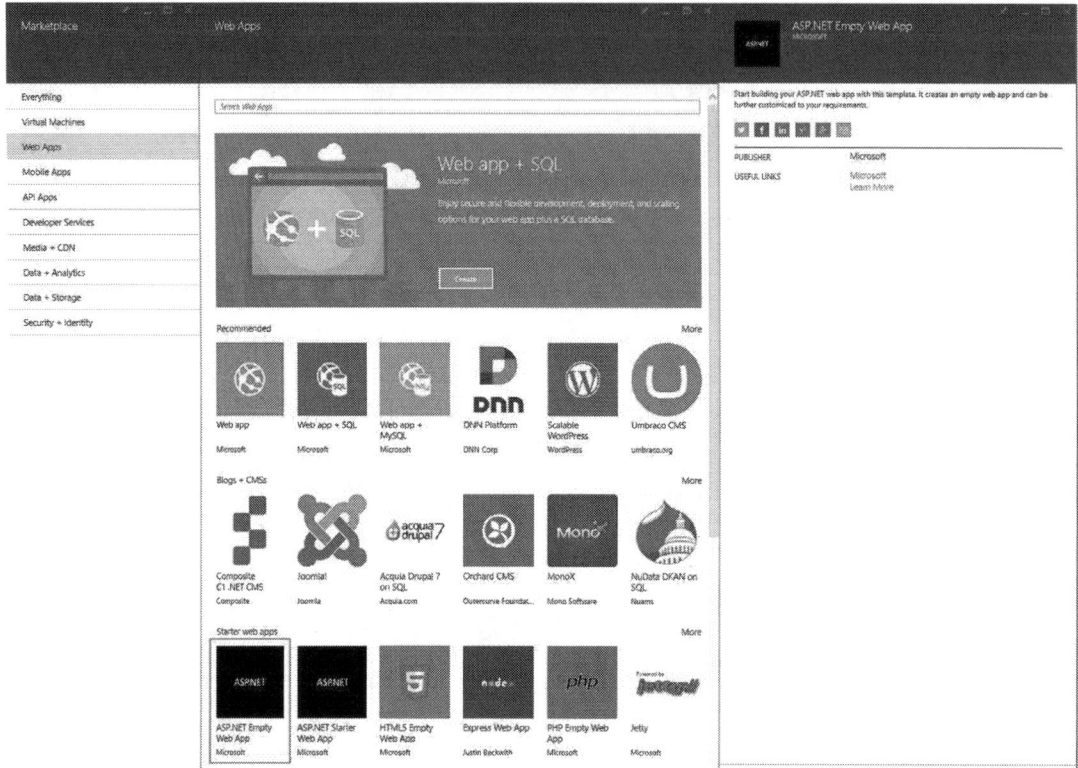

Figure 5-8. *The Azure Marketplace has several community and partner projects to help you get started*

In the ASP.NET pop-out window, click Create at the bottom of the page to create the new app. As shown in Figure 5-9, enter the ASP.NET empty site creation unique URL for the web site. As in the previous example, complete the rest of the settings by choosing a service plan or creating a new one, and select a pricing tier, subscription, and location.

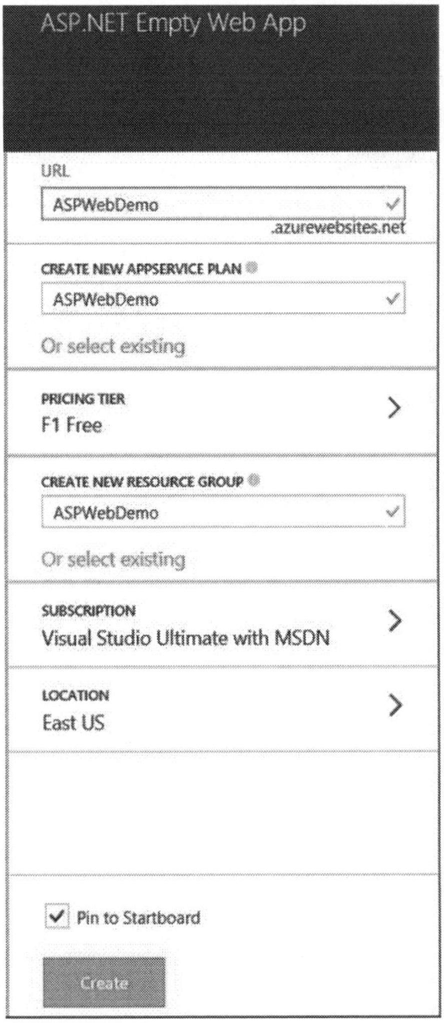

ASP.NET Empty Web App

URL
ASPWebDemo ✓
.azurewebsites.net

CREATE NEW APPSERVICE PLAN ◉
ASPWebDemo ✓
Or select existing

PRICING TIER ❯
F1 Free

CREATE NEW RESOURCE GROUP ◉
ASPWebDemo ✓
Or select existing

SUBSCRIPTION ❯
Visual Studio Ultimate with MSDN

LOCATION ❯
East US

✔ Pin to Startboard

Create

Figure 5-9. *Creating an ASP.NET empty site from the Azure Marketplace*

If you want to add the web site to your Azure Startboard, select the check box to do so and then click Create to create the web site.

Managing Your Azure Web Apps

Now that you've created a web app, you need to learn how to manage it from the Portal. Azure Web Apps is a very versatile platform that provides many features for configuring site settings, scaling, usage monitoring, and many other settings. If you choose to pin your web app to the Startboard, you can select it in order to load the web app dashboard into the Portal, as shown in Figure 5-10.

Figure 5-10. *Web app dashboard*

From the web app dashboard, you can control your site and modify its settings. If you click Settings in the dashboard, you see the Settings flyout in the Portal. As shown in Figure 5-11, it provides several options.

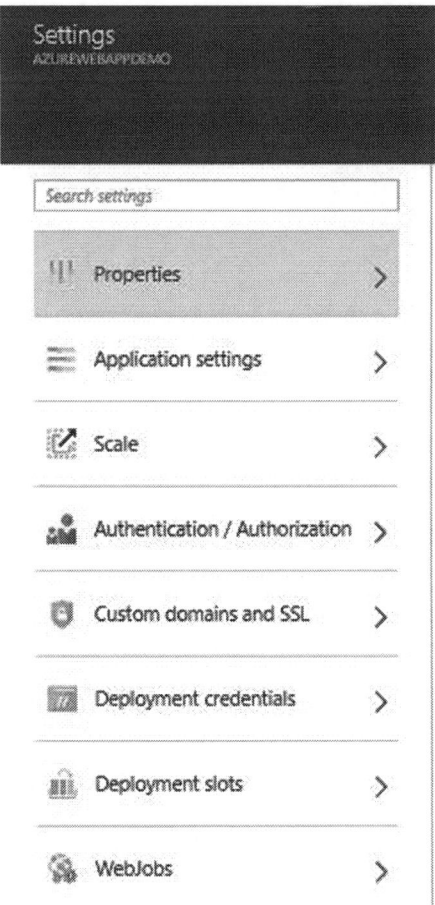

Figure 5-11. *All the settings for the web app are managed from the Settings flyout in the Portal*

In Figure 5-12, for example, the Web App Settings screen shows specific settings for the site. Here you can control application versions supported by the web app, including .NET framework, PHP, Java Python, and others. If you make any changes, be sure to click Save at the top.

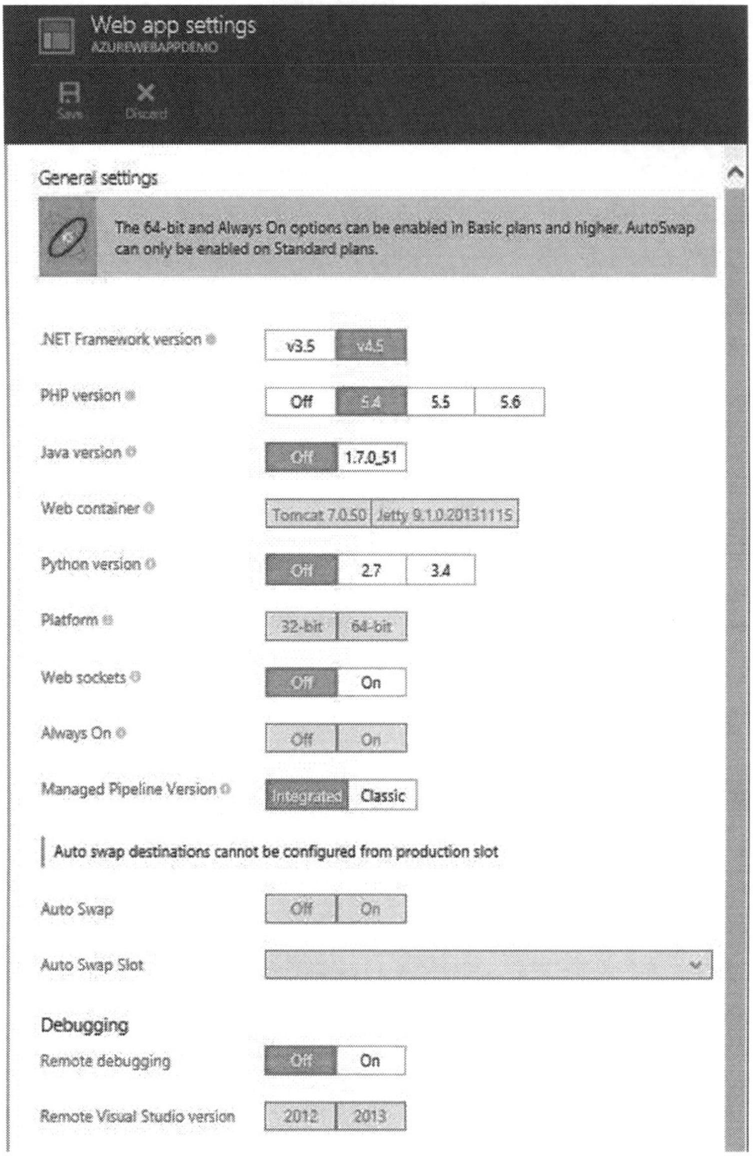

Figure 5-12. *Web app application settings*

Monitoring an Azure Web Site

Monitoring web app functionality is easy with Azure. You can add metrics to manage performance statistics. By default, when you create a web app in Azure, you can access the monitor from the site dashboard. There you can monitor CPU time, data in, data out, and HTTP server errors, as shown in Figure 5-13. You can also add metrics to measure things like response time and specific HTTP errors. Clicking the various items in the monitoring portal, such as Quotas, opens an additional window that gives you even more detailed information such as data out, memory used, file system storage used, and CPU usage for a given day.

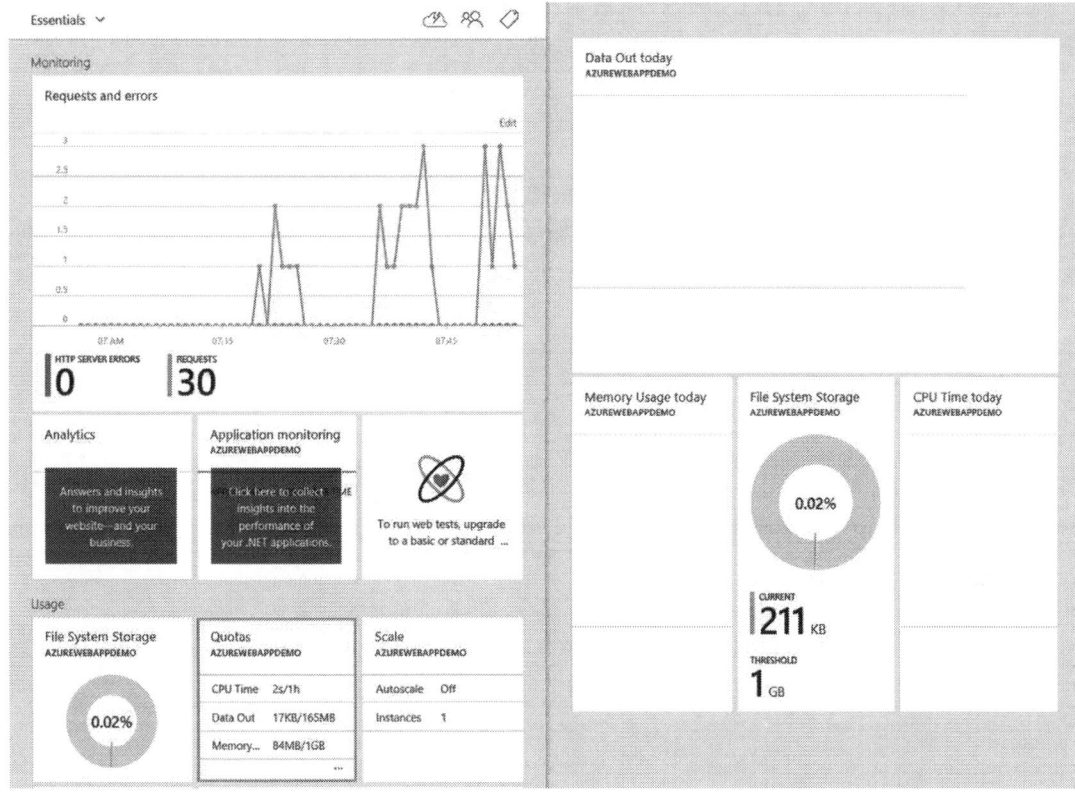

Figure 5-13. *Web app monitoring is set up by default*

Azure Web Apps Scaling

Scaling for Azure Web Apps gives you the option to increase the performance and throughput of your sites manually or automatically. Four service-level tiers are available in categories based on your needs: Free, Shared, Basic, and Standard. You can change the web app features at any time between those tiers to meet the demands of your business without incurring any downtime or service interruption.

The Free tier allows you to host up to 10 web apps in a shared environment. This tier does not offer any scaling. The Basic and Standard tiers run your web apps in private VMs, which are dedicated to you and your apps. You can host multiple web sites/domains in each Basic and Standard instance that you deploy.

The Free and Shared tiers are ideal for development and test scenarios; you can use the Free tier to evaluate the Azure platform quickly. When you've finished your evaluation or testing, you can easily convert the app to one of the paid tiers without delay or downtime in order to move your app into production so that it can begin serving customers. The Shared tier allows you to develop and test in an environment with features such as SSL, custom domain names, and more before putting your app into production, and it is suitable for low-traffic scenarios.

The Basic tier is designed for web apps with lower traffic requirements that do not need more advanced features like autoscale and traffic management. You can host unlimited web sites/domains using the Basic tier; pricing is based on the size and number of VM instances you run.

The Standard tier is designed for production web apps that are expected to see large amounts of web traffic or that require a higher level of performance. In this tier, you can host unlimited web sites/domains; just as with the other tiers, pricing is based on the size and number of VM instances you run.

In both the Basic tier and the Standard tier, built-in network load balancing support automatically distributes traffic across the VM instances to provide better performance as well as failover if one of your sites stops working. The Standard tier also includes built-in autoscale support that can automatically adjust the number of VM instances running to match your traffic needs, as shown in Figure 5-14.

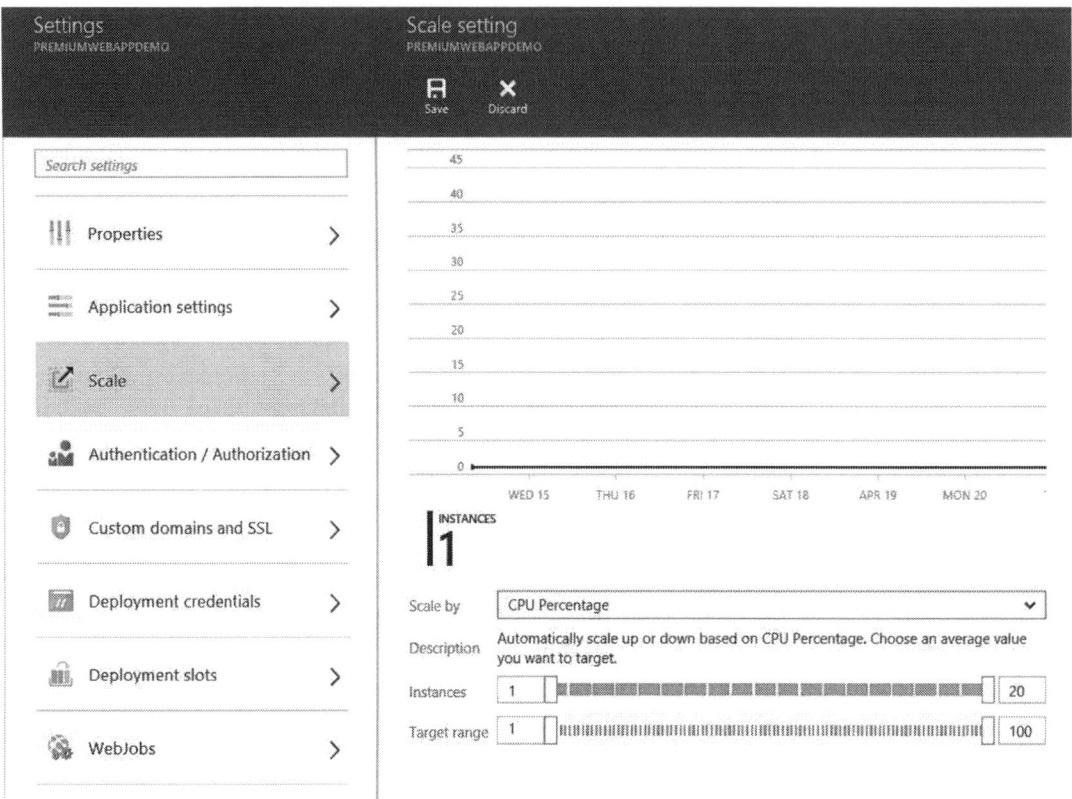

Figure 5-14. *Changing to the Standard tier allows you to change the scale based on resources you need. You can set the instances, or you can configure autoscale*

You can easily change and configure modes in the pricing tier portal in the Management Portal. You can scale up or down as required. These changes take only seconds to apply and affect all web apps within your web-hosting plan. They do not require your code to be changed or your applications to be redeployed.

When considering which web-hosting plan makes sense for your site, you must consider two related actions as you plan for your web app. The first is changing your web-hosting plan mode to a higher level of service; the second is configuring certain settings after you have switched to the higher level of service. Higher service tiers like Standard mode offer greater robustness and flexibility in determining the amount of resources, like the number of CPU cores, amount of memory, and storage deployed on Azure, as shown in Figure 5-15. In some cases, such as when you expect a greater-than-normal amount of traffic on your site due to a sale on your products, you also need to make sure you remove the spending cap on your Azure subscription so your site doesn't shut down automatically.

Figure 5-15. *Pricing tier plan for web apps*

Web Site Deployment with Azure Web Apps

There are many options for deploying your own content into Azure Web Apps. The easiest way is to deploy a web site that integrates with your source control system, such as Visual Studio. Automation makes the development process for continuous deployment easy. This is an efficient development and deployment method, but it also makes the backup and restore processes more manageable and reliable if you discover an issue with a change.

If you don't have source control set up yet, the easiest way to get started is to use a cloud-hosted source control system. Visual Studio and WebMatrix are Microsoft integrated development environments (IDEs) that you can use for web development. Both provide built-in features that make it easy to deploy to Azure Web Apps.

With Visual Studio, you can manage a full development environment, giving you the ability to create many different kinds of applications, including new web applications, and publish them directly to web apps. WebMatrix is free, easy to learn, and quick to install, but Visual Studio offers many more features for working with web apps. From within the Visual Studio IDE, you can create, stop, start, and delete web apps; view logs as they are created in real-time; debug remotely; and do much more. Visual Studio also integrates with source control systems such as Visual Studio Online, Team Foundation Server, and Git repositories.

You can deploy content to your site by using FTP with credentials that you create for your Azure web site regardless of what IDE you use. Additionally, from an on-premises source control system, you can use Team Foundation Service, Git, or Mercurial on-premises to deploy directly from your repository to Azure Web Apps.

For more information on deploying your web apps into Azure App Service, see `http://azure.microsoft.com/en-us/documentation/articles/web-sites-deploy`.

Azure App Service Migration Assistant

If you already have a large deployment of web sites that you wish to migrate to Microsoft Azure, Microsoft provides a tool called the *App Service Migration Assistant*, which greatly simplifies and speeds up the process. The tool requires that your web sites be running on Internet Information Service (IIS) 6 or later. The Migration Assistant analyzes your existing IIS server installation and identifies which sites can be migrated. It also identifies any items or elements that can't be migrated or are unsupported. With this information, you can make the necessary changes to your sites and migrate them to Azure when the updates are complete. The tool can be downloaded from `https://www.movemetothecloud.net`.

The Migration Assistant creates a readiness report, as shown in Figure 5-16, to identify any potential causes for concern or blocking issues that may prevent a successful migration from on-premises IIS to Azure App Service.

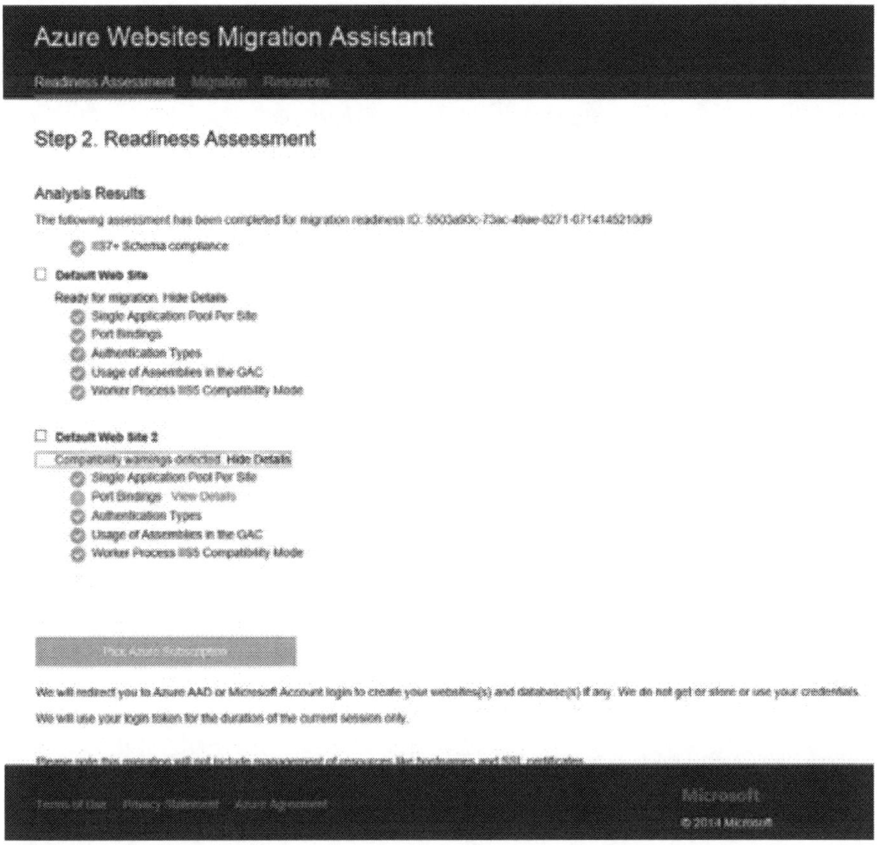

Figure 5-16. *Azure App Service Migration Assistant readiness assessment*

Some of the key items to be aware of are as follows:

- *Port bindings*: Azure App Service only supports port 80 for HTTP and port 443 for HTTPS traffic. Different port configurations are ignored, and traffic is routed to port 80 or 443.

- *Authentication*: Azure App Service supports anonymous authentication by default and forms authentication where specified by an application. Windows authentication can be used by integrating with Azure Active Directory and ADFS only. All other forms of authentication, such as basic authentication, are not currently supported.

- *Global Assembly Cache (GAC)*: The GAC is not supported in Azure App Service. If your application references assemblies that you usually deploy to the GAC, you will need to deploy to the application bin folder on Azure App Service.

- *IIS 5 compatibility mode*: This is not supported on Azure App Service.

- *Application pools*: In Azure App Service, each site and its child applications run in the same application pool. If your site has multiple child applications using multiple application pools, consolidate them into a single application pool with common settings or migrate each application to a separate web app.

- *COM components*: Azure App Service does not allow the registration of COM components on the platform. If your web sites or applications use any COM components, you must rewrite them in managed code and deploy them with the web site or application.

- *ISAPI filters*: Azure App Service can support the use of ISAPI filters. You need to do the following:

  - Deploy the DLLs with your web app.

  - Register the DLLs using `Web.config`.

  - Place an `applicationHost.xdt` file in the site root with the following content:

    ```
    <?xml version="1.0"?>
    <configuration xmlns:xdt="http://schemas.microsoft.com/XML-Document-
    Transform">
    <configSections>
        <sectionGroup name="system.webServer">
          <section name="isapiFilters" xdt:Transform="SetAttributes
          (overrideModeDefault)" overrideModeDefault="Allow" />
        </sectionGroup>
      </configSections>
    </configuration>
    ```

- Other components, like SharePoint, front page server extensions (FPSE), FTP, and SSL certificates will not be migrated.

RUNNING THE AZURE APP SERVICE MIGRATION ASSISTANT

To run the Migration Assistant, follow these steps:

1. On the IIS server or a client computer, browse to `https://www.movemetothecloud.net`.

2. Click the Dedicated IIS Server button to install Azure App Service Migration Assistant, as shown in Figure 5-17.

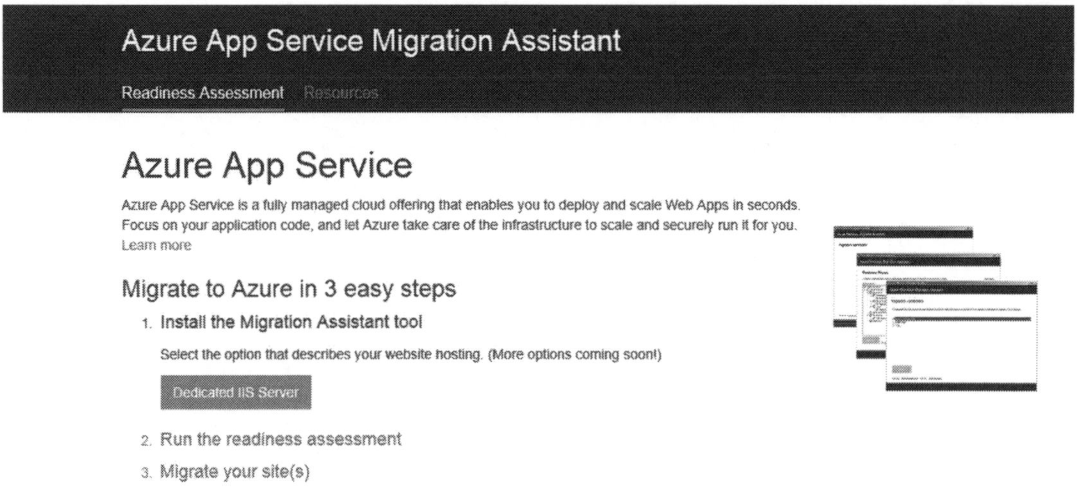

Azure App Service Migration Assistant

Readiness Assessment   Resources

Azure App Service

Azure App Service is a fully managed cloud offering that enables you to deploy and scale Web Apps in seconds. Focus on your application code, and let Azure take care of the infrastructure to scale and securely run it for you. Learn more

Migrate to Azure in 3 easy steps

1. Install the Migration Assistant tool

   Select the option that describes your website hosting. (More options coming soon!)

   Dedicated IIS Server

2. Run the readiness assessment

3. Migrate your site(s)

Figure 5-17. *When you connect to the Migration Assistant web site, you land on this screen*

3. Click the Install Tool button to install the Migration Assistant on your computer, as shown in Figure 5-18.

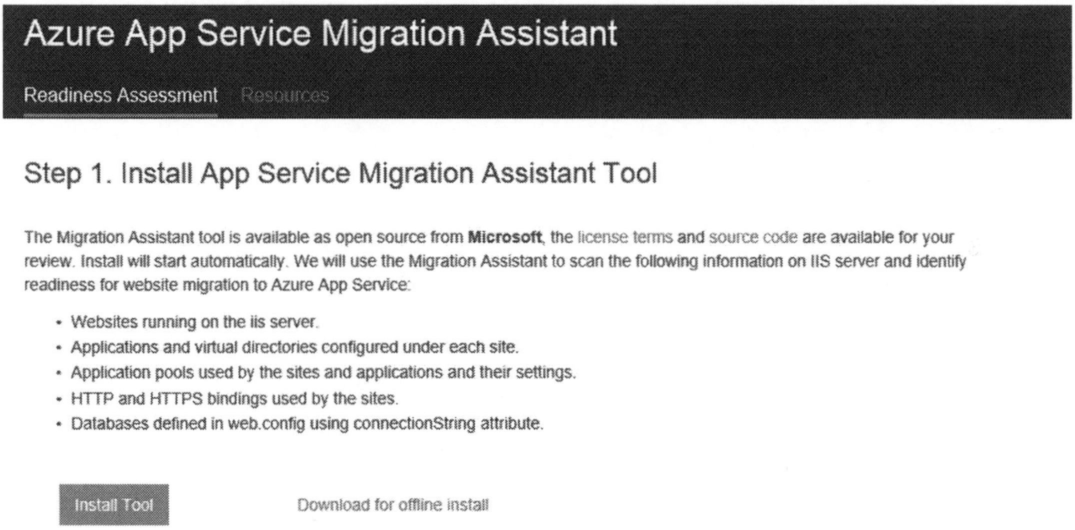

Azure App Service Migration Assistant

Readiness Assessment   Resources

Step 1. Install App Service Migration Assistant Tool

The Migration Assistant tool is available as open source from **Microsoft**, the license terms and source code are available for your review. Install will start automatically. We will use the Migration Assistant to scan the following information on IIS server and identify readiness for website migration to Azure App Service:

- Websites running on the iis server.
- Applications and virtual directories configured under each site.
- Application pools used by the sites and applications and their settings.
- HTTP and HTTPS bindings used by the sites.
- Databases defined in web.config using connectionString attribute.

Install Tool   Download for offline install

Figure 5-18. *Azure App Service Migration Assistant installation screen*

4. When the Application Install – Security Warning pop-up window appears, as shown in Figure 5-19, click Install to proceed with the installation.

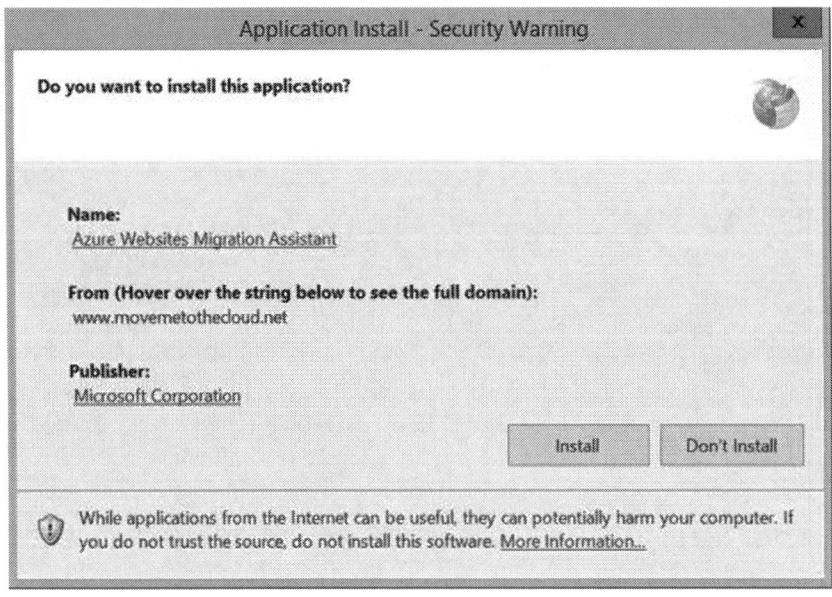

Figure 5-19. Application Install – Security Warning screen

5. In the Open File window, click Run to begin the installation, as shown in Figure 5-20.

Figure 5-20. Open File – Security Warning screen

6. The installer installs any required dependencies, such as Web Deploy, DacFX, and IIS. When the installation completes, you see a screen similar to the one shown in Figure 5-21.

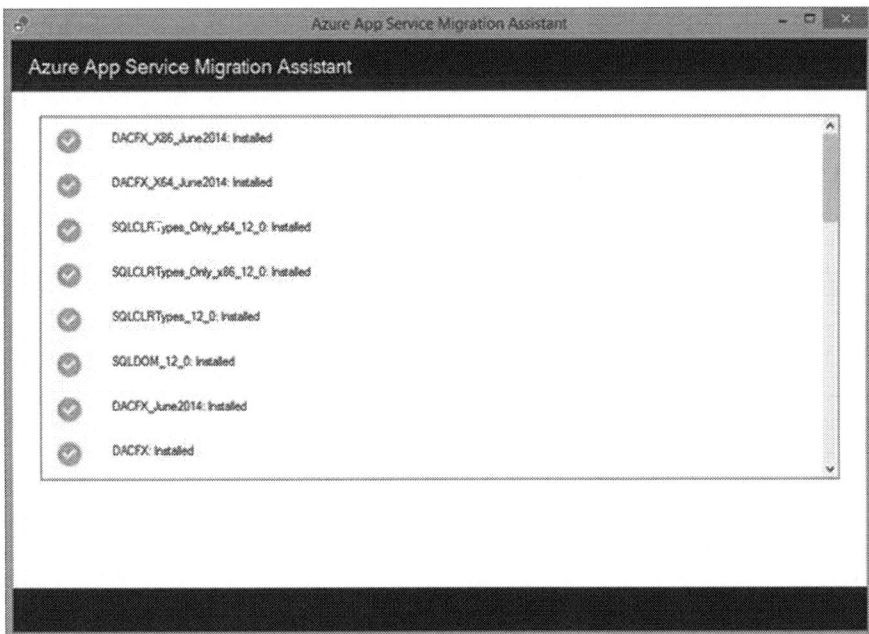

Figure 5-21. *Completed Migration Assistant installation*

When the installation completes, the tool starts automatically.

7. Depending on whether you installed the tool on your local IIS server or on a different computer, choose the appropriate migration option. You can choose any of the following options:

- Migrate sites and databases on the local server to Azure

- Migrate sites and databases from one or more remote servers to Azure

- Migrate a SCOM site and database from one or more remote servers to Azure

8. After choosing the appropriate migration option, click Continue, as shown in the example in Figure 5-22.

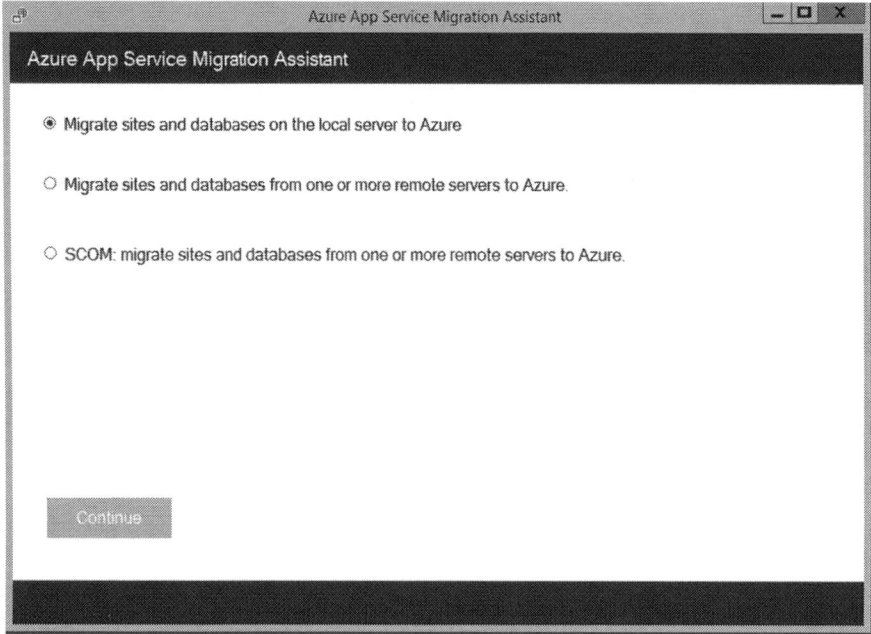

Figure 5-22. *Azure App Service Migration Assistant*

The Migration Assistant inspects your IIS server's configuration, looking at the sites, applications, and application pools—as well as any dependencies—to identify web sites that can be migrated.

9. Figure 5-23 shows three web sites: Default Web Site, WSUS Administration, and FTP. Each has an associated database that will also be migrated. Select some or all the sites you would like to assess, and then click Next.

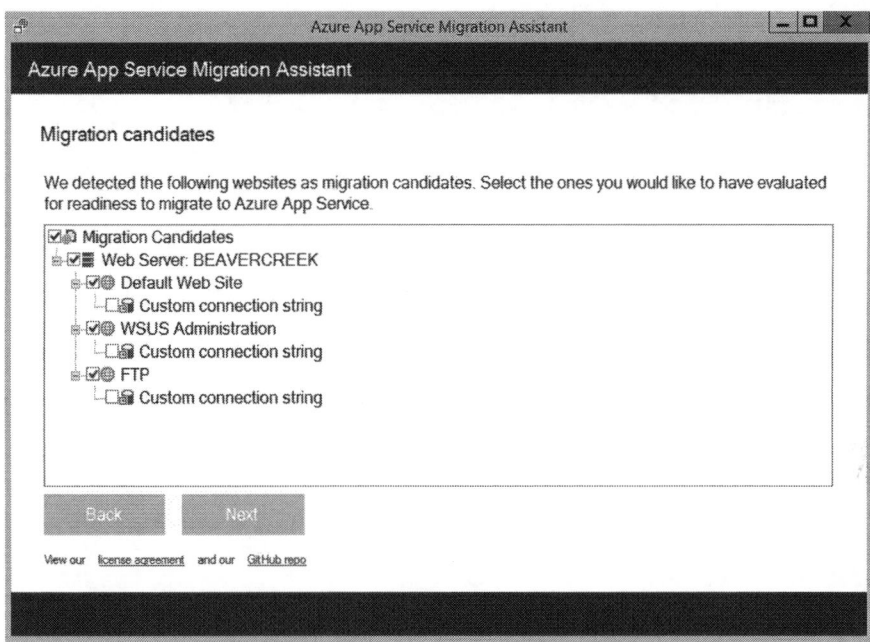

Figure 5-23. *Azure App Service Migration Assistant candidates*

10. When the assessment completes, click Upload to upload the readiness report, as shown in Figure 5-24. Optionally, you can choose to save the file on your local computer, run the migration tool later, and upload the saved readiness report when you are ready for it.

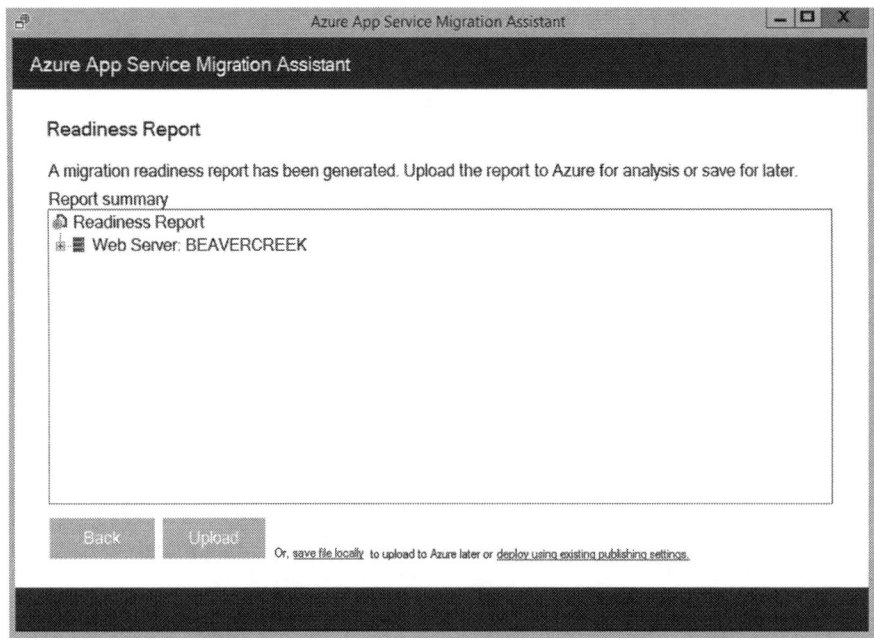

Figure 5-24. *Migration Readiness Report*

11. Once your readiness report has been uploaded, Azure performs an analysis and displays the results, as shown in Figure 5-25. Be sure to read the assessment details carefully for each web site, and make sure you understand and have addressed each of the reported issues before proceeding with the migration of your web sites.

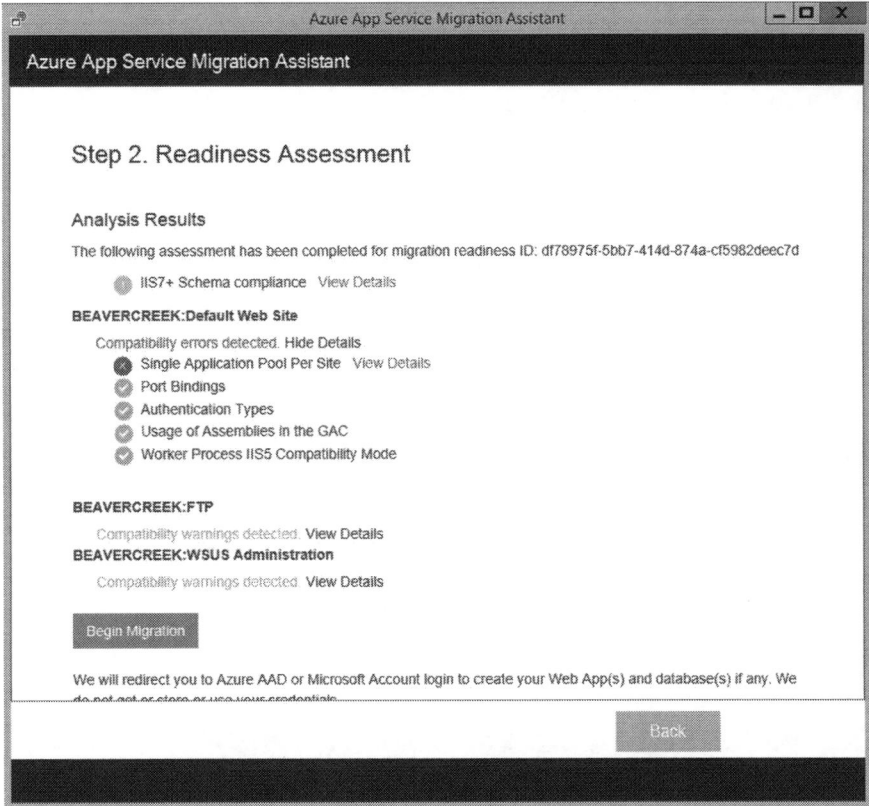

Figure 5-25. Readiness Assessment in the Migration Assistant

12. When you are ready to proceed, click Begin Migration, as shown in Figure 5-25. You are redirected to Azure to log in to your account, as shown in Figure 5-26. The account that you use to log in requires an active subscription, and it must be a global administrator in your tenant.

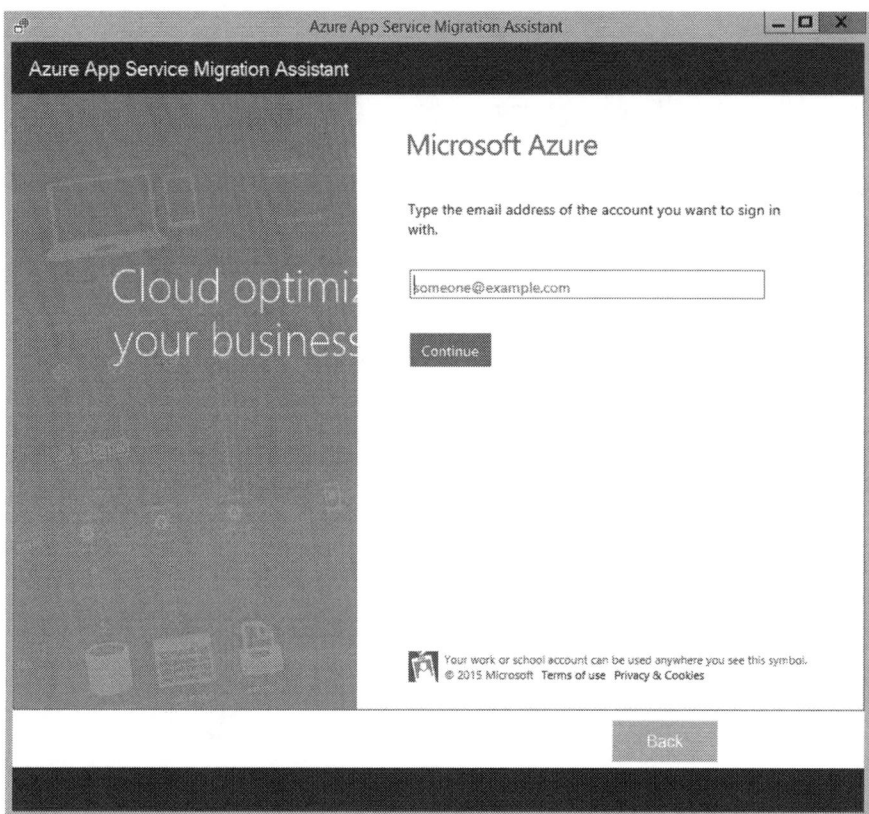

Figure 5-26. *Azure login screen*

13. Select your tenant account, the correct subscription (if you have more than one), and the region to use for your migrated app service and databases, as shown in Figure 5-27. Finally, click Start Migration.

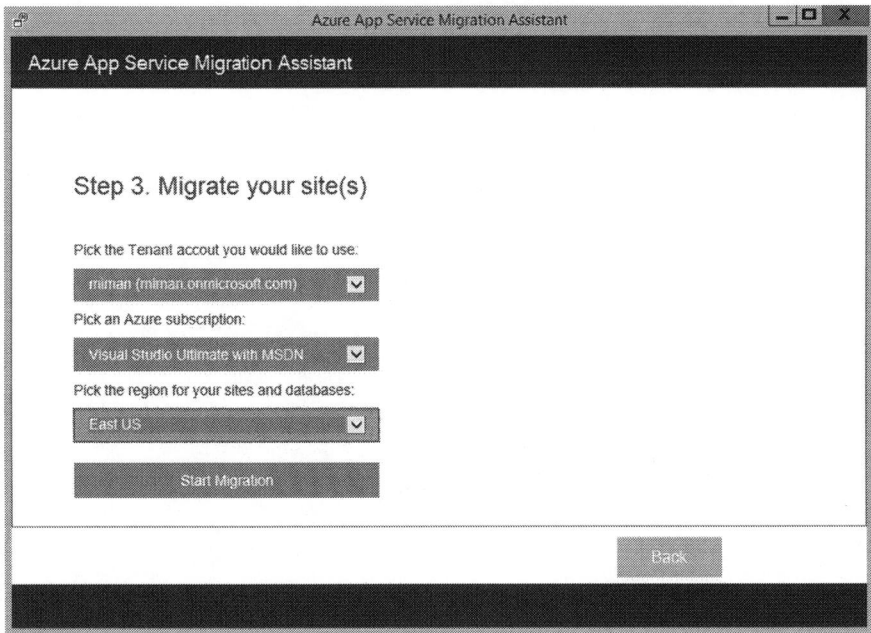

Figure 5-27. *Selecting the location in Azure for the migration*

14. On the Web Apps screen, you can choose to migrate any or all of the web sites that are on the server, as seen in Figure 5-28.

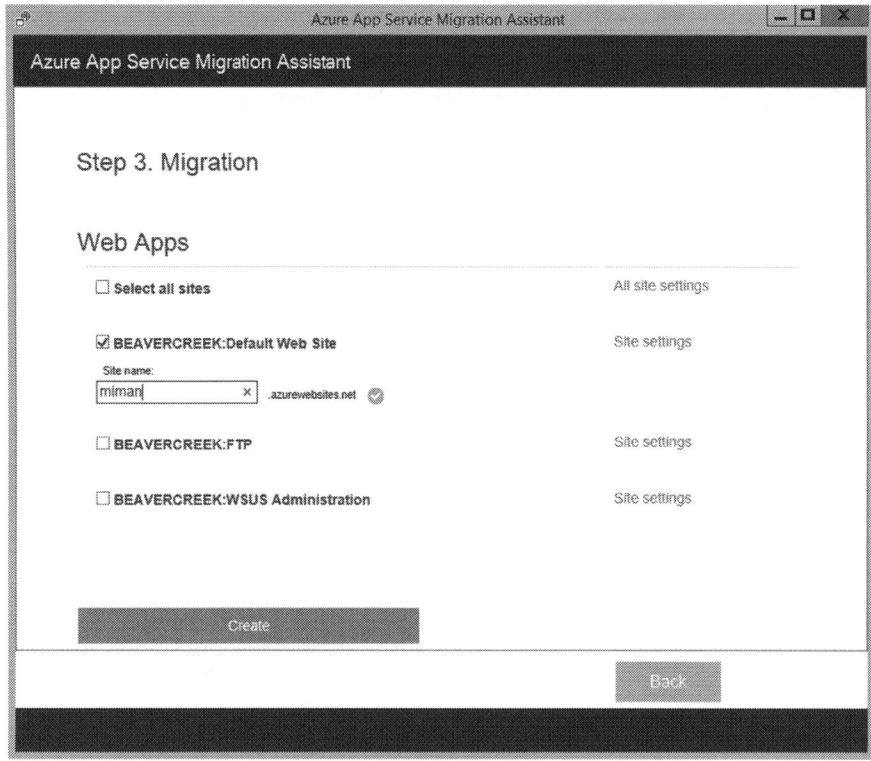

Figure 5-28. *Azure Web Apps migration screen*

15. There is a Site Settings link to the right of the site name, as you can see in Figure 5-28. Clicking this link brings up a page that allows you to configure settings for the site on that screen, as shown in Figure 5-29. You can make changes to the default migration settings, such as the following:

   a. Selecting a web site mode. The available modes are Free, Shared, Basic, and Standard, and they may vary depending on your subscription.

   b. The worker size of the web app. You can choose Small, Medium, or Large.

   c. App service plan.

    d.   Using an existing Azure SQL database or creating a new Azure SQL database.
            You can also choose a SQL edition: Basic, Standard, or Premium.

    e.   The database performance level. The choices are S0, S1, and S2.

    f.   The maximum database size. The sizes range from 100 MB up to 250 GB.

Figure 5-29 shows the BeaverCreek web site with the default settings.

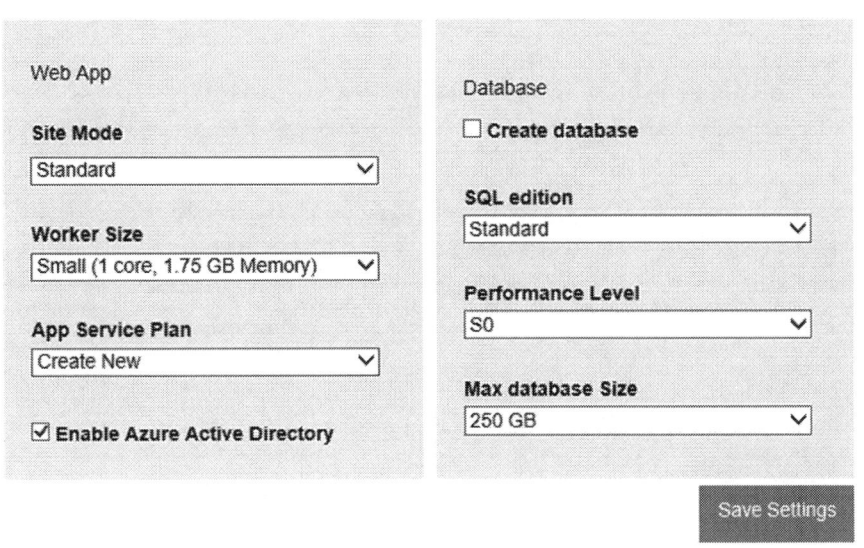

Figure 5-29. Web site settings screen

16. Once you have confirmed that the desired settings are selected, click Begin Publish, as shown in Figure 5-30, to start the migration process.

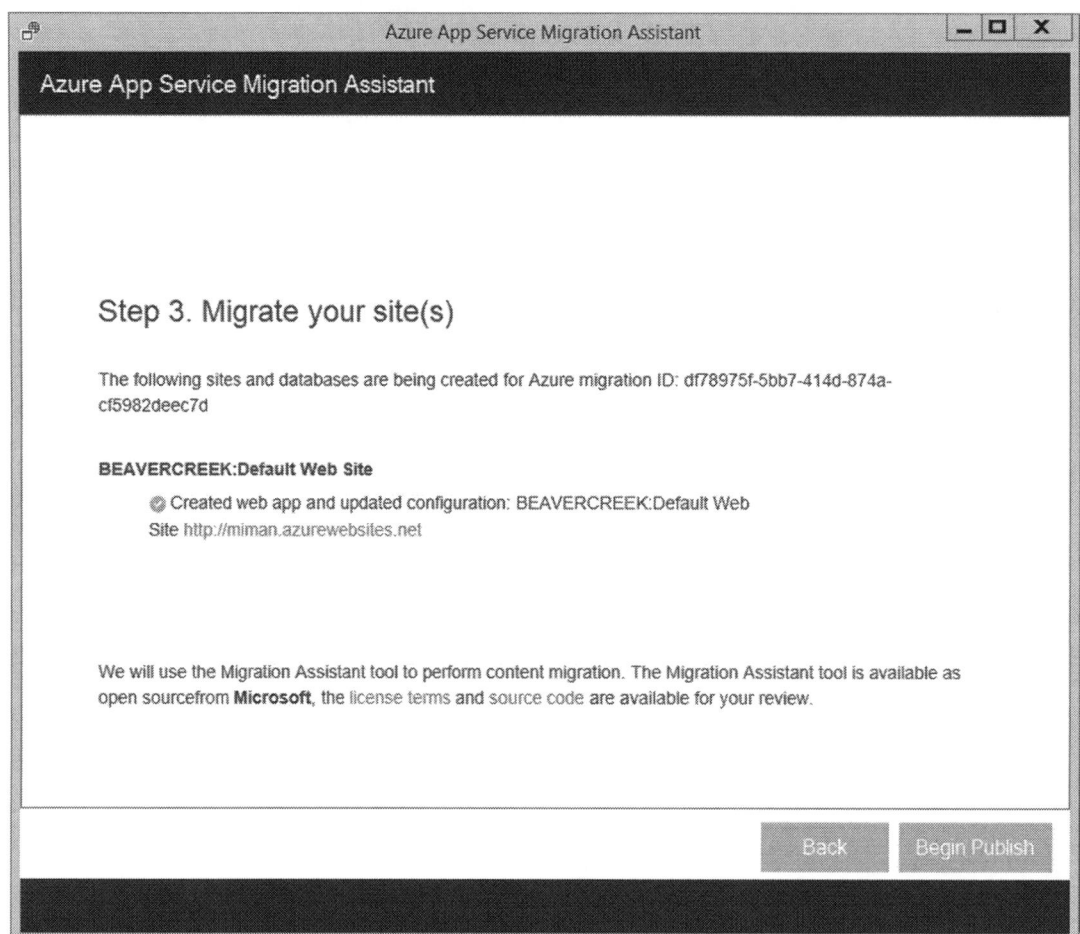

Figure 5-30. *App migration publish screen*

As you can see in Figure 5-31, the Migration Assistant creates the Azure SQL database, if selected, and the Azure app service if you chose to create a new one. It then publishes the web site content and databases. The progress of the migration is clearly shown in the tool.

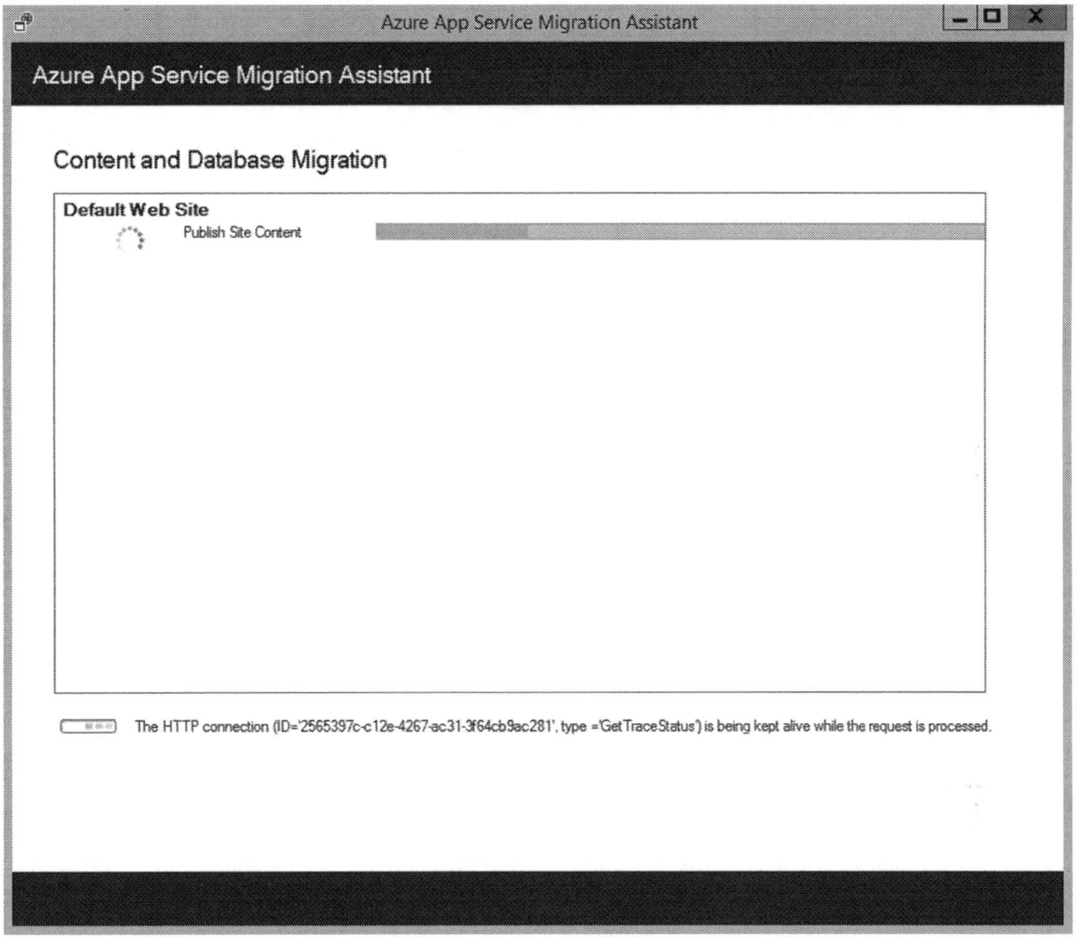

Figure 5-31. Azure App Service Migration Assistant progress screen

When the migration process completes, you see a summary screen similar to the one shown in Figure 5-32, which indicates whether the migration was successful and links to any newly created web sites.

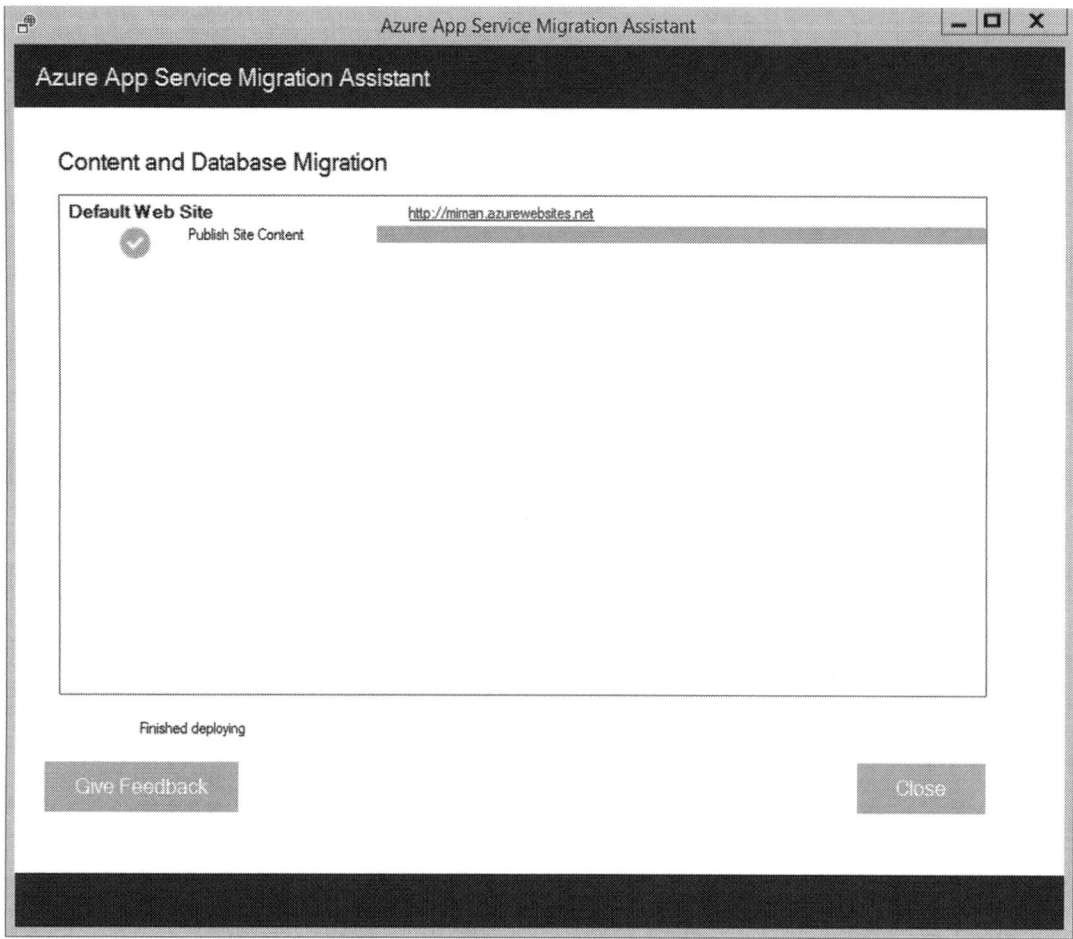

Figure 5-32. *Azure App Service Migration Assistant completion screen*

If an error occurs during the migration, the migration tool indicates the failure and rolls back the changes. You can also send the error report to Microsoft by clicking the Send Error Report button with the captured failure call stack and build message body.

When the migration completes, click the link to the Azure web sites to verify that the migration has succeeded. Browse your new Azure-based web site to make sure it functions as expected before changing your DNS settings to point to the new location of the site.

Now that you have migrated your web sites to Azure, you can manage them in the Azure Portal at
`https://portal.azure.com`. In the Azure Portal, open the App Service blade to see your migrated web
sites, and then click the site that you wish to manage, as shown in Figure 5-33. There you can manage
settings such as configuring continuous publishing, creating backups, autoscaling, and monitoring
usage or performance, as described earlier in this chapter.

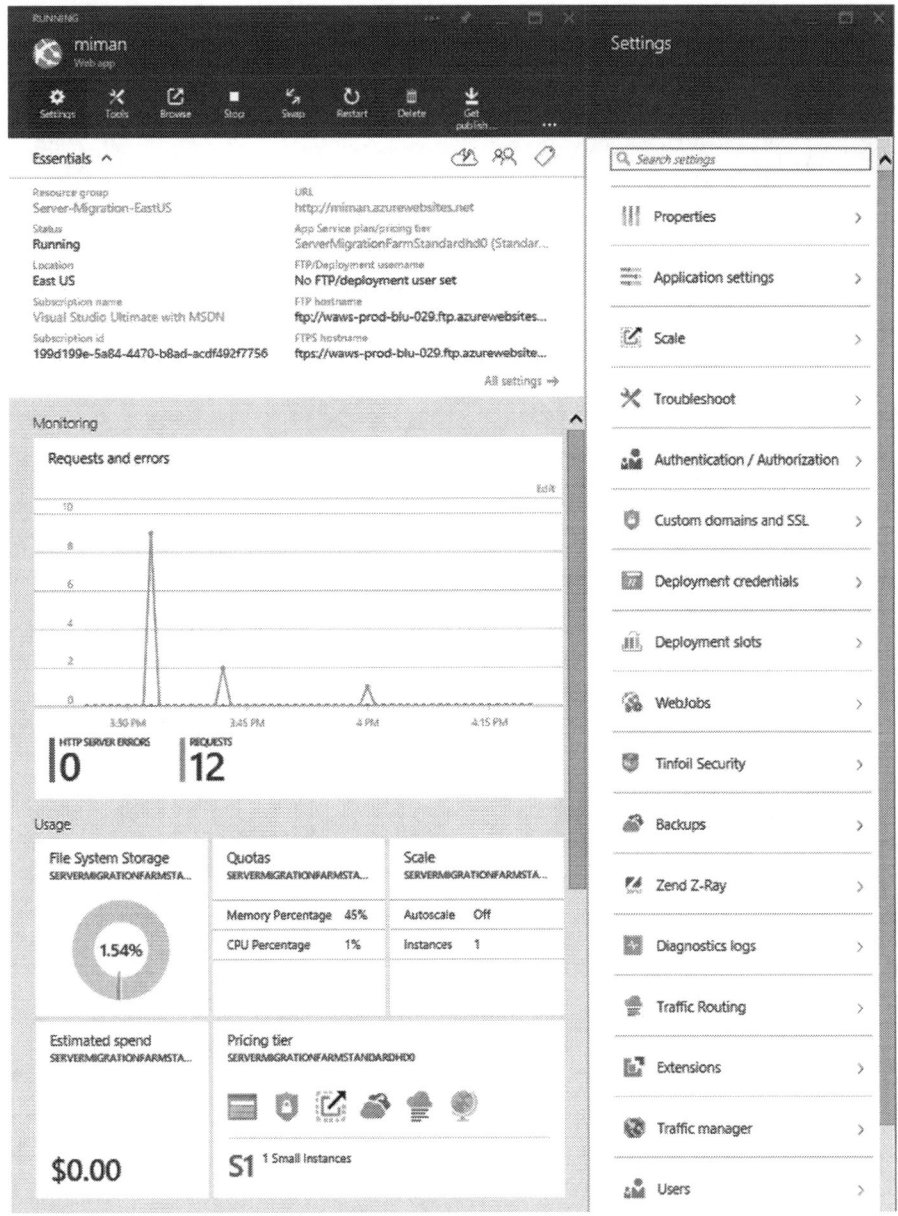

Figure 5-33. *Migrated web site, now an Azure web app*

Summary

In this chapter, you were introduced to the Azure Web Apps service and saw how easy it is to create and manage your web sites. Whether you are managing a small web site deployment or an enterprise deployment that needs to support a large retail operation, web apps can easily be scaled to suit your needs. Additionally, once your web sites are created in Azure, managing and monitoring them is simple with the available tools.

You also learned how easy it is to migrate your on-premises web sites into Azure Web Apps with the Azure App Service Migration Assistant. The Migration Assistant tool migrates your existing code and databases into Azure, allowing you to make the move to web apps quickly.

In the next chapter, you learn about the available storage options in Windows Azure. After finishing that chapter, you will have a good understanding of the options available in Windows Azure, and you can begin to plan your own Azure deployment.

■ ■ ■

## CHAPTER 6

Getting Started with Azure Virtual Machines

Introducing Azure Virtual Machines

Running numerous web sites from different customers on a single server has been well understood for the past 15 years or so, and it has been the mainstay of hosting providers worldwide. This model of web hosting allowed small businesses and individuals to create cost-effective online presences. In the last 10 years, however, emulating hardware to allow entire computer operating systems (OSs) to run has enabled hosting scenarios that, without virtualization, would previously have been too costly. Virtual machines (VMs) emulate the hardware required to run computer OSs. The VMs discussed in this book are all system virtual machines, not process virtual machines; process VMs are part of a detailed software development conversation. Only OSs supported on virtual hardware architecture can be run in a VM. Microsoft uses only x64 hardware for their hosts; hence any x86/x64 workload can run on the VMs running on these hosts. These VMs are also frequently referred to as *guests*. A VM is basically a software version of a computer's hardware onto which you can install an OS; the host slices its resources across all the VM guests it has running. For more information about VMs and how their abstraction works, see http://en.wikipedia.org/wiki/Virtual_machine. You can also download a copy of Microsoft's "Virtualization for Windows: white paper at http://download.microsoft.com/download/8/6/2/862032E0-9D03-4AB5-B033-E6022A6186B1/VirtualizationforWindows_a_Technology_overview.pdf.

Microsoft Hyper-V, released in June 2008, is a native or bare-metal Type 1 hypervisor, which means that it runs directly on the host hardware. Type 1 hypervisors don't exhibit the performance issues, vulnerabilities, and configuration challenges associated with Type 2 hypervisors, which run on a host OS (as another service) such as Windows Server or Linux. A comparison of Type 1 versus Type 2 hypervisors includes information regarding processes running in Ring 0; for more details, download the Microsoft Hyper-V white paper at https://www.microsoft.com/en-us/server-cloud/solutions/virtualization.aspx. Microsoft Azure uses as special OS built on Windows Server 2008 Type I hypervisors, called the *Microsoft Azure* OS; it runs the fabric layer of Azure. Microsoft calls Azure's hypervisor *Microsoft Azure Hypervisor*. Microsoft's *Azure Fabric Controller* controls all the scaling and reliability tasks needed in the environment. A frequent question is,

"What is the difference between Hyper-V and Microsoft Azure Hypervisor?" Microsoft Distinguished Engineer Hoi Vo provides the answer at http://azure.microsoft.com/blog/2009/01/29/design-principles-behind-the-windows-azure-hypervisor:

1. *Efficient*: Push work to hardware as much as possible. Any percentage gain once multiplied to tens of thousands of machines will be very significant for us. Consequently we can bet on new processor features to save CPU cycles for the hosted application.

2. *Small footprint*: Any features not applicable to our specific cloud scenarios are removed. This guarantees that we do not have to worry about updating or fixing unnecessary code, meaning less churning or required reboots for the host. All critical code paths are also highly optimized for our Windows Azure scenarios.

3. *Tight integration*: The Windows Azure Hypervisor is tightly optimized with the Windows Azure kernel. This is required to achieve the level of scalability and performance we want for our stack.

Azure VMs currently allow Microsoft customers to enable server-computing scenarios out of Microsoft's public or government Azure datacenters. Microsoft only supports x64 guest OSs in Azure. Azure datacenters are frequently referred to as Microsoft's public or government clouds. Customers can provision VMs from scratch using a variety of templates or even upload their own servers built on-premises in Azure into a VM. Azure datacenters allow Microsoft customers to control the networking, virtual hard disks, CPU, and memory resources allocated to any VM that they provision. Azure becomes an extension of the customer's datacenter infrastructure by providing computing, storage, and memory resources on demand. These resources can be scaled up or down as the customer's needs change. Auto-scaling and load-balancing VMs are a click away for a workload. This is the dynamic datacenter, with services scaling up and down as workloads demand and provisioning automatically as workloads or services require the infrastructure.

This chapter takes you through VM configuration and sizing, how to build and connect to VMs, and how to upload your own on-premises servers to Azure, regardless of the current hypervisor or physical server hardware.

Virtual Machine Configurations

Azure VMs include Windows and Linux VMs, both of which have Basic and Standard tiers. The key difference between the tiers is that the *Basic tier* lacks both auto-scaling and load-balancing capabilities. The same size VMs are available in both tiers, so if these capabilities are required, use the Standard tier. The Standard tier has different sizes of VMs broken out into series according to their configurations: A-series, D-series, DS-series, and G-series.

A-series is a basic, cost-effective option. D-series VMs should be considered by any business that needs to run applications that demand higher computing power and take advantage of faster disk performance. These VMs provide faster processors; the virtual cores (vCores) are approximately 60% faster than the A-series, and both the local disk and the temporary drive (D:\ on Windows) use a solid-state drive (SSD).

DS-series VMs can use Premium storage, which provides high-performance, low-latency storage for I/O-intensive workloads. These VMs use SSDs to host a VM's disks and offer a local SSD disk cache.

G-series VMs offer the biggest size and best performance, and they run on hosts with Intel Xeon E5 V3 family processors. These VMs are named for the world's most famous monster lizard, due to their size.

Sizing a VM correctly is important because its size has the greatest influence on its price. Size also affects the VM's processing, memory, and storage capacity. Storage costs are calculated separately based on pages used in the storage account. The following tables show the sizes and capacities offered by each series as of the time of this writing for US-based VMs. As time goes on, Microsoft will update these series specs and prices. For a complete breakdown by OS and Azure datacenter locations, refer to the Azure pricing guide at http://azure.microsoft.com/en-us/pricing/details/virtual-machines/#Windows.

A-series

The Basic tier is an economical, general-purpose option for development workloads, test servers, and other applications that don't require load-balancing, auto-scaling, or memory-intensive VMs, as listed in Table 6-1.

Table 6-1. *A-series Basic VMs**

Instance	Cores	RAM (GB)	Disk Size (GB)	Price
A0	1	0.75	20	$0.018/hr (~$13/mo)
A1	1	1.75	40	$0.077/hr (~$57/mo)
A2	2	3.5	60	$0.154/hr (~$115/mo)
A3	4	7	120	$0.308/hr (~$229/mo)
A4	8	14	240	$0.616/hr (~$458/mo)

*Prices include Windows Server licensing fee but not sales tax. Monthly Pay-As-You-Go estimates are based on 744 hours of continuous use.

The *Standard tier* offers the most flexibility. It supports all VM configurations and features, as itemized in Table 6-2.

Table 6-2. *A-series Standard VMs**

Instance	Cores	RAM (GB)	Disk Size (GB)	Price
A0	1	0.75	20	$0.02/hr (~$15/mo)
A1	1	1.75	70	$0.09/hr (~$67/mo)
A2	2	3.5	135	$0.18/hr (~$134/mo)
A3	4	7	285	$0.36/hr (~$268/mo)
A4	8	14	605	$0.72/hr (~$536/mo)
A5	2	14	135	$0.33/hr (~$246/mo)
A6	4	28	285	$0.66/hr (~$491/mo)
A7	8	56	605	$1.32/hr (~$982/mo)

*Prices include Windows Server licensing fee but not sales tax. Monthly Pay-As-You-Go estimates based on 744 hours of continuous use.

D-series

D-series VMs offer up to 112 GB of memory, utilize solid-state drives, and have faster processors than the A-series. The D-series can be used for more than Azure VMs; they can also be used for web or worker roles when you architect Azure Cloud Services. D-series VMs are ideal for high-performance, demanding workloads.

A variant of the D-series, called the DS-series, is specifically targeted for Premium Storage. The pricing and billing metrics for the DS sizes are the same as the D-series, as listed in Table 6-3.

Table 6-3. *D-series Standard VMs**

Instance	Cores	RAM (GB)	Disk Size (GB)	Price
D1	1	3.5	50	$.171/hr (~$127/mo)
D2	2	7	100	$0.342/hr (~$254/mo)
D3	4	14	200	$0.684/hr (~$509/mo)
D4	8	28	400	$1.368/hr (~$1,018/mo)
D11	2	14	100	$0.403/hr (~$300/mo)
D12	4	28	200	$0.806/hr (~$600/mo)
D13	8	56	400	$1.451/hr (~$1,080/mo)
D14	16	112	800	$2.611/hr (~$1,943/mo)

*Prices include Windows Server licensing fee but not sales tax. Monthly Pay-As-You-Go estimates based on 744 hours of continuous use.

G-series

G-series VMs are performance-optimized with the latest CPUs, memory, and storage, as detailed in Table 6-4. They feature the latest Intel Xeon processor E5 v3 family with two times more memory and four times more SSDs than the D-series. G-series VMs are the most powerful VMs available in Azure.

Table 6-4. *G-series Standard VMs**

Instance	Cores	RAM (GB)	Disk Size (GB)	Price
G1	2	28	384	$0.67/hr (~$498/mo)
G2	4	56	768	$1.34/hr (~$997/mo)
G3	8	112	1,536	$2.68/hr (~$1,994/mo)
G4	16	224	3,072	$5.36/hr (~$3,988/mo)
G5	32	448	6,144	$9.65/hr (~$7,180/mo)

*Prices include Windows Server licensing fee but not sales tax. Monthly Pay-As-You-Go estimates based on 744 hours of continuous use.

Network-Optimized VMs

Network-optimized VMs are only available in select datacenters. (See Table 6-5 for details.) These VMs add a 40Gbit/s InfiniBand network (a high-performance computing standard for high throughput and low latency), with Remote Direct Memory Access (RDMA) technology. They are ideal for Message Passing Interface (MPI) applications, high-performance clusters, modeling and simulations, video encoding, and other computing- or network-intensive scenarios.

Table 6-5. *A-series Network Optimized VMs**

Instance	Cores	RAM (GB)	Disk Size (GB)	Price
A8	8	56	382	$2.45/hr (~$1,823/mo)
A9	16	112	382	$4.90/hr (~$3,646/mo)

*Prices include Windows Server licensing fee but not sales tax. Monthly Pay-As-You-Go estimates based on 744 hours of continuous use.

Compute-Intensive VMs

Compute-intensive VMs are only available in select datacenters. (See Table 6-6 for details.) These VMs feature Intel Xeon E5 processors for high-performance clusters, modeling, simulations, and anything else that requires the highest level of computation today.

Table 6-6. *A-series Compute-Intensive VMs**

Instance	Cores	RAM (GB)	Disk Size (GB)	Price
A10	8	56	382	$2.45/hr (~$1,823/mo)
A11	16	112	382	$4.90/hr (~$3,646/mo)

*Prices include Windows Server licensing fee, but not the sales tax. Monthly Pay-As-You-Go estimates based on 744 hours of continuous use.

IP Addresses for Azure Virtual Machine and Cloud Service

Every Azure VM is automatically assigned a free virtual IP (VIP) address. For an additional charge, you can also get the following:

- *Instance-level public IP addresses*: These make a VM directly addressable by assigning it a public IP (PIP) address. Instance-level PIP addresses cost $0.004/hour per IP (about $3/month per IP based on 744 hours usage). You can assign up to five instance-level IP addresses per subscription.

- *Reserved IP addresses*: You can also reserve static PIP addresses for your VM. Reserved IP addresses allow you to reserve a public virtual IP address in Azure, which you can then associate with a new Cloud Service. The reserved IP address is *sticky*, meaning once it's associated with the Cloud Service, it won't change unless you decide to disassociate it. In a VM scenario, the reserved IP address remains associated with your Cloud Service even when all the VMs in the Cloud Service are stop/deallocated. At this time, you can't reserve an IP address for a Cloud Service that you have already created.

Virtual Machine Concepts

Virtual machines are a software version of computer hardware on which you can install OSs and which you can configure and use just as you would a traditional computer where the OS is running on actual hardware. Because the OS is separated from the hardware by a hypervisor, many challenges that used to exist no longer do, such as when the life of an OS was tied to the hardware on which it was installed or when a hardware failure caused a server to be rebuilt. VMs can run wherever there is a hypervisor, even with different CPU types. There is no dependency on the hardware.

You can create OS templates specifically for various server sizes as needed. Each template can have a specific number of virtual CPUs (vCPUs), RAM (vRAM), network interface cards (vNICs), and virtual hard disks (VHD or vDisk) sizes, which can be drives, disks, and images. All but the A8 and A9 VMs support only one vNIC. A8 and A9 support two vNICs.

vCPU

Virtual CPUs, or *cores*, are allocated when you select the size of the VM. The number of cores allocated to an Azure VM and the amount of vRAM allocated are coupled; that is, you cannot choose one without having the other preselected. This means you should consider the situation where you need a certain number of cores but a differing amount of RAM. A2/Medium is an example where two cores may be enough, but 3.5GB RAM is not. Choosing A3\Large is the next option, at four cores with 7GB RAM. RAM is usually more important than the number of cores. History has proven that most systems are not constrained by CPUs, but by RAM.

vRAM

Just like the RAM on a physical box, *vRAM* is the maximum amount of memory that a VM can use at any point in time. The amount of vRAM allocated to a VM can be changed while a VM is running, but a restart of the VM is required for the change to take effect. vRAM sizes in Azure range from 768MB, or 0.75GB, to 448GB, or 0.44TB, as of this writing.

Once an Azure VM is created, you can change the VM instance size in two ways: through the Azure Management Portal or using PowerShell.

CHANGING A VM'S SIZE THROUGH THE AZURE MANAGEMENT PORTAL

To change the VM's size through the Azure Management Portal, follow these steps:

1. Log in to your Microsoft Azure Management subscription using the Portal.

2. Choose the Virtual Machines option, and then select the VM whose size you want to change.

3. With the VM highlighted, select the Configure tab on the web page. Use the Virtual Machine Size drop-down list to select the new VM size.

4. Click Save to make the new VM size a permanent change.

CHANGING A VM'S SIZE VIA POWERSHELL

Perform the following steps to use PowerShell:

1. Create a PowerShell script using the following standard code (note that this stock PowerShell script requires you to edit some of the variables):

```
<#
.DESCRIPTION
This simple PowerShell scrip is used to create a function that can be used with
the standard PowerShell commands and pass in the parameters needed for the
function to change the VM size.
```

```
    .NOTES
        Variables to pass from the PowerShell command to the function include:
        MyAzureVM
        NEWVM-SIZE
    .WORK FLOW
        PowerShell cmdlets used in the PROCESS include
        Get-AzureVM = New Variable for the SERVICE
        The parameter passed to Get-AzureVM is SName (service name)
        PowerShell Update-AzureVM is then used to update the NEW SIZE of the VM
    .SECURITY
        Any input needs to be validated to prevent a "buffer overflow" or other
        security attack
        The ValidateNotNULL is necessary to make sure a parameter was passed.
        However,
        additional security validation steps would be required for production
    #>
    Function SetNEWAzureVMSizing{
        [CmdletBinding()]
        param(
            [parameter(Mandatory=$true)]
            [string]$MyAzureService,
            [parameter(Mandatory=$false)]
            [ValidateNotNullOrEmpty()]
            [string]$SName=$MyAzureService,
            [parameter(Mandatory=$true)]
            [string]$NEWVM-SIZE
        )
        PROCESS{
            Get-AzureVM –MyAzureService $ServiceName –Name $SName |
                Set-AzureVMSize $NEWVMSIZE |
                Update-AzureVM
        }
    }
    SetNEWAzureVMSizing –MyAzureService "<the-vm-name-to-change>" –NEWVM-Size "Small"
```

2. Edit the value of `<the-vm-name-to-change>` with the name of the specific VM.

3. Enter the new value of `NEWVMSize` for the parameter you want. The value must be a valid parameter such as small, medium through A7.

4. Save this PowerShell function and run it, passing in the necessary parameters.

Virtual Hard Disks

Virtual hard disks are often referred to as VHDs. Microsoft's VHD files include both VHD and VHDX formats. VHDs use the Windows Server 2008 and Azure file format only, (VHDX is not supported in Azure today, however, that may change in the future) whereas VHD and VHDX can use the Windows Server 2012 format.

If your VHD is a dynamic disk, convert it to a fixed disk first and then upload it. To do this, use Hyper-V Manager or the PowerShell cmdlet `convert-vhd`. Once you have uploaded a VHD, you can use it as a source to create a new VM; or, if it contains data, you can attach it to a VM as a data disk. For a step-by-step walkthrough, see the Azure blog post "How to Attach a Data Disk to a Windows Virtual Machine," at `http://azure.microsoft.com/en-us/documentation/articles/storage-windows-attach-disk`.

Microsoft Hyper-V supports three types of VHDs in either file format:

1. *Fixed disks*: These are usually thought of as providing the best performance. 100% of the size is allocated on the disk. These VHDs take the longest to migrate or back up because all blank space contained within the VHD (also known as *white space*) is written to the disk. This is the only VHD type supported in Azure.

2. *Dynamically expanding disks*: These are known as *auto-growing* or *thin-provisioned* VHDs. They provide the best balance of performance and size. With the VHDX file format, performance is close to that of pass-through storage to a SAN. With the VHD format, there is a performance hit; however, in most cases this is negated by the portability of the file because the size is limited to the data written to the VHD.

3. *Differencing disks*: This type of VHD is used in a parent-child relationship with another disk. It is great for testing changes such as a service pack or application install where the changes may need to be reverted. It is also good for application package testing when the user/admin needs to return to the state that existed prior to the install. Differencing disks and snapshots incur large performance penalties due to the nature of the reads being split across multiple files, and so forth. These are ideally suited for test/dev scenarios where performance is less of a priority than recovery.

■ **Note**   At the time of this writing, Azure only supports fixed VHD files.

VHD files are stored as page blobs in Azure. Blobs can be copied across storage accounts, allowing administrators to choose where they reside. You can use existing VHDs that contain an OS or VHDs that contain data by uploading the VHD to an Azure storage account. Use the `Add-AzureVHD` PowerShell cmdlet, available via the Azure PowerShell module, to upload a VHD to an Azure storage blob. If you don't have the Azure PowerShell module, you can download it from the Downloads page at `WindowsAzure.com`. For a step-by-step walkthrough, see the Azure blog post "Create and Upload a Windows Server VHD to Azure," at `http://azure.microsoft.com/en-us/documentation/articles/virtual-machines-create-upload-vhd-windows-server`.

■ **Note**   If you already own licenses for the software in a VM, it is cheaper to upload your existing images because the gallery images include the OS license costs in the hourly/monthly rate.

Sometimes you may need more details about specific topics. The Azure disk drives have not changed, so you can refer to this older blog post to review Windows Azure drives, disks, and images: `http://blogs.msdn.com/b/windowsazurestorage/archive/2012/06/28/exploring-windows-azure-drives-disks-and-images.aspx`.

All Azure VMs have at least two VHDs: one for the OS and one that is temporary. Additional data disks can be added to any Azure VM. Figure 6-1 shows the disks residing within an Azure VM.

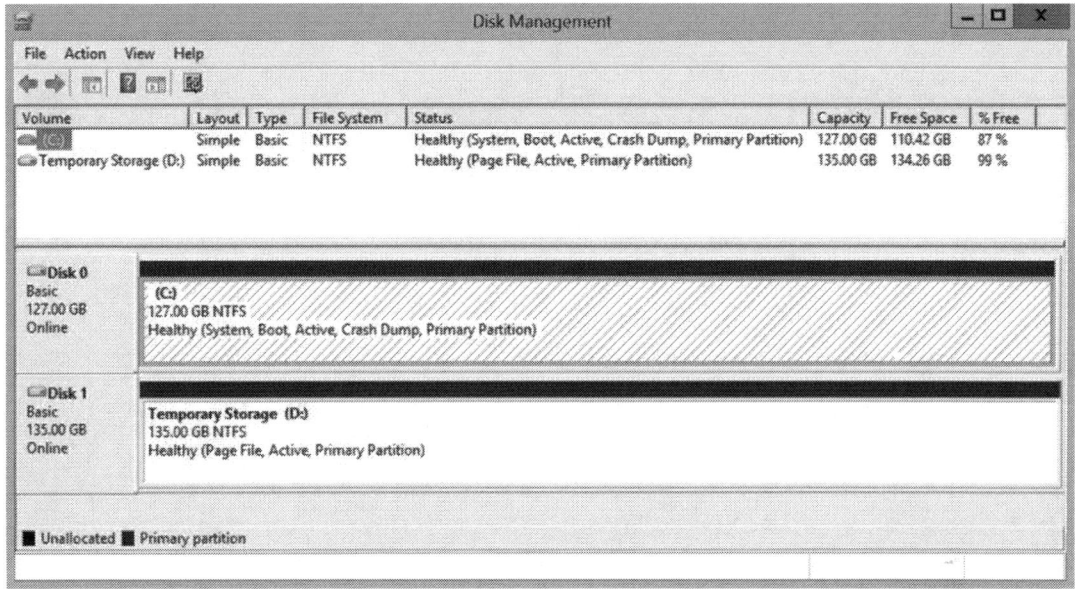

Figure 6-1. *Azure IaaS VM Disk Management console*

All of these disks are located in an Azure Storage account specified by the administrator or auto-generated by the portal as part of the provisioning process. Pay attention to where storage accounts and/or VMs are created. Most customers prefer to have the VMs reside in an Azure datacenter close to where the organization and/or users reside.

The Operating System Disk

Every VM created in Azure has the OS installed on the system disk, which is configured as a SATA disk, labeled as C:\, with a maximum size of 127GB. Whenever Azure stores data, such as VHDs in blob storage, the data is replicated in triplicate in the region selected during creation. This is done for redundancy in Azure in order to meet the required SLAs, and it does not serve as a backup for customers. If a customer chooses to geo-replicate this data, it is stored in another datacenter as part of the region you select that is more than 400 miles away, again in triplicate.

The Temporary Disk

Figure 6-1 shows the Temporary Storage disk, which is auto-generated as part of the provisioning process and always labeled drive D:\. On Linux VMs, this Temporary Storage disk is typically configured as /dev/sdb, and it is formatted and mounted to /mnt/resource by the Azure Linux Agent.

■ **Note**   Do not store data on the temporary disk! This disk provides temporary storage for applications and processes only.

The Data Disk

As shown in Figure 6-1, data disks are VHDs that are attached to any VM in order to store data that you need to retain. Data disks are registered as SCSI drives; hence they can be hot-swapped and labeled with a specific letter identifier that you choose. The size of the VM is the limiting factor on the number of data disks you can attach and the type of storage you can use to host the disks. Each data disk has maximum capacity of 1TB.

The operating system VHD and data disk VHD each have a *host caching* setting that can improve performance in some circumstances. In other cases, the host caching setting may degrade performance. Note that the default setting is Off for host caching for the read and write operations for data disks, and the default setting is On for read and write operations for the operating system VHD. To change the host caching setting, use the Set-AzureDataDisk cmdlet or the Set-AzureOSDisk cmdlet.

You can find the disks that are attached to a VM by using either the dashboard or the VM's Disks page in the Azure Management Portal, as shown in Figure 6-2.

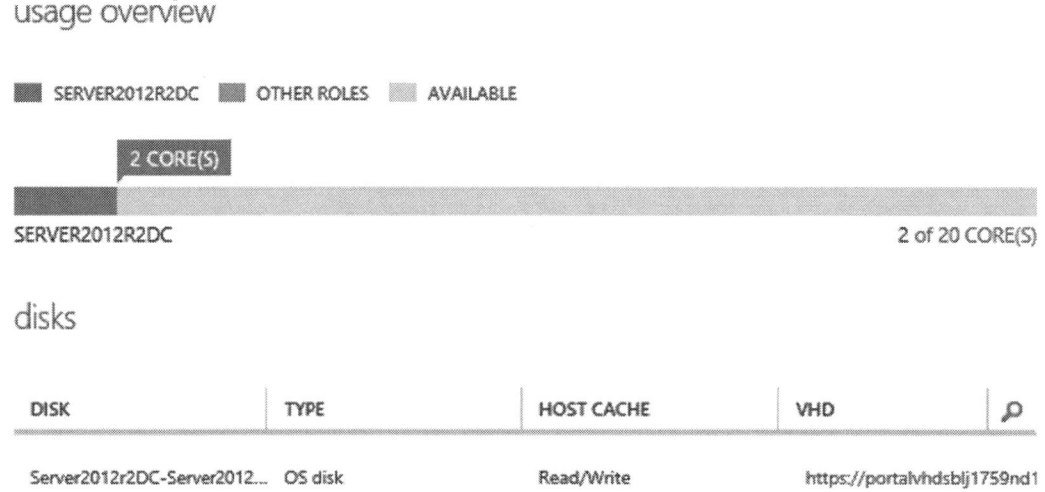

Figure 6-2. *Azure Management Portal VHD details*

Or, if you are using the new Azure Management Portal, the disks appear as shown in Figure 6-3.

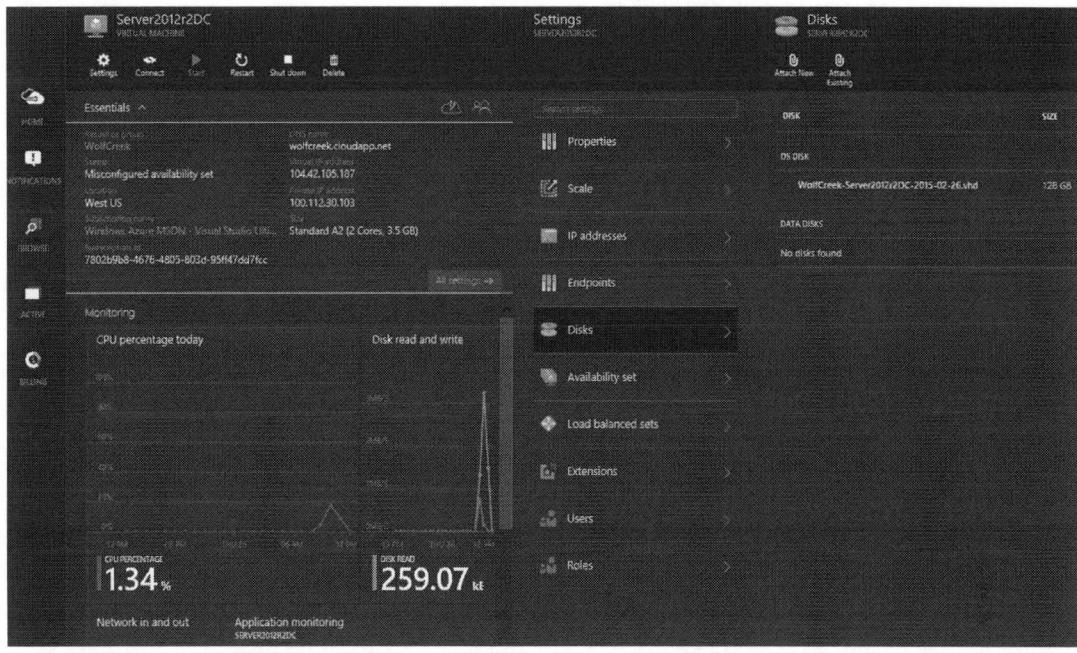

Figure 6-3. *New Azure Management Portal VHD details*

You can also use the Disks page of the Virtual Machines section of the portal to see all the disks deployed in your tenant, regardless of whether they are attached to a VM, as shown in Figure 6-4. This is an easy way to identify items that weren't cleaned up.

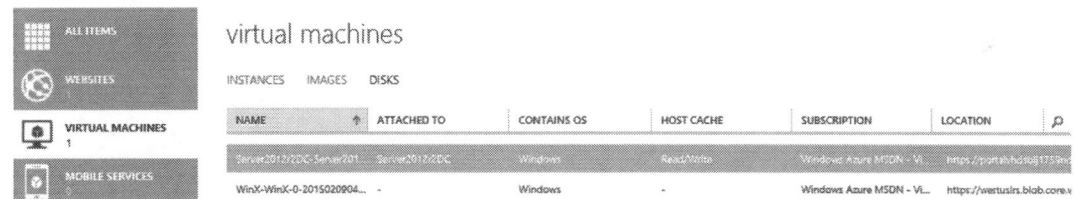

Figure 6-4. *Azure Management Portal VM disk details*

Or if you are using the new Azure Management Portal, the screen looks like the one in Figure 6-5.

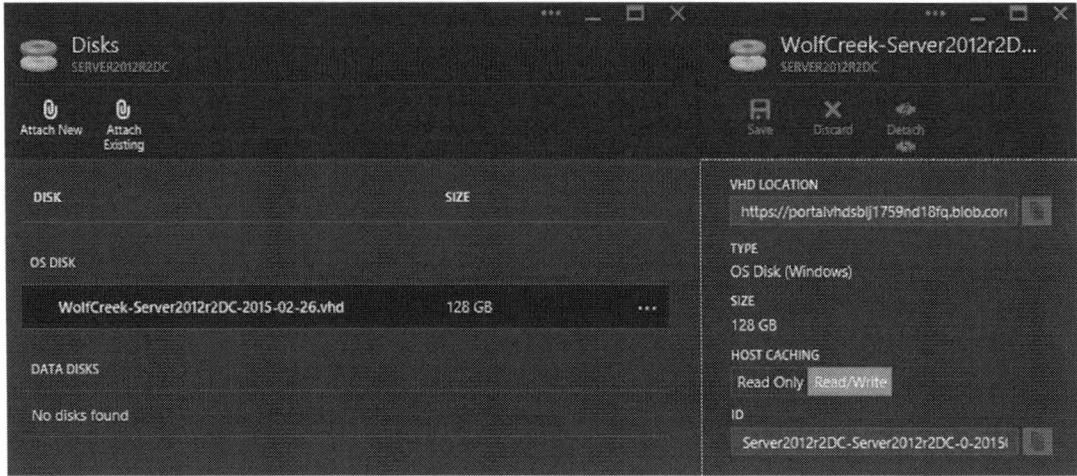

Figure 6-5. *New Azure Management Portal VM disk details*

You can delete disks through the Azure Management Portal, but the disks must first be detached from the VMs with which they are associated, as shown in Figure 6-6. Disks may also be deleted at the same time a VM is deleted, streamlining the process.

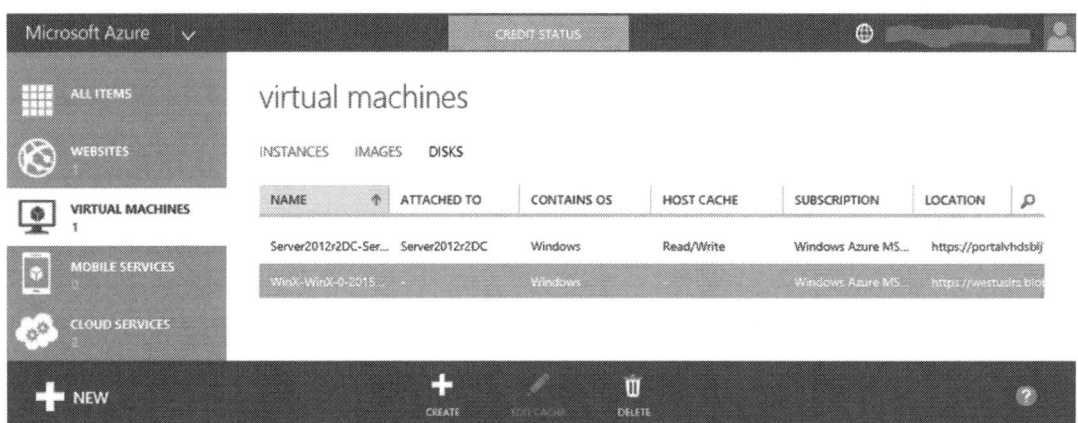

Figure 6-6. *Azure Management Portal VM disk deletion*

Azure offers Premium Storage: high-performance, low-latency disk for I/O-intensive workloads running on Azure DS-series VMs. Premium Storage requires a Premium Storage account and is locally redundant, meaning there are three copies of the data. You also have the option to attach multiple Premium Storage disks to your VM. Your VMs can have up to 32TB of storage and achieve 50,000 input/output operations per second (IOPS) with extremely low latencies for read operations. Premium Storage is currently available only for VMs.

vNIC

Virtual network interface cards (vNICs or vmNICs) provide connectivity to resources in the Azure Cloud Service in which the VM lives and the virtual network the VM is connected to by default. All but the A8 and A9 VMs support only one vNIC. A8 and A9 support two vNICs. Resources outside the Azure Cloud Service, whether in the same tenant or from the World Wide Web, must communicate with the VM via Azure endpoints, which should not be confused with Azure service endpoints. Azure endpoints are published ports that enable port forwarding on a firewall to allow traffic on that port into the system inside the firewall. Azure service endpoints determine whether your application is deployed to and managed by the global Azure platform, Azure operated by 21Vianet in China, or a private Azure platform. You can find more information on configuring Azure service endpoints at https://msdn.microsoft.com/en-us/library/azure/dn268600.aspx.

When a VMs is created using the Azure Management Portal, VM endpoints for Remote Desktop, Windows PowerShell Remoting, and Secure Shell (SSH) are automatically created, as you see later in this chapter when you create a VM. An important point for network communication is the fact that in the same Cloud Service or virtual network, individual VMs can automatically communicate with each other without the need for additional network changes. To communicate with systems on the Internet or on other virtual networks, a VM must use endpoints. Endpoints allow inbound network traffic to the VM. Think of endpoints like port forwarding on a firewall; they are how you allow traffic to reach the VM in Azure. Each VM endpoint has a public port and a private port:

- The Azure load balancer uses the *public port* to listen for incoming traffic to the VM from the Internet.

- The *private port* is used by the VM to listen for incoming traffic, typically destined for an application or VM service.

After you create an endpoint, you can use an access control list (ACL) to define rules that permit or deny the incoming traffic to the public port of the endpoint based on its source IP address. If the VM is in an Azure virtual network, you should use network security groups instead of ACLs. For more information on creating VM endpoints and managing the ACLs on them, refer to http://azure.microsoft.com/en-us/documentation/articles/virtual-machines-set-up-endpoints.

Microsoft Azure Virtual Network, not to be confused with Azure VM vNICs, is one of the several networking services available in Azure. Microsoft Azure Virtual Network allows customers to set up hybrid networks, extending their on-premises datacenter to Azure. By using the Azure VPN Gateway, customers can quickly connect their on-premises datacenter with the cloud. The VPN Gateway is just one of many methods for connecting on-premises to Azure; any of the connectivity methods allow VMs running in Azure to be joined to on-premises domains and connect to on-premises resources. For more information on extending your datacenter into Azure and available connectivity options, see Chapter 8.

Determining Your Virtual Machine Sizing

Earlier, this chapter discussed the different sizes of VMs available in Azure. VM size is the most significant factor that affects the price per hour to run that VM. Although it is easy to say you should select A-series VMs for most workloads, some workloads warrant higher levels of computing power, memory, or disk I/O. For example, whenever you are using SQL Server Enterprise Edition, you should select a VM with at least four or eight vCPUs or cores.

As VMs increase in size, so does the number of disks attached, resulting in higher disk I/O. Microsoft calculates 300 IOPS per disk for basic VMs and 500 for standard VMs. Multiply 300 by the number of disks, and you get the supported I/O of each disk that a VM can handle: for example, an A3 Basic VM has 8 disks, which will support 2,400 maximum IOPS. For a full list of the number of disks per VM and the supported disk I/O, see https://msdn.microsoft.com/en-us/library/azure/dn197896.aspx.

Be careful not to duplicate the hardware specs that you have in production in Azure from a sizing perspective. This statement may cause alarm, but one of the many benefits of Azure is the elasticity of resources. Conventional thinking for architecting solutions in a public cloud do not apply in this case:

- Azure can grow with the workload as needed. There is no need to architect for an end state or worst-case scenario. In other words, you don't need to build out 20 servers for a solution that may only need a few in the first year.

- Azure supports the auto-scaling of VMs to support high-demand spikes.

- Nowadays, CPU resources are over-allocated to many workloads, and carrying that architecture into Azure only increases the hourly/monthly cost with no added benefit.

- Storage is infinite, and you only pay for what you use, so current disk sizes don't matter—what's used on those disks is all you are billed for.

- RAM on physical systems includes drivers that won't be carried over to a VM in Azure. VMs use less memory than physical systems in general due to the generic Hardware Abstraction Layer (HAL) and lack of many unnecessary drivers or applets for the hardware.

Microsoft released the Microsoft Azure Cost Estimator Tool, which you can download at www.microsoft.com/en-us/download/details.aspx?id=43376. This 12MB tool lets you sample a single system or a number of systems, such as all the servers needed for a line-of-business (LOB) application. The Azure Cost Estimator Tool samples all the systems selected at the same time, so usage and resource needs can be accurately assessed. It then compares the hardware specs and resource usage, including disk I/O and network egress traffic, and recommends a VM size for each system sampled. This is a great way to know whether the existing workload is running on a system that is over-engineered for it.

The Azure Cost Estimator Tool prompts you, as shown in Figure 6-7, when an update is available. It is important to be aware of such updates, because they not only provide you with the latest VM options, but also include the latest pricing for the VMs and associated resources in multiple currencies. Remember, whenever you are comparing costs projected in the Azure Cost Estimator Tool, you are comparing the costs of the workload in Azure with on-premises running costs (hardware, power, cooling, building, security, and systems management among others).

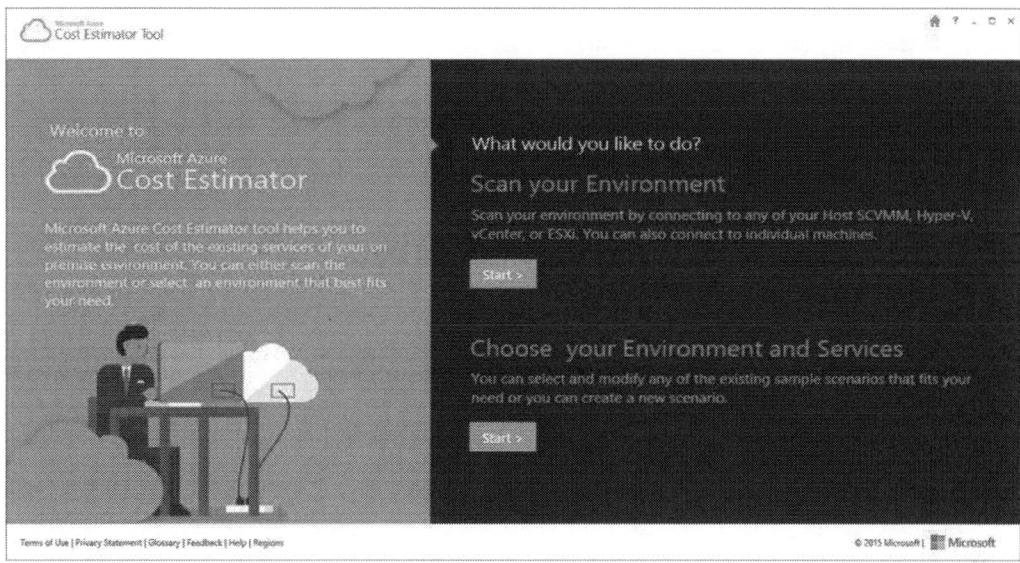

Figure 6-7. *Azure Cost Estimator Tool Home Page*

The Azure Cost Estimator Tool allows you to sample both physical and VMs, regardless of whether the VMs run on VMware or Microsoft. The VMs or physical systems can run Windows or various flavors of Linux OS, and the tool can sample their usage. No agent is required—the Azure Cost Estimator Tool, as shown in Figure 6-8, polls the systems remotely across the LAN or WAN from any system running Windows Vista SP2 or higher. Collection intervals can be set to a variety of days or weeks, all the way up to 31 days. As the collection window is lengthened, the collection frequency is shortened. For example, if your profiling duration is for 4 weeks, the maximum scanning frequency is every 12 hours.

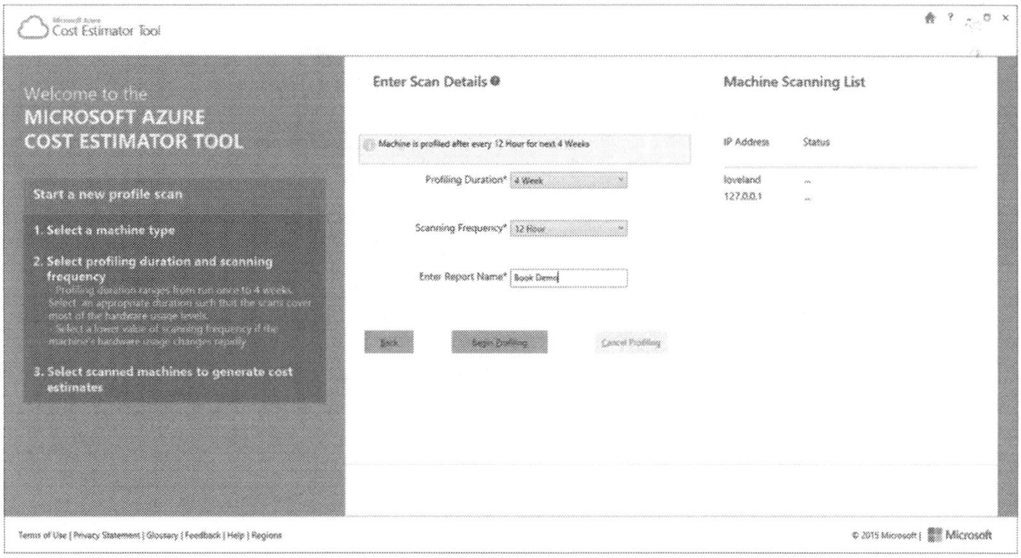

Figure 6-8. *Azure Cost Estimator Tool server selection*

Once the profiling is completed, the tool provides a report of the data sampled, as shown in Figure 6-9. To obtain and evaluate the cost to run a system in Azure, select the system in the report.

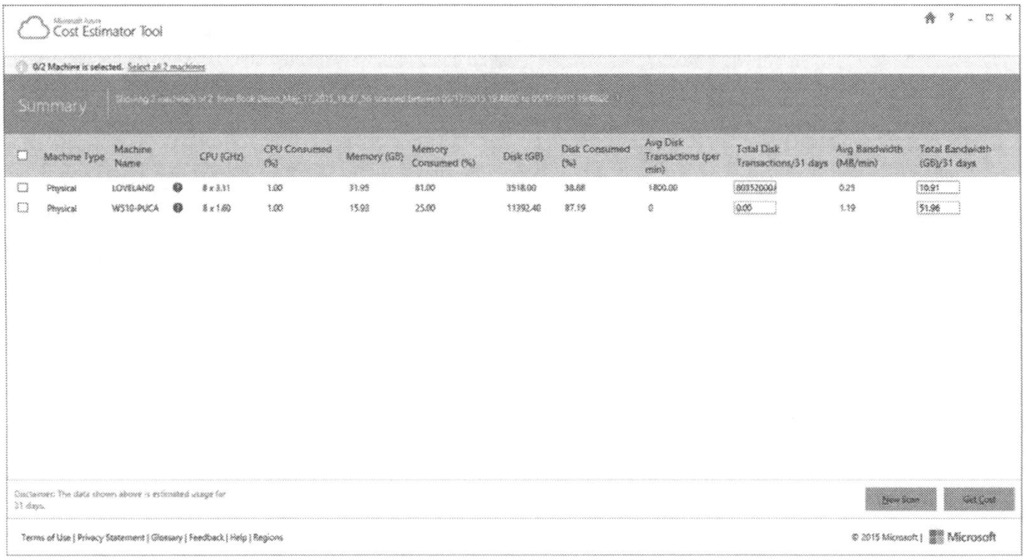

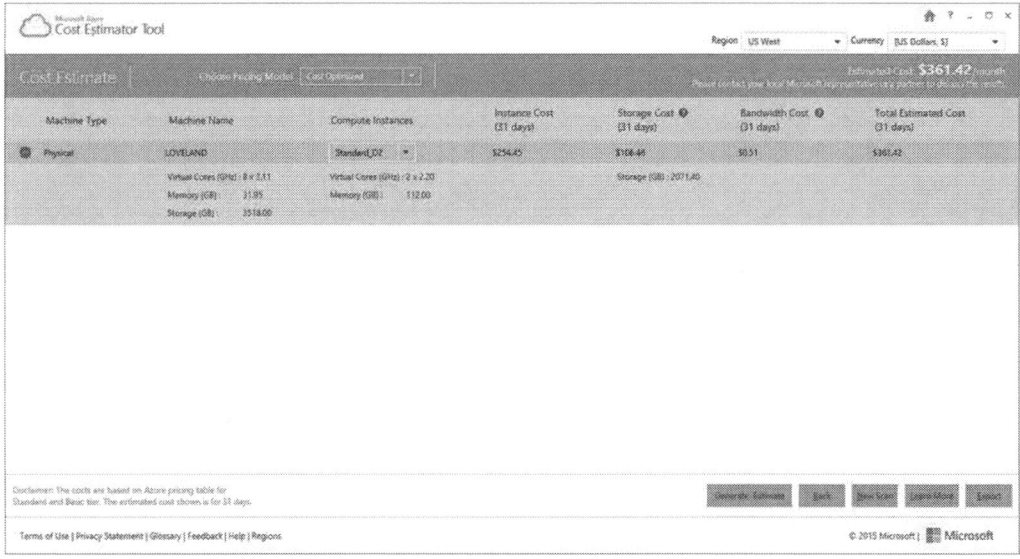

Figure 6-9. *Azure Cost Estimator Tool server profiling summary*

Figure 6-10 shows that the Azure Cost Estimator Tool selected an A4 VM, most likely due to the number of cores in the target system. Also note that the tool sees all the storage that the system has allocated to it at the current time. In the figure, it combines the locally used SSD storage and the Micro SD card used storage for the total.

Figure 6-10. *Azure Cost Estimator Tool cost estimate*

You can export the results of the tool for a single server or a number of servers in the Excel .csv format.

If System Center 2012 Operations Manager (SCOM) is deployed, you can import the Microsoft System Center 2012 Virtual Machine Manager (SCVMM) Management Pack (MP) from http://www.microsoft.com/en-us/download/confirmation.aspx?id=29679. This Management Pack has a report entitled "Virtualization Candidates," shown in Figure 6-11, which basically collects the same data you see in the Azure Cost Estimator Tool. This is another way to use existing performance data that is collected by System Center to make educated sizing decisions as you evaluate migration candidates. You can use the SCVMM MP even if SCVMM is not deployed. It is simply a method to use an existing report with many of these data points. The report can be used on any systems, physical or virtual, as long as they have a SCOM agent on them.

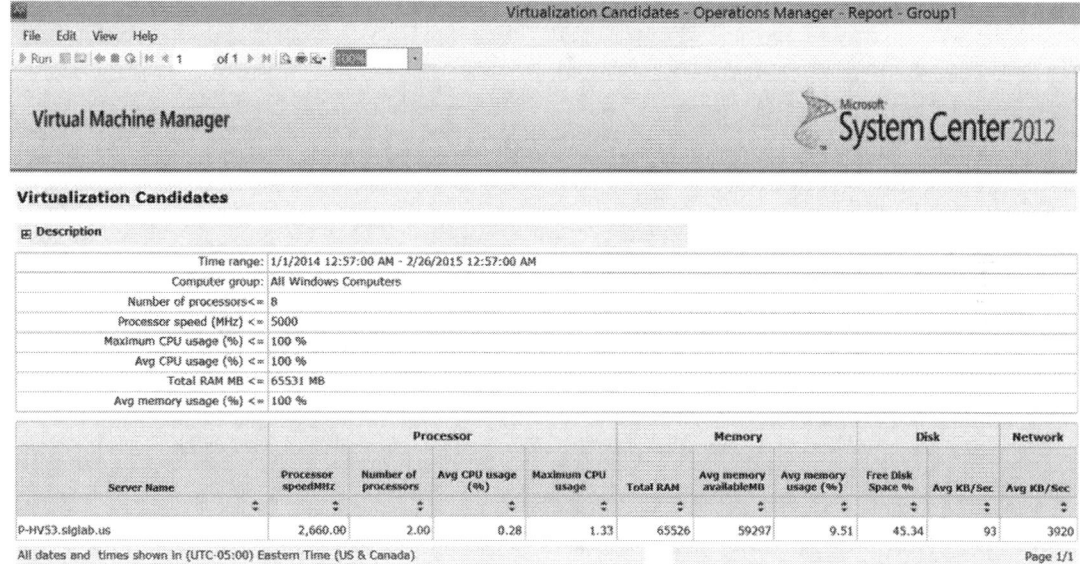

Figure 6-11. *Microsoft System Center 2012 R2 Operations Manager virtual machine manager report*

Determining the Operating System

When you deploy VMs from the Azure Gallery, you can choose from a large list including the OS and disk images of platform technologies such as SQL Server, BizTalk, Dynamics, and Oracle that are already installed. When deploying these image files, it is important to understand that the license costs for the OS and the associated technology in the VM are included in the hourly running rate. The Azure calculator details these costs; see http://azure.microsoft.com/en-us/pricing/calculator/?scenario=full. You can use licenses that you already own only if you upload your own image files.

Building Virtual Machines

In this section, you learn how to build a VM from scratch both in the current Azure Management Portal and also in the new Portal. You use VMs in the Azure Gallery, because doing so provides more configurable options than performing a quick create.

BUILDING A VIRTUAL MACHINE IN THE CLASSIC PORTAL

In these steps, you use the classic Azure Portal to create a VM:

1. Log in to the classic Azure Management Portal at https://manage.windowsazure.com. (the Azure Preview Portal URL is https://portal.azure.com and is used in another exercise later in this chapter).

2. Scroll all the way down the left side of the Portal, and select New.

3. Select Compute ➤ Virtual Machine ➤ From Gallery to start the VM Creation Wizard; see Figure 6-12.

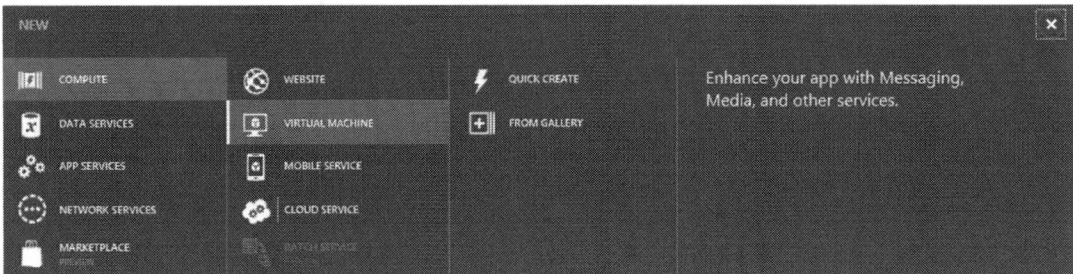

Figure 6-12. *Azure VM creation*

4. Choose which VM to create, as shown in Figure 6-13. Many different OSs are available, including many distributions of Linux. (Note: The number and types of images are updated often, and the specific types of images available to use depend on the type of Azure subscription. For example, an Azure subscription using MSDN provides different images than an Azure subscription enabled with an Enterprise Agreement.)

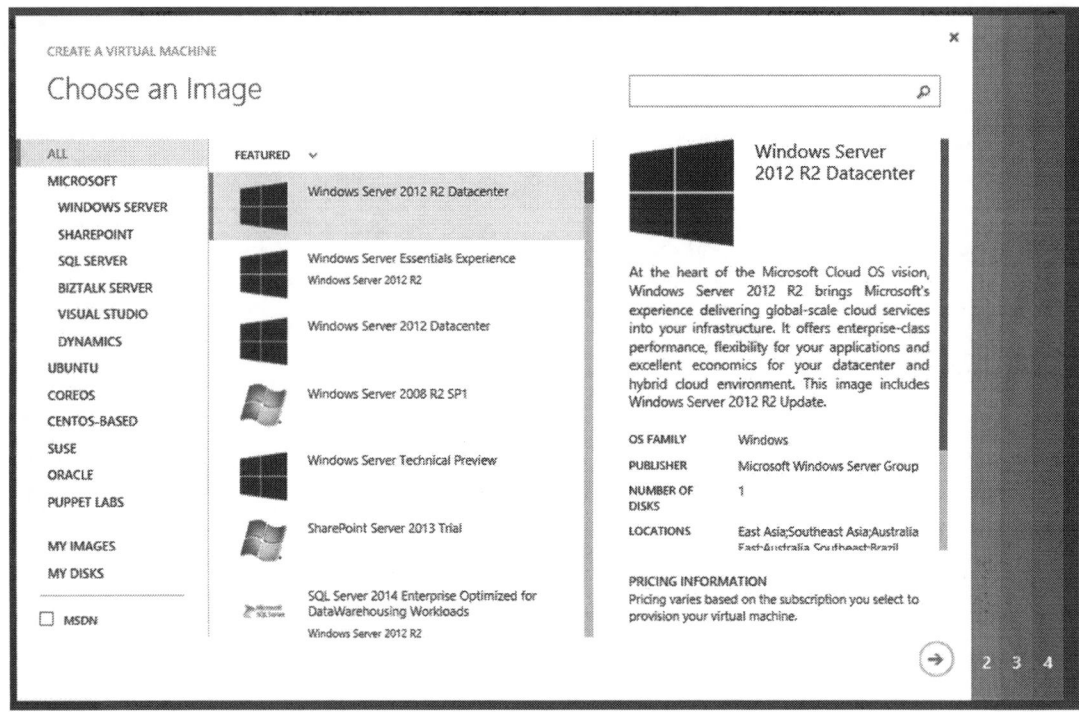

Figure 6-13. *Azure VM OS selection*

5. Because this is your first VM, select Windows Server 2012 R2 Datacenter, as shown
    in Figure 6-13. Click the arrow at bottom right to continue to the next screen of the
    wizard.

6. In this screen of the VM wizard, you enter some required parameters:

    •   Enter a unique VM name, and write it down for reference.

    •   Select the VM size using the drop-down. (The cost of the VM compute time is
        associated with the size of the VM. This is made clearer in the next exercise using
        the Preview Portal.)

    •   The New User Name is the administrator account used to log in to the VM once it is
        created. Every VM is required to have a New User Name; however, Administrator is
        not allowed.

    •   Note the Version Release Date. Microsoft and its partners, who provide disk images
        for the Azure Gallery, update the images routinely to keep them current with
        patches and various updates.

    Figure 6-14 shows ApressDemo for the VM name, and the VM size is set to A1. Click
    the arrow at bottom right to continue.

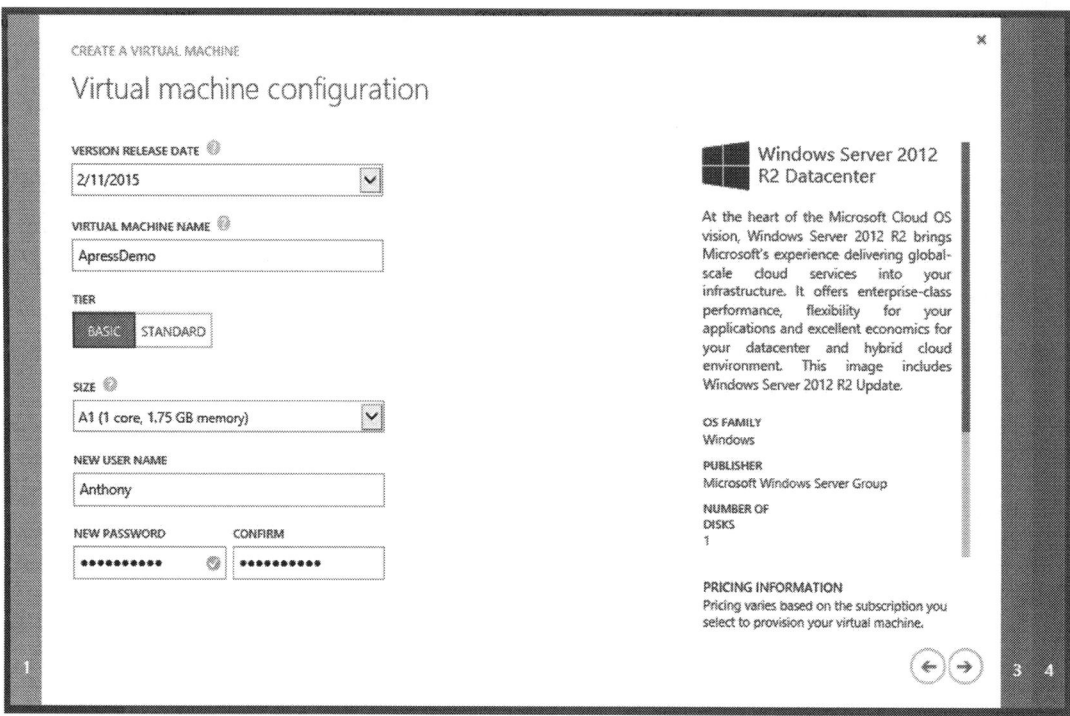

Figure 6-14. *Azure VM size and account configuration*

7. In this step, several additional parameters are required. Because this is your first VM, a new Cloud Service is created; just like the VM name, the DNS name for the Cloud Service must be unique. This is because this name is a public DNS namespace. You connect through the Internet to your VM through the Cloud Service. Later you learn how to make the necessary network changes to remove the Internet access and connect only from a site-to-site or point-to-site VPN.

8. Select the region where you want to build the Cloud Service and place this new VM. Leave the default settings for the other options, as shown in Figure 6-15. Notice in the figure 6-15 that you are selecting a preconfigured storage account in the West US using locally redundant storage. Also note the default ports that are open for the VM endpoints. Do not delete these as part of the provisioning process unless you have some other way of connecting to the VM. Deleting these as part of the provisioning process is the equivalent of painting yourself into a corner, and you will not be able to connect to the VM. Click the arrow at bottom right to continue.

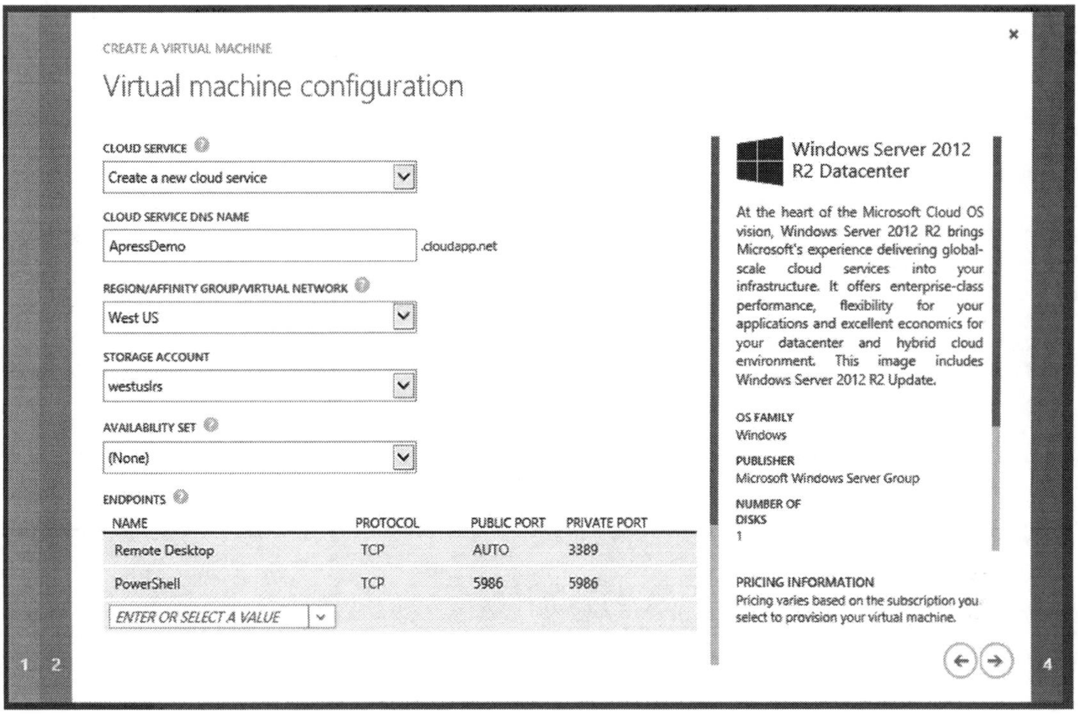

CREATE A VIRTUAL MACHINE

Virtual machine configuration

CLOUD SERVICE
Create a new cloud service

CLOUD SERVICE DNS NAME
ApressDemo   .cloudapp.net

REGION/AFFINITY GROUP/VIRTUAL NETWORK
West US

STORAGE ACCOUNT
westuslrs

AVAILABILITY SET
(None)

ENDPOINTS

NAME	PROTOCOL	PUBLIC PORT	PRIVATE PORT
Remote Desktop	TCP	AUTO	3389
PowerShell	TCP	5986	5986
ENTER OR SELECT A VALUE			

Windows Server 2012 R2 Datacenter

At the heart of the Microsoft Cloud OS vision, Windows Server 2012 R2 brings Microsoft's experience delivering global-scale cloud services into your infrastructure. It offers enterprise-class performance, flexibility for your applications and excellent economics for your datacenter and hybrid cloud environment. This image includes Windows Server 2012 R2 Update.

OS FAMILY
Windows

PUBLISHER
Microsoft Windows Server Group

NUMBER OF DISKS
1

PRICING INFORMATION
Pricing varies based on the subscription you select to provision your virtual machine.

Figure 6-15. Azure VM storage and networking configuration

9. The final page of the VM Wizard provides additional options that you should consider. The first option recommended, as shown in Figure 6-16, is to install the VM agent on this new VM. This agent provides remote PowerShell capabilities to change user passwords and IP addresses if necessary. The security extensions you select may depend on your choice for antimalware and antivirus. In this example VM, the extension for the Microsoft Antimalware option is selected. Click the check mark at bottom right to create this VM.

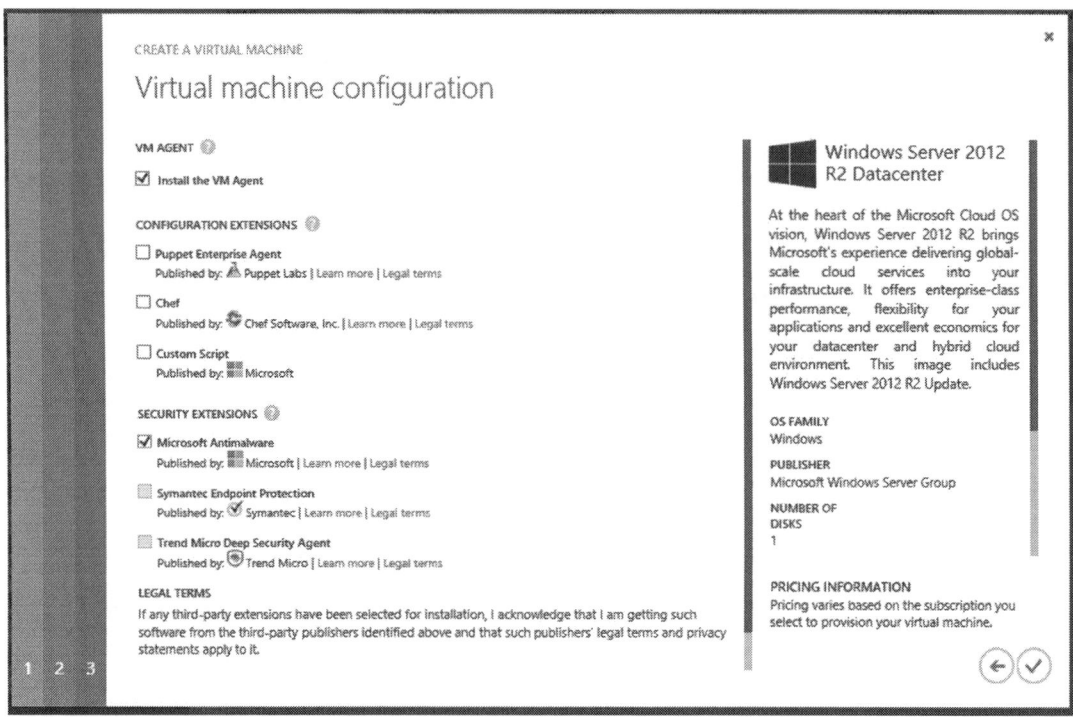

Figure 6-16. *Azure VM extensions configuration*

10. Your VM should be created in as little as six to eight minutes. Select the Virtual Machines service view in the Azure Portal to view the provisioning of your VM (see Figure 6-17). You cannot connect to the VM until it has been completely created.

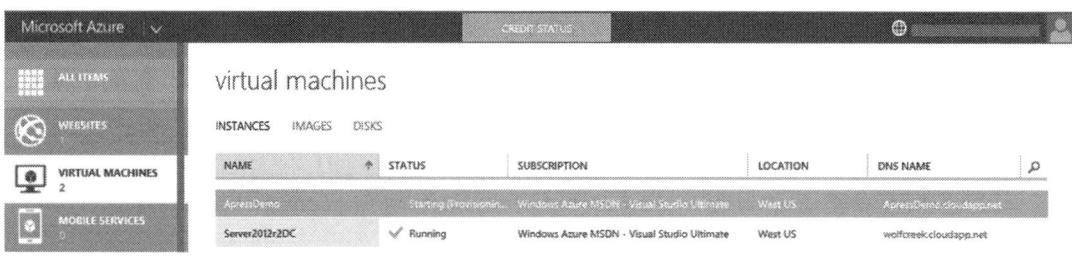

Figure 6-17. *Azure VM provisioning*

LOGGING ON TO YOUR NEW VIRTUAL MACHINE

Once your VM has been completely provisioned, you can log on to test it or continue with customization. (This exercise should be completed from a computer running a Windows OS or that supports a Microsoft Desktop Remote app.) Follow these steps:

1. From the Classic Azure Portal, click the Virtual Machines service view.

2. Select the VM that you just provisioned, as shown in Figure 6-18.

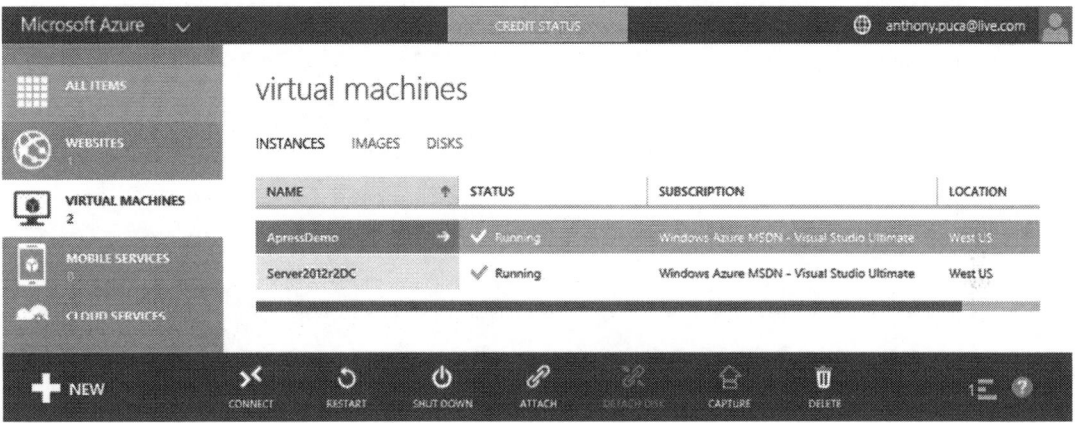

Figure 6-18. *Connecting to an Azure VM for the first time*

3. At the bottom of the page, click Connect to start the automatic creation of a Remote Desktop Connection.

4. The Remote Desktop Connection is created with all the necessary parameters to allow a connection from your Windows system to the newly created VM. The default connection for Windows VMs uses Remote Desktop Protocol (RDP). You should see a dialog box similar to the one shown in Figure 6-19.

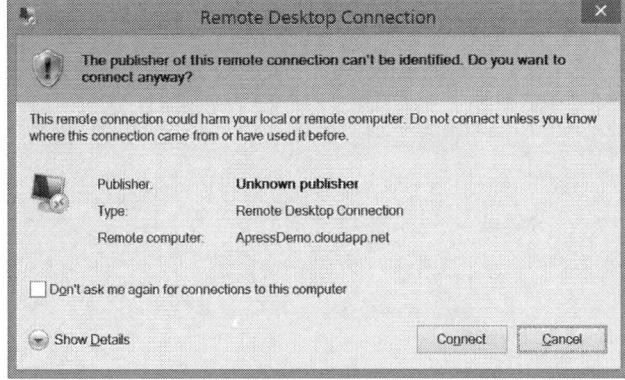

Figure 6-19. *An Azure VM remote desktop prompt*

5. Click the Connect button to continue.

6. Type the username and password created in step 6 of the previous exercise, and click OK to continue to connect using the Remote Desktop Connection.

7. Click Yes to verify the identity of the VM.

8. You are now able to log in to the VM and configure it as needed. Note that the VM is named as you configured it in step 6 of the previous exercise, but it is in a workgroup. The fully qualified domain name (FQDN) in the Remote Desktop title bar, shown in Figure 6-20, is how you resolve connecting to the VM until it is joined to a Microsoft Windows domain.

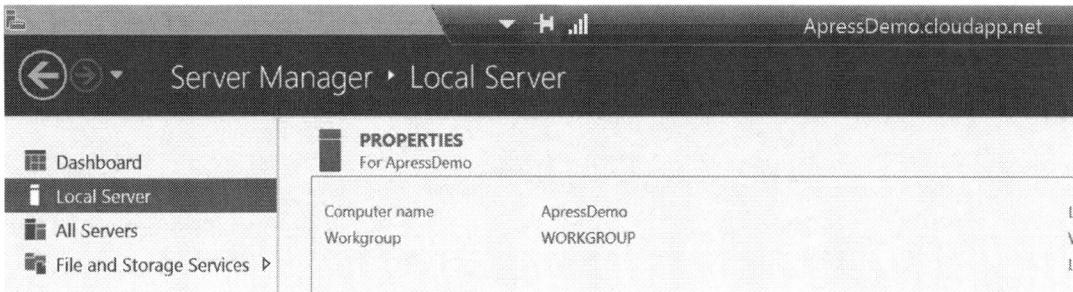

Figure 6-20. *An Azure VM Server Manager console*

BUILDING A VIRTUAL MACHINE IN THE NEW PREVIEW PORTAL

You need to become familiar with the new Azure Preview Portal and how to complete tasks like creating VMs. (The Preview Portal is scheduled to become the only portal in Azure; however, not all the Azure services are provided through the Preview Portal at the time of this writing.)

Create a new VM in Azure using the new Preview Portal by following these steps:

1. Log in to the Azure Preview Portal at `https://portal.azure.com`, as shown in Figure 6-21.

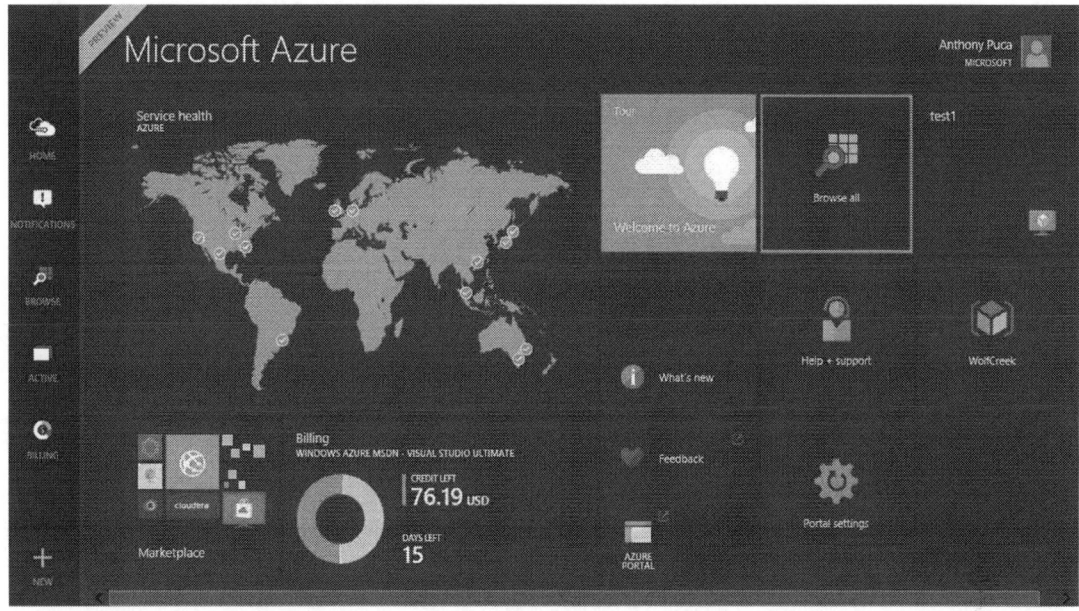

Figure 6-21. The new Azure Management Portal

2. To start the creation of the new VM, select the New option at bottom left in the Preview Portal. Your screen should look similar to Figure 6-22.

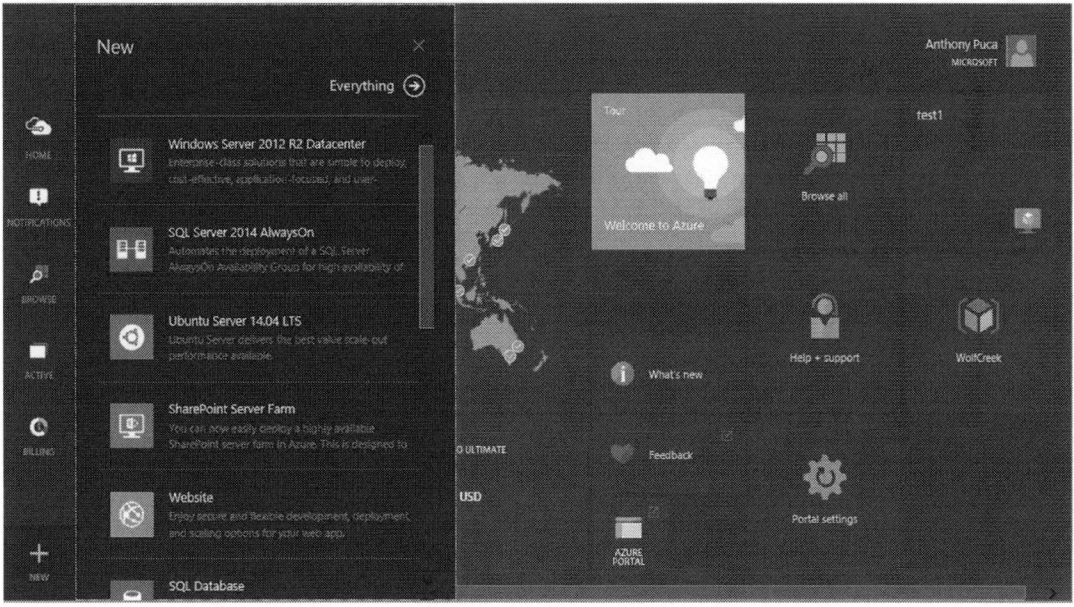

Figure 6-22. Provisioning a VM in the Azure Preview Portal

3. The Azure Preview Portal uses a windowing view called *blades* that provide a better perspective of the overall work being performed. Notice the new blade in Figure 6-22. Click Windows Server 2012 R2 Datacenter, and the screens shown in Figure 6-23 will be displayed. (The steps are similar to the previous exercise in which you created a VM in the Azure Classic Portal.) Enter your username and a strong password, select your location, select your VM series and size, and then click Create.

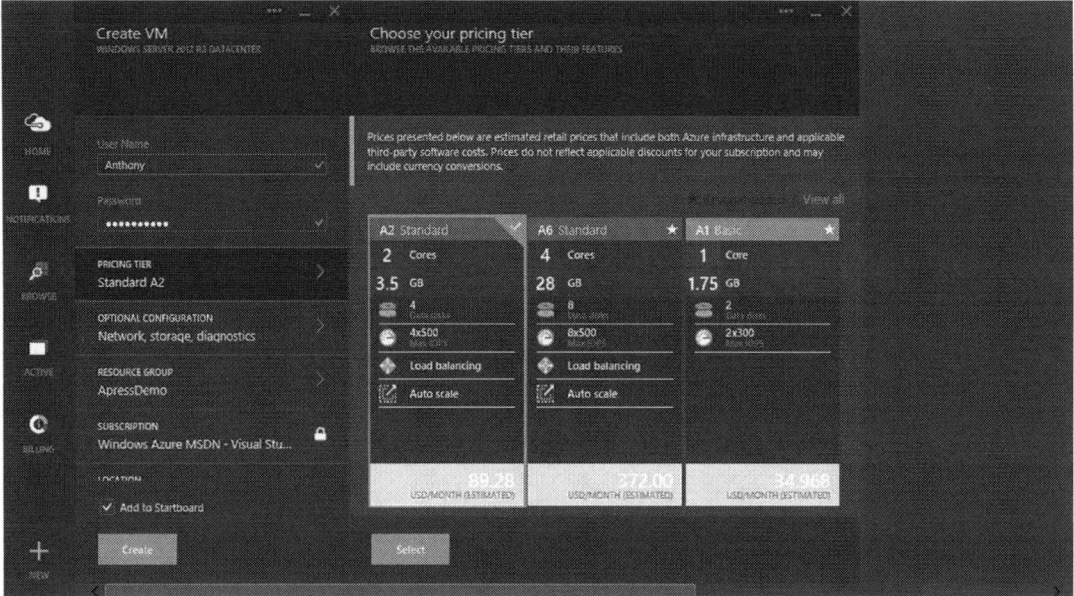

Figure 6-23. *Configuring the VM settings in the new Azure Management Portal*

Just like the previous exercise, New User Name refers to the local administrative account that will be created for you to manage the VM; this is just like the Windows 7, 8, and 10 desktop deployment experience where you are not allowed to use the local Administrator account. Create a strong password for this account. You need this user name and password to log on to the VM when the provisioning is completed. (When using the Preview Portal, you can see the cost of the VM size using the information in the blades.)

LOGGING ON TO YOUR NEW VIRTUAL MACHINE

Now that you have created a new VM using the Azure Preview Portal, you can log on to test it or complete the configuration. (This exercise should be completed from a computer running a Windows OS.) Follow these steps:

1. You should already be logged in to Azure from the Preview Portal at `https://portal.azure.com`.

2. Click your VM on the Startboard, as shown in Figure 6-24. If you need to find it, click Browse and then click Virtual Machines.

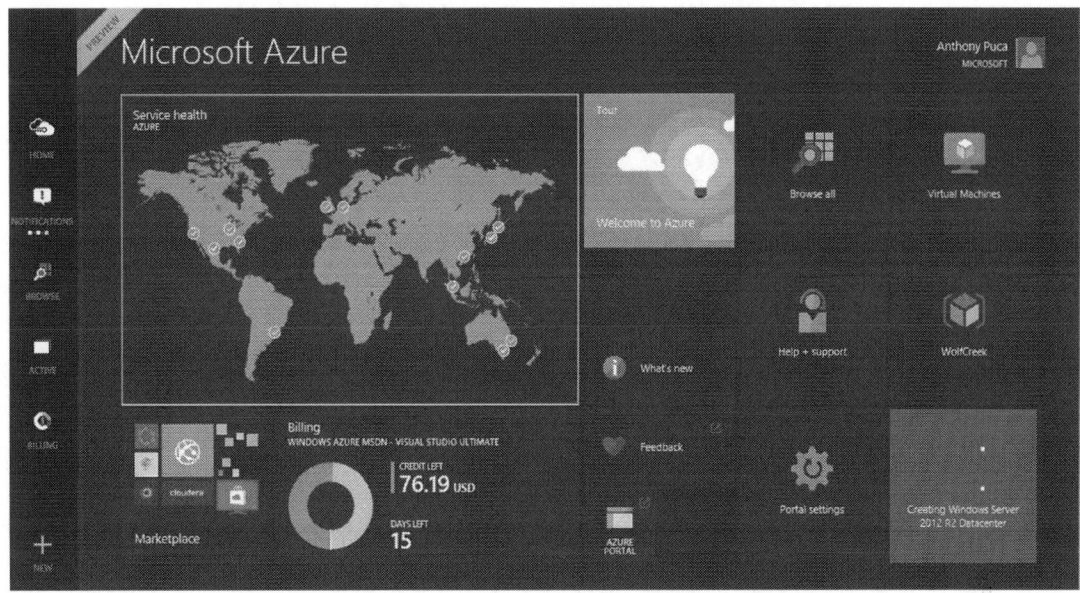

Figure 6-24. *Provisioned VM status on the new Azure Management Portal Startboard*

3. Select your VM from the list, as shown in Figure 6-25.

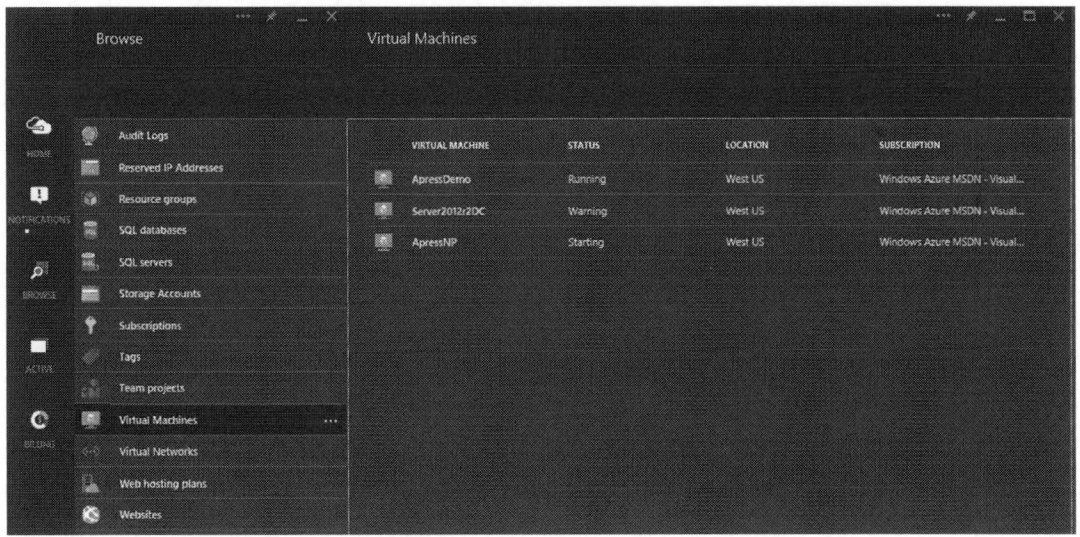

Figure 6-25. *VM list in the new Azure Management Portal*

4. On the Virtual Machines blade, shown in Figure 6-26, click Connect at upper right. (Note that in the previous exercise to create a VM using the Azure Classic Portal, the Connect option was at the bottom of the page.)

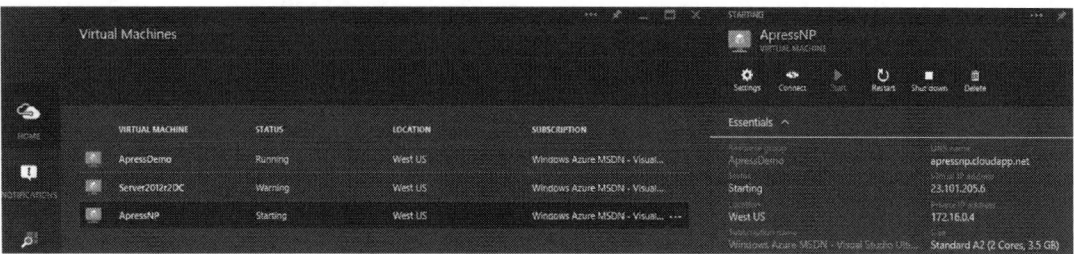

Figure 6-26. *VM details in the new Azure Management Portal*

5. Just as in the previous exercise, you need to click Open or Save to use the Remote Desktop Protocol file that was automatically created for this specific VM. You should see a Remote Desktop Connection window, as shown in Figure 6-27.

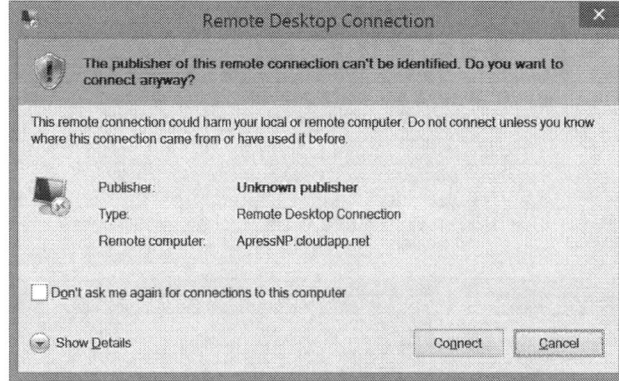

Figure 6-27. *VM Remote Desktop Connection prompt*

6. Click Connect to proceed with connecting to the VM.

7. Type the user name and password of the administrative account that you created in step 3 of the previous exercise for the VM, and then click OK.

8. You see a prompt to identify the VM: click Yes to continue.

9. Now you are able to log in to the new VM and configure it as necessary. Note that the VM is named as you configured it in step 3 of the previous exercise, but it is in a workgroup. The FQDN in the Remote Desktop title bar, shown in Figure 6-28, is how you resolve connecting to the VM until it is joined to a domain.

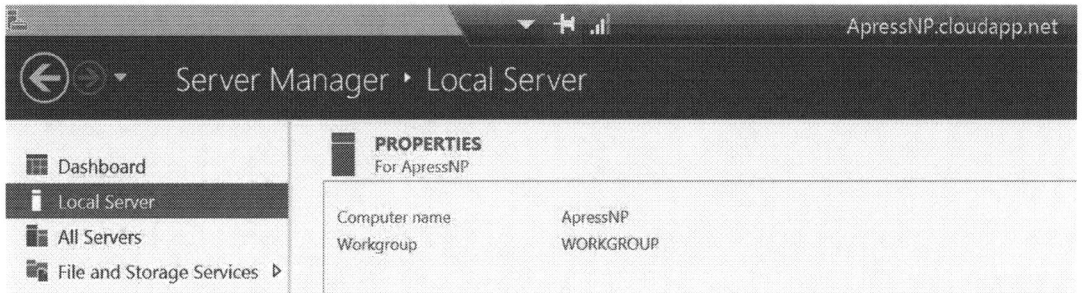

Figure 6-28. *An Azure VM Server Manager Console*

Virtual Machine Limits

Azure currently has a default and maximum limit of 50 VMs per Cloud Service. A VM must be in a Cloud Service; if there isn't one already created for the VM, one is created automatically. Cloud Services currently have a default of 50 VMs per subscription, with a maximum of 200 Cloud Services per subscription. There is a default and maximum limit of 150 input endpoints per Cloud Service to allow communication to the VMs in the Cloud Service from external sources. Input endpoints are like PIPs for VMs. VM-to-VM communication in the same Cloud Service doesn't require input endpoints. There is currently a default and maximum of 25 input endpoints per Cloud Service. For more information on VM limits, see `http://azure.microsoft.com/en-us/ documentation/articles/azure-subscription-service-limits`.

Microsoft Azure Virtual Machines, Networking, Cloud Service Support, and SLAs

Azure offers various support plans. Free billing and subscription management support is included with Azure subscriptions. Flexible support plans start at $29–$1,000/month. Azure support can also be added to Microsoft Enterprise Agreements as Premiere Support. For more information on Microsoft Azure Support, visit `http://azure.microsoft.com/en-us/support/plans`.

In order for Microsoft to provide a guarantee via service-level agreement (SLA), you must have more than one Azure service in specific configurations. The Azure web site states the following: "You deploy two or more role instances in different fault and upgrade domains for Cloud Services, your Internet-facing roles will have external connectivity of at least 99.95% of the time. For all Internet-facing Virtual Machines that have two or more instances deployed in the same Availability Set, Microsoft also guarantees that you will have external connectivity at least 99.95% of the time. For Virtual Networks, Microsoft guarantees a 99.9% Virtual Network Gateway availability." For more information on Azure SLAs, visit `http://azure.microsoft.com/ en-us/support/legal/sla`.

For current Azure status, refer to `http://azure.microsoft.com/en-us/status/#current`. A sample Azure status report is shown in Figure 6-29.

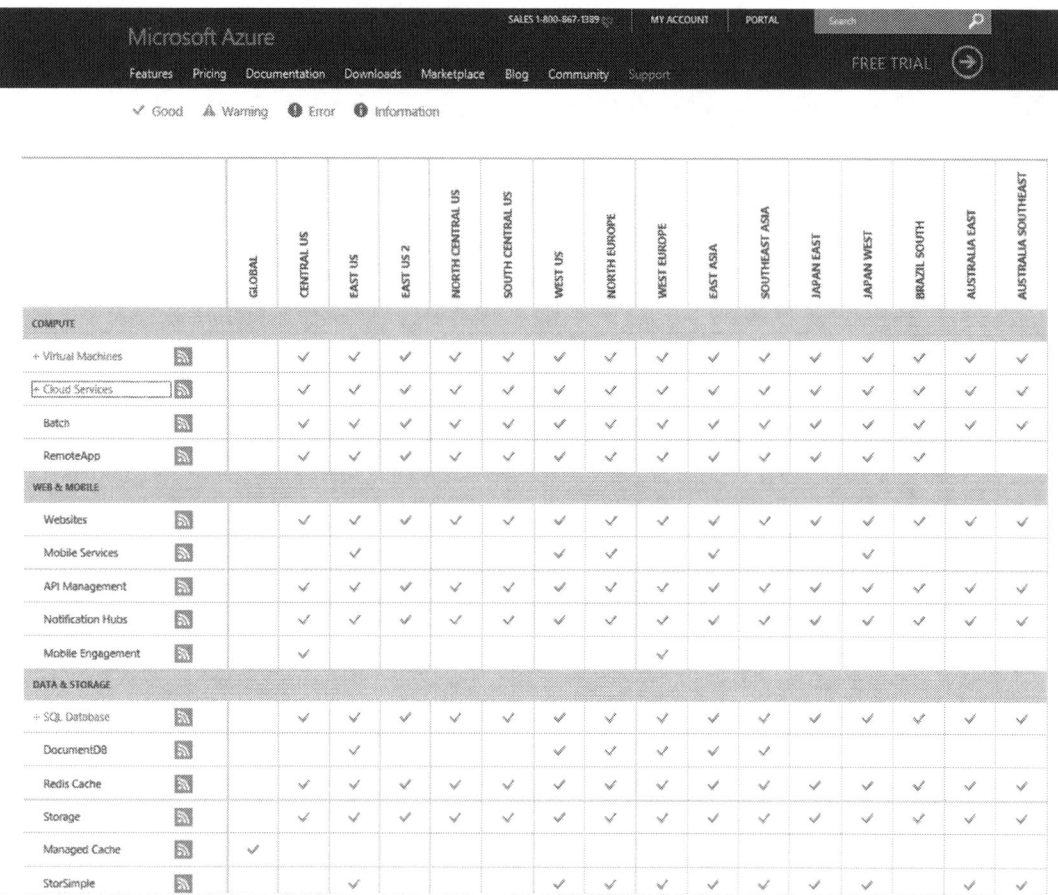

Figure 6-29. *Azure status web page*

Summary

As you have learned in this chapter, deploying VMs in Azure is simple. Analyzing your environment with the tools available today is also quite easy, and it will help you determine the sizes you need in Azure. Whether you use a credit card, an MSDN subscription, or the free Microsoft Azure Trial, or add Azure to your Select or Enterprise Agreement, it couldn't be easier to extend your datacenter beyond the constraints it has today.

The next chapter goes into much more detail regarding storage options in Azure. It addresses the cost, features, and performance differences between the various types of storage.

CHAPTER 7

■ ■ ■

Understanding Azure Storage and Databases

The computer storage pendulum has swung from people asking, "What would I do with all that storage?" about a decade ago to people now using personal storage media in amounts once only possible for the largest organizations in the world. As you are probably well aware, the average smartphone today has as much storage in it as a PC did in 1997. Data has proliferated in type, size, and audience over the last few years. This data proliferation over the last decade has jokingly been referred to as "datageddon." Data storage and data management have become a real challenge for organizations worldwide, as they struggle to keep up with webcam, voice, e-mail, transaction, and other data feeds that they are required to retain as part of their business's intellectual property or work product.

This chapter discusses the various types of storage available in Microsoft Azure. *Azure Storage* refers to long-term disk storage, not cache or RAM, which is closer to the processor and resides within the hosts running the virtual machines. Another key differentiator is that not all storage is created equal. There are capabilities to be considered, such as drive-access speed and redundancy. Because Azure is created to meet the needs of the enterprise, the type of storage used is enterprise grade as well. Therefore, at a minimum, these are physically 15K spindles and solid-state drives (SSDs) deployed in locally and geographically redundant setups.

Azure Storage is elastic, meaning it can grow and shrink with you, and you're only billed for what you are currently using. Even if a storage account or disk is provisioned at a substantially larger size than what is actually used, only the blocks used are counted for billing purposes.

Azure Storage is available from anywhere there is an Internet connection, like the rest of Azure. Many services already use Azure Storage, such as the Microsoft Windows Server 2012 native backup utility and the Microsoft System Center Data Protection Manager 2012. Azure Storage also uses a system that automatically load-balances your storage based on traffic, just like the most expensive storage area networks (SANs) on the market today. All of these Azure Storage capabilities can be provisioned quickly, and you can have customers up and running using them in about five minutes.

Azure Storage Services: Terms and Concepts

Microsoft's Azure Storage service is available in all Azure datacenters. In general, several types of Azure Storage options are available; they are defined after you create an Azure Storage account, with the exception of databases and StorSimple. The different types of storage are depicted in Figure 7-1.

- *Azure Storage accounts*: An Azure Storage account must be used to create blobs, tables, queues, or file storage services.

- *BLOB (binary large object) storage*: Blobs are generally used to store files accessed via a browser using the HTTP/HTTPS GET and POST methods.

- *SQL databases*: A SQL database is a type of storage used for structured data. But instead of managing a SQL server, Azure SQL Database is an alternative for consuming the database without having to manage the SQL server that is providing the service. This is different from consuming SQL Server as an IaaS, because in the latter scenario, you still need to manage and maintain the SQL Servers in IaaS.

- *Queues*: As the name implies, a queue provides messaging and communication between different applications. Queue storage provides such a mechanism without having to maintain a separate messaging bus.

- *Tables:* Azure Table Storage is a NoSQL key-value store that is useful for applications that must store large amounts of non-relational data without schemas. This is different from Azure databases in that table storage does not provide any way to represent relationships between data. It is a low-cost way to provide a fault-tolerant store for structured data that may not require the complexities of a relational database. For more information about the differences between Azure Table Storage and Azure SQL Database, see `https://msdn.microsoft.com/library/azure/jj553018.aspx`.

- *File storage*: File storage provides the ability to access files via standard SMB 2.1.

- *Hybrid storage (StorSimple)*: Microsoft acquired StorSimple, which is a storage solution that deploys on-premises 2U devices that use cloud storage for overflow, backup, and archiving capabilities. The StorSimple device is an ISCSI unit with SSDs and traditional drives for fast, low-latency access to frequently used files.

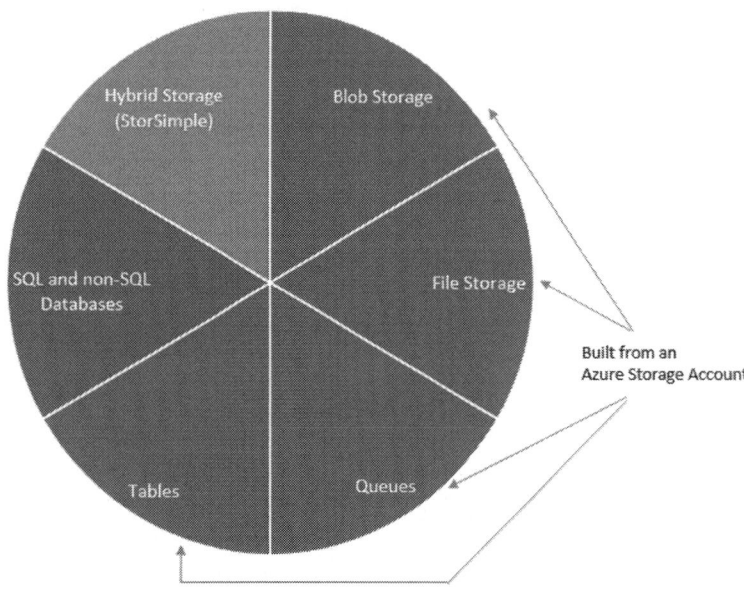

Figure 7-1. *Types of Azure storage*

Azure Storage Account

Before going into the details of the different types of storage, it is important to note that with the exception of StorSimple and Azure SQL Database, all storage types are created from an Azure Storage account. The Azure Storage account in turn determines certain characteristics for the storage, such as whether the storage is locally redundant or georedundant, and whether the storage is based on standard hard drives or SSDs.

Premium Storage

Azure Storage is generally provisioned on enterprise-class spinning hard drives. For higher performance, Azure offers Premium Storage. Premium Storage is provisioned on SSDs. As a result, Premium Storage delivers high-performance, low-latency disk support for I/O intensive workloads.

Locally Redundant Storage

Locally redundant storage (LRS), which is the base-level redundancy for storage, ensures that hardware is provisioned on three separate replicas in the same datacenter. This guarantees that no localized hardware failure results from an interruption in data services.

Georedundant Storage

Georedundant storage (GRS) takes LRS storage in one datacenter and replicates it to LRS in another datacenter that is more than 500 miles away. This ensures true georedundancy. Thus if an entire datacenter becomes unavailable, there is no interruption to data services because the second datacenter can continue providing services. Technically, GRS has six replicas of the data (LRS × 2).

CREATING AN AZURE STORAGE ACCOUNT

The following exercise walks you through the steps required to create an Azure Storage account. As part of this exercise, you see the different Azure Storage accounts and the storage types that each Azure Storage account supports:

■ **Note** Premium Storage is only offered as an LRS option and only supports page blobs, whereas non-Premium Storage provides LRS and GRS options and supports block and page blobs as well as tables and queues.

---

1. Go to the new Azure Management Portal at `https://portal.azure.com`.

2. Click New, select Data + Storage, and then select Storage, as shown in Figure 7-2.

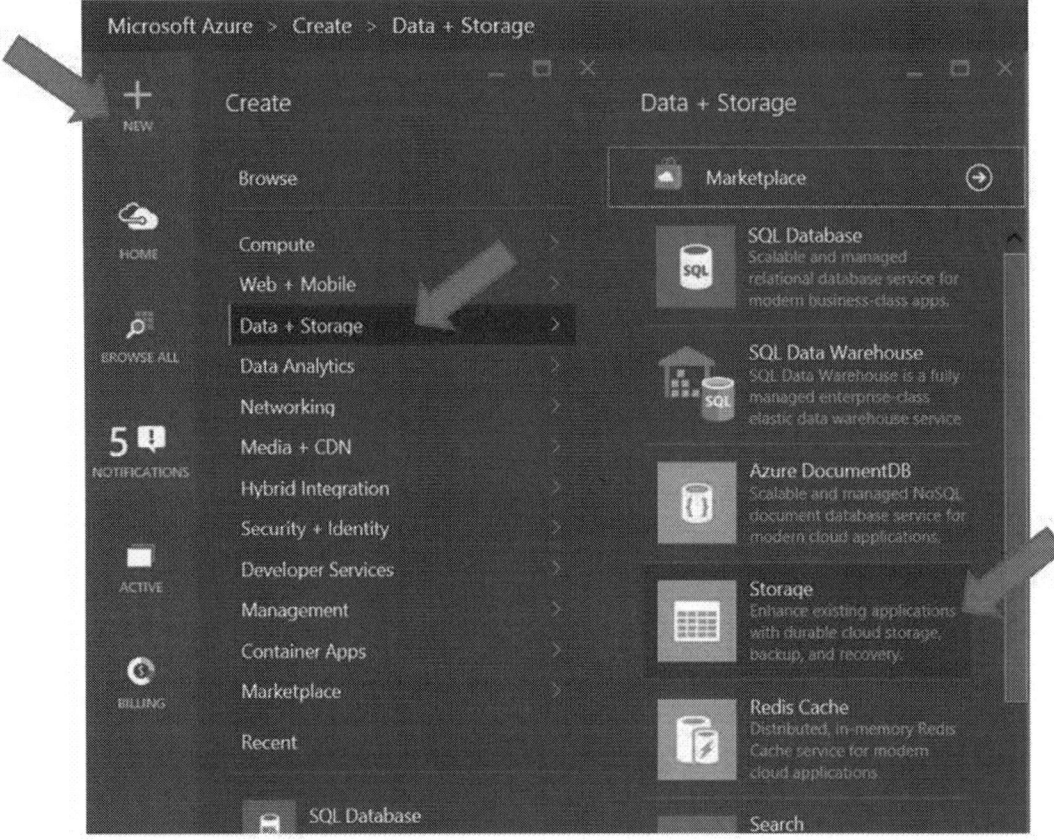

Figure 7-2. *Creating an Azure Storage account*

3. Provide a name for the Azure Storage account, and then click the Pricing Tier option, as shown in Figure 7-3.

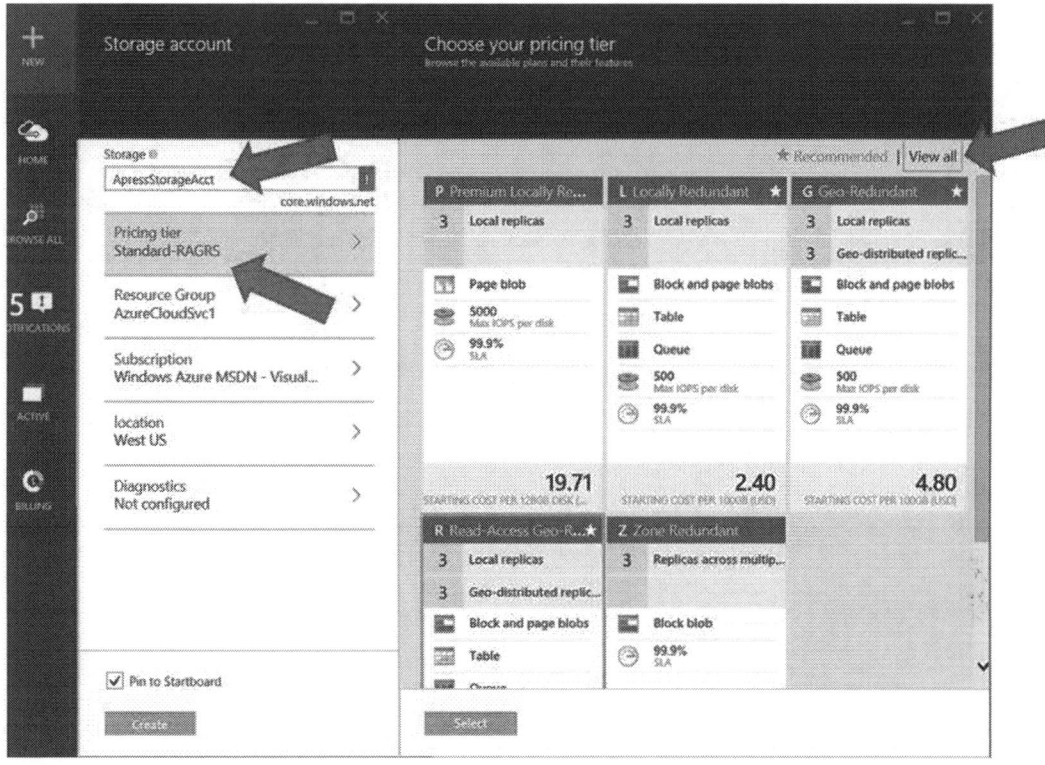

Figure 7-3. *Selecting the Azure Storage account type via the Pricing Tier option*

4. Click View All at upper right to see all available Azure Storage accounts, also shown in Figure 7-3.

5. Click Select to choose the pricing tier. Note the different types of accounts. For example, Premium Storage is only available in LRS and only supports page blobs with a 99.9% SLA, as shown in Figure 7-4. After selecting the type of account, click Create to create the Azure Storage account.

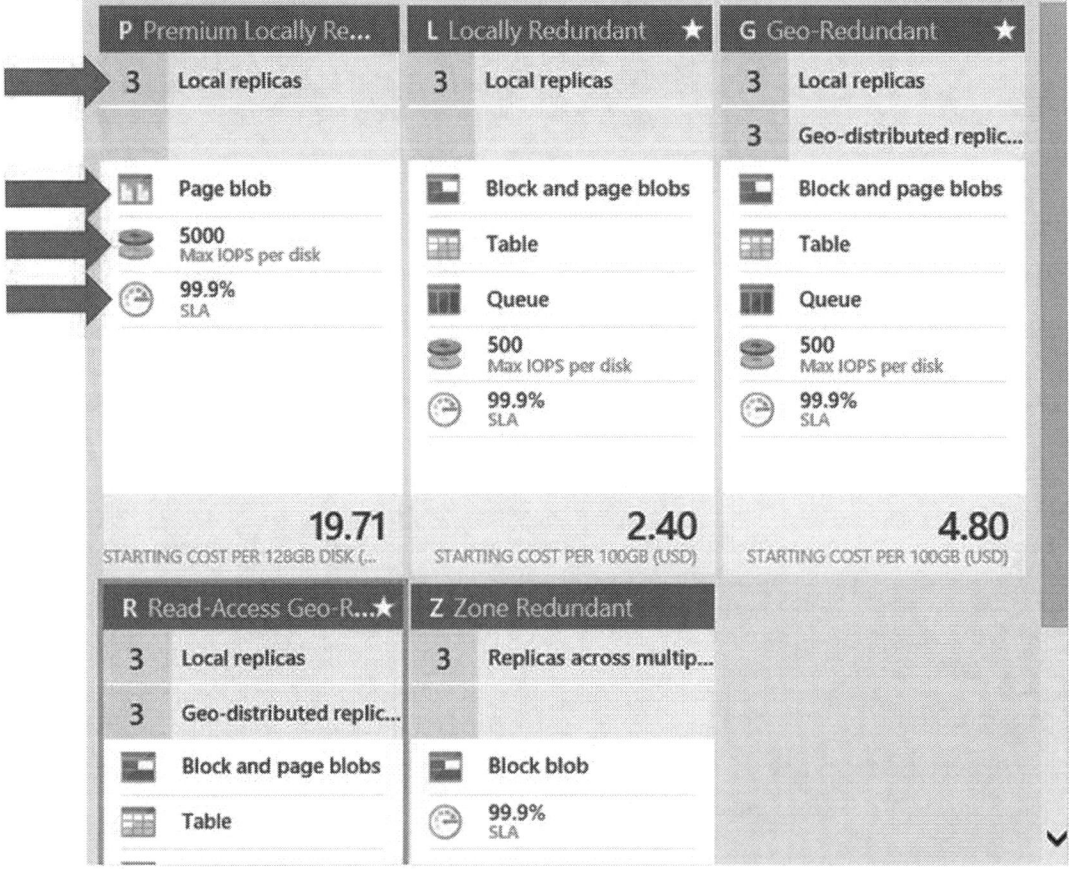

Figure 7-4. Characteristics of the different Azure Storage accounts

Now that you have created an Azure Storage account, you can use it to build block or page blobs, tables, queues, and file storage.

Queue Storage

Queues are used primarily for messaging between services and applications. Azure Queue is part of the Azure Storage family of services and uses REST-based protocols such as GET and PUT to transfer messages.

Azure provides two types of queue methods: Azure queues and service bus queues. Although both methods are messaging services, they have different features and capacities in terms of message size, maximum queue size, and message time-to-live (TTL). Application and service developers primarily use Azure queues, which are beyond the scope of this book. For detailed information about Azure queues and service bus queues, and the appropriate use-case scenarios for each, visit `https://azure.microsoft.com/en-us/documentation/articles/service-bus-azure-and-service-bus-queues-compared-contrasted`. You can also find a detailed discussion of Azure Queue storage at `http://azure.microsoft.com/en-us/documentation/articles/storage-dotnet-how-to-use-queues`.

File Storage

Azure File storage offers shared storage for applications using the standard Server Message Block (SMB) 2.1 protocol. Azure VMs and cloud services can share file data across application components via mounted shares, and on-premises applications can access file data in a share via the Azure File storage API. Azure VMs can connect to Azure Storage by simply mounting the file storage as a shared drive via the SMB protocol. Multiple clients can access the file storage via SMB simultaneously.

You can also achieve high-performance, low-latency file storage by building the file storage on the new Azure Premium Storage, which is based on SSD drives.

Blob Storage

Azure Blob storage is designed for storing unstructured data, such as data from backups, rich content such as images and streaming video or audio, text, or binary data. It is designed to be accessed over the HTTP or HTTPS protocol, which makes it ideal for anywhere access over the Internet. Because Azure Blob storage uses the HTTP/HTTPS standards, many third-party solutions use this storage option to offload the data that they generate.

▓ **Note** Although Azure Blob storage is usually accessed via a URL using the HTTP/HTTPS protocol, you can also access the contents via a number of APIs/SDKs that the Azure Team has created. These include .NET, Java, PHP, Ruby, and Python. For comprehensive documentation on using these SDKs/APIs, visit http://azure.microsoft.com/en-us/documentation.

The following are the core concepts of Azure Blob storage:

- There are two types of blobs:

  - *Block blob*: Comprises data blocks that are identified by their unique block ID. Blocks can be of different sizes, with a maximum of 4 MB per block. There is a maximum size of 200 GB for block blobs. As such, block blobs are ideal for large, efficient uploads; hence their use in backups. Files of up to 64 MB can be written in single-write operations.

  - *Page blob*: As the name implies, essentially a collection of 512-byte page files. A page blob can grow to a maximum size of 1 TB.

- You may define a blob as a block or page blob at the time of creation, but once it has been created, the blob type cannot be changed.

- All blobs reflect committed changes immediately.

- Blobs can be duplicated in a snapshot.

- To limit the risk of a blob being unintentionally overwritten, you can lease it for exclusive write access. When you do so, a lease ID is generated. Henceforth, any write requests that do not include the current or correct lease ID are not allowed to modify the blob's existing contents.

- Management of Azure Blob storage is done through an Azure Storage account, covered in the next section of this chapter.

- Azure Blob storage must reside in *containers,* which are groupings of Azure blobs. Containers can have unlimited blobs; likewise, Azure Storage accounts can contain an unlimited number of containers.

- Blobs are addressable using the following URL format: `http://<storage account>.blob.core.windows.net/<container>/<blob>`.

Figure 7-5 illustrates the concepts and relationships of the different Azure Blob components.

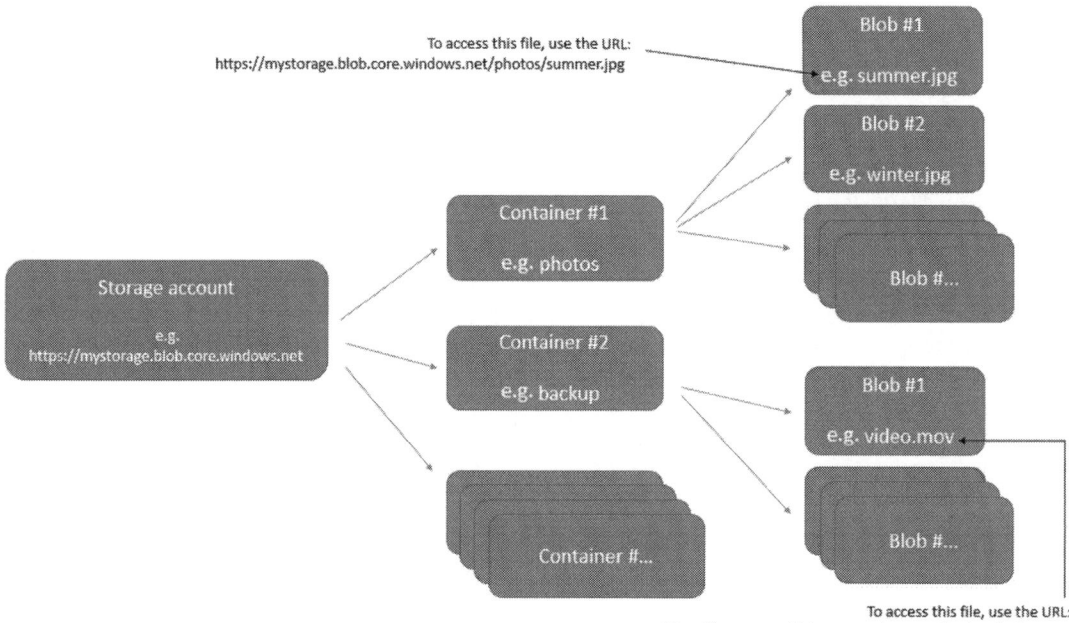

Figure 7-5. *Azure Blob components and access via HTTPS URL*

In addition to accessing Azure Blob storage through the browser, Microsoft also makes available a free Azure Storage Explorer through CodePlex. Azure Storage Explorer is a graphical user interface (GUI) application that provides user-friendly access to Azure Blob storage. You can download the Azure Storage Explorer at `http://azurestorageexplorer.codeplex.com`.

■ **Note**   Azure Storage performance metrics, such as IOPS and disk bandwidth, for the various VM sizes are available on the Azure Documentation site: `https://azure.microsoft.com/en-us/documentation/articles/storage-premium-storage-preview-Portal`.

Azure Storage Analytics

It is sometimes helpful to analyze how storage is being used. This is especially useful for optimizing the use of storage and finding opportunities to lower the cost of consumption or for troubleshooting purposes.

Azure Storage Analytics logs the access and actions of users accessing Azure Storage: for example, users storing content in Azure. Azure Storage Analytics then analyzes the logs to provide metrics data for a storage account.

To use Azure Storage Analytics, you must enable it individually for each service. You do so from the Azure Management Portal; for details, see Chapter 13. You can also enable Storage Analytics programmatically via the REST API or the client library.

The aggregated data is stored in a well-known blob (for logging) and in well-known tables (for metrics), which may be accessed using the Azure Table service APIs or through the Azure Management Portal. Storage Analytics has a 20 TB limit on the amount of stored data that is independent of the total limit for your storage account.

Storage Analytics logs detail information about successful and failed requests. This information can be used to monitor individual requests and to diagnose issues with a storage service. Requests are logged on a best-effort basis. Log entries are created only if there is storage service activity. For example, if a storage account has activity in its Blob service but not in its Table or Queue services, only logs pertaining to the Blob service are created.

Azure Storage Analytics is not enabled by default and can only be turned on by the storage account owner. Each write operation performed by Storage Analytics is a billable activity in addition to the amount of storage used to store metrics data.

All logs are stored in block blobs in a container named $logs, which is automatically created when Storage Analytics is enabled for a storage account. The $logs container is located in the blob namespace of the storage account, such as http://<accountname>.blob.core.windows.net/$logs. This container cannot be deleted once Storage Analytics has been enabled, although its contents can be deleted.

■ **Note**   At the time of this writing, capacity metrics are only available for the Blob service. Capacity metrics for the Table service and the Queue service will be available in future versions of Storage Analytics.

Azure Import/Export Service

The *Azure Import/Export service* allows you to transfer data to and from Azure by shipping hard disk drives. In scenarios with large amounts of data, shipping it via the Import/Export service may be faster and more cost effective than electronically transferring the data over the network or Internet. The hard disk drives that are shipped to or from Microsoft datacenters are encrypted.

Azure SQL Database

Azure SQL Database is a relational database-as-a-service type of storage for structured data.

■ **Note**   Azure SQL Database is based on Microsoft SQL Server database technology. This should not be confused with the similar Azure Table storage offering, which is a NoSQL datastore that allows authenticated requests for structured data. Because the concepts and capabilities in Azure SQL Database and Azure Table are similar, this chapter only covers Azure SQL Database. For information specifically about Azure Table storage, visit https://azure.microsoft.com/en-us/documentation/articles/storage-dotnet-how-to-use-tables.

The benefit of using the Azure SQL Database service is the ability to spin up and consume a relational database quickly; it can then easily be replicated for georedundancy without all the infrastructure deployment and management normally required. When you are considering whether to use Azure SQL Database for a solution, it is important to understand the SQL Server features that are *not* available. However, Azure SQL Database should be able to meet the needs of most solutions that require a relational database in the back end.

CREATING AND USING AN AZURE SQL DATABASE

The following exercise walks you through the steps required to create and access an Azure SQL database. You also use the new Azure Portal that is currently in preview:

▓ **Note**   You see in the Portal that you can create other types of databases, such as MySQL. Although this exercise is based on a SQL database, the concepts and steps are similar.

---

1. Go to the new Azure Management Portal at `https://portal.azure.com`.

2. Click New, select Data + Storage, and then select SQL Database, as shown in Figure 7-6.

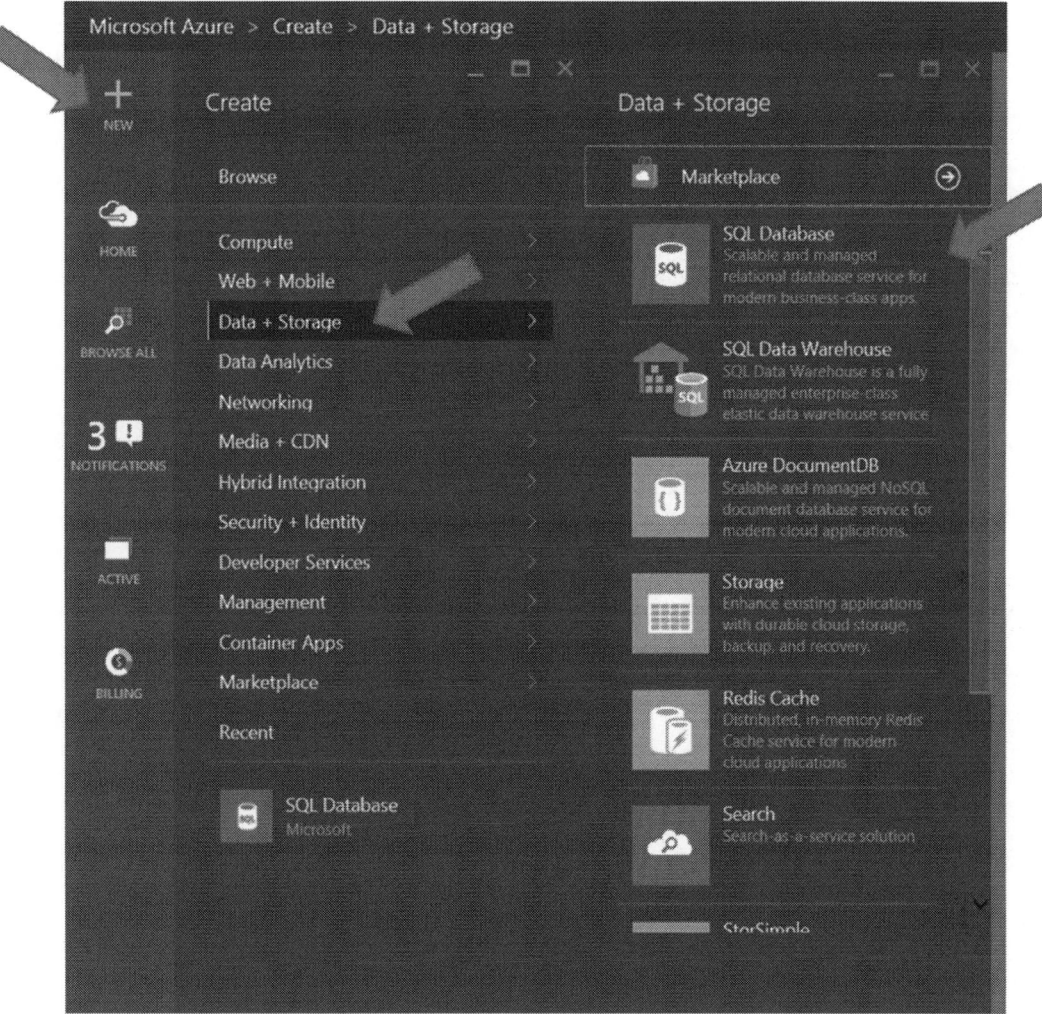

Figure 7-6. *Create a new Azure SQL database from the Portal*

3. Provide a friendly name for the SQL database. If your organization has multiple subscriptions, it is a good practice to change the subscription with which this SQL database is associated before making any other changes. At the bottom of the list, click Subscription to select the correct subscription for this database, as shown in Figure 7-7.

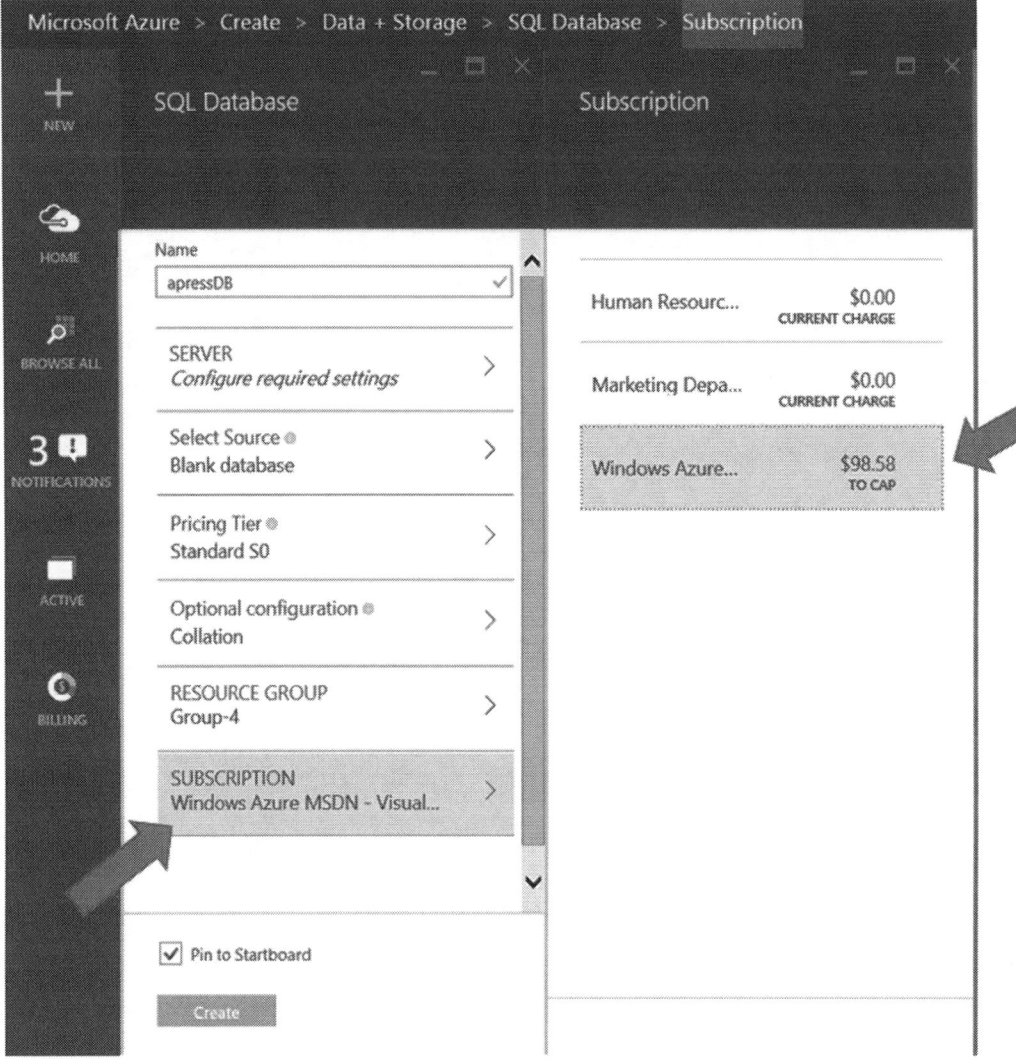

Figure 7-7. *Selecting the correct subscription*

4. Select the Pricing Tier menu, and choose the database type you wish to deploy. For this exercise, we selected Basic (5 DTUs), which has a maximum size of 2 GB.

5. Select Server, and then click Create A New Server, as shown in Figure 7-8. Provide information for the server name, server admin login password, and datacenter region where the database should be created. Click OK when you have finished configuring the database server, and then click Create to have Azure create the database.

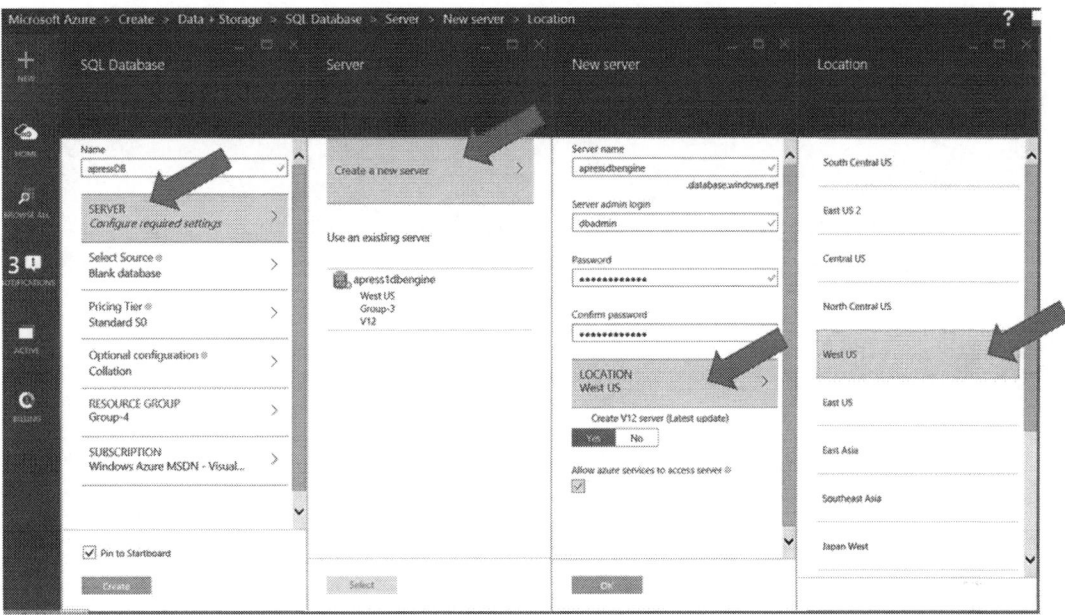

Figure 7-8. *Configuring the database server*

6. You are returned to the home page of the Portal. The status and progress of creating the new database are displayed on one of the tiles.

7. When the database has been created, you should automatically be directed to the SQL Database configuration screen, as shown in Figure 7-9. You can also get to the configuration screen by selecting the database from the Browse All menu option. Note that the status of the database is Online, and therefore it is ready for use.

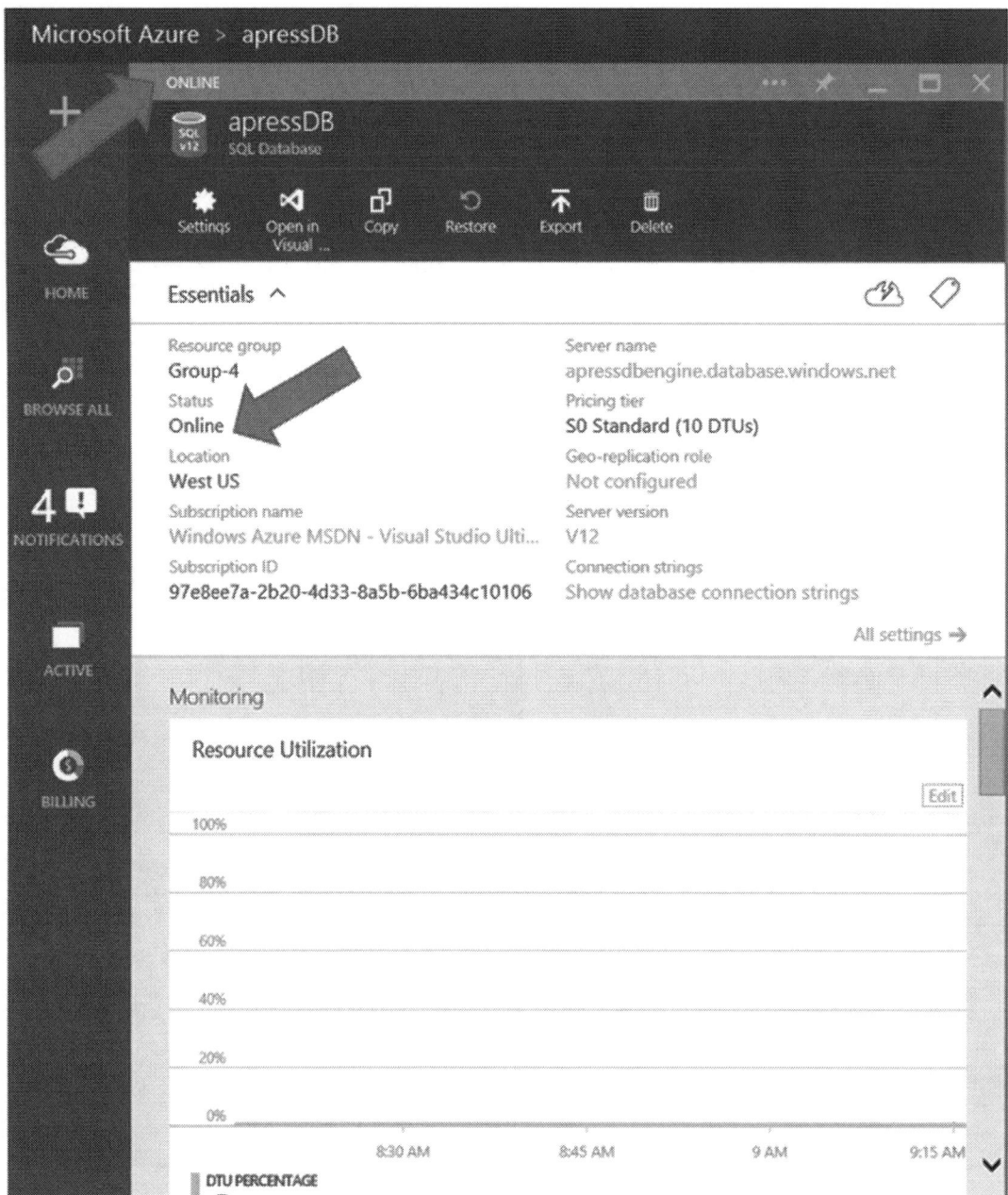

Figure 7-9. *Viewing the database properties*

8. As shown in Figure 7-10, click Settings to review and configure additional settings for the database, such as auditing and georeplication. This exercise does not go through all of these settings, because they are self-explanatory.

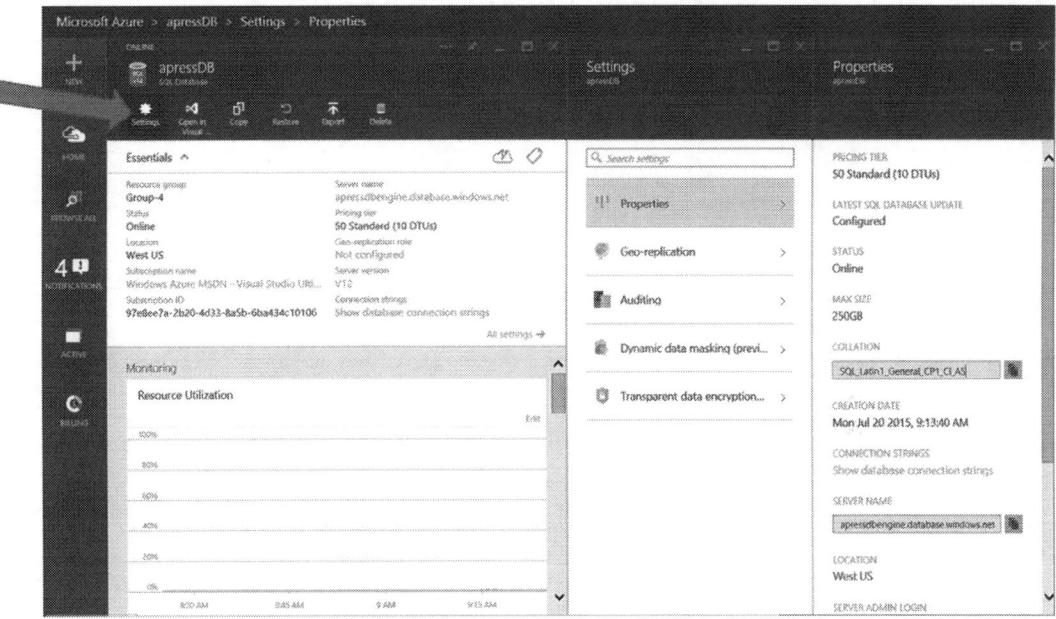

Figure 7-10. *Configuring additional database settings*

9. By default, the firewall settings for this database server would not allow you to connect to it directly from your client. In order to configure firewall settings so that you can connect to the database, click the server name and then select Show Firewall Settings, as shown in Figure 7-11.

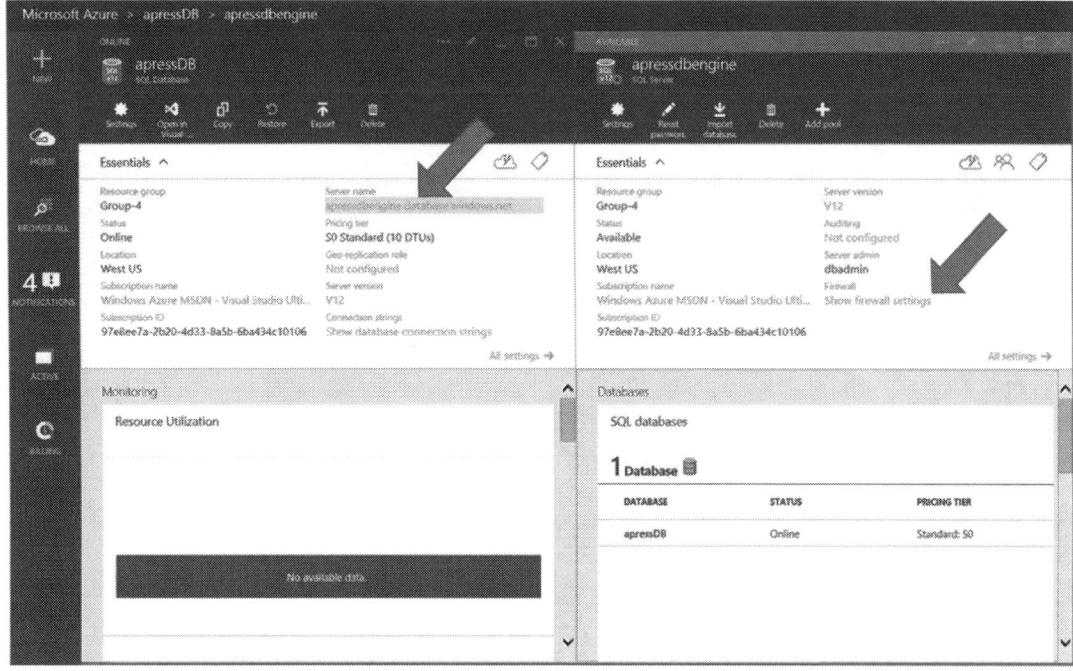

Figure 7-11. *Configuring the database server firewall settings*

10. The client IP address of the machine you are using to access this configuration should be detected. You have the option to add this IP to allow access by clicking Add Client IP; you can also specify ranges of IP addresses. Click Add Client IP, as shown in Figure 7-12. The IP address should be added to the access list.

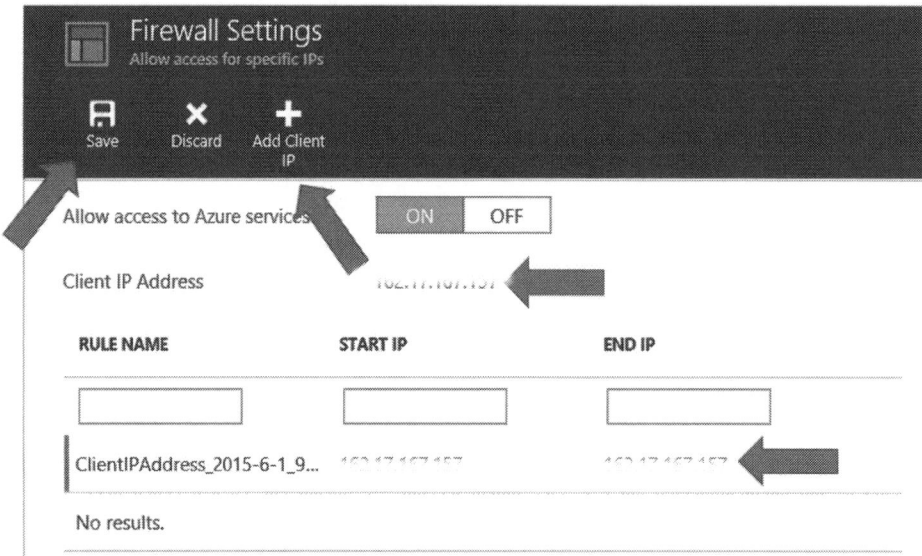

Figure 7-12. *Adding the client IP address to the access list*

11. Click Save to save the settings. The Portal says it may take up to five minutes for the settings to take effect, but it should happen immediately. If you have added the IP address to the access list and saved the settings but are still unable to connect to the database directly, wait a few minutes and then try again.

■ **Note**   It is important to save your firewall settings. It is not uncommon for administrators to add IP addresses to the access list and see them appear on the access list, as shown in Figure 7-9, but not save the settings. The firewall settings are not effective until you click Save.

You can now connect to the database to create tables and add data. Like any database, you can access it via a database-management tool like SQL Server Management or Visual Studio, or programmatically via database connection strings. The next part of this exercise show you the available connection strings and then demonstrates how to use Visual Studio to connect to the database:

12. From the SQL Database menu, click Show Database Connection Strings, as shown in Figure 7-13. Notice that there are four connections strings from which to choose, depending on what type of application you are developing. There is also a handy clipboard option that allows you to copy the connection string.

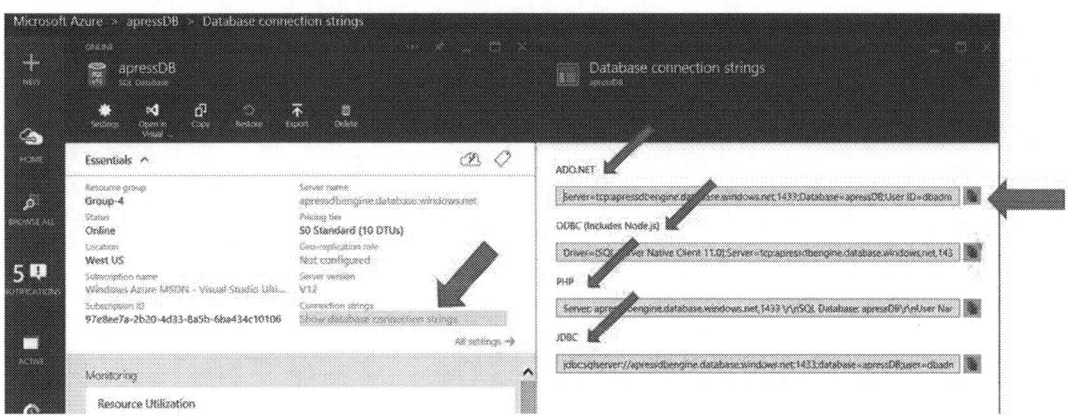

Figure 7-13. *Azure SQL Database connection strings*

13. Click Open In Visual Studio, as shown in Figure 7-14. Then select the option that is most applicable to your scenario. If you already have Visual Studio installed, you may need to get the latest update so that Visual Studio can connect to an Azure SQL database. Otherwise, you will get an error message that says Visual Studio does not recognize the database type. If you do not have Visual Studio, select one of the other options in order to connect to an Azure SQL database.

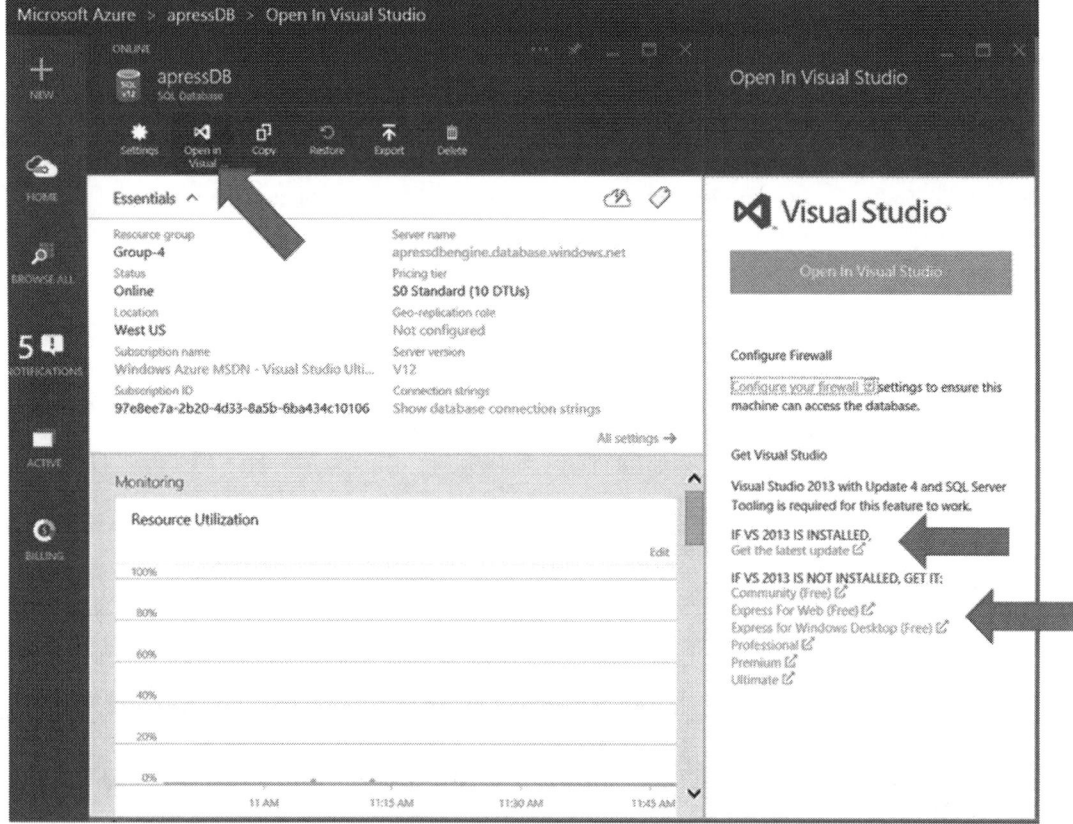

Figure 7-14. Download Visual Studio updates.

For this exercise, we downloaded and installed the updates for Visual Studio 2013.

14.　Launch Visual Studio.

15.　Click Tools from the menu, and select Connect To Database, as shown in Figure 7-15.

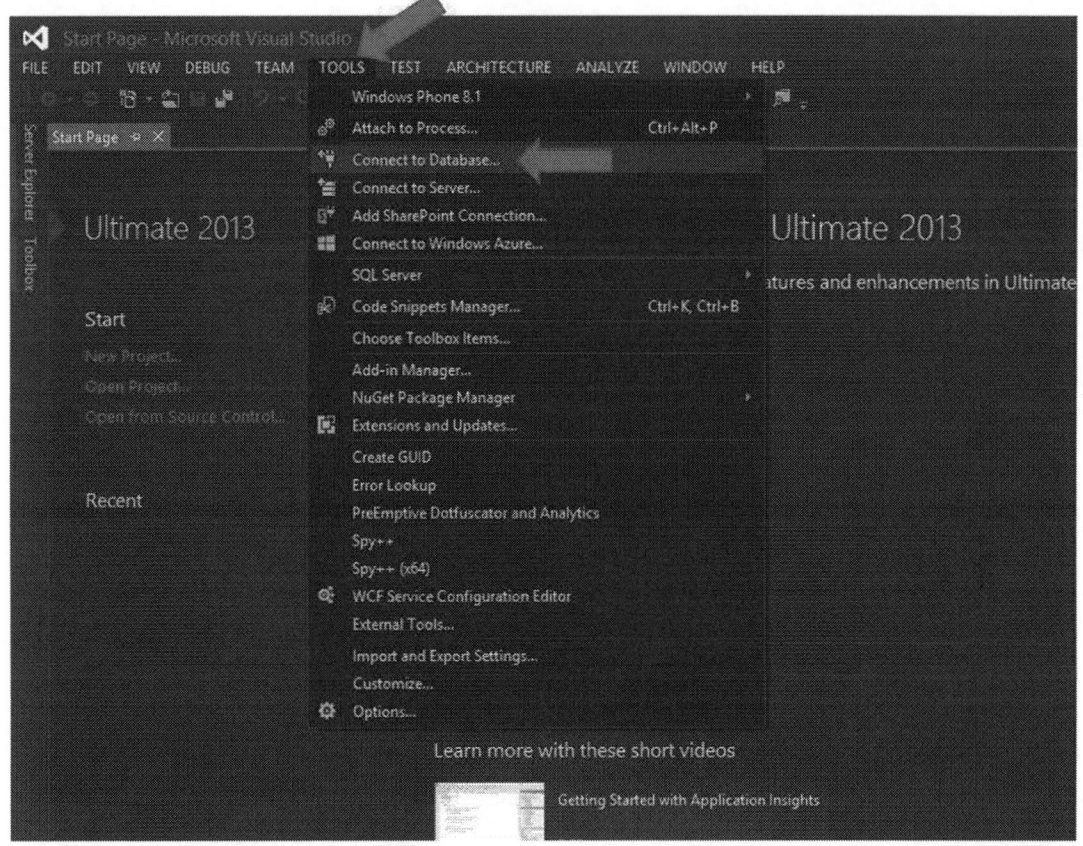

Figure 7-15. *Connecting to a database from Visual Studio*

16. Select Microsoft SQL Server as the data source, and uncheck Always Use This
Selection, as shown in Figure 7-16. Click Continue.

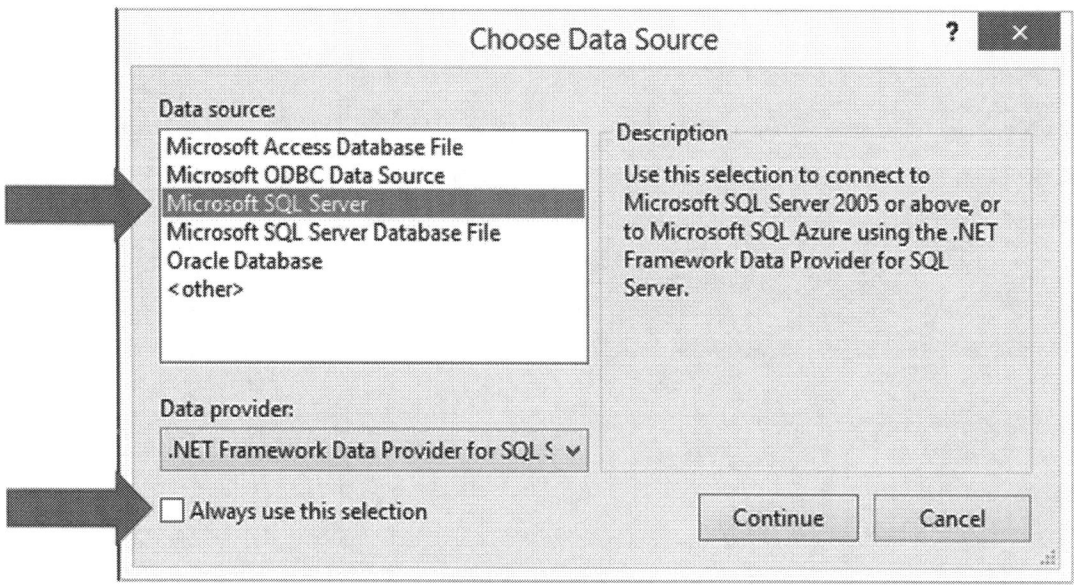

Figure 7-16. *Selecting a data source in Visual Studio*

17. From the Azure Management Portal, copy the server name, as shown in Figure 7-17.

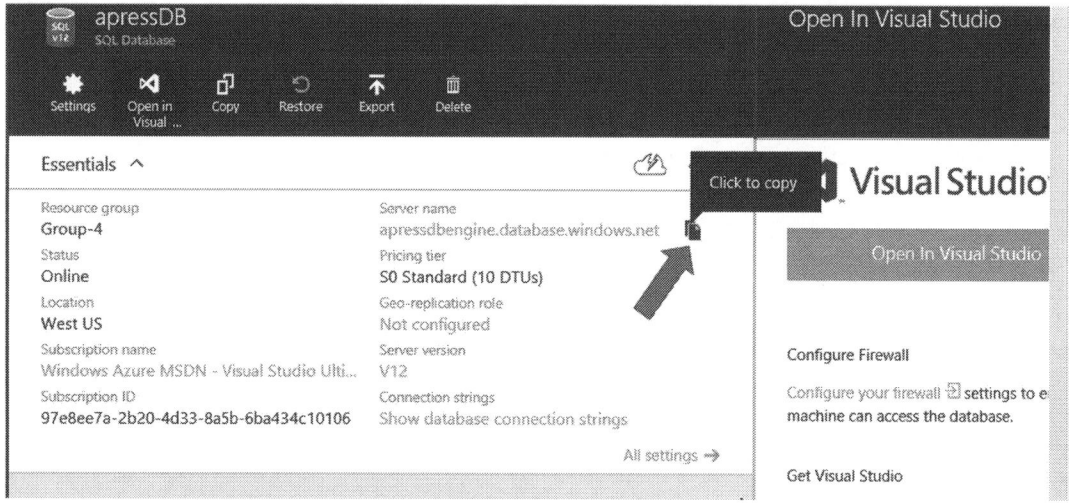

Figure 7-17. *Copying the Azure SQL database server name*

18. Paste the server name into the Visual Studio Add Connection dialog box, select Use SQL Server Authentication, and provide the required credentials, as shown in Figure 7-18.

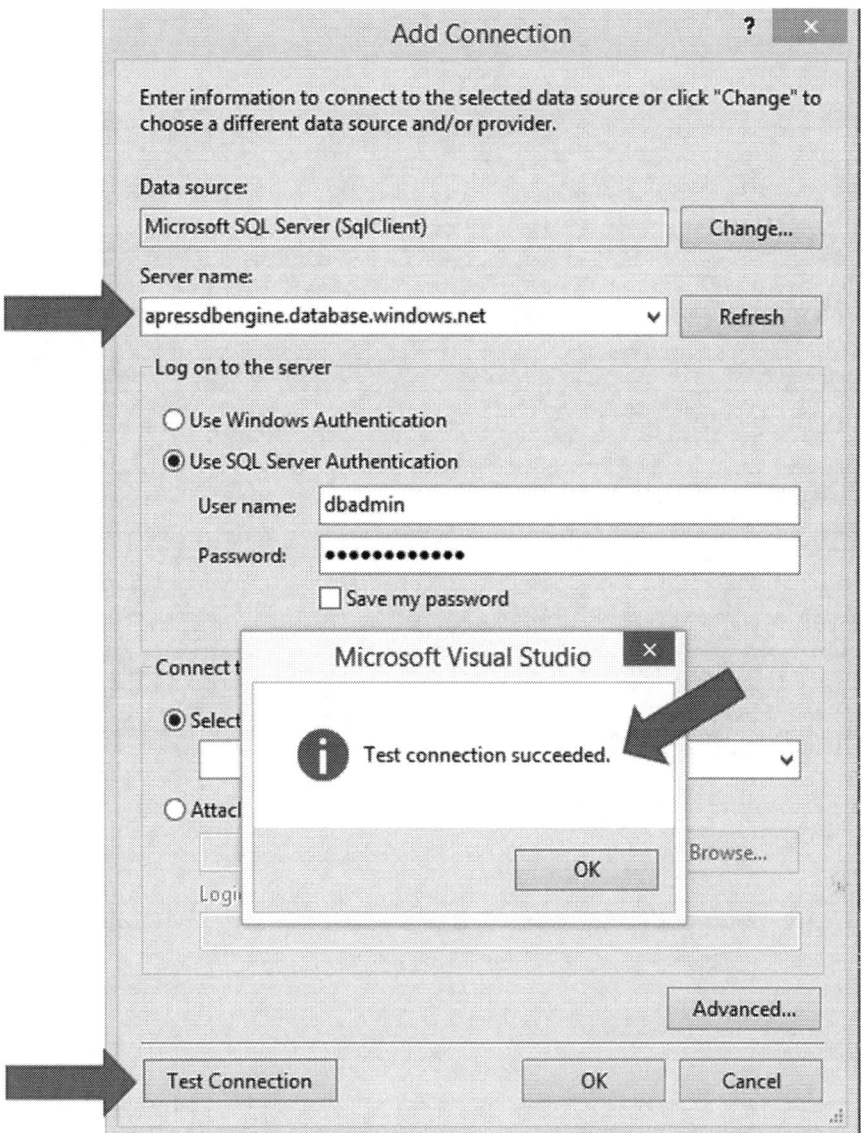

Figure 7-18. Testing the database connection

19. Click Test Connection to confirm that a successful connection to the database can be made, as also shown in Figure 7-18.

20. Click OK to close the dialog box indicating that the test connection succeeded.

21. Click OK again to close the Add Connection window.

22. A new database connection is now established. If you expand Data Connections, you should see the Azure SQL database server, as shown in Figure 7-19. Expand it, right-click Tables, and select Add New Table.

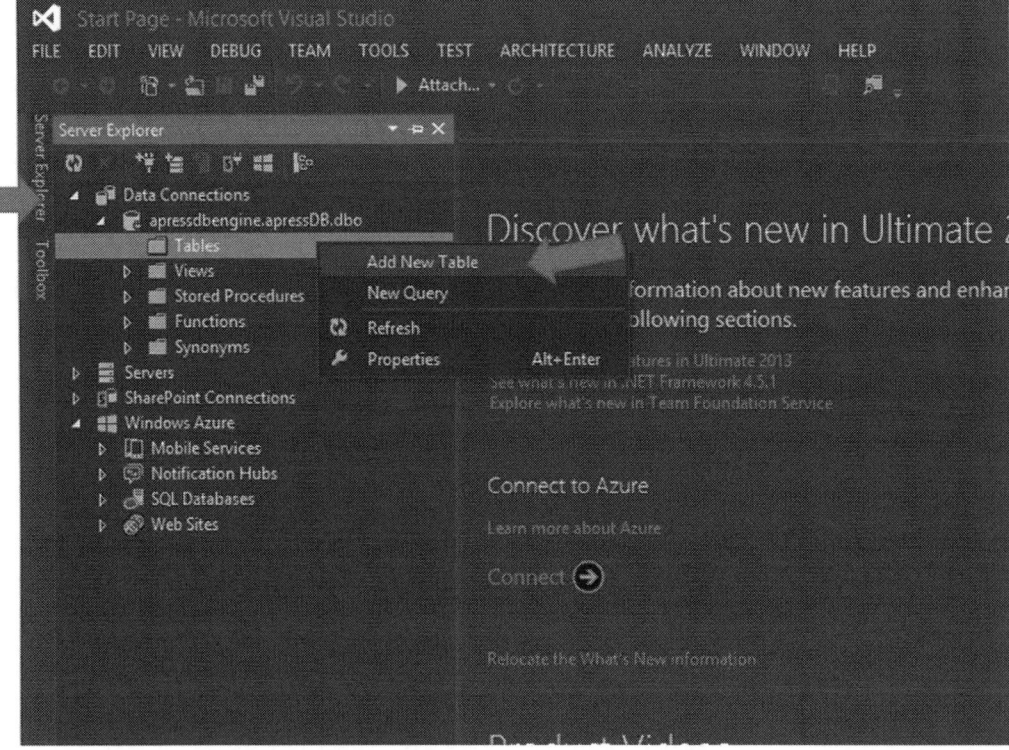

Figure 7-19. *Creating a new table in an Azure SQL database*

This concludes the exercise—managing databases and development are beyond the scope of this chapter. In this exercise, you saw how an Azure SQL database is created and how to access it via Visual Studio.

StorSimple

StorSimple is a hybrid on-premises and cloud storage solution. It consists of a 2U rackmount appliance that has SSDs, hard drives, and the ability to use Azure as a storage source. Figure 7-20 is a schematic of the rear panel of a StorSimple 8100 storage appliance.

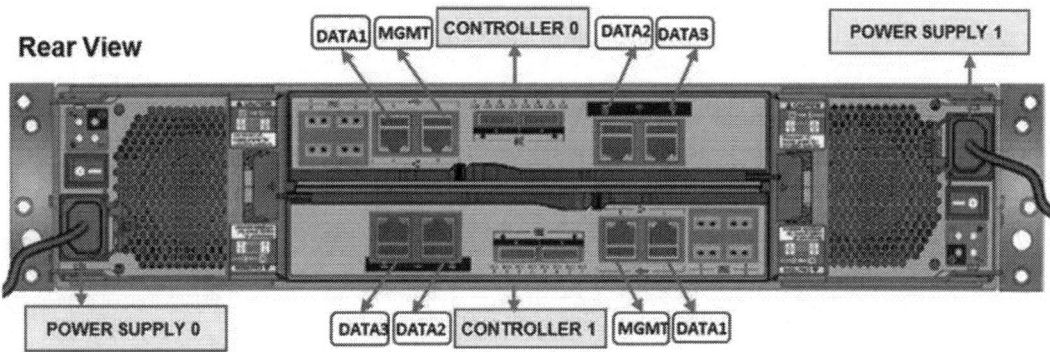

Figure 7-20. *Rear schematic of a StorSimple 8100 series storage appliance*

The idea behind StorSimple is the need for high-speed, low-latency access to frequently used data—hence the local storage on the appliance. Then, as data ages out, the StorSimple device moves the data from higher-speed local SSDs to the traditional hard drives that are also still on the appliance. Finally, once the device has reached 95% of capacity, as the data ages out even more, the content is moved to Azure storage. If the file is accessed after it has been moved to Azure storage, it is "promoted" back into the on-premises local StorSimple SSDs, and the aging process starts over. This entire process is transparent to the administrator and end user. It is depicted in Figure 7-21.

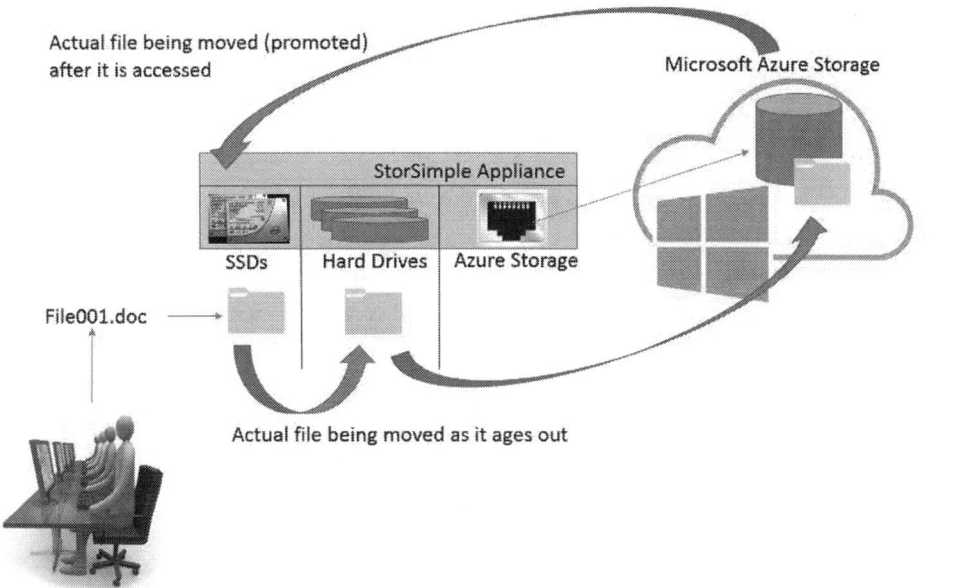

Figure 7-21. *How StorSimple's aging process for files works*

A StorSimple-specific storage account known as the *StorSimple Manager* is used to configure StorSimple. The StorSimple Manager is an extension of the Azure Management Portal. At the time of this writing, the new Preview Portal does not yet support the creation of a StorSimple Manager, so you need to use the Azure Portal. When you purchase StorSimple, this option becomes available, as shown in Figure 7-22. Also, at the time of this writing, Microsoft provides an onboarding service for StorSimple customers. As part of the service, Microsoft helps customers configure the StorSimple Manager and the appliance.

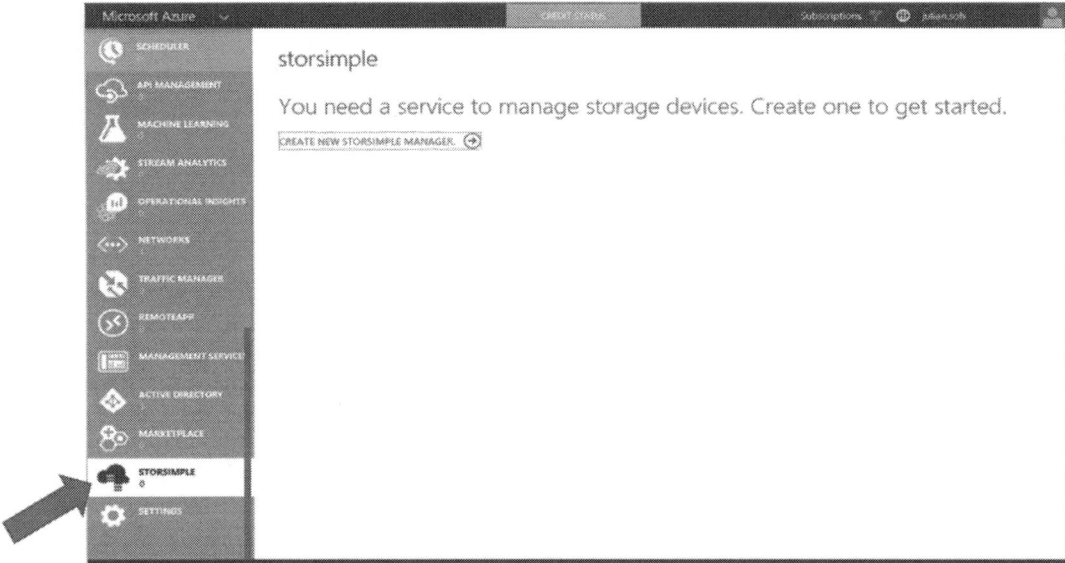

Figure 7-22. *Enabling the StorSimple Manager*

■ **Note**   At the time of this writing, the current hardware appliance versions for StorSimple are the 8000 series. The 7000 series of appliances is deprecated and superseded by the 8000 series, although the former can still be used with Azure. In some cases, such as Azure Government (MAG), only the 8000 series appliances are supported. StorSimple 5000 series hardware is no longer supported. For more information about StorSimple, visit http://azure.microsoft.com/en-us/documentation/services/storsimple.

StorSimple 8000 appliances provide automatic compression and de-duplication, so there is nothing for an administrator to configure with respect to these capabilities. The appliances have 10 GB Ethernet connections and come in two versions:

- *StorSimple 8100*: Provides 15 TB to 40 TB of storage on the appliance, depending on the level of compression achieved. The SSD on the 8100 is 800 GB in size. The maximum available storage that an 8100 appliance can handle, including Azure storage, is 200 TB.

- *StorSimple 8600*: Provides 40 TB to 100 TB of storage on the appliance, depending on the level of compression achieved. The SSD on the 8600 is 2 TB in size. The maximum available storage that an 8600 appliance can handle, including Azure storage, is 500 TB.

Summary

This chapter introduced the different types of Azure Storage accounts. These accounts determine certain hardware and deployment characteristics, such as LRS versus GRS, and standard HDDs versus high-performance SSDs.

Building on an Azure Storage account, you can define block blob, page blob, or file storage. You can also use storage accounts to create table and queue storage.

You were also introduced to relational databases as a service in the form of Azure SQL Database. But other non-SQL relational databases as a service, like MySQL, are also available.

Finally, you visited StorSimple as a hybrid on-premises and cloud storage solution. StorSimple is a unique solution that takes advantage of the best of on-premises and cloud storage.

The next chapter covers how to extend your network into Azure.

## PART III

Extending Your On-Premise Environment with Azure

CHAPTER 8

■ ■ ■

Extending Your Network with Azure

Introducing Azure Virtual Networks

Virtual networks (VNets, in Azure), maintain the same characteristics as physical networks. The processes of physical networks enable data from one computer to be transported over Transmission Control Protocol, Internet Protocol (TCP/IP) to another computer. The information, or data, is transformed so that TCP/IP *packets* can transport it efficiently; it is sent to another computer through hardware network interface cards (NICs) via physical network switches. To send the data to and from other buildings and other datacenters, network engineers use hardware devices referred to as *gateways*. Additionally, in datacenters today, the hardware provides network architects with the ability to virtualize physical networks or subnetworks (*subnets*) into a virtual network subnet called a *virtual LAN (VLAN)*. How would your budget be improved if Azure VNets reduced the need for a considerable amount of physical networking equipment?

This chapter provides you with a deep understanding of Microsoft Azure virtual networking components. You gain the insight needed for the planning considerations that let you use Azure Networks successfully. Finally, you walk through the steps required to build several VNet configurations used in Azure and study use cases for each option. One major arrangement provides steps for extending your current on-premises network infrastructure into Azure—what the industry refers to as a *hybrid network*.

Azure Networking Overview

An Azure VNet provides network engineers with the components to create virtual private networks (VPNs) that connect to your on-premises physical networks. VPNs allow computers to communicate using TCP/IP and reduce the need for physical networking hardware. This lowers the financial burden for items such as routers, switches, and gateway devices, not to mention the cost of maintaining and updating network hardware. The hardware components are virtualized to support Azure Cloud Services, and VNets are what you enable and configure through the Azure Portal or through PowerShell.

Remember that Azure is built on a modified version of the Microsoft virtualization platform, Hyper-V. The Microsoft hypervisor provides the virtualization of server hardware, including network adapters (NICs) and Hyper-V enabled virtual network switches. In your on-premises datacenter, physical network hardware is mixed with virtualized network hardware. In Microsoft Azure, only virtualized networking components are needed. You can use Hyper-V virtual network cards, virtual network switches, and gateways. In some of the Azure documentation, you may see the description "network overlay." This is because Hyper-V supports on-premises datacenter requirements to mix physical network hardware components with virtualized network components, or the entire network can be virtualized as in Azure. To support your understanding of Azure VNets, see Figure 8-1.

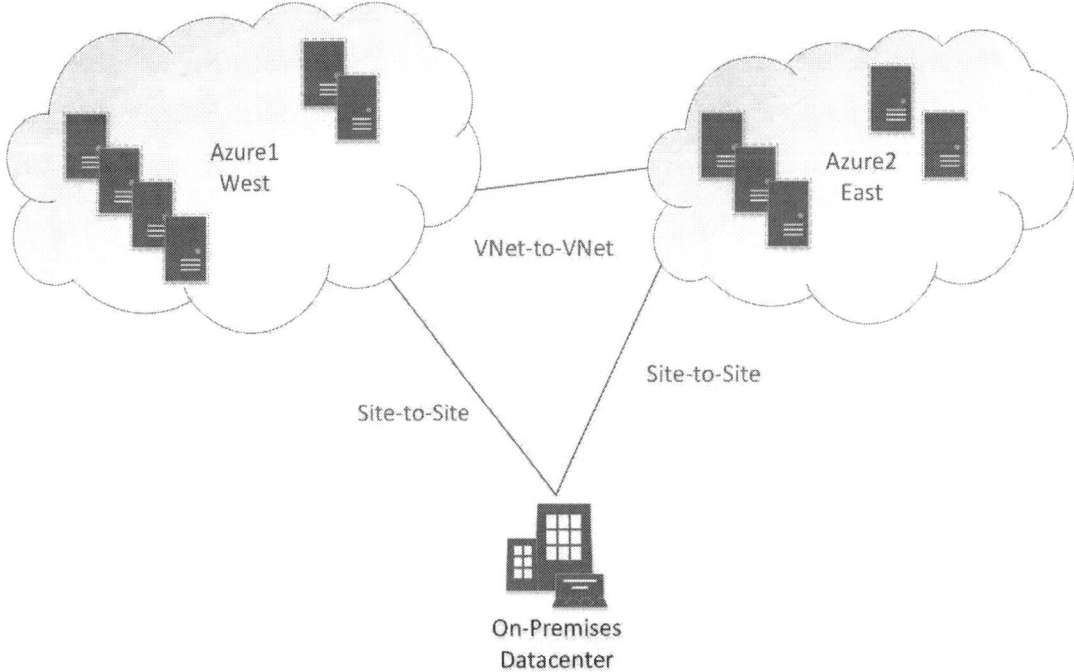

Figure 8-1. *Azure VNet and cloud services*

Areas of network condensation essential for successful network architecting are very similar to traditional hardware networking requirements, including the following:

- IP subnets
- IP addresses
- DNS name resolution
- Protocols

IP Subnets

IP networks are normally divided into subnetworks (subnets), which are smaller divisions of the overall IP network or local area network (LAN). In Azure, there is currently no limit on the number of subnets in the VNet address space, and there should not be any overlap between subnets.

Important considerations when planning subnets include the following:

- For each IP subnet in Azure, the first and last IP addresses are reserved when you create a new subnet (public or private). These two addresses equal all 0s (zeros) for the network address and all 1s (ones) for the broadcast address.

- IP addresses can be public or private, following the Request for Comments (RFC) standards.

IP Addresses

IP addresses used in Azure follow the specifications in *Classless Inter-Domain Routing* (*CIDR*, pronounced "cider"), which is a method of allocating IP addresses and routing IP packets. The Internet Engineering Task Force (IETF) introduced CIDR in 1993 as an IP version 4 (IPv4) standard. Planning for the use of IP address subnets using CIDR notation is another network architecture consideration when designing your Azure network.

CIDR notation consists of an IP address and a routing-prefix size expressed in decimal notation. The smallest subnet supported in Azure using CIDR notation is /29, and the largest subnet is /8. Here are some examples of CIDR notation:

192.168.1.0 / 29 (6 addresses, 8 subnets, range 192.168.1.0–192.168.1.7)

192.168.1.0 /24 (254 addresses, 256 subnets, range 192.168.1.0–192.168.1.255)

10.0.0.0 / 22 (1,022 addresses, 1,024 subnets, range 10.0.0.0–10.0.3.255)

10.10.0.0 /16 (65,534 addresses, 65,536 subnets, range 10.10.0.0–10.10.255.255)

98.245.0.0 /8 (16,777,214 addresses, 16,777,216 subnets, range 98.0.0.0–98.255.255.255)

The IP address is unique to a single device (server NIC, switch interface, or gateway). Azure VNets support public IP addresses and private (non-Internet-routable) IP address ranges, defined in RFC 1918, in the use of subnet address ranges (see Figure 8-2). The use of public IP addresses is a relatively new feature to provide broader options for your Azure services; it closes the gap between traditional network hardware and Azure VNet capabilities.

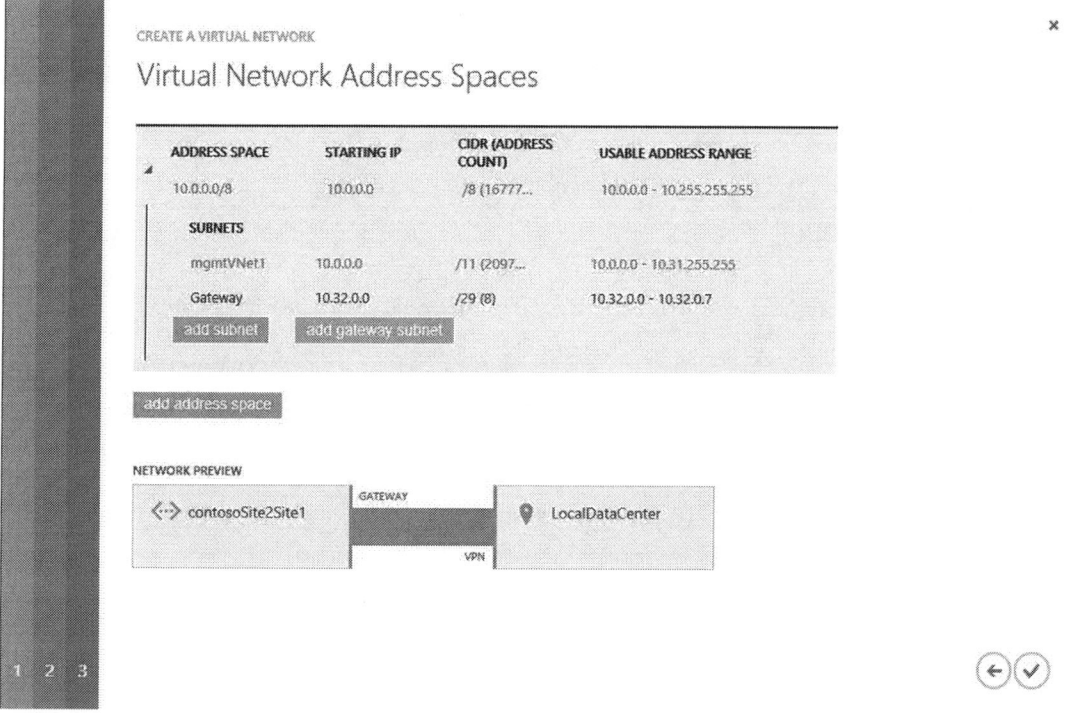

Figure 8-2. Azure VNet and subnets

Public IP address ranges and private IP address ranges are added to Azure the same way: by editing network configurations using the netcfg command with the appropriate switches, or by editing in the Azure Portal. You can enter the public or private IP address ranges when the subnets are created or edit them later.

Figure 8-3. *Azure VNet to VNet*

Other IP address considerations include the IP addresses assigned to virtual machines (VMs) or the cloud service. IP address are divided into the following three categories:

- DIP internal IP address from a DHCP pool of IP addresses

- VIP virtual IP, which is assigned to the cloud service where the VM resides and not assigned to the VM directly

- PIP instance-level public IP, which can be assigned directly to the VM but not to the cloud service

Public IP addresses and internal IP addresses are assigned when the service is created. The internal IP address DIP is a DHCP address assigned to the VM. The DIP is not designed for public-facing connectivity, and it is assigned to the VM based on the IP subnet from the Azure VNet that is created. If no VNet was created, then the VM is assigned a random IP address (from DHCP) until the VM is stopped and deallocated. The IP address that is assigned in this case is not part of your VNet, and therefore the VM to which this address was assigned cannot connect with your on-premises network.

DNS Name Resolution

Domain name system (DNS) is a naming system for computers and services used on the Internet or in an on-premises datacenter. It translates easily memorized names to TCIP addresses. The first Azure virtual server to boot in a subnet acquires the x.x.x.4 IP address. This server could be a stand-alone server, a stand-alone DNS server for your Azure VMs to use, or a DNS server that replicates DNS zones with your on-premises DNS server. The DNS is an essential component for effective functioning of most Azure services, on-premises datacenters, and Internet services around the world.

■ **Tip** To find out more about DNS and name resolution support in Azure, see the article "Name Resolution for VMs and Role Instances" at http://msdn.microsoft.com/en-us/library/azure/jj156088.aspx.

Protocols

Azure supports many of the foundational networking communication protocols, but a few are blocked. Broadcasts and multicast protocols are blocked in addition to IP-in-IP encapsulated packets. Again, referring back to the Hyper-V discussion in Chapter 1, Generic Routing Encapsulation (GRE) packets are also blocked. Many standard IP-based protocols used in VNets are supported. A few examples are

- TCP

- UDP

- ICMP

To support security in Azure VNets, you may perform standard testing such as pinging default routers in each subnet. This is also blocked. Additional blocked troubleshooting techniques include `tracert`, even for diagnostic support.

One other point in relation to the Open Systems Interconnect (OSI) model is that Azure VNets are on Layer-3, whereas traditional hardware VLANs are on Layer-2. Thus VLANs cannot cross from your on-premises datacenter into Azure.

Azure Networking Details

This section teaches you about the specifics of Azure VNets and when to use them. By default, every Azure cloud service allows VMs to communicate with each other. However, to communicate with other VMs in another cloud service, you use a VNet. VNets are also required when you extend your network from an on-premises datacenter to Azure cloud services.

The steps for networking are as follows:

1. Connect a single site or multiple sites.

2. Plan your IP networks.

3. Deploy and manage your networks.

Two types of VNet configuration are available in Azure:

- *Cloud-only VNet*: Lets you create an IP address space that allows VMs and PaaS entities to communicate with other IP addresses in the same Azure subscription or with another VNet in another Azure subscription. This provides subnet features to help coordinate and separately manage different business solutions in Azure, exactly as they are managed in an on-premises datacenter.

- *Cross-premises VNet*: Extends IP networks for many different configurations to support a requirement to extend your datacenter from a single building with limited resources to an Azure public cloud with unlimited resources. This is an amazing option for any network engineer—the ability to provide a secure VPN connection into a world-class, state-of-the-art datacenter.

With these two types of VNets, you can build many different types of IP subnet and networking configurations. Let's walk you through the steps to complete a few Azure VNet tasks, including the following:

- VNet in Azure (cloud only)

- VNet from Azure to a client computer (one or many)

- VNets from Azure to a local datacenter (hybrid)

- VNets into multiple Azure regions

There are more options than these four, but all Azure network configurations use one or more of these standard network connections to build larger networks.

■ **Tip** For a complete list of Microsoft Azure VNet configuration tasks, see http://msdn.microsoft.com/en-us/library/azure/jj156206.aspx.

Cloud-Only Virtual Network

Cloud-only VNets connect VMs and cloud services directly to other VMs and cloud services. Cloud-only VNets don't require a lot of detailed network architecture and don't use a VNet gateway to connect from one cloud service to another. Also recall the rule discussed earlier, that you must make sure the IP addresses used do not overlap other IP subnets.

Once the VNet is created, you can add new VMs and instances from a PaaS. All communication through the VNet is secure because the communication between two endpoints is carried over an Azure VNet.

CREATE A CLOUD-ONLY VNET

1. In the Azure Management Portal, click New in the lower-left corner, as shown in Figure 8-4.

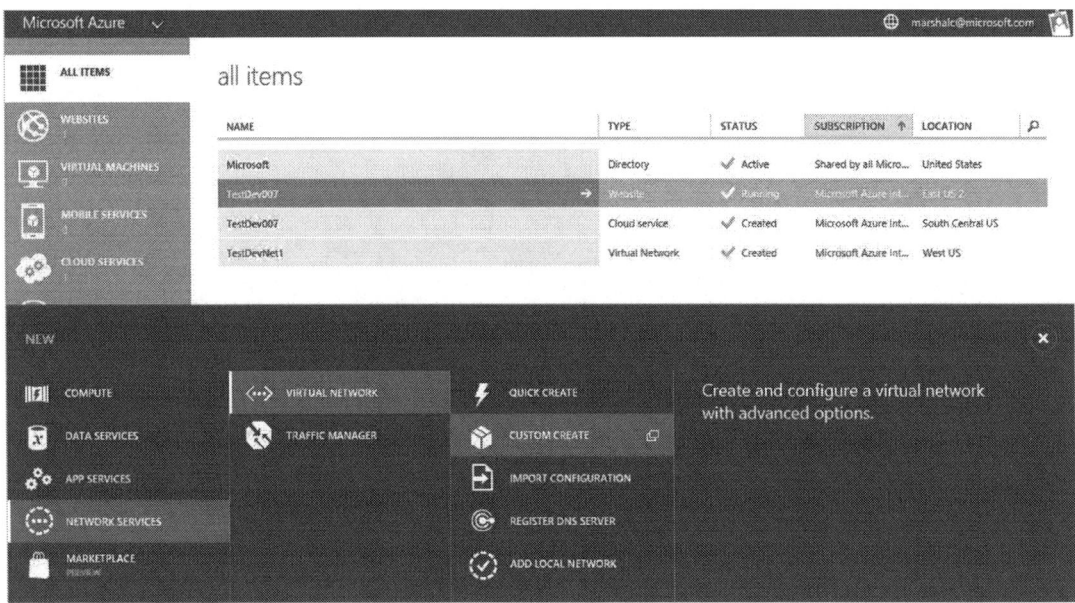

Figure 8-4. *Creating a cloud-only VNet using the Custom Create wizard*

2. Select Network Services ➤ Virtual Network ➤ Custom Create.

3. In the Create A Virtual Network Wizard, enter the following VNet details as shown in Figure 8-5:

   - Name (should be short and represent the service)
   - Location (Azure region)

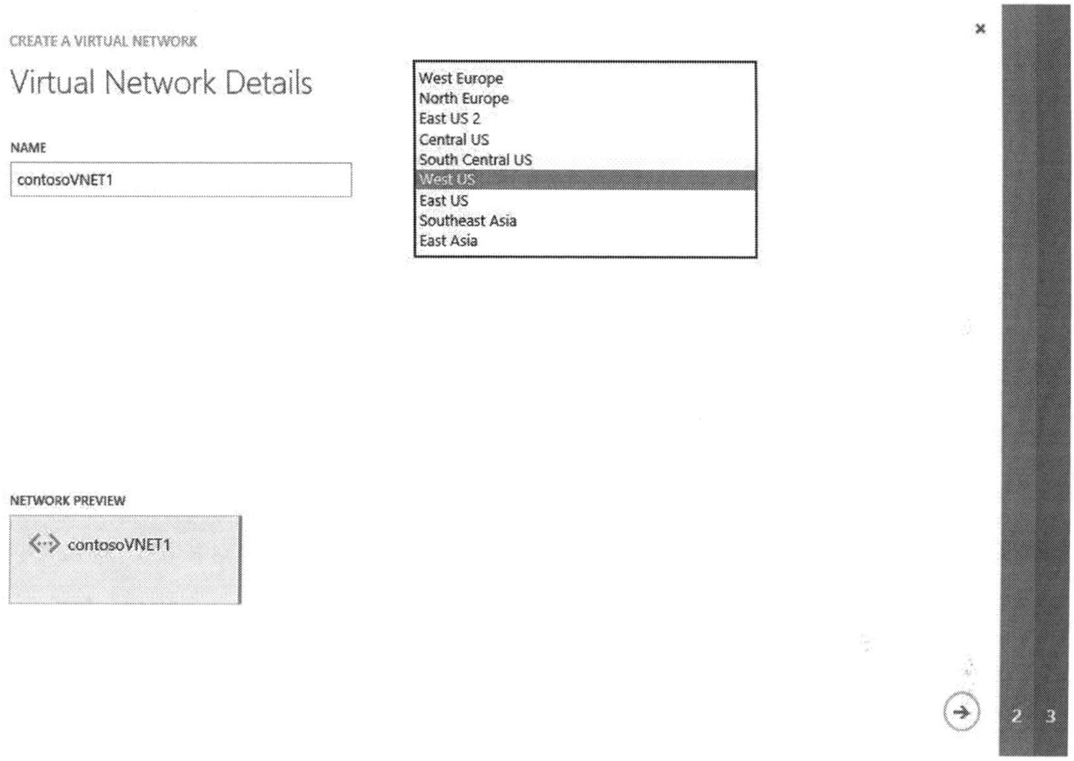

Figure 8-5. *Enter the server name and Azure region using the VNet wizard*

4. Click the arrow in the lower-right corner to proceed.

5. Leave the defaults on the DNS Servers and VPN Connectivity page empty for now. Azure provides DNS name resolution, but you can edit it later to add a dedicated DNS from your on-premises network. Click the arrow in the lower-right corner to proceed.

6. Leave the defaults for the current address space, unless you plan to use another IP address range.

7. Click the check mark in the lower-right corner to complete this wizard, as shown in Figure 8-6.

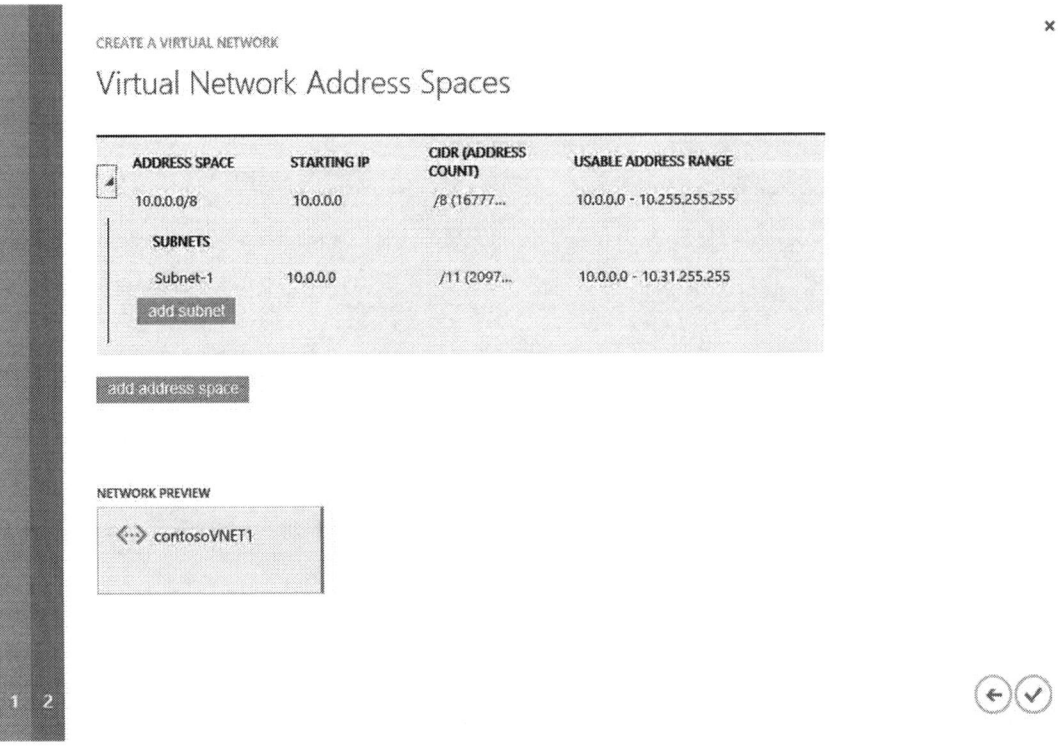

Figure 8-6. *Complete the wizard to create this VNet*

You can review the networks in the console. The final network settings should be similar to the final settings based on these steps.

Cross-Premises Virtual Network

There are differences between a cloud-only VNet and a cross-premises network connection. Currently, Azure supports three types of VPN connections:

- Point-to-site VPN
- Site-to-site VPN
- ExpressRoute

Point-to-Site Connections

This VPN type is used as a simpler connection from an on-premises computer to an Azure VNet. It does not require a VPN device. A VPN client is installed on the computer and establishes a connection to the Azure VNet. This VPN connection is best used when only a few clients need to connect to an Azure VNet.

If you roam from different sites in a city, state, or country, the point-to-site connection is generally the easiest to connect and maintain. Many smaller development shops that do not have an external-facing IPv4 address or VPN device use point-to-site VPNs. The process for enabling a point-to-site connection is provided in two parts. In Part 1, you use the Azure Portal.

CONFIGURE A POINT-TO-SITE CONNECTION: PART 1

1. In the Azure Management Portal, click New in the lower-left corner, as described in the "Create a Cloud-Only VNet" exercise earlier.

2. Choose Network Services ➤ Virtual Network ➤ Custom Create to start the wizard.

3. Provide the VNet details, including the name of the VNet and the location (Azure geographical region) where this VNet is to be enabled, as shown in Figure 8-7. Click the arrow in the lower-right corner to proceed.

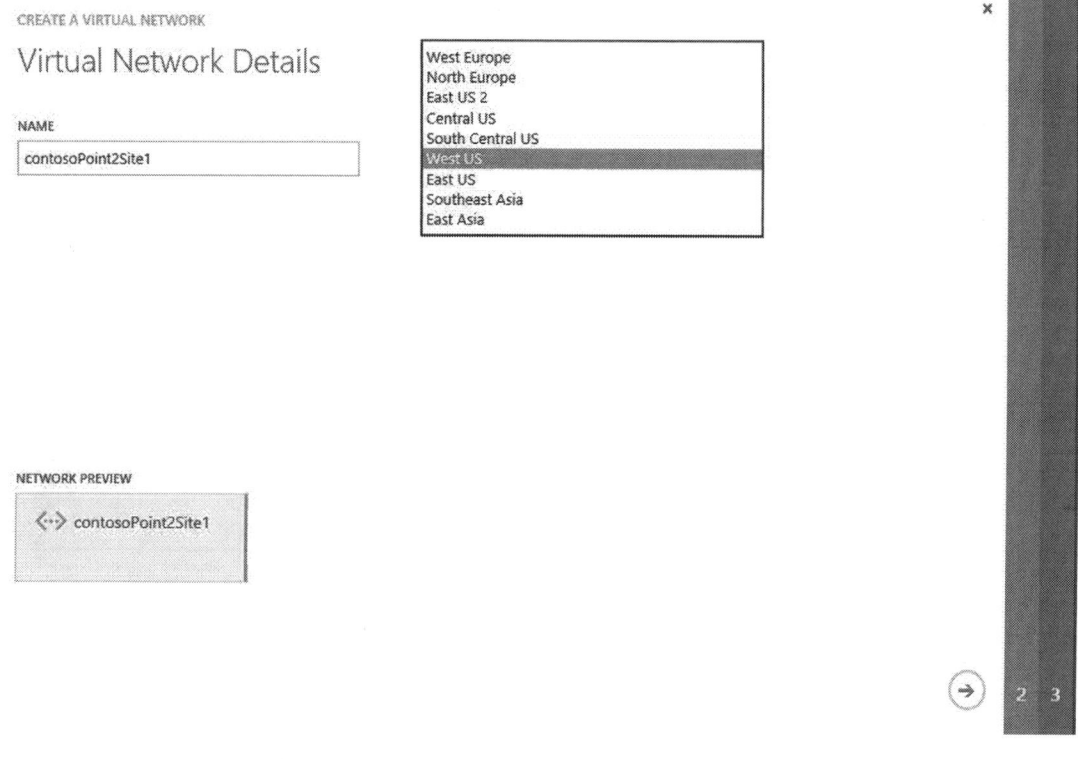

Figure 8-7. Creating a point-to-site VPN using the Virtual Network Wizard

4. On the DNS Servers and VPN Connectivity page, you have two options:

   a. Leave it blank, and allow Azure to perform name resolution.

   b. Fill in the DNS Server and IP address fields. This option does not create a DNS server, but it allows you to use another DNS resource.

For this example, you'll use Azure to perform name resolution.

5. On the same page, under the Point-To-Site Connectivity heading, click the check box to enable the option to configure a point-to-site VPN, as shown in Figure 8-8. When you enable this option, the Network Preview icon completes the visual indicator. Click the arrow in the lower-right corner to proceed.

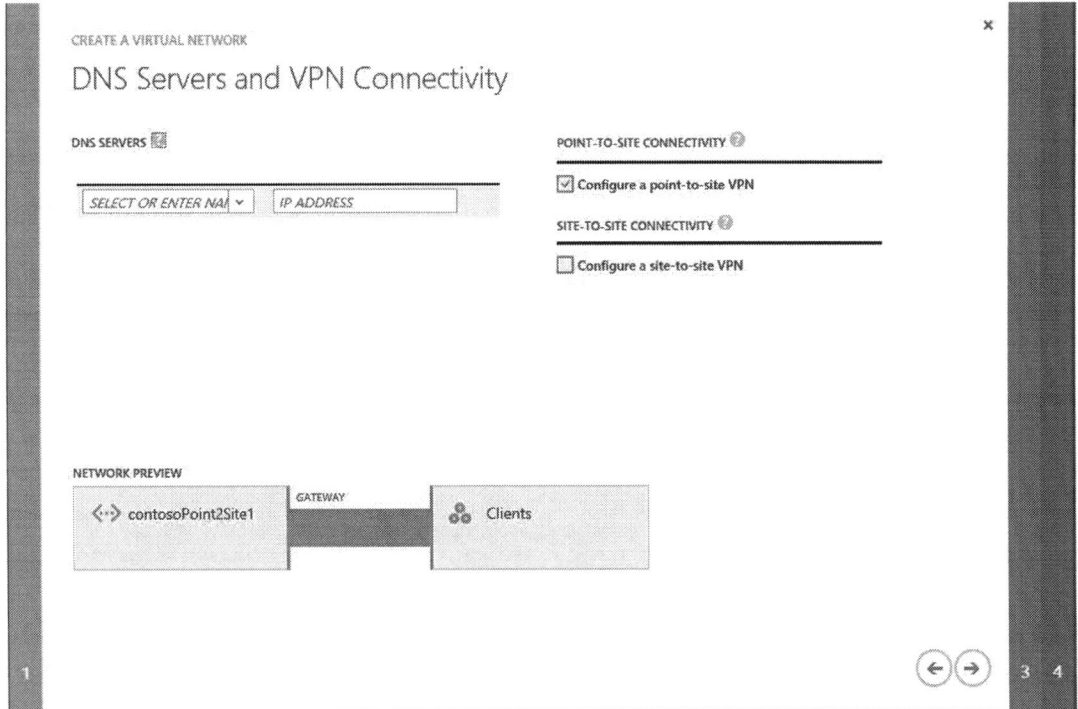

Figure 8-8. *Option to choose to configure a point-to-site VPN*

6. On the Point-To-Site Connectivity Page, the default address space is provided. If needed, you can edit the address space by moving the mouse over the Starting IP field and using the drop-down menu, as shown in Figure 8-9. You may also edit the number of CIDR addresses using the drop-down menu. This page of the wizard also lets you add other address spaces. Click the arrow in the lower-right corner to proceed.

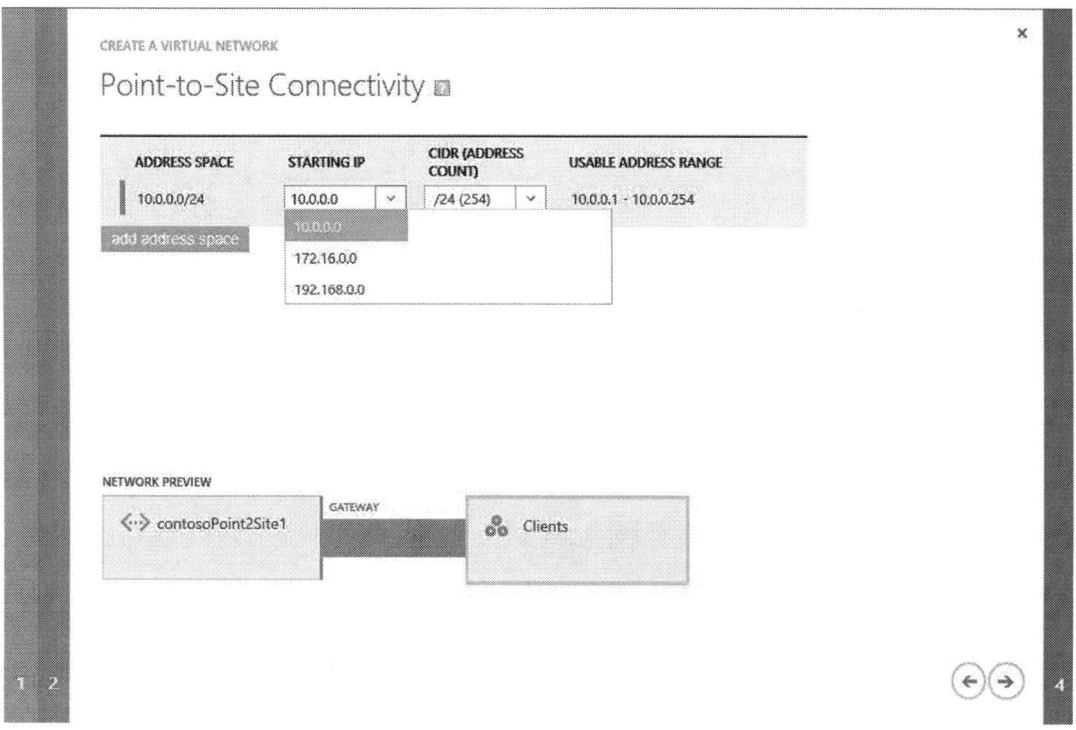

Figure 8-9. *Enter the starting IP address using CIDR notation*

7. The Virtual Network Address Spaces page lets you edit the address space, subnets, and CIDR (address count) . Click the button to add a gateway subnet, as shown in Figure 8-10, because you need one gateway for this subnet. Additional subnets help in the organization of VMs in a separate subnet based on their roles: DC, SQL, and so forth.

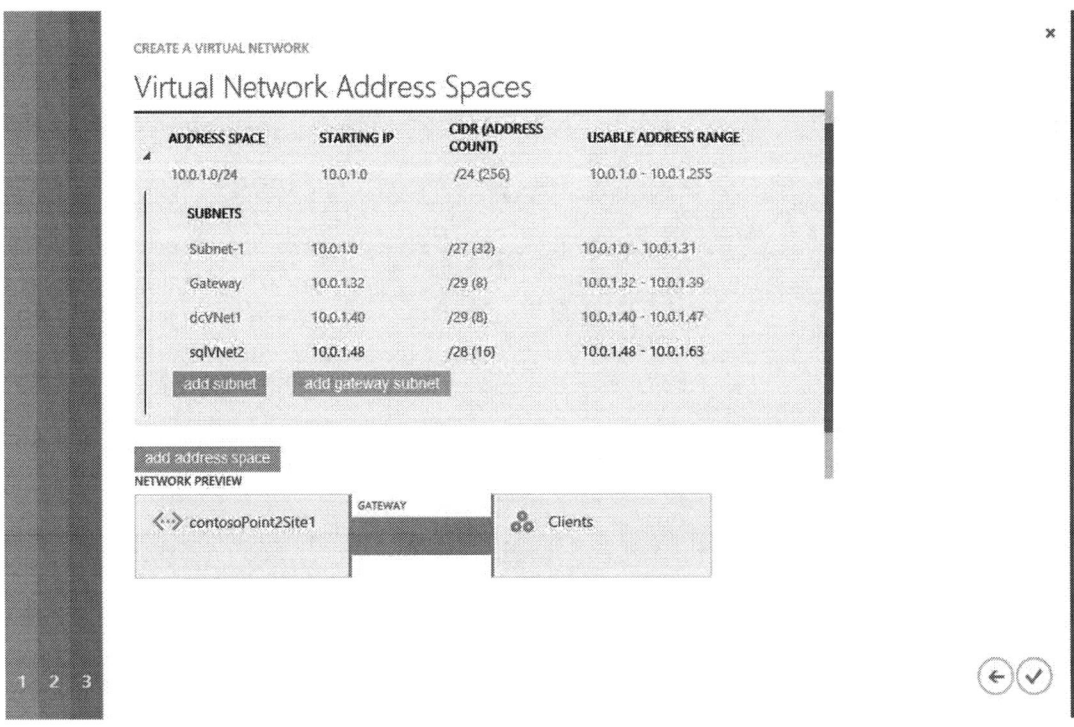

Figure 8-10. Final page to create the point-to-site configuration in the Virtual Network Wizard

8. Click the check mark in the lower-right corner complete the wizard.

9. In the Network pane view in your Azure Portal, select the point-to-site network that you just created, to view the dashboard.

10. At the bottom of the page, click Create Gateway (see Figure 8-11).

Figure 8-11. Point-to-site configuration from the dashboard view of the Azure Network pane

11. A gray pop-up window asks, "Do you want to create a gateway …?" as shown in Figure 8-12. Click Yes.

Figure 8-12. Pop-up window to create a gateway

It will take 15–20 minutes for the gateway creation to be completed. (Icons in the lower-right corner show the status of this process.)

Part 1 creates and enables a point-to-site VPN connection from the Azure Portal, but it is not the end of the entire process. Part 2 finalizes the secure client connection into Azure. The steps to do so are shown in the following exercise.

CREATE CERTIFICATES AND ENABLE THE CLIENT: PART 2

To authenticate the VPN client to the point-to-site VPN that you created in Part 1, you need to create an X.509 certificate root certificate that will be uploaded to the Azure point-to-site VNet. For lab purposes, you can use a self-signed certificate. The following steps describe how to create a certificate using the makecert utility that's available with the free version of Visual Studio Express 2013 for Windows Desktop:

■ **Note** Microsoft recommends using a self-signed certificate for lab testing only. When configuring point-to-site VPN connections in a production environment, we recommend purchasing a public certificate from a certificate provider. For testing, you can use the makecert utility that's available with Microsoft Visual Studio Express 2013 for Windows Desktop, which you can download from www.visualstudio.com/products/visual-studio-express-vs.aspx.

---

1. To create a self-signed certificate using makecert.exe, follow these steps:

    a. Download Visual Studio Express 2013 for Windows Desktop from www.visualstudio.com/products/visual-studio-express-vs.aspx, and install it by following the onscreen prompts.

    b. Once the Visual Studio Express for Windows Desktop installation is complete, open a developer command prompt for Visual Studio 2013.

    c. Run the following cmdlet, which creates the certificate in the CurrentUser personal certificate store and creates a corresponding .cer file and places it in the working folder:

    ```
    makecert -sky exchange -r -n "CN=P2SRootCert" -pe -a sha1 -len 2048
    -ss My "P2SRootCert.cer"
    ```

    d. While still in the Visual Studio cmd window, run the following cmd to create the required client certificate in the CurrentUser personal certificate store:

    ```
    makecert.exe -n "CN=P2SClientCert1" -pe -sky exchange -m 96 -ss My
    -in "P2SRootCert" -is my -a sha1
    ```

2. With all the necessary certificates created, go back to the Azure Portal. On the Networks tab, select the point-to-site VPN network you just created:

    a. If you wish to install the client certificate on multiple computers, export the client certificate from the computer on which it was created. You can use the following PowerShell cmdlet to do so:

    ```
    Get-ChildItem -Path cert:\CurrentUser\My
    ```

b. First you need to find the certificate's thumbprint. From the results, find the certificate that you created, and copy the thumbprint. Paste the thumbprint of the certificate into the next cmdlet:

```
$cert = (Get-ChildItem -Path cert:\CurrentUser\My\<Thumbprint>)

Export-Certificate -Cert $cert -FilePath c:\temp\certs\ P2SClientCert1.cer
```

c. You can now take the .cer file and install it on other computers that need to connect to your point-to-site VPN.

3. From the dashboard view, select the Certificates tab. Click Upload A Root Certificate to upload your certificate file to the Azure Portal.

4. On the Upload A Certificate page, browse to the location where the .cer file was created. Select the certificate file, and click Open. Click the check mark to upload the file.

5. From the dashboard view of the point-to-site VNet that you created in Part 1, in the quick glance menu on the right side of the Azure Portal screen, as shown in Figure 8-13, download the VPN client configuration package:

```
Download the 32-bit Client VPN Package
Download the 64-bit Client VPN Package
```

Supported operation systems include the following:

- Windows 7 (32/64)

- Windows Server 2008R2 (64)

- Windows 8 / 8.1 (32/64)

- Server 2012 / R2

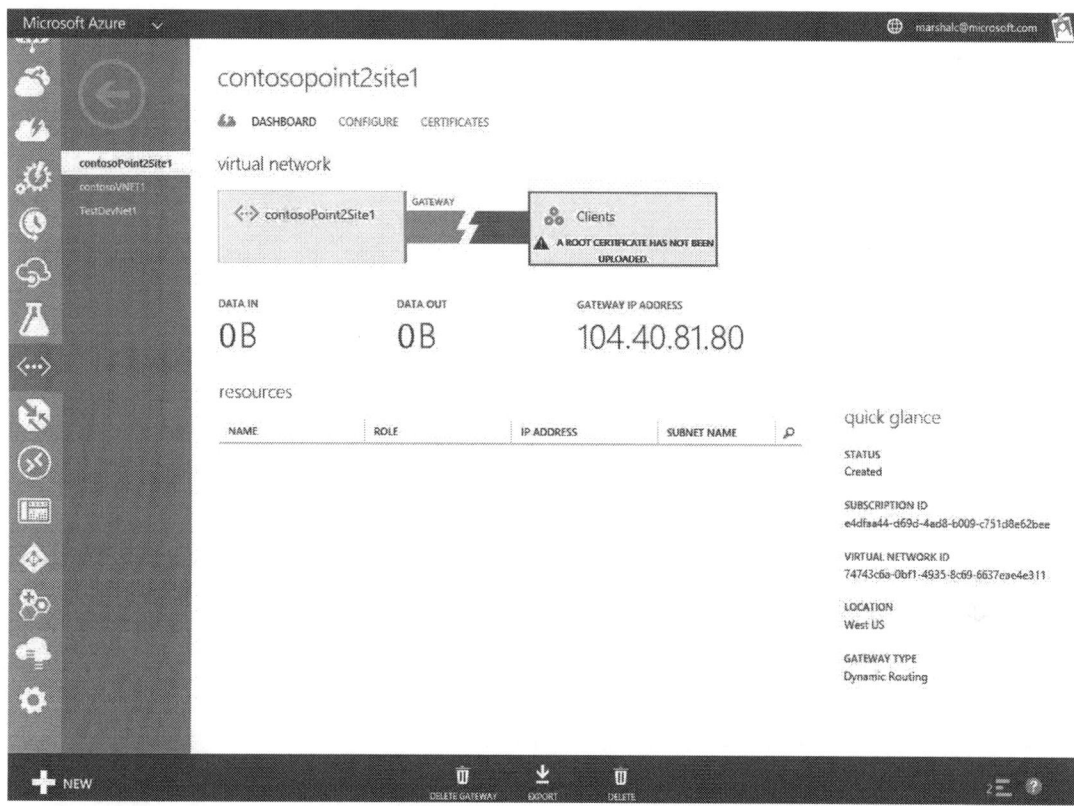

Figure 8-13. *Dashboard view of the Network pane in Azure Portal*

6. When prompted, choose to save the file on your local computer. When the download completes, run the .exe program on each client computer to connect to the Azure point-to-site VPN.

■ **Tip** The VPN client package is not signed by Microsoft or Azure. You can use the free SignTool to customize the package. This utility can be found at http://msdn.microsoft.com/en-us/library/windows/desktop/ aa387764(v=vs.85).aspx

---

7. After the package is installed, navigate to the VPN connection and connect. A message about the certificate appears. Click Continue to use elevated privileges. Click Connect. Your client is now connected through your Azure VPN point-to-site connection.

Open a command prompt, and run the IPCONFIG/ALL command to show the Azure VNet connection. Your results should be similar to the following:

```
PPP adapter VNetEast:

   Connection-specific DNS Suffix  . :
   Description . . . . . . . . . . . : contosoPoint2Site1
   Physical Address. . . . . . . . . :
   DHCP Enabled. . . . . . . . . . . : No
   Autoconfiguration Enabled . . . . : Yes
   IPv4 Address. . . . . . . . . . . : 10.0.1.4(Preferred)
   Subnet Mask . . . . . . . . . . . : 255.255.255.255
   Default Gateway . . . . . . . . . :
   NetBIOS over Tcpip. . . . . . . . : Enabled
```

Site-to-Site Connections

Using a site-to-site VPN allows the extension from your on-premises VNet to connect to your Azure VNet. This connection supports local on-premises resources, such as DNS and database servers, using the resources in Azure. The site-to-site VPN uses an on-premises VPN gateway device, which supports static and/or dynamic routing to connect to the Azure VNet gateway. A two-part procedure is required to complete the site-to-site connection.

In Part 1, you use a wizard in the Portal to configure the site-to-site connection in the Azure network. In Part 2, you complete the connection by creating a VNet gateway device in Azure and then download the configuration file to use with your on-premises VPN hardware.

■ **Caution**   Network engineers or the IT department normally manage on-premises gateway devices. Configuration of a gateway requires not only access to these devices, but also the experience to edit the configurations. If you do not currently manage these or other networking components, seek help from your peers to complete these exercises.

The steps to complete the site-to-site VPN connection include the following:

- Planning the IP subnet

- Enabling the Azure site-to-site connection

- Configuring the on-premises VPN device (public IPv4 IP)

- Enabling the gateway device

CONFIGURE A SITE-TO-SITE CONNECTION: PART 1

1. In the Azure Management Portal, click New in the lower-left corner.

2. Choose Network Services ➤ Virtual Network ➤ Custom Create to start the wizard.

3. On the Virtual Network Details screen, enter the name for the VNet and choose a location, as shown in Figure 8-14. Click the arrow in the bottom-right corner to continue.

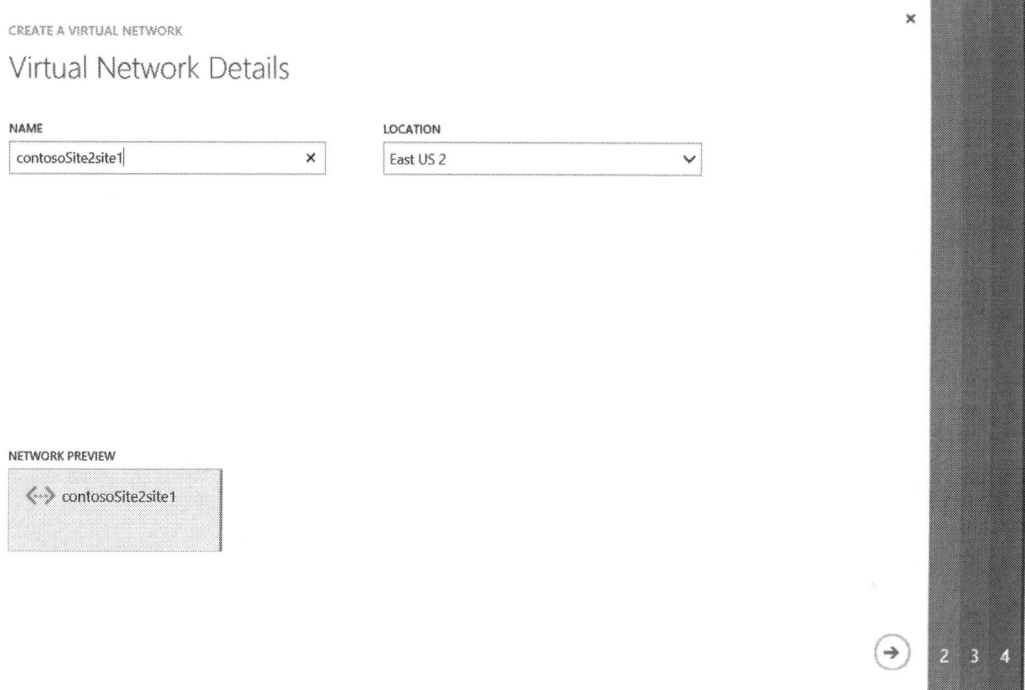

Figure 8-14. *Virtual Network Wizard to create site-to-site VPN*

4. On the DNS Servers and VPN Connectivity page, click the check box to configure a site-to-site VPN, as shown in Figure 8-15. As with the configuration of a point-to-site VPN, this does not create a DNS server; rather, it enables editing for on-premises DNS lookup. In this example, leave the DNS option blank. Click the arrow in the bottom-right corner to continue.

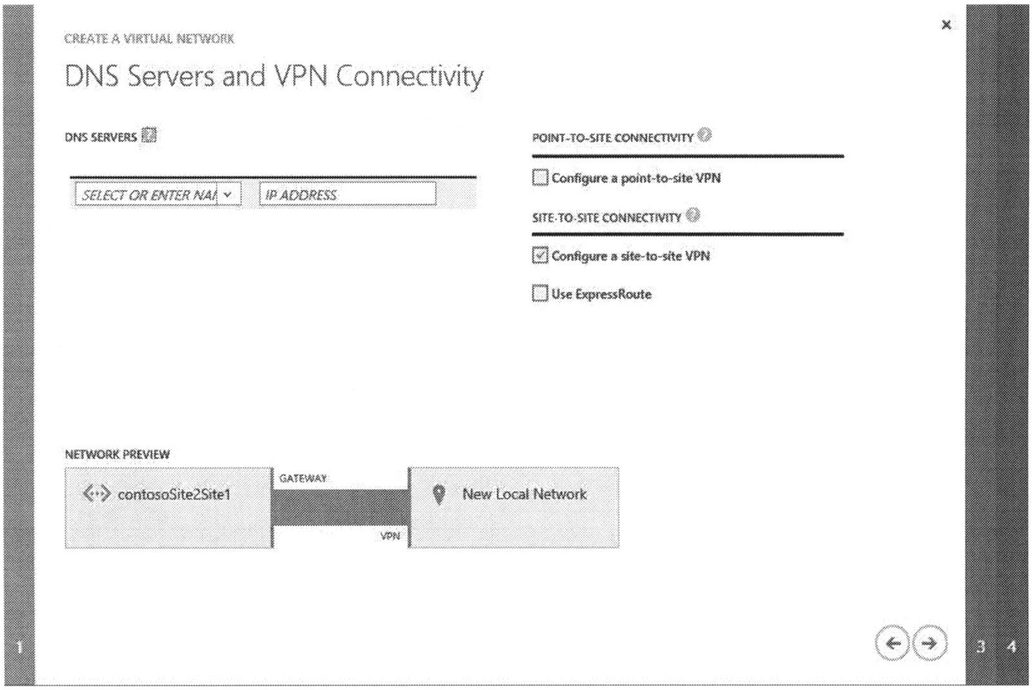

Figure 8-15. *Option to configure a site-to-site VPN in the Virtual Network Wizard*

5. On the Site-to-Site Connectivity page, enter a friendly name for your on-premises datacenter, the IP address information of your on-premises datacenter, and the external-facing IP address of your VPN device. For this example, enter the IP address 10.0.0.0 to complete the wizard, as shown in Figure 8-16. Click the arrow in the bottom-right corner to continue.

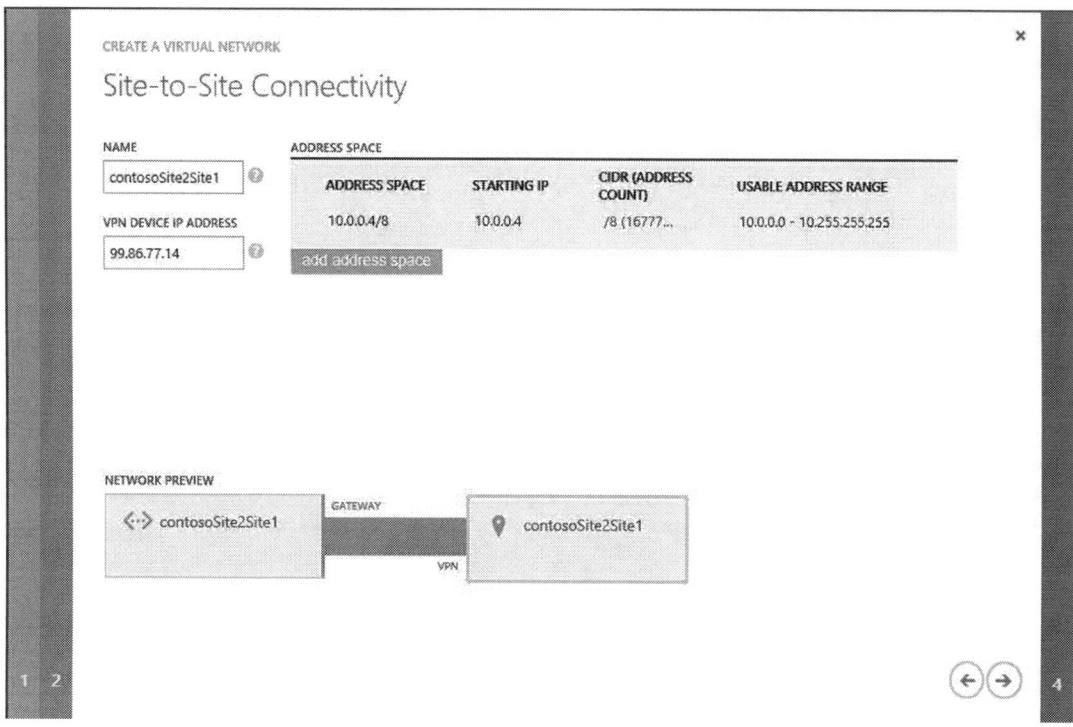

Figure 8-16. *Enter the VPN device IP address and address space in the Virtual Network Wizard*

The Virtual Network Address Spaces page shown in Figure 8-17 lists the Azure dynamic IP addresses (DIPs) discussed earlier in this chapter. The gateway is a required configuration: it must be added to the subnet to allow communication from on-premises networks to Azure VNets. Click the check mark in the bottom-right corner to complete these steps. Azure takes 15–20 minutes to create the VNet configuration.

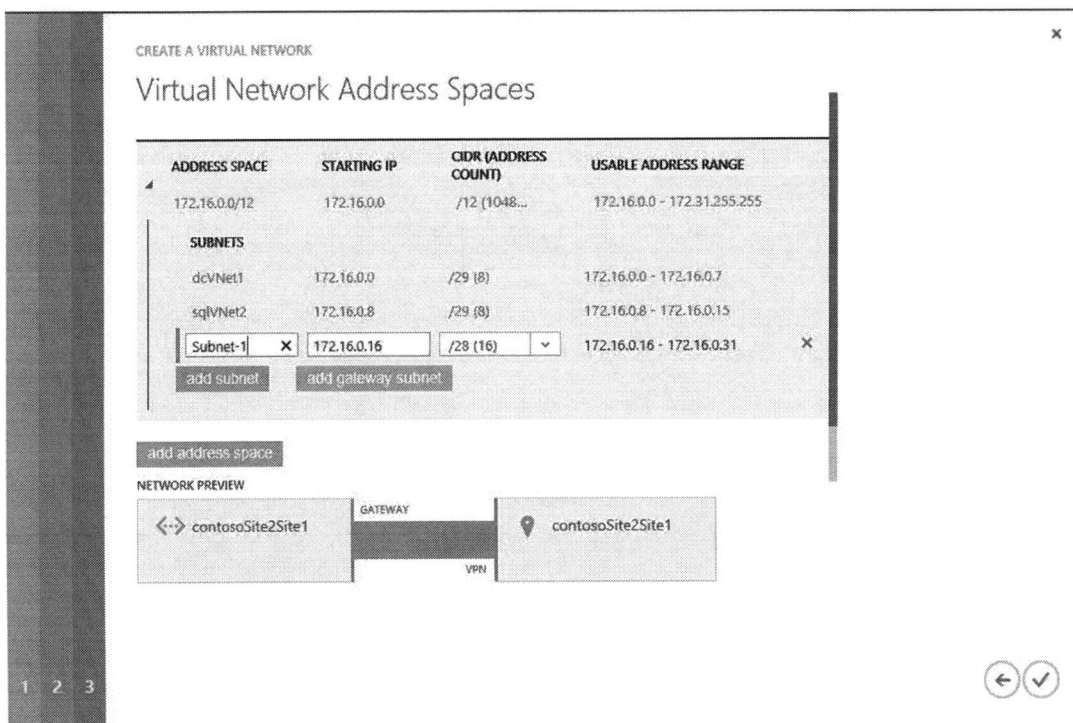

Figure 8-17. *Final page to create a site-to-site VPN in the Virtual Network Wizard*

This chapter has addressed using Azure VNet configurations, both in the cloud and extended into your on-premises datacenter. Network architects will agree that each of these configuration procedures is similar to that of physical networking on site.

In Part 2, you configure the VNet gateway both in Azure and on-premises in your datacenter. The gateway device in Azure supports connections using two types of routing: static and dynamic. If you would like to connect more VPNs to the end device, choose dynamic routing.

■ **Tip** Microsoft has worked diligently with many hardware OEMs to provide support for an ever-growing list of devices and OS versions, including Cisco, Juniper, Brocade, Barracuda, F5, Dell, and others. You can find the latest list of supported vendors at http://msdn.microsoft.com/en-us/library/azure/jj156075.aspx.

CONFIGURE A SITE-TO-SITE CONNECTION: PART 2

1. From the Azure Management Portal, return to the Network page to validate that the VNet was created. Click the name of the VNet, as shown in Figure 8-18.

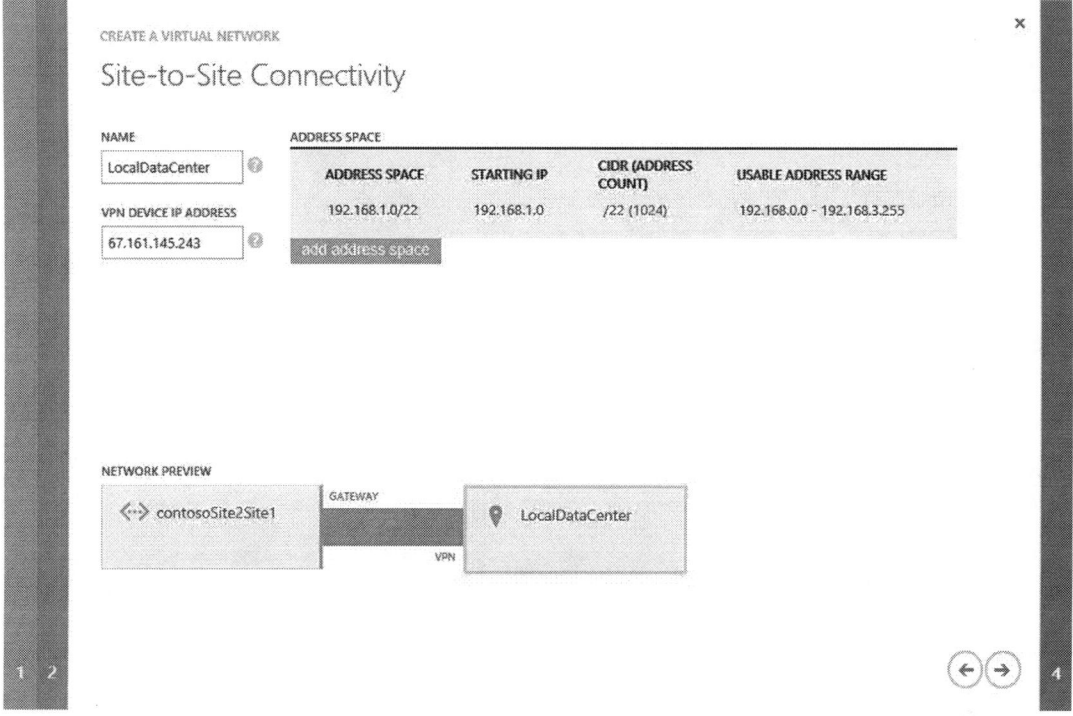

Figure 8-18. *Validating a site-to-site VPN using the Virtual Network Wizard*

Your view changes to the dashboard view. The VNet does not yet have a gateway configured, as shown in Figure 8-19.

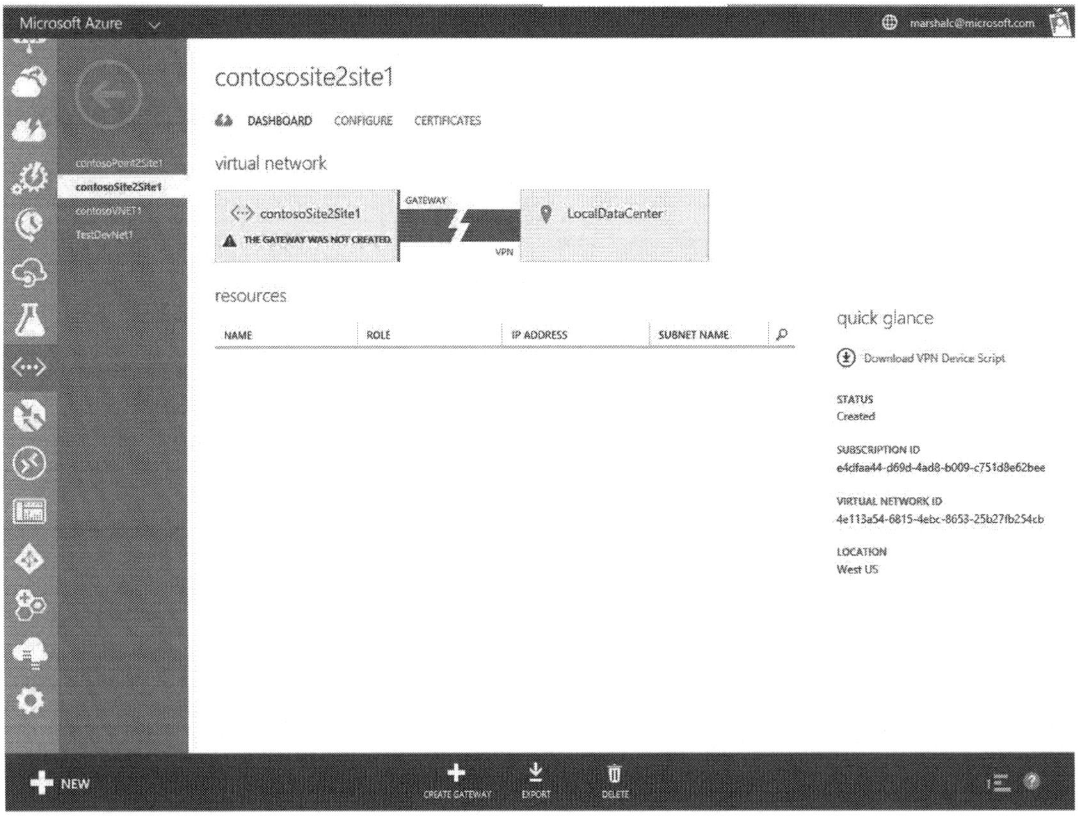

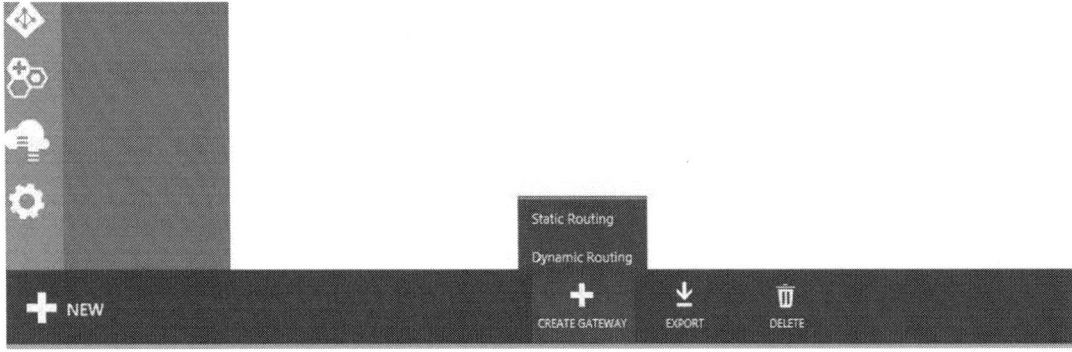

Figure 8-19. *Dashboard view of the Network pane in Azure Portal, showing that a gateway has not been configured for the VNet*

2. At the bottom of the page, click Create Gateway, as shown in Figure 8-20. Choose Static Routing or Dynamic Routing, based on your device support.

Figure 8-20. *Pop-up menu to create a routing gateway*

3. A pop-up asks if you want to configure the gateway, as shown in Figure 8-21. Click Yes. It may take 15–20 minutes to complete the gateway configuration.

Figure 8-21. Pop-up window confirming that you want to create a gateway

After the gateway device is created in Azure, there are many network components for which you need to collect information to supply to the supported VPN device in your local datacenter.

4. Click the Manage Key option at the bottom of the dashboard to copy the keys to the clipboard. Save the keys locally.

5. While in the dashboard view, in the quick glance section, select Download VPN Device Script. Select the vendor, platform, operating system, and version, as shown in Figure 8-22.

Download a VPN Device Configuration Script

Download a configuration script to help configure your local VPN device settings so that you can connect with the virtual network gateway.

VENDOR

| Cisco Systems, Inc. | ∨ |

PLATFORM

| ASA 5500 Series Adaptive Security Appliances | ∨ |

OPERATING SYSTEM

| ASA Software 8.3 | ∨ |

Figure 8-22. Options for downloading the VPN device on the local network

When prompted, choose to save the downloaded file to your local computer. After the download completes, this file is required to configure your on-premises hardware device, as shown in Figure 8-23.

Do you want to open or save **VpnDeviceScript.cfg** (3.77 KB) from **manage.windowsazure.com**?   Open   Save ▼   Cancel   ×

Figure 8-23. *Pop-up windows to save the configuration script based on the device option chosen*

6. Use the configuration information to complete the on-premises device configuration of the VPN appliance.

7. After the VPN device is configured, in the Dashboard view in the Azure Portal, you can validate that the network connection is made into Azure. Notice the traffic from Azure to your on-premises network.

■ **Tip**   If you do not see IP traffic flowing from on-site into Azure, check to verify the gateway IP address both in Azure and on-site. Also verify the subnet address range of your local networks.

The final topic in this chapter, multiple Azure locations, takes you through the combination of the previous three VNet configurations. Figure 8-24 portrays multiple datacenters connecting to multiple Azure locations.

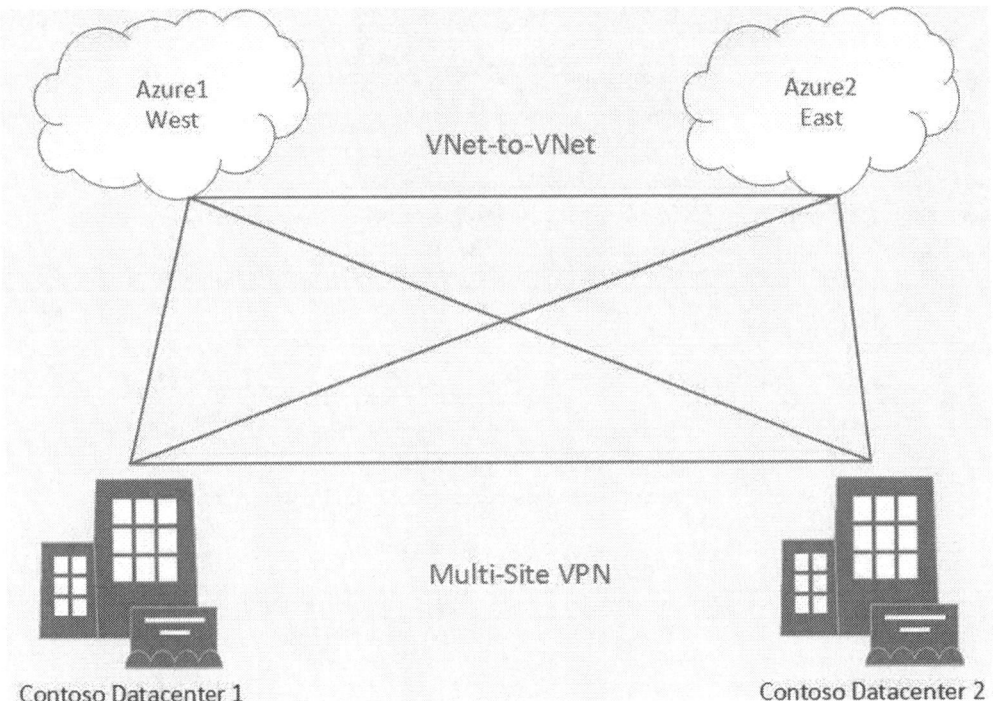

Figure 8-24. *Multiple datacenters connecting to multiple Azure locations*

Think about a business that uses two Azure locations to maintain redundancy or to reach another set of customers in a different geographic region. You can also use this type of connection if you have two on-premises datacenters and would like to connect to two Azure locations. Note that this configuration requires you to have selected a dynamic routing VPN option.

■ **Tip** If you selected static routing earlier, you can change to dynamic routing without removing any of the other configuration components by deleting the existing gateway and re-creating it with the other option. To help you decide what type of routing gateway you should choose, see the article "About VPN Devices and Gateways for Virtual Network Connectivity" at `https://msdn.microsoft.com/en-ca/library/azure/jj156075.aspx`.

Using this type of advanced connection into Azure and to multiple Azure locations provides redundancy for networks and Azure resources. To complete a multi-site VPN connection, you use XML files. The process currently is not completed using only the Azure Portal. This may change in the future, but today you'll create this configuration manually, as described in the following exercise. Many of the steps required for this configuration are based on the steps covered previously in this chapter.

CREATE AN AZURE MULTI-SITE VPN

This exercise uses Contoso locations to connect multiple Azure locations to two Contoso datacenters:

1. Create a site-to-site VPN, and select dynamic routing. Refer to the steps in the exercise "Configure a Site-to-Site Connection: Part 2."

2. In the Azure Portal, on the Network Management page, select the option to export the VNet configuration files. Click the check mark in the lower-right corner to proceed.

3. Save the `NetworkConfig.xml` file.

4. Open the `NetworkConfig.xml` file in an XML editor. The information should be similar to the following configuration file. In this case, you have two Contoso datacenters and two Azure locations:

```
<NetworkConfiguration xmlns:xsd="http://www.w3.org/2001/XMLSchema"
xmlns:xsi="http://www.w3.org/2001/XMLSchema-
instance" xmlns="http://schemas.microsoft.com/ServiceHosting/2011/07/
NetworkConfiguration">
  <VirtualNetworkConfiguration>
    <LocalNetworkSites>
      <LocalNetworkSite name="AzureSite1">
        <AddressSpace>
          <AddressPrefix>10.11.0.0/24</AddressPrefix>
          <AddressPrefix>10.12.0.0/24</AddressPrefix>
        </AddressSpace>
        <VPNGatewayAddress>131.2.3.4</VPNGatewayAddress>
      </LocalNetworkSite>
```

```
        <LocalNetworkSite name="AzureSite2">
          <AddressSpace>
            <AddressPrefix>10.12.0.0/24</AddressPrefix>
            <AddressPrefix>10.13.0.0/24</AddressPrefix>
          </AddressSpace>
          <VPNGatewayAddress>131.4.5.6</VPNGatewayAddress>
        </LocalNetworkSite>
      </LocalNetworkSites>
      <VirtualNetworkSites>
        <VirtualNetworkSite name="AzureVNet1" AffinityGroup="WestAfinGp1">
          <AddressSpace>
            <AddressPrefix>10.22.0.0/24</AddressPrefix>
            <AddressPrefix>10.23.0.0/24</AddressPrefix>
          </AddressSpace>
          <Subnets>
            <Subnet name="Azure-FE">
              <AddressPrefix>10.22.0.0/25</AddressPrefix>
            </Subnet>
            <Subnet name="Azure-BE">
              <AddressPrefix>10.22.0/25</AddressPrefix>
            </Subnet>
            <Subnet name="GatewaySubnet">
              <AddressPrefix>10.22.2.0/29</AddressPrefix>
            </Subnet>
          </Subnets>
          <Gateway>
            <ConnectionsToLocalNetwork>
              <LocalNetworkSiteRef name="AzureSite1">
                <Connection type="IPsec" />
              </LocalNetworkSiteRef>
            </ConnectionsToLocalNetwork>
          </Gateway>
        </VirtualNetworkSite>
      </VirtualNetworkSites>
    </VirtualNetworkConfiguration>
</NetworkConfiguration>
```

Edit the ConnectionsToLocalNetwork section, and add the multiple-site reference
to the network configuration file. In this case, you make the following two edits:

```
<Gateway>
        <ConnectionsToLocalNetwork>
          <LocalNetworkSiteRef name="AzureSite1"><Connection type="IPsec" />
          </LocalNetworkSiteRef>
        </ConnectionsToLocalNetwork>
      </Gateway>

    <Gateway>
        <ConnectionsToLocalNetwork>
          <LocalNetworkSiteRef name="AzureSite1"><Connection type="IPsec" />
          </LocalNetworkSiteRef>
```

```
    <LocalNetworkSiteRef name="AzureSite2"><Connection type="IPsec" />
    </LocalNetworkSiteRef>
  </ConnectionsToLocalNetwork>
</Gateway>
```

5. Save the edited version of the `NetworkConfig.xml` file. From inside the Azure Portal, navigate to Network Services and Virtual Network. Select the Import option. This import action reads the XML file changes and creates the additional network components.

6. New VPN tunnels are created and pass traffic for IP use. However, you need to use PowerShell to get the IPsec security keys for each tunnel and store them in a secure location. Use the following commands twice, because this exercise adds two locations and two datacenters:

```
PS C:\> Get-AzureVnetGatewayKey -VNetName "contosoVNet1"
-LocalNetworkSiteName "contosoDC1"

PS C:\> Get-AzureVnetGatewayKey -VNetName "contosoVNet2"
-LocalNetworkSiteName "contosoDC2"
```

7. Use PowerShell once more to verify that your connections were created correctly. Use the following command:

```
PS C:\> Get-AzureVnetConnection
```

The results should be similar to the following:

```
PS C:\Users\marshall\Azure> Get-AzureVnetConnection -VNetName
contosVNet1

ConnectivityState          : Connected
EgressBytesTransferred     : 661530
IngressBytesTransferred    : 519207
LastConnectionEstablished  : 12/12/2014 8:12:30 AM
LastEventID                : 23401
LastEventMessage           : The connectivity state for the local network
                             site 'AzureSite1' changed from Not
Connected to Connected.
LastEventTimeStamp         : 12/12/2014 8:12:30 AM
LocalNetworkSiteName       : Site1
OperationDescription       : Get-AzureVNetConnection
OperationId                : 7f68a8e6-51e9-9db4-88c2-16b8067fed7f
OperationStatus            : Succeeded

ConnectivityState          : Connected
EgressBytesTransferred     : 789398
IngressBytesTransferred    : 143908
LastConnectionEstablished  : 12/12/2014 8:12:30 AM
LastEventID                : 23401
LastEventMessage           : The connectivity state for the local network
                             site 'AzureSite2' changed from Not
```

```
Connected to Connected.
LastEventTimeStamp      : 12/12/2014 8:12:30 AM
LocalNetworkSiteName    : Site2
OperationDescription    : Get-AzureVNetConnection
OperationId             : 7893b329-51e9-9db4-88c2-16b8067fed7f
OperationStatus         : Succeeded
```

ExpressRoute

Microsoft ExpressRoute takes advantage of the large number of partners that are Microsoft Network Service Providers to support connectivity from on-premises datacenters or co-locations into Azure. Figure 8-25 illustrates the traffic flow from an on-premises data center to Azure over an ExpressRoute connection.

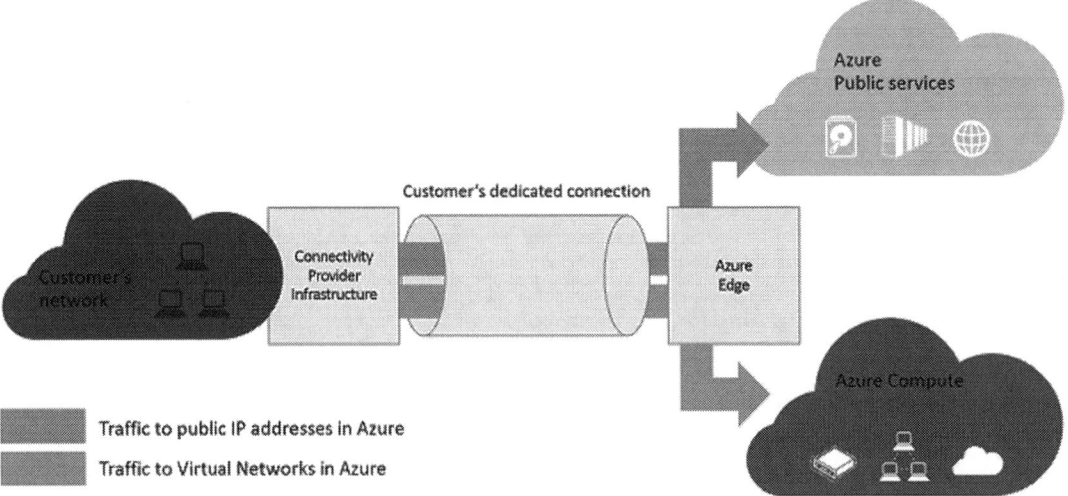

Figure 8-25. *ExpressRoute provides network connectivity with guaranteed bandwidth backed by an SLA*

Microsoft Network Service Providers support much greater bandwidth speeds and offer an SLA to support your business needs. Table 8-1 provides more detail about the ExpressRoute services.

Table 8-1. *A Few of the Microsoft Network Service Providers that Provide Microsoft Azure ExpressRoute Connectivity*

Properties	Network Providers	Exchange Providers
Supported service providers	Level 3, AT&T, Verizon, British Telecom, SingTel	Equinox, Level 3, TeleCityGroup
Bandwidth options	10Mbps, 50Mbps, 100Mbps, 500Mbps, 1Gbps	200Mbps, 500Mbps, 1Gbps, 10Gbps

---

▓ **Tip**   You can learn more about Microsoft security and compliance support at the Microsoft Azure Trust Center: `http://azure.microsoft.com/en-us/support/trust-center`.

Summary

This chapter introduced you to the many types of Microsoft Azure networking options and how they are virtually the same as their physical on-premises counterparts. Throughout the chapter, you were exposed to standard network connection components, such as IP addresses, IP subnets, network gateways, and VPNs.

In this chapter, you learned how to create many different types of Azure-to-Azure network connections (VNet-to-VNet connections). You went through the steps required to create a VNet connection from a client computer (point-to-site VNet connection). Finally, you learned to edit an XML file that used some of the other connection types to create multiple redundant connections. This multi-site VPN connection provides the largest number of connections from two or more datacenters to two or more Microsoft Azure locations.

The next chapter introduces you to identity management with Azure Active Directory, an Azure security feature. Security is a major focus of Microsoft Azure, and you learn more about Microsoft's Trustworthy Computing initiative.

CHAPTER 9

■ ■ ■

Identity Management with Azure Active Directory

Introducing Azure Active Directory

Azure Active Directory (AAD) is a service made available through Microsoft Azure for Microsoft cloud-based identity management and access capabilities. You can use this service to authenticate with other clouds. It is similar in function to Active Directory (AD), which is a service that runs in an on-premises datacenter on Windows Server.

AAD is the foundation for identity management in Office 365, and it can be used to provide single-sign on (SSO) access to more than 2,400 other cloud-based services such as Box, Dropbox for Business, and Salesforce, to name just a few.

Azure Active Directory Versions

AAD is available in three versions: Free, Basic, and Premium. The features of each version of AAD are included in the next higher level, as shown in Table 9-1.

Table 9-1. *AAD Features by Version*

Feature	Free	Basic	Premium
Price (per user)	Free	Contact your enterprise agreement representative.	Contact your enterprise agreement representative.
Directory as a service	✓	✓	✓
User and group management	✓	✓	✓
Directory objects	500K	Unlimited	Unlimited
End user access panel	✓	✓	✓
SSO for SaaS applications	10 applications / user	10 applications / user	Unlimited
Directory synchronization	✓	✓	✓
User-based access management and provisioning	✓	✓	✓
Basic security peports	✓	✓	✓

(*continued*)

Table 9-1. (*continued*)

Feature	Free	Basic	Premium
Logon/Access panel branding customization		✓	✓
Group-based access management and provisioning		✓	✓
Self-service password reset for cloud users		✓	✓
Self-service password reset for users with writeback to on-premises directories			✓
Self-service group management for cloud users			✓
Multifactor authentication (for cloud and on-premises applications)			✓
Advanced usage and security reports			✓
Microsoft Identity Manager server and iuser CAL			✓
Service-level agreement		99.90%	99.90%

With the Free version of AAD, you can manage user accounts that are cloud-based accounts or synchronized with your on-premises AD. You can also use the Free version to enable SSO with up to ten of the software as a service (SaaS) application providers with whom Microsoft has partnered.

AAD Basic Features

AAD Basic provides all the features that are available in the Free version and also introduces the ability to customize some of the pages with which users regularly interact. With the Basic version of AAD, you can customize the sign-in page and the access panel. This feature allows you to brand the portal with your company logo, which gives the service a personal look and feel.

The default sign-in page, shown in Figure 9-1, lets users access SaaS applications, such as when signing into Office 365.

Figure 9-1. *Default Office 365 sign-in page*

Figure 9-2 shows a customized Office 365 Portal sign-in page. Notice how support contact information is provided. Another common sign-in page configuration includes a legal disclaimer.

Figure 9-2. *Customized Office 365 sign-in page*

The access panel page in the Portal provides links to the SaaS applications to which a user has been granted access. You also get group-based access management and provisioning, which greatly simplifies the management of application access. By assigning access to SaaS-based applications to a single group, you only need to manage the membership of the group to provide access to the application to individual users.

The two biggest differences between the Free version and the Basic and Premium versions of AAD are the number of supported objects and the SLA. With the Free version, the default object quota is 150,000. It is possible, however, to go above this limit by contacting Azure support; they will increase the quota to a maximum of 500,000 on request. The Basic and Premium versions both support an unlimited number of objects. Also with the Free version, there is no SLA for the service; SLAs of 99.9% are available only when you purchase the Basic or Premium version of AAD.

AAD Premium Features

The highest level of AAD is the Premium version. With AAD Premium, Microsoft provides the following features in addition to those found in the Free and Basic versions.

Password Write-Back

Password write-back is an Azure Active Directory Synchronization Services (AAD Sync) tool feature that, when enabled, is used by your users to change a forgotten on-premises password in the cloud. It lets you configure your Azure tenant to write passwords back to your on-premises AD. When it's configured, it provides a simple cloud-based way for users to reset their on-premises passwords without needing to be in the office or call the helpdesk.

Password write-back is supported for resetting passwords for users regardless of whether you use Active Directory Federation Services (AD FS) or another federation technologies for SSO and whether you are using password synchronization. With password write-back, as long as the user accounts are synchronized into your AAD tenant, the on-premises passwords can be managed from the cloud.

Enabling password write-back does not change your on-premises AD password policies. In the same manner as a user changes their password on-premises, when a user resets their password, AAD ensures that it meets the on-premises AD policy before committing it to that directory.

Password write-back doesn't require any inbound firewall rules to work with your on-premises AD. It uses an Azure service bus relay as the communication channel into AD. This means you don't have to open any inbound ports on your firewall for this feature to work.

■ **Note**   Password write-back is not supported for user accounts that are members of protected groups in your on-premises AD. For example, members of the Domain Administrators security group can't use this feature.

Self-Service Group Management for Cloud Users

Self-service group management lets users create and manage security groups in AAD and provides them with the ability to request security group memberships, which can then be approved or denied by the owner of the group. By using self-service group management features, you can delegate daily control of group membership to people who understand the business need for membership requests.

A benefit of self-service group management is that it removes the burden of a group manager having to know who requires access to a group and who does not. For example, if you have many SaaS applications and use the access-management feature, by using self-service group management, users can submit requests to join groups as they need. The group owner then approves or denies the membership based on the business need for joining the group.

Multifactor Authentication (for Cloud and On-Premises Applications)

Azure *multifactor authentication (MFA)* provides a second level of security when signing into cloud-based or on-premises applications. When enabled, Azure MFA can be configured to verify a user's identity using a mobile app, a text message, or a call to a mobile or landline phone.

■ **Tip** Using a mobile device for MFA allows you to use this second level of authentication when signing in to Azure while working remotely.

You can use Azure MFA to secure cloud-based SaaS applications when authenticating with AAD or when using AD FS by configuring the AAD user account to require MFA. AAD security groups can also be configured to require MFA, which greatly simplifies its management, especially if you are also using the previously discussed self-service group management.

The MFA feature can also be used to secure on-premises applications. Doing so requires an MFA server to be installed and configured in your datacenter. MFA for on-premises applications provides the same MFA experience as Azure MFA when configured to provide a second layer of security to on-premises resources, such as IIS or AD.

When a user attempts to sign in to an on-premises application that has been configured to require a second level of authentication, the on-premises MFA server makes a call to the Azure MFA authentication service, which contacts the user by whatever method has been configured (mobile app, phone call, or text message).

Advanced Usage and Security Reports

All versions of AAD provide access and usage reporting to help administrators understand where potential security risks exist. The Azure Management Portal provides reports on five separate categories:

- Anomalous activity (an activity, such as a sign-in from an unknown source, that is inconsistent with what is normally expected)

- Activity logs

- Integrated applications

- Error reports

- User-specific reports

AAD Free Reports

AAD Premium offers more advanced reporting than the Free version. The following lists provide information about each of the reports that are available with AAD Premium:

- *Sign-Ins from Unknown Sources*: Indicates users who have successfully signed in to your Azure tenant while assigned a client IP address that is recognized by Microsoft as an anonymous proxy IP address. Users who want to hide their computer's IP address often use these proxies. They may be used for malicious purposes. For example, hackers sometimes use these proxies. This report shows the number of times a user has successfully signed in to your Azure tenant from that address and the proxy's IP address.

- *Sign-Ins After Multiple Failures*: Indicates users who have successfully signed in after multiple, consecutive failed sign-in attempts. It also shows you the number of consecutive failed sign-in attempts made prior to the successful sign-in and a timestamp associated with the first successful sign-in. Possible causes include

    - A user who forgot their password

    - A successful password-guessing brute-force attack

- *Sign-Ins from Multiple Geographies*: Indicates successful sign-ins by a user originating from different countries when the travel time between those countries would prohibit the user from actually signing in from both places. Results of this report show the successful sign-in events, together with the time between the sign-ins, the countries from which the sign-ins originated, and the estimated travel time between the two locations. Possible causes include

    - User sharing their password

    - User using a remote desktop to launch a web browser for sign-in

    - A hacker signed in to the account of a user from a different country

- *Application Dashboard*: Indicates cumulative sign-ins to the application by users in your organization over a selected time period. The chart on the dashboard page helps you identify usage trends for that application.

- *Account Provisioning Errors*: Lets you monitor errors that occur during the synchronization of accounts from SaaS applications to AAD.

- *Activity*: Shows the sign-in activity for a user. The report includes information such as the application signed in to, device used, IP address, and location. Microsoft does not collect the history for users who sign in with a Microsoft account.

- *Audit*: Shows a record of all audited events within the last 24 hours, last 7 days, or last 30 days. The report includes events in the following categories:

    - Credential updates

    - Device management

    - Directory synchronization

    - Domain management

    - Group management

    - Partner administration

    - Policy management (MFA)

    - Role changes

    - User account changes

    - User licensing

    - User, group, and contact management

AAD Premium Reports

The AAD reports details the following:

- *Sign-Ins from IP Addresses with Suspicious Activity*: Includes sign-in attempts that have been executed from IP addresses where suspicious activity has been noted. Suspicious activity includes multiple failed sign-in attempts from the same IP address over a short period of time and other activity deemed suspicious, possibly indicating that a hacker has been trying to sign in from this IP address. The results of this report show sign-in attempts that originated from an IP address where the suspicious activity was noted, together with the timestamp associated with the sign-in.

- *Irregular Sign-In Activity*: Includes sign-ins that have been identified as irregular by the Azure machine-learning algorithms. Reasons for marking a sign-in attempt as irregular include unexpected sign-in locations or time of day and locations that could be an indication that a hacker has been trying to sign in using this account. The machine-learning algorithm classifies events as *irregular* or *suspicious*, where *suspicious* indicates a higher likelihood of a security breach. The results of this report show these sign-ins, together with the classification, the location, and a timestamp associated with each sign-in.

- *Sign-Ins from Possibly Infected Devices*: Shows sign-ins from devices on which malware (malicious software) may be running. A possible cause may be users with anomalous sign-in activity. Microsoft Azure correlates IP addresses of sign-ins against IP addresses from which an attempt was made to contact a malware server. Use this report when you want to view all user accounts for which anomalous sign-in activity has been identified. This report includes data from all other anomalous activity reports. The results show you details about the user, the reason why the sign-in event was flagged as anomalous, the date and time, and other relevant information about the event.

- *Users with Anomalous Sign-In Activity*: Lists accounts that have been flagged as having anomalous sign-ins. Anomalous sign-in activity includes sign-ins from unknown locations, multiple failed login attempts, sign-ins from more than one location, and sign-ins that are outside of the usual time of day.

- *Application Usage: Summary*: Shows summary usage data for all the SaaS applications in your directory. This report is based on the number of times users have clicked the application in the Access Panel.

- *Application Usage: Detailed*: Provides information on how often a specific SaaS application is being used. Like the Application Usage: Summary report, this report is based on the number of times users have clicked the application in the Access Panel.

- *Devices*: Shows the IP address and geographical location of devices that a specific user has used to access Azure AD.

- *Groups Activity*: Provides information on all the activity for the self-service managed groups in your directory.

- *Password Reset Registration Activity*: Shows all the password-reset registrations that have occurred in your organization.

- *Password Reset Activity*: Shows all password-reset attempts (both successful and failed) that have occurred in your organization.

Service-Level Agreement

Microsoft offers a financially backed service-level agreement (SLA) for AAD Premium customers for Azure services. Table 9-2 shows the financial credit for which Azure customers may be eligible based on the amount of time the service is unavailable.

Table 9-2. *AAD Service-Level Agreement Credit Scale*

Monthly Uptime Percentage	Service Credit
<99.9%	25%
<99%	50%
<95%	100%

The SLA is available on each of the following Azure services:

- Active Directory
- API Management
- Automation
- Backup
- BizTalk Services
- Cache
- CDN
- Cloud Services
- ExpressRoute
- HDInsight
- Media Services
- Mobile Services
- Multifactor Authentication
- RemoteApp
- Scheduler
- Service Bus
- Site Recovery
- SQL Database
- Storage
- StorSimple
- Traffic Manager
- Virtual Machines

- Virtual Network

- Visual Studio Online

- Web sites

The monthly recovery time objective (RTO) and SLA for on-premises-to-Azure failovers for the site recovery service includes an additional metric for determining the amount of credit for which you could be eligible. The formula for determining this credit is shown in Table 9-3.

Table 9-3. *AAD Recovery Time Objective Schedule*

Protected Instance	Monthly Recovery Time Objective	Service Credit
Unencrypted	> 4 hours	100%
Encrypted	> 6 hours	100%

The full Azure SLA document is available for download at www.microsoft.com/en-us/download. Search for "Microsoft Azure SLA" at the Microsoft download site, and download the most current version of the document.

Adding and Managing Accounts in Azure Active Directory

AAD provides a great deal of flexibility in terms of adding and managing accounts. Adding accounts to AAD can be accomplished in a few ways.

MANUALLY CREATING USER ACCOUNTS

The first and most basic way to add an account to AAD is to do so manually in the Azure Portal. To add user accounts to AAD, do the following:

1. Open the Azure Management Portal, click the Active Directory link, and then click the directory to which you wish to add the user, as shown in Figure 9-3.

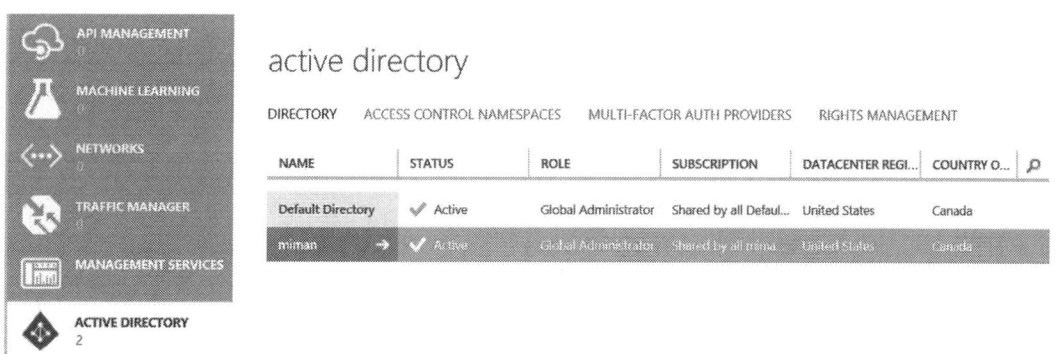

Figure 9-3. *AD domains*

2. In the directory Management Portal, click the Users tab, as shown in Figure 9-4.

Figure 9-4. Users tab

3. In the Users Management Portal at the bottom of the page, click Add User as shown in Figure 9-5.

Figure 9-5. Add User button

4. In the Tell Us About This User window, shown in Figure 9-6, select New User In Your Organization.

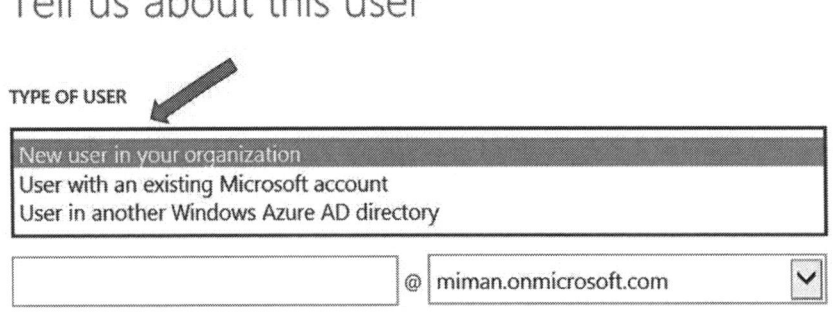

Figure 9-6. Selecting the user type

5. Enter a user name, as shown in Figure 9-7. The user name may only contain alphanumeric characters. Spaces and symbols are not valid characters.

After entering a user name, select the appropriate domain for the user. If you have added a *vanity domain* (also known as a *custom domain name*, such as contoso.com) to your Azure tenant, you have a default domain that ends in `.onmicrosoft.com` as well as your own domain. Once all of this information is set, click the arrow to advance to the next step.

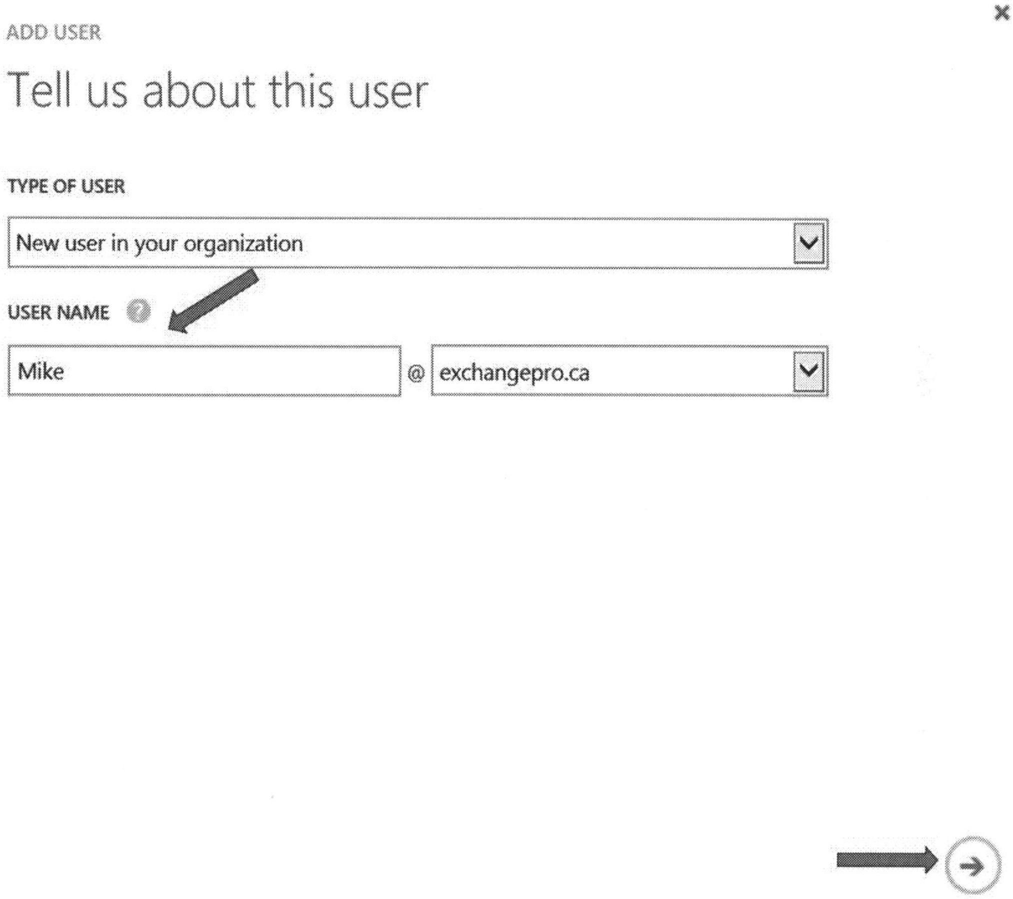

✕

ADD USER

Tell us about this user

TYPE OF USER

New user in your organization ⌄

USER NAME ?

Mike @ exchangepro.ca ⌄

→

Figure 9-7. Adding the user name and selecting a domain

6. At this point, you have the option to assign roles to the new user. As shown in Figure 9-8, there are many roles from which to choose. For more information about Azure administrator roles, see the MSDN article "Assigning Administrator Roles in Azure AD," at `http://msdn.microsoft.com/en-us/library/azure/dn468213.aspx`.

ROLE
User
Global Administrator
Billing Administrator
Service Administrator
User Administrator
Password Administrator

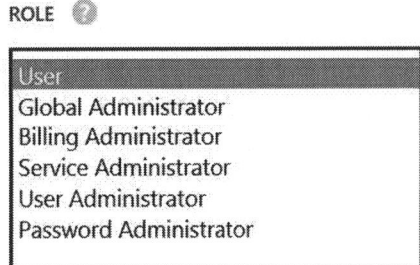

Figure 9-8. *Available Azure roles*

7. Also at this point in the new user-creation process, you have the option to enforce MFA for this new user, as shown in Figure 9-9. This chapter doesn't go too deeply into MFA, as it is discussed further in the next chapter.

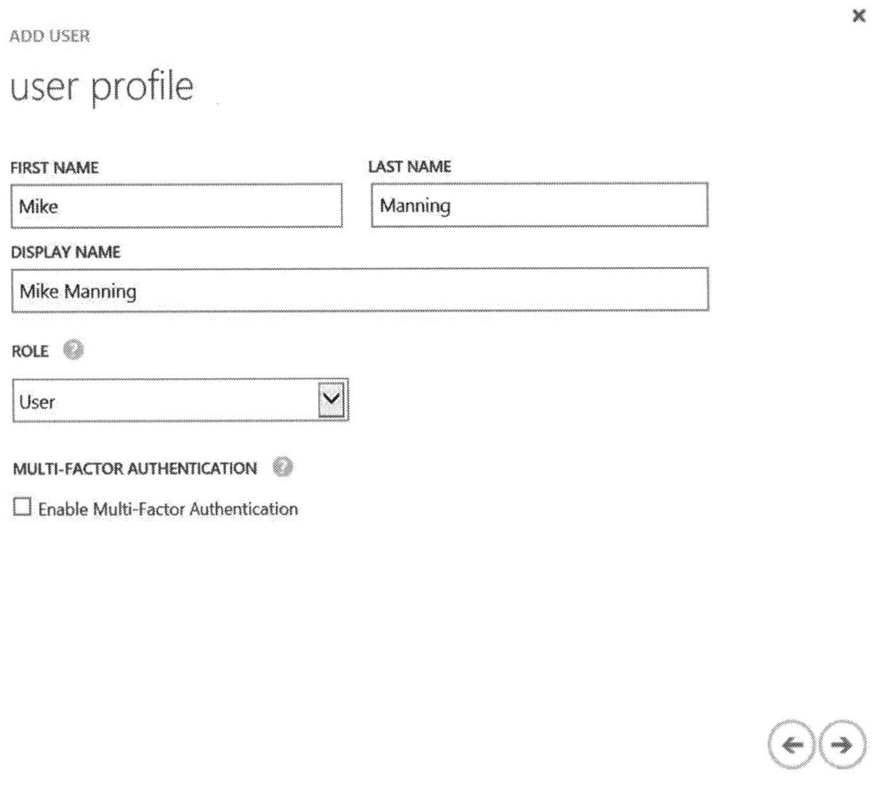

ADD USER
user profile
FIRST NAME
Mike
LAST NAME
Manning
DISPLAY NAME
Mike Manning
ROLE
User
MULTI-FACTOR AUTHENTICATION
Enable Multi-Factor Authentication

Figure 9-9. *Filling in the user profile information and selecting a role*

8. After completing all the necessary fields, you can create the user account. Clicking the create button, as shown in Figure 9-10, generates the user account and assigns it a temporary password.

ADD USER

Get temporary password

The new user 'Mike@exchangepro.ca' will be assigned a temporary password that must be changed on first sign in. To display the temporary password and to create the account, click Create.

Figure 9-10. *Creating the user account*

9. With the user account and password created, as shown in Figure 9-11, you have the option to record the password in a spreadsheet or other file. You also have the options to e-mail the password to a user account or to an administrator so that it can be shared with the user at a later time.

✕

ADD USER

Get temporary password

Successfully created user 'Mike@exchangepro.ca' with the following new password

NEW PASSWORD

| Jazo8052 | 📋 |

SEND PASSWORD IN EMAIL

The password will be sent in clear text

Maximum of five email addresses separated by semi-colons.

Figure 9-11. *Displaying the temporary password*

Bulk User Creation

Adding users manually into AAD is convenient and simple, but it can be very time-consuming if there are a large number of users to be added. In cases where hundreds or even thousands of users need to be added in a single event, importing user accounts from a .csv file is quick and easy.

The bulk import option is not available in the Azure Portal or with Azure PowerShell. To perform these steps, a subscription to Office 365 is required. This book does not cover Office 365, but for the purposes of this exercise, you require an Office 365 subscription. You can obtain a trial Office 365 subscription at https://products.office.com/en-us/business/office-365-enterprise-e3-business-software.

■ **Note** If you had a previous Office 365 trial subscription that has expired, it is recommended that you create a new one to complete this exercise.

It is assumed that you already have an Azure subscription. If you need to sign up for an Office 365 trial tenant as well, you can use the same ID that you use to manage Azure. Office 365 and Azure share the same AD space, so when you add users via the Office 365 bulk-import processes, the accounts will also appear in your Azure Portal under the Users tab in the Domains window.

After you create your Office 365 tenant, you can use the bulk-import process through Windows PowerShell. To do so, you first need to download and install the Azure Active Directory Module for Windows PowerShell cmdlets (pronounced *command-lets*). These cmdlets let you perform and automate user- and domain-management functions with AAD.

The first step in using the AAD PowerShell module is to install it on a computer that will be used for AAD management. The Azure AD Module is supported in Windows 8.1, Windows 8, Windows 7, Windows Server 2012 R2, Windows Server 2012, and Windows Server 2008 R2. The default versions of .NET Framework and Windows PowerShell are required to be installed on the management computer as well.

The Microsoft Online (MSOL) Services Sign-In Assistant must also be installed on the computer. The Sign-In Assistant is available from the Microsoft Download Center at http://www.microsoft.com/en-us/download/details.aspx?id=41950.

After downloading and installing the Sign-In Assistant, the next step is to download and install the Azure Active Directory Module for Windows PowerShell. The module is available at: http://go.microsoft.com/fwlink/p/?linkid=236297.

■ **Note** As of October 20, 2014, the 32-bit version of the AAD Module has been discontinued. All AAD Module installs should be done using the 64-bit version.

Now that the necessary components have been installed, you can connect to AAD using Windows PowerShell. First you need to connect to AAD. Use the following cmdlets to establish the connection:

```
$cred = get-credential
connect-msolservice -credential $cred
```

The first part of the cmdlet produces a credentials dialog window, as shown in Figure 9-12, where you enter your tenant Global Administrator or User Administrator name and password. These credentials are stored in the $cred variable, which is used by the second cmdlet to connect to Microsoft Online.

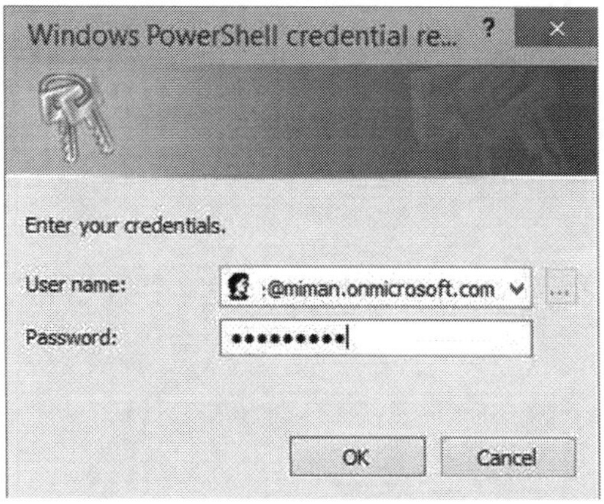

Figure 9-12. *Credentials entry form*

Once the connection to the MSOL service has been established, you can use other PowerShell cmdlets to manage your users and domains. To perform the bulk import, you first need to populate a .csv file with the required columns, as follows:

UserPrincipalName

FirstName

LastName

DisplayName

A good recommendation, as shown in Figure 9-13, is to add the UsageLocation field to the .csv file as well. Doing so removes the prompt for the user to set it when they sign in for the first time or for the administrator to have to do this when licenses are applied. Additionally, the user's preferred language can be set in advance of them logging in, which saves a mouse click.

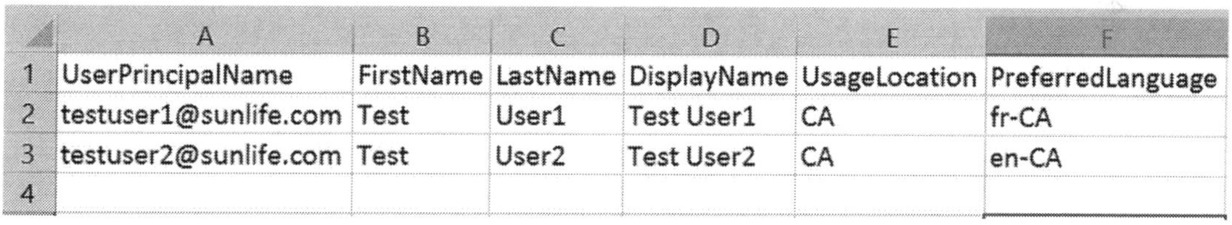

	A	B	C	D	E	F
1	UserPrincipalName	FirstName	LastName	DisplayName	UsageLocation	PreferredLanguage
2	testuser1@sunlife.com	Test	User1	Test User1	CA	fr-CA
3	testuser2@sunlife.com	Test	User2	Test User2	CA	en-CA
4						

Figure 9-13. *Sample .csv file*

You use two cmdlets to bulk-create the users in AAD from the .csv file: Import-csv and New-MsolUser. The following example imports users from a .csv file into a variable and then cycles through the information in the variable to create the accounts:

```
$users = Import-Csv C:\temp\O365Users.CSV

$users | ForEach-Object {

New-MsolUser -UserPrincipalName $_.UserPrincipalName -FirstName $_.FirstName -LastName
$_.LastName -DisplayName $_.DisplayName -UsageLocation $_.UsageLocation}
```

The accounts are populated with the information in the .csv columns by reading the individual variables and then writing that information to the attributes in AAD.

Although you can't do this in the Azure Portal, in Office 365 it is possible to add users via a .csv file import through a graphical user interface (GUI). This can be done by signing in to Office 365 as a Global Administrator or User Administrator, navigating to the Users ➤ Active Users page, and clicking the Bulk Add link, as shown in Figure 9-14.

Figure 9-14. *Bulk-import link*

Directory Synchronization

In addition to manually creating individual user accounts in Azure or bulk-creating them from a .csv file, another method in AAD to create them is through directory synchronization. With directory synchronization, objects are synchronized from your on-premises AD into AAD with the Azure Active Directory Synchronization Services (AAD Sync) tool, available free of charge from Microsoft. User objects, security groups, and distribution groups are synchronized with this tool.

The latest release of AAD Sync, released in the fourth quarter of 2014, offers many improvements over the previous version of the Directory Synchronization tool, known as DirSync. These improvements include an increase in the number of objects that can be synchronized before requiring a full SQL server installation from 50,000 to 100,000. Also, in the initial release of AAD Sync, password sync was not available; the current version makes this feature available.

PREPARING TO INSTALL AAD SYNC

To install AAD Sync, the computer on which it is to be installed must be running one of the following versions of Windows Server:

- Windows Server 2008

- Windows Server 2008 R2

- Windows Server 2012

- Windows Server 2012 R2

The computer can be standalone, a member server, or a domain controller with the following components installed:

- .NET 4.5.

- PowerShell (PS3 or better is required).

- The account to which you will install AAD Sync needs to be an administrator on the local machine.

Directory integration must be enabled on the Azure tenant:

1. To enable directory integration, log in to the Azure tenant with a Global Administrator account.

2. Go to the Active Directory tab, select the directory for which you are enabling integration, and click the Directory Integration tab, as shown in Figure 9-15.

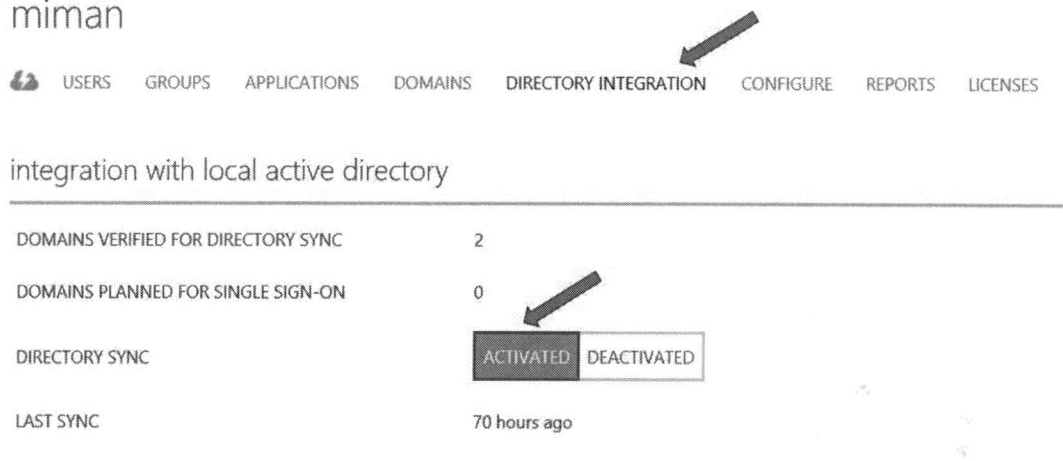

Figure 9-15. *Activating directory integration*

3. Under Integration With Local AD, click Activate.

AAD Sync Operational Accounts

The prior version of the Directory Synchronization tool, DirSync, required that an Enterprise Administrator account be used for the installation. This permission level was required so that installation operations, such as setting permissions for password sync or hybrid-enabled write-back, could be set. This level of permission was seen as excessive by many organizations' security teams, because the credentials for an Enterprise Administrator account are often a closely guarded secret.

The AAD Sync tool today no longer requires these permissions for installation. Instead, you are now required to set these permissions manually before installing AAD Sync. In organizations where the Enterprise Administrator permissions are known by only a few AD administrators, the installation permissions can be set by those administrators and then the installation of AAD Sync can be carried out by another server administrator without the need to grant that person Enterprise Administrator permissions first.

It is recommended that you create an AAD Sync service account for connecting to your on-premises AD as well as one for connecting to AAD. The account requirements for each are as follows:

- *AAD*: This must be a Global Administrator account, and it should have the password set never to expire.

- *On-premises AD*: This can be a standard user account. If password sync, hybrid, or password write-back is required, the permissions must be applied to the service account separately for those features to work properly.

▓ **Note**   To complete the steps that follow, you need to create a user account so you can apply the required permissions to it.

The permissions required for password synchronization are as follows:

- Replicating Directory Changes
- Replicating Directory Changes All

MODIFYING PERMISSIONS FOR PASSWORD SYNCHRONIZATION

Follow these steps to modify the permissions required to enable the account to read the password hashes from the on-premises AD.

To set the permissions for password synchronization, do the following:

1. Open Active Directory Users and Computers.

2. On the View menu, click Advanced Features.

3. Right-click the domain object, and then select Properties.

4. On the Security tab, shown Figure 9-16, if the desired user account is not listed, click Add; if the desired user account is listed, proceed to step 7.

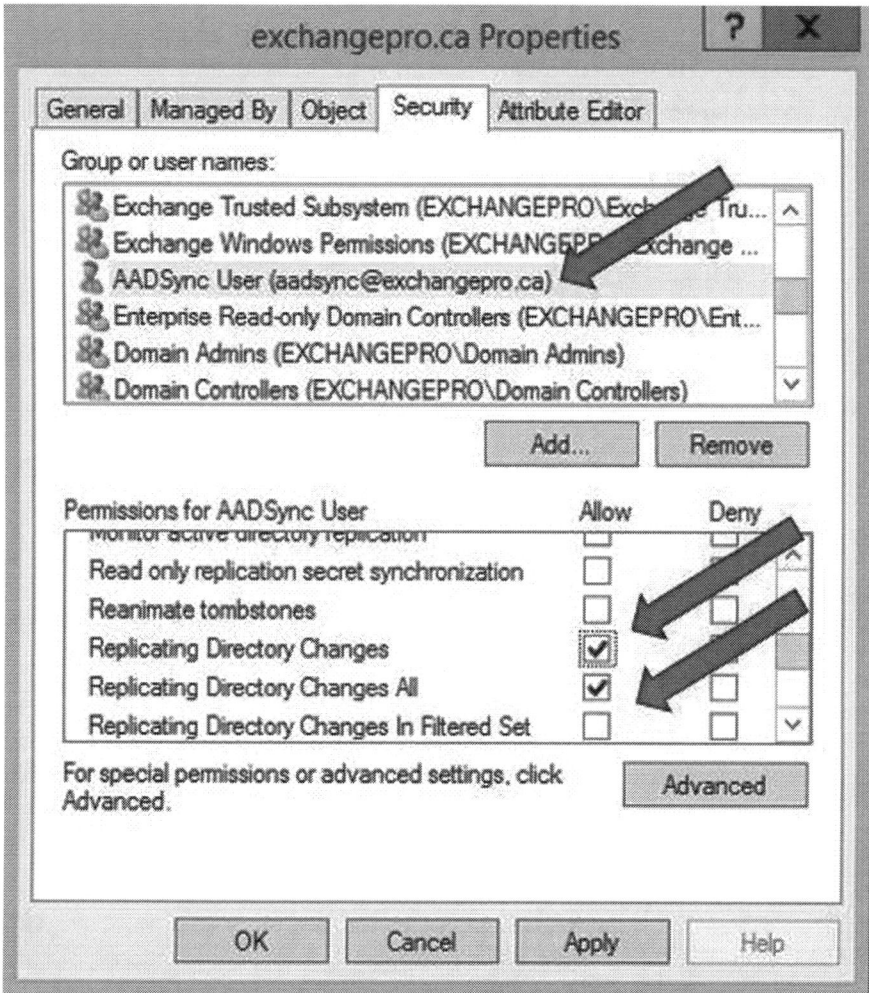

Figure 9-16. *Setting permissions to read the password hash*

5. In the Select Users, Computers, Or Groups dialog box, select the desired user account, and then click Add.

6. Click OK to return to the Properties dialog box.

7. Click the desired user account.

8. Click to select the Replicating Directory Changes and Replicating Directory Changes All check boxes from the list.

9. Click Apply, and then click OK.

If a hybrid configuration is required for using the rich co-existence functionality with an Exchange on-premises server, the permissions shown in Table 9-4 are required.

Table 9-4. Hybrid permission requirements

Object Type	Data Source Attribute
Contact	proxyAddresses
Group	proxyAddresses
User/InetOrgPerson	msExchArchiveStatus
	msExchBlockedSendersHash
	msExchSafeRecipientsHash
	msExchSafeSendersHash
	msExchUCVoiceMailSettings
	msExchUserHoldPolicies
	proxyAddresses

■ **Note**   For each object type, the Permission/Access right must be Write. Inheritance must be set to The Child Objects Only.

These permissions are required to enable AAD Sync to update the on-premises objects when Exchange online makes changes to the objects in the cloud.

■ **Note**   Although it's not a requirement, it is recommended that you keep your Exchange schema version close to that of AAD. As of this writing, the Exchange Online schema version is Exchange 2013, Service Pack 1.

To set the permissions for hybrid write-back, follow these steps:

1.   Open the ADSIEdit MMC snap-in.

2.   On the View menu, click Advanced Features.

3.   Right-click the domain object, and then click Properties.

4.   Click the Security tab, as shown in Figure 9-17.

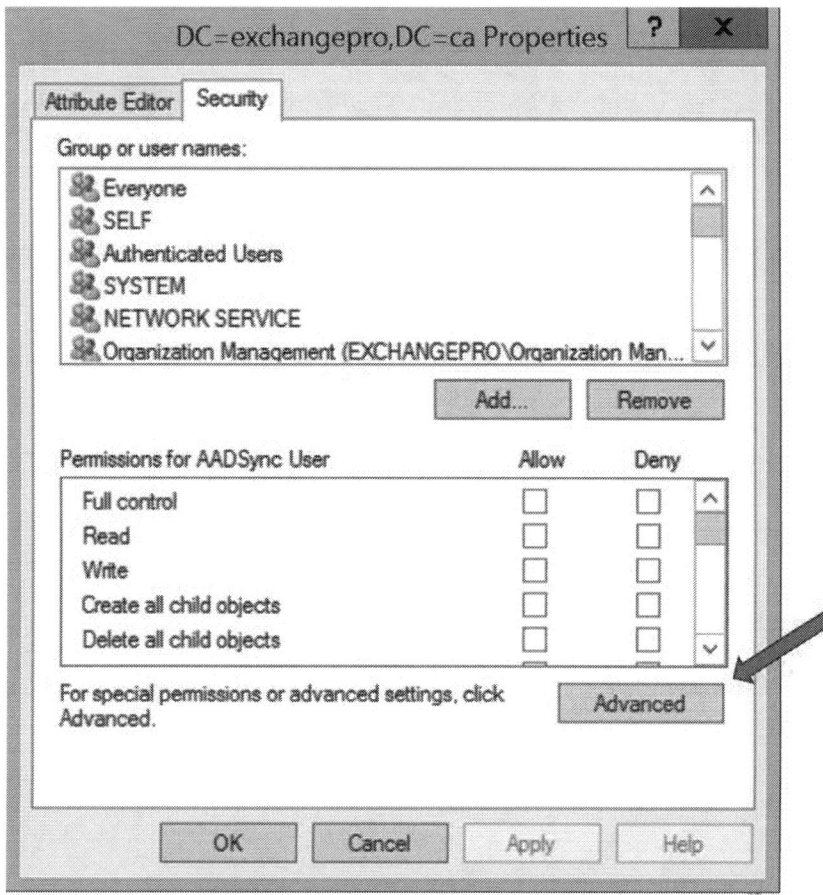

Figure 9-17. Accessing Advanced permissions

5. Click the Advanced button.

6. In the Advanced Security Settings window, click Add.

7. In the Permission Entry window, click Select A Principal, as shown in Figure 9-18.

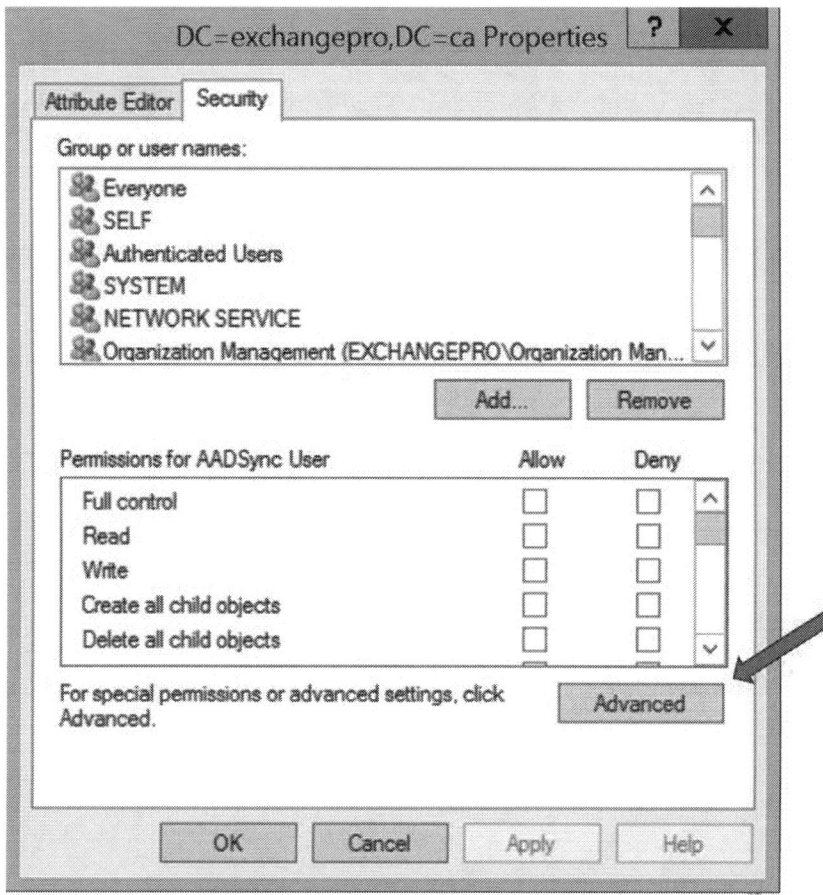

Figure 9-18. Selecting the account principal

8. In the Select User, Computer, Service Account Or Group window, enter the name of the AAD Sync service account that you created previously, click Check Name, and then click OK.

9. Following the permission requirements described in Table 9-4, select the object to which you will apply the permissions, as shown in Figure 9-19. The required objects are

    a. Descendant Contact Objects

    b. Descendant Group Objects

    c. Descendant InetOrgPerson Objects

    d. Descendent User Objects

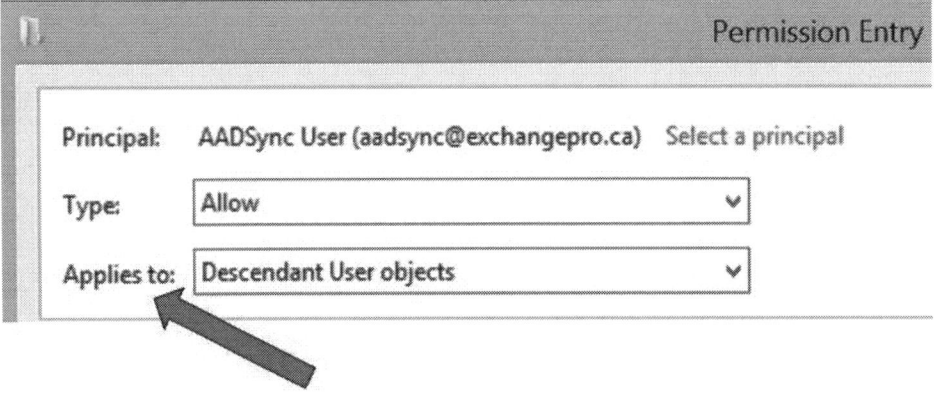

Figure 9-19. *Selecting objects the permissions apply to*

10. Set write permissions to enable the hybrid write-back permissions. For example, in Figure 9-20, the Write msExchArchiveStatus permission is enabled on the Descendant User object.

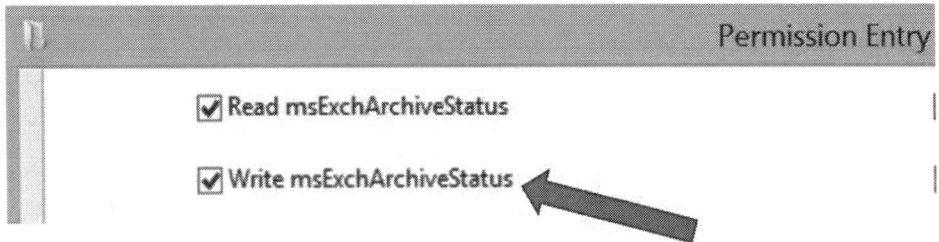

Figure 9-20. *Setting Exchange hybrid permissions*

11. Complete the preceding process for all the remaining permissions listed in Table 9-4.

12. When all the permissions have been applied, click Apply, and then click OK (twice).

13. Close ADSTEdit.

If you wish to use the password write-back feature that is included with AAD Premium, your AAD Service account requires permissions to reset and change the on-premises password. You can grant these permissions by following these steps, as shown in Figure 9-21:

1. Open Active Directory Users and Computers.

2. Make sure Advanced Features are turned on.

3. Right-click the domain, and select Properties.

4. Select the Security tab, and click Advanced.

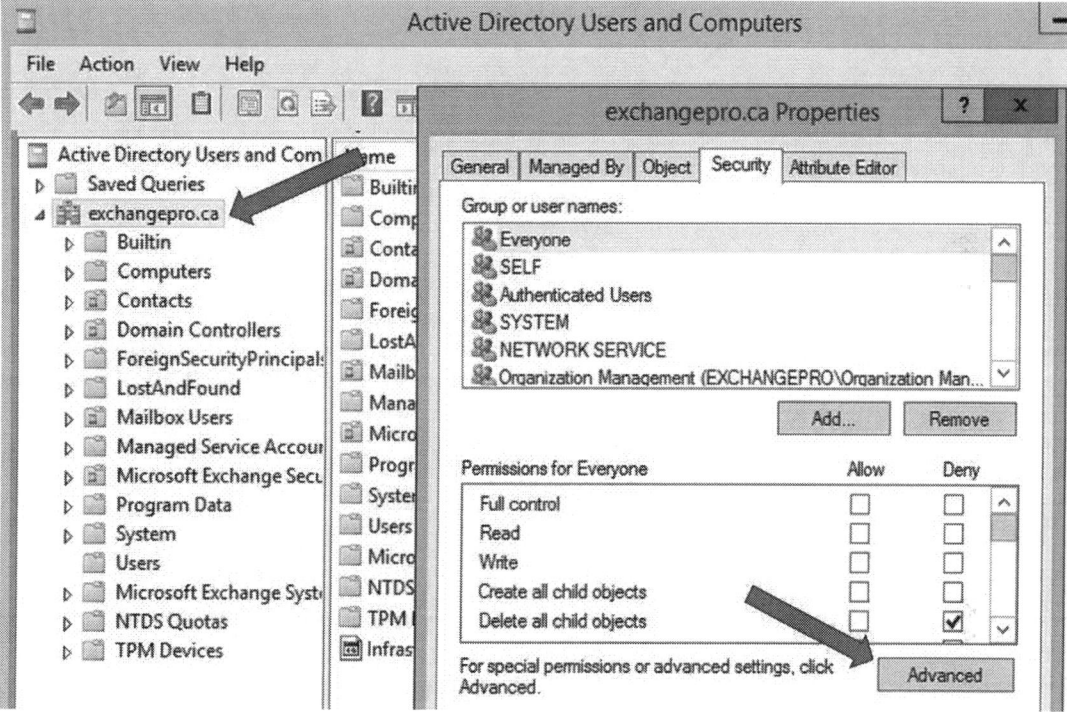

Figure 9-21. Accessing the Advanced permissions

5. On the Permissions tab, click Add.

6. Click Select A Principal, and select the AAD Sync service account, as shown in Figure 9-22.

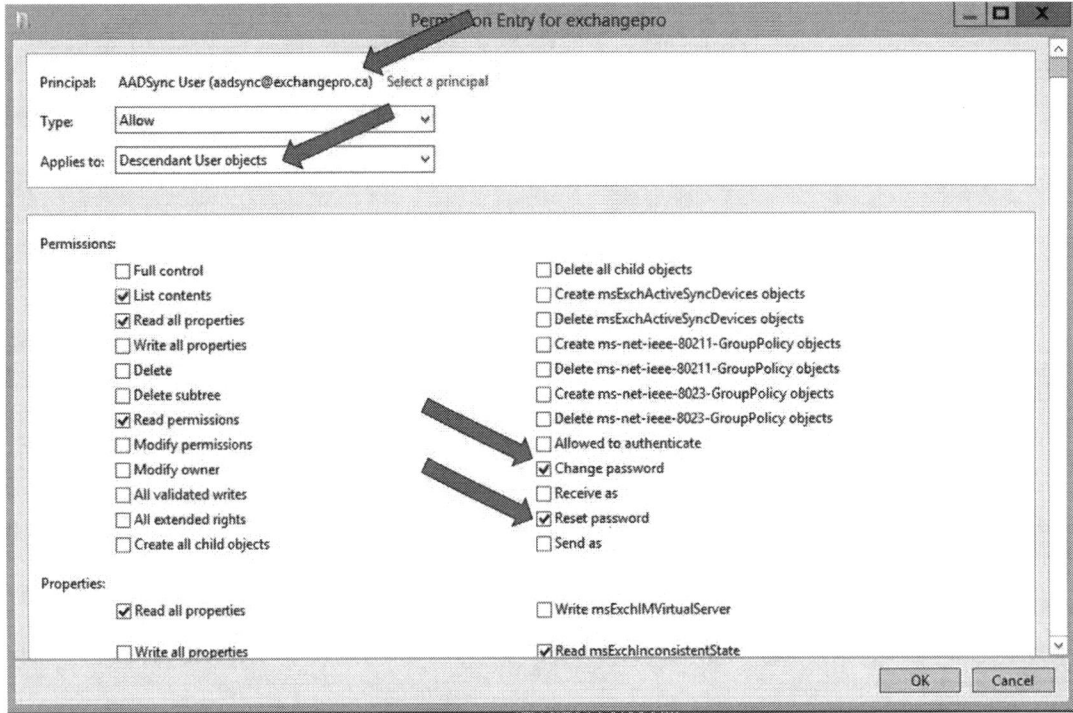

Figure 9-22. *Setting password write-back permissions*

7.   In the Applies To drop-down, select Descendant User Objects.

8.   In the Permissions section, select Reset Password and Change Password.

9.   Click Ok. Click Apply. Click OK.

Installing the Azure Active Directory Synchronization Service

Now that all the permissions for installing AAD Sync have been configured, you can proceed with the installation. Microsoft has worked hard to simplify the installation, whether it's for a single forest or a multiforest environment. The installation is straightforward and easy to follow for most deployments.

INSTALLING AAD SYNC

You can download the current version of AAD Sync from www.microsoft.com/en-us/download/details.aspx?id=44225. Then follow these steps:

1.   After downloading the AAD Sync installer, double-click the executable MicrosoftAzureADConnectionTool.exe.

    The executable is a self-extracting file that loads the binaries into a default folder called Microsoft Azure AD Connection Tool on the system drive. After the extraction completes, the actual installation launches.

2. The Welcome window is displayed, as shown in Figure 9-23. Here you have the option to select the installation path if the default path is not to your liking. You also must accept the license agreement in order to proceed with the installation. After agreeing to the End User License Agreement (EULA), click Install.

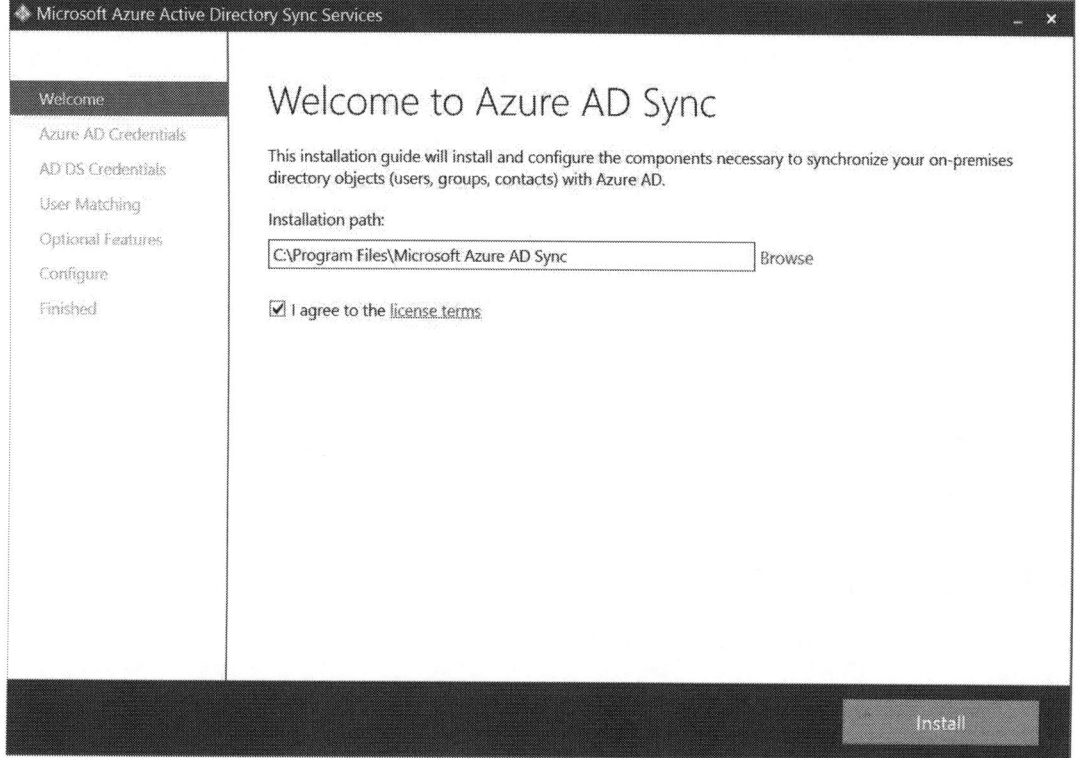

Figure 9-23. *AAD Sync Welcome window*

3. The installation begins installing the AAD Sync binaries into the folder you chose, as shown in Figure 9-24. When the installation is complete, the Connection wizard launches. There you complete the steps required to configure AAD Sync to suit your environment.

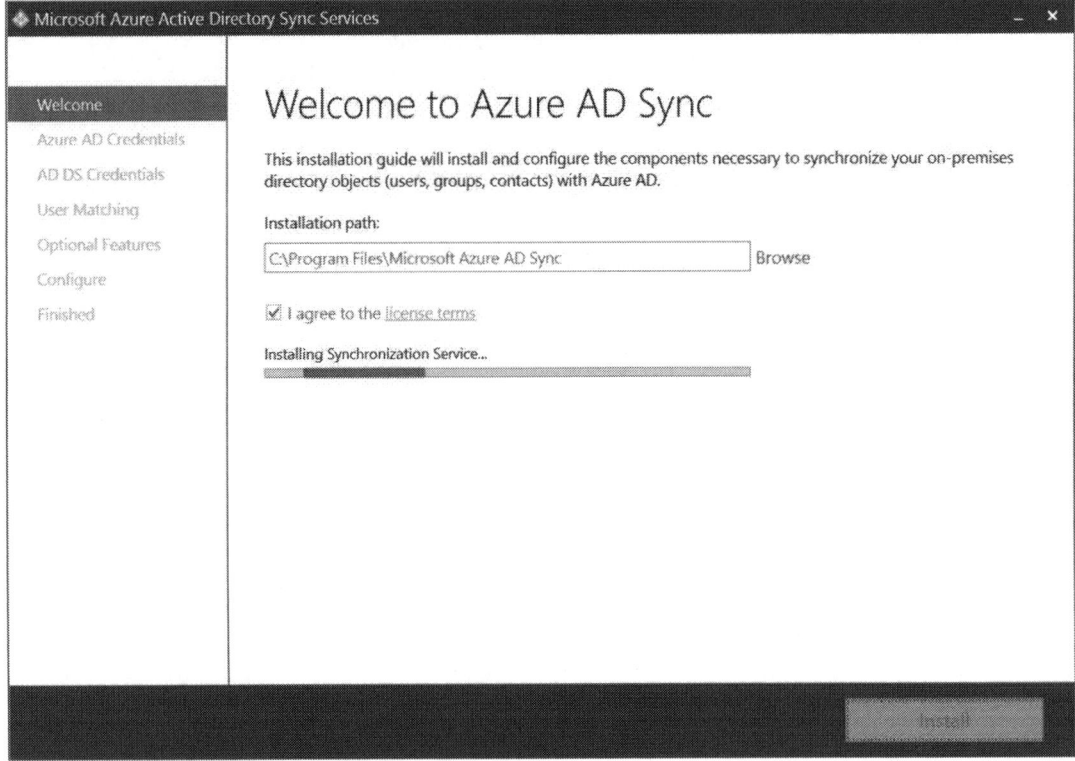

Figure 9-24. *Installing the AAD Sync service*

4. The first configuration step is to enter your tenant Global Administrator user name and password, as shown in Figure 9-25. Then click Next.

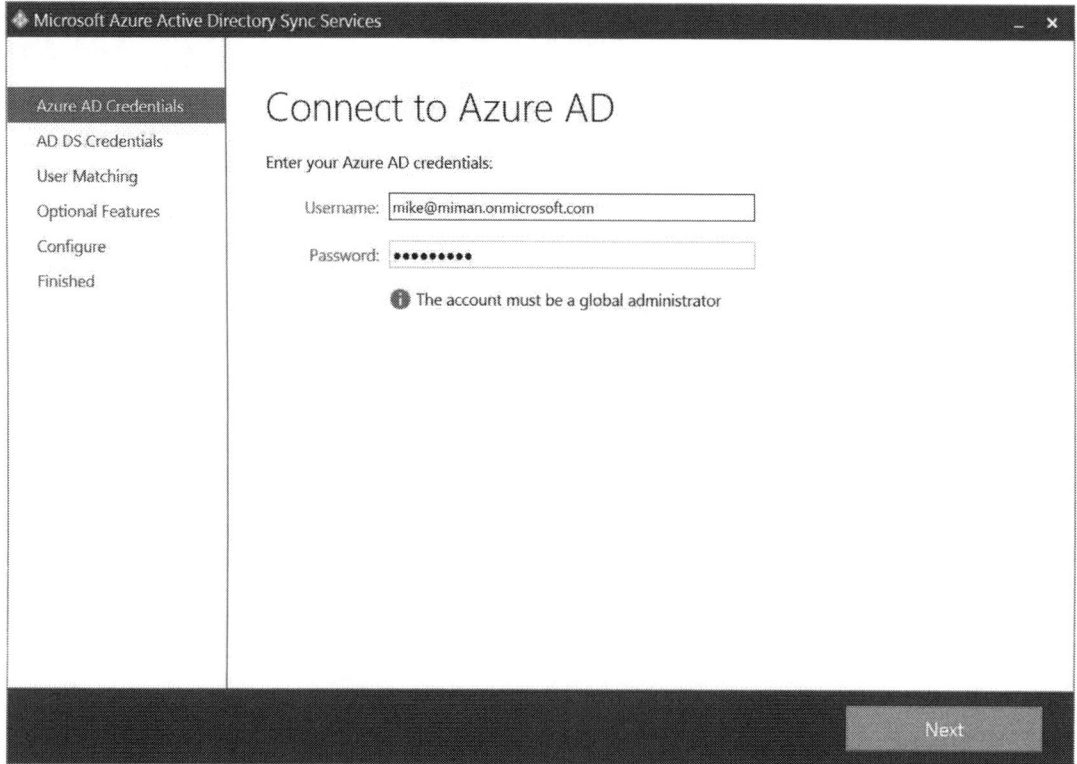

Figure 9-25. *Connecting to Azure AD*

5. After the wizard verifies the credentials and connects to your Azure tenant, it moves
    to the on-premises AD connection page, as shown in Figure 9-26. On this page,
    enter the credentials of the AAD Sync service account for which you configured
    permissions previously to enable password sync, hybrid write-back, or password
    write-back.

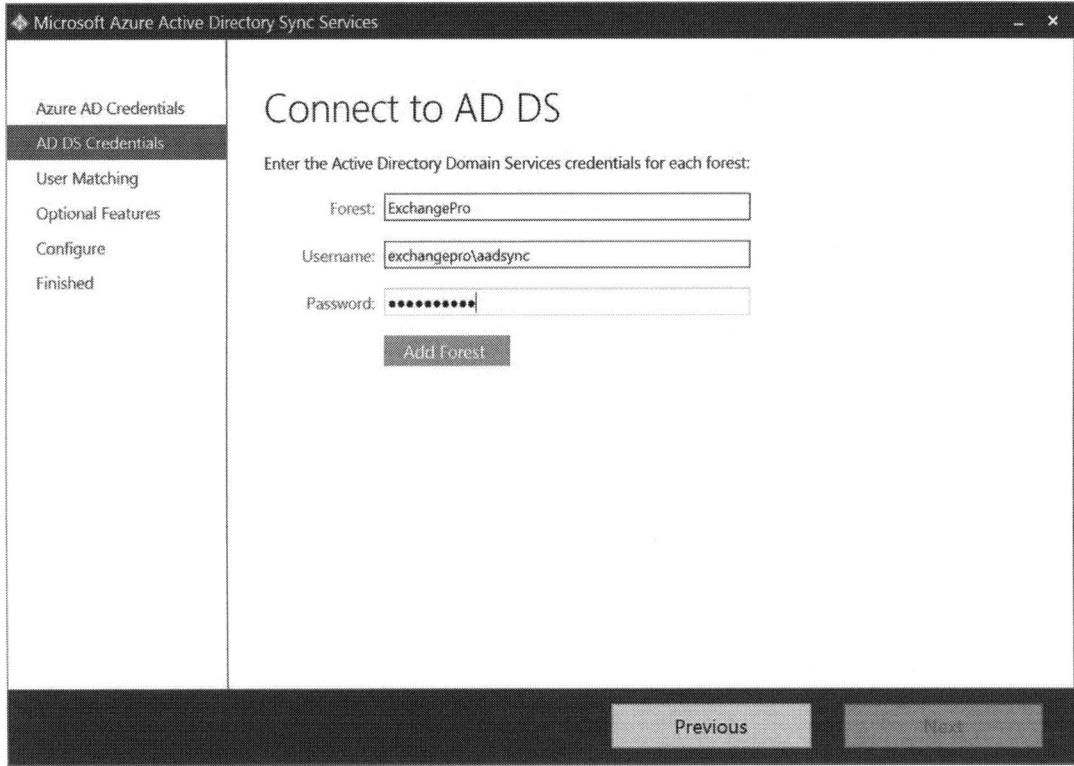

Figure 9-26. *Connecting to the first AD DS forest*

6. In this example, you're going to connect to a second on-premises AD forest, to illustrate the simplicity of using the new AAD Sync tools to do this. After entering the credentials for the first forest, as shown in Figure 9-25, click the Add Forest button; then repeat the same steps to connect to the second forest, as shown in Figure 9-27.

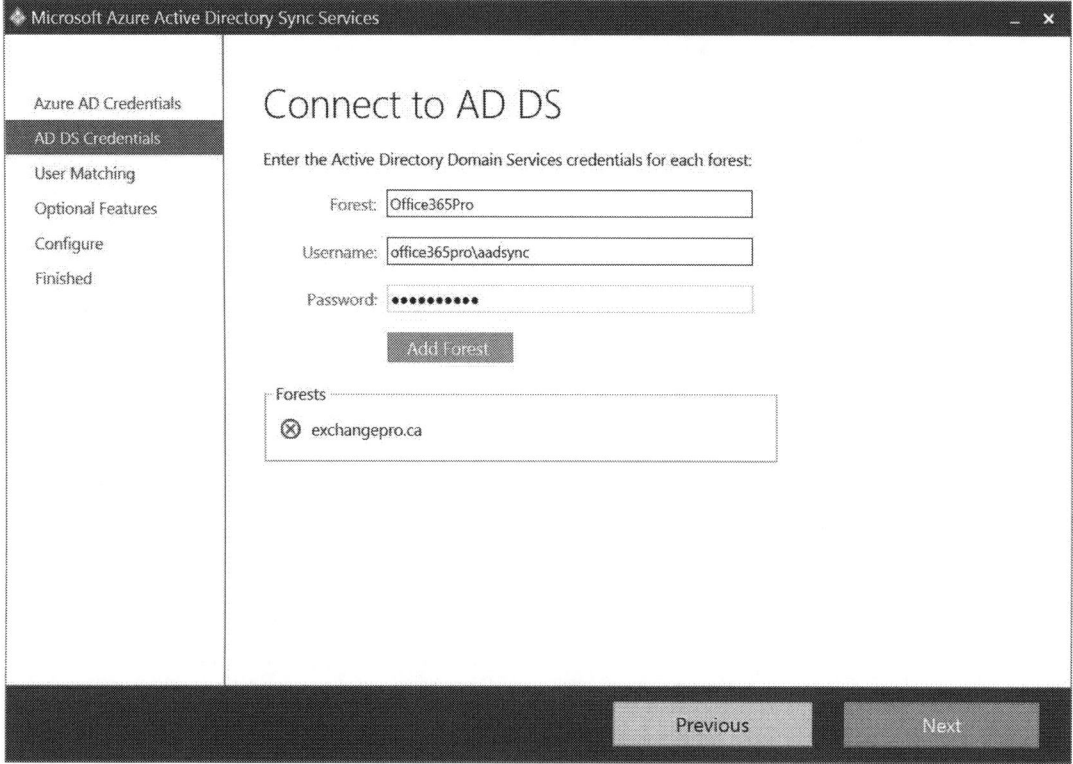

Figure 9-27. *Connecting to the second AD DS forest*

7. After entering the AAD Sync service account information for the second forest, click the Add Forest button. With both AD DS forests added to the AAD Sync configuration wizard, click Next to begin the next step in the configuration procedure, as shown in Figure 9-28.

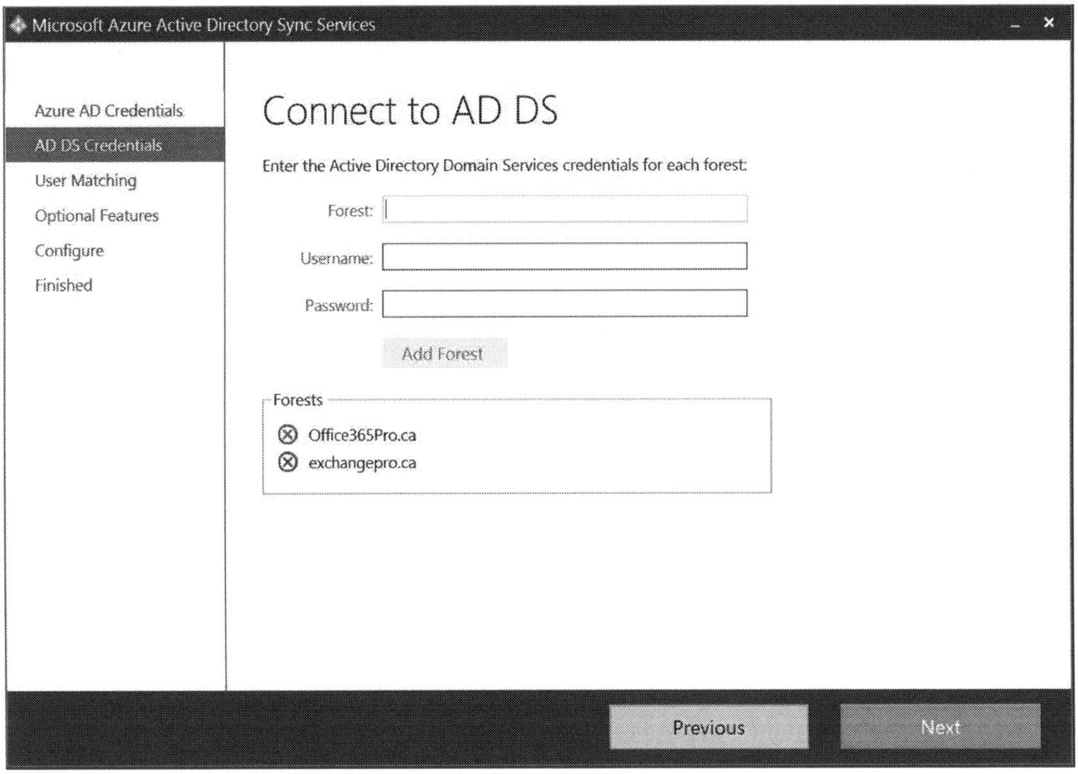

Figure 9-28. *Completed AD DS window*

Now that both forests are connected to AAD Sync, the next step is to configure user matching. *User matching* is the process that joins user objects, if they exist in multiple forests, into a single object for synchronizing to AAD. When user objects exist in multiple forests, such as in a resource forest model, AAD Sync needs to be able to match the objects in each forest before synchronizing them to AAD, to prevent the creation of duplicate objects in the cloud. If the object exists in one forest only, then matching is not required.

■ **Caution**   If a user object is to be moved across forests, then selecting a sourceAnchor attribute other than the default of objectGUID is recommended. The reason is that when an object moves across forests, the objectGUID changes. When the objectGUID changes, it no longer matches cloudAnchor or immutableID in AAD. immutableID is an AAD attribute that, by definition, never changes. This attribute is the security identifier in AAD in the same way the objectGUID is an object identifier in an on-premises AD.

The result of this mismatch is that a new user object is created in AAD, and the user loses access to the previous resources in the cloud. A good alternative sourceAnchor attribute would be one that is likely never to change, such as an employee ID.

8. In this example, users will not move across AD forests, so leave the default selections, as shown in Figure 9-29, and click Next.

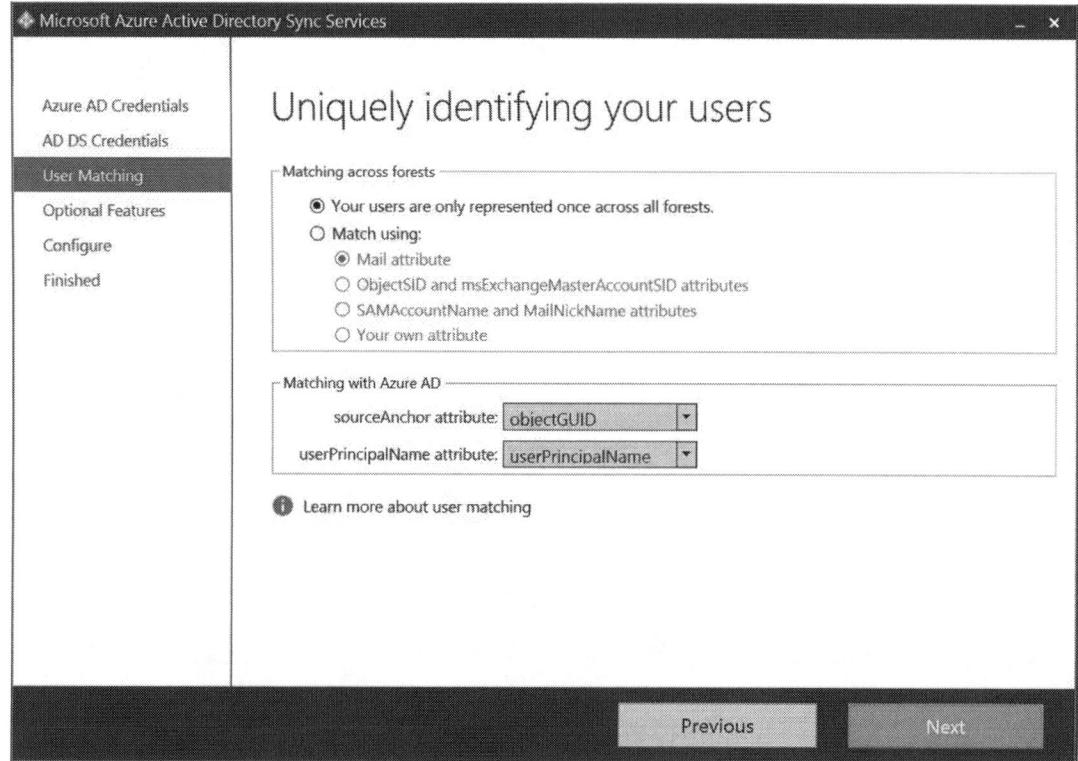

Figure 9-29. *User matching*

9. The Optional Features page, shown in Figure 9-30, is where you select features like Exchange hybrid, password synchronization, password write-back, and AAD app and attribute filtering. App filtering lets you reduce the number of attributes that are being synchronized to AAD. For example, if you aren't planning to use Exchange online, you may choose not to synchronize the attributes associated with Exchange on-premises to AAD.

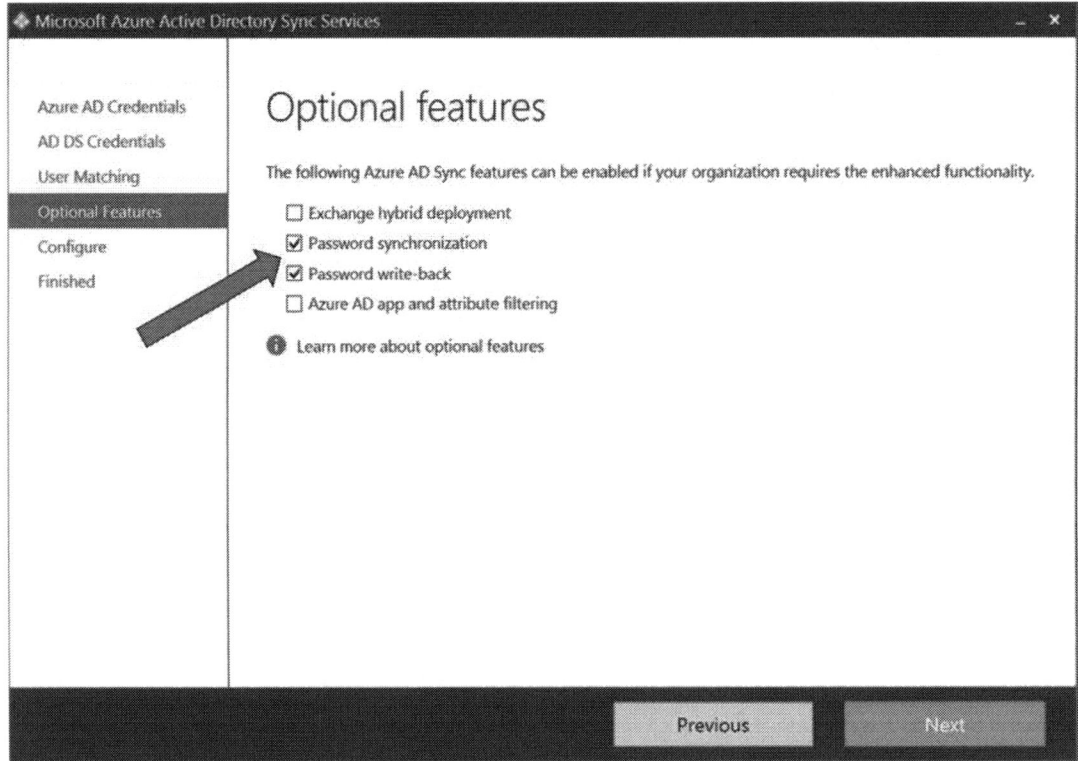

Figure 9-30. Optional features

10. Synchronizing all attributes, and enable the password synchronization and password write-back features. Click Next.

11. At this point, AAD Sync is ready to complete the configuration for synchronizing your on-premises objects into AAD, as shown in Figure 9-31, so click Configure.

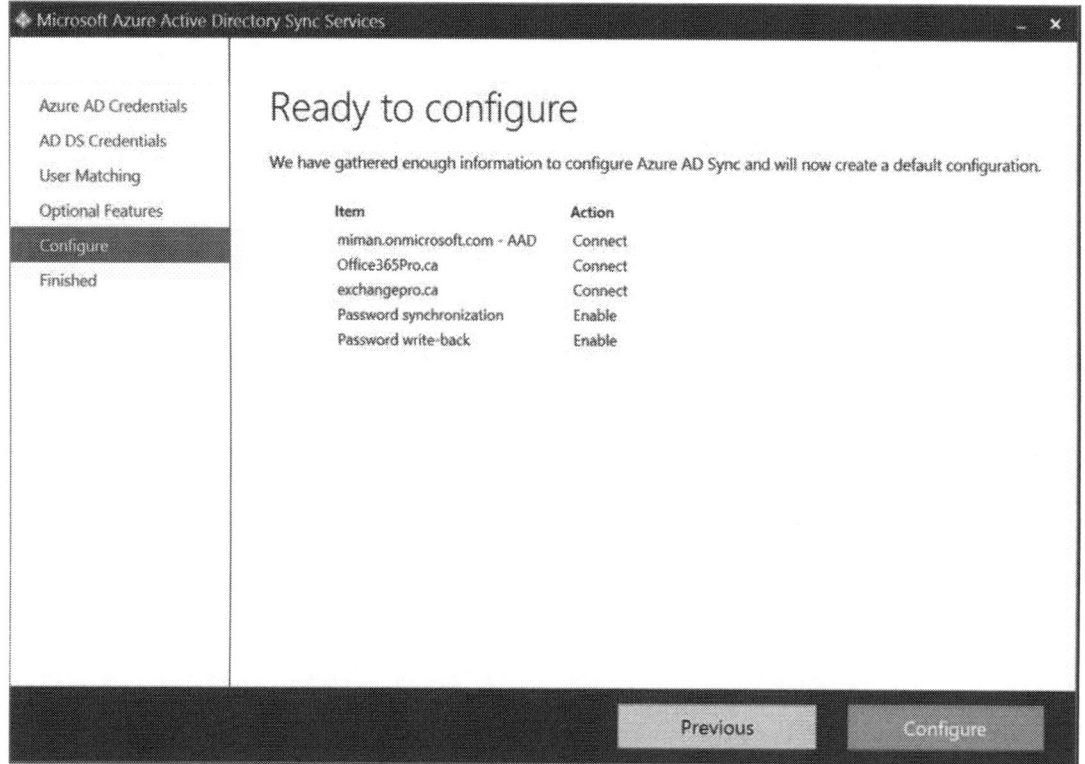

Figure 9-31. Ready to configure

12. The application takes a few minutes to configure the settings based on the selections you made, as shown in Figure 9-32, but it finishes fairly quickly.

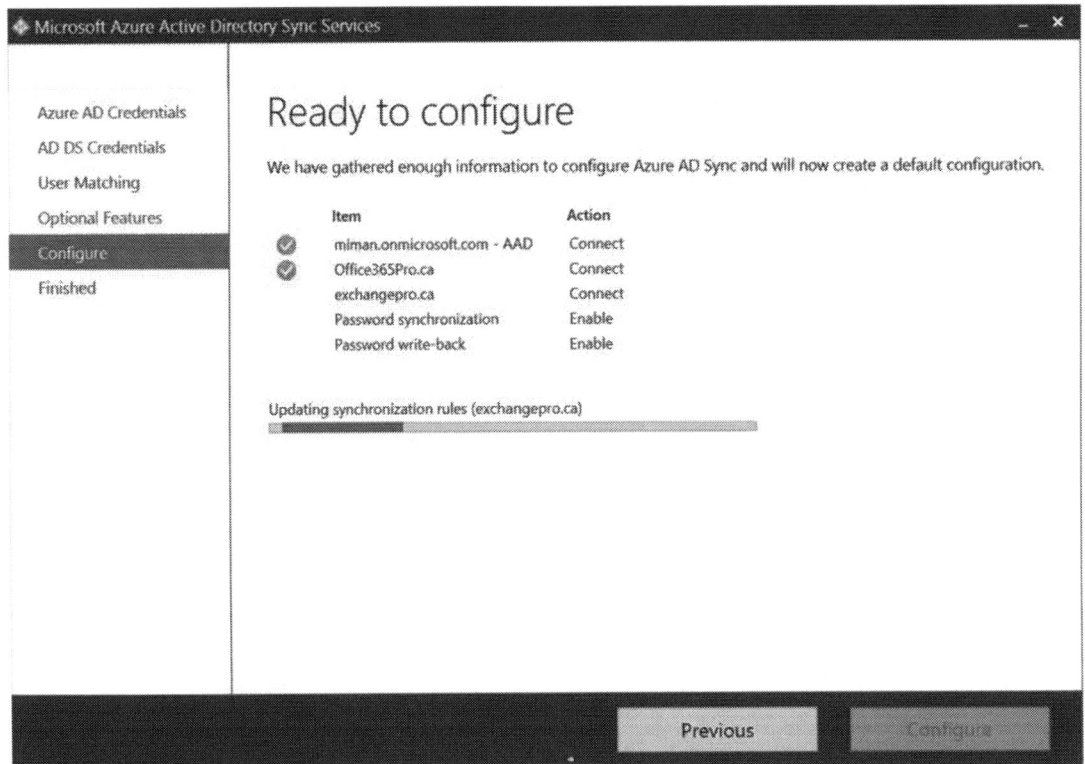

Figure 9-32. *Performing the configuration*

13. Once the configuration completes, as shown in Figure 9-33, you have the option to synchronize your on-premises objects. You're going to configure some filtering before synchronizing for the first time, so leave the Synchronize Now check box unchecked.

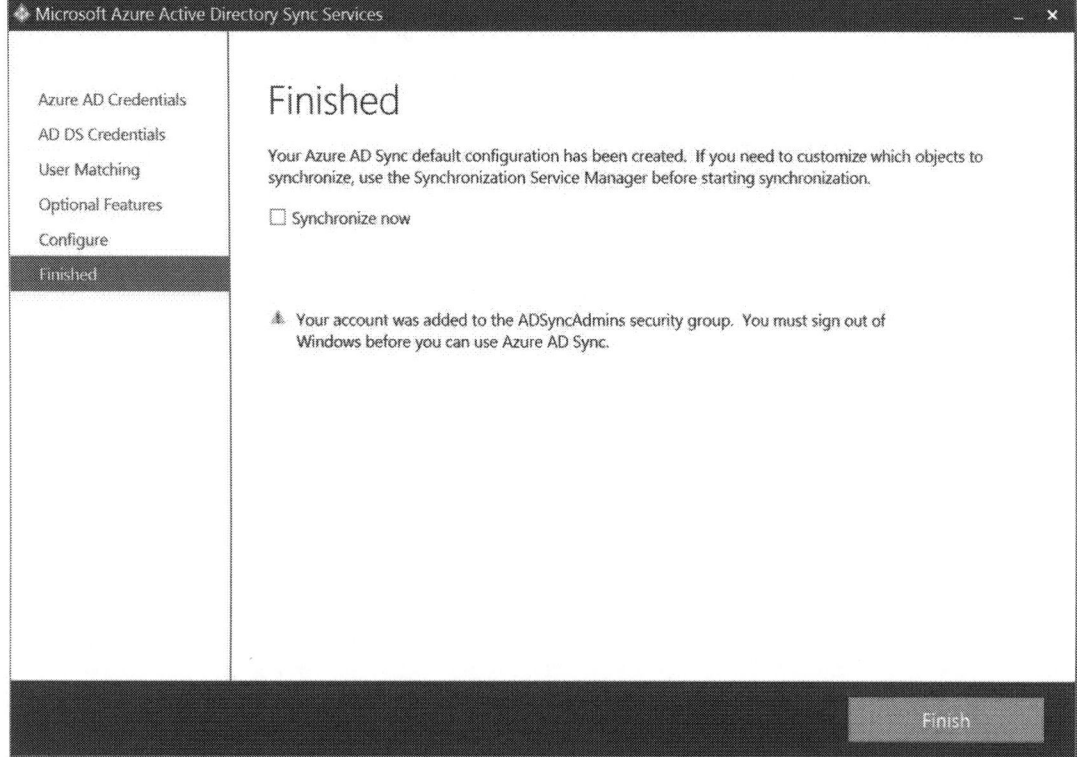

Figure 9-33. *Finishing the installation and configuration*

Be advised that one of the things the AAD Sync installation does is to create a scheduled task on the local computer that runs the Delta synchronization jobs every three hours. Unchecking the Synchronize Now check box causes the scheduled task to be created in a disabled state. In order to have the Delta synchronization jobs run as scheduled, you must enable the scheduled task once you have completed all the configurations.

■ **Note** The warning on this page is about the need to sign out and sign back in to the computer before you can use AAD Sync. This is due to the installation creating some security groups on the local server and adding the account that you used for the installation to the ADSyncAdmins local group. Only members of this group have the permissions to manage AAD Sync, so before you can configure the filtering, a sign out is required.

14. Click finish, and then sign out of the server.

■ **Important**   The AAD Sync installation creates a user account on the local server that is used as the service account for the Microsoft Azure AD Sync service. The account that is created starts with *AAD*, followed by randomly generated characters. The account also has the password set never to expire. If you chose to change the password or remove the password expiration setting, it is important to monitor the account password change frequency to avoid an interruption in the synchronization service.

■ **Tip**   If you want a deeper understanding of the steps the AAD Sync installation performed, the installation and configuration log files are located in the `C:\Windows\Temp\AADSync` folder.

Filtering AAD Sync

As in previous versions of the Directory Synchronization tool, there are three options for filtering objects to prevent them from synchronizing to AAD:

- *Domain-based*: Excludes an entire domain from your on-premises AD forest from synchronizing to AAD.

- *Organizational unit-based filtering*: Excludes an entire OU from synchronizing to AAD. As an example, you may have an OU that is specifically used for service accounts that don't need to be synchronized to AAD.

- *Attribute-based*: Prevents accounts that have specific data in a certain attribute. For example, you can put "on-premises only" into an account attribute and then filter on that data within that attribute to prevent accounts with this data from synchronizing to AAD.

CONFIGURING DOMAIN-BASED FILTERING AAD SYNC

Domain-based filtering and OU-based filtering have not changed since the previous versions of the synchronization tool. They are still managed in the Synchronization Service Manager tool. To configure domain-based filtering, follow these steps:

1. On Start, tap or click Synchronization Service to open the Synchronization Service Manager.

2. Click Connectors in the Tools menu.

3. In the Connectors list, select the connector that has AD Domain Service as Type.

4. Click Properties in the Actions menu, or right-click the connector and select properties.

5. Click Configure Directory Partitions.

6. In the Select Directory Partitions list, shown in Figure 9-34, verify that only the partitions you want to synchronize are selected.

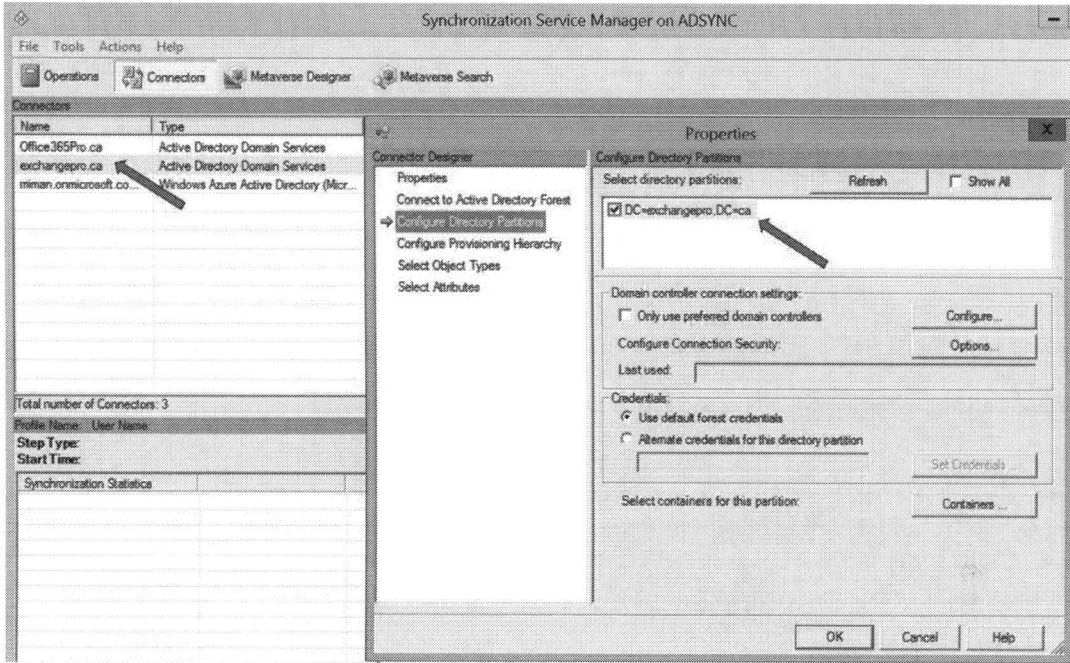

Figure 9-34. *Selecting the domains to synchronize*

7. To remove a domain from the synchronization process, clear the domain's check box.

8. Click OK to close the Properties window.

9. After updating the domain filter, you also need to update the following run profiles to remove the domains that were synchronizing previously:

    a. Full Import

    b. Full Synchronization

    c. Delta Import

    d. Delta Synchronization

    e. Export

■ **Note**   If you have removed a partition from the directory partitions list, you need to make sure all run profile steps that are referencing this partition are also removed. For example, if there was a second domain in the example forest, you would see two domains to synchronize when looking at the domain partitions in Figure 9-33. If you only wanted to synchronize one of the domains, you would remove the second one from the domain partitions and from the run profiles that control what is synchronized, as shown in Figure 9-35.

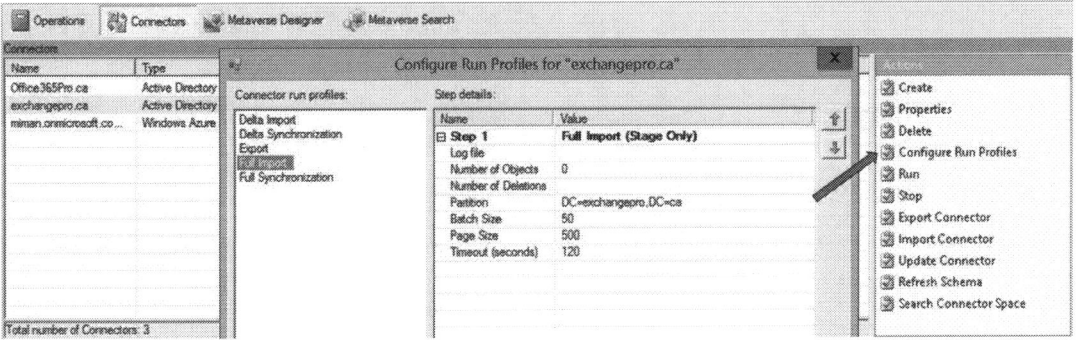

Figure 9-35. *Configuring run profiles*

CONFIGURING ORGANIZATIONAL UNIT–BASED FILTERING AAD SYNC

With AAD Sync, you also have the option not to synchronize individual OU's. You might choose to do this if you have an OU that contains contact objects that you don't want to synchronize into AAD. To configure domain-based filtering, follow these steps:

1. On Start, tap or click Synchronization Service to open the Synchronization Service Manager.

2. In the Synchronization Service Manager, click Connectors and then double-click the SourceAD management agent that you are filtering.

3. Click the Configure Directory Partitions link, select the domain you want to configure (if you have more than one), and then click the Containers button.

4. When prompted, enter your AD domain credentials.

■ **Note**   When the credentials dialog box opens, the account used to import and export to AD DS is displayed. If you do not know the password for the account, you can enter another account to use. The account you use must have read permissions to the domain currently being configured.

---

5. In the Select Containers dialog box, shown in Figure 9-36, clear the OUs that you don't want to sync up to AAD, and then click OK.

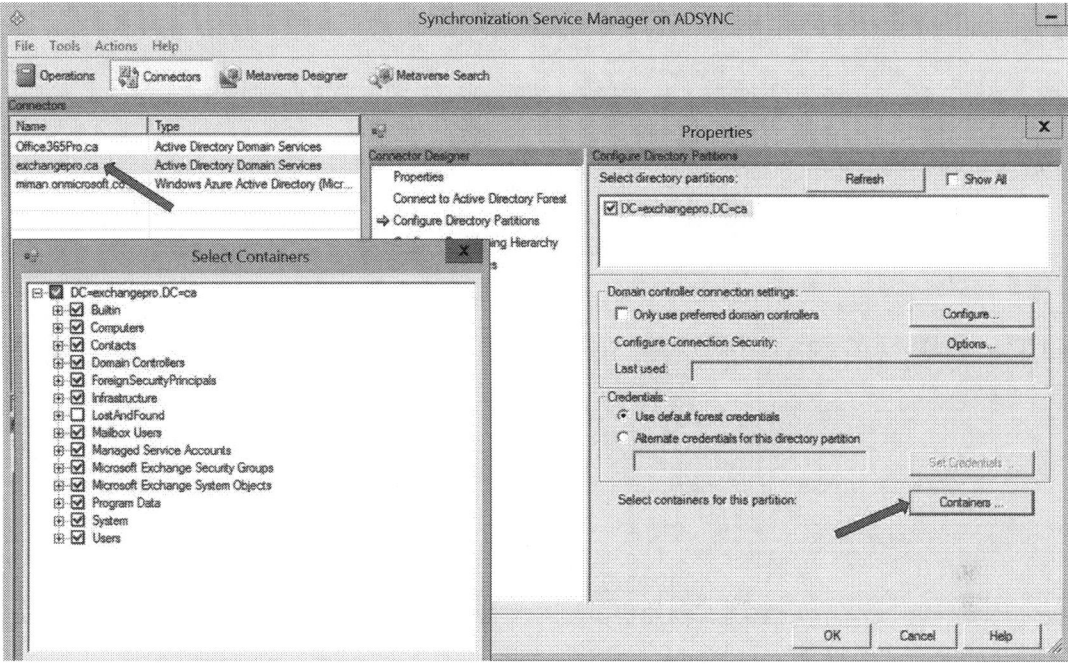

Figure 9-36. *Selecting the organizational units to synchronize*

6. Click OK on the SourceAD Properties page.

7. Right-click the SourceAD management agent, and select Run.

8. Run a full import and a Delta synchronization.

Configuring Attribute-Based Filtering

There are several ways to configure filtering based on AD attributes. Configuration on inbound synchronization from AD is recommended because these configuration settings will be kept even after upgrading to a newer version. Configuration on outbound synchronization to AAD is supported, but these settings will not be kept after upgrading to a newer version; they should be used only when required to view the combined object in the metaverse to determine filtering. For this reason, this section only discusses inbound filtering.

■ **Note** The *metaverse* is part of the AAD Sync database that is the staging area for objects being synchronized. As objects are pulled into AAD Sync from different sources, they are stored in the metaverse, where they are processed. For example, if a user has an account in two different forests, the accounts need to be joined before the final, single account is exported to its final destination.

Inbound-based filtering is accomplished by using the default configuration, where objects going to AAD must not have the metaverse attribute `cloudFiltered` set to a value and the metaverse attribute `sourceObjectType` is set to either User or Contact.

When you are filtering objects so that they don't synchronize to AAD, the attribute `cloudFiltered` must be set to True. In all other cases, the value should remain empty. This method is used to prevent synchronizing an object to AAD. This type of filtering is known as *negative filtering*.

In the following example, you filter out all contact objects that have an SMTP address ending in `office365pro.ca`. In the lab used in this example, there are two forests, and in each forest there are mailbox users who have contact objects in the other forest. Thus users in each forest are visible in the Global Address List.

CONFIGURING ATTRIBUTE-BASED FILTERING AAD SYNC

To configure attribute-based filtering, follow these steps:

1. Open the Synchronization Rules Editor.

2. Make sure that Inbound is selected, and click Add New Rule, as shown in Figure 9-37.

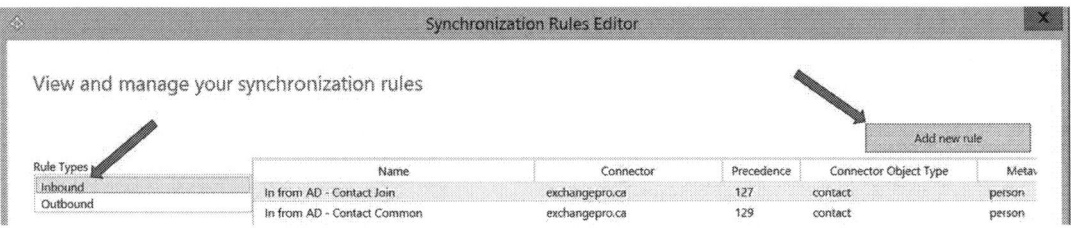

Figure 9-37. *Creating a synchronization rule*

3. Give the rule a descriptive name, such as *Filter out office365pro.ca contact objects*. Also provide a description of the filter, such as *Filter to prevent office365pro.ca contact objects from synchronizing to AAD*, so it's clear what the rule is doing.

4. On the Create Inbound Synchronization Rule page, shown in Figure 9-38, for Connected System, select the correct forest, which is one of the forests that was added when AAD Sync was installed.

   a. For Connected System Object Type, select Contact.

   b. For Metaverse Object Type, select Person.

   c. For Link Type, select Join.

   d. For precedence, type a value currently not used by another synchronization rule—for example, **10**. Click Next.

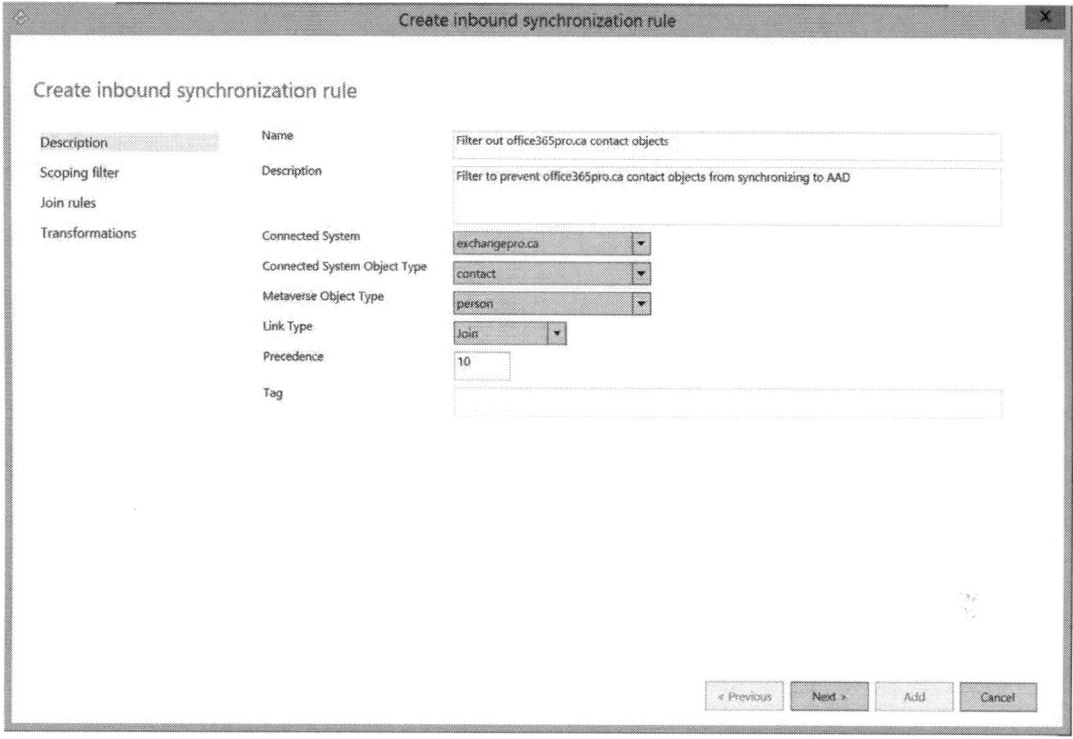

Figure 9-38. *Selecting the objects to filter*

5. On the Scoping Filter page, click Add Group, click Add Clause, and for Attribute, select `mail`, as shown in Figure 9-39.

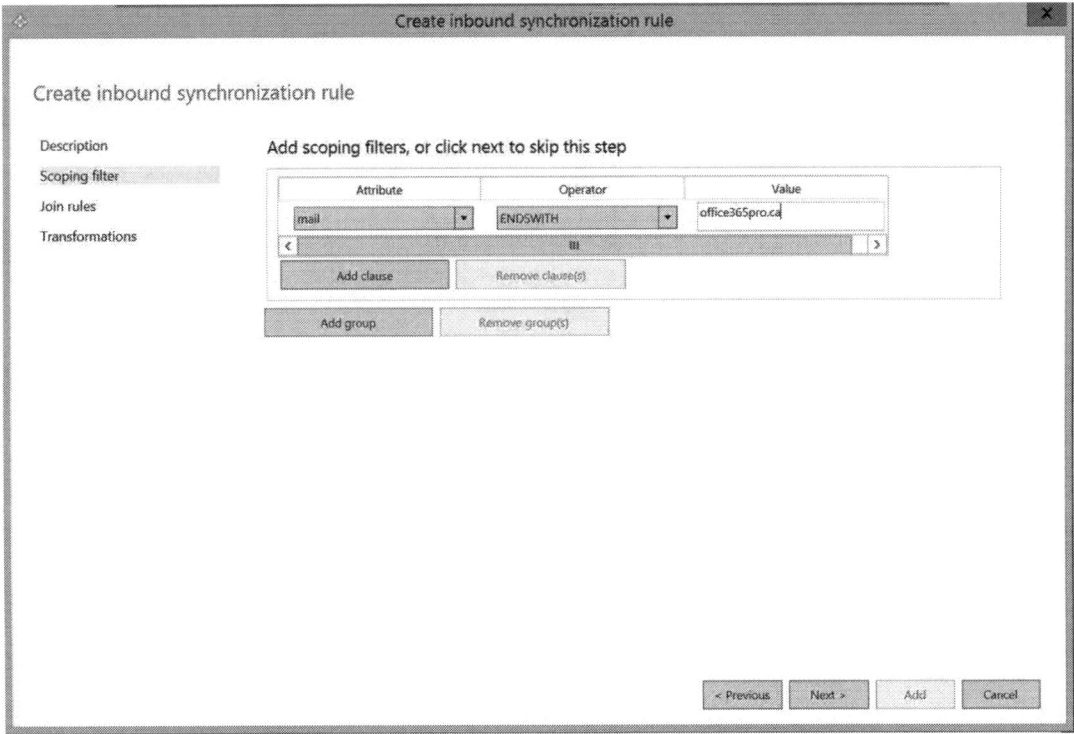

Figure 9-39. *Scoping the filter*

6. Make sure Operator is set to ENDSWITH, and type the value **office365pro.ca** in the
    Value box. Click Next.

■ **Note**　When practicing these steps in your own lab, instead of using office365pro.ca for the values,
use your own domain for filtering objects.

---

7. Leave the Join rules empty, and click Next.

8. On the Transformations page, shown in Figure 9-40, click Add Transformation.

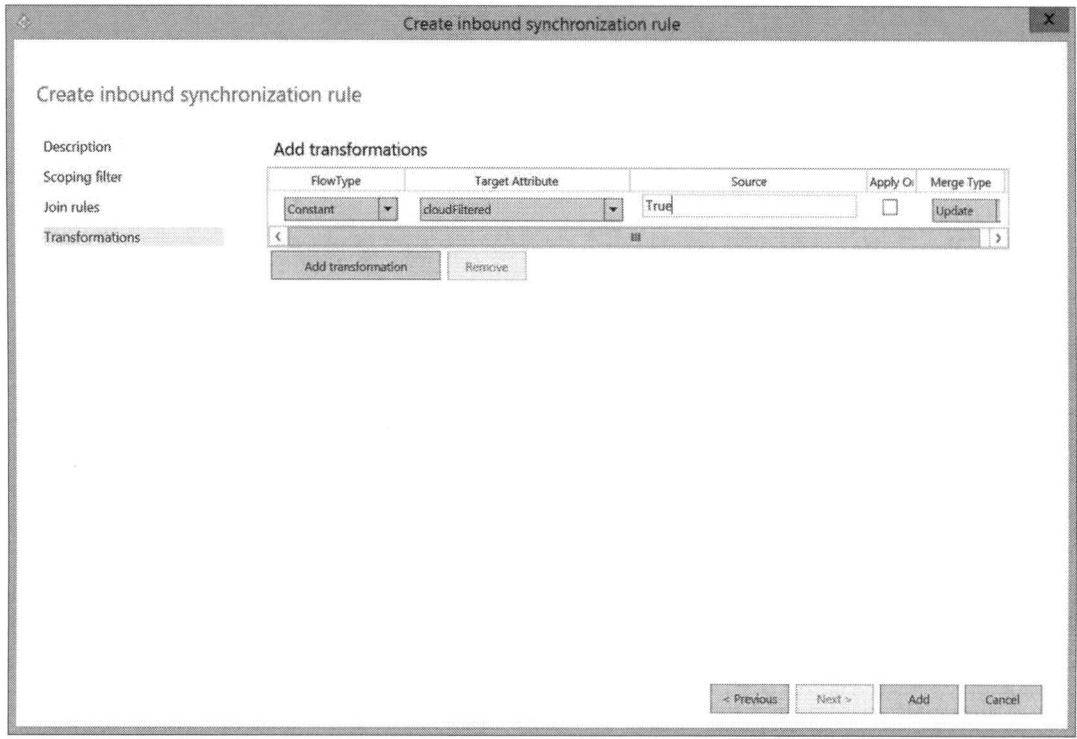

Figure 9-40. *Adding a transformation*

9. For FlowType, select Constant:

   a. For Target Attribute, select cloudFiltered.

   b. In the Source text box, type **True**.

   c. Click Add to save the rule.

10. A quick look at the inbound filters, shown in Figure 9-41, reveals that the newly added filter is present in the list. Now that you have your filtering in place, you can finally perform a synchronization.

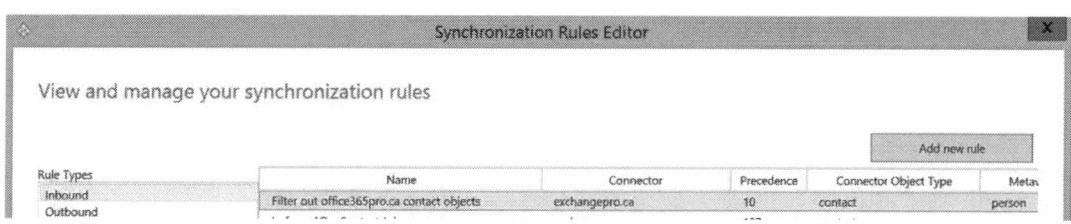

Figure 9-41. *Viewing the completed rule*

11. To force a synchronization of the objects, open a cmd window and navigate to the %ProgramFiles%\ Microsoft Azure AD Sync\Bin folder. There is a tool in the folder called DirectorySyncClientCmd. You have three options for running it:

- *Nothing*: Don't supply any parameters.

- *Initial*: This is used to force a full import, full sync.

- *Delta*: This is used to force a Delta Import, Delta sync

Because this is the first synchronization you're doing, use the initial parameter, as shown in Figure 9-42.

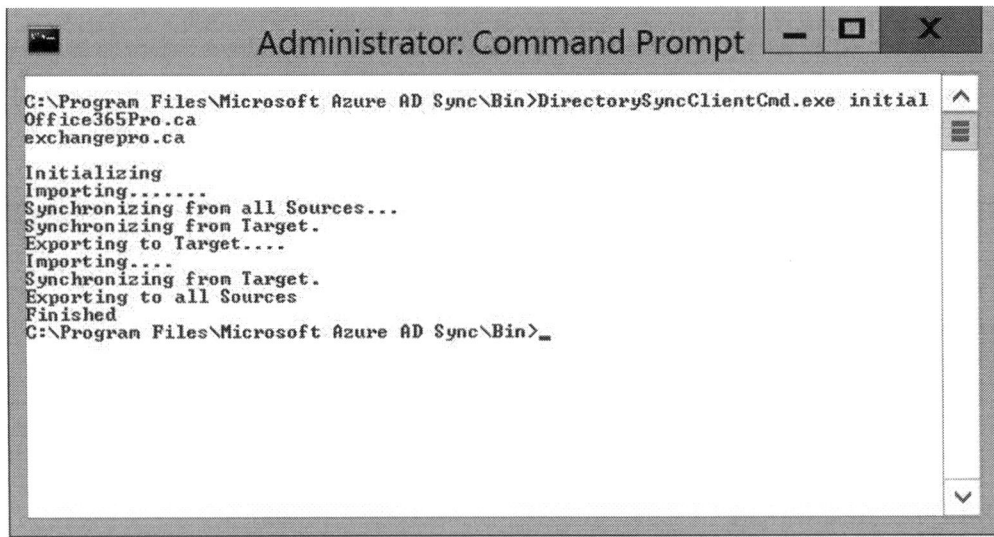

Figure 9-42. Forcing the initial synchronization

A look at the Synchronization Service Manager shows that the full import from one of the AD DS forests completed successfully; see Figure 9-43.

Profile Name: Full Import User Name: EXCHANGEPRO\miman					
Step Type: Full Import (Stage Only)			**Partition:** DC=exchangepro,DC=ca		
Start Time: 12/12/2014 2:07:16 PM			**End Time:** 12/12/2014 2:07:19 PM **Status:** success		
Synchronization Statistics			Connection Status		
Staging			DC01.exchangepro.ca:389		success
Unchanged	0				
Adds	87		Synchronization Errors		
Updates	0				
Renames	0				
Deletes	0				
Discovery					
Filtered Objects	0				

Figure 9-43. Viewing the synchronization results

You can also see in Figure 9-44 that the second AD DS forest import completed successfully.

Profile Name: Full Import User Name: EXCHANGEPRO\miman			
Step Type: Full Import (Stage Only)		**Partition:** DC=Office365Pro,DC=ca	
Start Time: 12/12/2014 2:07:12 PM		**End Time:** 12/12/2014 2:07:16 PM **Status:** success	
Synchronization Statistics		Connection Status	
Staging		O365DC01.Office365Pro.ca:389	success
Unchanged	0		
Adds	54	Synchronization Errors	
Updates	0		
Renames	0		
Deletes	0		
Discovery			
Filtered Objects	0		

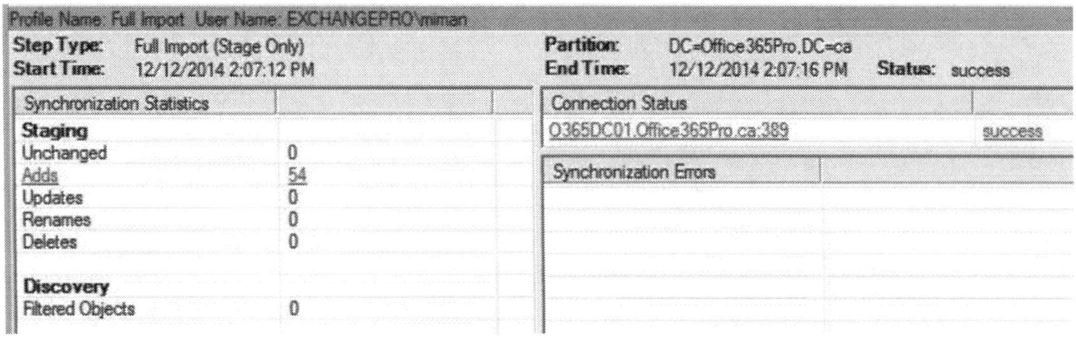

Figure 9-44. *Viewing the synchronization results*

Finally, in Figure 9-45, you can see that the export to AD AS completed successfully as well.

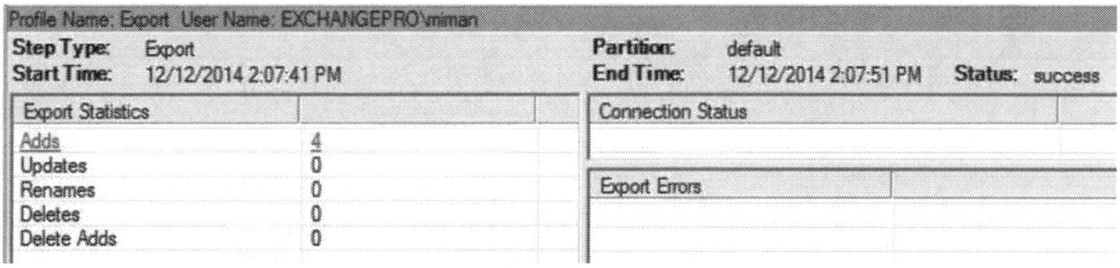

Profile Name: Export User Name: EXCHANGEPRO\miman			
Step Type: Export		**Partition:** default	
Start Time: 12/12/2014 2:07:41 PM		**End Time:** 12/12/2014 2:07:51 PM **Status:** success	
Export Statistics		Connection Status	
Adds	4		
Updates	0		
Renames	0	Export Errors	
Deletes	0		
Delete Adds	0		

Figure 9-45. *Viewing the synchronization results*

As you can see, a large number of objects were pulled in from each of the on-premises domains, but only a small number of objects were pushed out to AAD. This is caused by some of the filtering done on the inbound filtering rule, as well as by some of the on-premises objects that were previously synchronized.

In this release, version 1.0.470.1023 of Microsoft's directory synchronization tool, the object-filtering component is separated from the synchronization service manager, where it was previously. The filtering rules are now created and managed in a new tool called the Synchronization Rules Editor; it is located in the C:\Program Files\Microsoft Azure AD Sync\UIShell\ folder, and it is called SyncRulesEditor.exe. A number of default rules are designed to prevent objects, such as system objects, from synchronizing to AAD.

AZURE AD CONNECT TOOL

Microsoft is currently working on a new tool called Azure AD Connect (AAD Connect). This tool is in the public preview stage as of this writing.

AAD Connect is designed to simplify the installation of the tools required to synchronize and authenticate with Windows AAD, whether you are using a single or multiple AD forests, password sync, or AD FS. The wizard deploys and configures all components required to get the connection up and running, including synchronization services, AD FS, and the Azure AD PowerShell module.

With the new AAD Connect tool, customers can connect their on-premises infrastructure to AAD in a single, wizard-driven procedure. Based on your selections in the wizard, the tool does the following:

- Connects to your on-premises AD FS servers and downloads and installs the prerequisites, including the .NET Framework, Azure AD PowerShell Module, and Microsoft Online Services Sign-In Assistant

- Connects to your on-premises web application proxy (WAP) servers and downloads and installs the prerequisites, including the .NET Framework, Azure AD PowerShell Module, and Microsoft Online Services Sign-In Assistant

- Installs AAD Sync and configures the sync options such as password sync, password write-back, and Exchange hybrid mode, depending on your deployment requirements

- Helps to verify that everything is working properly

You can download the public preview tool and AAD Connect documentation from
`http://connect.microsoft.com/site1164/program8612`.

Summary

In this chapter, you were introduced to Azure Active Directory. You learned about the different versions of AAD and what each version offers. You also learned about the different methods used to add user accounts to AAD, along with how to install AAD Sync and how to configure the different filtering options.

In the next chapter, you learn about extending your on-premises AD to Azure by using the site-to-site VPN and installing a Windows server on an Azure virtual machine that will be configured as a domain controller in your domain.

CHAPTER 10

■ ■ ■

Extending Azure Active Directory

The Azure Active Directory Story

Chapter 9 introduced Microsoft Azure Active Directory (AAD) as the identity management (IDM) solution for cloud services like Office 365. AAD has continued to evolve to become a fully featured identity as a service (IDaaS) platform.

This chapter introduces the extension of AAD beyond Microsoft Office 365. AAD can be used to incorporate SSO and provisioning/de-provisioning of third-party SaaS offerings. You can unlock these extended capabilities by acquiring Azure Active Directory Premium (AADP) and using its licensing model.

As a SaaS, Office 365 needs an IDM platform. Azure AD is that IDM platform; it allows you to create and manage users in the Cloud. For enterprise customers with on-premises Active Directory (AD), the Office 365 Directory Synchronization (DirSync) tool was provided to replicate on-premises AD accounts to AAD. DirSync was later renamed Azure Active Directory Sync (AAD Sync), thus reflecting more accurately what the tool is designed to do.

Figure 10-1 depicts the process of synchronizing user objects from on-premises IDMs like AD to AAD via AAD Sync or Forefront Identity Manager (FIM).

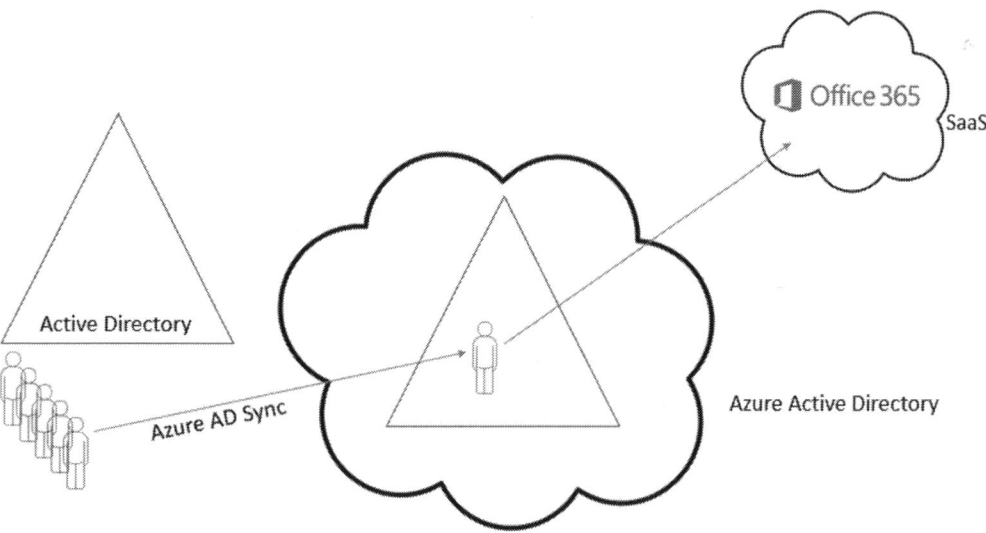

Figure 10-1. *User accounts synchronized with AAD for use in Office 365*

■ **Note**   Microsoft AAD is already in use if an organization is an Office 365 customer. The next version of FIM is called Microsoft Identity Manager (MIM). During this transition process, FIM and MIM are used interchangeably. AADP is the licensing model that unlocks additional AAD capabilities, which are explored in this chapter.

Single Sign-On (SSO) for Third-Party SaaS

This chapter explores the expansion of SSO through the use of AAD. As covered previously, a common enterprise architecture uses AAD to federate on-premises identities and consume claims-based authentication. Identities in AAD that are designated as federated identities trigger AAD to refer to a trusted claims authentication provider to carry out the actual authentication and consume the claims accordingly. As more and more enterprise customers have adopted Office 365, this has become a very common implementation of AAD and Active Directory Federation Services (AD FS).

CASE STUDY 1: SSO AND USER MANAGEMENT FOR THIRD-PARTY SAAS

In this case study, Adatum Inc. is an Office 365 customer. One of the departments recently selected Salesforce as its customer relationship management (CRM) solution. Adatum Inc. likes the turnkey nature of cloud-based SaaS so that it does not need to add and manage more on-premises infrastructure.

Challenge

Adatum Inc. faced two challenges with this decision. First, IT needed to manage Salesforce users separately in Salesforce. Second, Salesforce users needed to manage their own login credentials and passwords, which are separate from their AD credentials.

Resolution

Adatum Inc. chose to extend AAD to provide SSO for Salesforce. After all, users were already synchronized to AAD, and the company's SSO infrastructure was already deployed. Using an existing IDM was the best approach in this scenario. Figure 10-2 depicts how AAD will be used for Salesforce for Adatum Inc.

■ **Note**   Even if an organization is not currently using Office 365, AAD is still a viable IDaaS solution that can be the single IDM for cloud-based and claims-based applications.

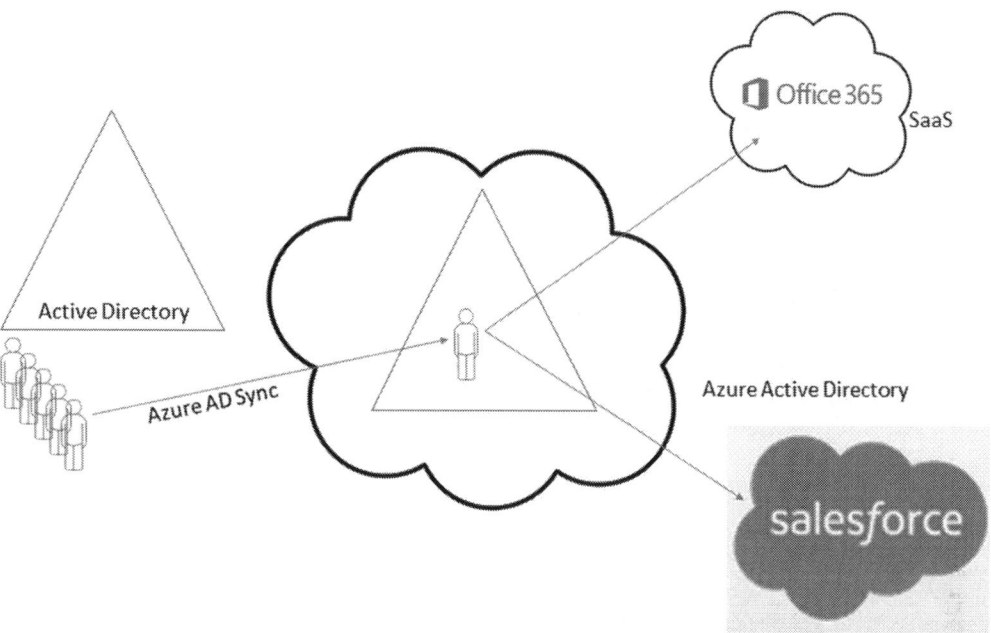

Figure 10-2. *Using AAD for Salesforce*

EXTENDING AAD FOR A THIRD-PARTY SAAS

The following exercise walks you through the steps that Adatum Inc. took to extend AAD to Salesforce. This exercise shows the steps of extending AAD for provisioning and authenticating Salesforce accounts. At the time of writing, the new Preview Portal does not include the ability to configure AAD, so this exercise uses the traditional Portal.

In order to configure Salesforce with AAD, you may need to go back and forth between Salesforce and AAD, so it is recommended that you open a separate browser window for the Salesforce configuration. Doing so minimizes confusion and will help you keep track of the configuration process. This exercise also assumes the following:

- AAD and AAD Sync have been configured, if you want to integrate third-party SaaS provisioning as part of your organization's AD account provisioning and de-provisioning (recommended).

- There is an existing enterprise Salesforce account.

- Your organization already has an Azure Active Directory Premium subscription, or you have signed up for a trial AADP subscription. If you do not have AADP, you may not be able to see some of the options described in the following exercises—for example, self-service password reset (SSPR).

■ **Note**   You can sign up for the Developer Edition of Salesforce in order to follow this exercise. To do so, visit https://developer.salesforce.com/page/Developer_Edition. Log in to the Azure Management Portal at https://manage.windowsazure.com.

Follow these steps:

1. Go to the AAD that will be used for Salesforce authentication, and click Applications, as shown in Figure 10-3.

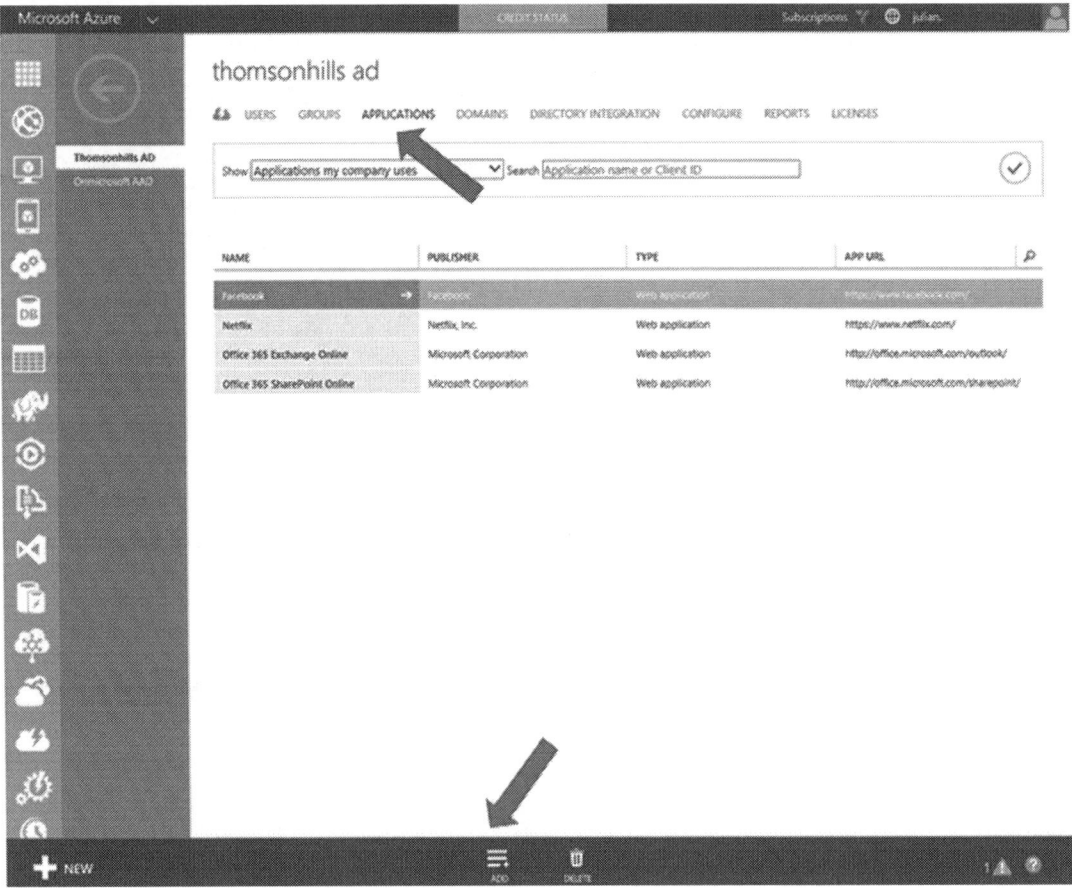

Figure 10-3.   *Adding a new third-party SaaS to AAD*

2. In the pop-up window, select Add An Application From The Gallery, type salesforce in the search window, and click the magnifying glass, as shown in Figure 10-4.

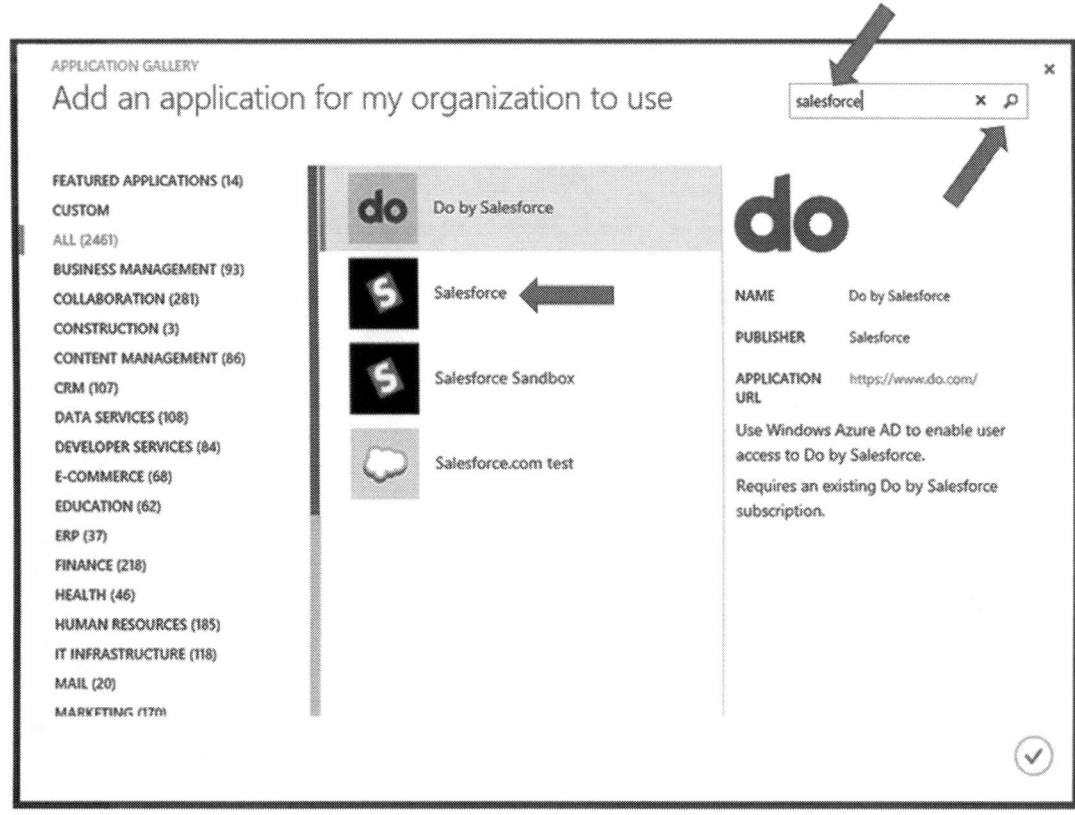

Figure 10-4. Adding Salesforce to AAD from the gallery

3. Select Salesforce from the search results, and click the check mark in the lower-right corner of the screen.

4. Once Salesforce has been added, under Step 1, click the green Configure Single Sign-On button.

5. For this exercise, select Windows Azure AD Single Sign-On, and then click the arrow in the lower-right corner.

■ **Note** In your organization's actual deployment scenario, select the SSO method that best matches your identity-management scenario.

---

6. On the Configure App Settings screen, click the Learn More link, and view the configuration instructions, as shown in Figure 10-5. Note that you need to do this each time you add a different SaaS application to AAD, because each application from the gallery has different steps and requirements; read the instructions so you have a better idea of what to expect. This exercise, however, walks you through the entire setup process.

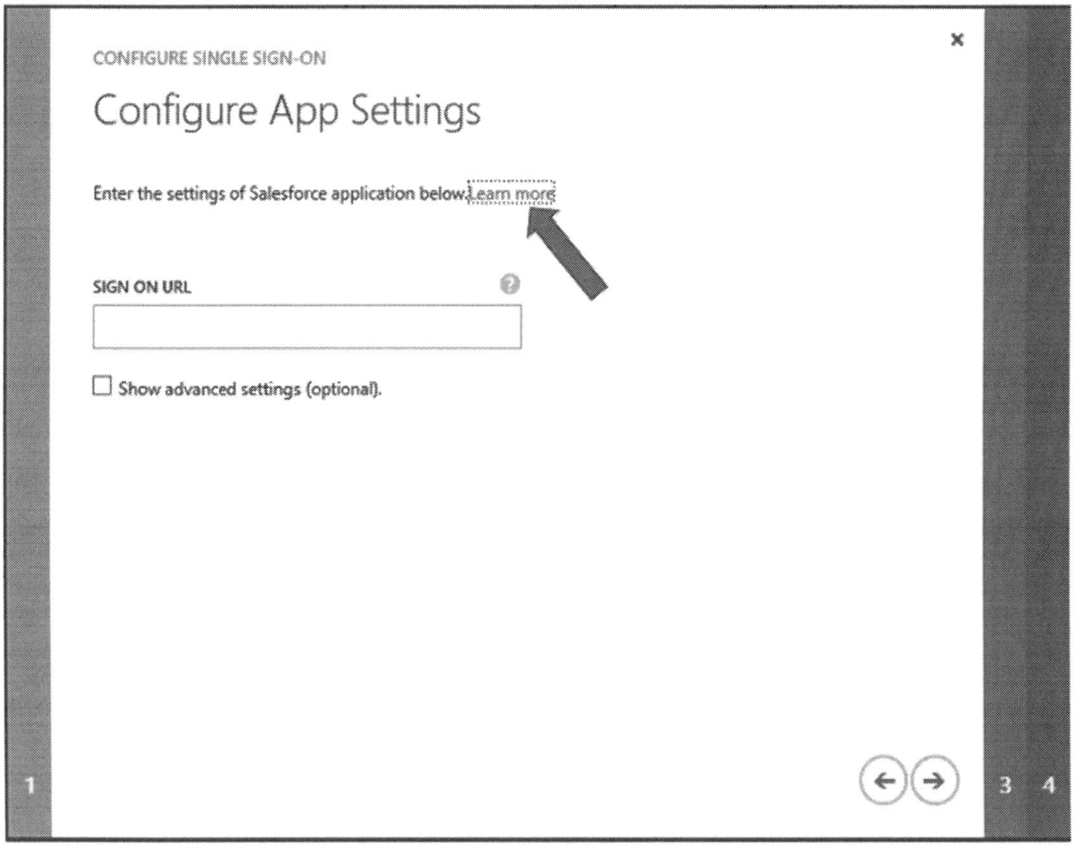

Figure 10-5. Viewing custom instructions to add Salesforce to AAD

7. Open a new, separate browser window, and log in to your Salesforce account at
   `https://login.salesforce.com`.

8. Along the left side of the screen, expand the Domain Management menu, and click
   My Domain, as shown in Figure 10-6.

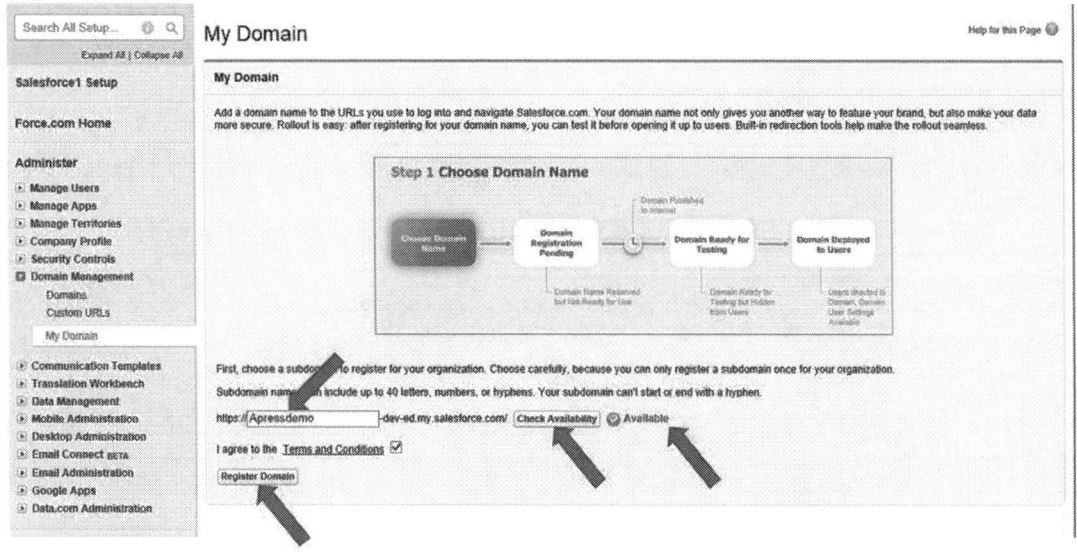

Figure 10-6. *Registering a Salesforce subdomain*

9. Enter a subdomain name, and click Check Availability. If the subdomain is available, a green Available notification appears, as shown in Figure 10-6. Read the Terms and Conditions, check the box to agree, and then click Register Domain. Make a note of your subdomain name, which you use in step 10.

10. Return to the AAD configuration browser screen, shown in Figure 10-5, and enter the Salesforce subdomain URL you registered in step 9, making sure you prefix the URL with `https://` (for example, `https://apressdemo-dev-ed.my.salesforce.com`). Then click the arrow in the lower corner.

11. In the Configure Single Sign-On At Salesforce page, click Download Certificate, as shown in Figure 10-7. Save the certificate to your computer. Make a note of the location and filename, because you will need to upload the certificate to Salesforce later. You can view the Salesforce configuration instructions, but this exercise walks you through the process.

Figure 10-7. *Downloading a certificate for Salesforce*

12. Return to the Salesforce browser window to continue with the Salesforce configuration.

13. Expand Security Controls in the menu on the left, and select Single Sign-On Settings, as shown in Figure 10-8.

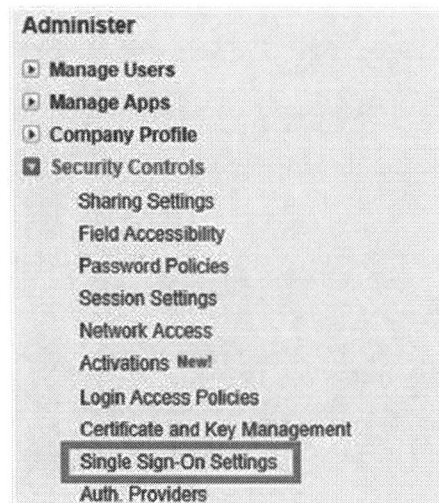

Administer

▸ **Manage Users**

▸ **Manage Apps**

▸ **Company Profile**

☑ **Security Controls**

      Sharing Settings

      Field Accessibility

      Password Policies

      Session Settings

      Network Access

      Activations **New!**

      Login Access Policies

      Certificate and Key Management

      Single Sign-On Settings

      Auth. Providers

Figure 10-8. *Configuring Salesforce SSO settings*

14. Click Edit to configure SAML.

15. Enable SAML by selecting the SAML Enabled check box. Click Save.

16. Click New under SAML Single Sign-On Settings.

17. Type in a name for this SAML configuration. Use the name `AzureSSO` for this exercise.

18. Return to the Azure AD configuration browser window, shown in Figure 10-7, and copy the issuer URL to the clipboard by clicking the icon located at the end of the URL, as shown in Figure 10-9.

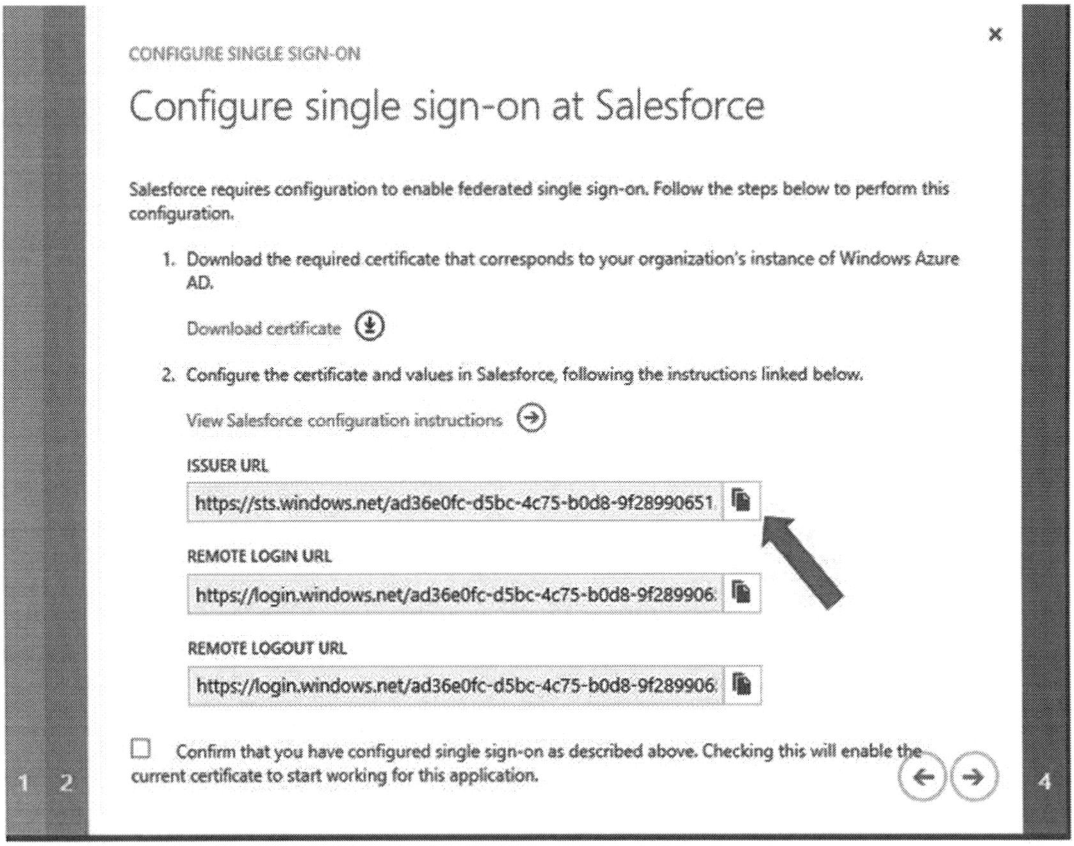

Figure 10-9. *Copying URLs from AAD to paste into the Salesforce configuration*

19. Return to the Salesforce browser where you're configuring the Salesforce SSO, and paste the URL into the Issuer field.

20. Repeat steps 18 and 19 to copy the remote login URL from AAD and paste it into the Identity Provider Login URL field in Salesforce.

21. Again, repeat steps 18 and 19 to copy the remote logout URL from AAD and paste it into the Identity Provider Logout URL field in Salesforce.

22. Still in the Salesforce SSO configuration browser, click the Browse button next to Identity Provider Certificate. Navigate to the certificate downloaded in step 11, select the certificate, and click Open.

23. In the SAML Identity Type section, select Assertion Sontains User's salesforce.com Username.

24. In the SAML Identity Location section, select Identity Is In The NameIdentifer Element Of The Subject Statement.

25. For Service Provider Initiated Request Binding, select HTTP Redirect.

26. In the Entity ID field, enter the Salesforce subdomain URL registered in step 10, making sure you prefix the URL with `https://` (for example, `https://apressdemo-dev-ed.my.salesforce.com`).

27. Click the Save button on the Salesforce SSO configuration screen to save the settings.

28. Click and expand the Domain Management menu in Salesforce, and select My Domain.

29. On the My Domain page in the Authentication Configuration section, click the Click Here To Login button.

30. After the login completes, make the custom Salesforce domain available by clicking Deploy To Users.

31. When you see the warning that the deployment cannot be reversed, click OK.

32. In the Authentication Configuration section, click Edit.

33. If you have a custom logo, you can choose to upload it to brand your organization's Salesforce subscription.

34. Select Azure SSO as an authentication service. Optionally, you can de-select Login Page if you only want to allow authentication through Azure SSO without the option of preventing a Salesforce-only account from logging in.

35. Click Save.

36. Return to the AAD configuration browser. You should still be on the Configure Single Sign-On At Salesforce screen. Select the "Confirm that you have configured single sign-on as described above. Checking this will enable the current certificate to start working for this application" check box at the bottom of the screen.

37. Click the arrow to advance to the next screen.

38. Verify and provide an e-mail address for notification of successful configuration, and then click the check mark at the bottom of the screen to complete the setup.

39. Click the Configure User Provisioning option in step 2.

40. Enter your Salesforce admin account and password.

41. For the User Security Token field, do the following:

    a. Go to the browser with your Salesforce configuration. Click the down arrow next to your name at upper-right, and select My Settings.

    b. Expand Personal in menu at left, and select Reset My Security Token.

    c. Click the blue Reset Security Token button.

    d. The new security token is e-mailed to you.

    e. Copy the security token string from the e-mail.

    f. Return to the Azure SSO User Provisioning configuration screen.

    g. Ignore the instructions to append the security token to your password. Instead, enter the security token string from the e-mail into the User Security Token field.

42. Click the arrow at the bottom of the screen.

43. If there are no errors, you see a confirmation screen. Click in the lower-right corner to complete the configuration for user provisioning.

44. Once AAD and Salesforce have been configured, you can test authentication to Salesforce through SSO. However, before doing so, you must assign users to the application:

    a. Click the Assign Users button in the Salesforce application configuration window.

    b. In the Users And Groups window, select the user or users to whom you want to assign access, and click Assign at the bottom of the screen, as shown in Figure 10-10.

    c. Select the appropriate Salesforce role for your users, and click the check mark in the lower-right corner.

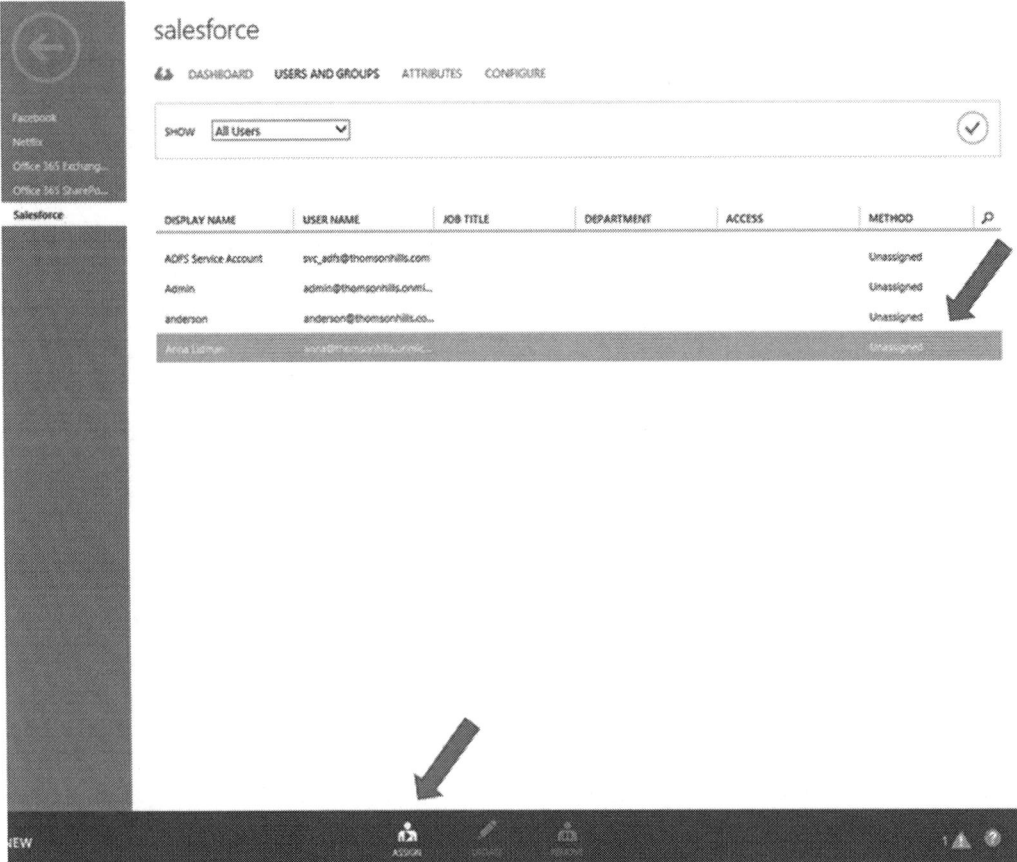

Figure 10-10. Assigning a user to an application

Users can now log in to Salesforce using their Active Directory credentials without being prompted for their user name or password.

End-User Experience

SaaS applications that have been assigned to users can be accessed directly via their respective URLs or via the Azure Access Panel at https://myapps.microsoft.com. The concept of the Access Panel is a single landing page where users can see and launch SaaS apps to which they have access without having to remember or bookmark each SaaS app's URL. Figure 10-11 shows the Access Panel.

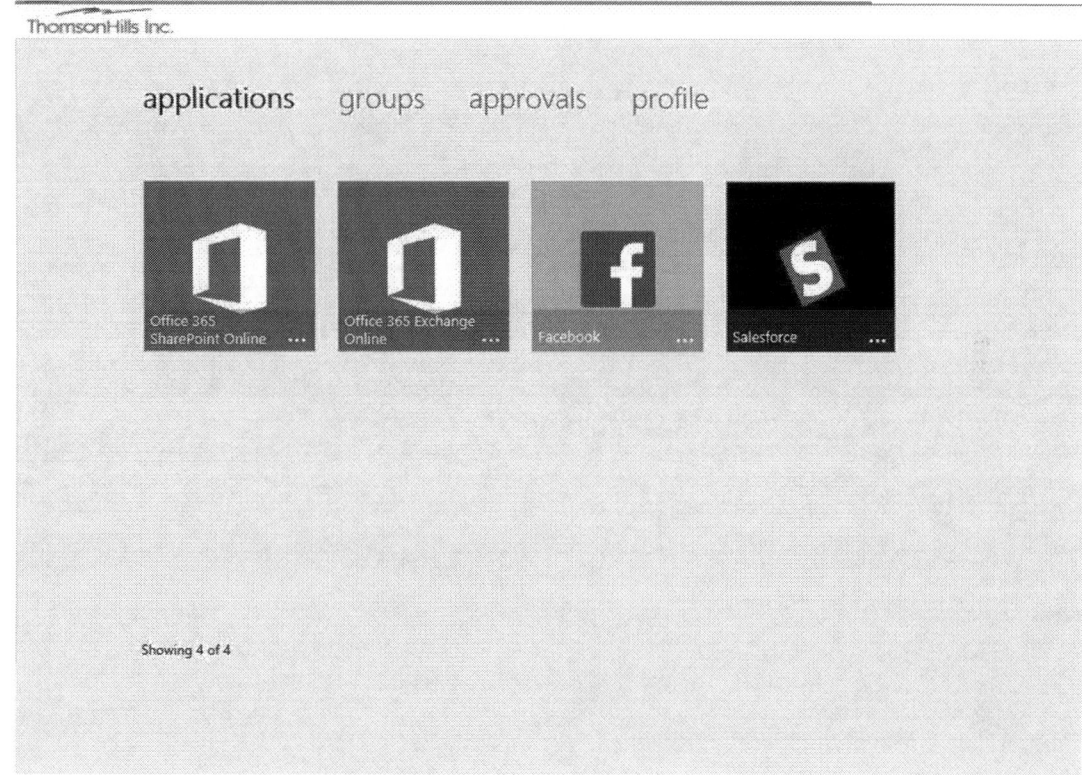

Figure 10-11. *The Azure Access Panel, showing all SaaS apps authorized for the user*

End-User SSO Experience with a Third-Party SaaS

This exercise demonstrates the user experience when accessing an application from the Access Panel:

1. Go to the Access Panel at https://myapps.microsoft.com, and log in when prompted. The user account used to log in displays the icons of applications to which the user has access, similar to the screen shown in Figure 10-11.

2. Continuing with the current scenario, click the Salesforce icon to launch Salesforce. The user is redirected to the Salesforce instance for Adatum Inc., as shown in Figure 10-12.

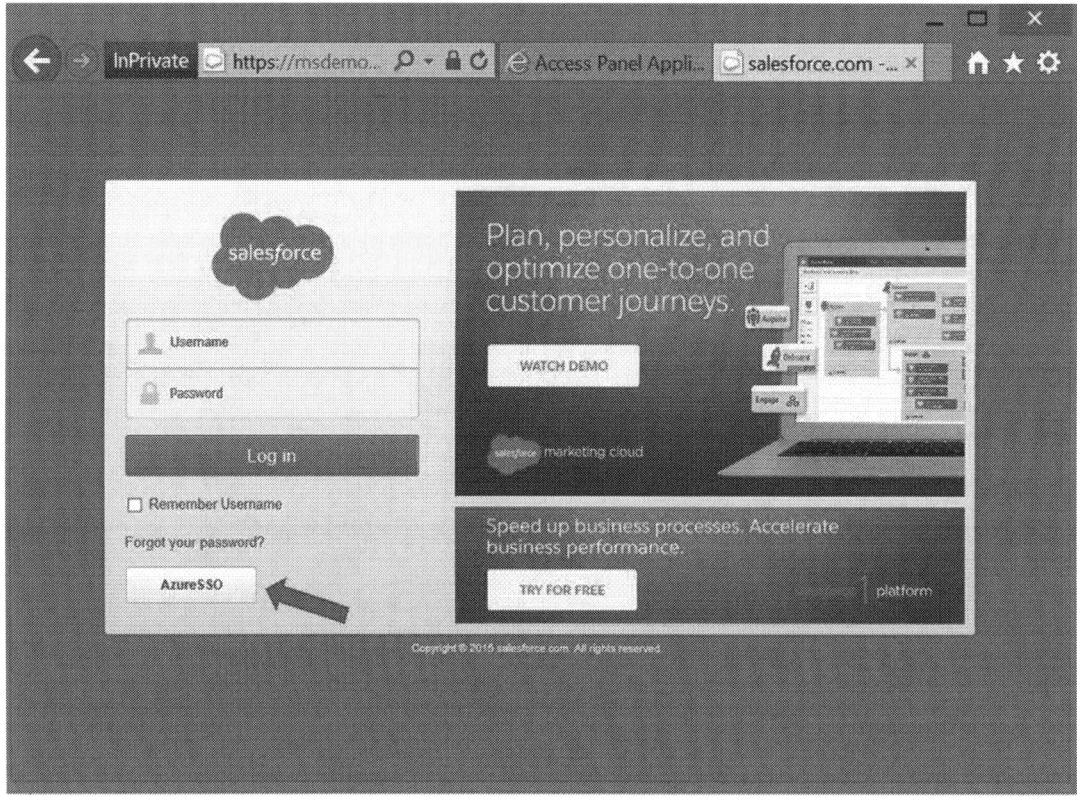

Figure 10-12. Redirected instance of Salesforce with the AzureSSO option

3. The user has the option to provide a username and password. Or if the user wants to use their credentials, as is the case in this exercise, click the AzureSSO button as shown in Figure 10-12.

4. The current user's authentication token is evaluated and, if it is still valid, the user is automatically authenticated to Salesforce. This experience is similar to other SaaS apps where AAD can provide SSO.

In this case study, AAD is used to provide SSO to a third-party SaaS, which was already pre-federated with AAD. The administrator for Adatum Inc. only needed to go through the configuration process once and assign users to the application before SSO could be established with Salesforce.

Once authenticated through AAD, there is no need for end users to supply their user credentials again in order to access Salesforce.

For the administrator, users of Salesforce or any third-party SaaS are managed through AD and AAD. There is no need to create, modify, or delete users as separate administrative processes for Salesforce or any SaaS that has been pre-federated with AAD.

CASE STUDY 2: SSO FOR CUSTOM DEVELOPED APPS

SSO for third-party SaaS was introduced in the previous case study. What about the case where in-house custom applications also require SSO?

Challenge

Adatum Inc. has several in-house custom line-of-business (LOB) applications, which are claims-based apps in the demilitarized zone (DMZ). Adatum Inc. would like to allow employees access to these applications from the Access Panel and to experience a SSO experience similar to that of third-party SaaS.

Resolution

The process to extend AAD to provide SSO for in-house custom applications is similar to the steps outlined in Case Study 1 for third-party SaaS. However, instead of selecting Add An Application From The gallery in step 3 of the exercise "Extending AAD for a Third-Party SAAS," choose the option Add An Application My Organization Is Developing, as shown in Figure 10-13.

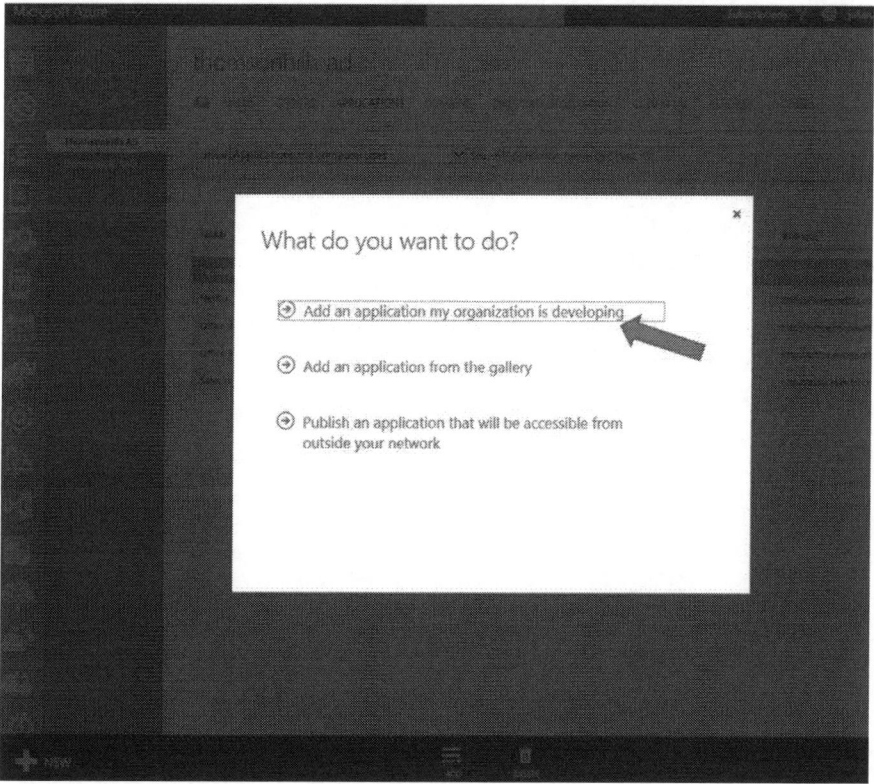

Figure 10-13. *Adding an in-house custom application to AAD*

Adatum Inc.'s developers must make sure custom in-house apps can federate and authenticate with AAD. Therefore, the developers need to understand the concept of claims-based protocols, such as SAML and OAuth, as well as security and access concepts, such as the Service Principal Name of an application. Going into the details about such developer-specific topics is beyond the scope of this book, but there are many good resources on this topic, including this blog post from Vittorio Bertocci, a Microsoft developer: `www.cloudidentity.com/blog/2012/07/12/single-sign-on-with-windows-azure-active-directory-a-deep-dive-2`.

AAD continues to evolve rapidly. You can keep up to date on all the new and upcoming features of AAD through the AD Team Blog: `http://blogs.technet.com/b/ad`.

In this case study, AAD is also used for in-house custom LOB applications. This provides SSO for most modern applications and thus provides users with a more seamless experience when accessing applications after the initial authentication. It also provides IT administrators with a single model to provision users through AD and AAD without having to manage disparate IDMs specific to individual applications.

CASE STUDY 3: SELF-SERVICE PASSWORD RESET (SSPR)

Adatum Inc. is exploring options to streamline IT operations by reducing the amount of busywork for IT administrators so that precious IT resources can be put to better use. Adatum Inc. would also like to provide better customer service for employees and 24×7 support for as many IT requests as possible.

Challenge

Adatum Inc. needs to optimize the use of IT resources in order to remain competitive. As a multinational corporation, Adatum Inc. has employees located throughout the world, and it may not be economical to have multiple Help Desks or even a single 24×7 Help Desk to support a global workforce. But whenever IT issues prevent employees from accessing Adatum Inc.'s systems, there is a loss of productivity that impacts revenues.

Resolution

Adatum Inc. discovered that, in addition to SSO for third-party SaaS, AAD also provides users with the self-service capability to reset passwords securely. With this ability, employees around the world can reset their passwords without contacting the Help Desk.

■ **Note** In addition to password reset, AAD provides user self-service for group-membership management. Configuring self-service group-membership management is similar to configuring SSPR and just as straightforward. Therefore, this chapter does not cover it in detail.

ENABLING USER SELF-SERVICE WITH AAD

This exercise demonstrates the steps required to configure user SSPR as well as the end-user experience. It also shows the steps to configure AAD SSPR:

1. Go to the Azure Management Portal at `https://manage.windowsazure.com`.

2. Select the desired directory in Azure, and click Configure, as shown in Figure 10-14.

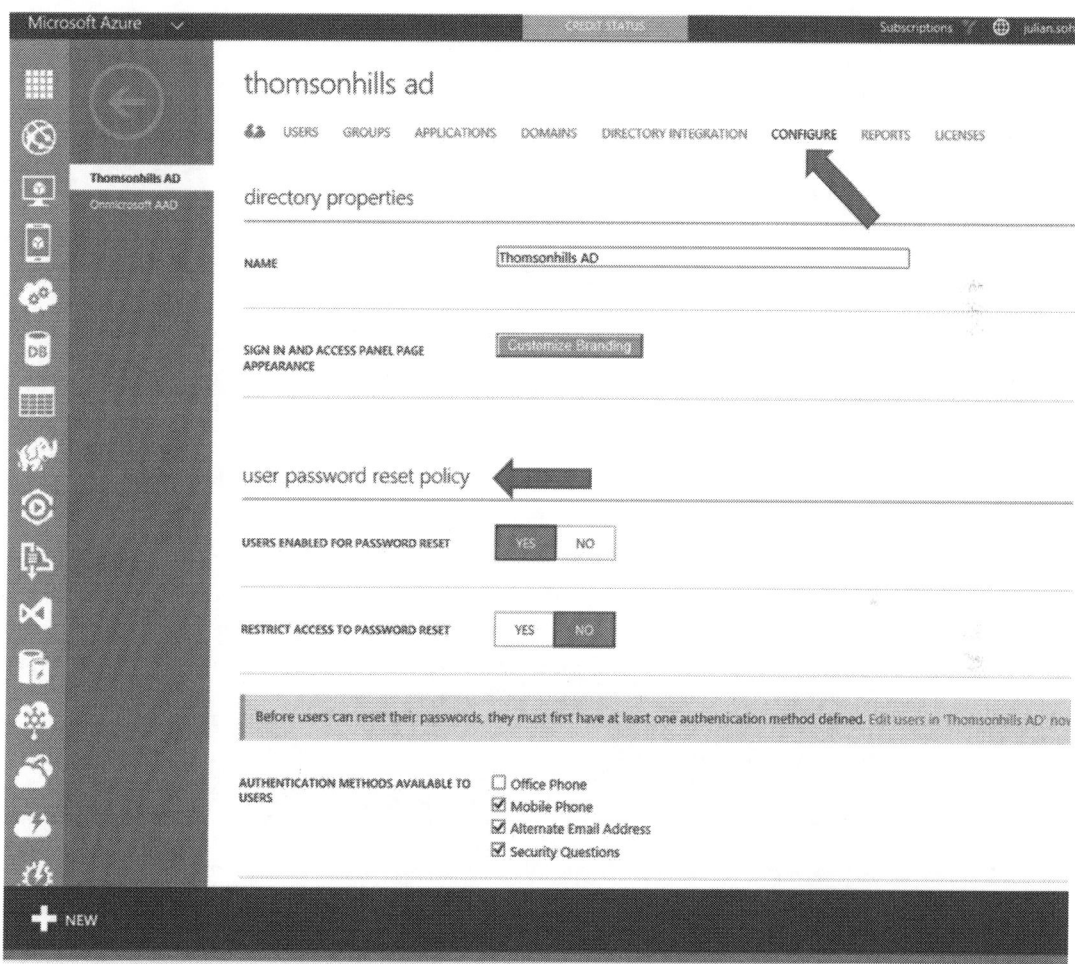

Figure 10-14. *Configuring a directory in Azure*

3. Configure the parameters under User Password Reset Policy, also shown in Figure 10-14. The options are self-explanatory, so it is left to you to finish configuring the password-reset policy based on the organization's needs.

4. Once the self-service password policy has been set, users must be provided with this link in order to be guided through a registration process to provide verification information: `http://aka.ms/ssprsetup`. This link can be sent via e-mail or placed on the organization's intranet page. Alternatively, you can turn on the option to require a user to be prompted automatically for the information upon initial login.

End-User Experience with SSPR

This example is based on the automatic verification option. When any one of the four options used to verify a user's identity is selected, the user is prompted to provide that piece of information when logging in to AAD, as shown in Figure 10-15 and Figure 10-16.

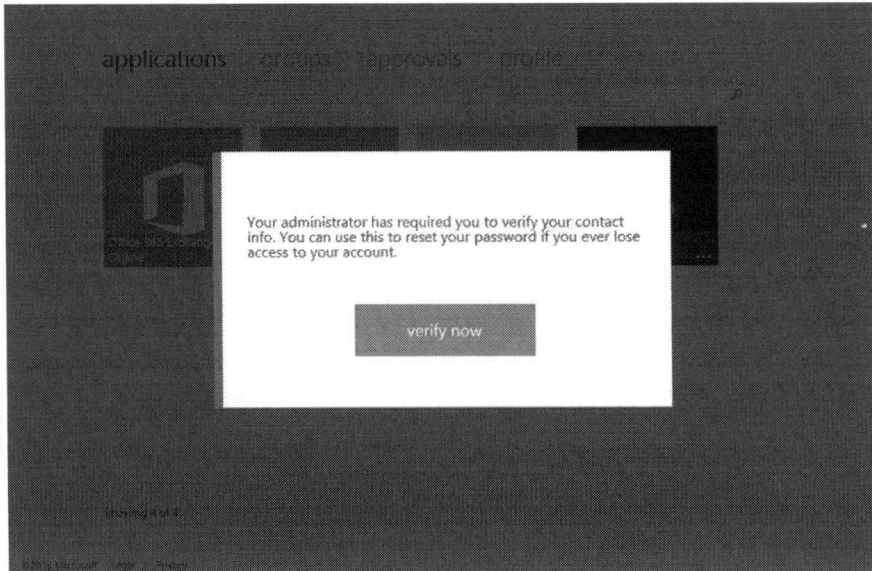

Figure 10-15. *The user is prompted to provide verification information upon login when an account does not contain information for a particular verification method*

don't lose access to your account!

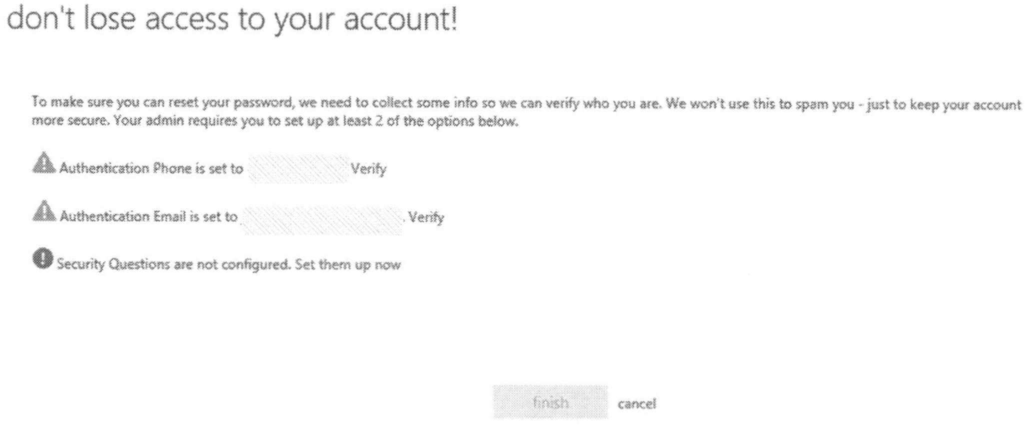

To make sure you can reset your password, we need to collect some info so we can verify who you are. We won't use this to spam you - just to keep your account more secure. Your admin requires you to set up at least 2 of the options below.

⚠ Authentication Phone is set to ▓▓▓▓▓▓ Verify

⚠ Authentication Email is set to ▓▓▓▓▓▓▓. Verify

🛇 Security Questions are not configured. Set them up now

finish   cancel

Figure 10-16. *The user is presented with information that needs to be verified or provided*

In the event that the user needs to reset their AAD password through the self-service process, they select the Can't Access Your Account link on the Azure login page, as shown in Figure 10-17.

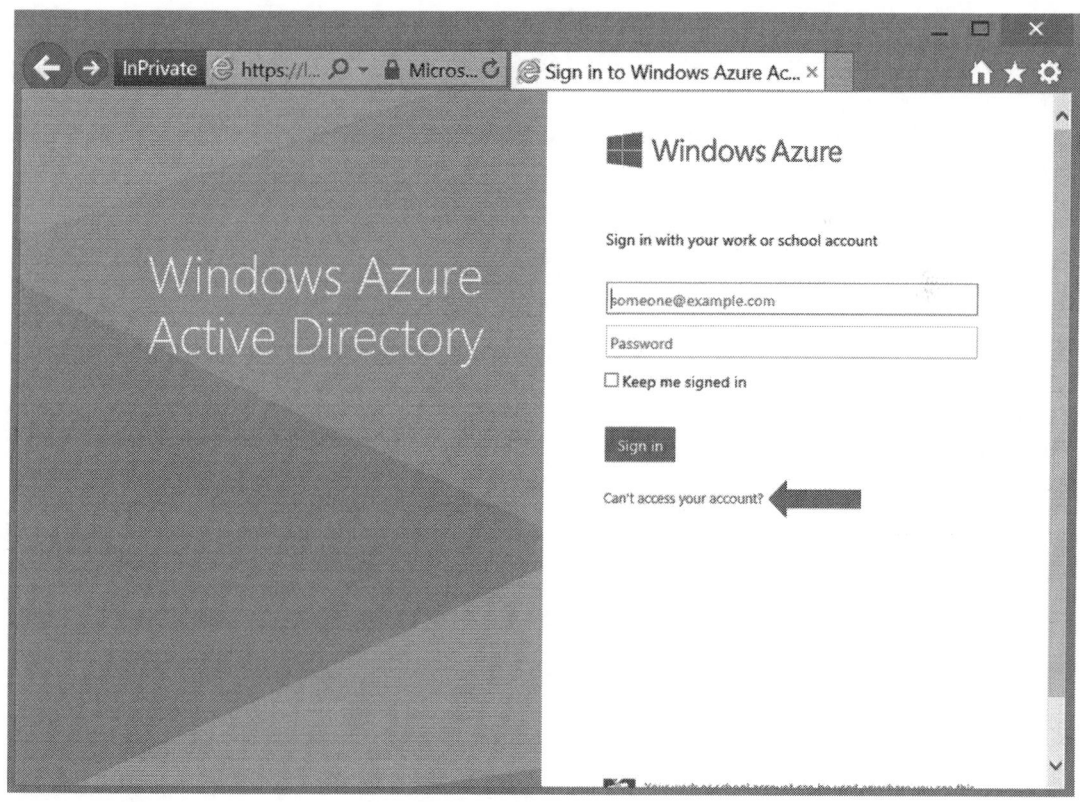

Figure 10-17. *The Can't Access Your Account link for SSPR*

Additional Information Regarding SSPR

AAD can also be configured with password write-back to on-premises AD. When this feature is configured, passwords that are reset in AAD are written back to on-premises AD so the user can authenticate through AD or AD FS after a password reset.

Another important point is that AADP or the Enterprise Mobility Suite, of which AADP is a part, also provides the licensing for an on-premises FIM server and user portal. This allows organizations to provide SSPR for users when they are not able to log into their domain-joined computers while on the corporate network. Configuring FIM is beyond the scope of this book, but this deployment guide details the steps to deploy and configure the FIM Portal for SSPR for domain-joined computers: `http://www.microsoft.com/en-us/download/details.aspx?id=29959`.

Summary

This chapter introduced the key features of AAD. Feature of AAD that were not covered include customizing the login page through branding (`https://msdn.microsoft.com/en-us/library/azure/dn532270.aspx`), security reports, and usage reports. You can learn about these capabilities of AAD at `http://azure.microsoft.com/en-us/pricing/details/active-directory`.

Chapter 11 examines a different set of Azure workloads and scenarios: Azure as an infrastructure as a service (IaaS) option for high-availability (HA) and disaster recovery (DR).

CHAPTER 11

■ ■ ■

Clusters, Regional VNets, High Availability, and Disaster Recovery

One of the key business features of Microsoft Azure is the ability to create or move virtual machines (VMs) into Azure, back out of Azure, and into another private or partner clouds when it makes sense for your business model, including the licenses you already own. Services create revenue, so the impact can be felt in client activity load, which in a traditional datacenter requires purchasing more hardware, "racking and stacking" systems, and weeks or months of preparation. Adding systems for improved performance or higher availability is built into Azure.

This chapter is about availability. It gives you a deeper understanding of Azure support for making systems highly available through Azure properties, infrastructure as a service (IaaS) in Azure, and other Azure services. Each of the topics covered addresses providing availability or redundancy for explicit business functionality. Specifically, this chapter provides you with guidance to plan for and architect business support using the following:

- Clusters

- Regional VNets

- High availability

- Disaster recovery

Failover Clustering in Microsoft Azure

The first availability service this chapter discusses—failover clustering—addresses the question, "Why would a business need a cluster to failover to the Azure cloud?" The answer is that failover, or availability, is often a business-driven response and not necessarily an IT-only requirement. The Azure cloud is always highly available, so this section looks at the requirements for enabling high availability (HA) services with Azure.

With nearly unlimited services, Azure subscriptions enable customers to scale down the size and cost of traditional on-premises datacenters. Chapter 8 discussed the flexibility of extending your traditional network into Azure IaaS by creating the exact type of IP networks in on-premises datacenters using Azure VNets. Hybrid cloud connectivity saves companies money while providing greater agility to create new business opportunities quickly, because Azure connects company services and systems using the same common tools and skills used with on-premises systems. With IaaS and Azure VNets enabled, you can extend clustering into or out of Azure.

▓ **Note**   One of our customers has offices and a small datacenter that they lease from the building owner. Power is often lost for the entire building, so this customer has architected its Azure subscription as the company's primary datacenter, with on-premises as the backup.

In this chapter's cluster example, Microsoft SQL Server is the database that the business needs to be highly available. Let's first discuss and walk through the options of the AlwaysOn Failover Cluster Instances feature and then discuss and provide steps for the AlwaysOn Availability Groups feature.

Why Choose Failover Cluster Instances?

Although all data is stored in triple redundancy in Azure, services hosted through Azure are not redundant by default. If an application's downtime is more expensive to the business than the cost of an additional server, *failover cluster instances (FCIs)* should be deployed. Your business may choose FCIs in Azure with the AlwaysOn Availability Groups feature because it is a relatively inexpensive and robust clustering solution that offers complete control over all services and databases on the server. One instance of Microsoft SQL server in Azure does not provide fault tolerance. Keeping servers in sync so that data is identical on each node using AlwaysOn FCIs is a great option. Service availability is necessary to keep one server online and responding to client requests if the other service is installed in an Azure upgrade domain while undergoing maintenance. Microsoft provides maintenance on one upgrade domain at a time to minimize disruptions. Fault domains and upgrade domains are discussed in greater detail in the section "High Availability in Microsoft Azure."

▓ **Note**   A *fault domain* in Azure is a rack of computers. During deployment of Azure services, you, the owner, cannot control the allocation of a fault domain. An Azure upgrade domain distributes services evenly into multiple upgrade domains so that disruption of services during a platform upgrade is minimal.

Failover cluster instances protect the entire instance of the server, system, and MSDB database. Availability groups only protect user-defined databases and not the complete system. There is a limit to the number of availability group worker threads to protect the number of databases.

ENABLING AN ALWAYSON FAILOVER CLUSTER

To successfully create a two- or three-node failover cluster between your on-premises datacenter and Azure, you need to have already configured Azure virtual networks (VNets) in your subscription and created a site-to-site virtual private network (VPN), as explained in Chapter 8. You also need to understand Windows Server 2012 R2 failover clustering, including using Windows Cluster Manager; this topic is outside the scope of this book.

Note Microsoft Virtual Academy has a free class that teachers Windows Server 2012 R2 cluster techniques. It is available at www.microsoftvirtualacademy.com/training-courses/failover-clustering-in-windows-server-2012-r2.

To create a failover cluster, follow these steps:

1. Create your VMs and storage in your Azure subscription, as described in Chapters 6 and 7.

2. Create a file-share witness for cluster voting, as described in this article: http://blogs.msdn.com/b/clustering/archive/2014/03/31/10512457.aspx.

3. Create a cluster, enable failover clustering for each node, and run the validation tests. This will take several minutes to complete. Create the cluster name and access point IP address.

4. Enable cluster volume replication.

5. Install SQL on the cluster nodes.

6. Enable load balancing.

Why Choose AlwaysOn Availability Groups?

Microsoft SQL 2014 enhanced the AlwaysOn Availability Groups feature introduced in Microsoft SQL 2012 by following through on the promise of manageability and a great user experience. AlwaysOn is integrated high availability and, as you see later in this chapter, disaster recovery (DR) in a single datacenter or across multiple datacenters. It would be unfair to think of AlwaysOn as a single feature, because the Microsoft SQL product team provides a suite of capabilities in this one solution.

If you are familiar with traditional database mirroring, then you are well on your way to understanding the HA of SQL Server AlwaysOn Availability Groups. This feature provides automatic or manual failover for a group of databases from one primary database server up to a group of eight secondary SQL replica database servers. With the use of availability groups, the failover to secondary targets provides for easy support for multiple secondary replicas and optional read-only access for backing up secondary databases. Additionally, availability groups no longer required shared storage, such as an expensive storage area network (SAN) or even a less expensive network attached storage (NAS) device, as discussed earlier.

You may be thinking that with the Azure SLA for cloud services uptime guarantee at 99.95% availability and VMs and virtual networks uptime guarantee at 99.9% availability, everyone should architect all business services in Azure and discontinue any on-premises datacenter services. We say not just yet, because of the potential downtime or outage of services of up to 43.2 minutes per month. See Table 11.1, later in this chapter, for details. How do you eliminate downtime completely? Let's answer that question by revisiting fault domains and upgrade domains, terms briefly discussed earlier in the chapter.

Table 11.1. *Azure Service SLAs and Downtimes*

Azure Service	SLA	30-day downtime (minutes)
Computing	99.95%	21.9
SQL Databases (Basic, Standard, or Premium)	99.99%	4.4
Storage	99.9%	43.8

To put things into perspective, the allowable downtime for a single SQL server running in Azure can be up to 43.2 minutes per month, and downtime for one VM (not platform as a service, PaaS), can be up to 21.3 minutes per month. These downtimes are the longest outages possible under the SLA guarantee for Azure

303

services. In a traditional on-premises datacenter, computers are placed into a rack, and AC power is applied to that rack. If power is removed from the rack, or if servers need to be upgraded, there is an outage. You need to install more than one instance on two fault domains.

To help you better understand AlwaysOn features, this discussion focuses on availability groups on two instances of Microsoft SQL Server from an on-premises datacenter to Azure, as illustrated in Figure 11-1. AlwaysOn allows services to remain running in order to reply to client requests and take advantage of the Azure 99.9% uptime. This example uses two instances of Microsoft SQL server in two different fault domains to prevent Azure rolling maintenance, or a security patch upgrade of only one upgrade domain at a time. This also provides you with the same 99.9% uptime for your SQL Server applications during required maintenance times, whether planned, or unplanned maintenance. With two different fault domains, you have the ability to maintain applications that provide fault-tolerance.

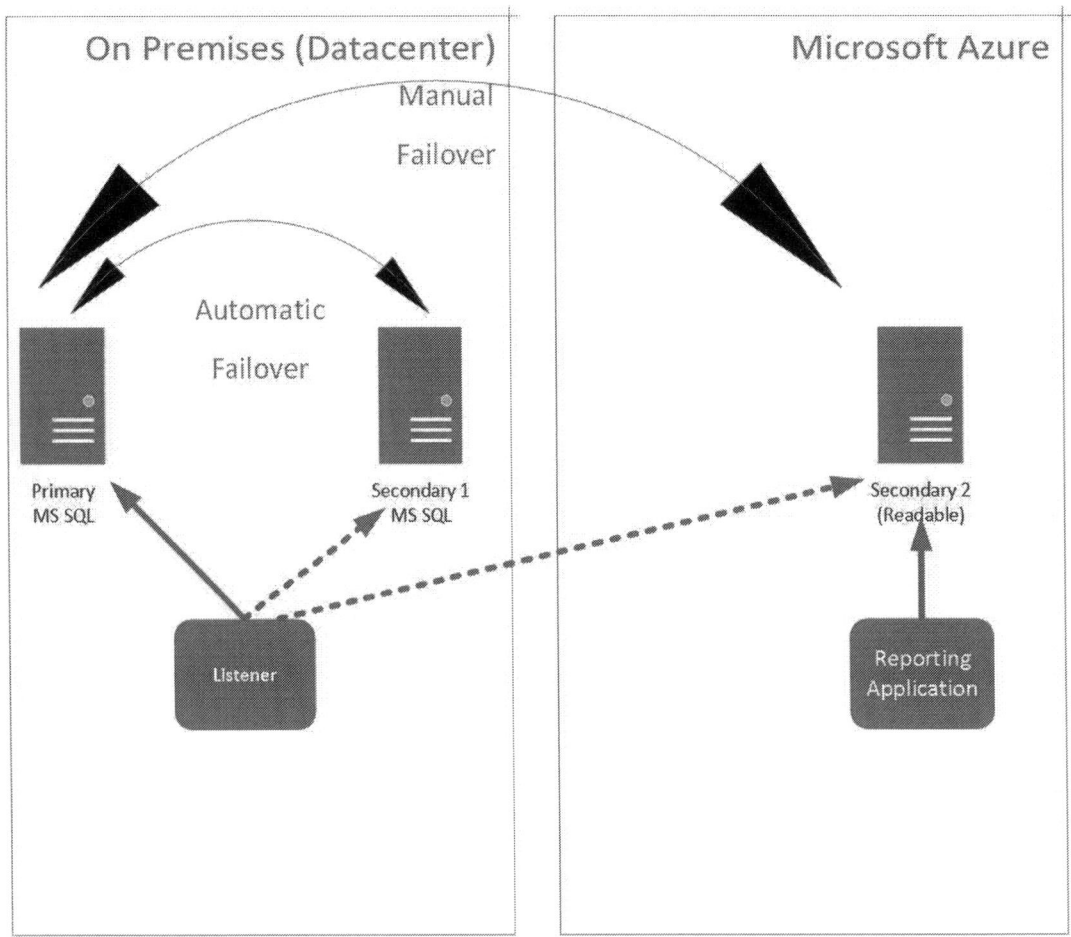

Figure 11-1. *AlwaysOn availability groups from an on-premises datacenter to Azure*

ENABLING ALWAYSON AVAILABILITY GROUPS

The prerequisites for enabling availability groups are not complicated, and many businesses realize the value in these features and implement them. To enable the AlwaysOn Availability Groups feature, you need to do the following:

- Configure Windows Server Failover Clustering (WSFC) on the node.

- Make sure your version of SQL Server supports AlwaysOn Availability Groups.

▓ **Note** The Azure gallery in the new Azure Portal has SQL images that have AlwaysOn Availability Groups already configured in the template from which it is provisioned.

- Enable availability groups on one server instance (node), one at a time.

- Make sure Administrator access to the WSFC cluster is enabled.

Follow these steps:

1. On the node you'd like to enable, choose Start ➤ All Programs ➤ Configuration Tools, and click SQL Server Configuration Manager.

2. In SQL Server Configuration Manager, click SQL Server Services, right-click the instance (node), and select Properties.

3. Select the AlwaysOn High Availability tab.

4. In the field containing the name of the local failover cluster, select the Enable AlwaysOn Availability Groups check box, and then click OK.

Regional VNets in Microsoft Azure

In this chapter, you've been introduced to many concepts relating to the deeper logical construction of an Azure datacenter. The racks of computers in an Azure datacenter are grouped to provide specific services like computing, storage, SQL Azure, service buses, and more. The services are arranged across the entire datacenter, and from one datacenter to the next.

When you are enabling services from your Azure Portal, as an IT administrator, you must be careful not to choose a storage account in one country and a hosted service in another country, assuming the datacenter is in another region. This type of configuration would have inherent latencies because of the networking requirement. When building services, conventional thinking says they should remain close— even within the same datacenter. Due to recent architectural improvements, Microsoft has increased the scope of network management to a region. This is achieved by using Azure regional VNets.

Affinity groups are no longer generally recommended for VMs and have been succeeded by regional VNets. You should only use an affinity group when a set of VMs must have the absolute lowest network latency between them. Placing VMs in an affinity group puts them in the same computing cluster or scale unit. It's important to note that using an affinity group can have two possibly negative consequences:

- The VM size options are limited to the sizes offered by the computing scale unit.

- There is a higher probability of not being able to allocate a new VM. This happens when the specific scale unit for the affinity group is out of capacity.

Regional VNets provide a method of placing services close to each other. This is an important option that, when overlooked, can create unwanted latency. To help you put the size of an Azure datacenter into perspective, the Chicago datacenter is the size of more than 12 football fields. The process of enabling a regional VNet provides guidance to the datacenter *fabric controller*, to group these services closer together to remove latency. The Azure *fabric controller (FC)* is the kernel of the Windows Azure platform. The FC provisions, stores, delivers, monitors, and commands the VMs and physical servers that make up Azure. Regional VNets allow the following:

- Lower latency

- Higher throughput

Regional VNets should be generated before you create computing or storage systems. Reserved IP, internal load balancing, and instance-level public IP are all managed at a regional level. If you will need any of these features, they must be deployed into a regional VNet.

ENABLING REGIONAL VNETS IN MICROSOFT AZURE

Now that you understand the value of using Azure regional VNets, the steps to enable them are easy. One of the key elements of planning is the need to use multiple datacenter regions. Then you must create a regional VNet for each region. The regional VNet currently cannot be created through the Portal workflow; this capability will be added in the near future.

To create a regional VNet follow these steps:

1. From the Azure Portal, select the Network option at left.

2. Select your Azure VNet, export the current network configuration file, and save it to disk.

3. Edit the file to add a new VNet, as follows:

```
<?xmlversion="1.0"encoding="utf-8"?>
<NetworkConfigurationxmlns:xsd="http://www.w3.org/2001/
XMLSchema"xmlns:xsi="http://www.w3.org/2001/XMLSchema-instance"xmlns="http://
schemas.microsoft.com/ServiceHosting/2011/07/NetworkConfiguration">
 <VirtualNetworkConfiguration>
 <VirtualNetworkSites>
<!- Regional Virtual Network Definition ->
<VirtualNetworkSitename="VNetUSWest"Location="West US">
     <AddressSpace>
       <AddressPrefix>192.168.50.0/24</AddressPrefix>
       <AddressPrefix>192.168.51.0/24</AddressPrefix>
     </AddressSpace>
```

```
    <Subnets>
      <Subnetname="frontendsubnet">
        <AddressPrefix>192.168.50.0/24</AddressPrefix>
      </Subnet>
      <Subnetname="backendsubnet">
        <AddressPrefix>192.168.51.0/28</AddressPrefix>
      </Subnet>
      <Subnetname="gatewaysubnet">
        <AddressPrefix>192.168.51.16/28</AddressPrefix>
      </Subnet>
    </Subnets>
  </VirtualNetworkSite>
 </VirtualNetworkSites>
 </VirtualNetworkConfiguration>
</NetworkConfiguration>
```

4. Go through the New Virtual Network Creation workflow in the Portal, select the edited file, and click OK. This completes the import process and creates the new regional VNet.

5. To do this via PowerShell, do the following:

    a. Run this:

    ```
    Get-AzureVNetConfig -ExportToFile "C:\Users\username\Documents\Netcfg.xml"
    ```

    b. Edit and save the file:

    ```
    Set-AzureVNetConfig –ConfigurationPath "C:\Users\username\Documents\Netcfg.xml"
    ```

This creates the Azure VNet.

Now, when you create VMs or storage services, you have the option to add the VM or storage pool to any regional VNet and enable it to be *georedundant* (geographically redundant). By enabling the services to support georedundancy, you add durability in case of a major disaster in an Azure region. Two systems are created in two different geographic regions, but note that there is a small up-charge for this availability feature.

■ **Note**   To gain a better understanding of geographically redundant storage, see http://azure.microsoft. com/en-us/pricing/details/storage.

High Availability in Microsoft Azure

Discussions in this chapter and throughout the book provide insights into the physical components of Azure as it relates to creating necessary virtual components. With virtualized networking capabilities to connect and isolate virtual servers for IaaS and PaaS, you should begin to see the economies of scale of using Azure. Many small and some medium-sized businesses do not maintain dedicated staffing for IT due to budgetary constraints, and most do not allocate funding for a primary or (especially) a secondary datacenter. Using the Azure cost model and highly available subsystems, businesses can start to plan, architect, and build a sustainable future, only paying for the IT resources that they need at a fraction of what it would cost to set up the equivalent technology on-premises.

High availability is not a single feature of Azure; it is architected in every service, every component, and every new provision of Azure. If we make the statement, "Microsoft Azure supports 100% high availability," then it is compelling to begin building your business on a highly available platform.

Microsoft has invested $20 billion US to date in 23 global datacenters. The Azure platform enables applications to be hosted and expanded worldwide, and to support client accessibility from the internet, corporate networks, or both. The Azure platform greatly simplifies, but doesn't completely remove, the complexity of cloud-only applications or integration of on-premises software with hosted services in your Azure subscription. It is a platform that was planned, architected, and built from the ground up to provide and support customers' demands for HA. Unfortunately, high availability is often viewed as a feature that can be added after a software application is finished. With Azure, high availability is the top feature required.

Azure IaaS now supports availability groups, as discussed earlier and illustrated in Figure 11-2. Availability groups in Azure provide the following services:

- Availability sets

- Management services

- Notification hubs (IOS, Android, and Microsoft)

- AutoScale (up and down)

- Virtual machines (load balancing)

- SQL Server AlwaysOn (clustering or availability groups)

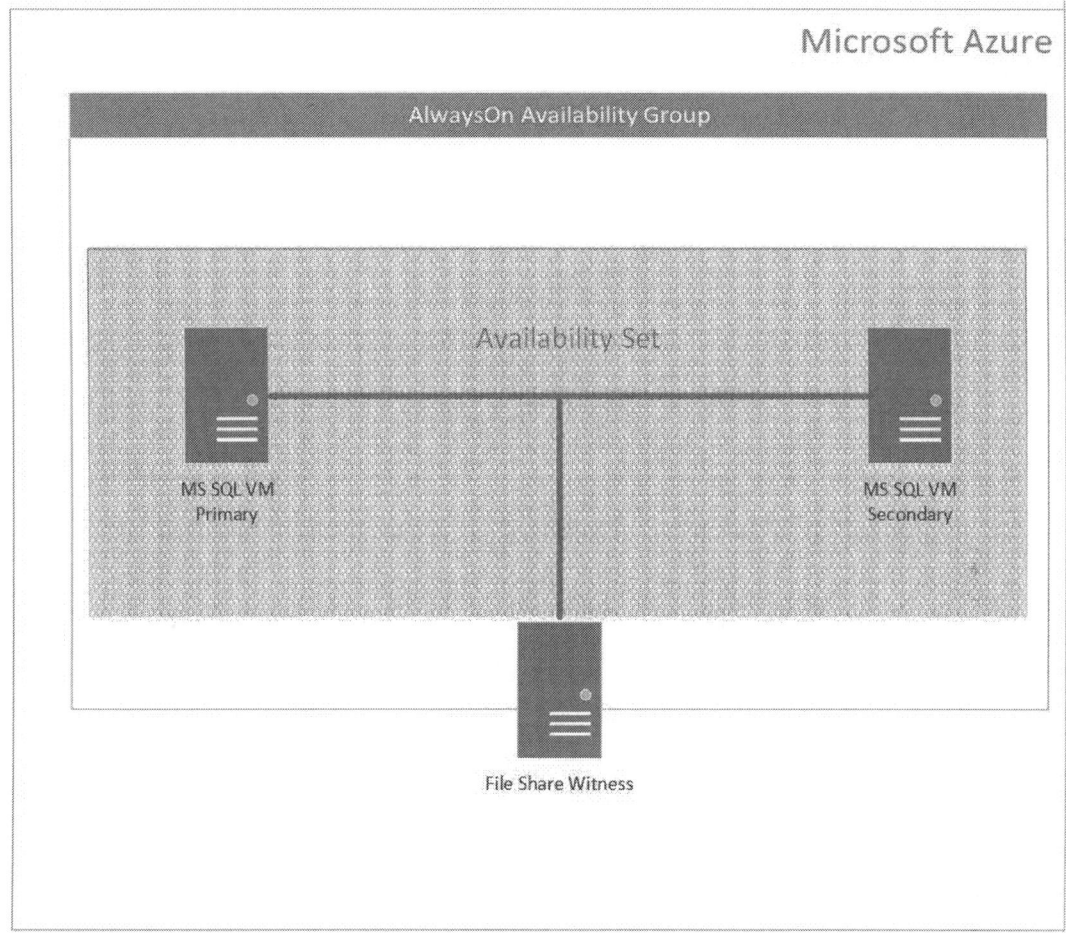

Figure 11-2. *Microsoft SQL AlwaysOn availability groups from inside Azure, using an availability set*

This section briefly highlights the Azure services that can help your business consume and take advantage of availability groups and then focuses on a detailed example of Microsoft SQL Server using availably groups.

Availability sets let Azure customers place workloads across multiple fault domains—which you can think of as being synonymous with racks—so that the failure of an entire rack does not bring down a service hosted in that rack. Placing VMs, for example, into an availability set, as depicted in Figure 11-2, avoids the possibility of a single outage impacting all the VMs supporting the service. Availability sets guarantee that not all VMs in an availability set will go down at the same time. If you're concerned about multiple racks going down at the same time, and hence multiple fault domains incurring an outage, georedundancy, covered in Chapter 7 and also discussed earlier in this chapter, and disaster recovery, covered later in this chapter, should be evaluated.

Management services have enhanced features that are supported in the Azure Portal with the ability to enable operation logs and alerts. The logs provide smart parameters that let you view specific log data criteria based on data range, service type, service name, or even statuses such as Failed or Succeeded. Alert notifications can be enabled for subscription owners, business owners who are on call, or any e-mail address, as discussed in Chapter 2.

A *Notification Hub* is a service that enables personalized, cross-platform broadcast push notifications. These notifications are pushed to Microsoft Windows 8, Windows Phone, IOS, and Android mobile devices. This service uses Azure global scale to enable low-latency push notifications to millions of users. The Notification Hub provides a secure process to relieve your onsite back end to handle platform notification services (PNSs) like WNS, MPNS, Apple PNS, and Google Cloud Messaging Service.

AutoScale is a service that reaches across many Azure services and easily enables automatic scale-up when services are needed and automatic scale-down so that you pay only for what you use. This feature provides configuration for automatically scaling web sites, cloud services, mobile services, and VMs. Chapter 5 introduced you to the Azure Websites feature, which supports automatic scale-up based on time or metrics. For example, you can create a rule to enable another web site from your template and join a number of instances into your web farm every time 75% utilization is realized on one or more web sites. An interesting capability lets you retest the metric or set a specific timeline to scale down automatically by removing web sites or to create a rule to have only three instances running at night.

The Virtual Machines service can use a no-extra-cost, built-in load balancer, as do Cloud Services, Websites, and Mobile Services. The Azure load balancer simply needs to be enabled on the service, and it can be configured to provide either scale or HA. VM balancing of network traffic enables scale-out across many VMs, as well as enabling HA across your applications in the Azure cloud. Chapter 6 introduced you to VMs and provided greater insight into this availability group feature.

The SQL Server AlwaysOn Availability Groups feature supports functionality similar to AlwaysOn failover clustering, discussed earlier in this chapter. Together, these features provide a comprehensive high-availability and disaster-recovery solution. Availability groups provide automatic or manual failover for a group of databases from one primary to a secondary SQL replica database server. With the use of availability groups, the failover provides painless support for multiple secondary replica databases. For more information on configuring Microsoft SQL Server 2012 AlwaysOn FCIs and availability groups, visit `https://technet.microsoft.com/en-us/library/jj822357.aspx`.

The SLAs listed in Table 11.1 are for three of the many other Azure services: Computing, SQL Databases, and Storage. For a full list of Azure SLAs, visit `http://azure.microsoft.com/en-us/support/legal/sla`.

FAULT DOMAINS AND UPGRADE DOMAINS

Azure creates and maintains high availability using the logical discernment of fault domains. Hundreds of thousands of physical computers in racks, and millions of virtual servers, are used to build and offer Azure services. Azure datacenters use Microsoft's Generation 4 datacenter best practices to run consistently at a power usage effectiveness (PUE) of 1.12–1.20 on the road to a PUE of 1.0, which will be possible in the future with Generation 5 datacenter best practices.

The scale of the servers in the Azure datacenter helps bring clarity to the understanding of fault domains and upgrade domains. Picturing a single rack of servers in an Azure datacenter, you can mentally visualize that group of computers as a fault domain. This is not how servers in the Azure Public or Government cloud are identified as a fault domain, but the image is necessary to help simplify your understanding.

When power is lost to a single server in the rack, all the VMs on that server and the applications on them are disrupted. This disruption can occur when the servers need to be updated with security patches and rebooted. The Azure Computer service SLA guarantees the level of connectivity uptime for a deployed service only if two or more instances of each role of a service are deployed.

Azure also uses the concept of an upgrade domain to ensure that applications running on the hundreds of VMs continue to process client requests without disruption. During the Azure service deployment, evenly distributed instances of multiple logical upgrade domains are performed. Then, when maintenance or security patches are required, they are completed one upgrade domain at a time. The upgrade process can be described as stopping instances (VMs) on one upgrade domain, upgrading applications or the physical server, bringing them back online, and then moving to the next upgrade domain. This is the least impactful way to upgrade systems, and it is why a minimum of two server instances are required to support the Azure SLA.

■ **Note**   The current Azure SLA for most services can be found at
http://azure.microsoft.com/en-us/support/legal/sla.

Disaster Recovery in Microsoft Azure

Due to recent global natural disasters, the need to prepare for DR is paramount. Every company realizes that this is a required part of their IT strategy. Many companies don't have an adequate DR solution in place because of complexity and cost. Azure reduces the complexity and high price of developing and implementing a DR solution with Azure Site Recovery.

Microsoft System Center Data Protection Manager (DPM) uses the Windows Server Volume Shadow Copy Service (VSS) by backing up blocks of data that have changed on the physical or virtual disks and copying that data to Azure BLOB storage. This process removes the need and cost for data tapes, tape drives, and offsite tape storage. Azure Backup has reduced the cost of long-term storage of data and the extreme cost of retrieving a backup set to recover a file or server. You can now architect DR scenarios using Azure's storage, confirming that disk is the new tape.

Why Choose Disaster Recovery as a Service in Microsoft Azure?

Azure Site Recovery provides DR-as-a-service (DRaaS). This section explores using this feature, which is needed by IT staff to support a customer's current configuration. As you walk through the different scenarios supported, keep in mind these two important terms related to restoring data and recovering from disaster: *recovery time objective (RTO)* and *recovery point objective (RPO)*. RTO is the targeted time duration in which a business process must be restored after a disaster; in other words, "How long will it take to restore?" RPO is the maximum-targeted period in which data might be lost from an IT service due to a major incident; in other words, "How much data can we afford to lose?"

Azure Site Recovery (ASR), previously known as Hyper-V Recovery Manager, supports recovery of simple to complex IT infrastructures on-premises, on-premises to Azure, or on-premises to on-premises. ASR simplifies DR by providing comprehensive, automated protection for VMware, Hyper-V, and physical servers in a single management solution. It provides the ability to meet stringent SLAs for availability, the recovery of files, or the need for physical and VM rebuilding. Customers have mixed hypervisors and use different management software suites to maintain availability. Many customers have deployed VMware or Citrix virtual infrastructures; however, they struggle to enable business continuity–disaster recovery (BC/DR) architectures. Most customers lack a BC/DR strategy that supports their business needs because of the high cost of custom or third-party solutions associated with these hypervisors, the limitations of other public cloud providers, and the extremely high cost of maintaining their own secondary datacenter.

Microsoft acquired the company InMage in July 2014. InMage supports BC/DR of VMware VMs between any number of on-premises locations or public clouds without stringent requirements or breaking the businesses' bank. The integration of InMage enables the use of the InMage Scout technology to support VMware's proprietary VMDK format for migration to different sites or on-the-fly conversions to Microsoft's open VHD format. InMage places entire VMs into Azure recovery services. The InMage technology allows Azure Site Recovery to support these sources and destinations:

- Enterprise
- Service provider

The purpose of the recovery vaults that can be enabled include the following:

- Production deployment
- Evaluating Azure Site Recovery
- Browsing Azure functionality

The datacenter environments are categorized in Table 11.2.

ENABLING DISASTER RECOVERY SERVICES

Azure recovery services provide DR support for many different IT datacenter configurations. Let's walk briefly through some of the options to enable on-premises to on-premises and on-premises to Azure.

The prerequisites for setting up and protecting an on-premises VMM site to Azure includes choosing a recovery target identified in Table 11-2 and creating an Azure storage account to store data replicated to Azure. This account requires that georeplication be enabled and in the same region as the Azure Site Recovery service associated with your subscription.

Table 11-2. *Disaster Recovery Sources and Targets with Azure Integration of the InMage Scout Solution*

Source Environment Type	Intended Target Environment Types
SCVMM site	Azure site
VMWare site	VMWare site
Hyper-V site	Hyper-V site SCCM site

This first exercise illustrates protecting an on-premises system running System Center 2012 R2 VMM Server.

Protection of an On-Premises VMM Site to Azure

1. Create an Azure Site Recovery vault. Provide a unique name for the site and its region, as shown in Figure 11-3.

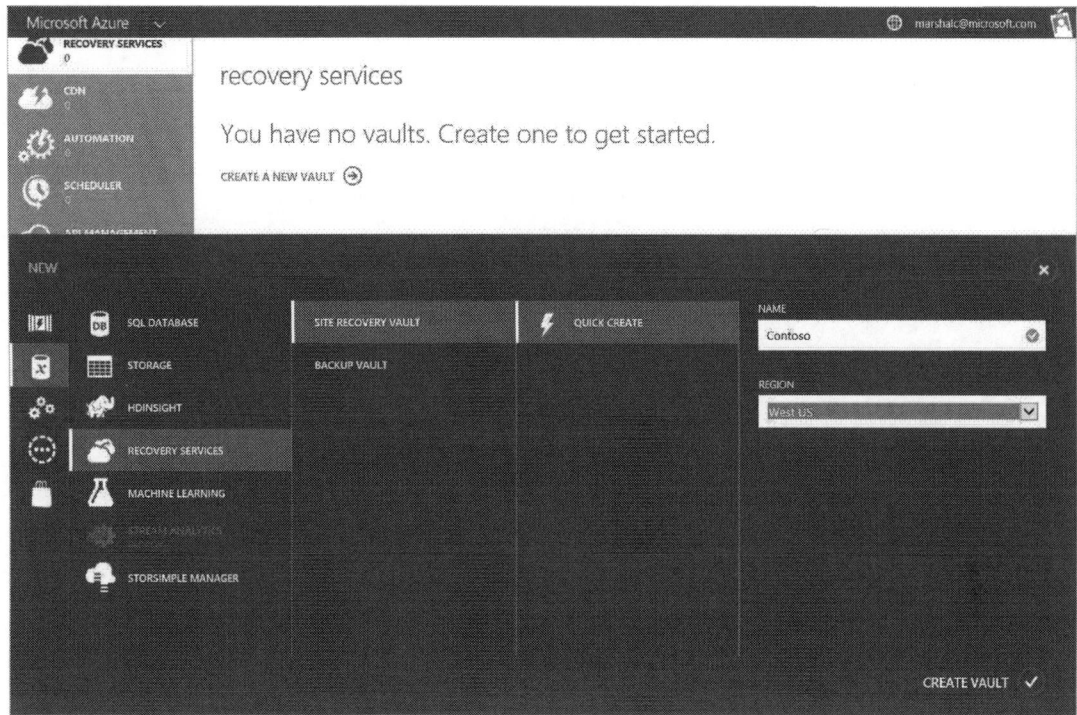

Figure 11-3. *Creating a DR site vault for Contoso*

2. Generate a registration key in the vault pane, and download the setup file. Run the installation program for the provider application on the VMM server on-premises.

3. Create the Azure storage account.

4. Install the Microsoft Azure Recovery Service agent on each Hyper-V host (each in the VMM cloud).

5. Configure the protection settings that are required.

6. Enable protection for each VM managed by the VMM cloud.

7. Run a test failover for a single VM to validate your recovery plan.

■ **Note** For a more detailed version of this exercise, visit https://azure.microsoft.com/en-us/ documentation/articles/site-recovery-vmm-to-azure/.

The prerequisites for setting up and protecting a VM with InMage in Azure Site Recovery between an on-premises VMWare site to a second on-premises VMWare site include a new vault name, as described in the first DR exercise.

Protection of a VMWare On-Premises Site to a VMware On-Premises Site

1. Download the registration key, as shown in Figure 11-4. This key is needed to install the InMage Scout agent.

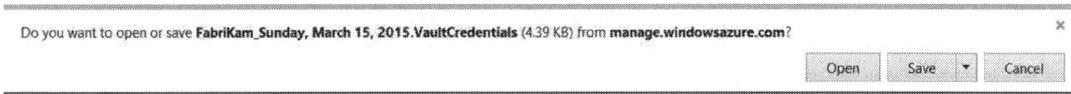

Figure 11-4. Download the registration key for use with the InMage Scout agent

2. Download the InMage Scout agent, as shown in Figure 11-5, and install it. (It is in a `.zip` file stored locally, and uncompressing is required.)

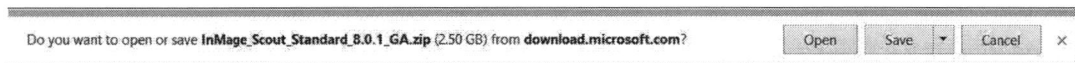

Figure 11-5. Download the InMage Scout agent `.zip` file

3. Prepare the Scout components, including the configuration server, Windows, and Linux vContinuum.

4. Install and configure the process server, and enable the mobility service on the source server.

5. Enable protection for the servers, and finalize the protection and recovery plan.

The prerequisites for setting up and protecting VMs between two on-premises VMM sites using SAN array replication include using System Center 2012 R2 VMM servers in each on-premises site with Hyper-V hosts deployed in the primary and secondary sites. From the VMM console, enable one cloud container from the primary server that you want to protect; also enable one on the secondary VMM server. Configure one of the two SAN arrays as primary and one as secondary. Configure networking between the Hyper-V host servers to support the storage LUNs.

Protection of a VMM On-Premises Site to a VMM On-Premises Site with SAN Array Replication

1. After you have created the Azure recovery vault, download the vault credentials, as shown in Figure 11-6.

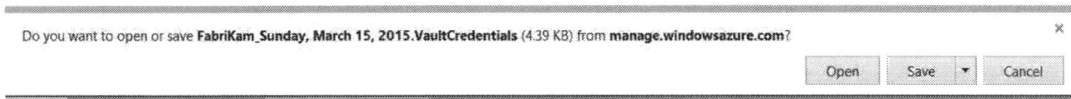

Figure 11-6. Download the Azure recovery vault credentials needed for the Provider install

2. Download the Microsoft Azure Site Recovery Provider, as shown in Figure 11-7, to be installed on the VMM's servers (install on the primary and secondary VMM servers).

Figure 11-7. *Download the Provider to install on the VMM server*

3. Download the update for VMM 2012 R2 and Update Rollup 5 for Microsoft System Center 2012 R2 VMM. (If you have not run the update before this step, you can find it at http://support.microsoft.com/en-us/kb/2822776.)

4. Remember, you registered your VMM clouds as part of the prerequisites for this exercise. Now you need to configure the cloud protection. Enable protection for replication groups and VMs. This completes your recovery plan.

■ **Note** For more information on how to use SAN replication, refer to https://azure.microsoft.com/en-us/documentation/articles/site-recovery-vmm-san.

The final exercise involves using Azure recovery services and the backup vault. This DR option provides a simple process to back up Windows servers, Windows essentials, and Windows clients from on-premises into Azure.

Backing Up Servers and Clients On-Premises to the Azure Backup Vault

1. Create your Azure recovery backup vault, as shown in Figure 11-8.

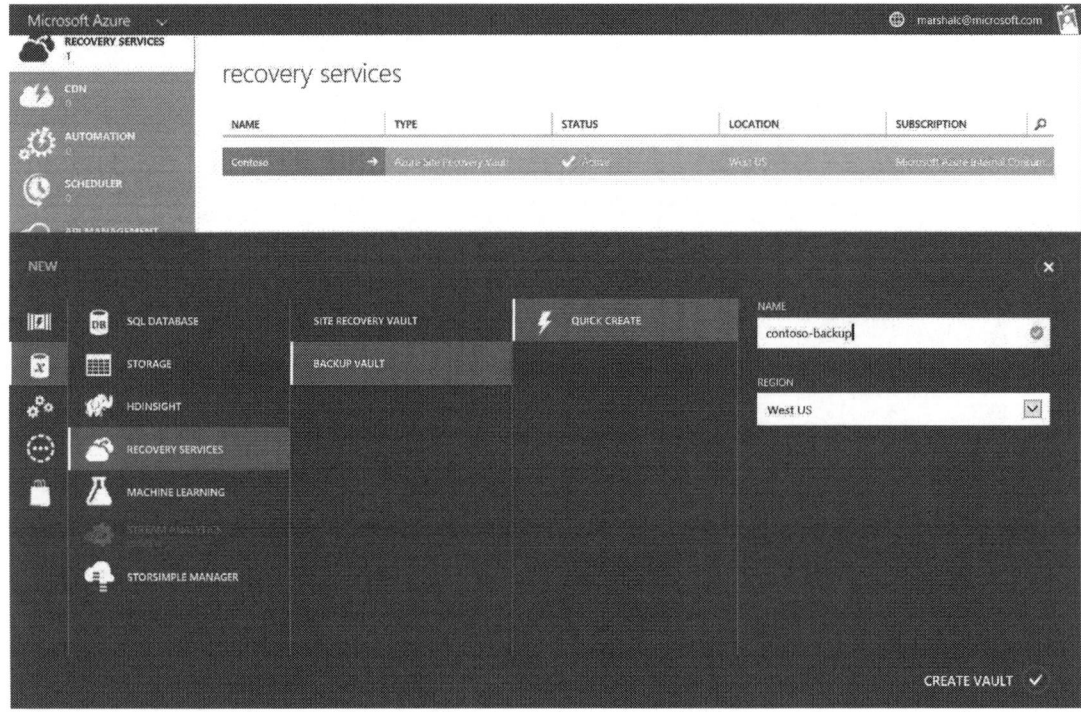

Figure 11-8. *Create the Azure recovery service Contoso backup vault container*

2. Download the vault credentials, as shown in Figure 11-9. (As a security precaution, you have two days to install the agent. If you don't complete the installation, you will need to repeat this step.)

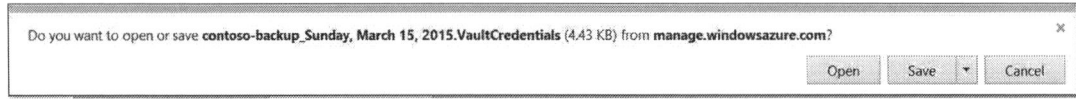

Figure 11-9. *Download the Contoso vault credentials with security support; they have a two-day expiration.*

3. Download and install the Azure Backup Agent on the servers, files, and folders that you want to protect, as shown in Figure 11-10.

Figure 11-10. *Download the Contoso Backup Agent installation for on-premises to Azure Backup*

4. The servers appear in the Register Items view in the Azure Backup view.

Summary

In this chapter, you've learned about the support for clusters and AlwaysOn Availability Groups in Microsoft Azure and how to enable systems to respond with more agility using regional VNets. You read about how every building block of Azure is planned, architected, and constructed to support the customer need for HA. Finally, you learned about Azure's many options for supporting DR plans and backing up from on-premises into Azure.

A final word and recommendation regarding using Azure for DR: with the lower price point of Azure, you can now create a cost-effective DR datacenter or DR site. Don't stop at creating a recovery scenario—you need to test the recovery of databases in order to ensure that you have the correct processes in place. Continue to use the scalability of Azure and its features to test failover plans and validate that the solution you architected provides the business-recovery results you expect. Nowadays, customers don't have to worry as much about the budget for geographically distributed datacenters with redundant capacity, because Azure provides the best price point, features, and scalability for DR requirements of businesses of every size.

■ ■ ■

## CHAPTER 12

Migrating Your Virtual Machines to Azure

The Microsoft Azure Virtual Machines (VMs) service can be used to help remove development or migration blockers of applications that depend on on-premises resources that require VMs. With Azure VMs, you can quickly migrate an existing application that currently runs on an on-premises VM. Additionally, you can connect different application models, such as web sites or Cloud Services web roles (VMs that have IIS installed) and worker roles (VMs that don't have IIS installed on them) with VMs, as discussed in Chapter 6.

This chapter explores how to determine which migration methods are best for your organization as well as some of the considerations involved when using Azure VMs. You also learn about establishing a migration life cycle for the applications in Azure. Finally, you see two methods for migrating your VM to Azure.

Migration Considerations when Using Azure Virtual Machines

When looking at a migration from on-premises applications to Azure, it's important to plan each of the migration phases carefully. A typical migration from on-premises to Azure includes an analysis phase, an application-migration phase, a data-migration phase, a testing and optimization phase, and an operations and management phase.

It's unreasonable to believe that you can shift masses of application data from on-premises to the Azure cloud without taking into account several migration factors. Whether you're considering a migration from a physical machine or an existing on-premises VM, or you're migrating VMware VMs or Amazon Web Services (AWS) workloads into Azure, you must first consider the application patterns and whether using a VM is the right choice. Applications or workloads that can easily use Azure Virtual Machines are as follows:

- Non-mission-critical database applications

- Development or test environments for database applications

- Backup solutions for on-premises database applications

- Applications or web sites that can scale on-demand easily in response to peak loads

- Database applications that will be deployed to SQL Server in VMs instead of using the Azure SQL Database service

This chapter does not go into specific details of how to move a SQL database. We recommend that you follow the detailed documentation regarding moving the database and data to a VM in Azure by visiting the Migrate a database to SQL Server on an Azure VM at this link: `https://azure.microsoft.com/en-us/documentation/articles/virtual-machines-migrate-onpremises-database/`.

Migration Options

One of the best features of Azure is the ability to move your on-premises servers easily into Azure and run them on Azure VMs. The biggest benefit of this feature is that you won't incur a lot of downtime to relocate your existing infrastructure to the cloud.

Azure has tools that enable you to migrate your existing Hyper-V, VMware, and AWS server workloads into Azure VMs. There are many tools that can be used for different purposes, such as migrating your organization's base server images so that you can create new Azure VMs that match your existing on-premises server builds.

This section introduces you to a few different methods for migrating your existing servers into Azure, whether they are running on VMware or Hyper-V in your existing datacenter or in another cloud service.

Disk2vhd

Azure only supports the virtual hard disk (VHD) format for disks connecting to Azure VMs. To move your physical servers into Azure, you need first to create VHDs of your existing physical disks so that they can be uploaded. Sysinternals offers a free tool for doing this, called *Disk2vhd*. Mark Russinovich, the Azure chief technology officer, wrote it.

Disk2vhd converts physical disks to the VHD format while the server is running. It uses the Windows Volume Snapshot technology to create a point-in-time snapshot of the disks you are converting. You can download Disk2vhd from `https://technet.microsoft.com/en-us/sysinternals/ee656415.aspx`.

CREATING A VHD FROM A PHYSICAL SERVER

Creating a VHD from a physical server is a quick and easy process, thanks to the free Disk2vhd tool. Follow these steps to create your VHD:

1. Download Disk2vhd, and launch the executable.

2. When the tool opens, make sure the Use Vhdx option is unchecked (because Azure VMs don't support this format), and click the ellipse button at the end of the VDH File Name field to select a location to save your file. Name your file something that will be meaningful to the server to which you are converting, so it is easily identifiable, as shown in Figure 12-1.

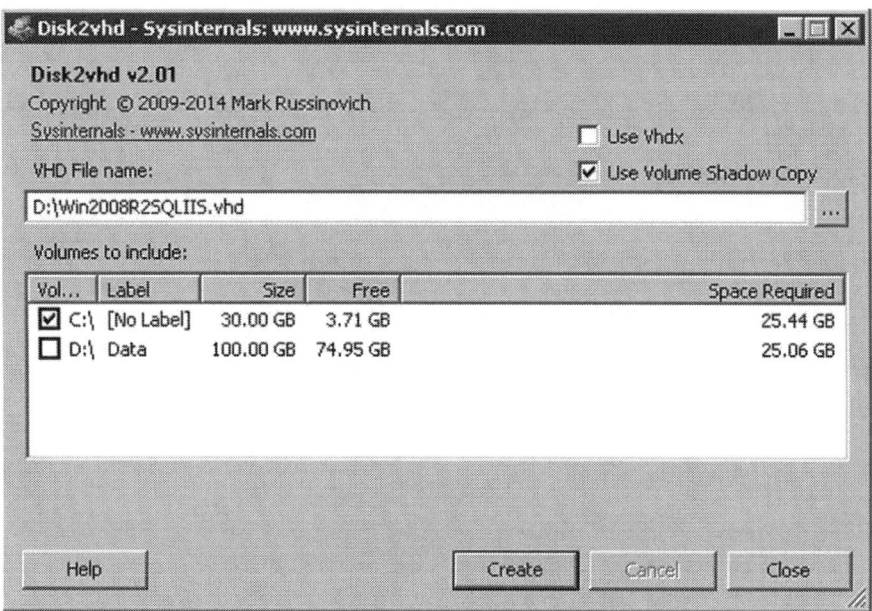

Figure 12-1. *Setting the Disk2vhd parameters*

3. Select the physical disk that you want to convert, and click Create. Keep in mind that the size of the disk you are converting for uploading into Azure must fit within the disk size allowed, based on the VM size to which you are migrating. For a list of VM sizes, see "Sizes for Virtual Machines" at https://azure.microsoft.com/en-us/documentation/articles/virtual-machines-size-specs.

As shown in Figure 12-2, the snapshot image is created and saved to the location you chose. The creation process is usually pretty quick.

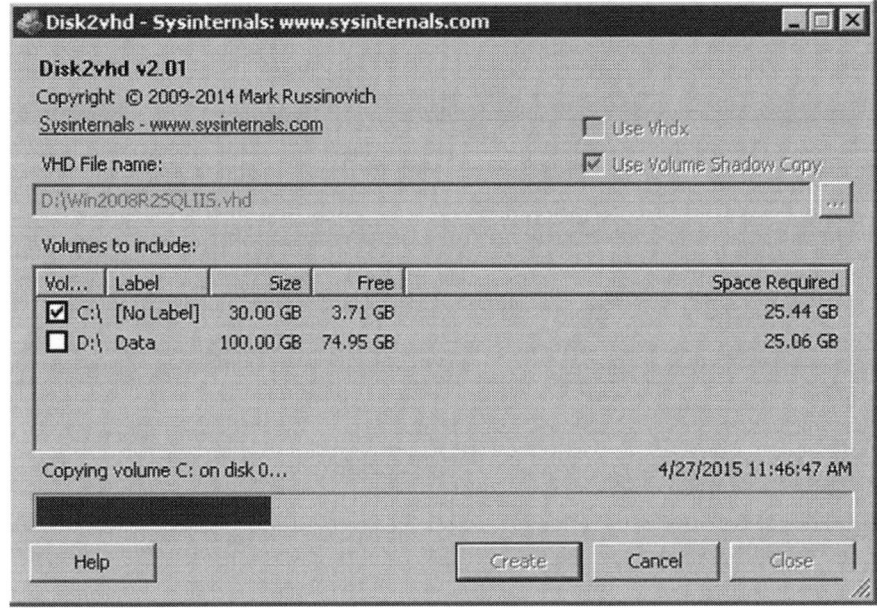

Figure 12-2. *The VHD is being created*

4. When the VHD creation is complete, the tool informs you that the VHD was exported successfully, as shown in Figure 12-3. Click the Close button to exit the tool.

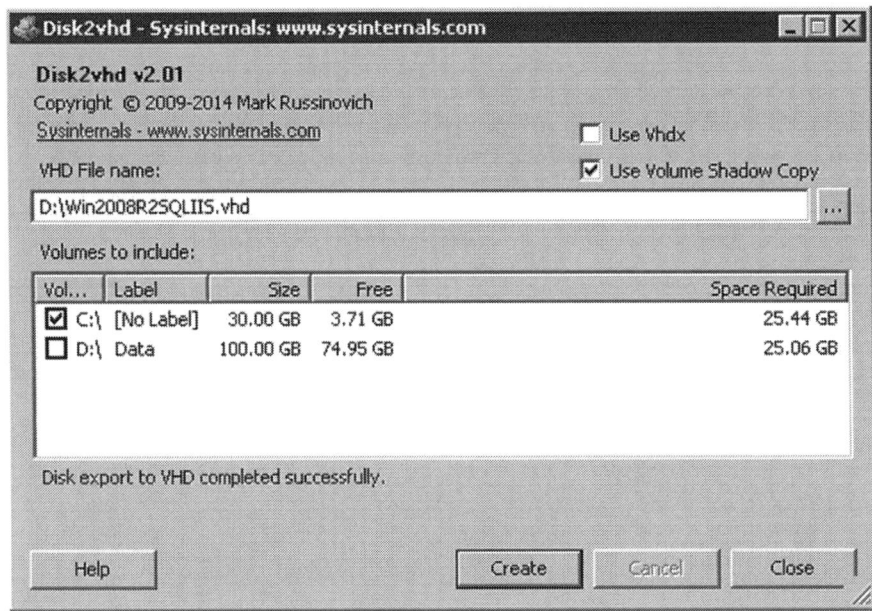

Figure 12-3. *The VHD creation is complete*

5. Open Windows File Explorer, and browse to the location to which you saved the VHD in order to verify that it has been created, as shown in Figure 12-4.

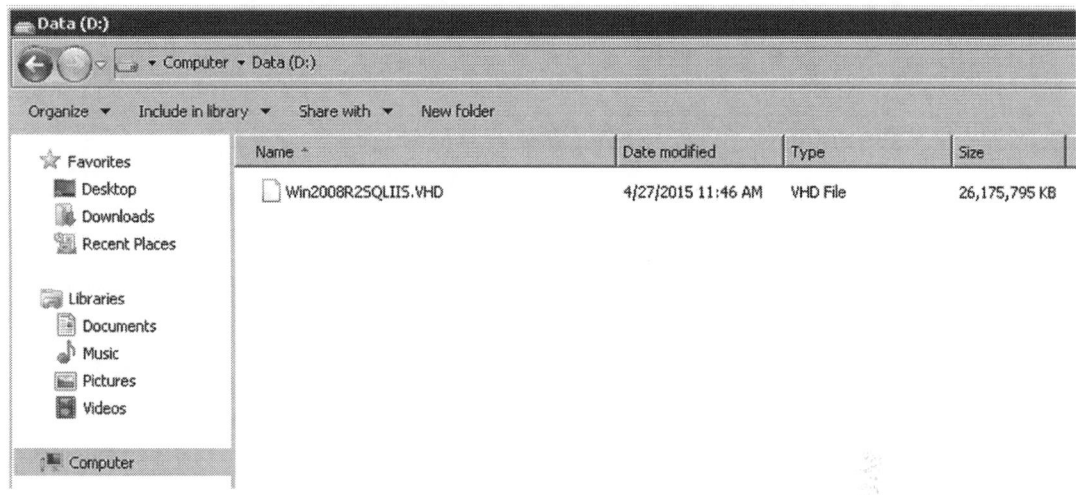

Figure 12-4. *Viewing the VHD file in Windows File Explorer*

Migrating Virtual Machines from Amazon Web Services to Azure

If your organization is currently utilizing Amazon Web Services (AWS)IaaS offerings to run production or lab VMs, you may be looking to move those VMs over to Azure. Moving VMs from AWS to Azure requires a number of manual steps; there is no method at present to move VMs automatically. Microsoft is currently previewing an Azure feature that will allow you to replicate VMs from other services, like AWS and VMware, which we touch on in the final section of this chapter. For now, however, VMs must be migrated manually, as demonstrated in the following exercise.

PREPARING THE AWS VM

The first step in preparing your VM to move from AWS to Azure is to create a VHD of the existing disks on your server:

1. Make VHDs of your server by following the steps in the earlier exercise "Creating a VHD from a Physical Server."

2. Once your VHDs are created, you need to upload them to AWS S3 storage. Before you can do so, you need to install the AWS PowerShell cmdlets on your server. You can download AWS PowerShell at `http://aws.amazon.com/powershell`.

3. To upload the files to AWS S3 storage, a storage bucket is required. If you don't have an existing storage bucket, open Windows PowerShell as an Administrator and create one with the following AWS PowerShell cmdlets:

```
Set-ExecutionPolicy RemoteSigned
Import-Module AWSPowerShell
Set-AWSCredentials -AccessKey AKIAIDQHZBB3FPPB7EAA -SecretKey NIQBKJAZ
vQ+LoYMqFHdbHwWZOu5jwwIpxxGuxzr5
New-S3Bucket -BucketName vmupload -Region us-west-2b
```

After running the cmdlets, you'll see that the bucket is created, as shown in Figure 12-5.

```
Administrator: Windows PowerShell (6)
PS C:\Users\Administrator> New-S3Bucket -BucketName d2dupload -Region us-west-2

CreationDate                                                    BucketName
------------                                                    ----------
4/28/2015 5:56:04 PM                                            d2dupload


PS C:\Users\Administrator>
```

Figure 12-5. *Creating a storage bucket in AWS*

4. Upload your VHD to AWS storage with a cmdlet similar to the following example and as shown in Figure 12-6, replacing the parameters with your own names and locations:

```
Write-S3Object -BucketName d2dupload -File D:\Win2008R2SQLIIS.VHD -Key
Win2008R2SQLIIS -CannedACLName Private -Region us-west-2
```

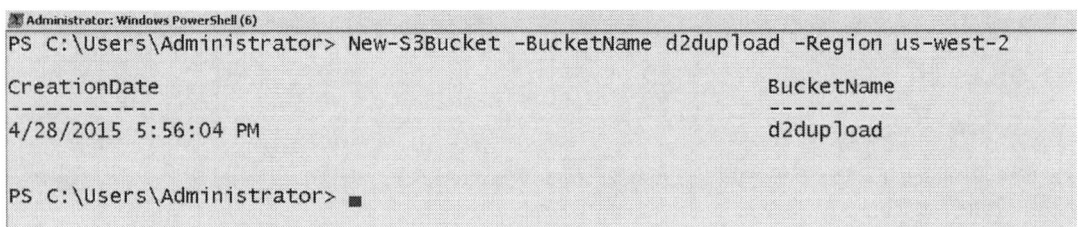

```
Administrator: Windows PowerShell (6)
PS C:\Users\Administrator> New-S3Bucket -BucketName d2dupload -Region us-west-2

Uploading
    File D:\Win2008R2SQLIIS.VHD...24%
    [oooooooooooooooooooooooooooo                                    ]
PS C:\Users\Administrator> Write-S3Object -BucketName d2dupload -File D:\Win2008R2SQLIIS.VHD -Key Win2008R2SQLIIS -Canne
dACLName Private -Region us-west-2
```

Figure 12-6. *Uploading the VHD into AWS storage*

5. You can browse your AWS storage to see the uploaded file in your new storage bucket, as shown in Figure 12-7.

Name	Storage Class	Size	Last Modified
Win2008R2SQLIIS	Standard	24.9 GB	Tue Apr 28 13:55:39 GMT-400 2015

AWS ∨ Services ∨ Edit ∨   Mike Manning ▾ Global ▾ Support ▾

Upload Create Folder Actions ∨   None Properties Transfers

All Buckets / d2dupload

Figure 12-7. *Viewing the VHD in the AWS storage bucket*

DOWNLOADING THE VHD FILE

Now that your VHD file has been uploaded to AWS, you need to download it onto your Hyper-V host, where you'll convert it to a fixed disk and install the Hyper-V integration service bits. To retrieve the file from your AWS storage bucket, you need to download and install the AWS PowerShell module on your Hyper-V host server, as you did on your AWS server:

1. Download the AWS PowerShell cmdlets from `http://aws.amazon.com/powershell`.

2. Open Windows PowerShell as an Administrator, and set the execution policy to `RemoteSigned`. Then import the AWS module and set your AWS credential in a variable with the following cmdlets, again using your own keys in place of what is shown in the example:

```
Set-ExecutionPolicy RemoteSigned
Import-Module AWSPowerShell
Set-AWSCredentials -AccessKey AKIAIDQHZBB4FPPB7EAA -SecretKey
NIJBKJAZvQ+LoYMqFHdbHwWZOu2jwwIpxxGuxzr5
```

3. Within the PowerShell environment, set your credentials (the Access Key and Secret Key, as you did in step 3 in the previous section), download the VHD using the following sample cmdlets:

```
$vhdPath = "C:\AWS VHD\Win2008R2SQLIIS.VHD"
Copy-S3Object -BucketName d2dupload -Key Win2008R2SQLIIS -LocalFile $vhdPath
```

The VHD downloads to your local Hyper-V host, as shown in Figure 12-8. This could take a while, depending on your Internet download speed and bandwidth.

Figure 12-8. *Downloading the VHD onto your Hyper-V host*

PREPARING THE VHD FOR AZURE

You need to convert the downloaded VHD from a dynamic disk to a fixed disk. This is necessary because Azure only supports fixed VHDs at this time. Use the following sample cmdlet to convert the disk, as shown in Figure 12-9.

```
Convert-VHD -Path $vhdPath -DestinationPath $vhdConvertPath -VHDType Fixed
```

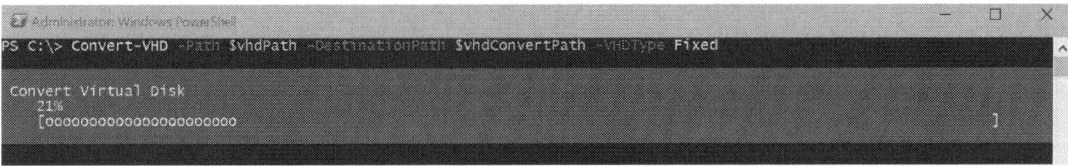

Figure 12-9. *Converting the downloaded VHD from a dynamic disk to a fixed disk*

Next you need to install the Hyper-V integration services so that Hyper-V drivers are installed. Use the cmdlets in the following steps to do this:

1. Store the location of the integration services ISO file in a PowerShell variable:

   ```
   $HVCabPath = "C:\Windows\vmguest\support\amd64\Windows6.x-
   HyperVIntegrationServices-x64.cab"
   ```

2. Mount the VHD, and store the disk number in a PowerShell variable:

   ```
   $diskNumb = (Mount-VHD -Path $vhdConvertPath -PassThru).DiskNumber
   ```

3. Verify that the VHD is mounted:

   ```
   Get-Disk $diskNumb).OperationalStatus
   ```

4. Store the VHD mounted drive letter in a PowerShell variable:

   ```
   $vhdDriveLetter = (Get-Disk $diskNumb | Get-Partition | Get-Volume).DriveLetter
   ```

5. Make sure the disk isn't read-only, so you can write the integration services files to it:

   ```
   Set-Disk $diskNumb -IsReadOnly $False
   ```

6. Install the integration services on the VHD. You can see the results of the preceding steps in Figure 12-10 and the final output of the Add-WindowsPackage cmdlet in Figure 12-11.

   ```
   Add-WindowsPackage -PackagePath $HVCabPath -Path ($vhdDriveLetter+":\" )
   ```

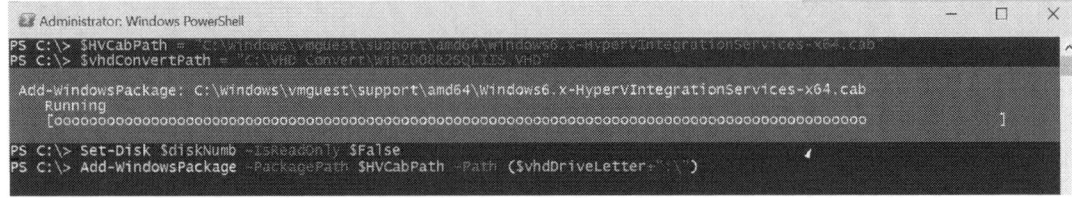

Figure 12-10. *The integration disk installing*

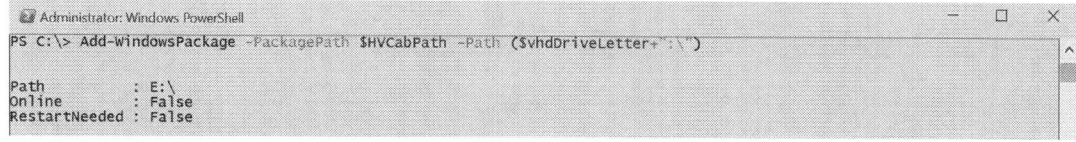

Figure 12-11. *The integration disk has been added*

With the integration services installed on the VHD, dismount the disk so that it can be copied into your Azure storage account:

```
Dismount-VHD -Path $vhdConvertPath
```

UPLOADING THE VHD TO WINDOWS AZURE STORAGE

Now that the VHD is ready for use in Azure, it's time to upload it. To do so, you need to set a few variables so that the file will be uploaded into the correct Azure storage container:

1. Select your Azure subscription, if you have more than one:

    ```
    Select-AzureSubscription "Your Azure Subscription"
    ```

2. Create and set a storage account. The storage account is a container in Azure Storage. You need to assign a name, label, and location for your account:

    ```
    New-AzureStorageAccount -StorageAccountName "awsvmstorage" -Label "AWSVmStorage"
    -Location "East US"
    $StorageAcct = "awsvmstorage"
    ```

3. Set the VHD file source and destination variables so that PowerShell can retrieve the file and copy it to your storage account:

    ```
    $SourceVHD = "C:\VHD Convert\Win2008R2SQLIIS.VHD"
    $DestVHD = "https://" + $StorageAcct + ".blob.core.windows.net/vhds/
    Win2008R2SQLIIS.vhd"
    ```

4. Upload the VHD to Azure:

    ```
    Add-AzureVHD -LocalFilePath $SourceVHD -Destination $DestVHD
    ```

As you can see in Figure 12-12, the first thing that happens is that Azure PowerShell calculates the hash for the file you are uploading.

Figure 12-12. *PowerShell calculates the file hash*

Next, as shown in Figure 12-13, Azure PowerShell finds the empty blocks in the file. This is done so that only blocks that contain data are uploaded. This makes uploading very efficient.

Figure 12-13. *PowerShell detects the empty blocks in the file*

Once the empty blocks are detected, the upload begins. As you can see in Figure 12-14, it can take a while for the upload to complete, depending on the size of the file and your Internet upload speed. In this example, the upload will take more than 5 hours. If you have an Express Route connection to Azure, your uploads will go a lot faster. (If you need a refresher on Azure Express Route, see Chapter 8.)

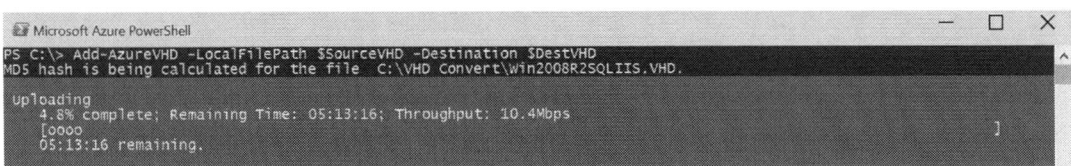

Figure 12-14. *The file upload begins*

After 5-1/2 hours, in the case of this example, the VHD has been uploaded to Azure, as shown in Figure 12-15. You need to complete just a few more steps before the file can be used to provision a VM.

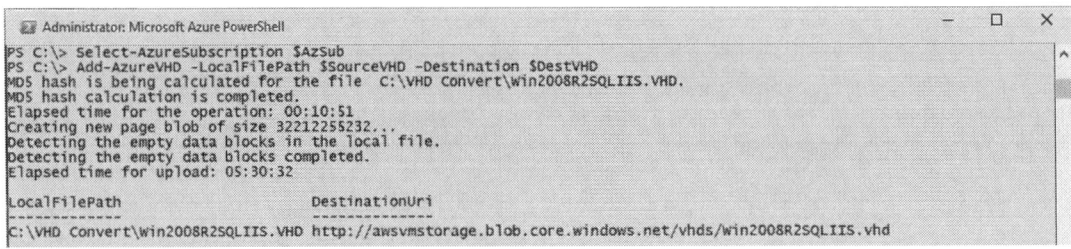

Figure 12-15. *The file upload is complete*

ADDING THE DISK TO AZURE SO IT CAN BE USED WHEN PROVISIONING A VM

Before you can create a new VM in Azure from the VHD file you just uploaded, you need to assign the disk as available for the VM in your subscription. Because this disk contains an OS and needs to be bootable, you need to use the -OS switch. If you don't use this switch, then the disk is stored as a data disk in Azure.

Use the following cmdlet to add the disk to your subscription. The results of the cmdlet are shown in Figure 12-16:

```
Add-AzureDisk –OS Windows –MediaLocation $DestVHD –DiskName $DiskName
```

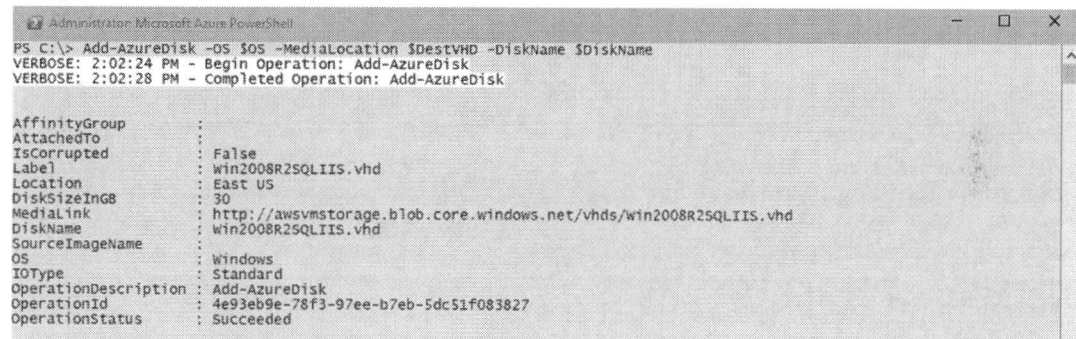

Figure 12-16. *Adding the disk to your Azure subscription*

With the disk added to your Azure subscription, you can now provision an Azure VM from it. The following cmdlet creates an Azure VM using the VHD you just uploaded, with configuration information from the New-AzureVMConfig parameters, and creates an endpoint of port 3389 on the VM so you can connect to it using Remote Desktop. You can see in Figure 12-17 that the cmdlet successfully creates the VM:

```
New-AzureVMConfig –Name $vmName –InstanceSize $instanceSize –DiskName $DiskName |
Add-AzureEndpoint –Protocol tcp –LocalPort 3389 –PublicPort 56290 –Name "Remote
Desktop" | New-AzureVM –ServiceName $serviceName –Location $location
```

```
PS C:\> New-AzureVMConfig –Name $vmName –InstanceSize $instanceSize –DiskName $DiskName | New-AzureVM –ServiceName $serv
iceName –Location $location
WARNING: The specified DNS name is already taken.
VERBOSE: 2:13:57 PM – Begin Operation: New-AzureVM – Create Deployment with VM Web01
VERBOSE: 2:15:01 PM – Completed Operation: New-AzureVM – Create Deployment with VM Web01

OperationDescription OperationId                              OperationStatus
-------------------- -----------                              ---------------
New-AzureVM          caf291fa-3b31-9ef5-b190-fb586c58e31c    Succeeded
```

Figure 12-17. *The new VM is created in Azure*

Log in to your tenant, and look at your VMs. You see the new VM in a running or starting state, as shown in Figure 12-18. Once it's running, you can connect to it and log in to it using the credentials you used when the VM was in AWS.

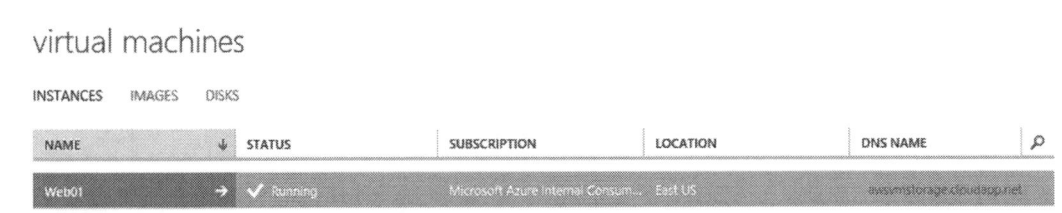

Figure 12-18. *The new VM has been provisioned and is running*

■ **Note**   If your computer was joined to a domain in AWS, and you haven't migrated your domain controller, you need to log on to the computer with a local administrator account to remove the computer from your old domain and join it to a new domain.

Working with PowerShell

As you saw in the previous section, Windows PowerShell is a great tool for working with Azure. Listing 12-1 contains all the cmdlets used in the previous example. You can save this code to your local machine for future use.

By changing the variables to match your systems, you can quickly download VHDs from AWS, prepare them to be usable in Azure, and then upload them into your Azure Storage account. Once the files are uploaded, the script adds the VHD to your Azure Storage account and registers it as a usable disk in your subscription. Finally, it provisions a VM for you to begin using.

Listing 12-1. Migrating a VM from AWS to Azure

```
# Set the execution policy in the PowerShell session so you can run the AWS PowerShell cmdlets
Set-ExecutionPolicy RemoteSigned

# Import the installed AWS PowerShell cmdlets
Import-Module AWSPowerShell

# Set your AWS credentials for logging into your AWS storage account
Set-AWSCredentials -AccessKey AKIAIDQHZBB3FPPB7EAA -SecretKey
NIQBKJAZvQ+LoYMqFHdbHwWZOu5jwwIpxxGuxzr5

# Create a new AWS storage bucket for uploading the saved VHD in
New-S3Bucket -BucketName d2dupload -Region us-west-2
```

```
# Upload the VHD into your AWS storage bucket
Write-S3Object -BucketName d2dupload -File D:\Win2008R2SQLIIS.VHD -Key Win2008R2SQLIIS
-CannedACLName Private -Region us-west-2

# Set the execution policy in the PowerShell session so you can run the AWS PowerShell cmdlets
Set-ExecutionPolicy RemoteSigned

# Import the installed AWS PowerShell cmdlets
Import-Module AWSPowerShell

# Set your AWS credentials for logging into your AWS storage account
Set-AWSCredentials -AccessKey AKIAIDQJTBB3FPPB7EAA -SecretKey
NIQBKJAZvQ+LoYMqDKdbHwWZOu5jwwIpxxGuxzr5

# Create the variable for the VHD download
$AzSub = "Microsoft Azure Internal Consumption"
$vhdPath = "C:\Users\azure\Downloads\AWSDownload\Win2008R2SQLIIS.vhd" # This is where the
VHD file will be downloaded to
$vhdConvertPath = "C:\VHD Convert\Win2008R2SQLIIS.VHD" # This is where the converted VHD
file will be saved to
$HVCabPath = "C:\Windows\vmguest\support\amd64\Windows6.x-HyperVIntegrationServices-x64.cab"
# This is the path to the Hyper-V integration disk
$diskNumb = (Mount-VHD -Path $vhdConvertPath -PassThru).DiskNumber # This will mount the VHD
to install the integration files onto
$vhdDriveLetter = (Get-Disk $diskNumb | Get-Partition | Get-Volume).DriveLetter # This is
the drive letter of the mounted disk
$subscriptionName = "Microsoft Azure Internal Consumption" # This sets the Azure
subscription that you'll upload the VHD into
$StorageAcct = "awsvmstorage" # Set Azure storage account name
$SourceVHD = $vhdConvertPath #Set the source and destination path of the disks
$DiskName = "Win2008R2SQLIIS.vhd"
$DestVHD = "http://" + $StorageAcct + ".blob.core.windows.net/vhds/" + $DiskNAme
$vmName = "Web01"
$instanceSize = "Small"
$ServiceNAme = "awsvmstorage"
$Location = "East US"
$OS = "Windows"

# Download the file from AWS
Copy-S3Object -BucketName d2dupload -Key Win2008R2SQLIIS -LocalFile $vhdPath

# Convert the dynamic disk to a fixed disk
Convert-VHD -Path $vhdPath -DestinationPath $vhdConvertPath -VHDType Fixed

# Install the Hyper-V Integration Services Drivers
(Get-Disk $diskNumb).OperationalStatus # This confirms that the VHD is mounted and available
Set-Disk $diskNumb -IsReadOnly $False # This ensures that the VHD can be written to
Add-WindowsPackage -PackagePath $HVCabPath -Path ($vhdDriveLetter+":\") #
Dismount-VHD -Path $vhdConvertPath # Now that the install is complete you need to dismount
it so it can be uploaded
```

```
# Prepare to upload the VHD to an Azure storage container
Select-AzureSubscription $AzSub # This sets the Azure subscription to use if you have more than one

# Upload the VHD to Azure
Add-AzureVHD -LocalFilePath $SourceVHD -Destination $DestVHD

#Assign the disk to Azure so it can be used to create a VM
Add-AzureDisk -OS $OS -MediaLocation $DestVHD -DiskName $DiskName

#Provision the VM in Azure from the uploaded disk
New-AzureVMConfig -Name $vmName -InstanceSize $instanceSize -DiskName $DiskName |
Add-AzureEndpoint -Protocol tcp -LocalPort 3389 -PublicPOrt 56290 -Name "Remote Desktop" |
New-AzureVM -ServiceName $serviceName -Location $location
```

MICROSOFT VIRTUAL MACHINE CONVERTER

Another good tool for preparing VHDs for uploading into Azure is the *Microsoft Virtual Machine Converter (MVMC)*. The MVMC is used to convert VMware-based VMs or VHDs into the VHD format used by Azure. It's also used to convert physical machines to VHDs or Windows Server 2012 VHDX format disks into VHD disks so that they can be uploaded into Azure.

The MVMC not only converts the disks that are running on VMware, but also migrates the rest of the VMware VM's configuration, including memory, the number of virtual processors, and network interface cards. In addition, it removes the VMware tools from the source VM and installs the Hyper-V integration tools on the destination VM. This allows for a complete migration from one platform to the other.

The MVMC is available for download at `https://www.microsoft.com/en-us/download/details.aspx?id=42497`.

There isn't enough space in this chapter to go through a step-by-step example of using the MVMC. Instead, review the TechNet article "Use Microsoft Virtual Machine Converter" at `https://technet.microsoft.com/en-us/library/dn874008.aspx` to walk through how to use it.

AZURE SITE RECOVERY

The final tool we'll introduce is the Azure Site Recovery tool. This tool is currently available in preview only for VMware and physical servers, but it is fully available to Hyper-V workloads.

The new features that are in development include the following:

- New heterogeneous workload support for various Windows and Linux editions with replication to and recovery in Azure

- New automated discovery of VMware vCenter Server managed VMs for replication to and recovery in Azure

- New continuous data protection with software-based replication to provide near-zero recovery point objectives (RPOs)

- New on-the-fly conversion of source VMware virtual machine disk (VMDK) files to bootable target Azure VHD files, ensuring low recovery time objectives (RTOs)

- New multi-VM consistency using ASR protection groups to ensure that all tiers in an n-tier application replicate consistently and fail over at the same time

- New failback to VMware infrastructure from Azure when an on-premises datacenter comes back up post disaster

- Enhanced active-passive replication that does not require running target Azure VMs at the time of replication, thereby reducing the total cost of ownership (TCO)

- Enhanced single-click failovers with ASR recovery plans to provide end-to-end workload-aware disaster recovery and orchestration at low RTOs

- Enhanced rich health monitoring for replication, failover, and failback with events and e-mail notifications

Because this feature is in preview mode and will likely go through many changes, we don't review how to set it up. Instead, see the Microsoft Azure Preview features web site at `http://azure.microsoft.com/en-us/services/preview`, where you can sign up to try it for yourself.

Once you sign up, you can follow the article "Set Up Protection Between On-Premises VMware Virtual Machines or Physical Servers and Azure" at `http://azure.microsoft.com/en-us/documentation/articles/site-recovery-vmware-to-azure` to begin using the recovery or migration capabilities.

Summary

As you learned in this chapter, migrating VMs into Azure is quite simple. Whether you use PowerShell, the free Microsoft Virtual Machine Converter, or one of the other migration methods, Microsoft has worked to make extending your datacenter beyond its current constraints a smooth a process.

The next chapter introduces to Azure monitoring and reporting. You learn how to monitor your web sites and VMs so that you can proactively prepare for potential problems. The reporting functionality allows you to keep an eye on your system's performance and access so that you can plan your needs according to the load on your applications or VMs.

■ ■ ■

## CHAPTER 13

Monitoring and Reporting

Introducing Azure Monitoring and Reporting

Monitoring IT services is critical to understanding how IT events impact the systems involved and to the users who rely on the IT services those systems provide. E-mail, although usually not a top-tier line-of-business application, is frequently monitored because outages and performance issues affect a large number of users in near real time. Organizations have embraced monitoring at various levels; some monitor everything and want deep insight into the errors that systems generate, whereas others just want to know that the systems hosting a service are up or respond to a ping.

The latter scenario doesn't provide much value. To be able to monitor technology proactively, IT administrators need to be able to identify trends and thresholds and alert the necessary individuals when those thresholds are exceeded. Identifying trends facilitates capacity planning and also helps identify workloads that are good use cases for cloud computing. If you can identify a system that is never used on a weekend, at certain times of day, and so forth, that system's services can be provided from the cloud and scale up and down as needed. To do so, you can use the auto-scaling capabilities provided by Azure, which would be cost prohibitive to set up on-premises.

The monitoring capabilities of Azure services vary, depending on the service you are examining. This chapter reviews Azure monitoring, logging, and alerting capabilities built into the following Azure services:

- Cloud Services

- Mobile Services (metrics for mobile endpoint availability only)

- SQL Databases

- Storage

- Virtual Machines

- Websites (metrics for web endpoint availability only)

This chapter is not designed to be a comprehensive guide to monitoring. Rather, it presents an overview of the built-in monitoring capabilities of Microsoft Azure for some of the mainstream services that consumers are using in Azure.

Monitoring a Microsoft Azure Websites

Microsoft provides a variety of web sites in Azure; at the time of this writing, there were 59 sites in the Azure Websites Gallery. Azure web sites, as shown in Figure 13-1 and Figure 13-2, are platform as a service (PaaS) offerings that run in a shared environment. Customers can set up their own Azure web sites on a number of different Windows OS versions or Linux OS version VMs, but the Azure Websites workspace provides PaaS web sites.

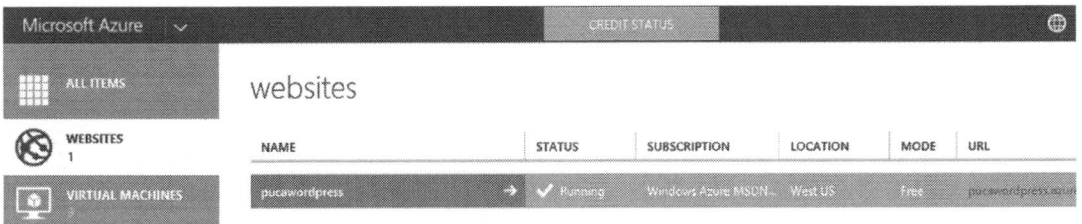

Figure 13-1. *Azure web site in the Azure Management Portal*

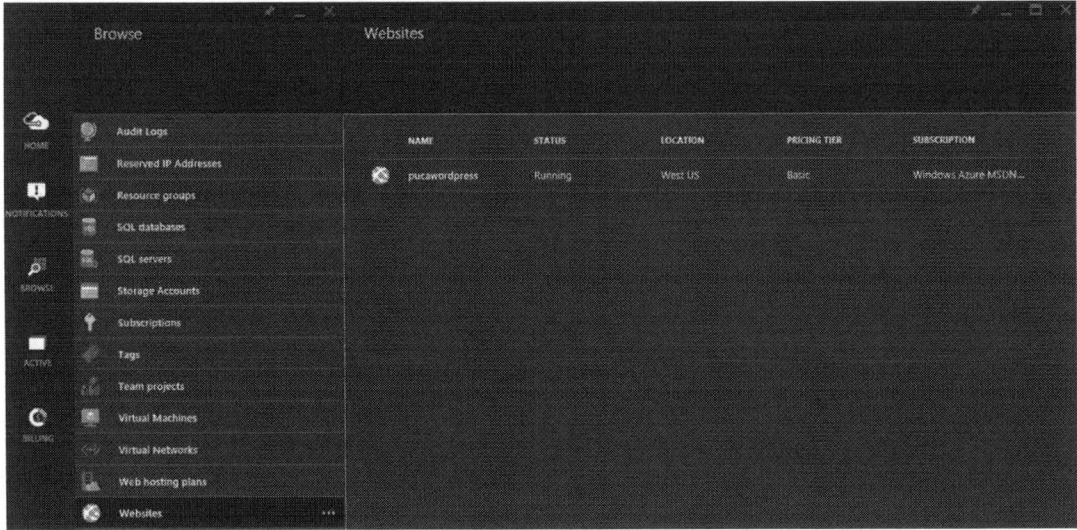

Figure 13-2. *Azure web site in the new Azure Management Portal*

To monitor availability information for web sites, you first need to enable endpoint monitoring for the appropriate resource. When you click the Azure web site that you wish to monitor, you are presented with a slew of options or *tabs* at the top of the page, including the dashboard and monitor.

■ **Note**   These tab fields are dynamic and updated as Microsoft releases new features into Preview. Look for the word *Preview* in green to identify newly released features. These features are not covered under the normal SLA until they are out of the Preview stage.

By clicking the dashboard tab on the Websites page, you can see how the following metrics are graphed:

- CPU Time
- Data In
- Data Out
- HTTP Server Errors
- Requests

Above the upper-right corner of the graph in Figure 13-3 are three items that allow you to configure the graph as you like. The first option specifies whether the graph is shown for ease of reading (Relative) or to the scale of the counters with a grid (Absolute). The second drop-down is the timeframe you wish to display: the last hour, the last 24 hours, or the last 7 days. The arrow in a circle acts as a refresh button for the graph data.

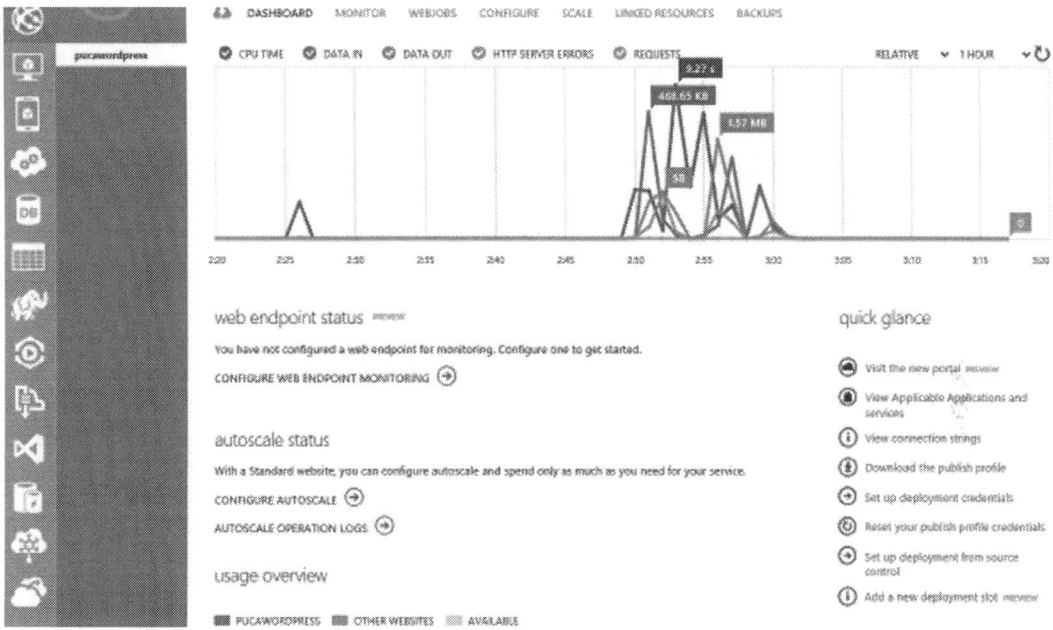

Figure 13-3. *Azure web site dashboard showing performance data*

These metrics are important to help you identify items such as how many hits your web site is getting and how much outbound traffic you are generating. Data Out is important because Azure customers pay for Data Out, or egress traffic, when they are not using ExpressRoute.

In Figure 13-4, you can see how different the new Azure Portal dashboard looks from the former one. This page scrolls down and provides quite a bit of additional data.

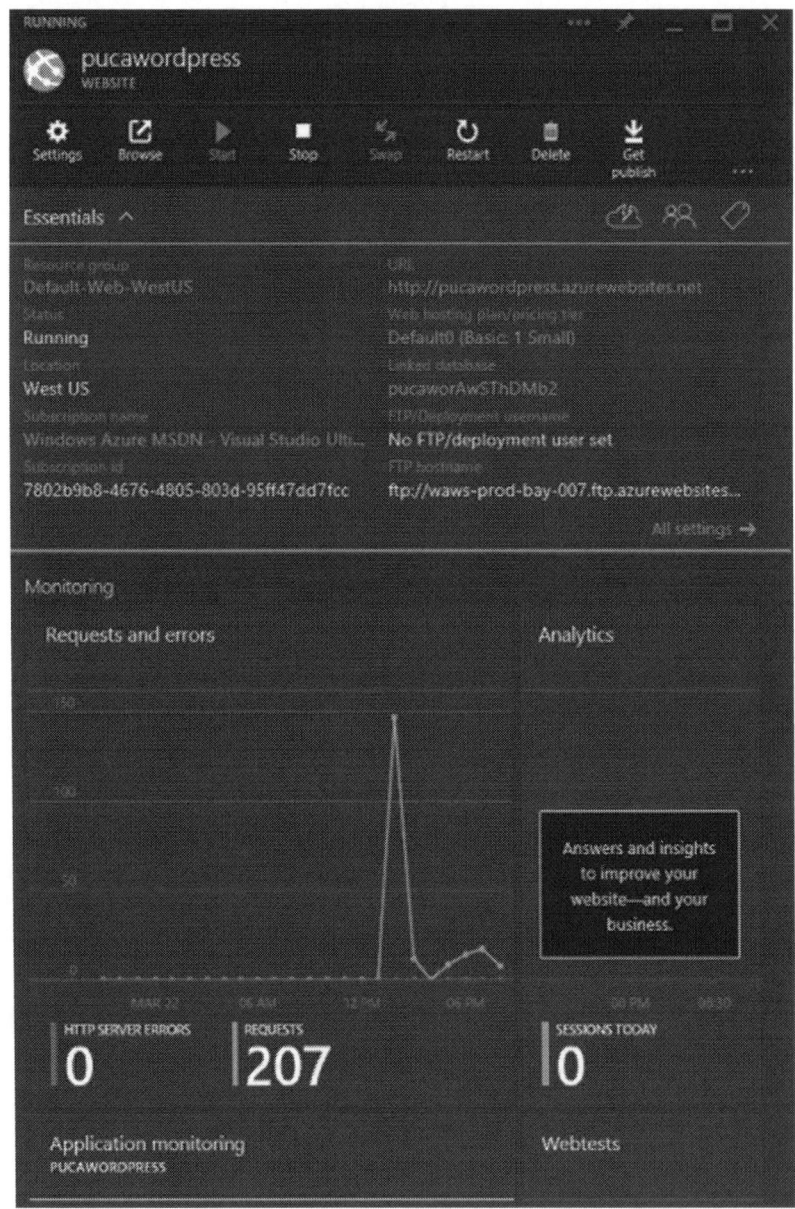

Figure 13-4. *Azure Websites dashboard in the new Portal, showing performance data*

Also notice that on the dashboard page, shown in Figure 13-5, you are presented with configuration items on the right, such as the connection strings, the site URL, and so on. Under Usage Overview is a series of graphs that represent near-real-time data metrics:

- *CPU Time*: Per day

- *CPU Time*: Per 5 minutes

- *Data Out*: Per day

- *File System Storage*: In GB

- *Memory Usage*: Per hour

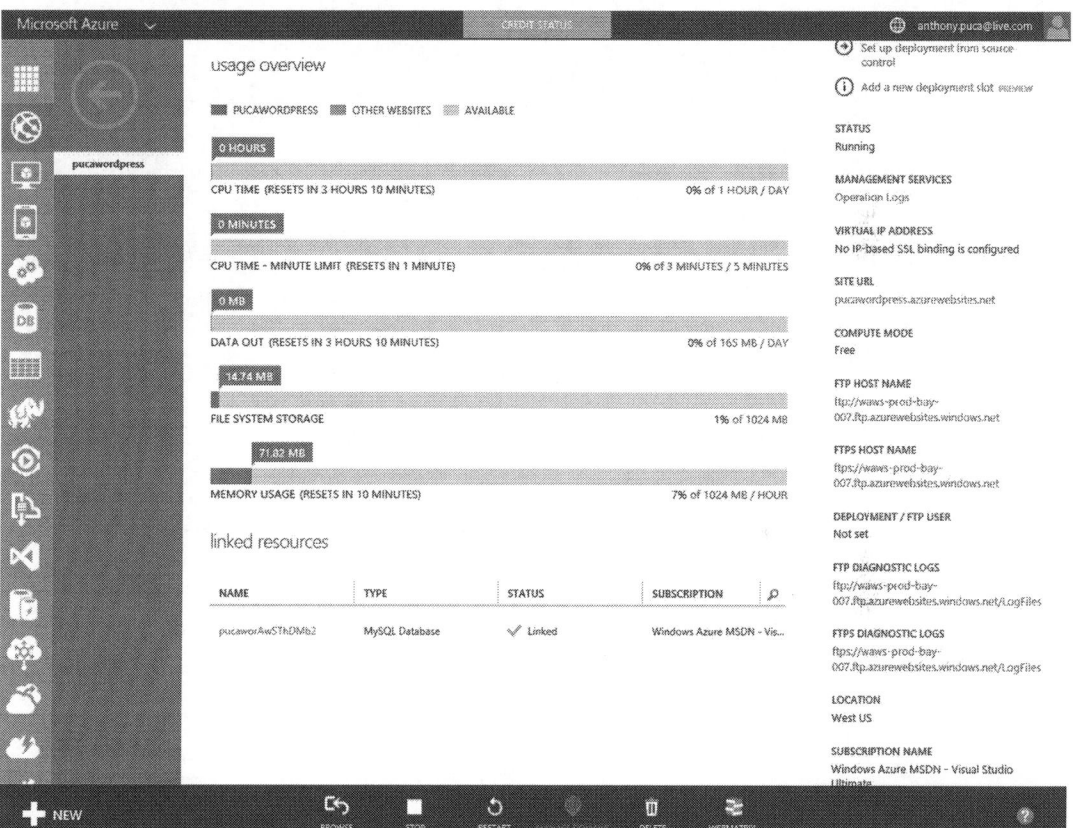

Figure 13-5. *Azure Websites dashboard, showing usage data*

In the new Azure Portal example in Figure 13-6, as you select or drill into items, fly-out menus and detail panes appear to the right.

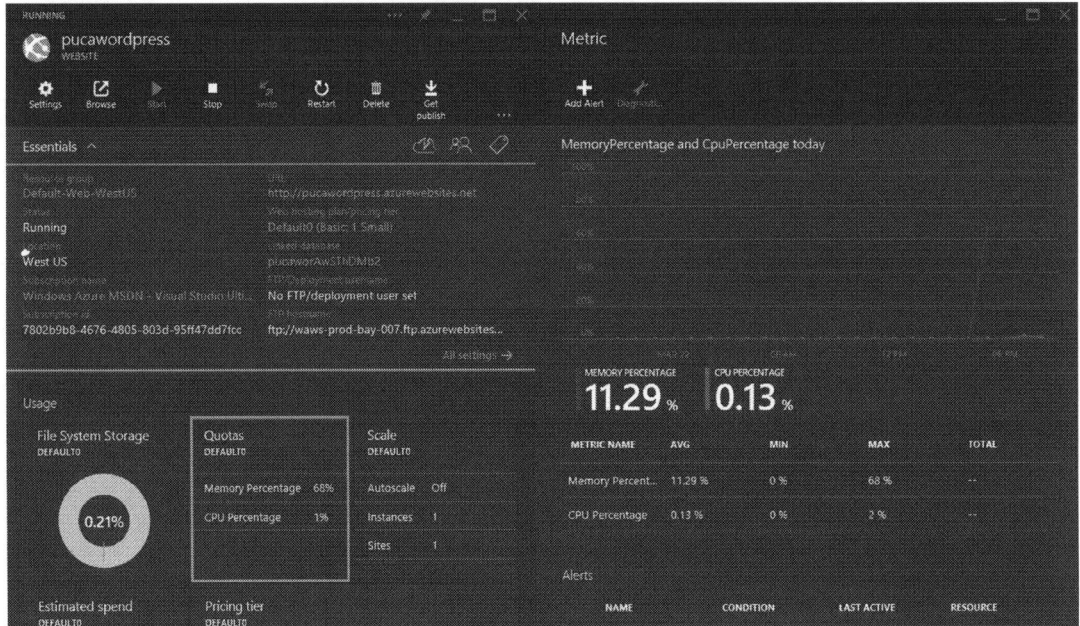

Figure 13-6. *Azure Websites dashboard in the new Portal, showing usage data*

When you click the web site's Monitor tab, you see the same five counters that are graphed on the dashboard tab; see Figure 13-7. Their corresponding Min/Max/Avg/Total values are displayed, as well as whether any alerts are configured.

Figure 13-7. *Azure web site in the Portal, showing the default monitors*

Because only six counters can be graphed at once, it is important to understand how to tailor the graph to your specific needs. To remove some of the counters from the graph, simply click the checkmark on the left side of each counter's line. The checkmark disappears, and the counter is grayed out, as shown in Figure 13-8.

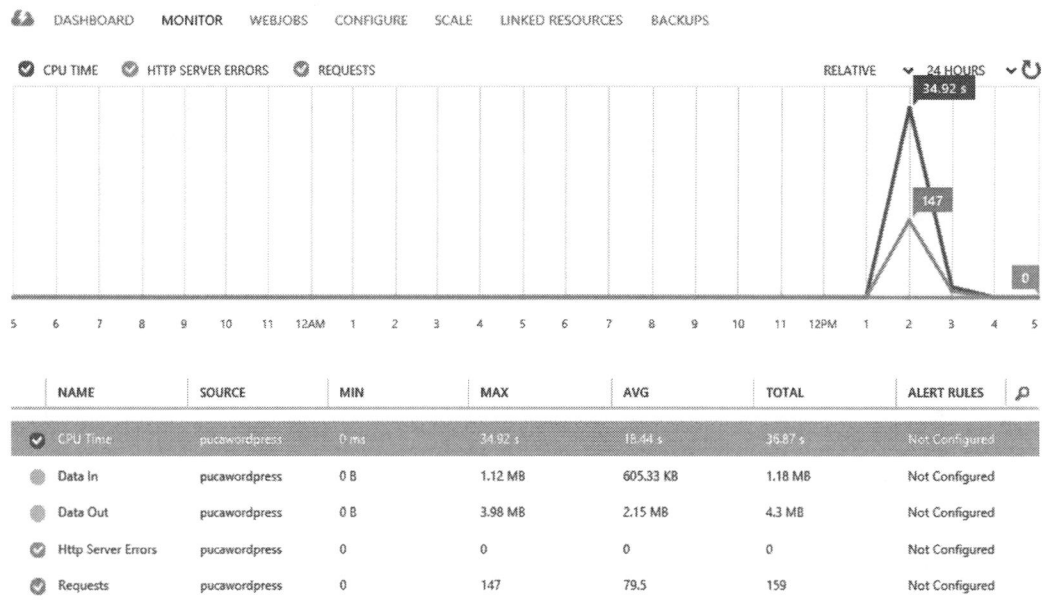

Figure 13-8. *Azure web site in the Portal, showing disabled monitors*

CREATING AN ALERT

Let's say that you want to know whenever Data Out is greater than a specific amount. You can set a threshold and have Azure send you an e-mail when it is exceeded. To set up a web site monitor, follow these steps:

1. On the Monitor tab of the web site you want to monitor, select the counter for which you want to create a threshold. In this example, use the Data Out counter.

2. Select Add Rule at the bottom of the browser window, as shown in Figure 13-9.

NAME	SOURCE	MIN	MAX	AVG	TOTAL	ALERT RULES
CPU Time	pucawordpress	0 ms	34.92 s	18.46 s	36.92 s	Not Configured
Data In	pucawordpress	0 B	1.12 MB	605.33 KB	1.18 MB	Not Configured
Data Out	pucawordpress	0 B	3.98 MB	2.15 MB	4.3 MB	Not Configured
Http Server Errors	pucawordpress	0	0	0	0	Not Configured
Requests	pucawordpress	0	147	79.5	159	Not Configured

Figure 13-9. *Configuring an Azure web site alert rule*

3. Give the alert a name and description, and then click the arrow in the lower-right corner, as shown in Figure 13-10.

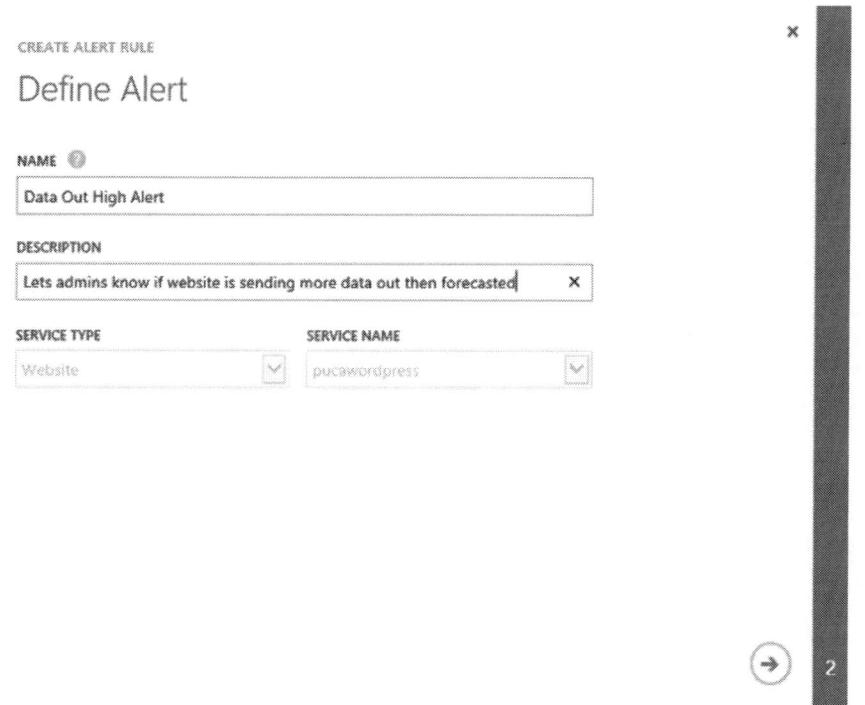

CREATE ALERT RULE

Define Alert

NAME
Data Out High Alert

DESCRIPTION
Lets admins know if website is sending more data out then forecasted

SERVICE TYPE
Website

SERVICE NAME
pucawordpress

Figure 13-10. *Azure web site alert-rule wizard*

4. Select the condition and threshold value, the window of time over which you want to evaluate the condition, and whom you want e-mails sent to, as shown in Figure 13-11.

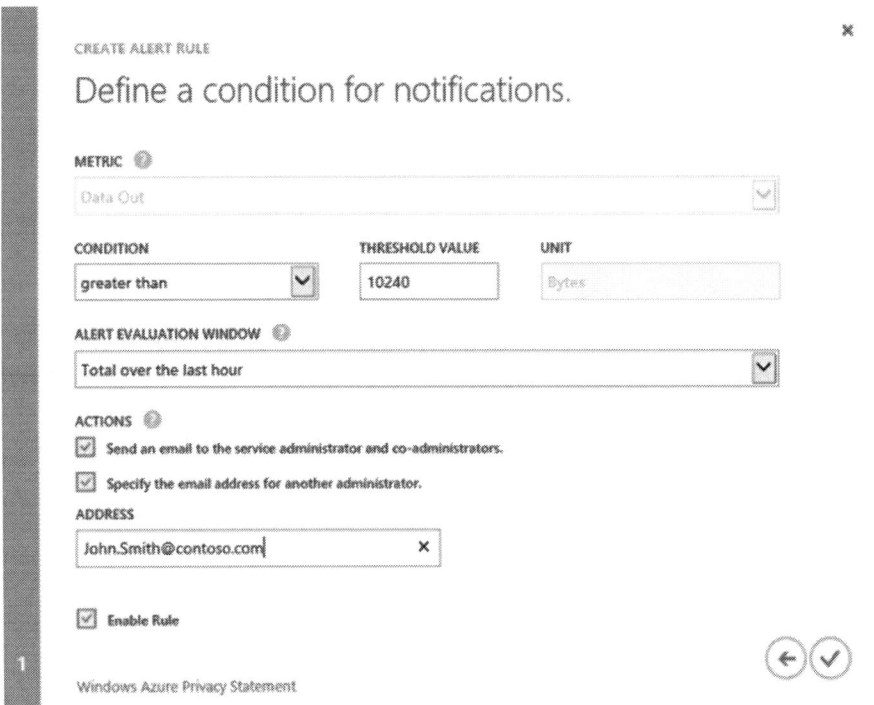

Figure 13-11. *Specifying Azure web site alert recipients*

5. After you see the success-notification ribbon at the bottom of the Azure Portal, notice that the Monitor dashboard now reflects the rule you created. Click the hyperlink in the Alert Rules column to jump to the Management Services section of the Azure Portal, as shown in Figure 13-12.

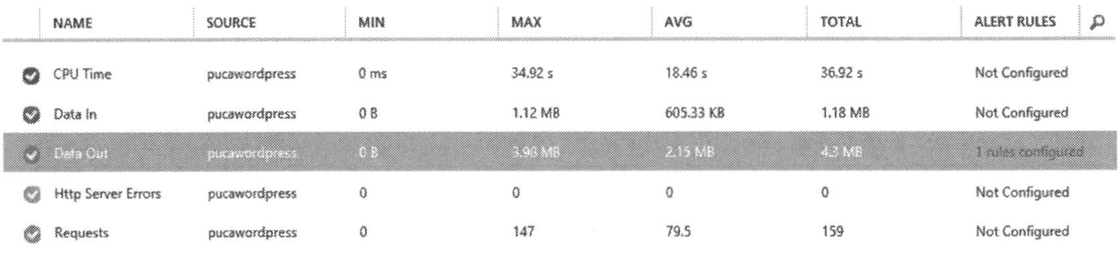

NAME	SOURCE	MIN	MAX	AVG	TOTAL	ALERT RULES
CPU Time	pucawordpress	0 ms	34.92 s	18.46 s	36.92 s	Not Configured
Data In	pucawordpress	0 B	1.12 MB	605.33 KB	1.18 MB	Not Configured
Data Out	pucawordpress	0 B	3.90 MB	2.15 MB	4.3 MB	1 rules configured
Http Server Errors	pucawordpress	0	0	0	0	Not Configured
Requests	pucawordpress	0	147	79.5	159	Not Configured

Figure 13-12. *Azure web site alert rule configured*

6. Once the alert becomes active, you can see when the threshold is broken. Figure 13-13 shows that the alert status is at a warning level.

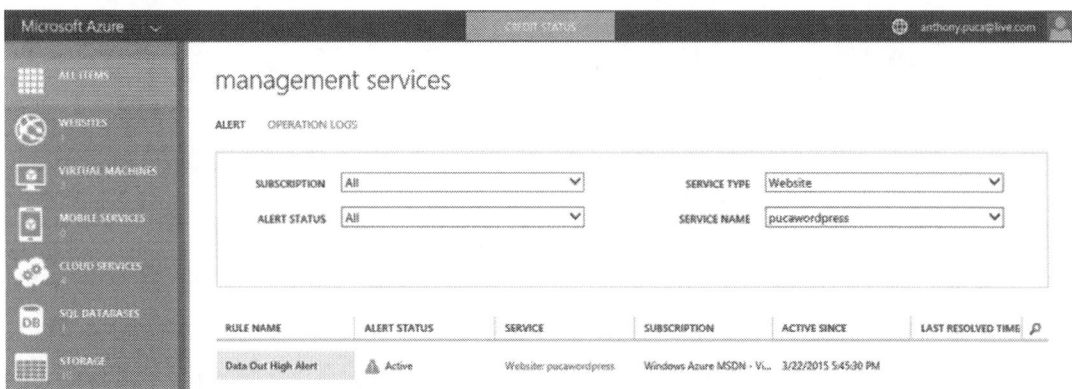

Figure 13-13. *Azure Management Services workspace*

7. Click the rule's name: in this example, it's Data Out High Alert. You see a detailed view of the monitoring-rule data, as shown in Figure 13-14.

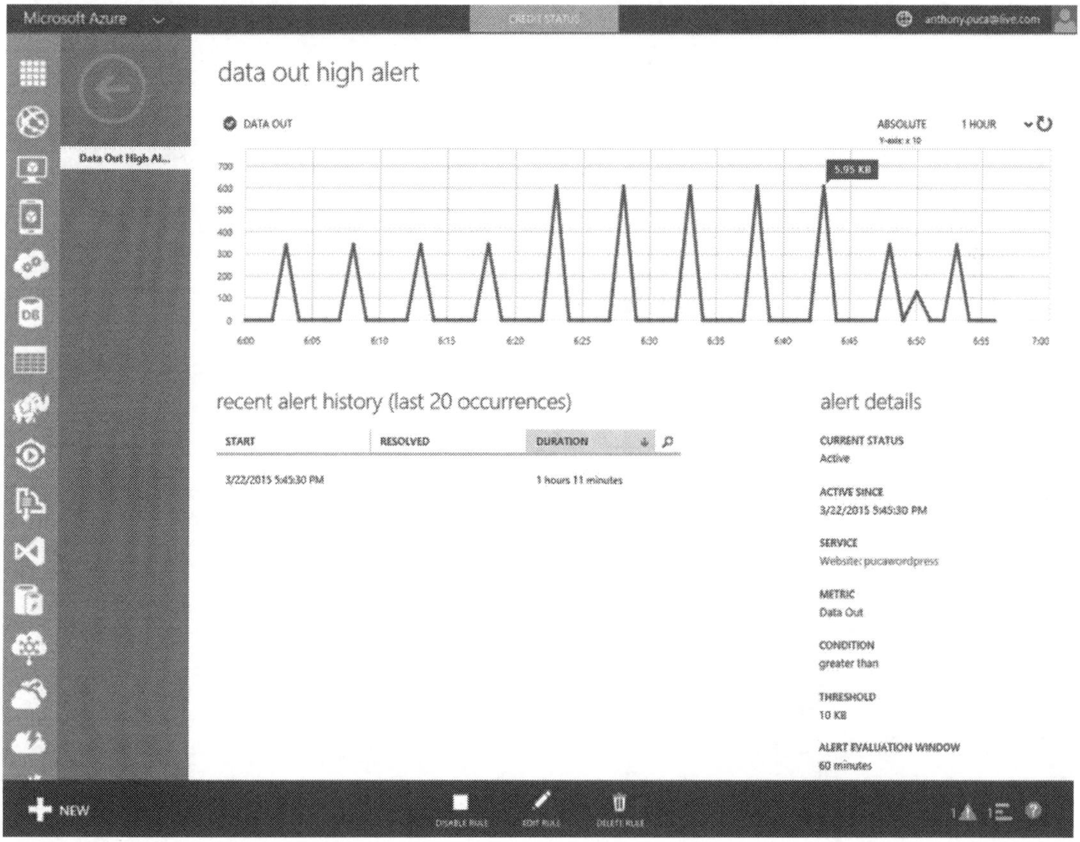

Figure 13-14. *Azure Alert History view*

345

Also notice in Figure 13-15 that at right, you can see the times the threshold has been exceeded and by how much it has been exceeded, as well as a number of attributes about this monitoring rule. The status of notifications and jobs appears in the lower-right corner of any screen in the Azure Portal.

Figure 13-15. *Azure alert notifications*

In the new Azure Portal, you create an alert rule by selecting Add Alert at the top of the metric graph. A flyout appears on the right, as shown in Figure 13-16, with all the necessary fields in one location.

Figure 13-16. *Adding an alert rule in the new Azure Portal*

346

Metrics to Monitor

You can monitor other metrics and set thresholds to generate alerts in Azure. Table 13-1 lists the web site metrics available at the time of this writing.

Table 13-1. *Azure Web Site Metrics*

Name	Unit
AverageMemoryWorkingSet	Bytes
AverageResponseTime	Milliseconds
CPU Time	Milliseconds
Data In	Bytes
Data Out	Bytes
Http 401 errors	Count
Http 403 errors	Count
Http 404 errors	Count
Http 406 errors	Count
Http Client Errors	Count
Http Redirects	Count
Http Server Errors	Count
Http Successes	Count
MemoryWorkingSet	Bytes
Requests	Count

Table 13-2 lists the SQL database metrics available at the time of this writing.

Table 13-2. *SQL Database Metrics*

Name	Unit
Blocked by Firewall	Count
CPU Percentage	%
Data IO Percentage	%
Deadlocks	Count
DTU Percentage	%
Failed Connection	Count
Log IO Percentage	%
Storage	Bytes
Successful Connection	Count

Table 13-3 lists the VM metrics available at the time of this writing.

Table 13-3. *Virtual Machine Metrics*

Name	Unit
CPU Percentage	%
Disk Read Bytes/Sec	Bytes/s
Disk Write Bytes/Sec	Bytes/s
Network In	Bytes
Network Out	Bytes

Endpoint Monitoring

Whenever you have services that are published via HTTP or HTTPS, you should use endpoint monitoring. *Endpoint monitoring* lets you monitor availability from geo-distributed locations. These tests will fail if the HTTP response code is 400 or greater or if the response time is greater than 30 seconds.

To configure endpoint monitoring, either select it from the dashboard or click the Configure tab and scroll down to the Monitoring section. As you can see in Figure 13-17, this is where you input a name, a URL, and up to three Azure locations from which you want to test connectivity.

Figure 13-17. *Configuring Azure endpoint monitoring*

The status of endpoint monitoring is available on the dashboard of any service that supports it, as shown in Figure 13-18.

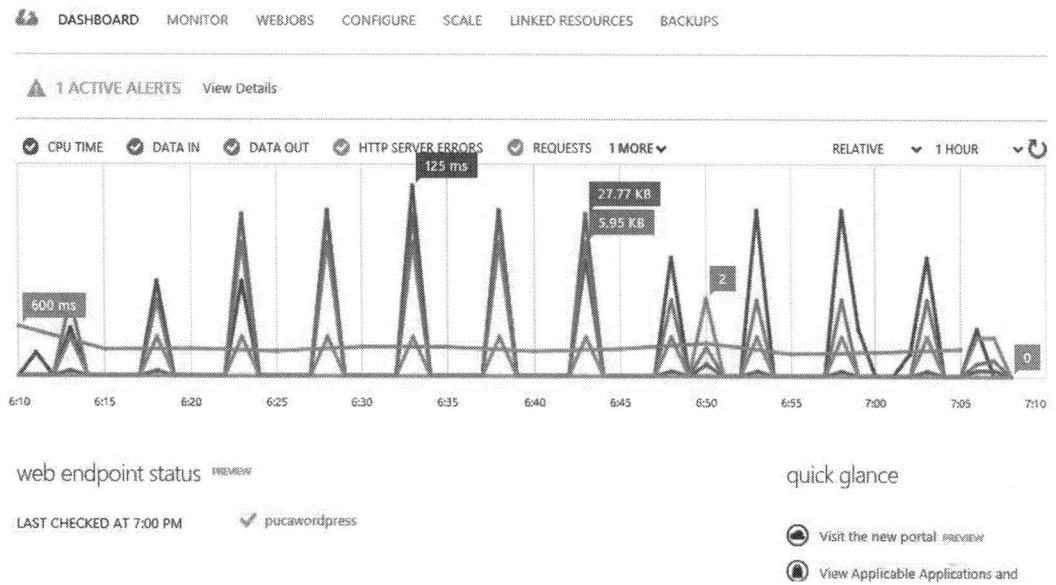

Figure 13-18. *Azure endpoint monitoring history view*

Endpoints currently support two metrics that you can monitor by creating a rule:

- Response Time in Seconds
- Uptime in Percent (%)

Monitoring Azure Virtual Machines

Azure VMs are monitored just like Azure web sites, with some small differences. For example, Azure VMs are provisioned with two endpoints already available. In Figure 13-19, port address translation is occurring through the Azure Management Portal to allow RDP access to the VM.

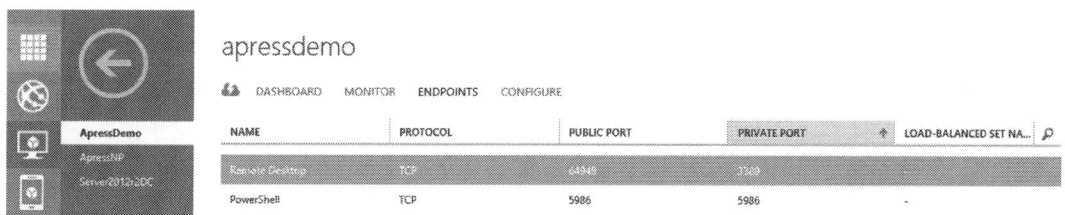

Figure 13-19. *Azure VM endpoint monitoring*

As you can see in Figure 13-20, the new Azure Portal provides much more information in a single pane. It shows the VM name, IP info, CPU performance trend, and endpoints that are published, as well as a slew of other attributes about the VM.

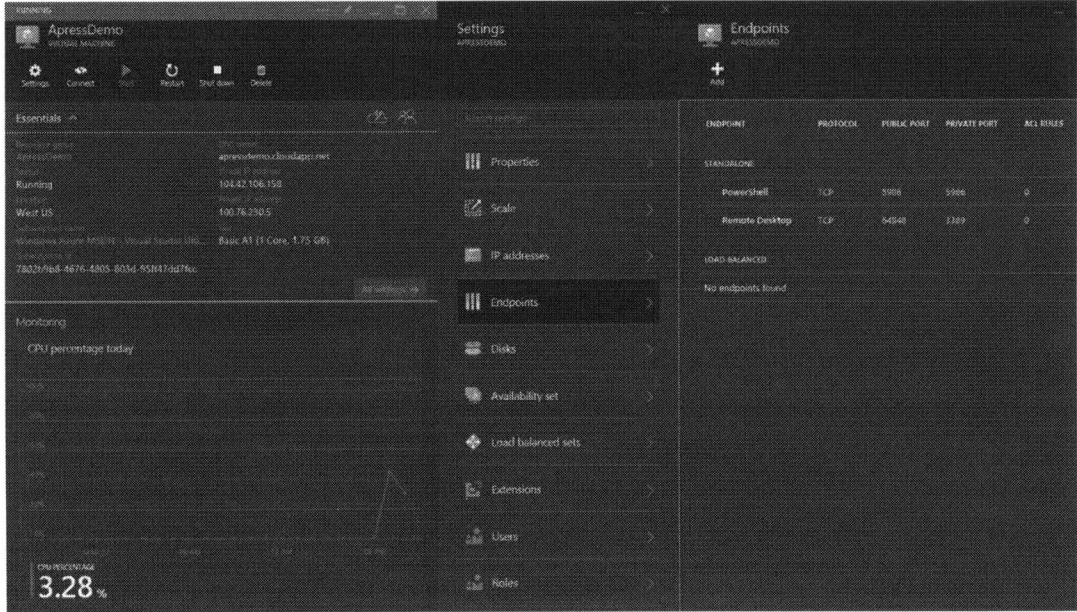

Figure 13-20. *Azure new Portal VM endpoint monitoring*

Minimal monitoring of VMs is available in Azure natively. For more detailed monitoring of VMs in Azure, Microsoft recommends using Microsoft System Center 2012 R2. System Center provides unified management across on-premises, service provider, and Azure environments. It provides VM portability between on-premises and Azure, as well as deep insight into the fabric, operating system performance, health, security, and service availability. System Center also gives you an outside-in view of the health and availability of the IT services you are providing, allowing you to configure your datacenter monitoring just as this chapter illustrated for endpoint monitoring of Azure web sites.

For more information on Microsoft System Center, visit `www.microsoft.com/systemcenter`.

Monitoring Storage

Azure supports monitoring blob, table, and queue storage. Storage monitoring includes aggregated transaction statistics and capacity data for a storage service. This data is aggregated at hourly or minute intervals for each storage service. Transaction data is recorded at the service level and the API operation level. At the service level, statistics summarizing all requested API operations are written to a table entity every hour, even if no requests were made to the service. At the API operation level, statistics are written to an entity only if the operation was requested within that hour.

When enabling storage monitoring, your options are as follows:

- *Off*: No storage monitoring occurs.

- *Minimal*: Collects data such as the amount of ingress and egress traffic, storage availability, storage performance, and success percentages. This data is then aggregated for the Blob, Table, and Queue services.

- *Verbose*: Includes all the data that is collected with the Minimal setting, along with the same metrics for each storage operation. This setting enables a closer analysis of issues that occur during application operations.

For each storage service that you monitor, you are asked to specify a retention period with a range of 0–365 days. It is recommended, as a best practice, that you specify a retention period slightly longer than you typically need to go back and look at performance data. Some organizations may only need a few weeks, whereas others may need 6–12 months.

■ **Note**   If you choose a retention period of 0, the system never deletes the analytics data, and thus it is your responsibility to do so.

To monitor Azure storage, it must be configured at the storage-instance level under the Configure tab of the Azure Management Portal. After you enable storage monitoring, it takes about an hour for the data to appear in the Portal. Figure 13-21 shows Blobs storage monitoring data being retained for 90 days.

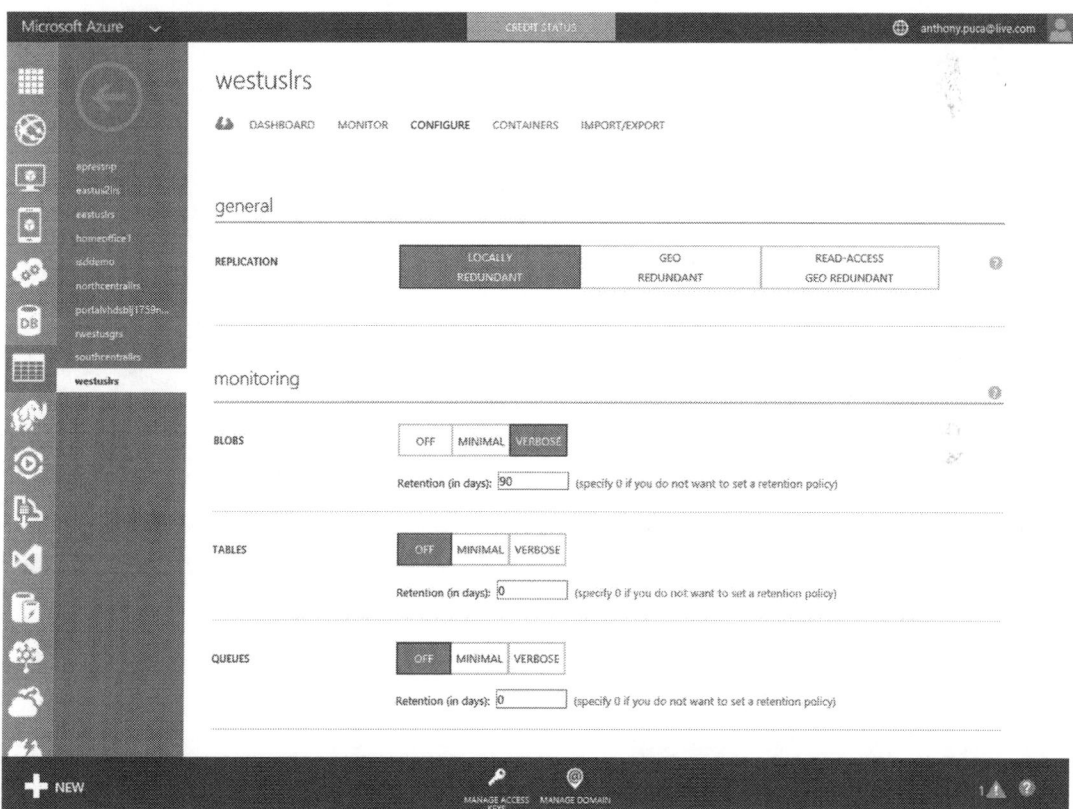

Figure 13-21. Configuring Azure storage monitoring

■ **Note**   At the time of this writing, capacity metrics are only available for the Blob service. Capacity metrics for the Table service and Queue service will be available in future versions of storage analytics.

Management Services

The Management Services section of the Azure Portal, shown in Figure 13-22, is essentially where all the monitoring rules you create are stored. From this workspace, you can see all the rules and the services to which they are linked, and you can jump right from the rule to the service using the hyperlink in the Service Name column. The Management Services workspace is also where you can view the operation logs for the Azure systems for which you have logging enabled.

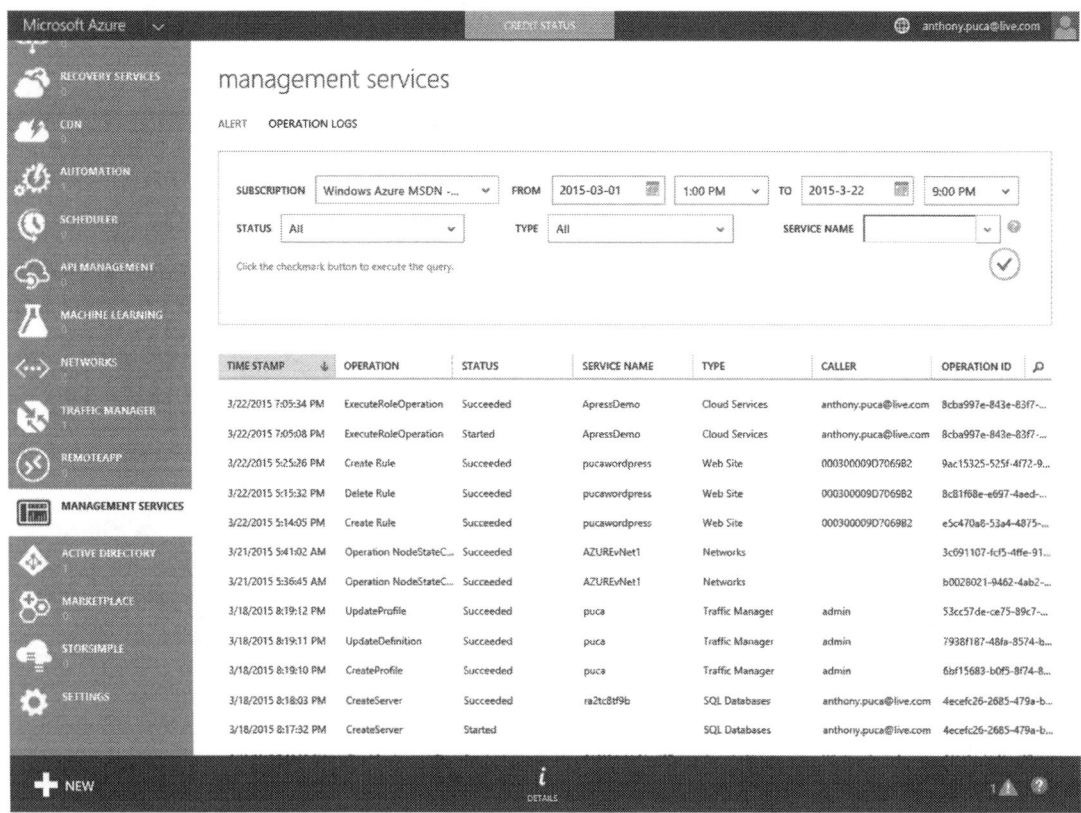

Figure 13-22. *Azure Management Services log view*

Summary

Azure includes the basic monitoring that most organizations need. Whether you want to see basic availability and performance data or you wish to perform more detailed synthetic transactions from outside the datacenter in which your systems reside, Azure monitoring exposes a rich list of attributes for monitoring and trending your systems. You should now have a good understanding of Azure monitoring, metrics, and endpoints; you can use these together to provide a monitoring framework or integrate them into your on-premises solution.

The next chapter introduces you to the Azure Machine Learning service. You learn what it is and how you can use it to recognize patterns based on historical data, which can help you predict trends.

## PART IV

Futures and Advanced Topics

■ ■ ■

## CHAPTER 14

Microsoft Azure Machine Learning

Machine Learning emphasizes the computational work of software to process sample and/or historic data with the goal of uncovering interesting patterns, identifying objectives, and predicting outcome. For example, machine learning might uncover that for the past 14 years of worker's compensation claims data, ear injuries in construction have an 88% chance of staying open for 180 days. Or when provided with juvenile offender historic data and recent juvenile crime data, machine learning might predict a 79% chance that a given juvenile's next offense will result in an assault.

What Is Microsoft Azure Machine Learning?

Microsoft Azure *Machine Learning (ML)* is an advanced analytics cloud platform that makes it easy to design, test, deploy, and share powerful and predictive analytics. Microsoft Azure Machine Learning lets you build analytical experiments and predictive models. A rich set of algorithms can be used to process data based on business needs. Azure Machine Learning also provides tight integration with the public domain languages R, Python, and SQLite. And because Azure Machine Learning lives in the cloud, the platform has inherent scalability, availability, and security.

R is an industry favorite of data scientists and statisticians. R includes a rich scripting language to manipulate, statistically analyze, and visualize data. Python is an open source programming language that makes it easy to develop powerful and comprehensive programs. SQLite, in addition to being a development platform, provides a SQL language with which most relational database administrators are already very familiar.

Once the Azure Machine Learning experiment has been tested and evaluated, you can deploy a fully managed web service with a few clicks and that can connect to data of all shapes and sizes. The Azure Machine Learning web services may be published to the Azure Marketplace, offering businesses the opportunity to provide predictive services for a fee.

Quick Hands-On Introduction

Before further education on the Azure Machine Learning capability it's important to get familiar with some basic terms and workflow using the platform.

Follow these steps to sign-up for your Azure ML subscription. If you don't have the time to do this now, the screen illustrations, descriptions, and walkthrough will still be educational:

1. Browse to *http://azure.com/ml* as seen in Figure 14-1, and either click on Get started now ➤ and sign-up for an Azure Machine Learning subscription or click on Pricing and get a free one-month trial.

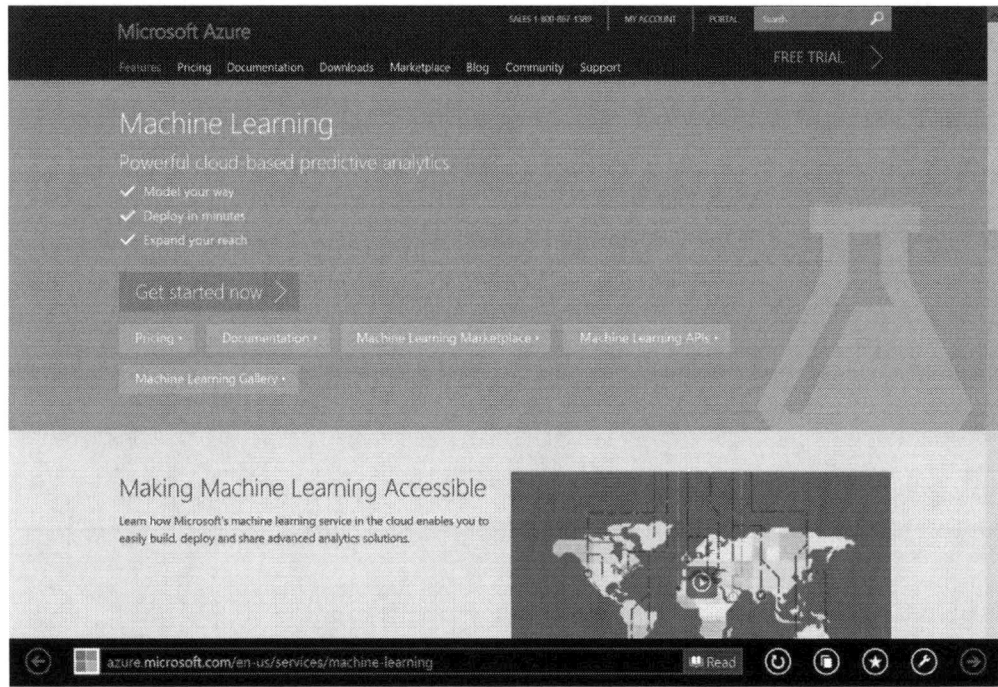

Figure 14-1. Azure Machine Learning Website

2. From the Azure Portal, you will find the Azure Machine Learning icon along the
    left side (you may need to scroll down). Click on the icon shown in Figure 14-2.

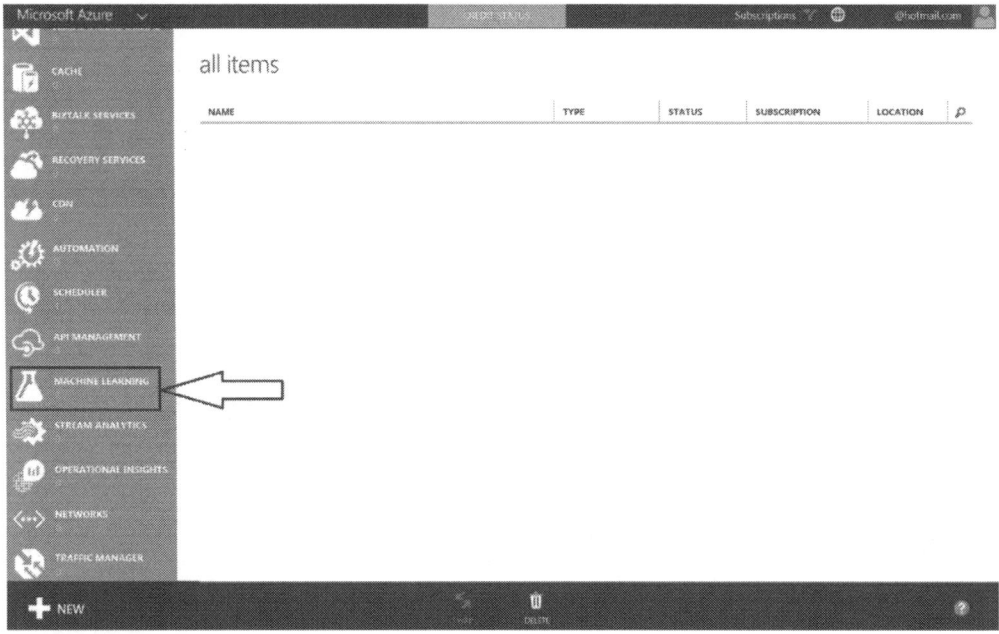

Figure 14-2. Azure Machine Learning in the Azure Portal

3. Once you have clicked on the Machine Learning Icon, click on +NEW in the lower-left corner and follow the steps, as shown in Figure 14-3, to set up and then access your Azure Machine Learning workspace. (The Hotmail address in masked in this figure.)

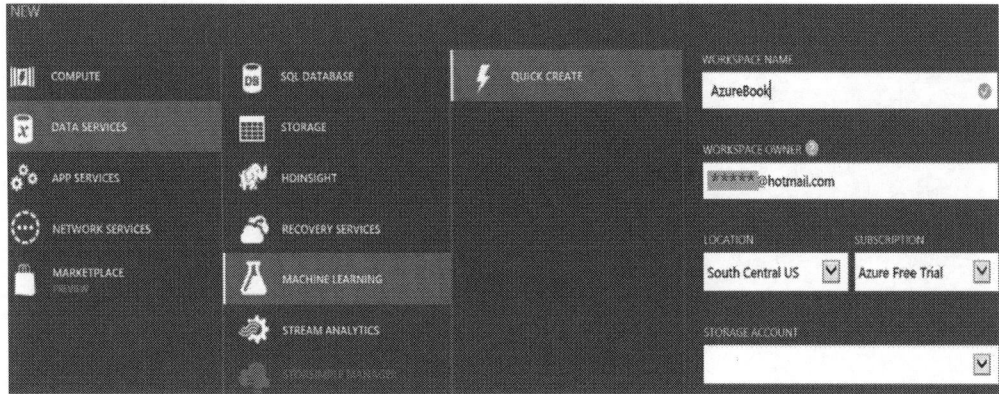

Figure 14-3. *Creating an Azure Machine Learning Workspace*

Once complete, you should see a screen similar to Figure 14-4.

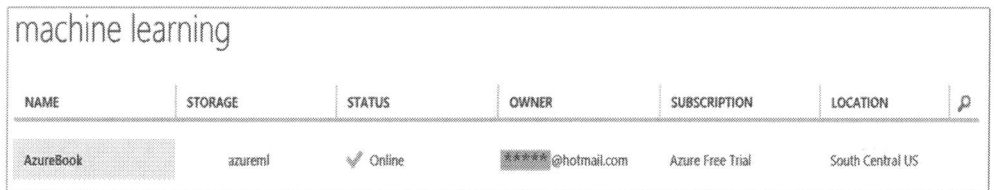

Figure 14-4. *Azure Machine Learning Subscription*

4. From here, highlight your Azure workspace and at the bottom of the screen, click **Open in Studio**. Figure 14-5 depicts Azure Machine Learning Studio (ML Studio).

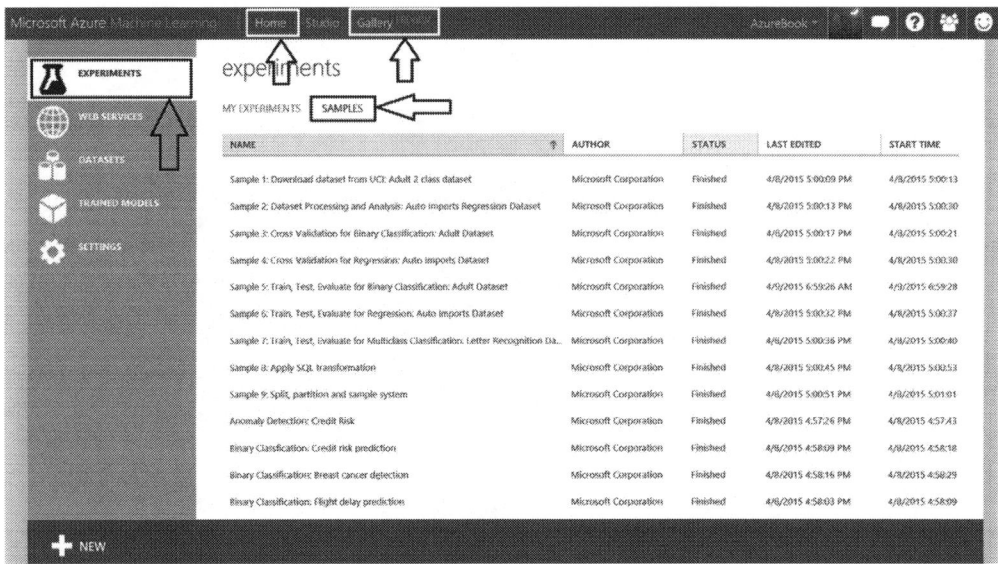

Figure 14-5. Azure Machine Learning Samples

■ **Note** ML Studio is where you will spend the vast majority of your time. This is where your Azure machine learning experiment authoring, analysis, and deployment takes place. An Azure Machine Learning experiment is an authoring "container", which encapsulates the data that you want to analyze, data cleansing you choose to perform, data feature selection, processing of algorithms against your data, validation of your analytics, prediction scoring and much more. You can copy, run, share experiments to other workspaces, and publish your experiment as a web service. Near the top of ML Studio you will find **Gallery**. This is where Microsoft and the Azure Machine Learning community (including you!) have shared experiments for others to investigate and incorporate. The experiments found in the gallery may include detailed write-ups, best practices and instructions for incorporating into your personal ML Studio workspace! Poke around in here and take a look at the various assets. Also near the top of ML Studio is where **Home** is. Go here to find a number of excellent learning resources.

5. You'll notice in Figure 14-5 that there are a number of sample experiments that Microsoft has provided. Scroll around, select an experiment or two and get familiar with the way the various experiments have been authored on the design canvas.

6. Now navigate to the experiment, "Sample 5: Train, Test, Evaluate for Binary Classification: Adult Dataset," as shown in Figure 14-6. This experiment will process adult census data and predict whether an individual, based on demographic attributes, will have an income greater than $50,000, or less than or equal to $50,000.

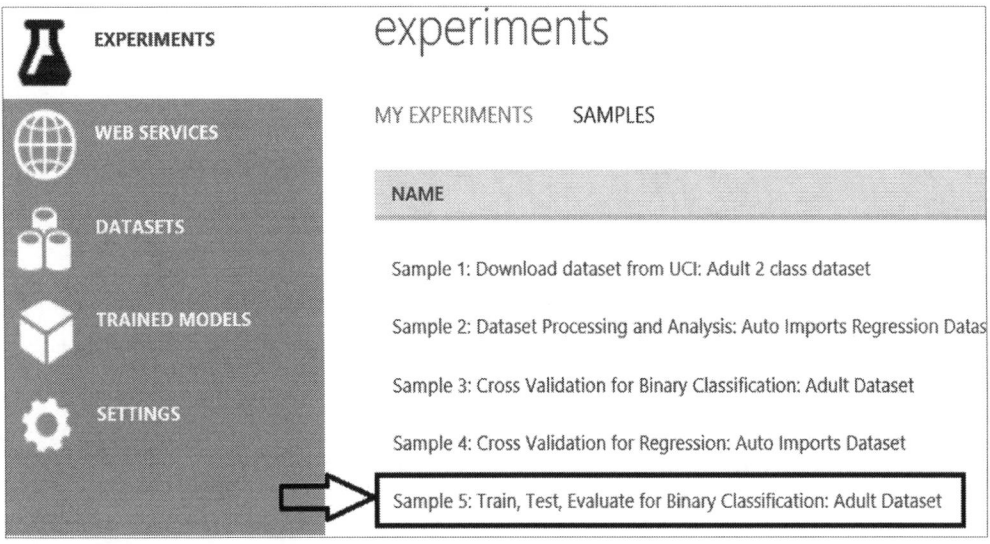

Figure 14-6. *Azure Machine Learning Sample Experiments*

7. Click to open the Sample 5 experiment. Then click Save As at the bottom of the screen, and name your experiment AdultCensusSalaryPrediction. You should see something that looks similar to Figure 14-7.

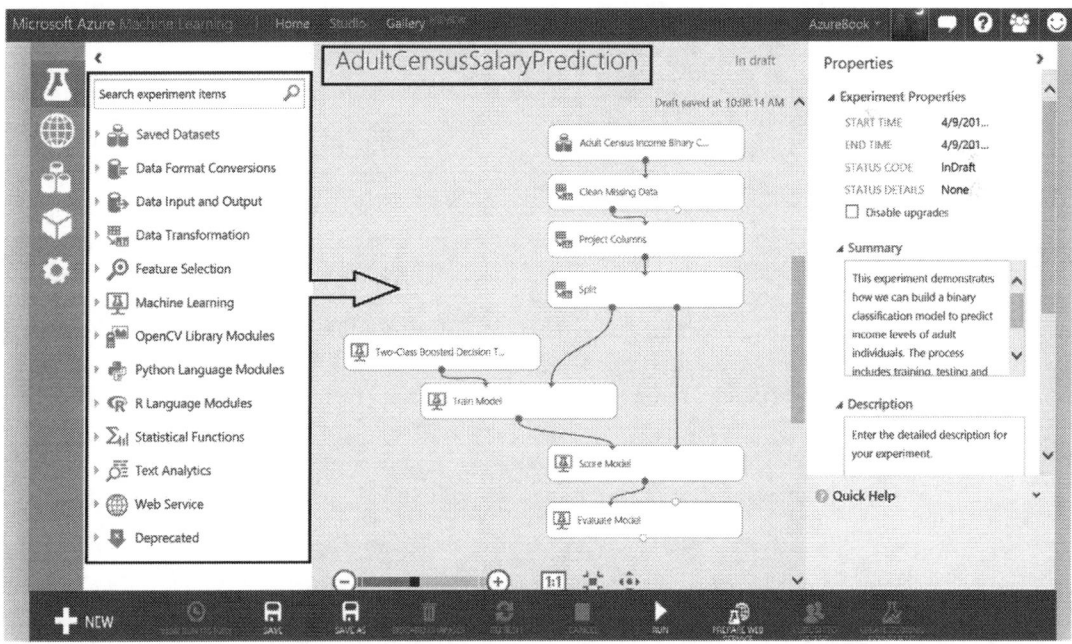

Figure 14-7. *Machine Learning Census Experiment*

8. Click RUN at the bottom of the experiment to have Azure Machine Learning process the census data and crunch the numbers as directed by the data process flow.

■ **Note** If you want to play around with this experiment before continuing, then work with your own copy by saving it under a different name. Be sure to open and return to the **AdultCensusSalaryPrediction** experiment when you are ready to proceed.

Now that you have the AdultCensusSalaryPrediction experiment created from the sample, you can't help but see the data flow and processing that is on the design canvas. What you are seeing on the canvas is called *modules*. These modules were dragged and dropped onto the canvas from the module list annotated in Figure 14-7 on the left side of the screen.

You can click on each major category of module and get a sense of the vast number of modules at your disposal. Once a module is dropped onto the canvas, you can connect their input and output ports to one another telling Azure Machine Learning how to process and direct the data as it winds through the data flow. Furthermore, you can have multiple independent data flow processing paths that will be run in parallel. You can cleanse data, split data, sample data, train algorithms on data, and score data with the probability of some desired outcome. You can also bring your favorite R scripts, Python, and SQLite into the mix.

9. Investigate a module further. Click on any module on the canvas, and notice that its properties appear on the right side of the canvas.

10. After an experiment is successfully run, the modules will have a green check mark status indicator at their right, as illustrated in Figure 14-8. If you do not see the green check marks in the modules, then click on **RUN** at the bottom of the screen.

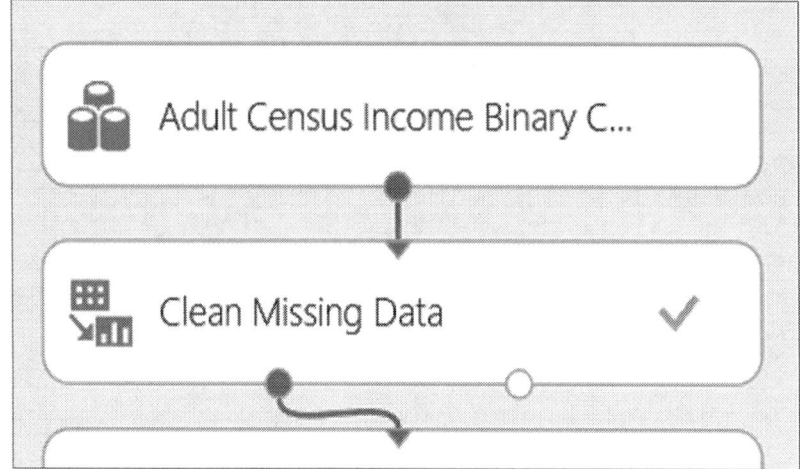

Figure 14-8. *Azure Machine Learning Module*

11. To see the dataset "Adult Census Income Binary..." that is being analyzed, click on its output port as illustrated in Figure 14-9.

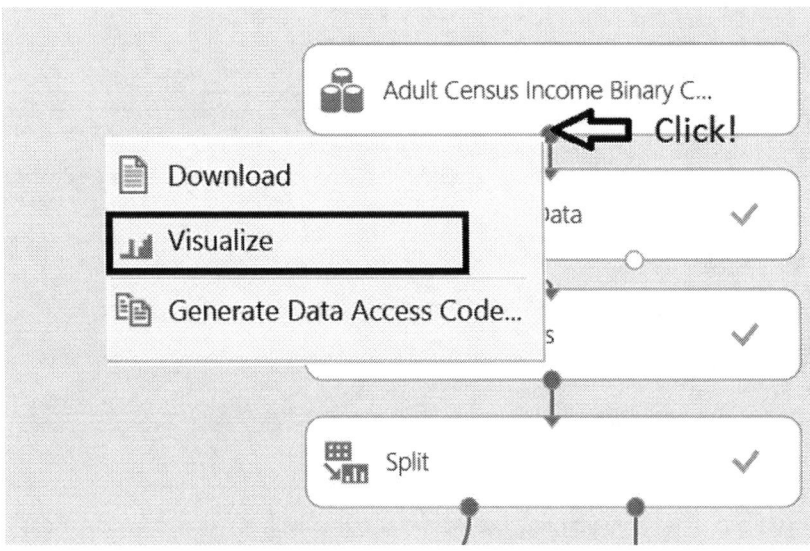

Figure 14-9. Machine Learning Data Cleansing Visualizations

12. To look closely at the data, click Visualize and you will see the rows, columns and some basic charting for the census data being processed, as illustrated in Figure 14-10.

The census data looks similar to what is shown in Figure 14-10.

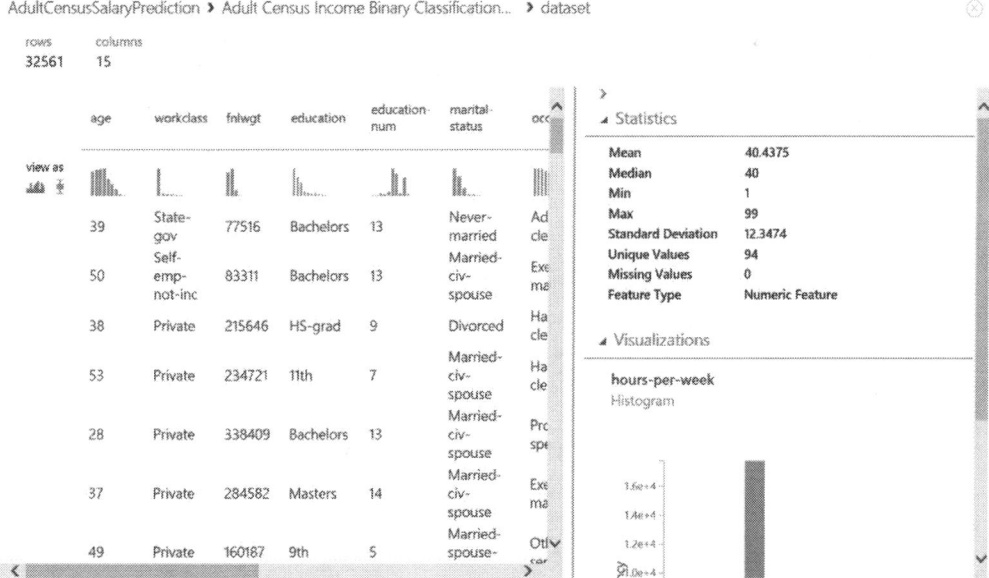

Figure 14-10. Census Data Visualizations

The census data incorporated in our experiment arrived there as a result of uploading a .csv file.

13. To create a dataset by uploading a .csv file, click +**NEW** from the Home page in ML Studio. Now click on the *three-cylinder DATASET* icon illustrated in Figure 14-11. From here you can see where you would upload from a local file. There is no need to proceed any further with this step as the dataset has already been created.

Figure 14-11. *Importing Datasets from CSV Files*

■ **Note** You can also bring data into an experiment using the Reader module. The Reader module can read data from Hadoop, SQL Azure Database, OData feeds, and so on.

The Reader and Writer modules, as seen in Figure 14-12, will be very valuable as you author and design more sophisticated Azure Machine learning experiments.

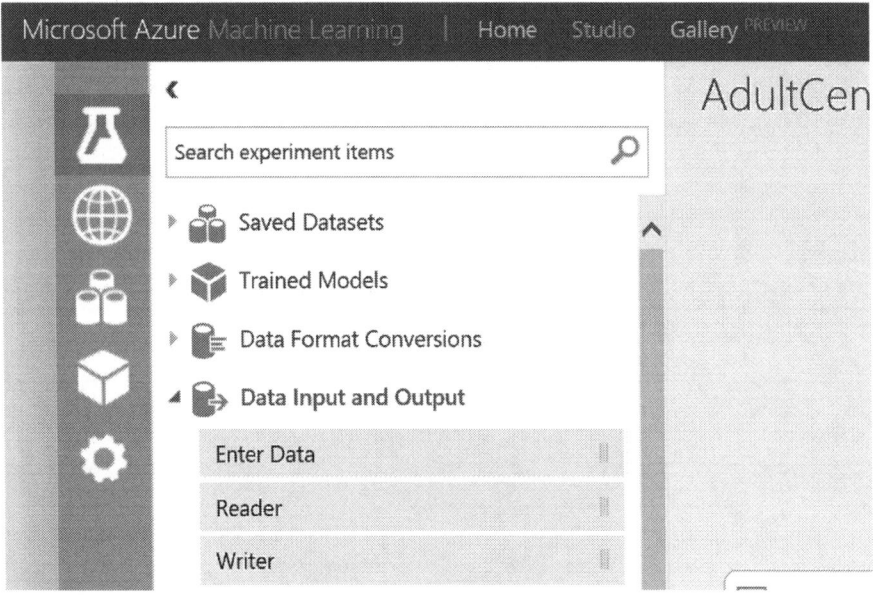

Figure 14-12. *Reader and Writer modules within ML Studio*

■ **Note** A dataset that is saved by clicking a module's output port and then selecting Save as Dataset can be accessed from any experiment, simply drop it onto the canvas as shown in Figure 14-13.

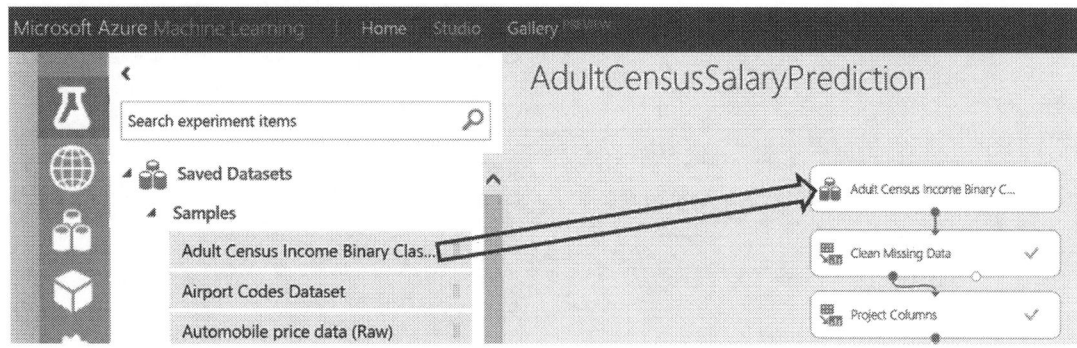

Figure 14-13. *Adding Datasets to an Experiment*

Now we will leave our quick hands-on peek into Azure Machine Learning and ML Studio. The experiment AdultCensusSalaryPrediction will be referenced as needed to support the educational process but it is not necessary for you to actively work in the experiment in ML Studio unless you would like to explore as we go along.

What Is a Good Machine Learning Problem?

The success of a machine learning solution is largely dependent on topical, consistent, and feature rich data. For machine learning to provide insight or predict outcome, it is very important to have quality representative data that captures past state for the predictions desired. Assume there is historical data for the income and demographics of people living between 1900 and 1920. The characteristics and demographics of a person making $50,000 dollars in the early 20th century would be of little value when faced with the exercise of predicting income for an individual living in 2015. Most predictive qualities around income for that data would be rather useless in predicting income today.

To predict the likelihood of an individual making more than $50,000 dollars, it will be necessary to have historical data that has a column representing the individual's annual income. In the census dataset the column income *classifies* the individuals as making less than or equal to $50,000 ("<=50") or greater than $50,000 (">50"). The column income in machine learning vernacular is called a *label* column. A label may have multiple classes. The label income has two classes ("<=50", ">50") and those two classes are what the experiment AdultCensusSalaryPrediction will try to predict. The census data also has columns that are *features* supporting the label income.

A feature is a machine learning term that represents the columns of data that each provide some unique or independent characteristic supporting the label(s). For example, if there was a column Occupation with the value "clerk" and another column JobId with the value "c" and they both represented the same thing, then it would suffice to choose either Occupation or JobId as a feature in the experiment, but not both. In the census dataset examples of featuresAzure ML:education features are: Gender, Age, Education, and Marital Status. When a feature is categorical it contains some limited set of domain values, for example, the categorical feature Education has values such as Bachelors, HS-grad, 11th, 9th and so on.

The experiment AdultCensusSalaryPrediction is supported by a census dataset that includes one label with two classes and multiple features with respective domain values. However, it's important to understand that machine learning problems and their associated Azure ML experiments can be extremely diverse. There could be experiments that operate on data that is highly numeric, or data that has multiple labels with numerous class values, perhaps data that is image data and so on. Figure 14-14 offers a glimpse into the csv file that makes up the census dataset. It has been annotated with machine-learning terms.

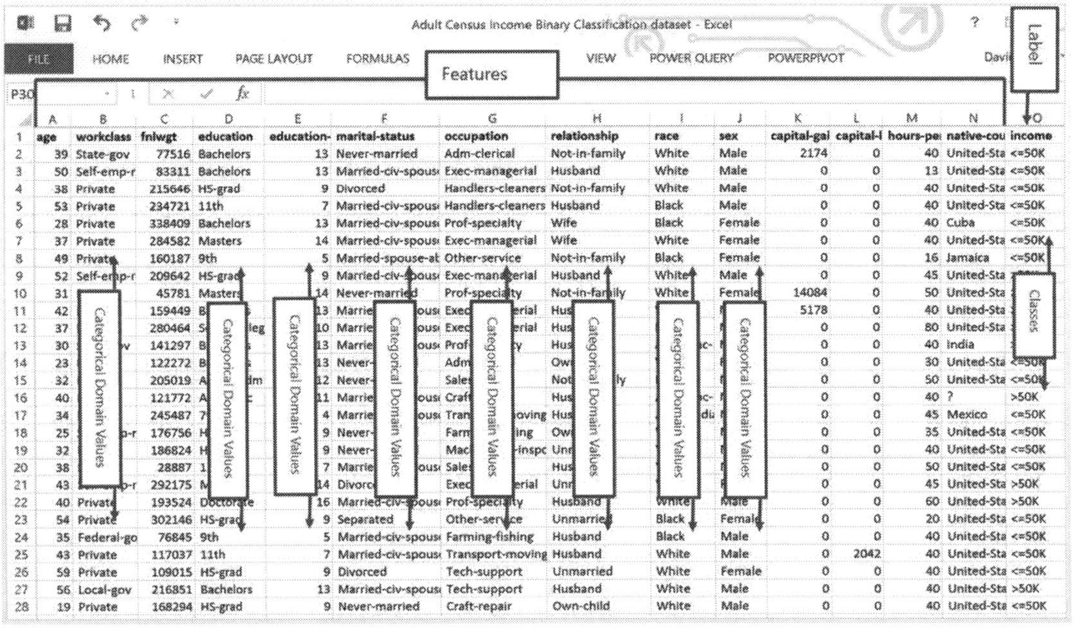

Figure 14-14. *Census CSV File Data*

Ideally the dataset that ultimately flows into the algorithm(s), as directed by the Azure Machine Learning experiment, is cleansed of errors, missing values and less important features. Given such a dataset it is possible to train a model to predict and identify disease risk, a product marketing opportunity, transaction fraud, or predict adult income.

Data Cleansing and Preparation

In the experiment AdultCensusSalaryPrediction, illustrated in Figure 14-15, some data cleansing takes place through the Clean Missing Data module that resides on the canvas. The Clean Missing Data input port is connected to the output port of the raw census dataset. The Clean Missing Data module properties can be configured to indicate what happens when missing values are encountered. The module can remove an entire row from the data flow if a given column has a missing value, replace a numeric column with the mean of the values, replace a missing value with a custom value, or even calculate a value. The author can configure the properties to indicate what minimum missing value ratio must be met before any action is taken, same behavior for maximum missing value ratio.

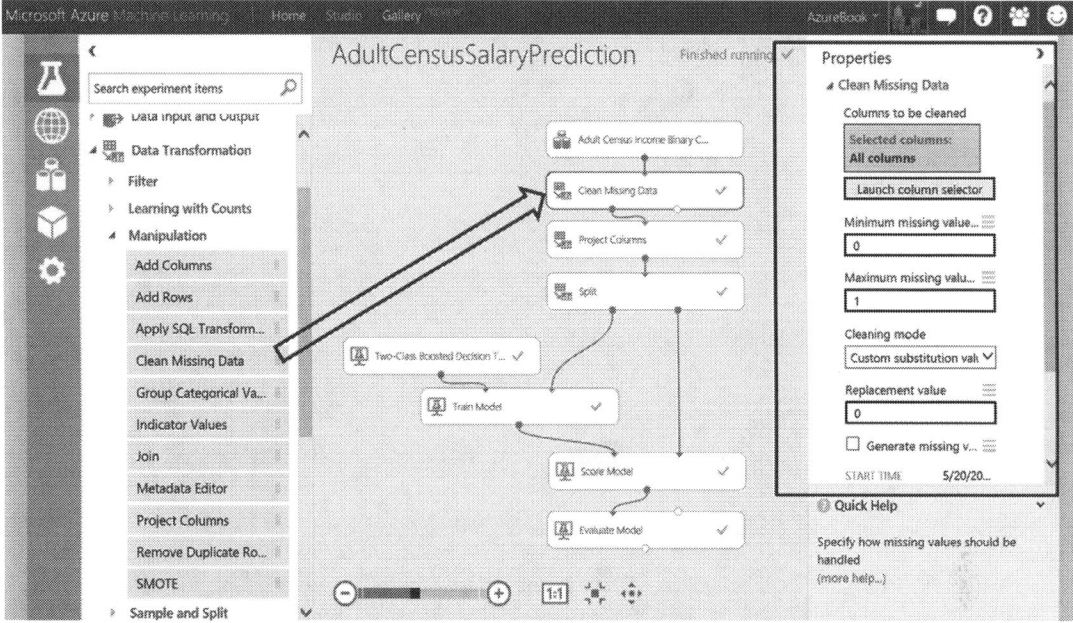

Figure 14-15. *Census Data Cleansing in ML Studio*

It is not uncommon that the majority of heavy lifting for a sound machine-learning project starts with data selection, feature engineering, data preparation and cleansing. This work can be done at the source, outside of Azure Machine Learning, or to some extent, inside the experiment using the various modules designed for data transformation. Data cleansing can also be carried out using the very powerful data manipulation aspects of the scripting modules for R, SQLite and Python.

There are a number of modules in ML Studio designed to cleanse and prepare data. For example, there is a commonly used module that allows the author to selectively pass along a subset of the columns to the data flow that might train an algorithm. The module to perform this operation is Project Columns and it is found on the AdultCensusSalaryPrediction experiment canvas. Notice how it has been hooked up to the data flow through its input and output ports respectively. The module's Launch column selector found in the property pane on the right side of the canvas, as shown in Figure 14-16, is used to identify which columns are excluded or included as the data flows through the experiment.

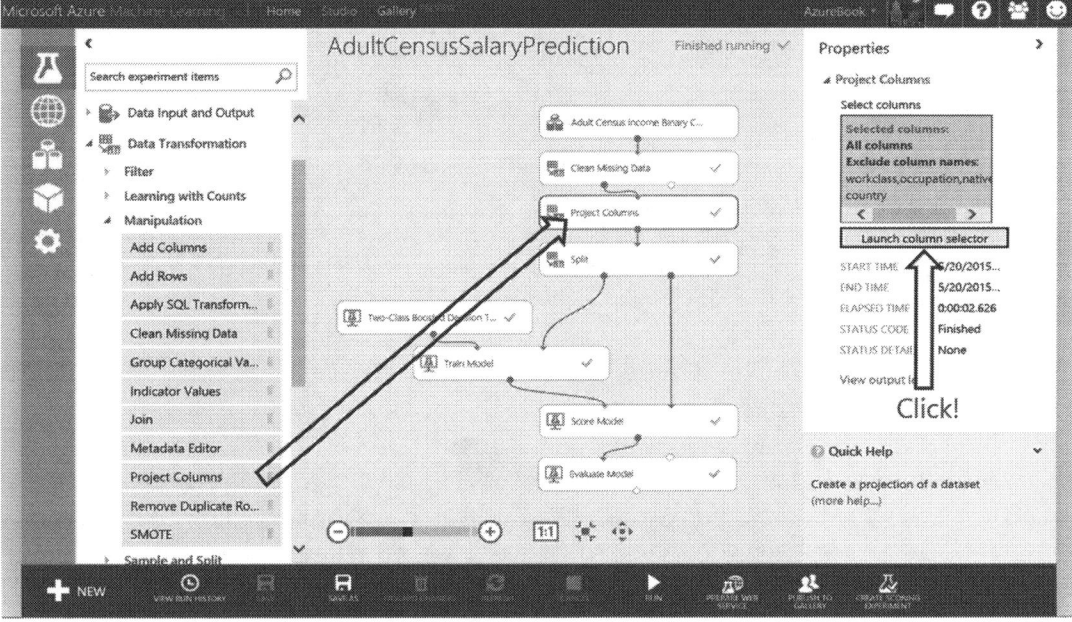

Figure 14-16. Projecting Columns in ML Studio

In this experiment, and for the subsequent data flow, the Project Columns module excludes the columns: workclass, occupation, and native-country, as seen in Figure 14-17.

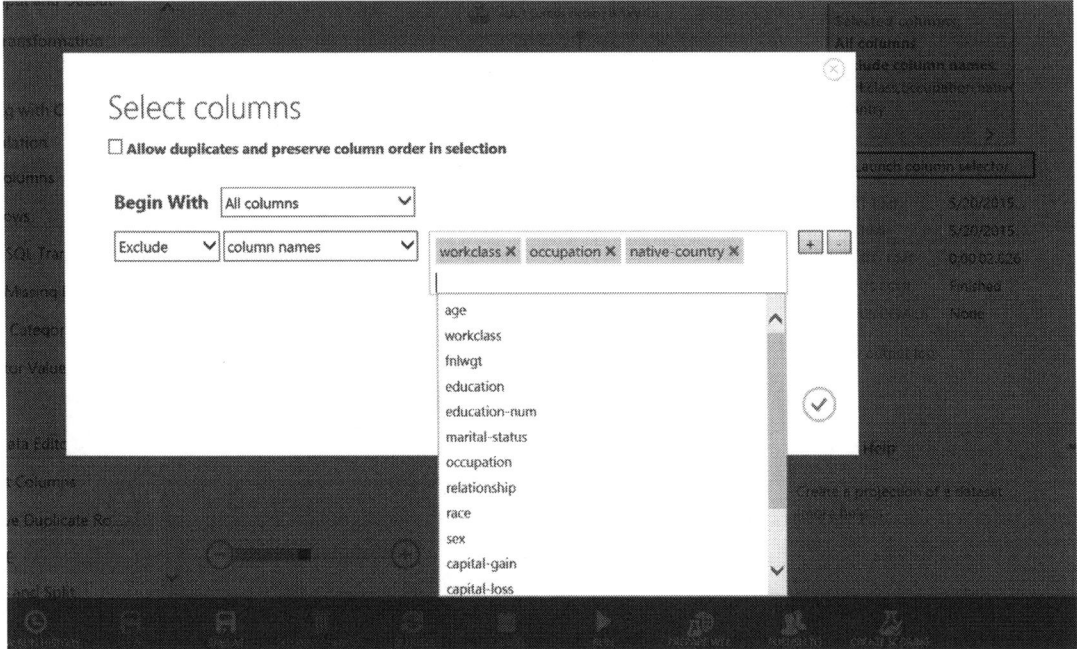

Figure 14-17. Excluding Columns in ML Studio

Choose an Algorithm and Train the Model

As a mental exercise and examining the census dataset, the goal is to predict an individual's likelihood of making more than $50,000 dollars. Assume nothing is known about the algorithms. Given the census dataset and the classes "<=50" and ">50" along with the desire to predict ">50", what would an approach be to look for aspects of the data that lean strongly to an individual making more than $50,000? One approach might be to use a tool like Excel and begin to chart, graph, grid, pivot, and group counts of features and their domain values until the most compelling features and values unveil themselves. Features and values that best influence the class ">50". With patterns and correlations uncovered in Excel and given an individual and all their features, it would be possible to now see how that individual's features and respective values fit into the hand-spun Excel analytics, which hopefully suggest a likelihood that the individual could be classified as ">50". It's important to point out that this Excel process could have been fraught with trial and error, human instinct, and false assumption. It is not to say that the conclusion of the Excel effort isn't valid, but it is possible that hidden and interesting correlations went undiscovered or obvious correlations (or dependence and causality) weren't accounted for. Machine learning will not only apply systematic and algorithmic mathematical rigor to this problem, it will do it in such a way that a person with Excel simply couldn't keep up with the computational processing as the data is sorted, branched, grouped, calculated and iterated over and over again. This is what Azure Machine Learning is doing. Of course the proper algorithms need to be chosen and configured as appropriate, but there is nothing like having a number crunching machine as your partner when analyzing data!

With the power of Azure Machine Learning and the right algorithms to do the heavy lifting, not only can millions of rows of data be crunched, but the effort in classifying and predicting each individual as "<=50" or ">50" will be carried out with the complexity and mathematical rigor required to arrive at an answer. The experiment author chooses the right algorithm and Azure Machine Learning does the rest of the work.

Choosing algorithms can be tricky but to understand some basic algorithm types, consider these three major areas:

- *Classification*: Classify each training instance (row) by assigning it to some set of fixed values. For example, for each individual their income is classified as "<=50" or ">50". For an insurance claim instance, it will be either TRUE or FALSE that the claim is open 180 Days. For street location and hour of day, the 911 event will be one of Disturbance, Violent, Liquor, Accident, or Other.

- *Clustering*: Partitions instances into similar groups. For example, group decedents based on cause of death, location, age, ethnicity, autopsy performed, and so forth. Within these groups, look for interesting patterns and correlations.

- *Regression*: Predict a real value for each instance. For example, predicting the speed for vehicle traffic, or predicting the cost of highway project types.

As the experiment AdultCensusSalaryPrediction is further inspected, notice that the data is split in Figure 14-18 so that the selected algorithm only uses a portion of the data. The remaining data will be used to evaluate the precision and accuracy of the model at a later point.

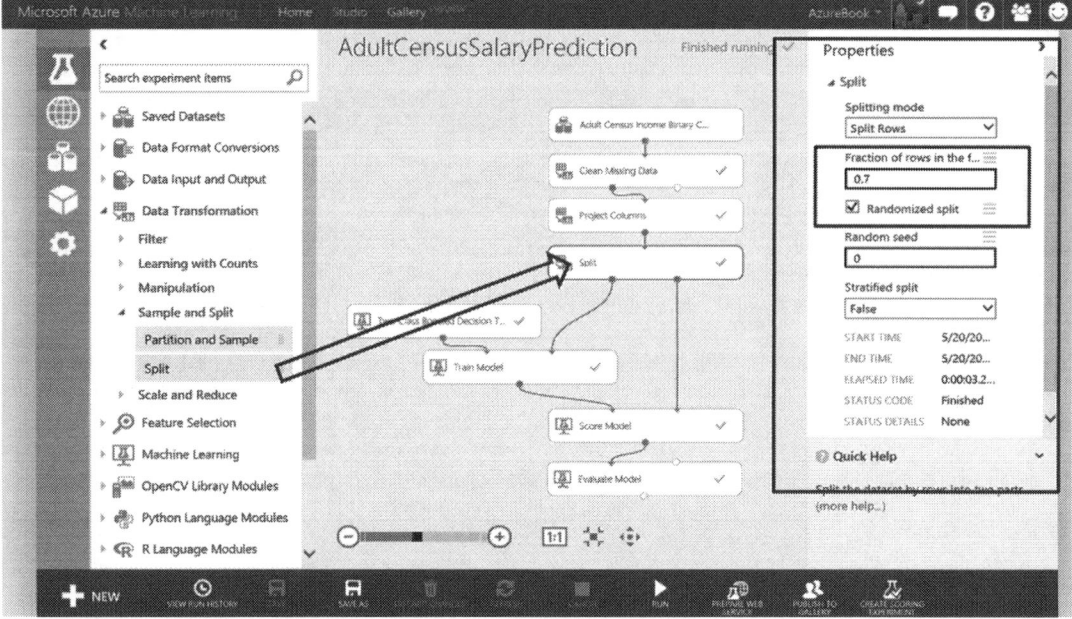

Figure 14-18. *Machine Learning Split Module*

The Split module's input port is connected to the output port of the Project Columns module. The Split module's property pane shows that 70% of the data will be sent through the first output port to train the model. The data selection to satisfy that 70% will be done randomly, as indicated by the presence of the checked box (see Figure 14-18). An experiment author will choose how much data to train the model with based on their understanding of the data. Perhaps the dataset is small and the author believes the best predictive results will come from training the model with a majority of the data. It is also very common to see a 50% split where half the data is used to train the model and the other half is used to test the model's effectiveness at prediction. In fact, the Split module's default property settings are preset to 50%.

An algorithm is chosen along with the Train Model module to crunch 70% of the census data. Because the dataset is classified with income as "<=50" and ">50", it would make sense to choose a classification algorithm. Since the dataset has 2 classes this helps to further limit the algorithm selection by looking for Two-Class algorithms. To this end, the Two-Class Boosted Decision Tree module is used in the experiment. The Train Model module is used to stitch 70% of the data together with the algorithm, as illustrated in Figure 14-19.

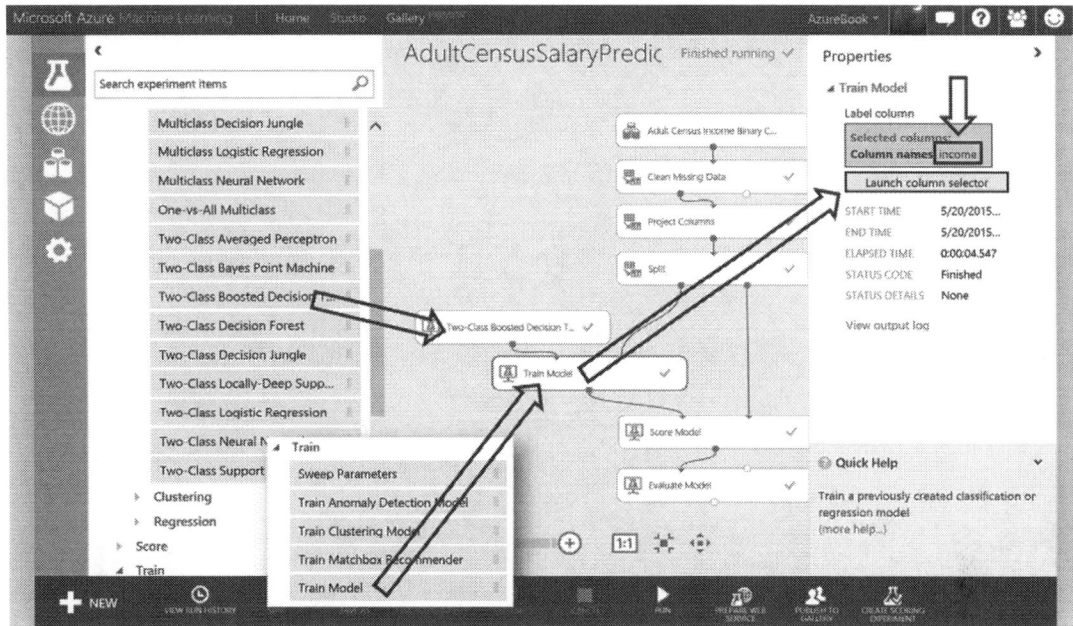

Figure 14-19. *Machine Learning Train Model Module*

■ **Note** For any module, and particularly useful for algorithm modules, there exists a "Quick Help" link at the bottom of the property pane. Click this link for technical documentation on a given algorithm. A useful algorithm selection decision tree can be found in the following blog entry authored by Brandon Rohrer from Microsoft, *https://azure.microsoft.com/en-us/documentation/articles/machine-learning-algorithm-cheat-sheet/*

The Train Model module, illustrated in Figure 14-19, initially has no idea about what the dataset label is required for training the Two-Class Boosted Decision Tree algorithm. The Launch Column selector button in the property pane for the Train Model module is used to choose column income as the label whose contents will be analyzed to train the model. The goal is to effectively predict the label classes "<=50" and ">50".

Once income is selected as the label column, the Two-Class Boosted Decision Tree algorithm module will use the other columns in the data flow as features (education, age, marital-status, etc.) as it teaches itself to predict ">50" and "<=50".

Score and Evaluate

After the model is trained, the results need to be evaluated. To test the model, new instances (rows) of individuals need to be introduced and scored. These will be the individuals representing 30% of the dataset based on the Split module configured earlier. Scoring the new individuals is essentially asking the trained model to only look at the individual's features and score them with the likelihood of ">50". This is akin to telling the trained model "given these individual's features, like age, education, gender and the like, calculate the probability that they will earn more than $50,000" In the experiment, the output port of the Train Model module coupled with the output port on the right side (30% of data) of the Split module are connected to the respective input ports of the Score Model module, Figure 14-20.

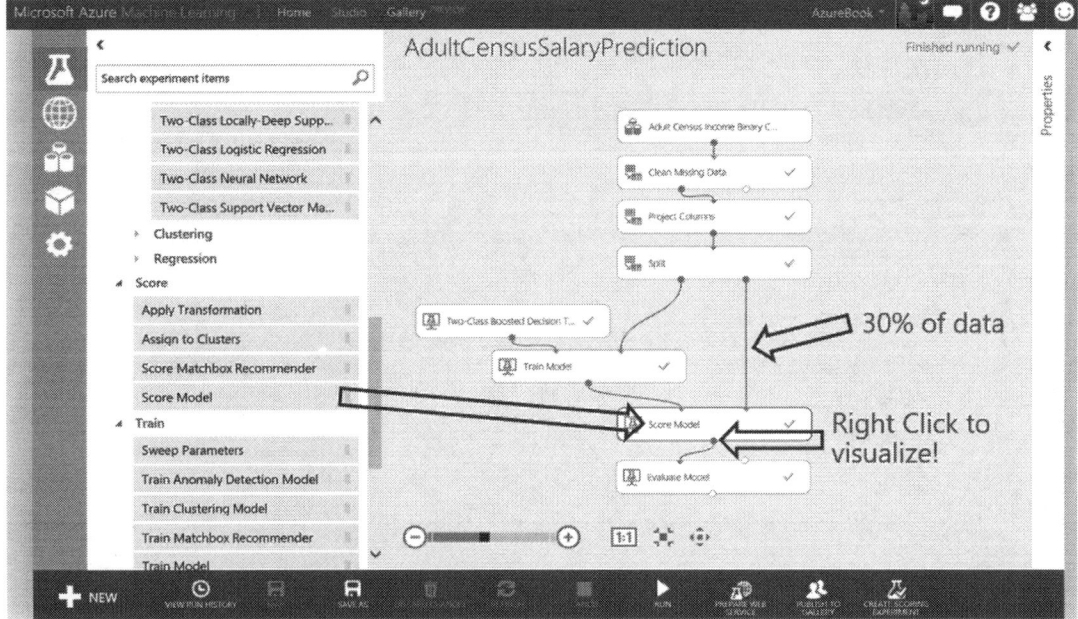

Figure 14-20. *Machine Learning Score Model Module*

After the "Score Model" module has RUN, two additional columns are added to the dataset that flows out of the Score Model module output port. The two columns show the probability of the likelihood that the individual will be ">50" as well as the predicted label itself ("<=50" or ">50"). This means that if a given individual is scored as 51.4568% probability, then the scored label would be ">50". Alternatively, if the individual was scored as 49.0934% probability that they would be ">50", then the scored label in this case would be "<=50". Another way to read the second example is that the individual has a 50.9066% (100 - 49.0934) probability of being "<=50". This is a little confusing, but since the focus is on whether the individual will make ">50", the scoring is relative to that class.

The ">50" is the *Positive* classification. If the algorithm indicates that there is a 50% chance (or better) that a given individual is ">50", and after peeking at the training data it finds that ">50" is the actual value, then that prediction outcome is a *True Positive*. Conversely, if the actual value is "<=50" then that would be a *False Positive*. It works the other way as well. If the algorithm indicates that there is a less than 50% chance the individual is ">50", then that is the *Negative* case and it would have the scored label "<=50". If the actual value for this individual in the training data was ">50", then a prediction of "<=50" would be a *False Negative*. If the actual value is "<=50", then a prediction of "<=50" is a *True Negative*.

To visualize the Score Model module dataset, the output port can be clicked followed by the selection of Visualize. Using arrow keys to scroll to the right within the viewer, 2 new columns are found: Scored Probability and Scored Label, see Figure 14-21. Notice in Figure 14-21 the column income has the actual income ("<=50", ">50") of the individuals. The Scored Labels column is what the Two-Class Boosted Decision Tree predicts for this individual after the model is trained. In some cases the actual value (in the income label column) is different than the algorithm's predicted Scored Labels column. An example of this is captured in Figure 14-21. The greyed rectangles illustrate False Negatives.

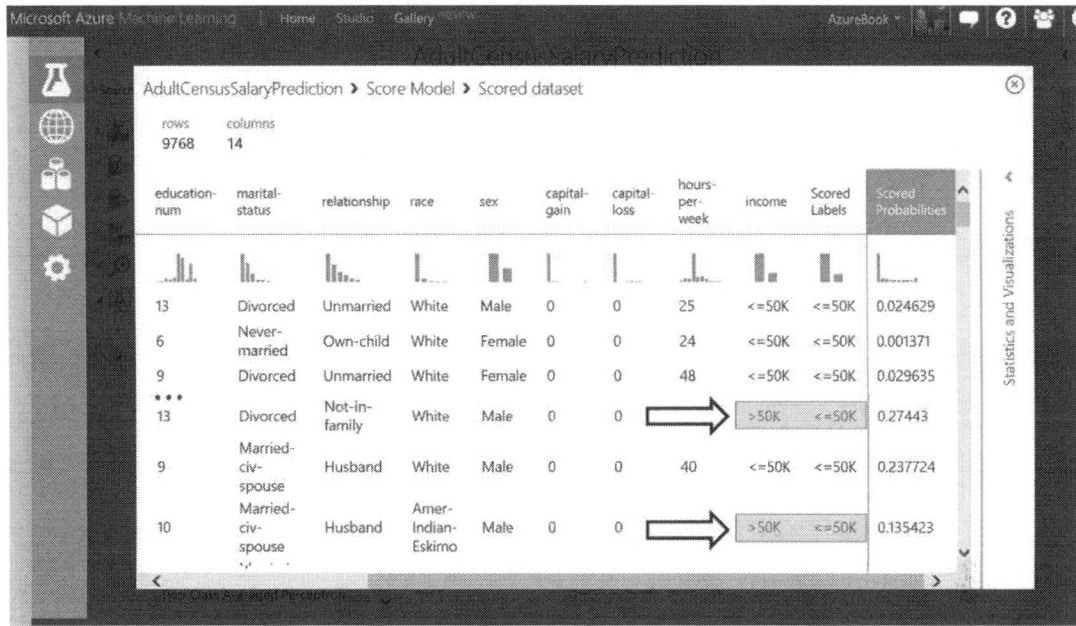

Figure 14-21. *Machine Learning Score Model Dataset*

With all of the True Positives (TP), False Positives (FP), True Negatives (TN) and False Negatives (FN) it is easy to see that tallying them up as they relate to the total count of individuals scored, could provide some insight into the effectiveness of the trained model.

For example, assume 10,000 individuals were scored and it was known that 100 of them had income ">50". If the algorithm scored 80 of those individuals correctly (it predicted 80 out the 100) and the algorithm's false positive calculation of ">50" was relatively high, say 35, then this would only be a somewhat precise model.

A common way to represent the counts of TP, FP, TN and FN is through a confusion matrix. A confusion matrix is a way to visualize the performance of the predictions, showing both what was predicted and what the actual value was during the scoring process. Figure 14-22 is a confusion matrix for the hypothetical 10,000-instance example.

		PREDICTED LABEL CLASSIFICATION	
		>50	<=50
ACTUAL LABEL CLASSIFICATION	>50	80 TRUE POSITIVE (TP)	20 FALSE NEGATIVE(FN)
	<=50	35 FALSE POSITIVE (FP)	9,865 TRUE NEGATIVE (TN)

Figure 14-22. *Machine Learning Confusion Matrix*

To calculate the overall accuracy of the hypothetical 10,000 individuals scored with the trained model, the calculation below is performed. Accuracy is to say "Of the entire data population, how good was the model at predicting either <=50 or >50?"

- Accuracy = (TP+TN)/(TP+FP+TN+FN)

- Accuracy = (80+9865)/(80+35+9865+20) = 99%

The following formula calculates the precision of the model (looking at true positive ratio). This calculation says "When the model predicts >50, how often is it right?"

- Precision = TP/(TP+FP)

- Precision = 80/(80+35) = 70%

Another performance metric is recall. Which is to say "With the total population of actual >50, how good is the model at predicting them":

- Recall = TP/(TP+FN)

- Recall = 80/(80+20) = 80%

In the example, when the model predicts the individual to have an income greater than $50,000 (>50), it is right 70% of the time. In other words, a prediction of ">50" comes with a 30% chance of representing a False Positive (actual of <=50). Generally speaking, whether the model predicts either "<=50" or ">50" the overall prediction accuracy is near perfect (99%). This is not hard to believe as the vast majority of the individuals in the example have actuals of "<=50" and with a TN rate that is in line with the actual count, it comes with little surprise that the accuracy is so high. The model does leave a few individuals with income greater than $50,000 left behind as false negatives, predicted as making less than or equal to $50,000. But, the recall is 80%, meaning when ">50" is predicted the majority of actual ">50" are being represented.

The confusion matrix is a powerful tool to visualize the performance of the Two-Class Boosted Decision Tree algorithm module. In ML Studio not only is it possible to view the model's confusion matrix, but a line chart is also provided where on the X axis the false positive rate is plotted and on the Y axis the true positive rate is plotted. The module that provides these performance metrics and visualizations is the Evaluate Model module as shown in Figure 14-23.

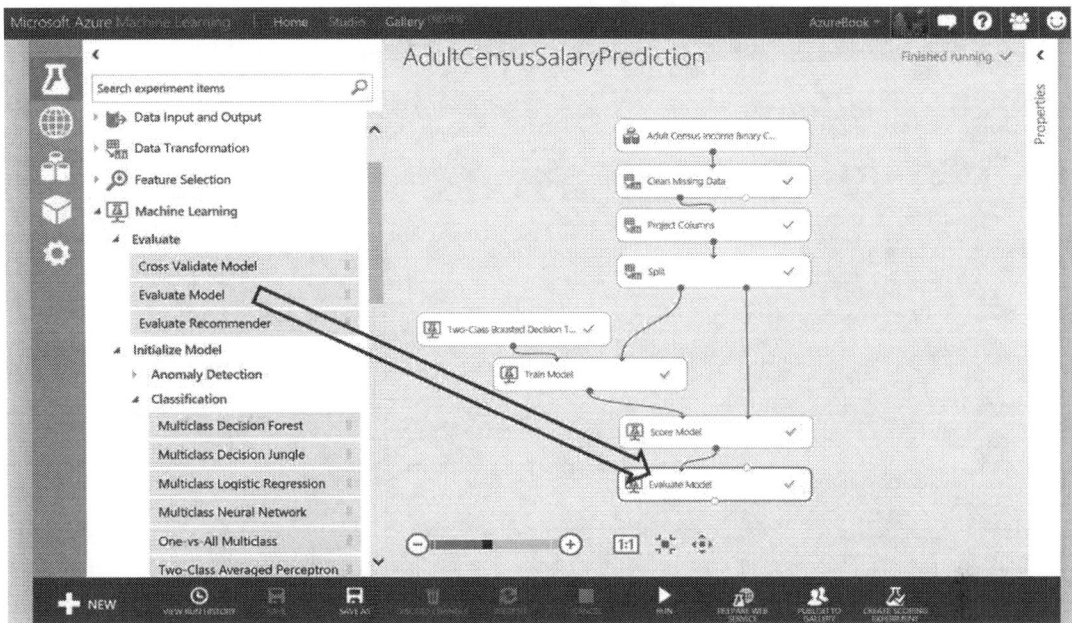

Figure 14-23. *Machine Learning Evaluate Model Module*

The Evaluate Model module has two input ports. Both are not required to be connected, but an interesting aspect of this module is that it can be used to compare the performance of two different scored datasets, perhaps the scored datasets came from different trained models that used different classification algorithms. In the AdultCensusSalaryPrediction experiment, only the first input port is connected to the previously scored dataset. The output of the Evaluate Model module is visualized by clicking its output port and then clicking Visualize. The results are shown in Figure 14-24.

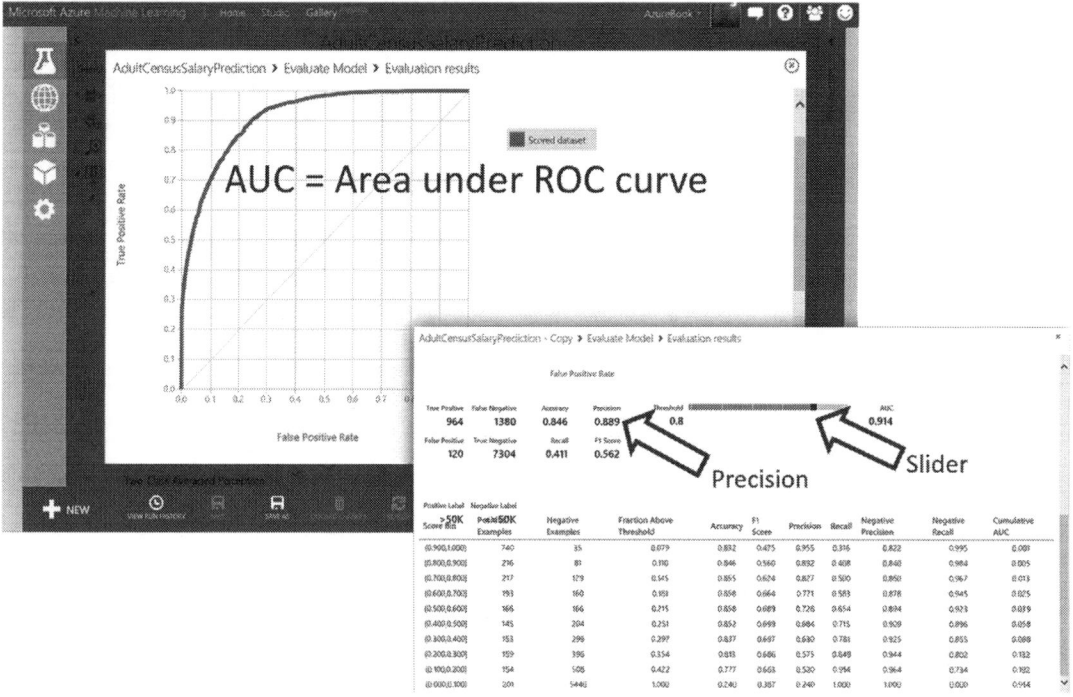

Figure 14-24. *Machine Learning Evaluate Model Visualization*

The curve is called an ROC curve. A model that performs well has a larger area under the curve (AUC) than above the curve. The closer the curve gets to the line diagonally cutting across the grid, the greater the chance that a random guess is just as good as the model. The confusion matrix is in the screen shot overlay as illustrated in Figure 14-24.

By dragging the Threshold slider to the right, the precision calculation typically improves. The threshold slider is a convenient way to assess precision as the probability of ">50" increases based on the value of the slider. The threshold slider calculates precision based on the count of true positives and false positives where ">50" is predicted at or above the percentage represented by the slider. If the slider was moved to .8, then the precision calculation would be based on the count of TP and FP where the likelihood of ">50" is 80% or higher. In this case, TP is 964 and FP is 120. The precision would then be 964/ (964+120) = .889 as illustrated in Figure 14-24.

The trained model in the experiment AdultCensusSalaryPrediction has accuracy, precision, and recall prediction results of 99%, 70%, and 80% respectively. These results are significantly better than a 50% random guess as to whether an individual will be "<=50" or ">50". Both from a precision and an accuracy perspective the evaluation of the model results in predictions that most organizations would be comfortable taking action on. The nature of a business problem and the benefit of the prediction coupled with the cost and risk of taking action on a false positive need to be weighed to determine if a model is considered viable. If the AdultCensusSalaryPrediction experiment and its trained model were used for shaping policy around fair wages or refining a marketing strategy, then it would be a sound experiment to operationalize.

Quick Hands-On Operationalizing an Experiment

If the experiment AdultCensusSalaryPrediction evaluates well and has been ascertained to effectively predict income, it would make sense to operationalize the experiment if appropriate business justification supports the effort.

An example of a business justification might include a marketing firm that wants to run the experiment against demographic data they have collected so that they can identify prospective customers that make more than $50,000 dollars. This kind of information could drive a marketing strategy. Another example could be a government entity that wants to ensure fair wages. In this case the experiment might be ran against new individual's data where their features could be tweaked (maybe change the feature Sex from "Male" to "Female") to see if the same income is predicted. If a disparity is found, then decisions might be made to correct a potential bias.

To prepare the Azure Machine Learning experiment to be operational, first the model must be saved as a self-contained unit of work encapsulating the algorithm, what features it expects, what label and associated classes are being predicted and so on.

The goal of this exercise is to create a web service that can be invoked from an application, from Excel, or from any system that can execute and report results for a web service.

In the marketing example, perhaps that organization wants to process all new customers that have entered their demographic data matching the features for the AdultCensusSalaryPrediction experiment. The organization's developer would have designed a weekly batch process that invokes a web service calling the experiment with the feature data entered by customers and getting predicted salary in return. The predicted salary results will establish which marketing campaign to assign to the each new customer.

The following steps walk through the exercise of configuring a web service for the AdultCensusSalaryPrediction experiment:

1. In the experiment AdultCensusSalaryPrediction, click the output port of the Train Model module and then click Save as Trained Model, as illustrated in Figure 14-25. Give the saved trained model a name, call it "Individuals50K".

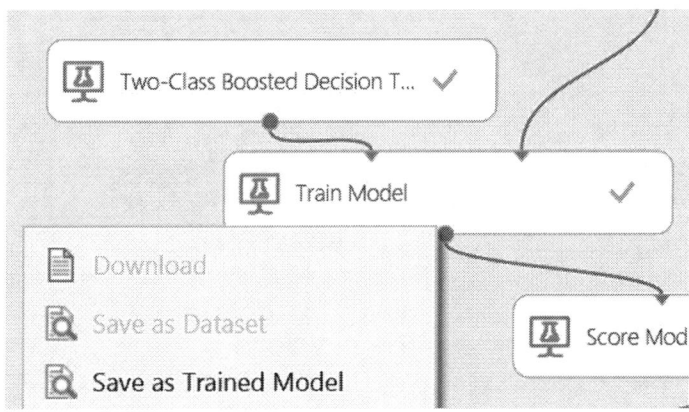

Figure 14-25. *Saving Machine Learning Train Models*

Next step is to copy the experiment AdultCensusSalaryPrediction to another experiment and name it so it can be recognized as an operational experiment. Perhaps precede the name with "prod" for production:

2. When the canvas is displaying the experiment AdultCensusSalaryPrediction, click Save As at the bottom of the screen and name the new experiment prodAdultCensusSalaryPrediction.

The following steps prepare the experiment prodAdultCensusSalaryPrediction to only contain what is necessary for production:

3. Right click and delete (or highlight and press del-key) the modules: Split, Two-Class Boosted Decision Tree, Train Model, and Evaluate Model.

4. In the left hand pane modules list and under the Trained Models heading, drag and drop the trained model you saved (Individuals50K) onto the canvas and connect the ports as illustrated in Figure 14-26.

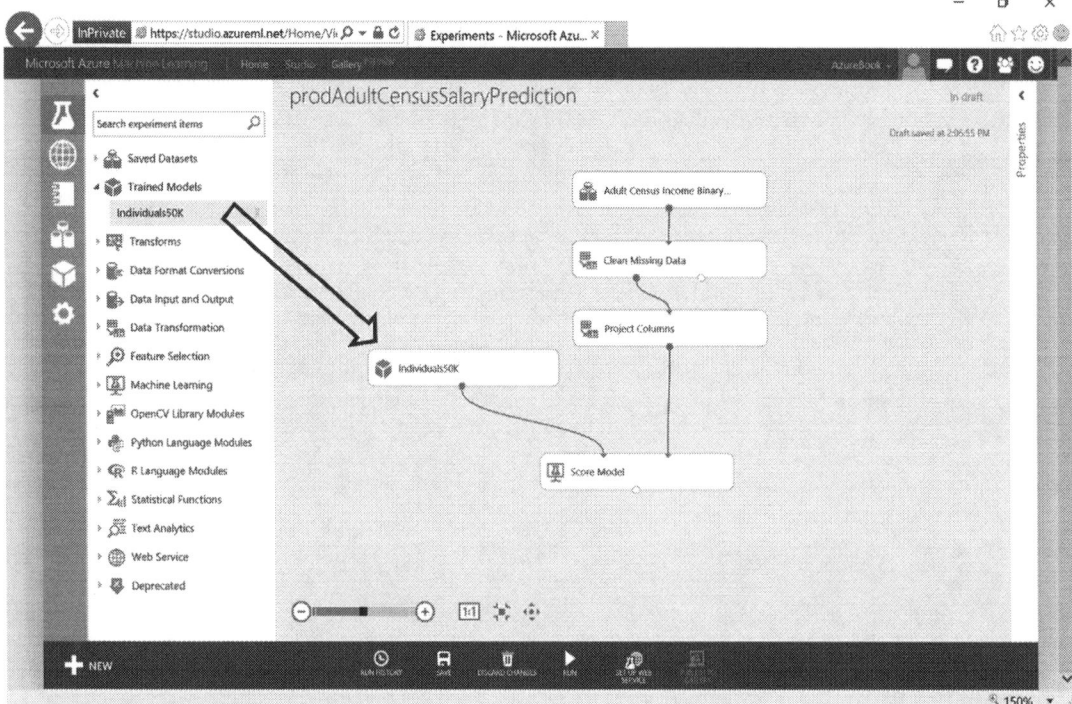

Figure 14-26. *Copying Machine Learning Experiments*

5. Click on SET UP WEB SERVICE at the bottom of the canvas.

6. Click on RUN at the bottom of the canvas.

7. Click on DEPLOY WEB SERVICE at the bottom of the canvas. You are now presented with the screen in Figure 14-27.

▓ **Note** There is tremendous power with the ease at which a web service can be created from an Azure Machine Learning experiment. When in the web service dashboard page as illustrated in Figure 14-27 and clicking on REQUEST/RESPONSE, all of the API Helper code is provided allowing the developer to easily deploy a web service that will execute the experiment prodAdultCensusSalaryPrediction.

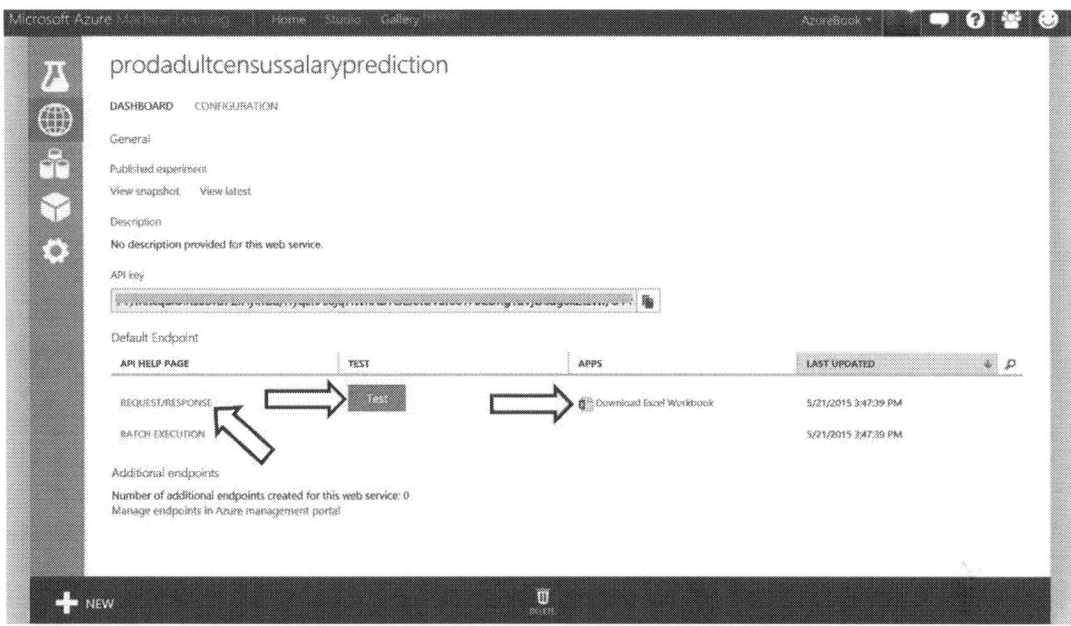

Figure 14-27. *Publishing a Machine Learning Experiment as a Web Service*

8. Test the web service by clicking on Test as shown in Figure 14-27 above. You are now presented with many of the features from the original census dataset as seen in Figure 14-28.

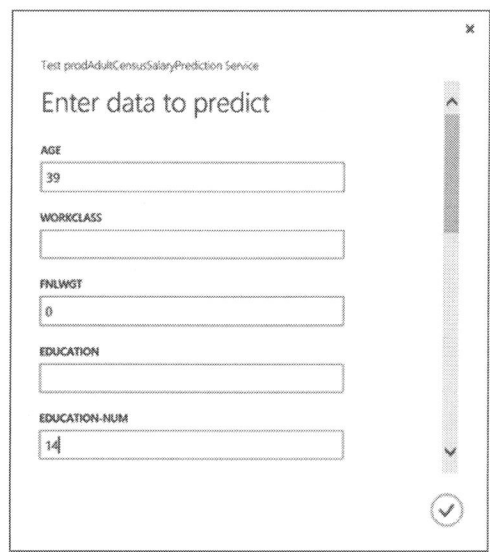

Figure 14-28. *Web Service "Test" Dialog with Features*

9. Enter the following feature values: age=39, education-num=14, married-status=Married-civ-spouse, relationship=Wife, race=White, sex=Female, hours-per-week=45, Figure 14-28.

■ **Note** By populating the Test dialog fields with categorical values relevant for the trained model, you will see some valid scored results returned. When entering the data, you ignore income as that is what the model is predicting.

---

10. Click on the check mark in the lower right corner of the Test dialog. You will see the web service results returned with the last element being the Scored Probability equal to ".88316..." and Scored Labels equal ">50K". Meaning, for this individual, the trained model predicts an 88% likelihood their income is greater than $50,000, Figure 14-29. You just invoked a web service that ran your experiment prodAdultCensusSalaryPrediction!

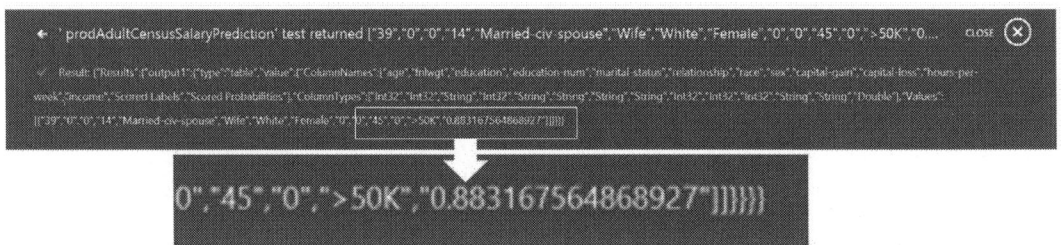

Figure 14-29. *Web Service Completion String*

The Azure Machine Learning web service dashboard illustrated in Figure 14-27 allows the user to download a sample Excel workbook that has been pre-wired with macros enabling it to execute the web service.

11. Click Download Excel Workbook and open the Excel Workbook, see Figure 14-30.

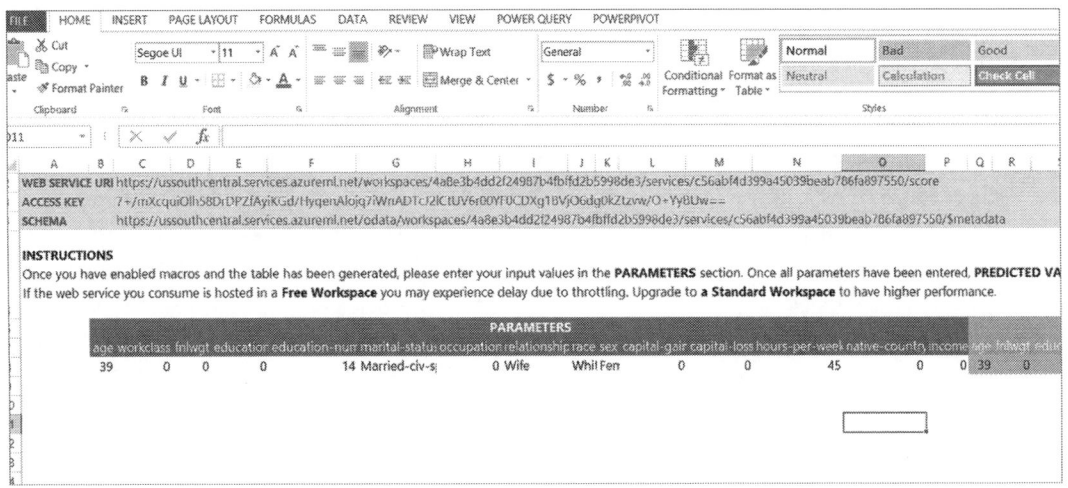

Figure 14-30. *Excel Workbook from Azure Machine Learning Studio*

12. Enable the content to allow macros. This will be a prompt Excel displays to the user. In Figure 14-30 the workbook has already been enabled.

13. Enter: age=39, education-num=14, married-status=Married-civ-spouse, relationship=Wife, race=White, sex=Female, hours-per-week=45 as seen in Figure 14-30.

14. Look at the scores on the right hand side of the matrix in Excel, you may need to scroll to the right. It should show around 88% as illustrated in Figure 14-31.

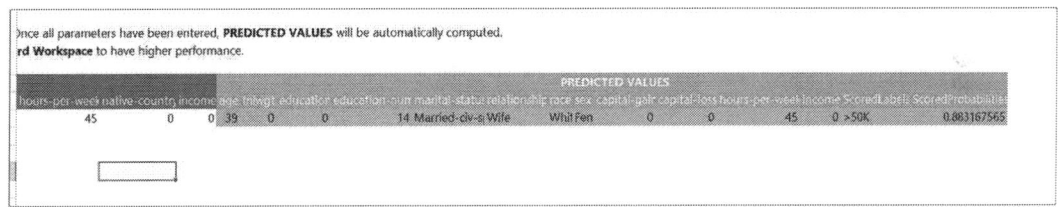

Figure 14-31. *Excel Workbook Predictions*

15. Now play around with the individual's features and categories to see what the web service experiment produces.

The ramifications of this simple exercise are profound. A business could publish the web service to the Azure Market Place, provide their business information and collect 10 cents every time someone executes the Azure Machine Learning web service to predict income.

The web service could be included in an organization's operational internal ETL (Extract Transform Load) processes, scoring data as it flows through a business data transform.

▓ **Note**   The web service could also have been deployed with neither inputs nor outputs. Consider a scenario where the experiment author dropped the Reader module onto the experiment canvas, configured it to read an Azure SQL Database staging table where the new individuals to be scored reside. The experiment processes what is in the stage table and writes the scored results to an Azure SQL Database reporting table that is accessed through the Writer module that was also dropped onto the canvas. The Writer module's input port would be connected to the output port of the Score Model module. In this hypothetical case, after the web service is created from the experiment and then invoked, it would simply read from a stage table and write to a report table. Using this strategy, the DBA has their role in setting up the stage and reporting tables in Azure SQL Database. The analyst simply reports against the report table and the data scientist did all of the Azure Machine Learning work. This scenario speaks to the ability to bring IT and business roles into a complete data analytics lifecycle, where any given person need not know what the others did, they each have their place and the whole of their efforts is much greater than the sum of their parts. Play this video to see such a scenario in action, *https://youtu.be/ABsOnmOzIUI*

Summary

With the ease, power, and flexibility of authoring experiments in ML Studio, coupled with the "click and go" web service integration of Azure Machine Learning, you have a cloud platform that is approachable to a broad audience of IT professionals, data enthusiasts, as well as traditional data scientists.

CHAPTER 15

Management and BI with HDInsight

Microsoft Azure HDInsight Overview

Under the leadership of new CEO Satya Nadella, Microsoft has become more supportive of collaborating with open source projects. Microsoft listens to customers that are building solutions, which in turn drives sales revenue. Microsoft's .NET Core server stack is open source, and it supports cross-platform development. Microsoft's Azure HDInsight is an example of this shift, with direct support of big-data analytics using the open source Apache Hadoop framework. In Microsoft Azure, this integration supports many languages including PHP, Node.js, Java, Python, Hadoop, and others. The change in Microsoft's support for the open source community has increased the number of open source solutions running on Microsoft Windows by 400%, from 80,000 applications in 2009 spiraling up to 350,000 applications by 2011.

This chapter gives you insight into the meaning of *big data* and how Azure supports Hadoop (a framework for distributed processing of very large data sets). You also learn how Azure HDInsight directly supports Hadoop. Specifically, you explore the support of Microsoft business intelligence (BI) and analytics for big data using HDInsight in the Azure model of paying only for what you use only when you need it. In addition, HDInsight is a great example of software as a service (SaaS): you can request a 2-node Hadoop cluster or a 100-node Hadoop cluster, and either request is available within 15 to 30 minutes. Azure deploys the cluster and manages it for you with a service-level agreement (SLA), so you don't have to worry about patching or uptime for the Hadoop service. By the time you reach the end of this chapter, you will have a deeper understanding of how to plan a Azure HDInsight solution to consume and visualize data for an end-to-end solution.

■ **Tip**   To learn more about the Microsoft shift toward open source projects and the company's support for open source solutions like Hadoop and MongoDB, as well as to review the open source project directory, go to the Microsoft Openness web site at `www.microsoft.com/en-us/openness`.

Big Data

Customers are requesting a supported, mature framework that does not lock businesses or developers into a primary development environment. This is one of the key design criteria of Azure HDInsight. Many companies employ database administrators (DBAs) who design, build, and use traditional database frameworks. Structured frameworks using relational data types for processing rows and columns of data in very large databases with a well-defined database structure are called the *database schema*. The concept of *big data* is better defined when the volume of data is too large for traditional relational database containment or when it contains a mixture of structured and unstructured data that doesn't follow the database schema.

To help you better understand the meaning of *big data*, we'll limit our definition to three attributes:

- *Velocity*: For example, global users posting to Twitter (this social network has tag tracking)

- *Variety*: Unstructured data (text, numerical, binary, images, and so on)

- *Volume*: Global server data (structured or unstructured)

Social media companies or products are an example of the complexity of large amounts of unrelated, or big data. Let's consider two examples of the significance of big data.

The first of two examples of big data is Twitter, which in 2015 will process more than 9,000 tweets per second and over 1 billon tweets in just 5 days. Twitter fits the model of big data by meeting the two-part definition of very large amounts of data and semi-structured or unstructured data, streamed in real time. If you examine the data structure of tweets, they consist of free-form text, including hash tags and shortened web links. A BI solution is needed to disclose patterns of customer satisfaction or dissatisfaction. What business doesn't need to know if their customers are happy with the company or unhappy with the products or services the company provides?

Consider the visual analysis shown in Figure 15-1. Here Twitter feeds for binge-watching tweets (vertical pegs) are overlaid with snowfall (geographical coverage) on the East Coast. Thus if a snowstorm is forecast, a hardware store may advertise on TV a special price on snow melt to clear driveways. Tracking weather and TV viewing patterns during major events can support sales of products related to those events.

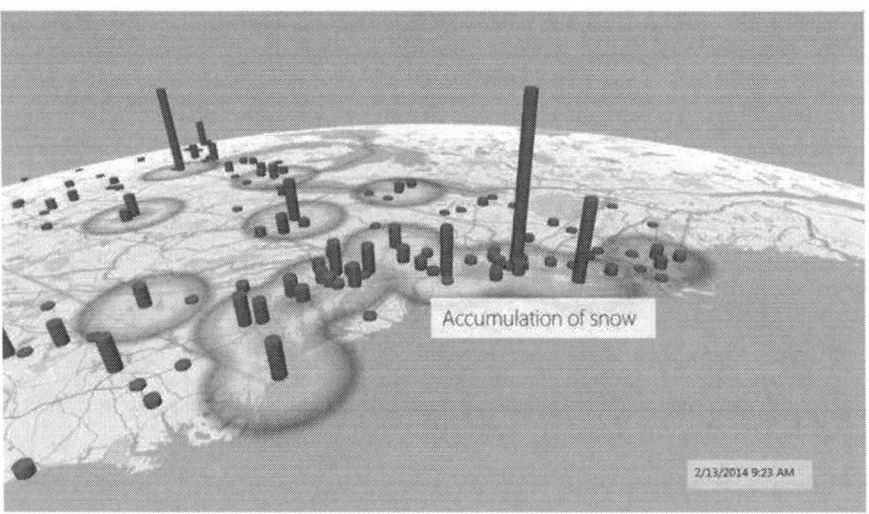

Figure 15-1. *Microsoft BI visual analysis of Twitter feeds, illustrating binge-watching of shows during a snow storm*

The second example of big data is a web server farm with many servers. A Microsoft BI solution can pull data from web logs on all the servers, scoping traffic in and out of the site server logs, and providing content characteristics including text, time, network addresses, logon identity, and other data to help identify patterns among visitors or consumers.

> ■ **Tip** For examples of big data on Azure, you can view some of the videos in the Azure HDInsight video library at `http://azure.microsoft.com/en-us/documentation/videos/index/?services=hdinsight`.

Now that you have a better understanding of big data, what is the role of Hadoop? Knowing this may help you to understand the financial gains available to companies that offer visual BI analytics such as those used in the Twitter example.

Hadoop

Hadoop, as stated earlier in this chapter, is a framework for distributed processing of very large data sets. Many traditional structured databases, like Microsoft SQL Server, can support very large data warehouses and massive data stores. If the data is massive, is streamed extremely fast (as in the Twitter example), and is un-structured—meaning it does not exactly match the criteria of text, binary, or numerical data that can fit into data tables—then some preprocessing must be applied to the incoming data. Normally this is not the best solution for traditional relational database design, so another approach must be used to sort the data for efficiency and speed.

A massive volume of disparate/different data requires a more efficient solution that provides multiple database nodes for processing the data. One node is the *name node*; you can think of it as the head node (main node) for splitting the workload across multiple nodes using NoSQL database technology. This is the framework for the Hadoop open source distributed processing technology. Figure 15-2 shows how it is architected.

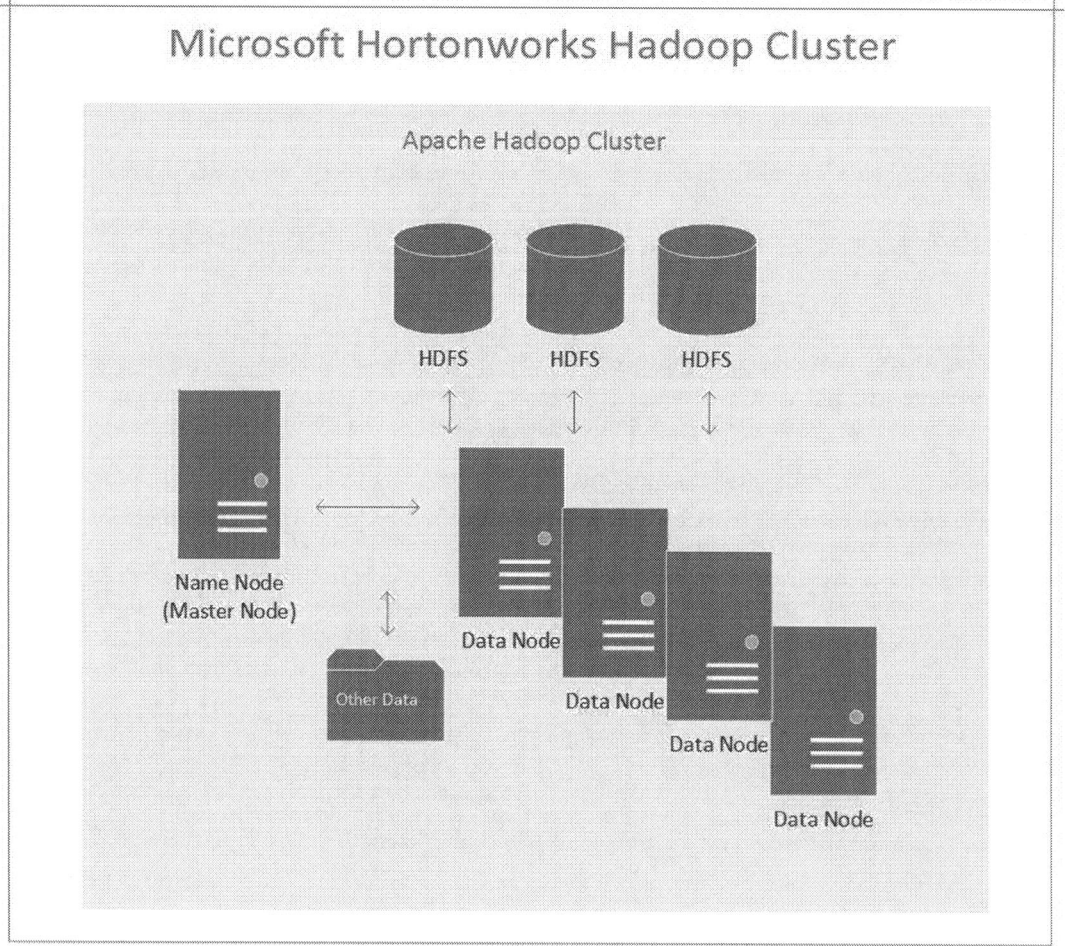

Figure 15-2. *Traditional Hadoop cluster showing the main name node and the supporting data nodes as part of the cluster*

You may know of additional Hadoop-related open source projects. Table 15-1 lists some open source technologies that work independently and also support Hadoop.

Table 15-1. *Open Source Related Projects that Work with Hadoop Frameworks*

Related Open Projects	Description
Ambari	Provides Apache cluster provisioning, management, and monitoring
Avro	Microsoft .NET library for Avro; used in data serialization
Hive	Works with data from the Hadoop Distributed File System (HDFS) source for queries (SQL-like queries)
HCatalog	Templeton (Butler) service for helping other technologies; provides coordination
HBase	Apache (NoSQL) non-relational database
Oozie	Used to coordinate workflows for multiple tasks and to maintain order
Pig	Can work with any data type; used with MapReduce functions
Storm	Apache Storm real-time computation system used to processes big data (like Hadoop)
Sqoop	Provides integration between data in HDFS tables and data in a traditional relational database
Zookeeper	Coordinates distributed processes

It is important to know that speed in BI analysis is achieved using a component function of Hadoop called *MapReduce* (sometimes written as Map/Reduce). MapReduce is a great feature for parallel processing that helps provide the speed and dexterity needed for the Hadoop processes.

To help you understand how the Hadoop architecture supports quick analysis of data faster than structured query databases, let's look at a simple example of a three-node MapReduce function. In Figure 15-3, the MapReduce workflow illustrates how this component is used in Hadoop.

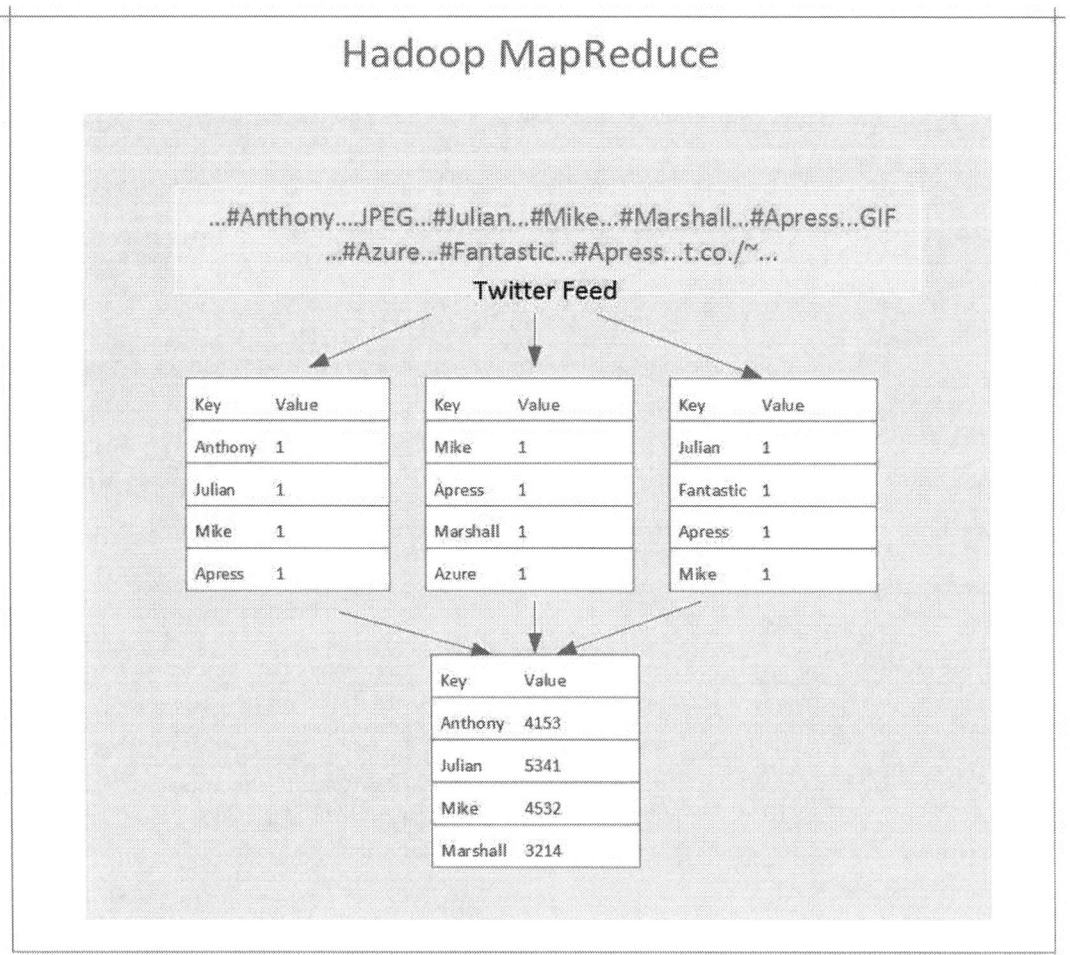

Figure 15-3. *MapReduce processing phase illustrating how Hadoop can improve processing speed over structured query databases*

How does Hadoop analyze all the data so quickly? The phase using the map reads a portion of the HDFS source data and generates a key value of the data, and it pairs the value by combining the key-value pairs at the reduce phase. If you look at the workflow in Figure 15-3, the different types of text are read from the HDFS source into more than one map node, so the process is very fast. The more nodes that are added to the map portion, the more quickly the analysis is completed. Each node then shares the key-value pair with the reduce node to gain aggregates for each item.

Each key and value is added at each map node and then passed in to the reduce node to provide the total value of each key. The reduce node provides a very specific function to maintain the key with a weighted value or summary.

HDInsight

HDInsight is Microsoft's managed Hadoop service in the cloud. One of the key advantages of Microsoft Azure is that you pay only for what you use and only when you need it. Let's take what you have learned about Hadoop and see how Azure HDInsight supports it.

Hortonworks is a vendor that directly supports Hadoop projects. The company worked directly with Microsoft engineers to build a partnership that created a Azure Hadoop solution called *HDInsight*. Figure 15-4 shows a logical view of HDInsight, which is designed to support the Hortonworks Hadoop architecture. Microsoft and Hortonworks built a 100% open source Hadoop solution on Windows and gave all the code back to the open source community.

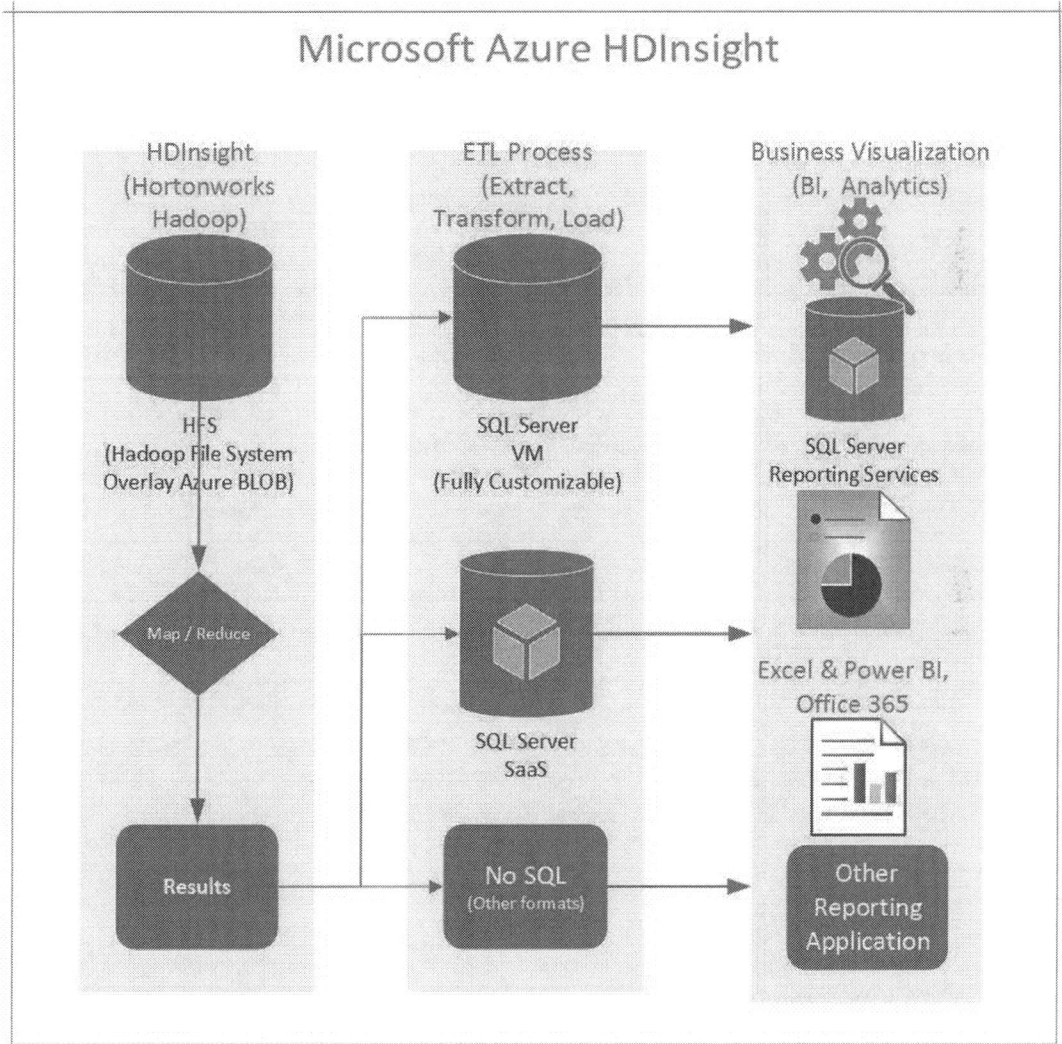

Figure 15-4. *Azure HDInsight Hortonworks architecture with support for NoSQL, business analytics, and other reporting applications*

In HDInsight, you can see how Hadoop clusters are represented in Azure. Chapter 7 introduced the many ways you can save money by using the Azure Storage service. Because Azure Storage relates to a big-data solution, HDInsight uses Azure blob storage. Specifically, the Azure team supports HDFS by using an HDFS-compliant software layer over Azure blob storage. This HDFS layer provides access to the terabytes and petabytes of Azure storage that some Hadoop applications require.

Many different versions of the Linux and Windows operating systems are available. Table 15-2 describes the versions of open source projects like Amari, HBase, Storm, and others available on these OSs.

Table 15-2. HDInsight Compared on Linux and Windows Platforms

Category	HDInsight on Linux	HDInsight on Windows
Cluster OS	Ubuntu 12.04	Windows Server 2012 R2
Cluster Type	Hadoop	Hadoop, HBase, Storm
Deployment	Azure Management Portal, cross-platform command line, Azure PowerShell	Azure Management Portal, cross-platform command line, Azure PowerShell, HDInsight .NET SDK
Cluster UI	Ambari	Cluster Dashboard
Remote Access	Secure Shell (SSH)	Remote Desktop Protocol (RDP)

In order for Azure to offer an SLA around HDInsight, a stable platform is configured, tested, and made available as an HDInsight offering. The HDInsight offering's version number is unique to Azure and not specifically related to a version of Linux, Apache, or Windows.

Table 15-2 shows the versioning control used to identify how the individual components are stacked together and offered as an Azure HDInsight version. It does not correlate with any current HDInsight version offering. The next section walks through the options to build an HDInsight deployment using Azure.

There is one final point to discuss about Hortonworks and the Hortonworks Data Platform (HDP) for Windows. This platform is a fully configurable big data cluster based on Hadoop, and it can be installed on physical on-premises hardware or on Hyper-V hosts with virtual machines on-premises. In addition, the HDP platform can be customized on VMs in Azure. But then it is not a SaaS solution, because it becomes an infrastructure as a service (IaaS) solution that can take on the administration of OS patching and Hadoop updates.

■ **Tip** To learn more about the Hortonworks and Microsoft partnership's support for the Apache Hadoop cluster on Azure, see the Hortonworks and Microsoft partner page at `http://hortonworks.com/partner/microsoft/`.

Deploying HDInsight

In this exercise, you walk through the steps necessary to deploy HDInsight in an Azure subscription. Options available in the deployment of HDInsight (SaaS) depend on the type of Azure subscription (Free Trial, MSDN subscription, or Pay-As-You-Go). The prerequisite for completing this exercise is to have a storage account available in one of the supported regions (West US and so on) to support the HDInsight deployment.

DEPLOYING HDINSIGHT

1. From your classic Azure Portal, select the HDInsight workspace, and choose the option to Create an HDInsight Cluster, as shown in Figure 15-5.

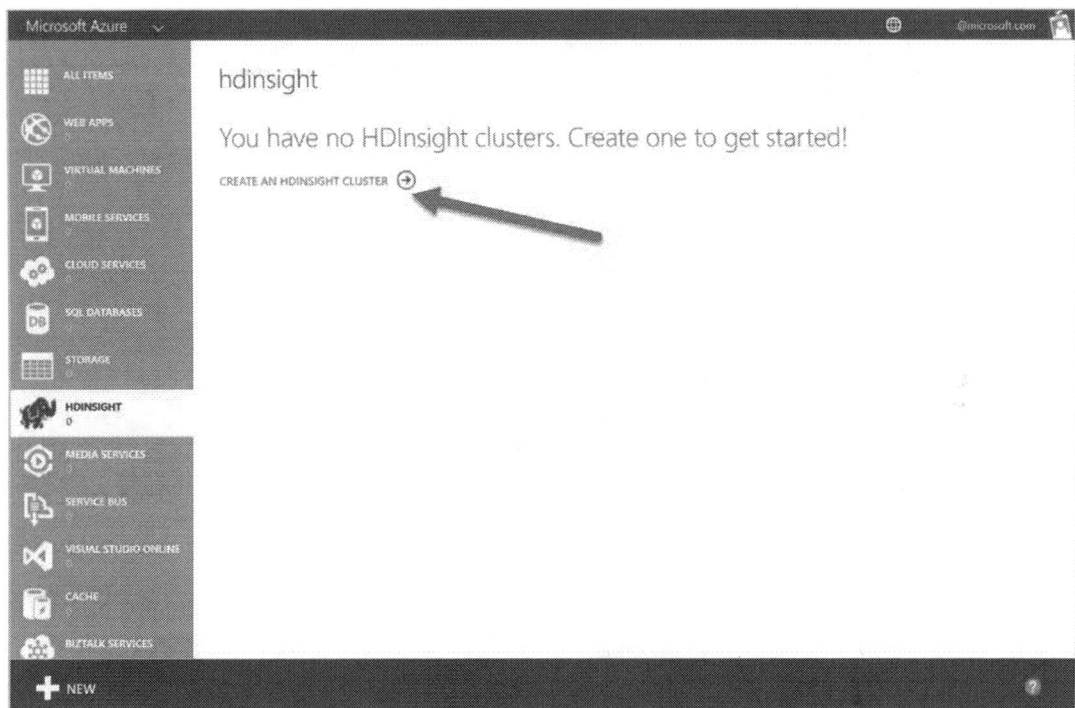

Figure 15-5. *Creating an Azure HDInsight cluster*

2. With this Azure subscription, the Hadoop options are preselected. Notice, however, that in Figure 15-6 the HDInsight options include HBase, Storm, and Custom Create. (Hadoop on Linux is not available for this subscription, but it may be available with your Azure subscription.)

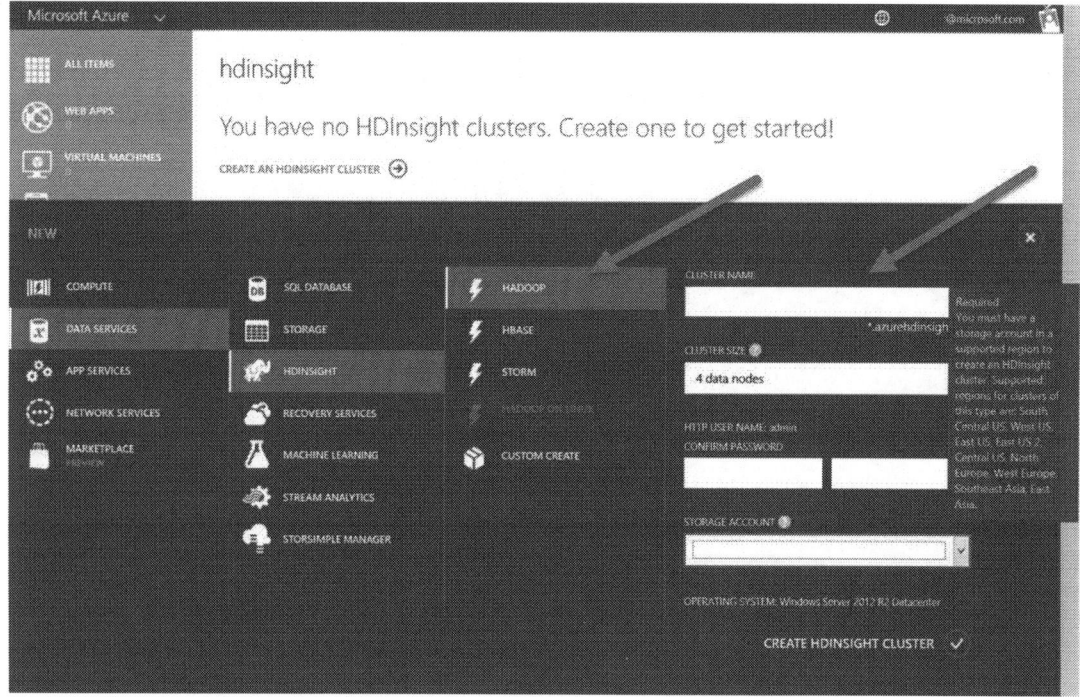

Figure 15-6. *Azure HDInsight open source selection*

3. The cluster name must be unique: use `contosohadoop.azurehdinsight.net` for this exercise. After you choose the name, you can select the Hadoop cluster size, as shown in Figure 15-7, from 1 node (for testing) up to a 32-node cluster (for production). Also note in Figure 15-7 the HDInsight supported storage account regions identified in the pop-up text window.

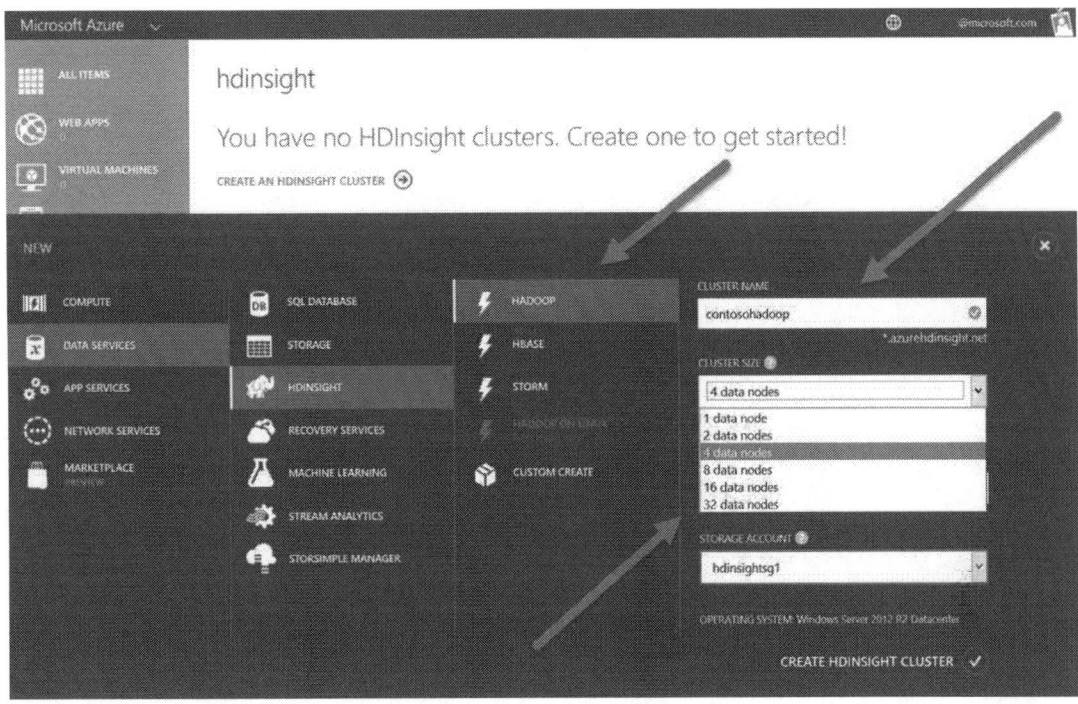

Figure 15-7. *Completed Azure HDInsight options*

■ **Tip** If your Storage Account entry has a red highlight around it, the storage account was not created in one of the supported Hadoop Azure regions. You cannot create the cluster until you select the correct Azure region for the storage account.

---

4. If you have created the storage account in one of the supported Azure regions, the new Hadoop SaaS cluster is created and displayed in the HDInsight workspace, as shown in Figure 15-8.

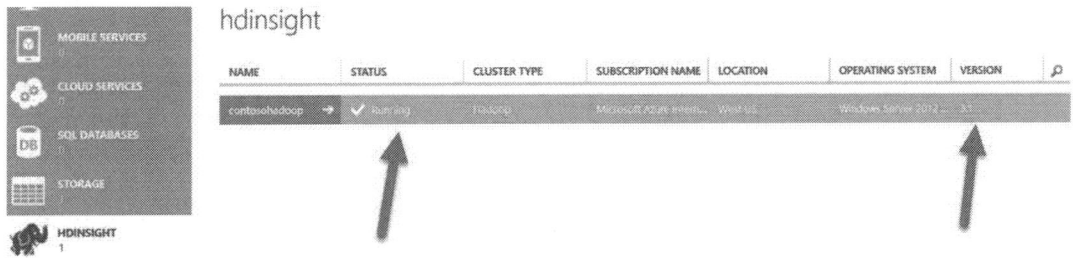

Figure 15-8. *Azure HDInsight version 3.1 SaaS cluster running*

■ **Tip**   In Figure 15-8, notice that the HDInsight version is 3.1. This is the Azure Hadoop SaaS version running on Windows Server 2012 R2 with an SLA for uptime.

5. Select the Get the Tools option shown in Figure 15-9 to install the Azure PowerShell SDK. This is a two-step process; selecting this feature starts the Web Platform Installer, shown in Figure 15-10, to download and install Azure PowerShell.

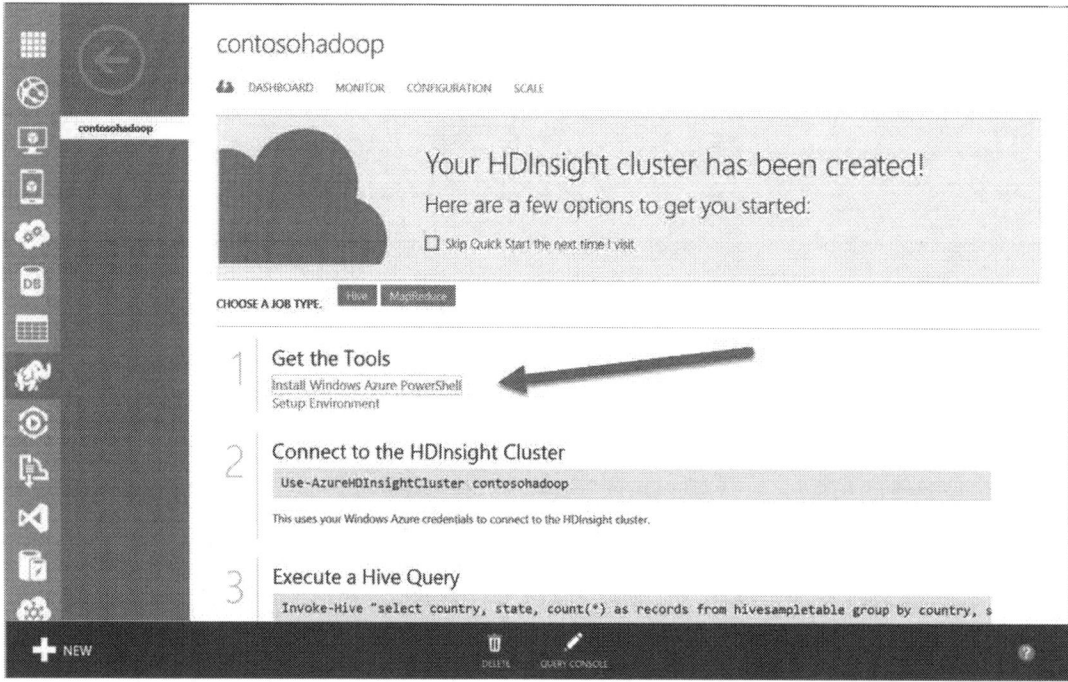

Figure 15-9. Get the Tools option to begin the Azure PowerShell install

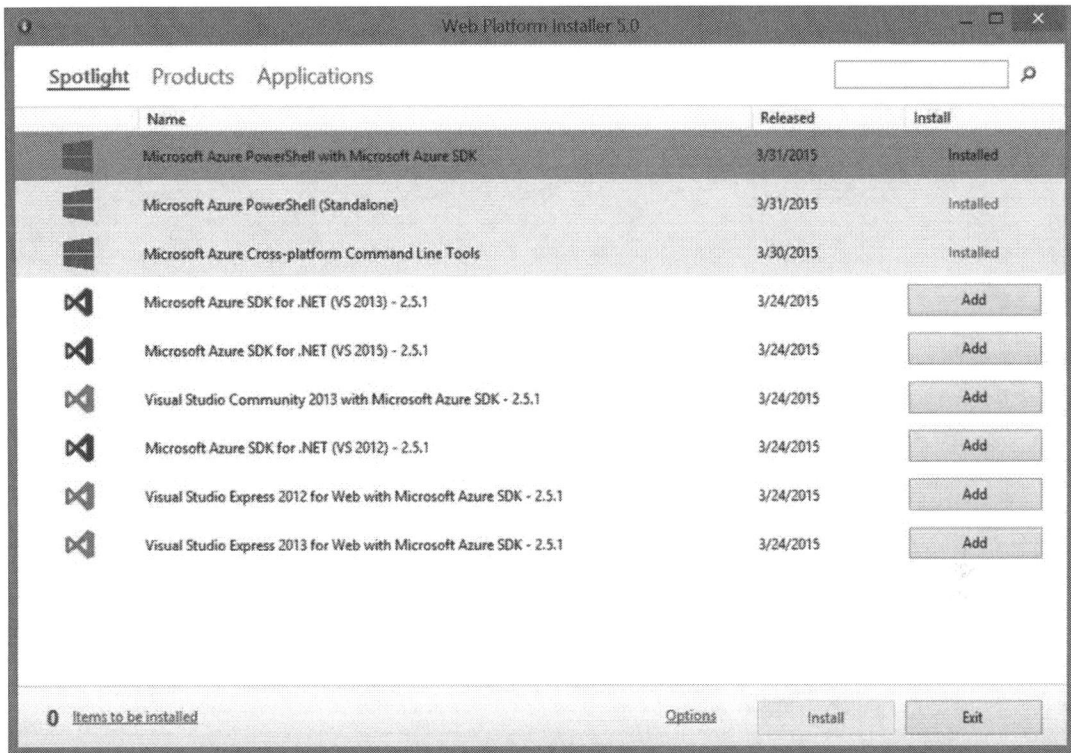

Figure 15-10. *Web Platform Installer used to install the Azure PowerShell SDK platform*

Defining Azure Business Intelligence

In this section, you learn about the options available to provide both business leaders and senior executives with visual reporting that is meaningful and actionable. Throughout this chapter, you have been introduced to multiple options for processing big data, such as using Pig with Hadoop in HDInsight or Hive, or many of the other projects identified in Table 15-1. Additional options are available for processing big data using traditional development code with Python, C#, C++, and other web-based languages like PHP and JavaScript.

It is also easy to provide BI with universal programs like Microsoft Excel, which provide the functionality needed to use Microsoft Power Query in business reports. The next exercise can be easily completed to produce beautiful reports using Hadoop big-data results.

MICROSOFT EXCEL POWER QUERY

■ **Note**   To complete this exercise, you must have permissions to install software on your computer.

---

1. Download Microsoft Power Query for Excel, as shown in Figure 15-11. It is located in the Microsoft Download Center at `www.microsoft.com/en-us/download/details.aspx?id=39379`.

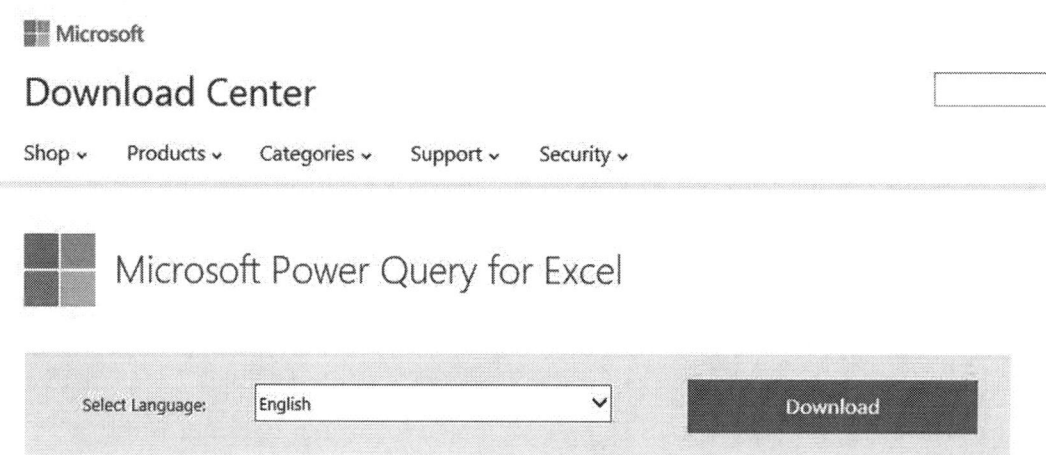

Figure 15-11. *Downloading Microsoft Power Query for Excel from the Microsoft Download Center*

2. Choose the correct version for your Microsoft Office installation: 32-bit or 64-bit. The OS version is not a factor in this decision. To validate what version you are currently running, open Microsoft Word and, in a new or an existing document, choose File ➤ Account.

3. Click the About Word icon. The version is displayed—32-bit or 64-bit—as shown in Figure 15-12. Follow the prompts to install Excel Power Query.

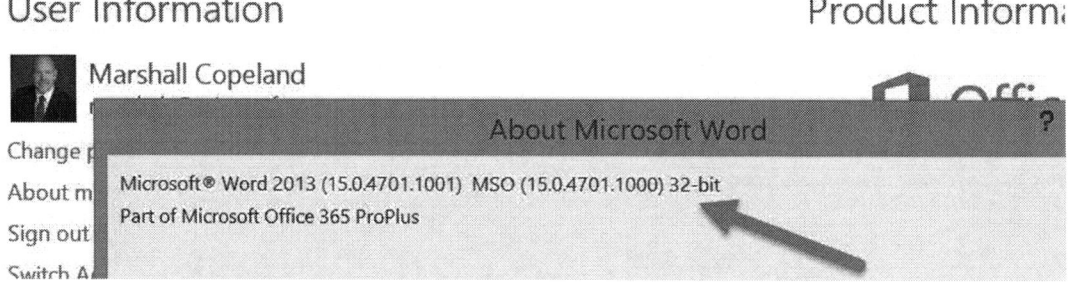

Figure 15-12. *Identifying the Office version: 32-bit or 64-bit*

4.   Once Power Query has completed its installation, open Excel, create a new blank workbook, select the Power Query tab, and choose From Other Sources ➤ From Hadoop File (HDFS), as shown in Figure 15-13.

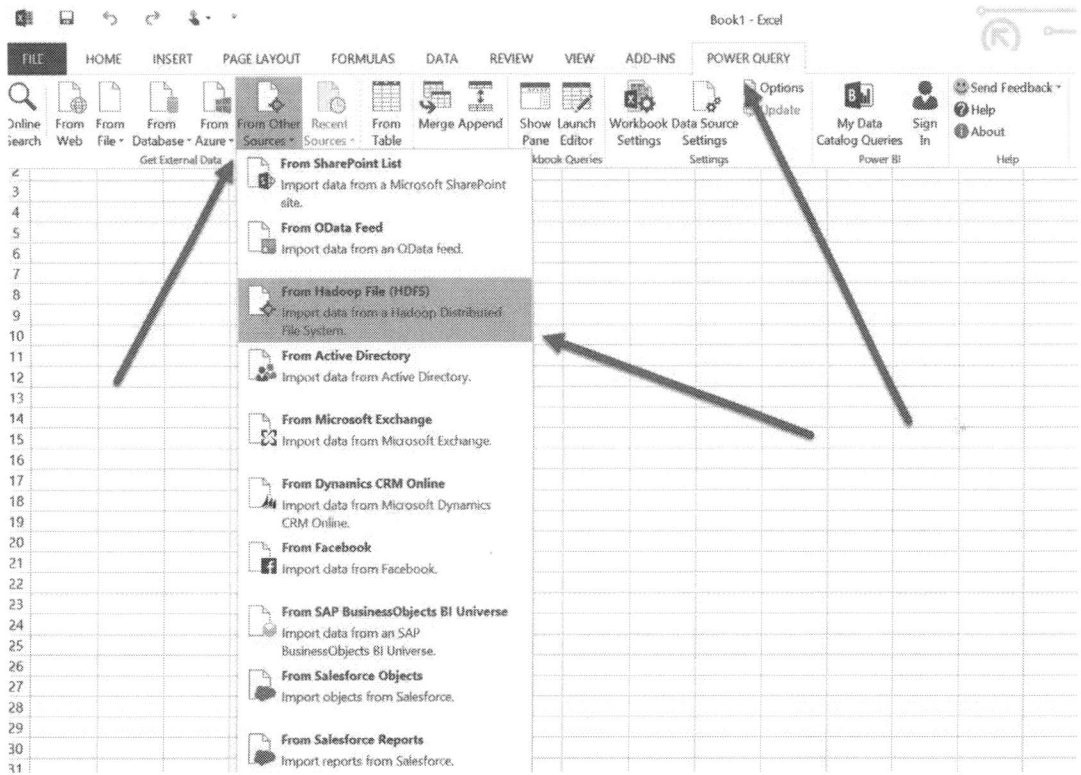

Figure 15-13. *Microsoft Excel Power Query add-in*

5.   Enter the name of the Hadoop cluster created in the previous exercise. In the example used for this chapter, the full name is `contosohadoop.azurehdinsight.net`, as shown in Figure 15-14.

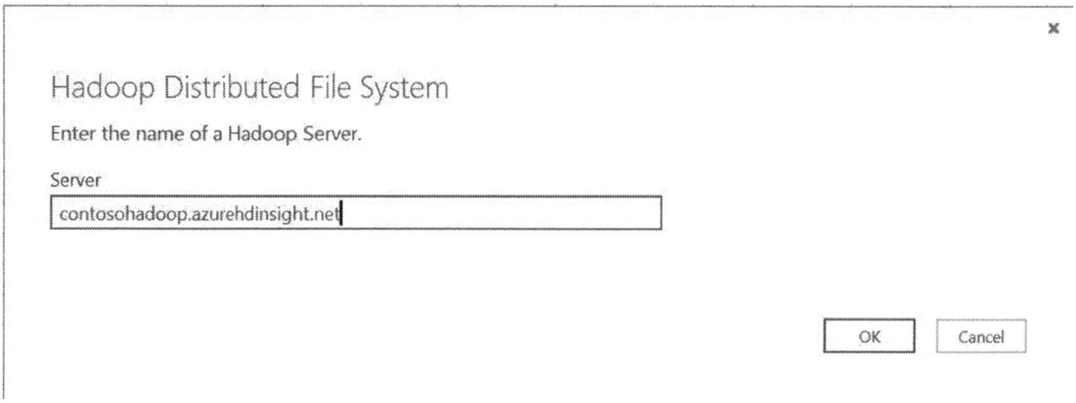

Hadoop Distributed File System

Enter the name of a Hadoop Server.

Server

contosohadoop.azurehdinsight.net

OK   Cancel

Figure 15-14. *Hadoop server name, built using Deploy HDInsight*

6. Connect to the Hadoop cluster using an anonymous logon or an account, as shown in Figure 15-15.

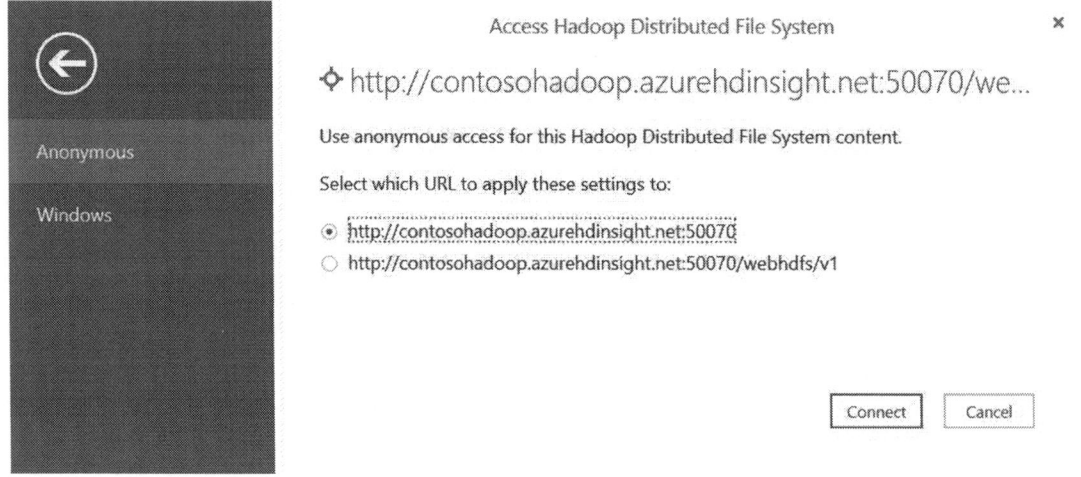

Figure 15-15. *Connecting Excel to the Hadoop cluster*

7. The Excel Query Editor opens, and you can start building Power Query reports from the HDFS data.

You can also connect Microsoft Excel to Hadoop using Microsoft Hive ODBC drivers. Other options are to use Office 365, to import and export data with Sqoop (listed in Table 15-1), and other methods.

■ **Tip**   You can learn more about Microsoft HDInsight and analytics by exploring the documentation and tutorials at the Azure Hadoop learning guide at `http://azure.microsoft.com/en-us/documentation/articles/hdinsight-learn-map`.

Summary

This chapter introduced you to the world of big data using a Microsoft Azure solution that supports the array of challenges that big data creates. You learned about Hadoop, an Apache open source project, and how Microsoft has partnered with Hortonworks to provide a 100% open source solution. Finally, you stepped though exercises to install HDInsight clusters into your Azure subscription and access the clusters using Microsoft Power Query in Excel.

The next chapter introduces you to configuring Microsoft Intune, which is another Azure solution. Intune supports Apple, Android, and Microsoft Windows phones, tablets, and portable devices. Discussion topics include the technology to support initiatives like bring your own device (BYOD) and how Intune protects corporate data. Additionally, Azure Rights Management Services (RMS) provide extended protection for documents with policy control, enabling end-to-end security of intellectual property mandated by both state and federal laws in order to protect privacy.

## CHAPTER 16

Working with Intune and RMS

Enterprise Management Suite

In Chapter 9, you were introduced to Azure Active Directory Premium (AADP). It is part of an Azure SKU called the Enterprise Management Suite. This suite also includes Microsoft Intune and Rights Management Services (RMS). These technologies can also be purchased individually, but you get a better value when purchasing the entire suite.

This chapter introduces you to Microsoft Intune and RMS. These technologies give you a greater level of control over your company's data, and they help prevent accidental leakage of your sensitive data.

Managing Mobile Devices with Microsoft Intune

Microsoft Intune is designed to help you protect and manage devices while, at the same time, allowing users to access company e-mail, data, and apps remotely. Because it is cloud-based, you can administer devices from any supported web browser. You can use Intune to manage many devices, including phones and tablets running the Android, iOS, Windows Phone, and Windows RT operating systems. Computers running Windows 8.1 can be managed as mobile devices or as computers using the Intune client software. To manage devices with Intune, open a web browser and browse to `https://manage.microsoft.com`.

Intune can manage mobile devices a number of ways:

- Intune on its own

- Intune with Configuration Manager 2012

- Intune with Exchange ActiveSync

▓ **Important**   This chapter assumes that Intune is managing devices alone, without System Center Configuration Manager (SCCM) integration or Exchange ActiveSync.

Supported Devices and Features

Intune mobile device management supports the following OSs:

- Apple iOS 7 and later

- Google Android 2.3.4 and later (includes Samsung KNOX)

- Windows Phone 8.0 and later

- Windows RT and later

- Windows 8.1 computers

For a list of features, see `https://technet.microsoft.com/en-us/library/dn600287.aspx`.

Preparing for Mobile Device Management

Before you can enroll mobile devices in Microsoft Intune, you need to prepare the Intune service by selecting the appropriate Mobile Device Management Authority setting on the Mobile Device Management page of the Administration workspace. The Mobile Device Management Authority setting determines whether you manage the devices with Intune or SCCM with Intune integration. This chapter assumes that Intune is used without SCCM, so the option should be set to Microsoft Intune, as shown in the example in Figure 16-1.

■ **Important**   Consider carefully whether you want to manage mobile devices using Intune only or by using SCCM with Intune integration. After you set Mobile Device Management Authority to either of these options, it cannot be changed.

SETTING THE MOBILE DEVICE MANAGEMENT AUTHORITY OPTION

1. In the Microsoft Intune administration console, shown in Figure 16-1, click Admin and then click Mobile Device Management.

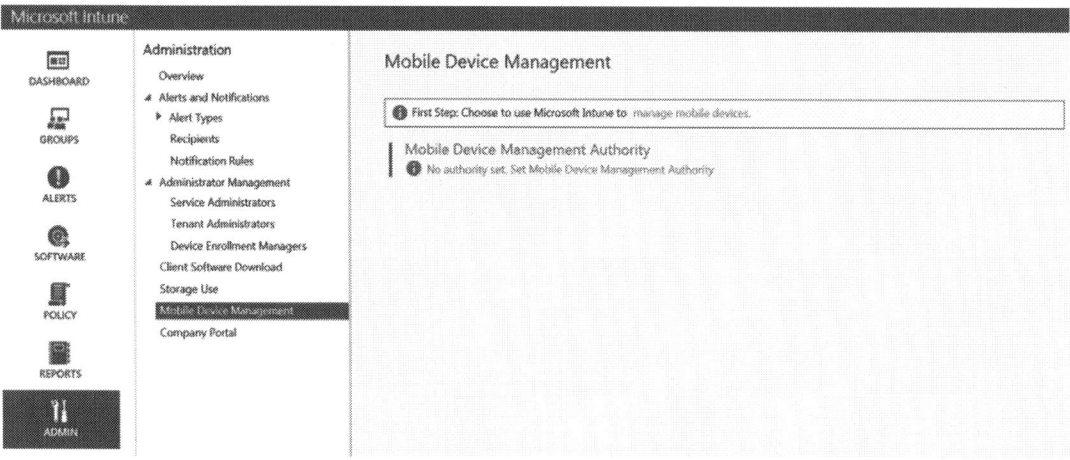

Figure 16-1. *Setting the Mobile Device Management Authority*

2. In the Tasks list, click Set Mobile Device Management Authority. The Manage Mobile Devices dialog box opens, as shown in Figure 16-2.

Figure 16-2. Confirming the mobile device management authority

3. Select the Use Intune To Manage My Mobile Devices check box, and then click OK.

■ **Important** Pay careful attention to the warning. Once the Mobile Device Management Authority option is set, it cannot easily be changed.

Configuring the Mobile Device Management Infrastructure

After setting the Mobile Device Management Authority, you are ready to start managing devices. As shown in Figure 16-3, some devices can be managed right away without requiring additional configuration. Windows, Windows Phone 8.1, and Android devices don't require additional configuration. iOS and Windows Phone 8 devices, however, require additional configuration before they can be managed.

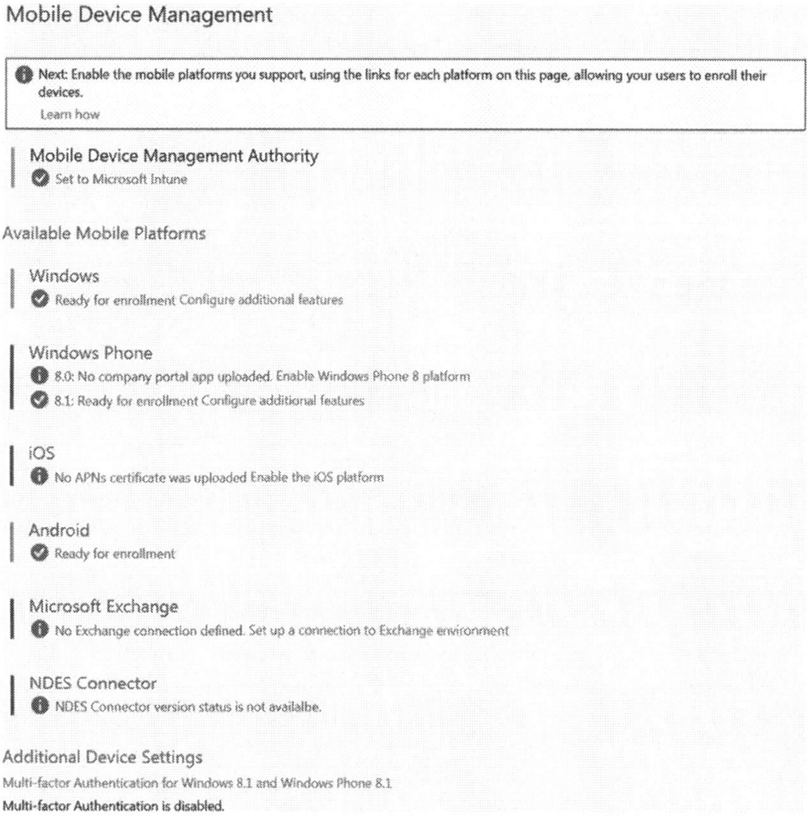

Mobile Device Management

> ⓘ Next: Enable the mobile platforms you support, using the links for each platform on this page, allowing your users to enroll their devices.
> Learn how

Mobile Device Management Authority
✓ Set to Microsoft Intune

Available Mobile Platforms

Windows
✓ Ready for enrollment Configure additional features

Windows Phone
ⓘ 8.0: No company portal app uploaded. Enable Windows Phone 8 platform
✓ 8.1: Ready for enrollment Configure additional features

iOS
ⓘ No APNs certificate was uploaded Enable the iOS platform

Android
✓ Ready for enrollment

Microsoft Exchange
ⓘ No Exchange connection defined. Set up a connection to Exchange environment

NDES Connector
ⓘ NDES Connector version status is not availalbe.

Additional Device Settings
Multi-factor Authentication for Windows 8.1 and Windows Phone 8.1
Multi-factor Authentication is disabled.

Figure 16-3. *Managing mobile devices*

Enabling iOS Mobile Devices Management

Each mobile device OS requires its own setup procedure. For example, to manage iOS devices, such as iPhones or iPads, you first need to install an Apple Push Notification service certificate from the Apple Push Certificate portal to connect iOS devices with your Intune account. Similarly, to manage apps for a Windows RT 8.1 device, you need to obtain side-loading keys and a code-signing certificate.

■ **Note** The Apple Push Notification certificate requires an Apple ID in order to complete the installation. If you don't have an Apple ID, create one before proceeding with the steps in the following exercise. This same Apple ID must also be used to renew the certificates. It is recommended that you create a corporate Apple ID for managing these certificates, rather than a personal ID.

ENABLING IOS MANAGEMENT

To enable iOS management, follow these steps:

1. On the Mobile Device Management page, click the Enable The iOS Platform link, as shown in Figure 16-4.

Figure 16-4. Enable The iOS Platform link

2. When the Enable page opens, click the Download The APNs Certificate Request button, as shown in Figure 16-5.

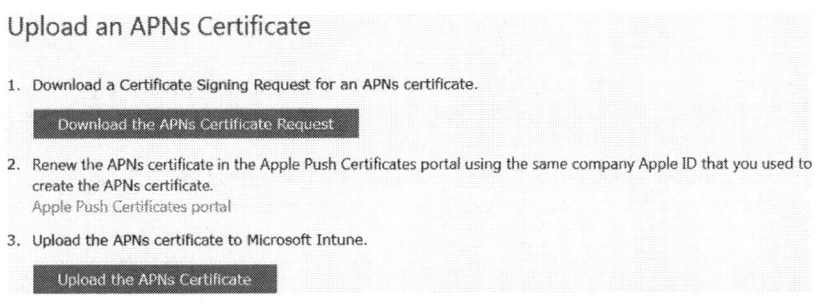

Figure 16-5. Downloading Apple Network certificate requests

3. A Save As dialog box opens, as shown in Figure 16-6, which allows you to save the certificate request file. Choose a location to save the file, give the file a meaningful name, and click Save.

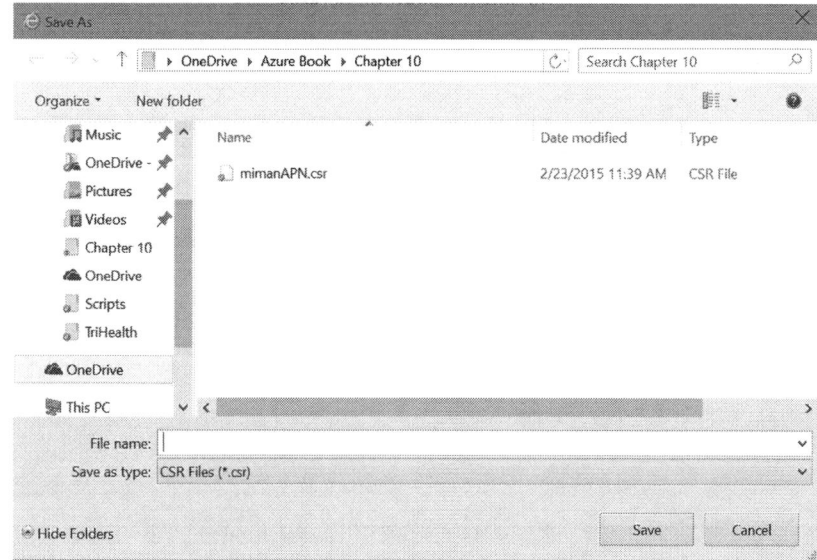

Figure 16-6. *Saving the certificate request file*

4. To create a new push certificate, click the Apple Push Certificates Portal link, as shown in Figure 16-7.

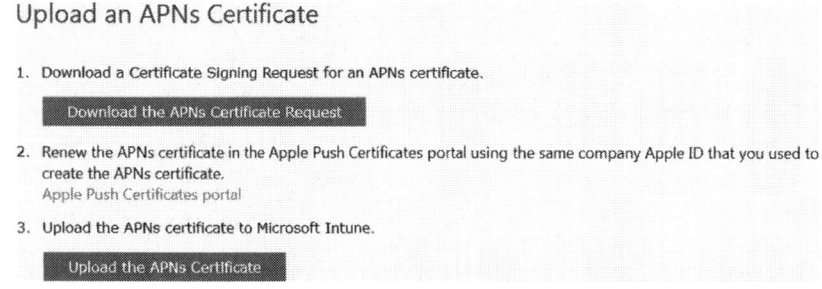

Figure 16-7. *Uploading an APNs Certificate*

5. The Apple Push Certificates Portal web site opens. Use your Apple ID to sign in to the portal, as shown in Figure 16-8.

Apple Push Certificates Portal

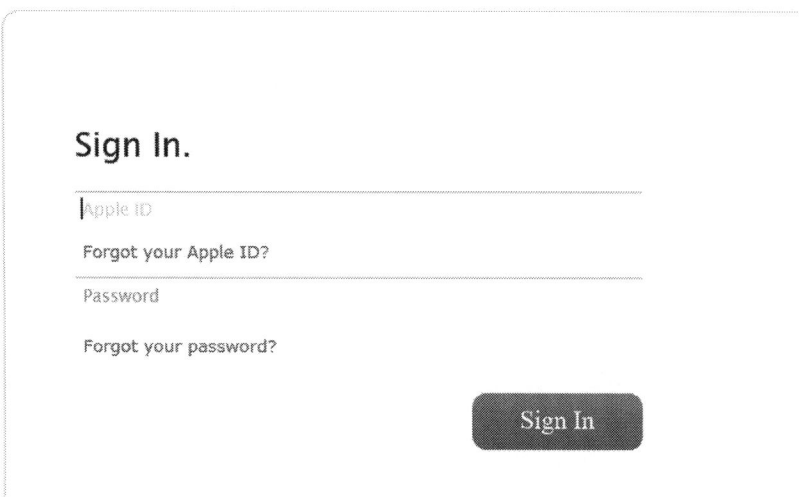

Figure 16-8. *Logging in to the Apple certificates portal*

6. On the Get Started page, click the Create A Certificate button, as shown in Figure 16-9.

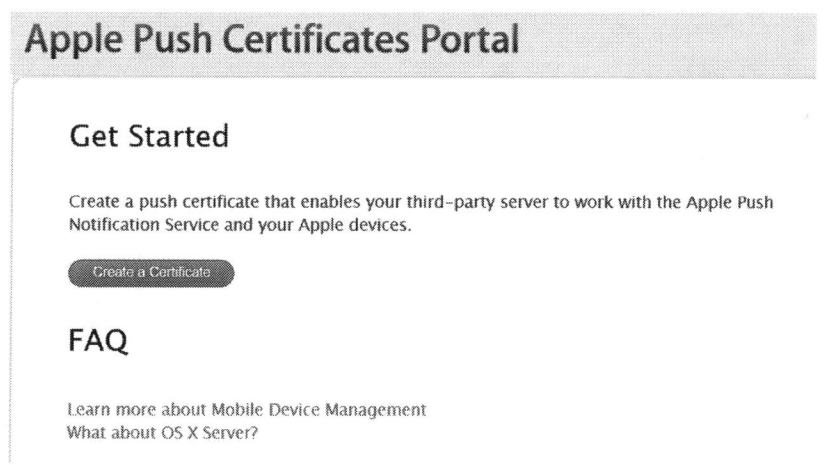

Figure 16-9. *Creating the certificate*

7. You are asked to accept the license agreement. Select the check box to indicate that you accept the terms of the agreement, and click Accept, as shown in Figure 16-10.

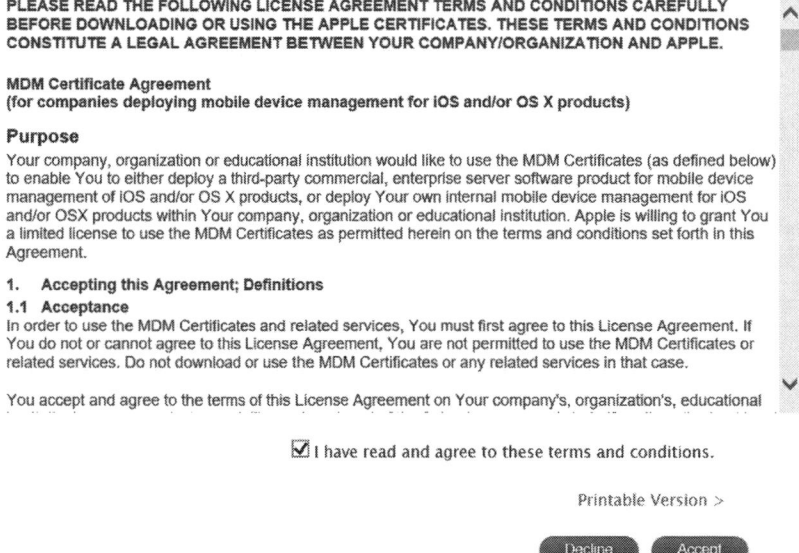

Figure 16-10. Accepting the terms of use

8. The Create A New Push Certificate page opens, as shown in Figure 16-11. In the Notes field, enter a comment that describes the use of the certificate. Click the Browse button to go to the location where you saved the certificate request file in step 1, and click Upload.

Create a New Push Certificate

Upload your Certificate Signing Request signed by your third-party server
vendor to create a new push certificate.

Notes

Cert for managing IOS devices in Microsoft Intune

Vendor-Signed Certificate Signing Request

C:\Users\miman\OneDriv   Browse...

Cancel   Upload

Figure 16-11. *Uploading the certificate request file*

9. You are asked to open or save the file. Choose to save the file to a secure location

10. To upload the certificate to the Apple Push Certificate portal network, click the
Upload The APNs Certificate button, shown in Figure 16-12. The Upload The APNs
Certificate dialog box opens.

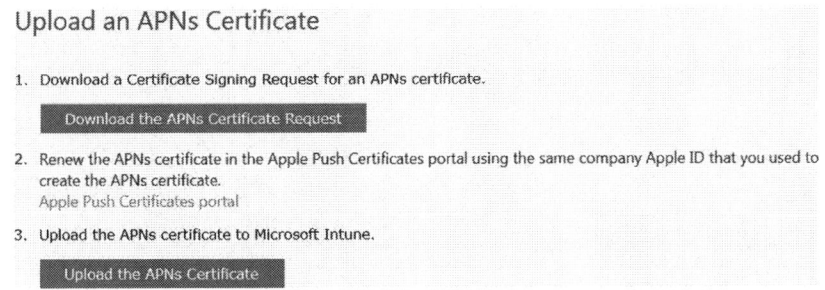

Upload an APNs Certificate

1. Download a Certificate Signing Request for an APNs certificate.

   Download the APNs Certificate Request

2. Renew the APNs certificate in the Apple Push Certificates portal using the same company Apple ID that you used to
   create the APNs certificate.
   Apple Push Certificates portal

3. Upload the APNs certificate to Microsoft Intune.

   Upload the APNs Certificate

Figure 16-12. *Uploading the certificate*

11. Click the Browse button, as shown in Figure 16-13, to locate the file you saved in step 9. Enter your Apple ID, and click Upload.

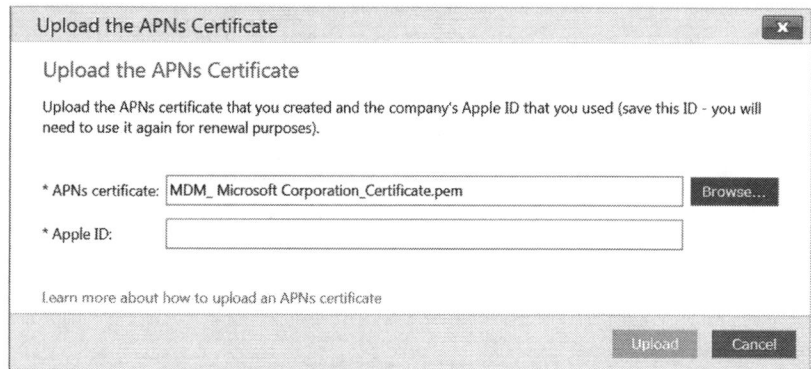

Figure 16-13. Completing the certificate upload

12. After the upload completes, you can manage iOS devices using Microsoft Intune, as shown in Figure 16-14.

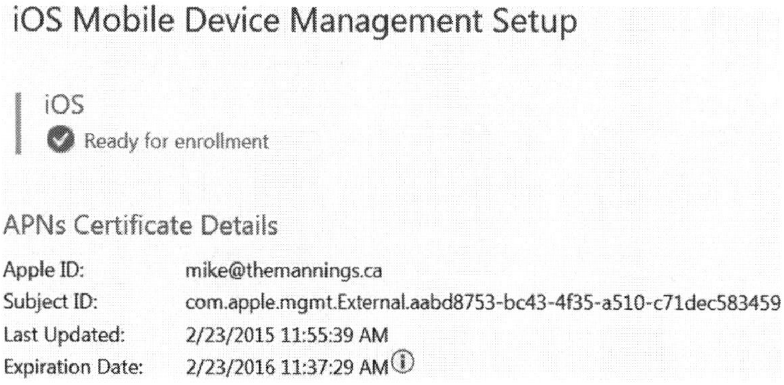

iOS Mobile Device Management Setup

iOS
✅ Ready for enrollment

APNs Certificate Details

Apple ID:	mike@themannings.ca
Subject ID:	com.apple.mgmt.External.aabd8753-bc43-4f35-a510-c71dec583459
Last Updated:	2/23/2015 11:55:39 AM
Expiration Date:	2/23/2016 11:37:29 AM

Figure 16-14. iOS mobile devices are now ready to be managed using Microsoft Intune

Enrolling Mobile Devices in Intune

When the Intune device-management infrastructure is in place, devices must be enrolled to enable device management and access to company resources. There are multiple options for device enrollment, as detailed next and in Table 16-1:

- *Bring your own device (BYOD)*: Users enroll their personal devices using a Company Portal app or setting. An administrator must license users for Intune, which is included in the Enterprise Management Suite SKU or as a separate license, to allow device management. Each user can have up to five devices managed by Intune.

- *Corporate-owned, choose your own device (CYOD) (iOS only)*: The company provides one or more devices from which employees may choose, while retaining administrative control of the device. These devices are owned and managed by the company and can be preconfigured to conform to company policies from their initial setup.

- *Corporate-owned shared devices*: These devices meet the need for equipment such as point-of-sale machines, kiosks, or tablets shared by multiple students in a classroom. Shared devices can be assigned to a device enrollment manager or can be userless:

  - *Device enrollment manager devices*: A special user account allows the administrator or their designee to enroll more than five devices. The administrator or manager takes ownership and can manage the device, its policies, and its apps.

  - *Userless devices (iOS only)*: The administrator enrolls the device with a device certificate, which restricts day-to-day users from modifying the device.

Table 16-1. *Mobile device management*

Enrollment Type	BYOD	CYOD	Shared Device With a Manager Account	Shared Device Without a User Account
Description	Personal device	Corporate-owned device for a single user	Corporate-owned device managed using a manager account shared by many users	Corporate-owned userless device used by many users
Device's user	Owner	Assigned user	No specific user	No specific user
Who enrolls	Owner	Administrator	Device manager	Anyone
Who un-enrolls	Owner or administrator	Administrator	Administrator	Administrator
Who can reset	Owner or Administrator	Administrator	Administrator	Administrator

Now that the Intune management environment is set up, you can begin enrolling devices. However, to do so, you first need to perform a few tasks.

Adding Intune Users

The first task you need to complete is to add your user accounts. Microsoft Intune can use an existing Azure Active Directory (AAD) tenant domain for user accounts, making adding accounts to Intune a simple process. To get your user accounts to appear in Intune when using directory synchronization, as in this chapter, you only need to assign an AAD Premium license to your users. Once they are licensed, they will show up in Intune, and you can begin to enroll devices.

Creating Enrollment Profiles

The next step is to create enrollment profiles. Profiles specify whether devices have user affinity (a user and device association) and assign a group for device management. At least one profile must be specified before company-owned devices can be enrolled in Intune.

CREATING ENROLLMENT PROFILES

1. In the Microsoft Intune administration console, choose Policy ➤ Corporate Device Enrollment, and then complete the following fields:

    -   *Name*: The profile name listed in the Intune administration console.

    -   *Description*: A brief summary of the purpose of the policy.

    -   *Enrollment Details:* Specifies whether to prompt the device user for credentials when enrolling the new device.

    -   *Assign devices to the following group*: Specifies a mobile device group for devices assigned this profile.

2. Click Save Profile.

Specifying Company Portal Settings

You can customize the Intune Company Portal for your company.

CUSTOMIZING THE INTUNE COMPANY PROFILE

1. In the Microsoft Intune administration console, choose Admin ➤ Company Portal and configure the following fields:

    -   Company Name

    -   IT Department Contact Name

    -   IT Department Phone Number

    -   IT Department Email Address

    -   Additional Information

- Company Privacy Statement URL

- Support Website URL (not displayed)

- Website Name (displayed to user)

2. You can also customize the Company Portal with your company logo, company name, company color, and background.

Setting Terms and Conditions

Optionally, you can publish terms and conditions that users see the first time they use the company portal. Once enrollment is set up, inform your users that device enrollment is now available. Instruct them to go to the device store and install the Company Portal, or go to Company Apps (Windows Phone 8.0 only). Users can enroll and manage their mobile devices with the Company Portal app. They can also use a Company Portal web site. Each device OS has its own Company Portal app:

- *Android*: Users install the Company Portal app from Microsoft on Google Play.

- *iOS*: Users install the Company Portal app from Microsoft from the App Store. Users can then view their devices to enroll their phones.

- *Windows Phone 8.1*: Users install the Company Portal app from Microsoft from the Windows Phone store.

- *Windows Phone 8*: Users choose System Settings ➤ Company Apps, and sign in using their user ID. The Company Portal app is deployed to users' phones.

- *Windows 8.1 and Windows RT 8.1*: Users install the Company Portal app from the Windows Store. The enrollment process is as follows:

  a. Choose PC Settings ➤ Network ➤ Workplace.

  b. Enter the User ID, and click Turn On.

  c. Select the Allow Apps And Services From IT Admin check box, and click Turn On.

When users open the Company Portal, they are asked for their credentials. The first time in the portal, users are asked to accept the terms—it doesn't matter whether the device is enrolled. The user either accepts or declines the terms. Upon accepting, they continue to the portal. If they decline, they are asked to confirm that they want to decline and are then given a link that instructs them on how to unenroll. Users are not automatically unenrolled, and until they unenroll, you can still manage the device.

At this point, the process is different for devices that have not yet been enrolled, depending on the OS of the device:

- For Windows and Windows Phone 8.1 devices, the Company Portal reminds the user to enroll. Windows Phone 8.1 has a link to enrollment settings, and Windows provides a link to Help content that describes how to enroll.

- For iOS and Android devices, the user is led through the enrollment process. Users still see a message from Microsoft about the impact of enrolling.

Getting Started with Azure Rights Management

Azure Rights Management Services (Azure RMS) is the security-control feature in Microsoft Azure that is used to protect company information, whether on a corporate device or a personal device. Azure RMS uses a combination of encryption, identity, and authorization policies to secure files and e-mail. When users share documents or e-mails that are protected with Azure RMS, the protection stays with the protected item.

In Figure 16-15, you can see how Azure RMS works as a rights-management solution for Office 365 as well as for your on-premises servers and services. You can also see that it supports most devices that run Windows, Mac OS, iOS, Android, and Windows Phone.

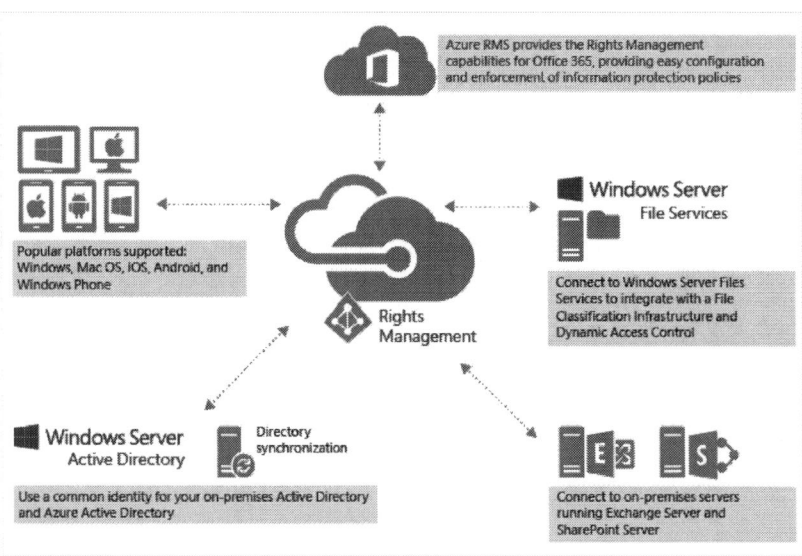

Figure 16-15. *Azure RMS*

Configuring Azure Rights Management

By default, RMS is disabled when you first sign up for Office 365 or AAD. To enable RMS for your tenant, you first need to activate it.

ACTIVATING RMS

To activate RMS from the Azure Management Portal, follow these steps:

1. Sign in to the Azure Management Portal.

2. In the left pane, click Active Directory.

3. On the Active Directory page, click the Rights Management tab.

4. Select the directory to manage, and click Activate, as shown in Figure 16-16, to turn on RMS.

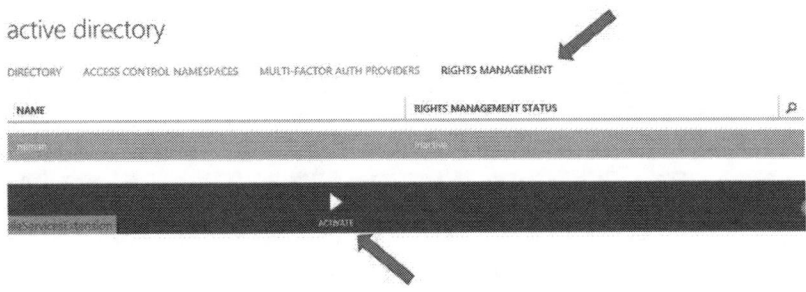

Figure 16-16. *Activating Azure RMS*

The Rights Management Status now displays as Active, and the Activate option is replaced with Deactivate.

After activating Azure RMS, you can begin using the two default templates to apply policies to sensitive files that restrict access to authorized users in the organization. These two templates have the following rights policy restrictions:

- Read-only viewing for the protected content:
  - *Display name: <organization name>*: Confidential View Only
  - *Specific permission*: View Content
- Read or Modify permissions for the protected content:
  - *Display name: <organization name>*: Confidential
  - *Specific permissions*: View Content, Save File, Edit Content, View Assigned Rights, Allow Macros, Forward, Reply, and Reply All

The default templates may be sufficient for most users, but if you want to create your own custom rights-policy templates, you can do that as well. Some of the reasons for creating custom templates are as follows:

- You need a template to grant rights to only some of your users instead of all users.
- You need only some of your users to be able to see and select a template (departmental template) from applications, instead of all users.
- You want to define a custom right for a template, such as View and Edit but not Copy and Print.
- You want to configure additional options in a template that include an expiration date or specify whether the content can be accessed without an Internet connection.

Before users can select a custom template that contains settings such as those listed here, you first need to create and configure it and then publish it to your tenant.

Creating, Configuring, and Publishing a Custom Template

You create and manage custom templates through the Azure Management Portal. You can sign in directly from the Azure Management Portal, or you can sign in to the Office 365 admin center and choose advanced features for Rights Management, which then redirects you to the Azure Management Portal.

CREATING A CUSTOM TEMPLATE

To create, configure, or publish custom templates for RMS, use the following procedures. Begin in the Azure Management Portal:

1. In the left pane, click Active Directory.

2. On the Active Directory page, click Rights Management.

3. Select the directory to manage.

4. Click Create A New Rights Policy Template.

5. On the Add A New Rights Policy Template page, choose a language, add a name and a description, and click the check mark.

After the template has been created, on the Get Started With Rights Management quick-start page, click Manage Your Rights Policy Templates. The template you just created is in the list of available templates, showing a status of Archived. At this point, the template is created but not configured, and it is not yet visible to users. The next step is to configure the template.

CONFIGURING AND PUBLISHING A CUSTOM TEMPLATE

On the Templates page, select the newly created template:

1. From the Your Template Has Been Added quick-start page, click the Get Started link, Configure Rights For Users And Groups, and then click Get Started Now.

2. Select the users and or groups who will have rights to use the content that is protected by the new template.

■ **Note** As a best practice, use groups rather than users, which simplifies management of templates.

---

3. Click the arrow in the lower-right corner to assign one of the listed rights to your selected users and groups.

4. When you have chosen all the rights that you want to apply to the template, click the check mark in the lower-right corner to complete configuring the rights to your template.

■ **Note**   You don't have to select one of the default rights to grant to your users or groups. Selecting Custom allows you to choose from the any of the following rights:

- View Content
- Save File
- Edit Content
- Copy and Extract Content
- View Assigned Rights
- Change Rights
- Allow Macros
- Export Content (Save As)
- Print
- Forward
- Reply
- Reply All
- Full Control

■ **Tip**   You can make templates visible to a subset of users when they see a list of templates in applications. To do so, click Scope, which is currently in Preview, to configure a template as a departmental template, and follow the same steps as in the "Configuring and Publishing a Custom Template" exercise to add a group or groups.

If you wish to configure additional options with your template, click the Configure link. On this page, you can add languages and the name and description of this template in that language. When you have users who speak multiple language, it's important to add each language they use and supply a name and description in that language. Users then see the name and description of the template in the same language as their client OS, which ensures that they understand the policy applied to a document or e-mail message. If there is no match with their client OS, the name and description they see falls back to the language and description that you defined when you first created the template.

Additionally, you can set the template expiration to one of the following options:

- Content never expires.
- Content expires. You can define for your templates when files that are protected can no longer be opened. You specify a date, or a number of days, starting from the time that the protection is applied to the file.

You can also configure offline access to the files protected by your templates. The configurable offline settings are as follows:

- Content is available only with an Internet connection.

- Content is always available.

- Content is available for a specified number of days without an Internet connection.

This setting can be used to control how users can access protected files. For example, if you specify that content is not available without an Internet connection, or that content is only available for a specified number of days, then when that threshold is reached, users must be re-authenticated, and their access is logged. When this happens, if their credentials are not cached, users are prompted to sign in before they can open the file.

In addition to re-authenticating, the policy and the user group membership are reevaluated. This means users could experience different access results for the same file if there are changes in the policy or group membership from when they last accessed the file.

Updating Templates

When RMS templates are updated, the updates first need to be downloaded before they can be used. Template updates must be downloaded for Exchange Online (EOL) and for Microsoft Office.

Forcing Exchange Online to Download Changed Custom Templates

If you've already configured Information Rights Management (IRM) for Exchange Online, custom templates will not download for users until you make the following changes with Windows PowerShell in Exchange Online.

▧ **Note** You must perform this procedure each time you change a template.

UPDATING TEMPLATES FOR EXCHANGE ONLINE

To update templates for Exchange Online, follow these steps:

1. Connect to Exchange Online using Microsoft Azure PowerShell. For detailed information on connecting to EOL, see this TechNet article: `https://technet.microsoft.com/en-us/library/jj984289(v=exchg.150).aspx`.

   Use the `Import-RMSTrustedPublishingDomain` cmdlet to reimport your trusted publishing domain (TPD) from Azure RMS. For example, if your TPD name is Cloud Protection, enter

   ```
   Import-RMSTrustedPublishingDomain -Name "Cloud Protection"
   -RefreshTemplates -RMSOnline
   ```

2. To confirm that the templates have imported successfully, wait a few minutes and then run the `Get-RMSTemplate` cmdlet and set Type to All. For example:

```
Get-RMSTemplate -TrustedPublishingDomain "Cloud Protection" -Type All
```

3. For each imported template that you want to be available in the Outlook Web App, you must use the `Set-RMSTemplate` cmdlet and set Type to Distributed:

```
Set-RMSTemplate -Identity "Cloud Protection" -Type Distributed
```

After you archive a template when using Exchange Online with Office 365, users will continue to see the archived templates when using the Outlook Web App or mobile devices that use the Exchange ActiveSync Protocol. To stop users from seeing these templates, connect to EOL with Microsoft Azure PowerShell and then use the `Set-RMSTemplate` cmdlet as follows:

```
Set-RMSTemplate -Identity "RMS Online: 1" -Type Archived
```

Forcing Microsoft Office to Refresh Updated RMS Custom Templates

By default, RMS templates are refreshed by Microsoft Office every seven days. By editing the local computer's Registry, you can change the automatic schedule so that changed RMS templates are refreshed more frequently. You can also force an immediate refresh by deleting the `templates` folder on a computer.

CHANGING THE AUTOMATIC RMS TEMPLATE REFRESH SCHEDULE

To change the automatic refresh schedule, follow these steps:

1. On the local computer, open `Regedit.exe`.

2. Expand the registry to the following key:

```
HKEY_CURRENT_USER\Software\Classes\Local Settings\Software\
Microsoft\MSIPC
```

3. Change the `TemplateUpdateFrequency` value to the number of days that you want the updates to download. For example, if template updates happen frequently, set the value to 3 to have the updated templates downloaded every three days.

You can also force the RMS templates to update immediately by deleting the templates folder in the registry.

4. Delete the following folder: `%localappdata%\Microsoft\MSIPC \Templates`.

Summary

In this chapter, you stepped through the process of preparing Microsoft Intune without integration with Systems Center Configuration Manager or with Exchange Active Sync, and of setting up the rest of the Intune device-management environment for your Intune subscription. You also worked through the process of enrolling mobile devices. After completing these steps, you should be able to begin managing your users' devices.

You also navigated the process of activating and configuring Azure RMS. With these two technologies activated and configured, you can confidently deploy mobile devices to your users with the knowledge that your corporate information is protected.

Index

▒ B

▒ C

Get the eBook for only $5!

Why limit yourself?

Now you can take the weightless companion with you wherever you go and access your content on your PC, phone, tablet, or reader.

Since you've purchased this print book, we're happy to offer you the eBook in all 3 formats for just $5.

Convenient and fully searchable, the PDF version enables you to easily find and copy code—or perform examples by quickly toggling between instructions and applications. The MOBI format is ideal for your Kindle, while the ePUB can be utilized on a variety of mobile devices.

To learn more, go to www.apress.com/companion or contact support@apress.com.

Made in the USA
Middletown, DE
19 May 2016